eBook and Digital Learning Tools

for

Global Politics
Applying Theory to a Complex World

MARK A. BOYER

NATALIE F. HUDSON

MICHAEL J. BUTLER

Carefully scratch off the silver coating with a coin to see your personal redemption code.

75 550819-GG8A-D7G8

This code can be used only once and cannot be shared!

If the code has been scratched off when you receive it, the code may not be valid. Once the code has been scratched off, this access card cannot be returned to the publisher. You may buy access at **www.oup.com/he/boyer**.

The code on this card is valid for 2 years from the date of first purchase. Complete terms and conditions are available at **https://oup-arc.com.**

Access length: 6 months from redemption of the code.

S0-BMV-325

Directions for accessing your eBook and Digital Learning Tools

VIA THE OUP SITE

Visit **www.oup.com/he/boyer**

⬇

Select the edition you are using and the student resources for that edition.

⬇

Click the link to upgrade your access to the student resources.

⬇

Follow the on-screen instructions.

⬇

Enter your personal redemption code when prompted on the checkout screen.

VIA YOUR SCHOOL'S LEARNING MANAGEMENT SYSTEM

Log in to your instructor's course.

⬇

When you click a link to a protected resource, you will be prompted to register for access.

⬇

Follow the on-screen instructions.

⬇

Enter your personal redemption code when prompted on the checkout screen.

For assistance with code redemption or registration, please contact customer support at **arc.support@oup.com**.

Global Politics

Applying Theory to A Complex World

Global Politics

Applying Theory to A Complex World

Mark A. Boyer
University of Connecticut

Natalie F. Hudson
University of Dayton

Michael J. Butler
Clark University

New York   Oxford
OXFORD UNIVERSITY PRESS

Oxford University Press is a department of the University of Oxford.
It furthers the University's objective of excellence in research, scholarship,
and education by publishing worldwide. Oxford is a registered trade mark of
Oxford University Press in the UK and certain other countries.

Published in the United States of America by Oxford University Press
198 Madison Avenue, New York, NY 10016, United States of America.

© 2020 by Oxford University Press

Library of Congress Cataloging-in-Publication Data

Names: Boyer, Mark A., author. | Butler, Michael J., author. | Hudson,
    Natalie Florea., author.
Title: Global politics : applying theory to a complex world/ Mark Boyer,
    Michael Butler, Natalie Hudson.
Description: New York : Oxford University, 2019. | Includes bibliographical
    references and index.
Identifiers: LCCN 2019020481| ISBN 9780190655600 | ISBN 9780190655532
    (paperback)
Subjects: LCSH: International relations. | World politics.
Classification: LCC JZ1305 .B69 2019 | DDC 327—dc23
LC record available at https://lccn.loc.gov/2019020481

Printing number: 9 8 7 6 5 4 3 2 1

Printed by **Quad Graphics**

Printed in the United States of America

Brief Contents

Table of Contents

CHAPTER 3   Interpreting Power: A Levels-of-Analysis Approach   53

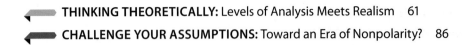

CHAPTER 6   **International Organization: The Evolving
Quest for Global Governance   157**

CHAPTER 7	War and Terrorism 193

CHAPTER 8 Pursuing Security   225

FEATURES

CHAPTER 9 International Law and the Search for Justice   257

FEATURES

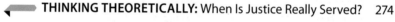

FEATURES

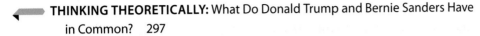

CHAPTER 11   # Global Political Economy: Searching for Equity in the Global South   333

FEATURES

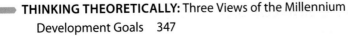

FEATURES

Preface

This book aims to educate young people for global citizenship. With this over-arching goal in mind, we will recurrently ask the reader to consider the challenges and opportunities faced in their immediate surroundings, those that transcend geographic and political boundaries, and perhaps most importantly, those that push their thinking about the world in new and interesting ways. We hope that this text will help students connect what they confront on a local level with broader trends and forces at work at the global level.

In a world that is more interdependent than ever before, we ultimately hope that students will consider what it means to be a global citizen and how best to engage in finding global solutions to complex problems that most often have global implications. But what does it mean to educate for global citizenship? While educating for global citizenship certainly involves providing baseline knowledge about global actors, international institutions, historical events, cultural dynamics, and urgent political challenges, it first and foremost requires students to think critically and theoretically about the world around them. For this reason, critical and theoretical thinking constitute the foundation of *Global Politics*. This contemporary presentation stresses the importance of global events and offers students a number of lenses through which to interpret the world around them. *Global Politics* challenges students to actually apply what they are learning throughout an integrated print and digital content program. This process of applied learning enables students to see themselves as empowered individuals and members of a global community with rights and responsibilities, guiding how they contribute to society.

Learning Goals

Geared toward undergraduate students taking a first international relations course, this highly accessible, comprehensive, yet concise and intellectually sophisticated text will help students develop a deep appreciation of global politics—equipping them to encounter the threats and opportunities of their generation. This requires a text that covers both a depth and breadth of course material but also a writing style that is straightforward and clear.

Most other texts relegate theory and history to stand alone chapters. Instead, we encourage students in every chapter to use theory as a tool, and to connect key historical moments to illuminate current political events. For us, theory and history matter greatly and must be integrated throughout the course rather than being relegated to a specific place within the course or book. This emphasis is essential for students to make sense of the world and to equip them with the tools needed to be global citizens. Additionally, for this same purpose, we introduce several innovative features within each chapter. These boxed essays highlight the unique perspectives of this book, pushing students out of their comfort zone, to consider practical theoretical applications to everyday interaction, and to reflect on the personal and individual implications of global politics for people all over the world—some that are like them and some that are not. In the current political climate, such integration of theory, history, reliable social science, and diverse perspectives have never been more important.

Pedagogical Features

- **Challenge Your Assumptions** These real-world scenarios prompt students to critically evaluate the highlighted case and form their own opinions and ideas, thus enabling them to analyze, evaluate, and apply course

CHALLENGE YOUR ASSUMPTIONS

Toward an Era of Nonpolarity?

The concept of *polarity* introduced in this chapter assumes the existence of one to several great powers. These actors possess significant military, economic, diplomatic, technological, and natural resource advantages over the rest of the international community. But what if we live in a world in which such clear advantages no longer exist? Richard Haass, the president of the preeminent foreign policy think tank in the United States, the Council on Foreign Relations, has raised this possibility. In his forecast for the direction of global politics in the 21st century, Professor Haass has introduced the idea of *nonpolarity*. Haass accepts the premise of a decline in US power but, at the same time, sees no rising power sufficient enough to surpass (unipolarity) or even balance (bipolarity) the United States. He also rejects the more common assertion that the decline in US power is bringing the United States "back to the pack" and ushering in a new era of multipolarity.

Haass envisions a future in which power is multifaceted and spread out far beyond the narrow scope of a few great powers. Although five states (China, India, Japan, Russia, and the United States) and one regional governmental organization (the EU) currently merit that distinction, there are also multiple regional powers with extensive internal power reserves (Brazil, South Africa, Mexico, and Nigeria, to name a few). The real key to

Haass' argument is his claim that the growing importance of new types of actors and issues in global politics draws influence from a wider array of (nonmilitary) power assets. In a nonpolar system, we can reasonably consider as important centers of power international and regional organizations, nongovernmental organizations, corporations, terrorist organizations and paramilitaries, major media outlets, and even states and cities within nation-states.

Nonpolarity is the by-product of globalization and transnational networks, and of the increased volume, velocity, and importance of cross-border flows of goods, services, money, and ideas moving along those networks. Yet it is important to recognize, as Haass does, that an emerging nonpolar system is likely to be a world of great disorder. In a system where power is widely diffused, resulting in a void "at the top," the prospects for order and an effective response to important global issues, such as climate change, terrorism, and the proliferation of WMDs, may be limited. In turn, in such a "flat," nonhierarchic system, it would seem that the importance of multilateralism, cooperation, and networked responses to networked problems would be magnified.

What do you think? Does the concept of polarity still matter? Or are we entering a new, "nonpolar" era. If so, how might this affect you?

content to their everyday lives. This feature aims at challenging conventional thinking on a range of global issues. For example, the Challenge Your Assumptions feature in Chapter 3 examines the concept of polarity and if it still matters. We ask students to consider whether or not we are entering a "nonpolar" era and how such a shift in the system of power might affect them. In Chapter 7, we challenge students to consider whether or not international courts are effective in limiting and responding to war and in Chapter 12, we raise questions about human rights advocacy being a new form of Western imperialism.

- **Thinking Theoretically** This feature highlights and applies significant international relations theories beyond the chapter content. Through the use of empirical, real-world cases, this feature enhances students' appreciation of the ways one can interpret and explain a political issue as well as an opportunity to formulate well-reasoned opinions. For example, Chapter 5 compares and contrasts the global views of Liberal Feminism and Radical Feminism, examining how each approach can have such different strategies to achieve the goal of gender equality. In the context of recent global women's marches, the #metoo movement, and advocacy around the gender pay gap, this feature pushes students to see variation within the theoretical construct and to consider what they think the best path to achieving equal rights for men and women is and why given recent history. This feature gives students a closer look at all five major schools of thought discussed in Chapter 2.

THINKING THEORETCIALLY

Liberal and Critical Feminist Perspectives on Gender Inequality in the Workforce

The global women's movement is committed to gender equality and the emancipation of all marginalized people. The movement is made up of many different kinds of feminists and women's groups, all with varying ideologies and perspectives on what equality means and how best to achieve it. The theories and ideologies that define the different approaches to feminist activism determine what these groups value and, subsequently, what they advocate. These different theoretical approaches greatly impact the goals and strategies associated with that activism.

Liberal feminism is rooted in the liberal philosophy that emerged during the Enlightenment, utilizing an individualist approach to equality (Peterson & Runyan 2010:81). Liberal feminists believe that women possess the capacity and abilities necessary to promote and bring about equality by working within existing structures to correct prior wrongs and bring about gender equality (Tickner, 2001). Such a perspective promotes social change through a greater representation of women within existing institutions (Peoples & Vaughn-Williams, 2014).

Critical feminists consider the problem to be the privileging and promotion of a particular conception of masculinity at the expense of other attitudes, values, and dispositions. As such, the focus of advocacy and action is on changing value systems and reforming existing institutions within society that promote males and "maleness" at the expense of women and other marginalized populations (Tickner, 2001).

These theories are not only different in the way they view the world and how gender is constructed in the world, they also inform activism in significantly different ways. These different constructions of gender and the power relations that follow from them impact the strategies feminists employ to influence global policies in order to make positive changes toward gender equality. One practical application of this theory-policy link would be the case of feminists' work toward equality of men and women in the workforce.

For their part, liberal feminists emphasize policy changes that would result in equal pay for men and women. The gender pay gap stands at 23% globally and 2% in the United States; that gap widens for women of color.[33] Liberal feminists focus on narrowing this gap, and activism for a liberal feminist might focus on promoting international legal standards requiring equal compensation for men and women in the same jobs performing the same tasks. Activists also might advocate having more women in positions of power in large corporations, particularly given that only 33 of the Fortune 500 companies are run by women.[34] In this case, liberal feminists might push for government-based incentive packages for companies that make a certain percentage of executive positions women's positions.

Conversely, critical feminists are less concerned with the wage gap and more concerned with the creation of a livable wage, as well as with the types of work available—or not available—to women. Critical feminists call attention to the fact that in many parts of the world, women are restricted to working insecure, low-paying, and unsafe jobs in the informal economy. Relatedly, women throughout the world are far more likely to undertake vital but unpaid (and, thus, economically devalued) jobs, such as caring for children and the elderly, collecting food, cooking, and maintaining the household. Critical feminists ask why this work in the "private" sphere is both unpaid and performed almost entirely by women, while work in the "public" sphere is monetarily compensated, socially valued, and—not coincidentally—disproportionately done by men.

This discussion of gender inequality in the labor market is just one example of the ways in which different schools of thought within feminism diagnose problems differently and, by extension, promote different solutions for them. Though feminist activism shares a similar concern with the elimination of gender inequality, it varies greatly on how best to work toward that goal (Sjoberg, 2017).

- **Personal Narrative** These stories allow students to take a closer look at individuals and how people from all walks of life are engaging in global politics. From activists to artists, to scholars to students themselves, these personalized narratives tell the story of global citizens who are thinking globally and acting locally. For instance, Chapter 12 highlights the inspiring work of Warsan Shire, a young African poet who writes primarily about the immigrant experience speaking from her life experience. Of her many published works, this feature focuses on "Home" which captures the stark reality of some of the horrifying decisions refugee parents must make. Her work is timely, relevant, and powerful. Her story, like others featured in the text, will inspire students and encourage them to engage especially through social media.

In addition to these boxed features, each chapter also contains more mainstream pedagogical tools that help guide student learning and their own assessment of their learning as they read each chapter. These tools are essential for today's college students as they learn to understand and apply new theoretical

Powerful Words, Pop Culture, and Poetry

Human rights advocacy often leads us to think about global NGOs like Amnesty International or Human Rights Watch. We focus on the ways these large organizations raise awareness about situations of human rights abuses and mobilize people and their governments to act. But in order for human rights advocacy to move people to act, stories must be told and human connections made. Advocacy work requires connecting people to the actual survivors of human rights abuse and allowing the stories of victims to be heard.

Warsan Shire, a young poet, educator, and African feminist, has a tremendous capacity to capture in words and verse the human experience, particularly for those who suffer, are marginalized, or are oppressed. Shire writes primarily about the immigrant experience and speaks from her life as an outsider, as an immigrant. Born in Kenya to Somali parents, Shire grew up in London, where she became the city's first Young Poet Laureate in 2014. She has given new understanding and feeling to how we think about belonging, displacement, love, and home. And although she doesn't use the language of human rights specifically, her talent takes her readers there.

She has written several collections of poems, including her first book, *Teaching My Mother How to Give Birth*, published in 2011 with flipped eye publishing. One of the poems in this book, entitled "Home," captures the stark reality of some of the horrifying decisions refugee parents must make. Shire writes:

> you only run for the border, when you see the whole city running as well
> you have to understand, no one puts their children in a boat unless the water is safer than the land
> I want to go home, but home is the mouth of a shark, home is the barrel of the gun, and no one would leave home, unless home chased you to the shore

This reading gives deep meaning and understanding to this chapter's discussion of the millions of people displaced across the globe. You can listen to a full reading of this hauntingly powerful piece, at https://www.youtube.com/watch?v=p50wrd2JiX4.

With over 78,000 Twitter followers (@warsan_shire), Shire represents a new genre of poets who can capture empathy and power, often in under 280 characters. Her quiet charisma and poignant lines have particular resonance in the digital age. Her international reach and capacity to cross into pop culture are impressive. Her poetry has been translated into Italian, Spanish, Portuguese, Danish, Estonian, and Swedish, and it was adapted for Beyoncé's album *Lemonade*. Check out her work, and consider how she uses words to explore memory, voice, trauma, healing, and belonging. How do those experiences relate to our understanding of those people forced to leave their homes?

frameworks, develop a sense of what it means to think critically about the world, and take seriously the notion of global citizenship.

- Each chapter begins with a **chapter-opening vignette**, which discusses a topic or event in the news that illuminates the chapter's major themes. The example outlined in the chapter opening is integrated throughout the rest of the chapter as a case study to help students better understand and apply theoretical frameworks and new concepts.

- **Learning objectives** describe the educational goals students are expected to come away with upon reading the chapter. Learning objectives are keyed to each chapter-ending summary, as well as the major headings within the chapters.

- **Key terms** appear in the chapter margins where terms are first used, as well as in a chapter-ending list to help students recall the important concepts covered in the chapter.
- A rich **graphics program** of photographs, figures, and maps that illustrate the latest concepts and help students explore essential chapter themes.
- End-of-chapter Critical Thinking Questions reinforce the concepts from each chapter and promote problem solving. For example, Chapter 6 covers international organizations. After reading this chapter, why do you think states choose to cooperate and form international organizations like NATO or NAFTA? What motivates choice? In your answer, consider which theoretical perspective informs your belief system. These questions also connect back to the **Student Learning Outcomes** that begin each chapter of the text.

Organization of Book

There are a few key organizational distinctions in this book. First, as outlined in the Table of Contents, there is no specific "history" chapter in this book. As mentioned, this text endeavors to integrate historical discussions and key moments of the past (even pre-1945) to better contextualize current discussions about arms control, climate change, human rights, economic development, and global monetary policy, just to name a few. The goal is to encourage students to always consider what historical events contributed to the current situation, and to be more keenly aware of the ways in which history can repeat itself and the dangers of making policy in an ahistorical context.

While the book also integrates theory throughout each chapter, Chapter 2 is uniquely dedicated to introducing students to the five essential bodies of political theory in IR. Unlike many IR textbooks, we believe students must be exposed to theoretical frameworks beyond realism and liberalism—although we do explore these two theories and their many variations in-depth. Chapter 2 also covers constructivism, feminism, and various approaches to world systems theory.

Third, this book takes a unique approach to teaching students about the levels of analysis. Chapter 3 uses the levels-of-analysis approach levels-of-analysis to explore and account for how power is at work at the individual, state, and system level. Connecting the most central concept in the study of IR (power) to the critical methodology for analyzing global politics (levels of analysis) provides students with both the breadth and depth they need for reading and understanding the more topical chapters that follow.

The remainder of the book (Chapters 4–13) cover the critical issues and fundamental questions that guide this field of study. From globalization and transnationalism to international and regional security, to terrorism and war to economic development, human rights and climate change, this text aims to introduce students to the complex issues that will define their era.

Supplements

Oxford University Press offers a complete and authoritative supplements package for both instructors and students. When you adopt *Global Politics,* you will have access to an exemplary set of learning resources to enhance teaching and support students' learning.

Companion Ancillary Resource Center (ARC) Website at www.oup.com/he/boyer

The Ancillary Resource Center (ARC) at "http://www.oup.com/he/boyer" www.oup.com/he/boyer is a convenient, single destination for resources to accompany *Global Politics.* Accessed online through individual user accounts, the ARC provides instructors with access to up-to-date ancillaries at any time while guaranteeing the security of grade-significant resources. In addition, it allows OUP to keep instructors informed when new content becomes available. The ARC for *Global Politics* includes:

- **Instructor's Manual:** For each chapter of the textbook, the Instructor's Manual includes chapter objectives, a detailed chapter outline, lecture suggestions and activities, discussion questions, video resources, and web resources.
- **Test Item File:** This resource includes over 1,000 test items, including multiple choice, short answer, and essay questions. Each question is coded to chapter learning objectives and section headings.
- **Computerized Test Bank:** The computerized test bank that accompanies this text is designed for both novice and advanced users. The system enables instructors to create and edit questions, create randomized quizzes and tests with an easy-to-use drag-and-drop tool, publish quizzes and tests to online courses, and print quizzes and tests for paper-based assessments.
- **PowerPoint Resources:** Each chapter has two slide decks to support your lectures. One deck includes the chapter outline and content; the other includes just the artwork included in the text.
- **Video Resources:** Offering recent clips on timely topics from network news programs, TED, and other well-known sources, clips are approximately 5–10 minutes in length providing a great way to launch your lectures about key concepts with real world issues and examples.

Digital Learning Tools

Global Politics comes with an extensive array of digital learning tools to ensure your students get the most out of your course. Developed exclusively to support OUP International Relations titles, these activities have been extensively reviewed by users of similar digital content in their classrooms. Several assignment types provide your students with various activities that teach core concepts, allow students to develop data literacy around important contemporary topics and issues, and to role play as decision makers to engage with problems that simulate real world political challenges. Each activity includes an auto-graded assessment so students can immediately see their level of knowledge of the content under study and is optimized to work on any mobile device or computer. For users of learning management systems, results can be recorded to the gradebooks in one of several currently supported systems. Access to these activities is free with purchase of a new print or electronic textbook. These and additional study tools are available at www.oup.com/he/Boyer, through links embedded in the enhanced eBook, and within course cartridges. The activities are described below:

Interactive Activities: Several activity types are included with this text's digital learning materials—whether putting students in the shoes of a decision maker in simulations of real world events, teaching them basic core content, or asking them to engage with data around contemporary global political issues, these features take your student's learning beyond the book. Designed to be assigned as homework, these activities take approximately 5 to 20 minutes to complete and conclude with assessments to show students their performance. These assessments can also be automatically recorded in an LMS gradebook when used in an interoperable way. Contact your local Oxford University Press sales representative for more information. Topics include:

> ***Stopping an Epidemic***
> ***Building the USS Relief***
> ***Intervening in Bhutan***
> ***Preventing World War***
> ***Keeping the Peace in Gineau-Bissau***
> ***Negotiating with China***
> ***Negotiating the Lisbon Protocol***
> ***Acting as President***
> ***Free Trade***
> ***Climate Change***

Video Activities: Each chapter incorporates several links to relevant, timely videos that allow students to see the real world relevance of the topics of their studies. Each video includes brief assessments to make the connection between course content and objectives and contemporary global issues.

Activities include:

Kinds of Bias That Shape Your Worldview

In Praise of Conflict

A Feminine Response to Iceland's Financial Crisis

Political Theory: John Maynard Keynes

Governments Don't Understand Cyber Warfare

Why Nations Should Pursue Soft Power

The Rise of Isolationism

How Nationalism and Globalism Can Coexist

How China Is (and Isn't) Fighting Pollution and Climate Change

The Intricate Economics of Terrorism

Terrorism as a Failed Brand

Inside the Mind of a Former Radical Jihadist

The Case for Optimism on Climate Change

100 Solutions to Reverse Global Warming

The Earth is Full

Online Study Tools: Many additional online study tools are available at www .oup.com/he/boyer for student's self-paced learning and assessment. For each chapter, these include interactive flashcards, chapter review PowerPoint slides, key terms quizzes, chapter quizzes, chapter exams, short answer essay tests, videos, web activities, and web links.

- **Learning Management System integration:** OUP offers the ability to integrate OUP content into currently supported versions of Canvas, D2L, or Blackboard. Contact your local rep or visit oup-arc.com/integration for more information.

Acknowledgments

The authors wish to thank all members of Oxford University Press, in particular executive editor Jennifer Carpenter, for her enthusiasm and support for this book project from the beginning. We are also grateful for the detailed guidance and feedback from Marian Provenzano, senior development editor, for the efficient work of Patrick Keefe to research art and security permissions, and the overall shepherding of production by Micheline Frederick. The OUP team has made this a better book and we hope we have upheld the high standards for which OUP is known.

Most especially, we would like to thank our students who continue to inspire us with their drive, passion, and curiosity about the world around them. Our students continue to shape and reshape our thinking on many of the themes and topics covered in this book. And we are grateful for the opportunity to learn alongside you in this ever-changing and complex world.

We are also thankful to the many reviewers who provided detailed edits and comments to early versions of this book project.

First Edition Reviewers:

Lauren Balasco, Stockton University

Michaelene Cox, Illinois State University

Robert Denemark, University of Delaware

Gigi Gokcek, Dominican University of California

Brian Greenhill, University at Albany, SUNY

Uk Heo, University of Wisconsin-Milwaukee

Derwin Munroe, University of Michigan-Flint

Angela D. Nichols, Florida Atlantic University

Jerry Pubantz, University of North Carolina at Greensboro

Clifton Sherrill, Troy University

Leslie Stewart, Delta State University

Jaroslav Tir, University of Colorado Boulder

Dr. John D. Van Doorn

Robert Weiner, University of Massachusetts Boston

About the Authors

Mark A. Boyer is a Board of Trustees Distinguished Professor at the University of Connecticut and serves as Executive Director of the International Studies Association (www.isanet.org). Throughout his career as a scholar-teacher, he has actively sought the integration of teaching, research, and service in all his professional activities. Public goods theory is fundamental to much of his teaching and research, as he seeks to bridge the theory-practice gap and help students to do so, as well. In addition to an array of journal articles, his books include *International Cooperation and Public Goods* (Johns Hopkins University Press, 1993) and *Defensive Internationalism* (University of Michigan Press, 2005; co-authored with Davis B. Bobrow). His most recent, and on-going, research project, *Adapting to Climate Change* is currently under contract with the University of Michigan Press. His professional awards include the UConn Honors Program Faculty Member of the Year (2015), the International Studies Association's Ladd Hollist Award for Service to the Profession (2009), the UConn Provost's Outreach Award for Public Service (2006), the UConn Alumni Association's Award for Excellence in Teaching at the Graduate Level (2004), the UConn Chancellor's Information Technology Award (2001), the American Political Science Association's Rowman & Littlefield Award for Teaching Innovation (2000), a Pew Faculty Fellowship in International Affairs (1992) and an SSRC-MacArthur Fellowship from 1986–88. He also served twice as editor for ISA journals: *International Studies Perspectives* (2000–2004) and *International Studies Review* (2008–2012; co-edited with Jennifer Sterling-Folker).

Natalie Florea Hudson is an Associate Professor of Political Science at the University of Dayton, where she also serves as the Director of the Human Rights Studies Program. She specializes in gender and international relations, the politics of human rights, human security, and international law and organization. Her book, *Gender, Human Security and the UN: Security Language as a Political Framework for Women* (Routledge, 2009) examines the organizational dynamics of women's activism in the United Nations system and how women have come to embrace and been impacted by the security discourse in their work for rights and equality. She has numerous articles appearing in journals such as *International Studies Quarterly, International Studies Review, Journal of Human Rights, International Journal, Simulation and Gaming,* and *Global Change, Peace & Security.* Her current research focuses on human rights and humanitarian advocacy campaigns focused on sexualized violence in conflicted-affected areas.

Michael Butler is an Associate Professor of Political Science and Director of the Henry J. and Erna D. Leir Luxembourg Program at Clark University in Worcester, Massachusetts. In 2014–15, he was a Fulbright Scholar at the Institute of International Studies, University of Wrocław (Poland). His research and teaching interests converge in the areas of conflict and conflict management, security studies, and foreign policy. He is the author of two books—*International Conflict Management* (Routledge, 2009), and *Selling a 'Just' War: Framing, Legitimacy, and U.S. Military Intervention* (Palgrave Macmillan, 2012), editor of a third, *Securitization Revisited: Contemporary Applications and Insights* (Routledge, 2019), with an additional monograph, *Deconstructing the Responsibility to Protect*, forthcoming (Routledge). He has published numerous articles in leading academic journals including *International Studies Quarterly,* the *Journal of Conflict Resolution,* the *Journal of Global Security Studies, International Studies Perspectives, International Studies Review,* the *Canadian Journal of Political Science, Global Change, Peace, & Security,* and *International Negotiation.* He has served on the editorial boards of *International Studies Review, Simulation & Gaming* and *International Studies Perspectives,* and is a member of the Governing Council of the International Studies Association-Northeast as well as a Senior Fellow at the Canadian Centre for the Responsibility to Protect (CCR2P) at the University of Toronto. Butler is series co-editor (with Shareen Hertel) of the International Studies Intensives book series (Routledge).

Global Politics
Applying Theory to A Complex World

Global Politics Matters

Every day, global challenges impact your life and your local community, either directly or indirectly. Maybe you decided to change your travel plans recently because of the threat of terrorist attacks or the potential health impact of the Zika virus in certain countries. Maybe you know someone whose work will be affected by Brexit, the 2016 British decision to leave the European Union. If you live in California, you may be thankful for the heavy rains in 2016 and 2017 that relieved the years-long drought, but those rains may also have sensitized you to the impact of climate change on your life and livelihood. You may even have a family member or friend who has been impacted by the travel restrictions on people from certain countries put in place by the United States through executive order in 2017.

Whatever the issue or situation, wherever it occurs, it will likely affect you or someone close to you. And in our ever-more interconnected world, the daily impact of global forces is growing. Each of the examples just mentioned illustrates how connected we are to events in the world well beyond our own control and how we must increasingly learn to manage global impacts in our everyday, seemingly local lives. The examples also help us think about what it means to engage as a global citizen, to act locally but think globally, and to constantly learn

In October 2018, thousands of men, women, and children, many of them Hondurans, gathered to journey north through Mexico to the US border to escape drug cartels, gang violence, and extreme poverty in their home countries. The attempt of these people to assert their right to seek asylum illustrates many concepts central to global politics, including the fluidity of borders, the history of migration, national and human security, and economic prosperity.

from our shared history and from the body of scholarship that continues to grow in this important field of study.

This book seeks to familiarize you with the history, theories, and practices of global politics as a distinct and increasingly interdisciplinary field of study. We also hope that this book develops your ability to think critically and theoretically about the complex world around you and the range of actors and institutions operating within it. Lastly, this book aims to equip you with the baseline knowledge to engage with and understand current events as an informed global citizen.

Learning Objectives

Discuss the ways that global politics directly and indirectly affects you and your world.

Discuss the complexity of global politics within the context of history and the changing types and roles of global actors.

🌐 Why Global Politics Matters

global politics Who gets what, how, and when around the globe. Used to describe the substantive focus of this book. Signifies that many interactions in today's world no longer fit with the term *international,* which implies that states remain the sole purveyors of global political activity.

Global politics, or who gets what, how, and when around the world, encompasses a wide range of issues that affect your financial health, the physical environment you inhabit, and your personal security. In many ways, economic impacts, such as those caused by unregulated trade and open borders, are the clearest and most acutely felt. Sometimes, specific events are economically costly. For example, in addition to the terrible human toll of the hurricanes Irma and Maria in 2017, the Puerto Rican government has estimated that it will cost $139 billion for the island to make a full recovery in terms of replacing destroyed property and infrastructure, restoring basic social services like schools and health care, and meeting other costs.[1]

Global economic issues often affect national affairs, and vice versa. For instance, the 2015 Canadian election, the 2016 Brexit vote in the United Kingdom, the 2016 US presidential election, and the 2018 election of Jair Bolsonaro in Brazil all centered to a large degree on national economic challenges that were caused in part by (or at least were perceived to be caused by) international processes and global institutions. Indeed, the interconnections between national and global affairs are so close that many social scientists now use the term **intermestic** to symbolize the intersection of international and domestic concerns.

intermestic Characterized by interconnectedness of international and domestic concerns. In decision-making, used to signify the merger of international and domestic concerns.

Global politics affects not only your economic well-being but also your physical environment—the quality of the air that you breathe and the water that you drink, how you get your food and clothing, and many other aspects of the world that you inhabit. One global environmental challenge involves climate change, which affects individuals, cities, and states in ever-expanding ways as sea levels rise and natural disasters (e.g., the hurricanes just mentioned) become increasingly common.

The 2018 report from the United Nations' (UN) Intergovernmental Panel on Climate Change (IPCC) indicates that even warming of half-a-degree Celsius could expose tens of millions of people to life-threatening heat waves, water shortages, and coastal flooding. Another important environmental challenge is the enormous growth of the world's population and its pressure on resources, which threatens to change the quality of life as we know it. It took 100,000 years of human existence for the world popula-

The devastation from Hurricane Maria is obvious in this picture. What seems less obvious to some decision-makers in the United States is the link to climate change and how it can dramatically impact the daily life of people around the world.

tion to reach 1 billion. Now, only a little more than 200 years later, the population numbers 7.7 billion people.[2] As Figure 1.1 shows, each additional billion people have been added more quickly. Although growth rates have been declining slightly, the UN Population Fund predicts that world population will reach over 11 billion by 2100.[3] Later in the book, we will discuss the concept of carrying capacity and how population pressures interfere with the ability of the Earth to sustain so many inhabitants. Beyond the pressures on natural resources and the diversity of our ecosystem, we also have to think about how our global community will prepare to educate and create jobs for a growing youth population as well as how best to take care of an aging population across the world.

Finally, global politics also affects your personal security. Disease and the potential for violence are just two threats to life that are connected to global politics. Although these threats are unlikely to affect you personally, they represent what are often called **high-value, low-probability problems.** Such problems are not very likely to occur but will be extremely serious if they do. Low-probability problems can become much more urgent if policy-makers do not deal with them. The 2015 Iran nuclear deal is an example of this kind of challenge. Under the agreement with the United Kingdom, France, Russia, China, Germany, and the United States, Iran agreed to limit many of its nuclear activities and allow international inspectors access to ensure compliance in return for the lifting of crippling economic

high-value, low-probability problems The nature of most problems or threats, in which the likelihood of a given individual being impacted is very low but the consequences if it occurs are very serious.

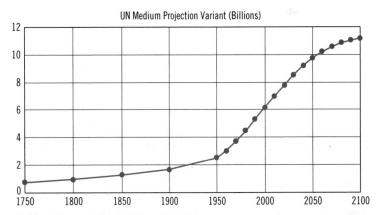

Figure 1.1   Global population will continue to grow for most of the next century, putting even more stress on the ability of Earth to sustain life as we know it.

Averting conflict in the global system depends heavily on building relationships of trust and predictability where possible. In this 2015 photo, US Secretary of State John Kerry speaks with Hossein Fereydoun (center), the brother of Iranian President Hassan Rouhani, and Iranian Foreign Minister Javad Zarif (right), before they announce the 2015 Iran nuclear deal, signed by the United Kingdom, France, Russia, China, Germany, and the United States. Under President Trump, the United States is no longer a party to the agreement.

3 Kinds of Bias
That Shape Your
Worldview

sanctions that Iran has long endured. (In 2018, President Donald Trump withdrew the United States from the agreement.)

As we move through the chapters of this book, one central theme emerges: we are facing complex problems that do not lend themselves to simple solutions. These problems affect us individually but also as a collective. It is important to consider both our own interests and shared interests in addressing and responding to the challenges our world faces. Ultimately, we study global politics because it allows us to grapple with interesting, complex, and consequential questions about ourselves and our world. In the next section, we will start to unravel the complexity that defines global politics.

Grappling with Global Complexity

Global politics is multifaceted and often overwhelmingly complicated. Why, for instance, were many of America's European allies much less supportive of US military actions in Iraq and Afghanistan in the early 2000s compared to the military intervention in the 1990s? Why do many countries support environmental sustainability with words and even signatures on environmental agreements but fail to live up to their commitments? Why is consensus on economic policies nearly impossible to achieve, even among the world's most developed countries? Although domestic politics is increasingly polarized, complex, and stalemated, global politics brings complexity to even higher levels. In this section, we address various aspects of this complexity. We then lay out some frameworks for understanding global politics from a diverse set of theoretical perspectives.

The Study of Global Politics

Before we go any further, it is worth spending a few moments discussing the recent evolution of the field you are now studying. Many topics of study in international relations (IR), such as the role of economic and cultural exchange in reducing conflict, can be traced back at least a millennium to Sanskrit discussions of ancient India, or even as far back as biblical times with the Book of Exodus and reflections on the role of diplomacy (Trushcke, 2016). For our purposes, however, we are going to focus on the modern study of IR, which arguably originated in response to the horrors of World War I with the establishment of the first chair in the field at the University of Wales, Aberystwyth, in 1919 (Carlsnaes, Risse, & Simmons, 2002). Since that time, scholarly interest in the causes of war and the conditions needed for peace has continued to evolve and grow into an interdisciplinary field of academic inquiry.

While IR is closely connected to the field of political science, the two are increasingly distinct. IR is informed by studies of diplomatic history, how culture affects international interactions, how our leaders think about and perceive the situations they confront, how economic forces constrain the actions of countries throughout the world, and how social structures around gender, class, and race reinforce patterns and trends of IR. Thus, any good student of IR must account for the fact that many academic disciplines inform our understanding of the world. For instance, within the International Studies Association (ISA; www.isanet.org), a leading forum of the study of global affairs, you can find special study sections on diplomatic studies, feminist theory, global health, history, technology, communication, law, sociology, economics, demography and geography, religion, and more. The eclecticism within the ISA is evidence of the varied perspectives that can be brought to bear on the topics in this book and in academic and policy studies as well.

The world itself is also constantly changing, which means that the tools used to analyze it must change. Decades ago, as the field of IR was developing, most of the interactions that took place in the world were between states, as we will discuss in more detail in later chapters. Today, however, the types of actors in world affairs are greater in number and more varied in type. As a result, the term *international relations* is sometimes viewed as anachronistic and inaccurate for studying today's world. We, the authors of this book, prefer the term *global* as more inclusive of the types of interactions that take place in today's world and the scope of the spaces where such interactions take place. This term better accounts for the multifaceted and dynamic processes of **globalization**, the increasing integration of economics, communications, and culture across national boundaries that will be discussed in Chapter 5. Thus, we use the term *global* most of the time in this book unless there is a specific reason not to do so, such as when we talk about a bilateral relationship (which, indeed, may remain international).

Similarly, we have chosen not to use the term *international relations* as the title for this book. Instead, we use *global politics*. But why keep *politics* in the terms we use and the title of the book, you may ask? Why not *global relations,* or *global affairs,* or even *world affairs?* Very good question. Some of it has to do with our own educational backgrounds (we all earned our PhDs in political science); some of it has to do with which classes will find this book a helpful educational tool; and some of it has to do with the linguistic conventions that still keep most academic study tied to specific disciplines each often having its own language, theory, and methods. It also has a lot to do with our desire to keep questions about power—who has it and who does not—as a central theme of this book. (We will take up the concept of power in great detail in Chapter 3.)

Global Actors

As testimony to the movement away from the international to the global, this section focuses on the diversity of actors that now populate global politics and are the focal points of this book. Unlike the actors in most of your

In Praise of Conflict

globalization A multifaceted concept that represents the increasing integration of economics, communications, and culture across national boundaries.

state A political actor that has sovereignty and a number of characteristics, including territory, population, organization, and recognition.

sovereignty The most essential defining characteristic of a state and perhaps the global system. The term strongly implies political independence from any higher authority and also suggests at least theoretical equality.

anarchy A fundamental concept in global politics identifying the lack of a governing authority in the global system and the implications it has on global interactions.

international organizations Organizations with an international membership, scope, and presence. There are essentially two types of international organizations—intergovernmental and non-governmental organizations.

daily interactions, most actors involved in global politics are organizations, not people. This does not mean that we should downplay the influence of individuals in global politics, but rather that we need to recognize organizations as groups of people with established practices of interaction that condition the impact of individuals. In other words, groupings of people often act not merely as collections of individuals, but behave in their own ways. This is why we have psychologists (who study individuals) and sociologists (who study groups).

States (or countries) are one type of organizational actor, and they are the primary actors in global politics. Currently, the global community includes almost 200 states, but as is obvious when you read any newspaper or watch the news, some states are more involved in global politics (or seem to matter more) and some less so. A variety of factors including (but not limited to) power, history, and geographic location dictates this level of involvement. Regardless of a state's power and position relative to others, states' central organizing principle is that of **sovereignty**. Sovereignty is the authority of the state to govern itself autonomously and is based on recognition by other states and nonstate actors. Even though sovereignty is not always enjoyed equally by all states, this sovereign status separates states from other actors in world affairs.

State sovereignty also means that no world government controls the actions of states in the way that a federal government controls lower governmental units within its borders. This lack of central governing authority—a condition called **anarchy**—has varying consequences for state interactions, not the least of which is a system where states and other global actors are often in conflict with one another. Although all states are legally equal, the reality is that states participate in the global system in different and asymmetric ways. The United States is among the few states that hold a position of privilege and therefore power, exercising significant influence over global interactions. Other states in privileged positions include China, Russia, Japan, and Germany. Conversely, countries like Andorra, Vanuatu, and Gambia have much less power and influence over global interactions—and in some cases even over their own affairs. For all states, state sovereignty is often viewed as eroding because of such sociopolitical forces as the Internet, social media, and global financial markets, just to name a few.

Even though states hold the global legal status that sovereignty brings, **international organizations,** groupings of actors that often center around a particular issue, are playing increasingly significant roles in contemporary global politics. The most prominent of

The UN General Assembly plays an agenda-setting role in global politics. So even without compulsory authority to enforce its decisions, it has successfully promoted issues to the global forefront over the past decades. The agenda-setting role has become even more important with the growth of former colonial Global South countries that became UN members from the later 1950s onward.

these are the 300 or so **intergovernmental organizations (IGOs)**, which are comprised almost entirely of states. Some are global, like the UN (see Figure 1.2) and the World Trade Organization; others are regional, like the European Union, the Organization of American States, and the African Union.

Even more numerous are transnational actors, such as Amnesty International, Greenpeace, and Oxfam, that reach across and even permeate states. One prominent example, **nongovernmental organizations** (NGOs), are formal legal entities distinct from the state, often operating not for profit, and primarily composed of individuals. Thousands of NGOs exist today, and their concerns touch virtually every aspect of international politics, ranging from the AIDS crisis (the International AIDS Society) to zero population growth (Population Connections) to human rights (Amnesty International).

Multinational corporations (MNCs) are private enterprises that have production subsidiaries or branches in more than one country. The energy company ExxonMobil and the agribusiness Monsanto are another prominent type of transnational actor. The annual earnings of some of these companies often rival the economic output of midsize states and dwarf most of the smaller ones. In a largely unregulated world economy where money is the source of power, MNCs are important players to consider.

Finally, individuals are also important actors on the world stage. Individuals usually exercise their influence on global politics as decision-makers, protesters, voters, or some other role within the bounds of a state, IGO, or NGO. Sometimes, however, individuals play roles that transcend national and other institutional

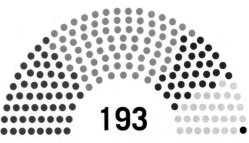

193

Division of the General Assembly by membership in the five United Nations Regional Groups.

▮ The African Group
▮ The Asia-Pacific Group
▮ The Middle and Eastern European Group
▮ The Latin American and Caribbean States (GRULAC)
▯ The Western European and Others Group (WEOG)
▮ No group

Figure 1.2   In contrast to the UN Security Council, the General Assembly is a universally representative body, with regional groupings shown here.

intergovernmental organizations (IGOs) Organizations that are global or regional in membership and scope and whose members are states.

nongovernmental organizations Formal legal entities distinct from the state, often operating not for profit, and primarily composed of individuals.

multinational corporations Private enterprises that have production subsidiaries or branches in more than one country.

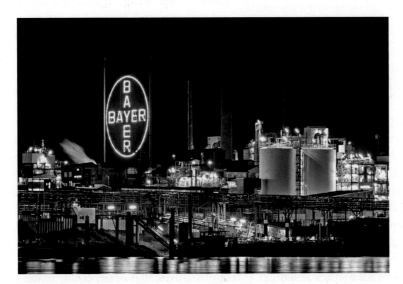

Multinational corporations play important roles in global affairs, especially when you consider their market dominance. The German chemical and pharmaceutical company Bayer acquired agricultural giant Monsanto in 2018, giving it even more influence in a broader set of global markets.

Edna Adan Ismail, Somalia's first qualified nurse-midwife, had a career with the World Health Organization. When she returned to Somalia, she donated her personal assets to help build the country's first maternity hospital.

boundaries. The Irish rock star Bono has made significant waves in crusading for various causes of importance to global affairs, including debt relief for the developing world and the HIV/AIDS crisis—a type of activism sometimes called "celebrity diplomacy" (Cooper, 2009; Matijasevic, 2015).

Ordinary people can also make a difference in the way the world works every day. Take Edna Adan Ismail, a Somalian woman who with great persistence obtained an education—a rarity for girls like her—and became her country's first qualified nurse-midwife. After working for the World Health Organization, Edna returned to Somalia to build the country's first maternity hospital. With the help of supportive donors, Edna completed her maternity and teaching hospital (Kristof & WuDunn, 2009). In a world where over 300,000 women die in childbirth each year—over half of them in Africa—maternal mortality is a critical area (*Maternal Health*, 2016). Starting with Chapter 3, each chapter will include a *Personal Narrative* feature that highlights the impact that individuals can and do have on global politics. We hope that you will be able to connect with these stories, perhaps seeing aspects of yourself in ordinary people across the globe doing extraordinary things.

Global History in Context

American philosopher and poet George Santayana wrote, "Those who cannot remember the past are condemned to repeat it."[4] His off-quoted statement provides a number of ideas that we will develop throughout this book. First, Santayana tells us that leaders must know something about history in order to learn, grow, and evolve, both as individuals and for their communities. Understanding history is essential to effective governance, citizenship, and democratic participation and choice. Second, Santayana implies that for us to understand the world around us, we must understand how it got to be this way. In other words, how has our history shaped what exists today, and how does it constrain what might emerge in the political world tomorrow? History provides us with many critical details of specific events, which we can often use to identify patterns and even make generalizations. While we can learn many lessons from history, however, we must avoid drawing simple conclusions from historical cases and be wary of using oversimplified political analogies to understand the complex dynamics of IR.

Following up on Santayana's thinking, this book will make a point of identifying the relevant historical context as it applies to each chapter's focus. In each chapter, it will be important to think about how history impacts the relevant actors in IR and the development and veracity of the theories that help us understand the patterns of global interactions we observe every day. As one IR scholar argues,

"History does not simply provide us with the story of our past, prudential truths, and antidotes to hubris, but perhaps more significantly, a greater capacity to craft our own collective and individual life stories, political or otherwise, as we strive to join the past and provide for the future" (McKeil, 2015). We encourage you to take seriously the historical context that is integral to all chapters that follow.

A key moment in this history is the **Peace of Westphalia** of 1648, which ended the Thirty Years War. This event is widely recognized by scholars as the birth of the modern nation-state system. The Treaties of Westphalia granted sovereignty to virtually all the small states in Europe, effectively ending the rule of the Holy Roman Empire or any other higher authority, such as the Church. The monarchs governing these new states were able to determine their own domestic policies, including the sect of Christianity practiced in a country and the development of national militaries.

The emergence and eventual triumph of the state as the dominant mode of governance and organizing principle had profound consequences for the nascent global system. One of these consequences was that states became the primary actors in the post-Westphalian international system, and they remain dominant, though increasingly challenged, today. Central to this state-centric system is the guiding norm of sovereignty, which is one of the most basic factors impacting state behavior.

The dominant place of the sovereign state in IR is a central reason why realism, one of the IR theories discussed in Chapter 2, has long been the dominant lens through which to analyze it. Realism's focus on the state as the primary actor in world affairs and on the state's monopoly of power allows the theory to provide powerful and logical explanations for much of what we will discuss throughout this book and observe every day in the news. From this perspective, we often explain the international system in terms of **polarity**, or concentrations of state power, such as the bipolar system that defined the Cold War or the evolving multipolar system that characterized the 1990s and beyond. But realism's dominance began to break down with the emergence of new thinking about the future of diplomacy and IR in the early 20th century, which focused on the rise of economic issues in global affairs and the growing role of nonstate actors in the system.

We suggested earlier that the historical dominance of the state is increasingly challenged today. One change has involved the weakening of the Western orientation of the international system as a result of an expansion in the number and power of non-Western states. The colonial empires established by the imperial Western powers collapsed after World War II, and in the ensuing years over 100 new countries gained independence. The vast majority of these new countries, as evident in Map 1.1, are located in the Global South, a term used to note that most former colonies and now developing countries are located south of the countries in the industrialized north. A few, like China, have achieved enough power to command global attention and challenge the United States for global leadership. Even the smaller Global South countries have gained a stronger voice through their membership in international organizations. For example, Global South countries now command a majority in the UN General Assembly, where all 193 member-states have one vote regardless of wealth, population, or geographic size (see Chapter 6). As discussed in greater detail in Chapter 9, the **Global North–Global South divide** is still a

Peace of Westphalia
The peace agreement signed in 1648 to end the Thirty Years War, effectively removing papal authority for dispute settlement in Europe. Viewed as the starting point for the modern nation-state system.

polarity The number of predominantly powerful actors in the global system at any given point in time.

Global North–Global South divide (or North-South divide) The economic disparities between the developed North and underdeveloped South that are the roots of tension in global forums. To a large degree, this cleavage is a legacy of colonialism.

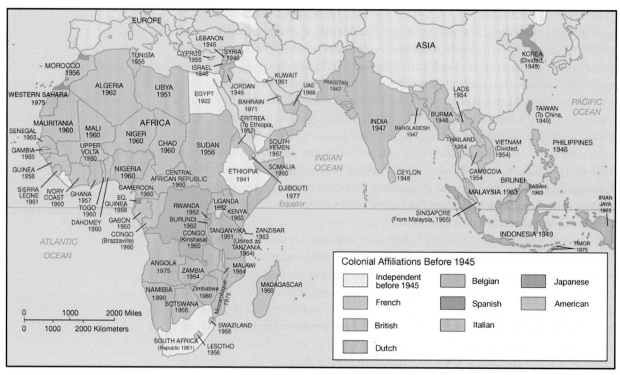

Map 1.1   Decolonization led to creation of many new countries in the Global South. This maps shows the progression of decolonization and symbolizes the rise of development issues onto the global political agenda.

relevant organizing principle for understanding politics, economics, and culture. This divide mostly exists because of inequalities across the economically developed North and the less developed South.

Underlying these empirical observations are some of the fundamental questions that guide this book: In an increasingly globalized world, what is the nature of the international system and the humans who live in it, how did we get here, and what is the future? How do we understand change versus continuity? For example, how do we interpret and analyze the fact that North Korean and South Korean leaders recently pledged to rid the peninsula of nuclear weapons and officially end the Korean War, which began shortly after World War II? The adjacent photo depicts a breakthrough peace summit between the two Korean leaders in 2018, an interaction that had not happened since 2007. The meeting produced five specific promises aimed at reducing military tension between the two states, which include holding high-level talks,

The symbolism in this photo is manifest. The leaders of North and South Korea are reaching beyond their country's boundaries to shake hands in disputed territory. But this meeting was indeed a breakthrough simply by the fact that the two leaders met face-to-face after many years of hostile diplomacy in various forms.

establishing a joint liaison office, destroying or moving back guardposts along the border, and facilitating meetings for families separated by the demilitarized zone (DMZ). According to a South Korean newspaper, *Hankyoreh*, more than one third of those promises have been kept.[5] Is this an instance of great change and a cause for hope in world affairs, or is it politics as usual? These are the kinds of questions that this book will examine to help you better understand, contextualize, and analyze current events.

Along with the rise of non-Western states, the fact that—as noted earlier—nonstate actors are rising to the fore in many IR venues is also affecting the system in the 21st century. The processes of globalization and the blurring of national boundaries have opened up new spaces for nonstate actors to grow, connect, and make a difference in global society. Nonstate actors range from humanitarian organizations and churches to foundations and businesses to terrorist networks and human smuggling rings. It is critical to consider nonstate actors operating in both official and illicit ways, along with whom these actors claim to represent and how much power they wield in the system. Globalization has empowered nonstate actors in both positive and negative ways, sometimes simultaneously. The Internet, along with innovations in technology, transportation, and even finance, make the world a place where states seemingly have less control over their citizens than was the case even twenty years ago. This is particularly important as we consider the role of nonstate actors, which we discuss in greater detail in Chapter 5.

In the end, then, the historical evolution of IR and the interactions that it entails impact which theoretical lenses are most valuable and accurate in their explanations of world affairs. In the next section, we will discuss why understanding theory matters. Then, in Chapter 2 we will examine five perspectives that are widely used in the study of IR.

Interpreting Global Politics

We have seen that considerable transformation is taking place around how the world is organized and how global politics proceeds. Long-dominant structures, ideas, and practices have changed substantially and at an increasing rate during the past century. Traditionally, global politics has been tumultuous and often violent, centering on independent and self-interested countries using their power to compete against other countries in a largely anarchic global system where there is no central authority to set and enforce rules and resolve disputes. Although this remains a central characteristic of global politics, new trends and forms of interaction are emerging, and it is critically important to examine which states are reinforcing which trends. For instance, according to the 2017 report from the Global Peace Index, the world is getting more peaceful, with 93 countries seeing improvement. The data, which take into account everything from wars to the level of government weapons purchases to homicide rates, incarceration rates, perceptions of criminality, political repression, and suppression of free speech, shows 68 countries actually getting worse; these include the United States and the Middle East.[6] Some of the differences that distinguish the traditional conceptions of global politics from evolving trajectories are shown in Table 1.1.

You might note that the evolving trajectories shown in Table 1.1 suggest growing complexity in the global system, and there is tangible evidence of this

CNN Asks Egyptians

Table 1.1 Traditional Conceptions and Evolving Trajectories

ATTRIBUTE	TRADITIONAL CONCEPTIONS	EVOLVING TRAJECTORIES
Human organization	National societies	Multiple identities and community affiliations: global, regional, local; religious, ethnic, race, gender, class
Interests	National interests	Global and regional interests; local identity-based interests
Predominant interactions	Competitive zero sum	Mixture of cooperation and competition; not zero sum
Pursuit of security	Focus on the national	Multiple focal points of security across actors and issues
Pursuit of prosperity	Economic nationalism	Mutual effort; recognition of interdependence; management of globalization
Locus of authority	Sovereign states	Many, including international organizations, individuals, nongovernmental organizations, subnational groups, and more
Conflict resolution	Power-centric	Law- and norm-centric in addition to power-centric

trend. First, the evolving trajectories in global politics reflect how we interact as individuals inside our own countries. Certainly, we pursue our own interests in domestic systems, with considerable freedom to do so, and we partly rely on ourselves for our own safety and welfare. In domestic political systems, however, individuals also recognize rules and norms, are accountable for obeying them, and have some sense of common identity and shared responsibility to achieve the common good and help struggling members of society.

Second, although the traditional conceptions continue to be essential to the way we analyze global politics, they are not as dominant as they once were in academia or in the policy community. If a century ago a professor had written a global politics book predicting a world organization with 193 countries as members (the UN), a legal community of 28 European countries (soon to be 27 with Brexit), the virtual disappearance of tariff restrictions under the World Trade Organization, or tens of billions of dollars a year in economic aid flowing from rich to poor countries, that book, if printed at all, would have been consigned to the fiction section of the library.

Exploring and comparing the traditional conceptions and the more complex evolving trajectories underlies almost all the content of this book. In Chapter 2, we will consider several ways to think about global politics theoretically, some of which map closely to the traditional and evolving columns of Table 1.1.

Thinking Theoretically: Tools for Studying Global Politics

Organizing our thinking about world events is important because it allows each of us to make sense of what is going on in the world—recurrent terror attacks in Europe, the Middle East, and the United States; the spread of the Zika virus (among other communicable diseases); the rise of computer hackers as new actors in world affairs; or the ebb and flow of the global economy. Given the impact that seemingly random events have on our daily lives, organizing our thinking about them gives us a chance to plan and act in ways that help us live productive and secure lives.

To get a better perspective on these and other stories, we must put them in both historical and theoretical context. Several theoretical perspectives will be developed in more detail in Chapter 2, and we will draw on theory throughout the book to help analyze events from diverse perspectives. This often means melding current happenings with theoretical lenses and historical context. For example, in the ongoing Brexit situation, it is worth noting the United Kingdom's historically conflicted re-

Even with NAFTA, free trade hasn't really been all that free. Until recently, Mexican trucks had to unload their goods into US trucks to cross the border. Now, Mexican trucks can cross with their goods and travel into the United States for their deliveries, making trade a little freer in the process.

lationship with the European project from the 1950s onward, as well as the struggle between state sovereignty and evolving supranationalism among the European Union countries. We will cover the history of the global system in later chapters and also set up relevant historical backdrops necessary to understand the issues, concepts, and theories in each chapter. As you will see throughout the book, we need to draw on both history and theory to help us better understand and think critically about the world around us.

As we seek to explain and think systematically about global politics and all its complexities, the use of theories becomes an indispensable tool in our toolbox. **Theory** allows us to describe, explain, and even predict phenomena. Theories help us distinguish which facts are important, what questions we should be asking, and who really counts. For instance, theories have allowed some analysts to argue that the spread of Zika is evidence of lax health standards in many developing countries and a lack of effective global health institutions. Some might argue that the spread is also an artifact of problematic immigration and travel medicine standards. Map 1.2 illustrates the spread of Zika in a relatively short time period from locales in South America throughout much of the Western Hemisphere.

With these aspects of theory in mind, consider, as you begin to think theoretically, this advice from James Rosenau (2004:330):

> [Thinking theoretically] is a technique that involves making a habit of asking a six-word question about anything we observe. . .—. The six-word question seems quite simple at first glance. It is: "Of what is this an instance?"

The "this" in the question is anything you observe (be it in world or personal affairs), and it is a powerful question because it forces you to find a larger category in which to place what you observe. That is, it compels you to move up the conceptual ladder and engage in the theoretical enterprise. There are many

theory An interconnected set of ideas and concepts that seeks to explain why things happen and how events and trends relate to one another. Theories allow us to explain and even predict the occurrence of various phenomena.

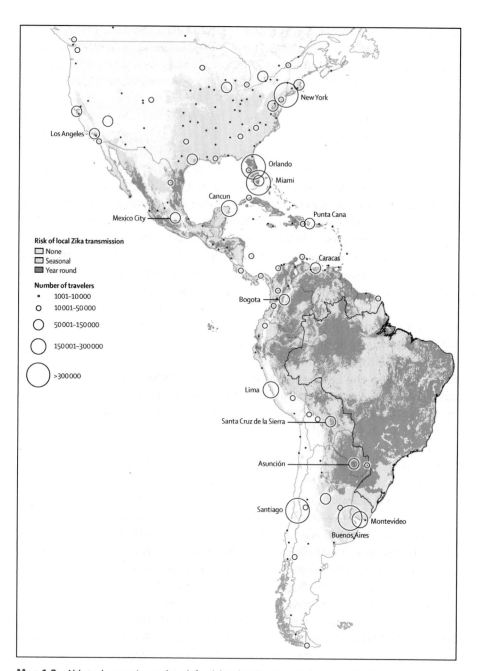

Risk of local Zika transmission
☐ None
☐ Seasonal
■ Year round

Number of travelers
· 1001–10000
○ 10001–50000
○ 50001–150000
○ 150001–300000
○ >300000

Map 1.2   Although countries work to defend their borders, health threats don't abide by national boundaries and carry no passports. The spread of Zika in recent years illustrated on this map presents a case in point.

advantages to thinking theoretically, but perhaps the most important one is that it will help you to better understand your own underlying assumptions and more critically analyze why you think what you do.

Other reasons for thinking theoretically include the simple notion that such thinking helps us build knowledge. If we confine ourselves to treating every event as unique, then our past and present are little more than a complex jumble of seemingly random events. By thinking theoretically, we look for patterns that help us understand more clearly what has occurred and, perhaps, even predict what may occur. Thinking theoretically also gives us a better chance of evaluating policy. One example is assessing the debate over whether the democracies in the Global North should work to promote democratization throughout the Global South. Chapter 9 provides some insight into the exploration of the "democratic peace theory," which is the idea that democratic states seldom, if ever, go to war with one another (Chernoff, 2004). If this theory is correct, then the path to world peace may be through democratization throughout the world. This would make promoting democracy not simply an altruistic ideal but also a significant contribution to global security. Lastly, thinking theoretically pushes us to think more critically about our own biases and assumptions as we examine our world. In this way, "thinking about how we think" helps us to ask new questions and opens our minds to alternative perspectives.

As you begin to think about events and to decide "of what is this an instance," do so expansively, and do not worry at least for now whether your ideas seem controversial or even contradictory. James Rosenau (2004) once ended up with 23 answers when he thought about one event and then asked himself "of what it was an instance." From such beginnings, you can test and refine your thinking to see what seems to hold up and what does not.

You will encounter discussions of various theories throughout this book. A good place to start in these discussions is to consider a range of ideas that have been put forth to address the study of global politics in its most general terms. To that end, as mentioned previously, Chapter 2 presents five different theoretical perspectives. Two, realism and liberalism, are arguably the dominant schools of thoughts in IR. The other three, world systems, feminism, and constructivism, present thought-provoking challenges to their dominant counterparts. That said, there is increasing theoretical diversity in our field, and Chapter 2 reflects that intellectual and academic reality and the cognitive diversity that each of us, as an observer and a participant in global politics, brings to the game. Also watch for the *Thinking Theoretically* features that start in Chapter 2. These features will focus your attention on theory applied to real-world settings and will help you develop the analytic tools you need to make your own critical decisions about global politics.

Before we take up these schools of thought in detail, several intellectual caveats are in order. First, none of the theories discussed in Chapter 2 are truly comprehensive. Some scholars argue that even realism and liberalism are "best described as paradigm[s]" rather than full-scale theories (Geller & Vasquez, 2004:1).

Second, each theoretical perspective has numerous variations because "[i]f you put four IR theorists in a room you will easily get 10 different ways of organizing theory, and there will also be disagreement about which theories are relevant in the first place" (Jackson & Sørenson, 2003:34). There are, for instance, classical realists, neoclassical realists, offensive realists, defensive realists, and other kinds of realists (Schmidt, 2004). We will briefly note some of these subdivisions in the sections of Chapter 2 but mostly concentrate on the major premises of the theories discussed.

Third, do not be fooled by the connotations of realism and liberalism. Realists do not necessarily see things as they "really" are. Also, do not equate the use of "liberal" here with left-of-center political parties in American domestic politics. In this context, liberalism is more closely tied to the writings of 18th- and 19th-century political philosophers like Jean-Jacques Rousseau, Adam Smith, Immanuel Kant, and Thomas Hobbes than it is to US politics and policy implementation. For example, someone might consider President Barack Obama to be a liberal in American politics, but one might better understand his approach to some foreign and security policy situations through a realist lens.

Fourth, try to focus on what each theory has to offer rather than its shortcomings. Each of these approaches helps us to better understand world politics. Each also has its weaknesses and biases, as you will come to understand throughout this book. There are considerable overlaps among theories as well, not only in terms of what they try to explain but even in the manner by which they try to explain it and some of their key assumptions about human behavior and social structures.

Lastly, and perhaps most importantly, recognize that the theories presented in Chapter 2 are not the hypothetical ramblings of abstract scholars in the field of IR. Rather, they result from years of concept development, rigorous critique, and empirical testing by both scholars and practitioners. As a result, every time a theory is used by an analyst, it is refined both conceptually and empirically. This is one reason why so many variations exist within a given approach. This community of scholar-analysts undertakes theory development to advance knowledge and understanding to (hopefully) improve the world around us. Thus, theory does not just emerge out of someone's imagination or mere opinion. Rather, it is the product of engagement with the field of study and the long-term observation of actors, processes, and issues, as well as their interactions.

Ultimately, the goal of this book is to help you see the value and relevance of IR theories in trying to analyze historical and contemporary events and explain decision-making processes in thoughtful ways. Such an empirically based and theoretically sound approach will allow you to better understand how globalizing processes and forces are transforming world politics and what these economic, political, social, and cultural shifts mean for states and individuals. As mentioned, it will also allow you to better understand your own biases and perspectives on the world around you. One feature that starts in Chapter 2 is *Challenge Your Assumptions*; the goal here is to push you to think critically and raise questions

It may be hard to imagine that four deceased white men continue to have such an impact on world affairs and your daily life. In clockwise order from the upper left, Jean-Jacques Rousseau, Adam Smith, Thomas Hobbes, and Immanuel Kant were some of the seminal thinkers who helped shape the development of democracy and capitalism several centuries ago. Their writings remain relevant to our understanding of domestic and global society and politics today.

about certain subjects that are often beholden to conventional thinking, long-held stereotypes, and even misperceptions. We hope this feature encourages you to be curious about your own belief system and that which you hold to be true. With that said, we now move to the theories in Chapter 2.

Chapter Summary

- It is important to think about the many ways global politics directly and indirectly affects your daily lives, from your environment and health to your wallets and the clothes you wear to the places you go and the social networks you engage with.

- While the global system is most often characterized by sovereign states existing in a state of anarchy, nonstate actors and globalizing forces are increasingly exerting power and influence, moving us away from IR to global politics.

- In addition to states, which have traditionally been the focus of IR, new actors have arisen within the global arena. These include intergovernmental organizations (IGOs), nongovernmental organizations (NGOs), and multinational corporations (MNCs).

- We improve our understanding of world politics by putting events within the context of history and applying various theories to see patterns and make generalizations about the conduct of global affairs.

Critical Thinking Questions

1. Consider how your life is impacted by the world around you. What do you see as the most important way your life is affected by global affairs? How is your life most regularly affected?

2. For many college students, studying theory might sound boring. Explain to your roommate at least three reasons why thinking theoretically is important.

3. Draw global politics *or* international relations. Don't worry about your artistic ability, but think carefully about who and what is emphasized in your drawing, the issues you see as central, and the nature of the system. What does your drawing say about your worldview and basic assumptions of the way the world works? Compare your drawing with those of others in the class, and hypothesize about their worldviews.

Key Terms

anarchy	high-value, low-	international	Peace of Westphalia
Global North–Global	probability problems	organizations	polarity
South divide	intergovernmental	multinational	sovereignty
global politics	organizations	corporations	state
globalization	intermestic	nongovernmental	theory
		organizations	

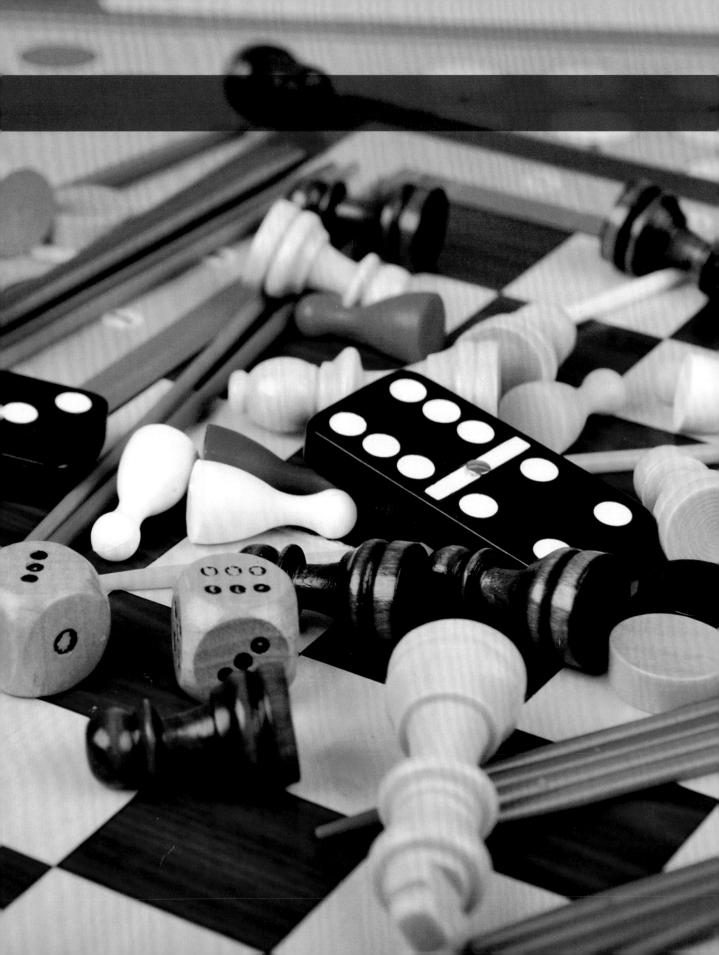

Theory Is Everywhere

Theory is everywhere. This is because a theory—or the lens through which we see and interpret global politics—in the social sciences is largely a composite of a set of assumptions about how the world works. Almost everyone has some conception of how global politics works (or should work), some set of guiding assumptions or preconceived notions, and none of those conceptions can be scientifically proven to be "true" or "false." Taking those two considerations into account, the statement that "theory is everywhere" makes a lot of sense. Multiple competing explanations, drawing on a wide range of assumptions, are constantly being advanced from all corners as a way of claiming "truth" about the "facts" of global politics.

The main goal of this chapter is to provide a basic roadmap to navigate this complex and sometimes messy landscape of IR theory. As such, this chapter gives you initial exposure to the basic logic of the five most prominent and enduring theories or "lenses" in the field of IR. The chapters that follow will return consistently to these theories to help deepen your understanding of them by providing examples of how they have been used to understand the "real world" of global politics. Though none of these theories individually provides a complete or perfect explanation of the way global politics works, each plays an important role in helping all of us process information and systematically organize our thoughts about some

Some theories approach the world as a game, where strategy and moves can be predicted with some degree of confidence. In our diverse world, though, there are many games from many countries, with strategies and tactics that are often conditioned by centuries of culture, history, and sociopolitical interaction.

aspect(s) of it. You may find one or more—or none—of these theories convincing. More important from our standpoint is that you gain a familiarity with the main competing lenses used to interpret and explain the nature of global politics, so that you too can analyze the world around you in a systematic and evidence-based way.

Learning Objectives

Identify five theories that help to improve our understanding of global politics and to interpret the behavior of states, societies, and individuals.

Explain the principles of realist theory and the focus on the self-interest and promotion of the state and nation.

Outline the principles of liberalism and how the world has moved in this direction during the past century.

Discuss world systems theory and its challenge to the paradigms of realism and liberalism.

Describe constructivism and impact of ideas, norms and identities.

Discuss feminist theory and the way in which global politics is structured around socially constructed conceptions of gender and the intersection with political and economic power.

Theoretical Perspectives: Diverse Views on Global Politics

What is your own worldview with respect to global politics? Do you think that military power is the primary means that states use to pursue their goals in the world? To what extent should considerations of justice and fairness factor into your understanding of global political processes and outcomes? What issues and which actors do you think are the most important in contemporary global politics (and even in domestic politics, remembering that domestic concerns mix with global issues)? What views do your parents have about global politics? (Yes, believe it or not, one of the most accurate—though imperfect—ways to understand what you think is to understand what your parents think!) How have your views on global politics changed from when you were in high school? These types of questions should help you reflect on your implicit and explicit assumptions about the way the world works. We ask that you keep these questions in mind as you read this chapter (and those that follow). Think about the theories we introduce in this chapter, and consider which of the five best fit your own perspective. Maybe none of them do, or maybe aspects of all of them do. For now, though, try to keep an open mind about all of them.

Along these lines, theories generally have both empirical (factual) and normative (value-based) aspects. Empirically, any good theory should provide an insightful description and explanation. That is, the theory should help interpret past and current events in a way that tells you "of what is this an instance of" (to recall Rosenau's standard from the closing section of Chapter 1). A more difficult but still valid test of the empirical worth of a theory is how well it enables accurate prediction. So, one thing that you can do to evaluate the different theories is to watch developing events, think about how each theory would predict their outcomes, and then see which one proves most accurate. The predictive power of theory has been central to debates in social sciences about the value of theory for decades. As we will see throughout this book, however, there is little consensus about whether prediction is possible—and about whether analysts should even pursue prediction as part of theory.

Prescription is another, and related, attribute of many theories. Prescription involves policy advocacy, arguing what policy should be on the basis of a set of theoretical principles about how things work. In this way, prescription takes the analytical strength of a theory and uses it not only to advance predictions about behavior, but also to offer recommendations about the best responses to cope with or manage that behavior. The prescriptive use of theory is one answer to the question "Why does theory matter?" But it also reveals challenges and problems. The recurring policy challenges posed by the North Korean nuclear crisis are in part a product of the shortcomings of theory. Without a theoretical "lens" that can effectively and consistently predict the behavior of the North Korean regime, decision-makers from Clinton to Bush to Obama to Trump have often been left to make educated guesses about the intentions, assumptions, and interests of Kim Jong-Un or his predecessor and father, Kim Jong-Il. Here, one can see the utility of theory in application, as a guidepost for effective policy-making—or, in its absence, as a limiting factor.

In most instances, you can use the prescriptive aspect of theory to organize your views about what your country's foreign policy, and the future course of world politics, should be. If you do so starting with a solid grounding in theory, you will begin to see each event and situation as part of the ongoing patterns of events connected to human nature, value systems, and key historical events. And as we discussed at the close of Chapter 1, it is helpful to remember that each of the perspectives discussed here is the product of years of rigorous intellectual theorizing and empirical analysis. That doesn't mean they are perfect or even mostly correct; no social theory is designed or should be expected to predict 100% of outcomes. But it does mean that significant numbers of scholars and practitioners use these approaches to analyze world affairs and see value in using them to organize their thinking, analysis, and conclusions about global politics.

Ultimately, one of the goals of this chapter—and of this entire book—is to help you work through the process of what James Rosenau (2000) called "thinking theory thoroughly." One of the ways in which we hope to achieve this goal is through the recurring *Thinking Theoretically* features in this book (see Table 2.1).

Table 2.1 **Thinking Theoretically**

CHAPTER	CHAPTER TITLE	FEATURE TITLE
Chapter 1	Global Politics Matters	Tools for Studying Global Politics
Chapter 2	Theory Is Everywhere	Playing the Prisoner's Dilemma Game
Chapter 3	Interpreting Power: A Levels-of-Analysis Approach	Levels of Analysis Meets Realism
Chapter 4	Nations and States: Past, Present, and Evolving	Contending Views on Nationhood
Chapter 5	Globalization and Transnationalism: Forces of Integration and Disintegration	Liberal and Critical Feminist Perspectives on Gender Inequality in the Workforce
Chapter 6	International Organization: The Evolving Quest for Global Governance	The Neoliberal Legacy of Dag Hammarskjöld
Chapter 7	War and Terrorism	Clausewitz, War, and Realism
Chapter 8	Pursuing Security	The Drug War in Mexico
Chapter 9	International Law and the Search for Justice	When Is Justice Really Served?
Chapter 10	Global Political Economy: Protecting Wealth in the Global North	What Do Donald Trump and Bernie Sanders Have in Common?
Chapter 11	Global Political Economy: Searching for Equity in the Global South	Three Views of the Millennium Development Goals
Chapter 12	Human Rights: A Tool for Preserving and Enhancing Human Dignity	Explaining Where Human Rights Come From
Chapter 13	Global Political Ecology	Your World, Your Worldview

We now turn to the five major theories that we will draw upon recurrently throughout the book: realist theory, liberal theory, world systems theory, constructivism, and feminist theory. In the rest of this chapter, we will discuss the logic of each of these theoretical perspectives, document their major contributions, and consider the similarities and differences between and among them. But this is just a starting point—both with respect to this book and to your consideration of global politics going forward. Together, we will continue to encounter and grapple with these and other theories in later chapters where they are most relevant and can lend insight regarding the substance of that chapter. And undoubtedly, you will continue to encounter and grapple with them on your own, as you navigate global politics throughout your life. We also encourage you to ponder the argument and questions posed in the *Challenge Your Assumptions* feature, especially as it highlights the foundation of rationality that underlies several of the theories discussed in this chapter.

🌐 Realist Theory

realism The view that world politics is driven by competitive self-interest and that the central dynamic of the global system is a struggle for power among states as each tries to preserve or improve its military security and economic welfare.

Realism is based on the view that competitive self-interest, given the preeminent goal of survival, drives global politics (Morgenthau, 1946). Following from the basic assumption that anarchy reigns in IR, realists believe that the decisive dynamic among countries is a struggle for power in an effort by each to preserve

CHALLENGE YOUR ASSUMPTIONS

IR Theory and the Role of Rationality

The role of rationality is central to debates over IR theory. In basic terms, rationality can be understood as the process of systematic intellectual reasoning based on logic and information. This is a process we all undertake thousands of times every day as we navigate the major and minor decisions in our lives. Indeed, because it is such a (seemingly) basic and fundamental element of human existence, the two dominant paradigms discussed in this chapter—realism and liberalism—place a premium on the role of rationality in the decision-making of individuals (classical realism and classical liberalism) and in the behavior of states (neorealism and neoliberalism).

The assumption of rationality shared by realists and liberals points the two theories in very different directions. Realists assert that individuals will (individually or collectively) prioritize self-interest and survival; indeed, this is crucial to the belief on the part of realists that states are unitary rational actors (Waltz, 1959). Liberals also point to the very same reason, asserting that the rational faculties and capacities of human beings explain why people will (again, individually or collectively) learn to cooperate and seek out opportunities to collaborate.

Other theories place less emphasis on the assumption of rationality in their explanations for how global politics works, with some calling into question the assumption outright. Neo-Marxists and world systems theorists see rationality as quite powerful in explaining global politics, due in no small part to its central position in microeconomic reasoning about economic agents (firms and consumers). Capitalists and the "core" states that support them are behaving rationally as they seek out the highest rate of return through the means of global expansion and exploitation (Wallerstein, 2004).

The focus of constructivism on the power of norms explicitly calls into question the influence of human rationality relative to social forces. Whether an idea attains normative status or not has little to do with whether that idea is "rational"—that is, based on a systematic process of reasoning steeped in the unbiased consideration of evidence (Onuf, 1989). Feminist IR theorists have convincingly argued that the priority status leant to rationality is itself a highly gendered outcome rooted in the socially constructed idealizations of "masculinity" as inherently rational and "femininity" as inherently emotional, making it no surprise that rationality is touted by mainstream theories long dominated by men (Tickner, 2001).

What do you think? How important is rationality in explaining global politics? Are people—and, by extension, states, international organizations, nongovernment organizations, and the like—"rational"?

---

or, preferably, to improve its military security and economic welfare in competition with other countries. This competition for power takes place among all states (big and small, rich and poor) as they seek to improve both their absolute and relative security in an environment where they are uncertain of others' intentions (Mearsheimer, 2001). The result of such a competitive dynamic is, perhaps unsurprisingly, an IR prone to and rife with conflict and war, as well as oriented around arms races, competing alliance structures, espionage and intelligence gathering, and economic nationalism.

In light of this, it is not at all surprising that realists see this struggle for power as a **zero-sum game**, one in which a gain for one country is inevitably a loss for others. Realists also tend to see humanity as inherently divided by national loyalty to countries or to some other source of political identity, such as religion, ethnicity, or culture. Because these identities are best protected and realized through government, realists focus on states as the primary, if not

zero-sum game A contest in which gains by one player can only be achieved by equal losses for other players.

▲ **THINKING THEORETICALLY**

Playing the Prisoner's Dilemma Game

Although we do not consider it directly in this book, yet another theory of global politics deserves mention: rational choice theory. Rational choice theory in IR is specifically concerned with explaining decision-making as the microfoundation of all global political behavior. Grounded in microeconomics, rational choice theory assumes that every decision a person makes is informed by instrumental rationality—a process of rank-ordering one's preferences and seeking outcomes that provide for the greatest marginal utility (gain in well-being). Applied to global politics, this means that some actors will achieve such outcomes, while others will not. Rational choice theorists refer to these one-off interactions as "zero-sum" games. These interactions or "games" are further complicated by the imperfect information and uncertainty that surrounds them, leaving actors to make decisions that seem rational but turn out to be suboptimal. This concept of "bounded rationality" was identified long ago by the Nobel Prize–winner Herbert Simon (1976), and it lies at the heart of the most famous examples of game theory: the prisoner's dilemma, chicken, ultimatum, and various repeated interaction games

(Zagare, 2013). However, such suboptimal and conflicting outcomes can be overcome in structured, long-term interactions in which reciprocity influences strategic choices toward cooperation (Axelrod, 1984).

Rational choice theory is a fundamental element of game theory. For a social scientist, game theory models that explain and predict outcomes can be classified into three groups: purely cooperative games, in which players prefer and jointly benefit from the same outcomes; purely competitive games, in which one person's gain is another's loss; and mixed games, including the prisoner's dilemma, that involve varied motives of cooperation and competition. The prisoner's dilemma, for example, demonstrates how two rational individuals might not cooperate even if it appears to be in their best interests to do so. In what ways do we presume rationality in politics, in economics, in life? What are the limits to rationality? How would the outcome vary if the situation was repeated over time, building certain expectations and even trust between individuals? How do human relationships, such as those in foreign policy decision-making, affect rationality?

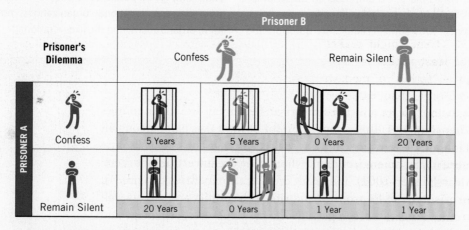

The Prisoner's Dilemma has been applied to many situations in social scientific study. Fundamentally, it illustrates the tension between personal self-interest and collective interest. That tension is often left unresolved with outcomes that are less than optimal for society.

the only, legitimate actors in IR. Considering states to be the only actors that "matter" stems, again, from anarchy and the survival imperative. To the extent that individuals and societies have any hope for survival at all within the "dog eat dog" international system—a "war of all against all" (*bellum omnium contra omnes*)—it is only through the mechanism of the sovereign state. Indeed, the primacy of the state in realist thought draws largely on Thomas Hobbes' presumption that the state (like the Leviathan) is willing and able to identify and undertake appropriate actions to ensure its own survival. As a result, the state is the actor best suited to provide stability and order to its citizens and subjects, and doing so in turn requires the state to protect its citizens and subjects from external threats as well as internal upheaval (Hobbes, 1651). In this way, states are the fulcrum on which all international interactions turn. One game theoretical approach and its relationship to IR theory is discussed further in the *Thinking Theoretically* feature.

Realism: An Emphasis on Power

Realists contend that struggles between states to secure their frequently conflicting national interests are the main impetus for foreign policy actions. Given this view, realists maintain that countries should, and usually do, base their foreign policy on the existence of what they see as a Darwinian world in which power is the key to national survival of the fittest. In the words of one scholar, "[i]n an environment as dangerous as anarchy," those who ignore realist principles will "ultimately not survive" (Sterling-Folker, 1997:18). From this perspective, realists define national interest mainly in terms of whatever enhances or preserves a state's security, influence, and military and economic power. We will explore this realist concept of power in depth in Chapter 3.

For realists, then, might makes right—or it at least makes for success. Indeed, the "father" of modern realism, Hans Morgenthau, reasoned that it is unconscionable for a state to follow policy based on such principles as justice and morality. He argued that "while the individual has a moral right to sacrifice himself" in defense of an abstract principle, "the state has no right to let its moral [views] . . . get in the way of successful political action, itself inspired by the moral principle of national survival" (1948:38). This statement does not imply that realists are amoral, however (Williams, 2004).

Power projection is an important indicator and symbol of influence in the world. Chinese naval personnel and vessels, shown here, give China a growing role in global political military affairs well beyond its borders.

A realist might argue that the highest moral duty of the state is to do good for its citizens. More moderate realists contend that surviving and prospering in a dangerous world requires that we weigh morality prudently against national interest. One scholar has summed up this realist rule of action with the maxim, "Do 'good' if the price is low" (Gray, 1994:8). In other words, don't let a desire to do good in the world get in the way of the state's pursuit of power maintenance and accumulation as it relates to other actors in the system. This type of calculation has been at the heart of many military interventions at least since the end of the Cold War. And in many respects, the "do good at low cost" adage is one reason why some realists strongly opposed American intervention in both Iraq and Afghanistan throughout the 2000s. In both cases, the costs were very high and the outcomes ambiguous.

Classical Realism and Neorealism

As realist theory evolved, it split into two schools of thought based primarily on different views about the root cause of the perpetual conflict that realists of all types believe defines IR. Classical realism emerged from the contributions of Thucydides, Machiavelli, and Hobbes (among others), and was synthesized for modern application in the early and mid-20th century by scholars such as E. H. Carr (1939), George Kennan (1951, 1954), and especially Hans Morgenthau (1946, 1948). Morgenthau distilled the insights of centuries of realist thinking in his "Six Principles of Political Realism," stressing in no uncertain terms that politics was a unique endeavor that turned exclusively on power and interests and in which morality and legalism had no place.

classical realism A branch of realist thought that believes the root cause of conflict is the aggressive nature of humans.

Classical realism fuses together assertions and beliefs, drawn from centuries of thinking about the human condition, regarding the primacy of self-interest over values, the obligation of the sovereign to rule with force when necessary, and the propensity of humanity toward violence when confronting scarcity, seeking prestige, or facing uncertainty. Tying these lessons together is a general pessimism about human nature. Indeed, the central theme of classical realism is that political struggle among humans is inevitable because of the inherently selfish nature of human beings.

To this point, Hobbes argued in *Leviathan* (1651) that humans have an inherent urge to dominate, which often causes them to "become enemies and . . . [to] endeavor to destroy or subdue one another." Similarly, Morgenthau (1945:17) described "the lust for power" in humans as a "ubiquitous empirical fact." For classical realists, these are enduring constants that no social arrangement can change—and we should expect conflict and violence to remain the enduring constant in IR as a result. Therefore, classical realists believe that it is foolhardy to trust other countries and their people (Brewer et al., 2004). As one realist puts it, "The sad fact is that international politics has always been a ruthless and dangerous business and it is likely to remain that way" (Mearsheimer, 2001:2).

neorealism A branch of realist thought that attributes the self-interested struggle for power among countries to the anarchic nature of the global system.

Neorealism also portrays global politics as a struggle for power, but neorealists believe that the cause of conflict is not human nature per se, or the individual choices and preferences that follow from it, but rather the anarchic (unregulated) structure of the global system (James, 2002). This central assumption explains why neorealists are sometimes called "structural realists." For neorealists, the lack of any effective central governing authority in the international system means that states, with no "higher" authority to turn to, are locked in a self-help struggle for survival at all times. The result of such a self-help system is that every country must rely on its own strength for security. However, because "there is no authoritative, impartial method of settling these disputes—i.e., no world government—states are their own judges, juries, and hangmen, and often resort to force to achieve their security interests" (Zakaria, 1993:22). In this structure, no state can be trusted; therefore, in making policy decisions, states must assume worst-case scenarios about one another.

The two schools of realism also disagree on how countries determine their foreign policies (Cozette, 2008). Classical realists prescribe that states and their leaders should suspend value judgments and instead follow the dictates of power, but they concede that they may not always do so (Williams, 2004). Instead, classical realists believe that national leaders can and do err by allowing morality, ideology, or considerations other than power realities to govern foreign policy (Kennan, 1951). In contrast, because neorealists believe that countries are **rational actors** and therefore will react similarly and predictably to power realities in a given situation no matter who is in office, they pay little attention to internal policy-making in countries (Waltz, 1979). Rather, these theorists are interested in ascertaining rules about how states react under the different sets of circumstances that arise in an anarchic global system.

rational actors The idea that people in general aim to maximize their utility and profit from action taken rather than acting against their self-interest.

Within the realm of neo- or structural realism are further important differences. Perhaps the central one for our consideration here is the difference between offensive and defensive realism. Both offensive and defensive realists emphasize the dominant role that the anarchic structure of the international system plays in explaining outcomes in IR. They also share the view that some **balance of power** among the great powers is the best (most stable) arrangement possible in an anarchic system, given the unlikelihood of achieving world government (Weiss, 2009) or hegemony (Kindleberger, 1973). Offensive and defensive realists differ significantly, however, with respect to how exactly anarchy impacts states.

balance of power A concept that describes the degree of equilibrium (balance) or disequilibrium (imbalance) of power in the global or regional system.

For defensive realists like Kenneth Waltz (1979), Barry Posen (1984), and Jack Snyder (1991), states are essentially status quo actors in a defensive posture. In this view, states undertake actions necessary to ensure their own survival but otherwise seek to avoid generating instability and disruption. While states may engage in war and conflict with one another, this is primarily the by-product of attempts to ensure their own survival—that is, to defend themselves—rather than to dominate other states. In the view of defensive realists, states do not necessarily desire or seek out war and conflict, but with nothing to stop this from happening, anarchy creates a permissive environment for war and conflict to occur as a by-product of the efforts of states to secure themselves.

A competing point of view among neo- or structural realists is that of offensive realism, as articulated by scholars such as John Mearsheimer (2001).

From this standpoint, the anarchic structure of the international system is, again, the most important consideration, but here, it is important for the opportunity it provides states to pursue war and conflict for opportunistic reasons—that is, to go on the "offensive" and capture gains so as to improve their relative position and better ensure their survival. In Mearsheimer's (2001: 31) words, "for every neck, there are two hands to choke it," which is a rather blunt way of saying that the lack of central governing authority under anarchy supports and even encourages states to behave aggressively toward one another, even to the point of actively seeking war for relative gain.

Uniting realists and neorealists of all stripes is the doubt that there is any escape from an IR defined by persistent conflict. Classical realists focus on the immutability of human nature, while neorealists focus on the characteristics of the international system. Yet both remain skeptical about the ability of interdependence or international organizations to promote cooperation (Sterling-Folker, 2002). It is also worth noting that another strand of realism—neoclassical realism—has been put forth as a way of unifying the classical and neorealist arguments (Foulon, 2015). First introduced in a seminal article by Gideon Rose (1998), neoclassical realism advances a synthesis of the neorealist emphasis on anarchy and the classical realist emphasis on human nature—focusing in particular on how individual perception and cognition as well as social dynamics at the domestic level impact how decision-makers understand, process, and interpret the actions and intentions of other states in an anarchic environment. This "guesswork" is imprecise and even risky, but it is also commonplace since few, if any, useful mechanisms exist for information gathering, exchange, and communication between and among states (at least in the realist view).

The dominance of realism as a theoretical lens for the analysis of global politics is well-established and is certainly manifest in the history of our field of study. The contributions of realist theory are many and varied, particularly with respect to the study of war and security. Realism has introduced and/or informed crucial concepts including polarity, the balance of power, the security dilemma, deterrence, alliance formation (balancing, bandwagoning, and buck-passing), and numerous others discussed throughout this book. Some would take this dominance and these contributions even further by arguing that realism is also a belief system that underlies thinking on the part of most everyday citizens (Kertzer & McGraw, 2012). We can even find realist thinking in the 2018 US National Defense Strategy that identifies great powers, like China and Russia, as greater threats to US national security than terrorist organizations, like ISIS. Yet as the rest of this chapter demonstrates, many IR scholars (and policy-makers) reject the central tenets of realism and its singular focus on states and material power, finding it insufficient to explain much of what transpires in contemporary global politics. These challenges have resulted in the development of various other theories, including the oldest and most prominent alternative to realist theory: liberalism.

🌐 Liberal Theory

Liberalism has long been the primary counterpoint to realism in IR theory. Liberals reject the realists' contention that politics is inherently and exclusively a zero-sum struggle for power. While liberals do not dismiss power and interests as factors explaining the conduct of IR, they do add morality, ideology, emotions (e.g., friendship and mutual identity), habits of cooperation, and even altruism as additional factors that may influence the behavior of global actors and the course of world politics.

Liberalism also holds that global politics need not be a zero-sum game and can in fact be a **positive-sum game**. In other words, it is possible to have win-win situations where the gains of one or more countries do not have to come at the expense of others and where mutual interests can be identified and achieved in ways that satisfy all parties. Liberals also are proponents of **cosmopolitanism** and, as such, are prone to think that all humans have a common bond they can draw on to identify themselves beyond the narrow boundaries of their country or identity group and to identify and forge ties with people around the world in ways that enhance the collective good.

liberalism The view that people and the countries representing them are capable of cooperating to achieve common goals, often through global organizations and according to international law.

positive-sum game A contest in which gains by one or more players can be achieved without being offset by losses for other players.

cosmopolitanism An understanding and appreciation of the shared human experience and the ties that bind people together across nations, borders, and cultures.

Liberalism: An Emphasis on Cooperation

Unlike realists, liberals do not believe that acquiring, preserving, and applying power for self-interested gains must be, or even always is, the essence of global politics. Instead, liberals argue that states can and do identify areas of mutual interest with other states and behave in a cooperative fashion to pursue and attain those interests. For instance, the growth and expansion of global commerce was born largely of a widely shared desire by the vast majority of states and their leaders to expand and diversify their economies and improve their material standards of living through international trade, investment, and consumption (as discussed in Chapter 10). Where this has been achieved, according to liberals, it is largely because states identified areas of shared interest and opportunity, cooperated in those areas, and created international institutions and agreements to sustain and deepen that cooperation (Moravcsik, 1997).

Similarly, the global expansion of democracy in three distinct "waves" (Huntington, 1991) since its emergence in the French and American revolutions is both a by-product of shared interests and cooperation and a means to the end of further and deeper cooperation, at least among democracies. To the extent that democracy is understood (especially by liberals) as the most effective and representative form of government, it promotes the interests of democratic nations and their citizens collectively and simultaneously. At the same time, liberals contend that the expansion of democracy provides additional opportunities for collaboration between those nations and their citizens due to their mutual respect and regard for the values, norms, and institutions around which their societies are built (Doyle, 1983).

Political Theory: John Maynard Keynes

It is important to note that liberals do not reject the importance of material gain and power, even within a cooperative international order. As discussed previously, material gains are actually a crucial catalyst for international economic cooperation, as reflected in the expansion of capital and trade flows over the past century (Russett & Oneal, 2001). But liberals also accept the continued (if declining) utility of military power in global politics. Indeed, liberals themselves are sometimes willing to use military force or other forms of coercion—though typically as a later if not a last resort—for the purposes of self-defense or in response to overt international aggression (Walzer, 1977). Many liberals also favor the use of military force, especially if authorized by the United Nations, to prevent or halt genocide and other gross violations of human rights and consider such occasions legitimate grounds for the use of military power, perhaps to the extent of constituting a "responsibility to protect" innocent people experiencing intense hardships or atrocities (Bellamy, 2009).

Beyond such clear-cut examples, though, liberals differ with respect to how material power should be used, and to what end. Some favor a concerted and assertive effort to expand and promote liberalism, even forcibly if need be—a strand known as **liberal internationalism**. It was this version of liberalism that led Woodrow Wilson to send American troops to Europe in an effort to "make the world safe for democracy" in a "war to end all wars," and that arguably led George W. Bush to invade Iraq to overthrow the authoritarian regime of Saddam Hussein in the hopes of fostering democracy. This school of thought hews more closely to classical liberal thought, and the views of Enlightenment thinkers such as Immanuel Kant (1795) and John Stuart Mill (1859), in arguing that liberal values and institutions should be left to emerge organically, without undue outside interference.

liberal internationalism   A theoretical perspective that seeks to transform international relations to emphasize peace, individual freedom, and prosperity by replicating models of liberal democracy globally through various foreign policy objectives.

CNN Video: Realism, Liberalism, the USA, and India.

Whatever the exact formulation, liberal thought has had a clear influence on the actions of some post–Cold War leaders, particularly in the United States. This influence is largely rooted in the conviction of most liberals that national interests and global interests can be, and oftentimes are, identical and interchangeable. Thus, for liberals, promoting improvements in global economic conditions, human rights, and democracy is very much in the national interest of the United States and other economically developed and democratic countries. Why? Because civil and political rights, democracy and free market capitalism are considered by most liberal thinkers to be universally and inherently appealing and beneficial (Fukuyama, 1989). Liberal internationalists consider it something of a "duty" for countries like the United States—that is, those with a democratic political system and market-based economy—to promote those arrangements in other countries (Miller, 2010).

Liberals tend to dismiss the realists' warning that pursuing ethical policy often works against the national interest. The wisest course, liberals contend, is that countries recognize that their national interests and the common interests of the world are inextricably tied. This liberal expansionism can take on an imperial, even messianic tone at times; echoing Wilson's resolve to make the world safe for democracy, President George W. Bush pledged that "America will . . . support democratic movements . . . with the ultimate goal of ending tyranny in our world."[1] The goal of "helping" others in ways that are beneficial to the United States as well provided the rhetorical foundation for President Obama's commitment in Afghanistan and in the fight against ISIS, as exemplified by his claim that "I've been very clear that we are going to move forward on a process of training [local citizens] so that they can provide for their own security."

Such views do not mean that Presidents Bush and Obama, and other decision-makers with liberal views, do not also pursue realist policies oriented around coercion and self-interest. In fact, during the George W. Bush administration, expansionist aspects of liberal internationalism were merged with a realist emphasis on military force in what is sometimes called "neoconservatism" (Goldberg, 2003). Thus, for many in the Bush administration, one stated purpose of the war in Iraq was to promote democracy, while another, less publicized rationale was to stabilize the geopolitics of the region and secure access to cheap oil for the United States and other advanced industrialized countries. Liberal internationalism was key to this doctrine, in that it helped underwrite the assumption that the global interest and the US national interest were in fact indistinguishable (Daalder & Lindsay, 2003).

Classical Liberalism and Neoliberalism

As with realism, we can divide liberalism into two main schools of thought. Similar to classical realism, **classical liberalism** is based on its proponents' views of human nature. In contrast to the pessimism of classical realists, however, classical liberals—heavily influenced by and indebted to Enlightenment-era thinking and its emphasis on the rational and perfectible human—are optimistic about human nature (Rousseau, 1750). They contend that, while still in many cases self-interested, our possession of rational faculties means that human beings are able to learn and, by extension, that society can evolve. As a result, people can come to appreciate the benefits of cooperation with one another as well as the risks and hazards of conflict—and in the process seek out opportunities for cooperation and collaboration for personal and collective gain. This idea is captured in Immanuel Kant's concept of "asocial sociability," whereby humans may not be inherently sociable but can and do learn to live collaboratively in society when incentives and opportunities to do so exist (Schneewind, 2009).

Undoubtedly, contemporary classical liberals trace their intellectual lineage to Enlightenment political philosophers such as Jean-Jacques Rousseau (1712–1778) and Immanuel Kant (1724–1804). Rousseau argued in *The Social Contract* (1762) that humans had joined together in civil societies because they found it easier to improve their quality of life and secure physical protection through cooperation than through competitive self-reliance. This stands in direct contrast to Hobbes' account that the social contract was maintained primarily through the overarching enforcement and control of the state ("the Leviathan"). Kant advanced perhaps the most vital contribution to classical liberal IR theory through his landmark work *Perpetual Peace* (1795). Sketching out a vision for

classical liberalism A branch of liberal thought that attributes cooperation to human nature and the understanding that people can achieve more collectively than individually.

an enduring peace in IR, Kant outlined three "Definitive Articles" that would provide the sure foundation: first, the civil constitution of every state should be republican; second, the law of nations should be founded on a federation of free states; and third, the law of world citizenship shall be limited to conditions of universal hospitality.

Individually and collectively, Kant's definitive articles provided a lasting blueprint for classical liberalism, in which liberal republics—the preferred form of government—gradually come to associate collectively and to cooperate, with that cooperation being knitted together and underwritten by cosmopolitan ideals and commercial and cultural exchange. It is not hard to see evidence of Kantian logic in popular examples of classical liberal thought such as Fukuyama's famous proclamation of an "End of History" and the triumph of liberalism (1989), or in the robust arguments in support of the democratic peace thesis, which argues that democracy is the key to peace given the "iron law" that no two democracies have gone to war with one another over the past two centuries (Levy, 1988) and the pacific tendency of democracies that this allegedly reflects.

neoliberalism The branch of liberalism that recognizes the inherent conflict in an anarchic global system but asserts it can be eased by building global and regional organizations and processes that allow actors to cooperate for their mutual benefit.

Neoliberalism, sometimes called neoliberal institutionalism (NLI), emerged in the 1970s and 1980s in a manner somewhat parallel to the emergence of neorealism, sharing the latter's emphasis on the international system rather than the individuals and states that comprise it. Accordingly, the "inside-out" emphasis of classical liberals on international cooperation emerging from the learned behavior of (liberal) states and the rational decision-makers and citizens who populate them is replaced with an "outside-in" explanation, in which cooperation is sustained and encouraged by international institutions (treaties and organizations).

Like neorealists, neoliberals also place a decided emphasis on the structure of the international system, and they agree with neorealists that competition among sovereign states in an anarchic world system causes conflict. Neoliberals, however, contend that as a result of the proliferation of international institutions, the structure of the system is not nearly as anarchic as neorealists claim; rather, these institutions coordinate and regulate the behavior of states and enhance cooperation between them, providing an increasing degree of global governance in the process. But how did we get to this point in which governance is beginning to supplant anarchy, at least in the minds of neoliberals?

complex interdependence The broad and deep dependence of issues and actors in the contemporary global political system that many scholars believe is a by-product of globalization.

According to neoliberals, the international system is defined by **complex interdependence**, the notion that countries are tied together through trade and many other global economic and social exchanges that both increase cooperation and limit conflict (Keohane & Nye, 2012). The linkages and exchanges characterized by complex interdependence are long-standing, varied, and leave states in a position where they are both vulnerable to shifts and disturbances in the global order and dependent on one another (Keohane & Nye, 2012). This vulnerability and dependency, though, is precisely what provides the incentives necessary for cooperation between and among states and other interested groups. Groups have cross-national ties and build relationships that don't rely on the relations of states. Since the problems and challenges are too big for states to manage individually, and the opportunities and benefits associated with cooperation too great for states to pass up, states have every incentive to explore cooperation.

The main thing stopping states from doing so is what economists call "transaction costs"—impediments to cooperation resulting from a concern about the enforceability of agreements, or the inability to communicate and coordinate positions in order to create those agreements in the first place. In the case of global politics, this is where international organizations come in, both as a means of providing for communication and coordination of positions and as a way of ensuring

South Korean farmers protest in the streets of Hong Kong against the World Trade Organization. Over the past two decades, protests against the role and power of global and regional organizations have remained potent as the tension between national interests and global trends plays out in the streets and even through voting.

the treaties and other cooperative arrangements that states enter into will be enforced and that defection and cheating will be discouraged and punished. An organization like the World Trade Organization is illustrative; created in 1995, it adjudicates trade disputes and ensures compliance with international trade agreements (e.g., the General Agreement on Tariffs and Trade) by parties to those agreements, even imposing financial penalties when violations of those agreements were identified.

Like classical liberalism, neoliberalism favors democratic political arrangements at the national level as a means to promote democracy at the global level. It also promotes the development and application of international law and the proliferation of stronger international organizations to manage the expanding ties among countries. Finally, neoliberalism also places special emphasis on international commerce as the area where cooperation between and among states and nonstate actors alike (corporations, nongovernmental organizations, international banks, and so forth) has progressed the farthest. Many neoliberals consider these three areas of activity not only related but mutually reinforcing, as reflected in Russett and Oneal's (2001) concept of the "Kantian triangle" (see Figure 2.1). The interactions between international organizations and law, democratic governance, and economic interdependence are viewed as key mechanisms for reducing anarchy and, by extension, conflict in the international system.

Liberal thinkers (both classical and neo-) apply the contributions of Enlightenment thinkers such as Rousseau and Kant to global society and argue that people and their countries can better

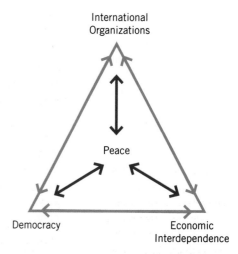

Figure 2.1   This image illustrates how the three elements of economics, democracy, and international organizations are mutually connected in the pursuit of world peace. Together these liberal approaches form the "Kantian tripod" resulting in the "Kantian peace."

their existence by extending liberal norms and institutional arrangements from the domestic to the international arena, joining together to build a cooperative and peaceful global society. Clearly, realists differ with this perspective, but so too do proponents of other theories who question liberal assumptions about the upward linear trajectory of "progress" and the prospects for global governance, the alleged universal appeal of democracy and capitalism, and the fairness, transparency, and equality of liberal political and economic arrangements. Where do you stand? Do you believe that your state's interests—or yours personally—are tied to those of other nations and societies? Does human nature push individuals and states toward greater and deeper cooperation? Are international organizations and agreements evidence of an emerging system of global governance, or even of "perpetual peace," as liberals claim?

World Systems Theory

In some ways, liberalism is the "yang" to the realism "yin." While contradictory or oppositional in many ways, to the extent that both theories provide differing accounts of the same phenomena, they are complementary too. Given their head start on the field, as well as the limiting nature of the "grand debate" between them, it is not a surprise that realism and liberalism have risen to the position of dominant paradigms (Dunne, Kurki, & Smith, 2013). Yet even while dominant, realism and liberalism have not gone unchallenged—with those challenges mounting in recent years. The first such challenge to the dominant paradigms of realism and liberalism that we will explore here is world systems theory.

World Systems Theory: An Emphasis on Inequality

world systems theory The view that global politics is an economic society brought about by the spread of capitalism and characterized by a hierarchy of countries and regions based on a gap in economic circumstance.

World systems theory is perhaps the best umbrella term or approach for a group of theories applying and extending Marxist thought to contemporary global politics. Advocates of this perspective believe that economic structure and forces are a primary factor in shaping global political relationships and the power they engender. World systems theorists contend that the world-system (defined as a capitalist world economy) has replaced the nation-state as the central unit of concern for understanding global politics. As a result of its capitalist orientation, the contemporary world-system is steeply divided between "have" and "have-not" countries in what the leading world systems theorist Immanuel Wallerstein (2004: 98) describes as an "international axial division of labor." This division is perpetuated through the concerted efforts of the haves (the economically developed countries of the Global North, also known in world systems theory as the "core") to keep the have-nots (the Global South, also known in world systems theory as the "periphery") weak and poor in order to exploit them. Some goods, like industrial products, help generate higher levels of technology, employment and profits; others, like agricultural or mining products, do not. Producing core goods helps states grow economically and politically in ways that the production of peripheral goods simply does not.

The skyline pictured here is not in the Global North, but rather is testament to the remarkable economic success that Singapore has had through playing by rules largely set by the Global North. Not all economically aspiring countries are able to replicate the success of Singapore and others like it.

Core states are often charged with keeping peripheral countries poor. Poorer states only achieve success by dutifully serving the Global North's interests. So, while South Korea and Singapore have achieved considerable prosperity, world systems theorists would argue that these semi-peripheral states have only slightly altered their structural position.

Why does a capitalist world economy create and sustain this structured inequality? World systems theorists explain the unequal nature of the world-system as an inevitable outcome of capitalism's logic rather than as a by-product of any moral defect per se. To do so, world systems theorists draw on the concept of "monopoly capitalism," in which the natural end-state of capitalism is seen as total domination of the means of production (labor and natural resources as well as capital [financial and technological]) in each and every industry (Baron & Sweezy, 1966). This is done through accumulation and control of land, labor, resources, money, and machines in the hands of an ever-smaller group of ever-larger corporations. To get to this point, according to world systems theory, capitalists must naturally expand their reach globally in search of opportunities to exploit and control labor and raw materials wherever they are cheapest (Wallerstein, 2004).

Of course, as a theory used to explain global politics, world systems theory must provide some account for the role of states in the world-system. And indeed, states are hardly irrelevant in the creation and perpetuation of a capitalist world economy, playing a crucial role in supporting bourgeois capitalism. Primarily, this support comes through policies and actions that help promote capitalist expansion not only domestically but also—and especially—internationally. Indeed, as Wallerstein (2004) has argued, a capitalist world economy would not have been possible without the support that states have provided to the capitalist class in its pursuit of global exploitation and domination.

From the early 18th through the mid-20th century, state support for the creation and promotion of a capitalist world economy took place largely through colonialism and imperialism. Today, world systems theorists contend that this support is largely translated through business-friendly policies by states and international organizations, which have created a largely deregulated global economy favorable to multinational corporations. And on some occasions, both past and present, world systems theorists argue that state support for capital expansion has come through war. Whether to "open up" closed societies for capitalist activity (particularly those with abundant natural resources and/or a cheap supply of labor) or to "punish" states and societies that resist engaging and participating in the capitalist world-economy, military force is seen by world systems theorists as one option in the toolkit states use to ensure the smooth functioning of global capital expansion.

World systems theorists contend that the evolution of the Western-dominated capitalist system has distorted development and left vast economic, social, and political disparities between the core (the Global North) and the periphery (the Global South) of the international system. To change such a starkly unequal world system, world systems theorists generally favor a restructuring of economic relations domestically and internationally to end the uneven distribution of wealth and power—before the inherent flaws in that system lead to its ultimate collapse.

Marxism and Dependency Theory

Several strands of thought concerned with the role the unequal global political economy plays in explaining global politics can be associated with world systems theory. The first of these strands, **Marxist theory**, is based on the ideas of Karl Marx, who with Friedrich Engels in *The Communist Manifesto* (Marx & Engels, 1848) depicted the essence of politics as the struggle between the propertied and powerful bourgeoisie and the poor and oppressed proletariat over the distribution of wealth. The first Soviet Communist Party chief, Vladimir Ilyich Ulyanov (better known as Lenin), applied Marxism to global politics. Prior to the Bolshevik Revolution that catapulted him to power, Lenin argued in "Imperialism: The Highest Stage of Capitalism" (1916) that bourgeois (middle- and upper-class) capitalists had consciously misled proletariat workers in prosperous countries into supporting the exploitation of other workers in poor regions through **imperialism**. Indeed, in Lenin's view, it was just this imperialist impulse that led to World War I—an argument he used to successfully launch a revolution against the Tsarist regime in Russia in 1917.

Marxists following in Lenin's wake have continued to extend Marx's views concerning the implications of the unequal distribution of capital for society to the global arena. With their focus on the material foundation of global politics and the nature of imperialism, the Global North has come to be seen in world systems theory as the **center/core** of exploitation throughout the world, with both the northern ruling and working classes complicit in the exploitation of the **periphery** countries and peoples of the Global South.

Marxist theory The philosophy of Karl Marx that the economic order determines political and social relationships. Thus, history, the current situation, and the future are determined by the economic struggle, which is termed *dialectical materialism.*

imperialism A term nearly synonymous with *colonialism,* recalling the empire building of the European powers in the 19th century. The empires were built by conquering and subjugating Southern countries.

center/core The focal points of global politics according to world systems theory, which encompasses Global North countries around which global economic and political power revolve as a result of an overwhelming concentration of capital.

periphery Countries in the Global South that are exploited by the countries in the Global North (center/core) for their cheap labor, natural resources, or as dumping grounds for pollution or surplus production.

Another strand contributing to world systems theory is **dependency theory**. The foundations of the theory of dependency emerged in the 1950s from the research of the Economic Commission for Latin America and the Caribbean, a United Nations–established body concerned with the challenges of economic development in that region. Highlighting the important limiting factor of inequality, members of this commission (most notably Raul Prebisch) inspired like-minded thinkers such as Andre Gunder Frank, Fernando Henrique Cardoso, Enzo Faletto, and others to develop an explanation for economic underdevelopment from the perspective of semi-peripheral and peripheral countries (Foster-Carter, 1973). Here, dependency theory highlighted some

Mining for gold in the Congo highlights the dark irony of extractive industries in the Global South. While the workers pull a highly valuable commodity out of the ground, they live in poverty and the corporations and elites that control the operation receive great economic benefits. Sadly, this is too often a reality of economic development in the Global South.

key and, to that point, overlooked aspects of global capitalism. The existence of a global capitalist order means that the study of underdevelopment will not make sense if we try to understand why one country is "peripheral" by comparing it to another country that is "developed." The reasons for underdevelopment do not reside inside the underdeveloped countries. The global capitalist order promotes subordination of the periphery to the core as the path to economic development; in places like Latin America, economic development is actually greatest when ties to the core are lessened (Gunder Frank, 1967).

dependency theory The view of global politics as an economic system in which the Global South is dependent upon and disadvantaged by the Global North as a perpetuation of the imperialist relationships established in previous centuries.

Like the original versions of Marxist theory, dependency theory holds that underdevelopment and poverty in the Global South are the result of exploitation by the Global North. Unlike Marxists, however, dependency theorists do not believe that the workers of the world will unite if freed of their respective bourgeoisie masters; rather, they focus on greater state involvement in creating self-sustaining national economies with an equitable distribution of wealth (Cardoso & Faletto, 1979). Dependency theorists contend that the Global North's exploitation of the Global South is driven by the Global North's need for cheap primary products (e.g., oil), large external markets for the Global North's expensive manufactured goods, profitable investment opportunities, and low-wage labor. Because this economic system enriches the Global North and impoverishes the Global South, dependency theorists argue that the Global North follows policies designed to keep the Global South dependent. For this reason, world systems theorists call the created system *neocolonialism* because it operates without colonies but is nevertheless imperialistic. (We will explore world systems theory and its application to today's political economy in Chapter 11.)

The dependency of the Global South is maintained in a number of ways. Some are subtle, such as giving rich countries much greater voting and decision-making power in the International Monetary Fund (IMF) and some other IGOs, thereby allowing the Global North to manipulate the world economy to their advantage. More specifically, it has been customary for the managing director of the IMF to be selected from a European country. Christine Lagarde from France, a lawyer and former politician, just left this position in September 2019. And the president of the World Bank has always been an American, with David R. Malpass, former Under Secretary of the US Treasury for International Affairs, taking over in April 2019.

Other techniques are less subtle. These include corrupting and coopting local elites in the Global South by allowing them personal wealth in return for governing their countries to benefit the Global North or, if the local elites are defiant, using military force to overthrow them and replace them with friendlier regimes. These tactics have long been highlighted by accusations of weak governance, corruption, and collusion across the Global South, and they fit quite squarely with the implications of how the center relates to the periphery, as mentioned earlier. As for countries such as South Korea or Singapore, which have achieved considerable prosperity, world systems theorists are apt to argue that these **semi-periphery** states have achieved success only by dutifully serving the Global North's interests.

semi-periphery Those countries that do not occupy a commanding position in the global economy but that serve an important function or fill an important niche in the global system, supporting the primacy of the center/core countries.

Neo-Marxist schools predict or favor dramatic changes to the prevailing economic model of capitalism. Orthodox Marxists predict the radical overthrow of the capitalist system, and advocate toward that end. Dependency and world systems theorists, however, focus much less on wiping away capitalism. Some strands of dependency theory argue that peripheral countries should cut their ties with core countries, or work to manage those ties in such a way that allows more technologically sophisticated production. Others contend that we can improve capitalism by radically reforming it, a perspective that recognizes the practical advantages of ensuring at least minimally acceptable economic and social conditions for all. What do you think? Is economic inequality—directly caused by the natural workings of capitalism itself—the single factor that explains the workings of global politics today? Are multinational corporations more important than states and international organizations? Or does world systems theory perhaps fall into the similar trap of realism and neorealism, by offering grand theoretical pronouncements based on broad patterns of behavior and material forces rather than examining the origins and underpinnings of those patterns and forces?

Constructivism

constructivism The view that changing ideas, norms, and identities of global actors shape global politics.

Whereas theories such as realism, liberalism, and world systems theory explain the behaviors and interests of actors in the global system as shaped by tangible and measurable forces and factors (e.g., military power or wealth accumulation), constructivism "flips the script." **Constructivism** holds the view that changing ideas, norms, and identities of global actors shape global politics. In the words of one prominent constructivist (Wendt, 1999), the key to understanding global politics lies in looking at "ideas all the way down"—that is, ideas fundamentally define identities, which in turn shape interests, which in turn produce behavior. This focus stands in marked contrast to materialist and behavioralist theories, which look no further than interests when seeking to explain behavior and which consider ideas or identity as matters of secondary importance (Hopf, 1998). In the view of constructivists, such approaches provide only a superficial understanding of that behavior by failing to account for the core ideas and self-identities that actually explain it (Onuf, 1989).

Nuclear weapons remain a potent real and symbolic measure of global power. The fact that North Korean leader Kim Jung-Un is personally monitoring a missile test bears out this reality and symbolism and forces others to account for North Korea in global decision-making.

As a school of thought with deep roots in social science disciplines such as sociology and psychology, constructivism rests on the assumption that social life and social behavior are "constructed"—that is, our collective reality is just an evolving by-product of our interpersonal interactions and communication of ideas with others in our social domain (Checkel, 1998). This social domain can be our community, our state, our nation, or the whole world. Perhaps the singular maxim of constructivist IR—Alexander Wendt's (1992) pithy statement that "anarchy is what states make of it"—captures this description well. For constructivists, the material factors of our lives matter less, and explain far less, than do ideas conveyed through discourse. In other words, social context matters, and "anarchy is what states make of it" (Wendt, 1992). Consider, for example, the fact that many states have nuclear weapons; in 2018, France had 300, Pakistan had 145, China had 280, and Russia had 6,850. And yet, the approximately 15 nuclear weapons that North Korea has are what pose a threat to US national security. The social relationship between countries matters; the ideational structure (bilateral relationships) gives meaning to the material structure (nuclear weapons).

Constructivism: An Emphasis on Norms

Applied to the study of global politics, constructivism contends that we can best explain the behaviors and interests of actors in global politics if we understand and appreciate the underlying ideas driving the behaviors and defining the interests of the majority of those actors. Such ideas are what sociologists call **norms**, and constructivism seeks to identify which ideas constitute norms as well as how such norms emerge and spread or are "diffused" (Finnemore & Sikkink, 1998).

norms Ideas that come to be shared by the majority of the population in a given society, such that they become the basis for assessing and regulating social conduct and behavior.

The emphasis on ideas as the primary explanation for behavior might be easy to grasp when we think about a highly ideologically motivated actor such as ISIS. The interests and behavior of ISIS clearly are little more than manifestations of a deep-seated apocalyptic ideology shared by the group's core adherents—and those ideas tell us far more about ISIS than any stated interests or evident behaviors (McCants, 2015). Yet for constructivists, the same logic applies just as seamlessly to explaining the behavior of the United States in responding to ISIS. Given the extent to which the ideology of ISIS stands in direct opposition to the core ideas and national (self-)identity of the United States and its citizens, the confrontation between the United States and ISIS has very little to do with competing interests and nearly everything to do with incompatible ideas.

Here is where norms come into play, as a means of determining which idea from among a set of contending ideas is most acceptable and appealing to the majority in society. In the case of international society today, clearly the ideas espoused by the United States—while not above criticism—are more broadly appealing than those promoted by ISIS. As such, the behavior of the United States can be said to be more in line with global norms than the behavior of ISIS. This is reflected by the relative difference in the perceived legitimacy of the normative (US) versus non-normative (ISIS) actor, as well as by international society's strong opposition to and rejection of ISIS' behavior.

Another focal point of constructivism is identity, including how individual and collective identities are formed and how they direct and reinforce conceptions of interest and behavior on the part of states and other actors. Constructivists are hardly the first scholars of global politics to consider the role of identity. Constructivism's take on identity is a bit different, however, from that of realists and liberals. As the direct by-product of ideas, constructivists contend that identities—ethnic, religious, linguistic, and gender, as well as national—are causal factors that produce certain conceptions of interest and types of behavior. At the same time, constructivists contend that identities, given their origins in ideas, are fluid and subject to change, making shared understandings of interest that follow from them subject to change as well. From a constructivist position, it is entirely possible—if not likely—for a country's "national interest" and behavior toward other countries to change and evolve over time as its national identity changes and evolves as a consequence of the emergence and appeal of different ideas (Neumann, 2016).

Even in a country like China with a relatively coherent ethnic identity rooted in the Han Dynasty, ethnic divisions exist. These Malaysian men are protesting the oppressive treatment of Uyghur Muslims at the hands of the Chinese government.

Consider, for example, the extent to which ideas of European community made inroads in France and Germany after World War II, changing the national identities of both countries and, by extension, their interests, behaviors, and mutual relationship. Similarly, China's unique path to global economic and political prominence in recent decades has been explained by some scholars, such as the British academic Martin Jacques (2009), as the product of the powerful cohesive force of Chinese ethnic identity springing from the Han Dynasty. In both examples, and in numerous others, identity is the driving force.

English School and Critical Theory

Like the other theories considered in this chapter, constructivism has different strains. One of these is really the forerunner of constructivism in global politics: the so-called "English School" of IR. The English School came into being in the late 1950s in the United Kingdom through the efforts of the British Committee on the Theory of International Politics (funded in part by the US-based Rockefeller Foundation). Seeking to develop a theoretical alternative to realism and liberalism, this committee, chaired by the historian Herbert Butterfield and with other prominent members, including Martin Wight and Hedley Bull, placed particular emphasis on the social aspects of interstate relations.

Constructivism was greatly influenced by the English School's emphasis on the fundamentally social basis of international politics. Constructivist insights regarding the nature and conduct of global politics, however, extend far beyond the English School, which basically accepted the main premises of the dominant paradigms (realism and liberalism) while seeking to synthesize and nominally revise them. Though the English School proved crucial during the evolution of IR theory in advancing the claim that the international arena was in fact a "society of states" (Bull, 1977), constructivism in IR has advanced broader assertions and critiques, in large part due to the influence of critical theory.

The main concern of constructivism lies in identifying those ideas that take root and spread widely in our global society, thereby shaping the thinking and perception of what constitutes appropriate and inappropriate (or "deviant") behavior. Building on this fundamental sociological and psychological concern with legitimacy and (collective) perception, constructivism in IR drew momentum from what is sometimes called the "Third Debate" of the 1970s and 1980s and the emphasis of critical theorists such as Anthony Giddens, Jurgen Habermas, and Michel Foucault on interpretation and discourse (Price & Reus-Smit, 1998). Though some critical theorists have rejected (and continue to reject) the premise of constructivism as critical theory due to its empirical focus, to the extent that constructivism is concerned with issues such as agency, legitimacy, sovereignty, and most of all, power in society—including who has it, who uses it, and the implications of those two questions for society at-large—it is hard to argue that constructivism has not at least been influenced by critical theory (Onuf, 2013).

Debate continues (even sometimes among the authors of this book!) over whether constructivism should be considered a full-fledged theory of global politics. Can constructivism provide a complete explanation of how global politics works, or a systematic approach for studying the workings of IR? One could argue that constructivist concepts underlie each of the other four perspectives discussed in this chapter. Yet many argue that constructivism has expanded the palette of IR scholarship by revealing the importance of ideas and norms as primary forces in shaping social interactions and, by extension, political behavior itself. What do you think? Do evolving norms, interests, and identities fundamentally shape relationships between global actors? Or are core attributes of the global system, such as the scarcity of resources or the concentration of material power, more important factors in determining the outcome of events?

Feminist Theory

feminist theory A collection of theoretical approaches that analyze the role of gender in global politics.

Like world systems theory—and unlike any of the other theories considered in this chapter and in this book—**feminist theory** considers one particular factor to have disproportionate explanatory power and, thus, to demand analytical inquiry. Whereas for world systems theory that factor was class inequality, for feminism it is gender—and in particular, the way in which every aspect of global politics is structured around socially constructed and idealized conceptions of gender and gender roles and their intersection with political and economic power.

Feminist scholars of global politics generally reject realist and liberal understandings of IR as centering on power struggles between sovereign states in an anarchic world (Tickner, 1992). Those two mainstream approaches assume that power involves one person or organization that is able to coerce another to do something he/she/it would not otherwise do. This coercive capability usually stems from one individual's greater material capabilities. For example, "I have power over you because I have a bigger army, and therefore, I can conquer you." Feminists understand power in a much broader and more complex sense. Power, as a socially constructed concept, is not only about power over, but also about power with and power through.

Feminists are most interested in how the everyday interaction between people and communities is a social exercise of power relations, and this focus is critical to understanding macroglobal processes like war, trade, and diplomacy (Enloe, 1989). Like constructivism, feminist theory emphasizes the role of language in constructing and performing certain narratives about the way the world works (Cohn, 1987). For example, consider the concept of "cheap labor" (Enloe, 2004). Feminists would interrogate this concept and argue that a better way to phrase it would be "labor made cheap." This latter approach encourages us to ask questions about how the labor was made cheap, who made it cheap, and for what purpose it was made cheap:

- How are men and women affected differently by the demand for and supply of cheap labor, say, in textile factories?

This well-known photo from the G-20 Summit meeting in Hamburg, Germany in July 2017 was striking for two reasons. First is the overwhelming number of men among the G-20 leaders. Second is the symbolic marginalization of the United States in this multilateral forum as President Trump is positioned (perhaps ironically) on the far left.

- What kind of labor do we pay for (e.g., skilled or unskilled, unionized or not, or sweatshop or more regulated), what kind of labor do we not pay for (e.g., child care), and how are these differences gendered?

- Which labor is considered masculine, which is considered feminine, and which professions are more lucrative?

- What is the effect of such divisions of labor on decision-making power and access to resources?

When you ask these sorts of unaskable questions, you are asking feminist questions, expressing a feminist curiosity, and taking women's lives seriously. You are making sense of how we produce, construct, and contain knowledge about global politics (Zalewski 2007). These are essential aspects of feminist theorizing and can be applied to all of the essential issues of global politics, from war and peace to human rights and the environment.

Halla Tómasdóttir: A Feminine Response to Iceland's Financial Crisis.

Feminism: An Emphasis on Gender

Not so long ago, gender was considered irrelevant in IR. Indeed, even as recently as the late 1990s, one of the leading scholars of IR theory questioned whether feminist theory really had a research program at all (Keohane, 1998a). But now, gender analysis constitutes an accepted, although sometimes misunderstood,

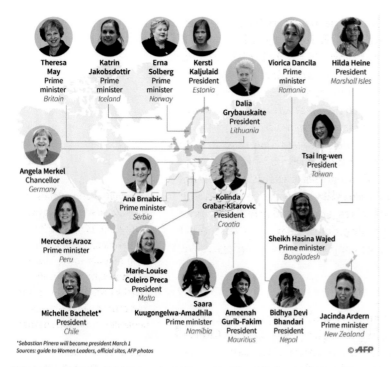

Theresa May Prime minister *Britain*
Katrin Jakobsdottir Prime minister *Iceland*
Erna Solberg Prime minister *Norway*
Kersti Kaljulaid President *Estonia*
Viorica Dancila Prime minister *Romania*
Hilda Heine President *Marshall Isles*
Dalia Grybauskaite President *Lithuania*
Angela Merkel Chancellor *Germany*
Ana Brnabic Prime minister *Serbia*
Kolinda Grabar-Kitarovic President *Croatia*
Tsai Ing-wen President *Taiwan*
Mercedes Araoz Prime minister *Peru*
Sheikh Hasina Wajed Prime minister *Bangladesh*
Marie-Louise Coleiro Preca President *Malta*
Michelle Bachelet* President *Chile*
Saara Kuugongelwa-Amadhila Prime minister *Namibia*
Ameenah Gurib-Fakim President *Mauritius*
Bidhya Devi Bhandari President *Nepal*
Jacinda Ardern Prime minister *New Zealand*

Sebastian Pinera will become president March 1
Sources: guide to Women Leaders, official sites, AFP photos

© AFP

Although women leaders have made strides around the globe in recent years, those pictured here still only represent a small percentage of the leaders of the nearly 200 UN member countries. And subtracting from this small percentage, Theresa May, pictured here left office in June 2019.

part of IR inquiry, and we see gender analysis as not only a central feature of feminist IR theory but also as a factor being incorporated into global policy-making by the United Nations, the European Union, the North Atlantic Treaty Organization, and many other IGOs (True, 2003).

Gender and women, of course, are not one and the same, and they should not be used interchangeably (even though they often are in global policy-making). Gender refers "to the socially learned behaviors, repeated performances and idealized expectations that are associated with and distinguish between proscribed gender roles of masculinity and femininity" (Runyan & Peterson, 2013:2). This means that gender is not the same as sex, the biological and anatomical characteristics of men's and women's bodies, and while gender is sometimes related to sex, sometimes it is not. Gender is really about the socially constructed categories of "men" and "women" as well as masculinity and femininity.

Not surprisingly, feminist analysts have been successful at making gender a legitimate category of analysis in the study of global politics. Gender analysis in global politics, as implied previously, is based on the examination of two basic but complex questions: "Where are the women (and where are they not)?" and "How is the power of gender at work?" To answer the second question, we must answer the first. The first question focuses on where women are, and are not, in global politics; what positions they hold and do not hold; and what women's social locations say about power, privilege, and visibility. For example, why are we just now seeing the first female leader of the IMF (Christine Lagarde of France), and how has her approach looked different (if at all)? Or, what effects do gender **quotas** have on increasing women's participation in politics? The *power of gender* refers to the ways in which we constantly "gender" our social, political, and economic worlds and the ways in which this social practice of gendering has implications for who has power and who does not, for who counts and who does not. When looking at women and gendered experiences in war, why has the international community made sexual violence in conflict a priority over other forms of violence experienced in conflict by women and men, and over other gendered issues like women's right to participate in the peace process? How does dichotomous gendered thinking affect how we conceptualize

quotas Gender quotas are used to create balanced (e.g., gender, race, ethnicity, region, etc.) representation within legislative bodies of national governments and can be mandated by the constitution or electoral laws.

who are victims (i.e., female civilian) and who are perpetrators (i.e., male combatant) in sexual- and gender-based violence (Baaz & Stern, 2013)?

One of the primary ways we gender our world is through dichotomous thinking. This sort of either-or thinking helps us to organize the world into certain categories: autonomous-dependent, public-private, leaders-followers, rational-emotional, and objective-subjective (to give just a few examples). Although these categories can be helpful in processing information, they usually tend to create a conceptual hierarchy, and this hierarchical thinking can be an oversimplified and often problematic way of viewing the world. Feminist theory also encourages us to think about other social categories of exclusion, exploitation, and oppression. This focus on **intersectionality** allows us to think about socially constructed categories, such as race, class, and sexual orientation, and how these other identities interact with gender identities in ways that affect one's access to power and how one experiences oppression and privilege in the international system.

Strands of Feminism

Like the other theories outlined in this chapter and throughout the book, there are different strands within feminist thought (Dietz 2003). **Liberal (or orthodox) feminism** tends to focus on the position of women in existing power structures. It asks questions about why so few women are present in political leadership and what gender equality would mean for world peace (Hudson et al., 2012). Although the number of women in decision-making bodies has increased at national and international levels (ipu.org), they are still largely underrepresented. **Critical (or radical) feminism** is less concerned with adding women to existing structures of power and privilege and more concerned with asking questions about why those structures exist in the first place (Sylvester, 1994; Zalewski, 2007) and how such systems, particularly **patriarchy**, continue to persist in the 21st century. Thus, it focuses on how global politics is gendered and how masculinity and femininity (not male and female), gender roles, and culture intersect in ways that determine what a society values. Though any one person could fulfill both gender roles, many cultures—historically and currently—associate masculinity with traits such as being aggressive, outgoing, and strong. But in many situations even today, if a woman were to appropriate these masculine attributes, she would be considered too bossy and aggressive, but her male counterpart would simply be seen as an assertive man who knows what he wants. In this way, the system has limited the roles that women can legitimately play and thus has limited their power. For radical or critical feminists, the problem is not too few women, but rather what the system actually values and promotes via culture and social rules.

Feminist theory challenges you to consider not only how seemingly far-off and distant global processes and institutions are structured unequally in accordance with idealized conceptions of gender, but also how your own political community, and indeed your own values and worldview, may also be gendered. The implications of a society structured along gender lines, with power distributed and applied accordingly, are real for all people, regardless of sex and gender.

intersectionality Refers to the ways in which multiple institutions of oppression (e.g., racism, sexism, homophobia, transphobia, ableism, xenophobia, and classism) are interconnected and cannot be understood separately from one another.

liberal (or orthodox) feminism The belief that gender equality is best achieved through political and legal reform so that women have equal access and equal opportunity in the workplace, politics, and other public spaces.

critical (or radical) feminism The belief that gender equality is best achieved when we restructure the system in order to change what society values in terms of work, leadership, and politics and what society constructs as normal.

patriarchy The system of gender-based hierarchy in society that assigns most power to men, uses male(ness) as the norm, and places higher value on masculine traits.

Utilizing a gender lens is not as easy as it sounds, and many don't see it without a feminist push. Once some start looking, however, they see it everywhere. How does gender inform your own interpretations of global politics—and the very way in which global politics itself is studied, including what questions do (and don't) get asked? Are those behaviors, activities, and roles traditionally defined as "masculine" or "male" rewarded and promoted more than those traditionally defined as "feminine" or "female"? How does this impact your country's foreign policy behavior and conception of the "national interest," as well as how power is distributed within your society and globally?

CNN Video: Women and Microcredit.

🌐 Where Do We Go from Here?

Building on what we have laid out in this chapter, you probably recognize that IR is a diverse and contentious field, perhaps because of the very complexity of its focus of study: global politics. In the coming chapters, we will lay out a variety of aspects of global politics and present you with both the information and the tools to form your own views on global events and processes.

The theories we discuss in this chapter and across the rest of this book can be compared along several fronts. As you can see in Table 2.2, there are major differences between these five theories. For instance, how does a theory view relationships and interactions in global politics—as contentious (realism), collaborative (liberalism), unequal (world systems theory, feminism), or dynamic and context-dependent (constructivism)? Who are the predominant actors—states (realism), international institutions (liberalism), socioeconomic classes (world systems theory), or the proponents and beneficiaries of particular norms, ideas, and social arrangements (feminism, constructivism)?

At the same time, there are some interesting areas of overlap. For example, realism and world systems theory are exclusively concerned with examining and explaining material power and social conflict (though for different reasons). Conversely, liberalism and constructivism share a common emphasis on ideas and cooperation, though constructivism is more inclined toward the former and liberalism toward the latter. For its part, feminism has different "strands" of thinking that focus on material and ideational power, and on which is deserving of more immediate attention and revision.

As you read about these theories, you can return to this table to compare the theories and examine your own views. Along these lines, it is important to distinguish between theory and ideology. Theory is the lens that helps you understand the complexity of global politics. Ideology is that idea that some theory is objectively true—basically by virtue of the fact that you believe it to be true. As you consider the following questions, don't let a particular ideology inhibit your ability to use various lenses to generate insight and uncover new understanding of the issue in front of you. Do you, for example, see global politics as a zero-sum or positive-sum game? What actor or actors are most important? Is conflict inevitable or avoidable? As you proceed through the rest of this book, think about your answers to these questions, whether they

Table 2.2 Theories of IR

ISSUES	REALISM	LIBERALISM	STRUCTURALISM/ WORLD SYSTEMS	FEMINIST	CONSTRUCTIVISM
Chief architects	Thomas Hobbes, *Leviathan*; see also Thucydides and Machiavelli	Immanuel Kant; see also Grotius	Karl Marx; see also Lenin, *Dependencia* School (Presbich, Cardoso, Gunder Frank, Wallerstein)	Ann Tickner; Cynthia Enloe; Cynthia Weber; Christine Sylvester	J. G. Ruggie; Martha Finnemore; Alexander Wendt
Essence of system	Conflictual	Cooperative	Unequal	Gendered	Socially constructed
System M.O.	Anarchy; self-help	Institutions facilitate collaboration	Capitalist exploitation	Patriarchal subordination	Temporal and contingent anarchy
Amount of inherent conflict in system	Large amount due to security dilemma	Minimal as states see value of cooperation	Potentially large— hegemonic wars and conflict; structural violence	Extensive, with disproportionate effects on women	None inherent
Dominant unit	Rational, self-interested states	International institutions and organizations	Owners of capital; "core" versus semi-periphery and periphery	Constructed gendered hierarchies of power	Status quo actors and institutions
Ultimate goal for actors in system	Stability; self-preservation	Order; fuller future integration	Dependent on position; preserving status quo, or revolution	Preservation of patriarchal status quo	Preservation of dominant paradigm and conventions
Main obstacle to ultimate goal	Weak or ineffectual states	Strong, self-interested states	Nature of system	Structured inequality and discrimination by sex/gender	Non-normative actors, institutions, and behaviors
Nature of power	Material/relational (coercive)	Moral/rhetorical (compelling)	Economic	Male, only "power over is seen"	Ideational
Vision of the future	Similar to past; states remain dominant, though power distribution may change	State power will wither away as benefits of cooperation become apparent	Continuation of three-tiered system until inherent contradictions become unsustainable	Varies, depending on "strain" (liberal, critical)	Maintenance and expansion of status quo likely
Relationship of economics to politics	Politics drives economics	Should be separated as much as possible	Interwoven— seamless web of forces and concepts	Subordinated; complementary in sustaining patriarchy	Contingent on position of actor relative to status quo

change, and how different lenses help you think differently about the world around you.

Throughout the text, keep in mind the theories you have encountered in this chapter as you are introduced to numerous examples helping you put the perspective into a larger theoretical context. Hopefully, by the end of this book, you will have thoughts about which (or even perhaps all) of these theories fit best with your worldview and the evidence we will discuss throughout the book.

Chapter Summary

- Five theories that help to improve our understanding of global politics are realist theory, liberal theory, world systems theory, constructivism, and feminist theory. We improve our understanding of global politics by putting events within the context of theory to see patterns and make generalizations about the conduct of international affairs.

- Realist theory focuses on the self-interested promotion of the state. Realists believe that power politics is the driving force behind global politics. Thus, realists believe that both safety and wisdom lie in promoting the national interest through the preservation and, if necessary, the application of the state's power.

- Liberal theory holds that humans are capable of cooperating out of enlightened common interests in an orderly, humane, and just world, and that the world has moved significantly in that direction during the past century. Liberals also see the policy prescriptions of realists as dangerous.

- World systems theory argues that economic structure is a primary factor in shaping political relationships and the power they reflect. World systems theorists contend that the world is divided between have and have-not countries, and that the haves (the economically developed countries of the Global North) work to keep the have-nots (the Global South) weak and poor in order to exploit them.

- Constructivism rests on the assumption that social life and behavior are "constructed"—that is, our collective reality is really just an evolving by-product of our interpersonal interactions and communication of ideas with others in our social domain. This social domain could be our community, our state, our nation, or the whole world.

- Feminist theory generally rejects traditional understandings of IR as being about power struggles between sovereign states in an anarchic world. Feminists understand power in IR in a much broader and more complex sense. Power is not only about power over, but also about power with and power through.

Critical Thinking Questions

1. What are theories, and why do they matter in the study of global politics?

2. Explain a current event from two different theoretical perspectives. In terms of each theory's explanatory power, consider the strengths and weaknesses of the lenses in understanding this particular current event.

3. Choose a political leader, past or present. Is this leader best described as a realist, a liberal, a Marxist, or a feminist? Give at least three specific examples (e.g., character traits and decisions made) to support your argument.

4. Constructivists assert that interactions shape identities and ideas about those identities, which in turn shape interests. Find an example where the United States interacted differently with another state (e.g., Russia, China, North Korea, or Mexico) in a way that reshaped both states' interests, and explain the process of how the interaction reshaped identities and/or ideas and thus changed interests.

5. How does feminist theory help us better understand the concept of power in global politics? Why is this important?

Key Terms

balance of power
center/core
classical liberalism
classical realism
complex
   interdependence
constructivism
cosmopolitanism

critical (or radical)
   feminism
dependency theory
feminist theory
imperialism
intersectionality
liberal (or orthodox)
   feminism

liberal internationalism
liberalism
Marxist Theory
neoliberalism
neorealism
norms
patriarchy
periphery

positive-sum game
quotas
rational actors
realism
semi-periphery
world systems theory
zero-sum game

rdian
cret files
han war
White House condemns Pakistan over aid for Taliban

Interpreting Power: A Levels-of-Analysis Approach

What is power in global politics—and who has it? These are among the most fundamental questions to consider when embarking on the study of this field. We can apply these questions to a variety of situations, whether they include a state's ability to convert its military power to achieve its strategic objectives, such as Russia's March 2014 annexation of Crimea, or an international court's ability to advance international norms, such as the International Criminal Tribunal's March 2016 conviction of Bosnian Serb leader Radovan Karadžić for war crimes.

The increasing power of nongovernmental actors is also important to consider. One example is the infamous "WikiLeaks" case. Premiering on the Internet in December 2006, WikiLeaks was the brainchild of the enigmatic Australian Julian Assange, a one-time publisher and journalist turned "Internet activist." Assange is committed to exposing what he perceives as the duplicity and short-sightedness of many powerful states and their political leaders. WikiLeaks challenges the ability of states to conduct their foreign policy ventures under a cloak of secrecy—and in doing so reflects the old adage that "knowledge is power."

Julian Assange, founder of WikiLeaks, addresses assembled media in London in July 2010. This simple photo reflects the influence of individuals (Assange), the state (here, the US and UK governments he was targeting), and the global political system (technology and the globalized media) in International Relations. Assange remains a pivotal figure in light of WikiLeaks' alleged interference in the 2016 US presidential election.

Interpreting the nature and application of power in global politics requires us to take into account not only what power is and where it comes from, but also who has it and how they use it. In this chapter, we look at how global politics allows us to account for power at the individual, state, and systemic levels and how these shape the course of events.

Learning Objectives

Define the concept of power in global politics.

Describe the levels-of-analysis approach.

Identify the main characteristics of individual-level analysis.

Discuss the structure and dynamics of state-level analysis.

Identify the structures, patterns, and interactions among actors in systems-level analysis.

Defining Power in Global Politics

Power is an elusive concept. As former Harvard University dean and top US National Security Policy Advisor Joseph Nye has put it, power "is like the weather. Everyone talks about it, but few understand it" (2000:55). The prominent political scientist Harold Lasswell (1936) famously defined political power as the factor that explains who gets what, when, and how. And while much has changed in the world since Lasswell's writing in contemporary global politics, power remains the primary mechanism used by actors of various types to pursue their interests and agendas.

Power can have many different sources and translations. Consider, for example, the threat that WikiLeaks poses to many states and their leaders, by grasping for power in the form of information to reveal to the public details of many major foreign policy decisions as well as the petty aspects of international diplomacy, such as revealing that US diplomats referred to Italy's then–Prime Minister Silvio Berlusconi as feckless, vain, and ineffective. WikiLeaks even has the potential to alter the balance of American politics, such as in its October 2016 release of thousands of emails sent and received by Hillary Clinton on her private server while she was US Secretary of State. The fact that numerous governments have sought to restrict the site, deprive it of a host server, block Assange's access to the Internet, or even deny him diplomatic sanctuary, as Ecuador did when it expelled him from its embassy in London, turning Assange over for arrest by British authorities in April 2019—is evidence of the "threat" that WikiLeaks—and Assange himself—poses.

Characteristics of Power

Defining power is challenging, since it has many seemingly contradictory faces. This section introduces the character of power in global politics as well as those apparent contradictions.

POWER AS ASSET AND ASPIRATION.   Power is both an asset (something an actor possesses) and an aspiration (something an actor seeks). Most discussions look at power solely as an asset helping an actor achieve its goals. In this sense, power is like money—something that is **fungible** and can be converted into some other desired good or end (Baldwin, 1979). But such an analogy is limited, since political power is far less fungible than money (Nye, 2004). Consider, for example, that US military spending has long exceeded the military budget of the rest of the major military powers combined, yet the United States has in recent years struggled to fully realize its aims in recent wars in Iraq, Afghanistan, and in military counterterrorism operations against ISIS in Syria and Iraq.

Power is also an aspiration. In a world of competing interests, it makes sense to seek, acquire, or preserve sufficient power to pursue one's own agenda. As introduced in Chapters 1 and 2, realists in particular view the aspiration to power by states as "natural" given the constant danger and instability associated with an anarchic international system (Schweller, 2004). From a realist perspective, the problem is not the aspiration to obtain ever-increasing reserves of power, but rather the temptation to squander power on marginal goals or the reluctance to utilize it to protect or advance vital interests. Conversely, liberal and critical theorists question whether this aspiration is beneficial, both because of the costs of acquiring power and because of the threat that doing so poses to others. These theorists also conceive of power as not only tangible or material but also something with a basis in ideas. Liberals, constructivists, and feminists differ among themselves in how they conceive of power, who has power, and what they see as its ultimate purpose. However, they share a concern with the implications of a theory—realism—that considers a constant quest for power to be the most important factor driving global politics.

HARD AND SOFT POWER.   As we saw in Chapter 2, the prevailing understanding of power as advanced by realists is that it is coercive—that is, something used to force other actors to do something. Often called **hard power**, this type of power relies on the delivery of credible threats, such as the threat or use of military force or the threat to levy economic sanctions. Crucial to hard power is the skillful linking of those threats to tangible and material factors of power like a state's military or a nation's economy.

It would be a mistake to equate power with coercion, however. If you recall Lasswell's earlier definition of power, it refers to anything used by an actor to achieve its desired goal. As such, there is another dimension to power in global politics, one that has little to do with threats and everything to do with incentives. This is called **soft power**, which depends largely on the ability of an actor to persuade others to follow. This can be done by offering positive incentives,

fungible The idea that power of one type (e.g., military power) is not necessarily transferable or applicable to other policy areas. Thus, military power might not prove helpful in the financial or environmental sector.

hard power The use or threatened use of material power assets by an actor to compel one or more other actors to undertake or not undertake a desired action. Hard power relies on coercion.

soft power The use or prospective use of material or ideational power assets by an actor to induce another actor or actors to undertake a desired action or not undertake an undesirable one. Soft power relies on persuasion.

Shashi Tharoor:
Why Nations Should
Pursue Soft Power.

such as foreign aid or cultural exchanges, or by representing an appealing and attractive example or ideal. As the leading architect and proponent of soft power, Joseph Nye, puts it, "A country may obtain the outcome it wants in world politics because other countries—admiring its values, emulating its example, aspiring to its level of prosperity and openness—want to follow it" (2004:5).

Hard power is easier to grasp because its results are more obvious—and because, as the litany of wars and arms races throughout history shows, it has been used more often. Realists tend to dismiss soft power, arguing that countries follow other countries' leads if they share the same interests, not because they admire them. Conversely, liberals and others who believe that soft power can be potent point to the negative impact that the 2008 global financial crisis, largely triggered by a lack of US oversight of shoddy financial practices in the financial and housing markets, had on US soft power. The results greatly diminished the US image abroad (Friedberg, 2010).

ABSOLUTE AND RELATIVE POWER.   In global politics, power also has an absolute dimension. One example of absolute power is the US stockpile of 6,800 nuclear warheads—a figure which the Trump Administration seeks to increase and of which about 2,800 are currently slated for decommissioning.[1] The destructive capability of these weapons has an absolute quality, affording the United States greater power and influence in global politics than it otherwise would have. This power accrues regardless of what other states and nonstate actors do, which partially explains why other states have also obtained them and still others continue to pursue them.

At the same time, power does not exist in a vacuum. Assessing any actor's power also requires one to take into account the power of the adversary or competitor with which it is engaged. Thus, when attempting to accurately assess an actor's capabilities, we must consider relative power. The fact that China has the largest army in the world and the highest constant level of economic growth over the last two decades makes China powerful in absolute terms. However, it provides a more useful and practical appraisal if we talk about China's power in relation to other specific actors. Whatever the sources and extent of China's power, they afford China greater influence over a relatively small neighbor such as Vietnam than over a regional power such as Japan or another global power such as the United States.

CAPABILITIES AND CREDIBILITY.   Material factors shape every actor's power. For states, important assets include military strength, economic assets, technological and physical infrastructure, demographics, and natural resources. For nonstate actors such as international or nongovernmental organizations, the capability of the organization's leaders, the size and source of its budget and staff, and its organizational efficiency and adaptability matter.

Material assets may translate into capabilities, but they do not automatically equate to a powerful global presence. That presence depends not only on capabilities but also on credibility—that is, an actor's willingness and/or ability to utilize its material power in the pursuit of its interests. The fusion of material capabilities with political will is what together equates to the effective use of power, a fact that highlights the political and perceptual as well as material aspects of power in global politics. India's 1998 decision to publicly test nuclear weapons, thereby announcing to the world its status as a nuclear weapons state, illustrates how these two aspects of power are linked. Although India first tested a nuclear warhead in 1974, it did so covertly for both strategic and ideological reasons (Mistry, 2004). When domestic debate within India turned to the prospect of conducting a public test in the mid-1990s, a significant amount of opposition came from more hard-line elements in the military and defense establishment. This opposition stemmed from the view that any enhanced influence associated with revealing that India possessed "the bomb" would be offset by the reality that few other actors perceived that India would actually use it.

OBJECTIVE AND SUBJECTIVE POWER.   Just as power in global politics flows from an actor's ability and willingness to convert its own assets into action, it is also in part determined by how others perceive that actor's assets. Objective power consists of assets that an actor not only possesses but is ready and willing to use, and thus can be a major factor in determining whose interests prevail. One example was the period leading up to the US invasion of Iraq in 2003. While much of the international community—including many close US allies—opposed the decision, their diplomatic rebukes were little match for the Bush administration's desire to use the United States' massive military arsenal to overthrow Saddam Hussein.

Like hard power, objective power is easy to understand. And the converse of objective power—subjective power—is no less important. Again, remember Lasswell's insight that political power is something used within a social context. For an actor to be truly powerful, other actors must perceive it to be powerful; reputation matters. One study of the subjective aspect of power found that a state's power diminishes, and the possibility of future aggression against it increases, if other states perceive it as lacking the ability and willingness to follow through on commitments or to maintain a strong and consistent position in crisis settings (Foster & Palmer, 2006).

Power as the Production of Effects

It is worth exploring one additional conceptual framework that understands power as the production of "effects that shape the capacities of actors to determine their circumstances and fate" (Barnett & Duvall, 2005:42). This framework focuses on the constraints that shape the behavior and capabilities of actors within the global system and how those constraints condition the possible outcomes. Barnett and Duvall (2005) go on to discuss four types of power: compulsory (direct control over another actor), institutional (control over socially distant actors), structural (how structures define the range of social interactions), and productive (similar to structural power but focusing more on production and reproduction of hierarchy in the system). Although they delve into much greater detail and nuance, the main takeaway is the complexity and fluidity of power both as it operates in the global system and in how scholars struggle to understand it and teach it to students.

From Ordinary to Extraordinary: Malala's Journey

Analysts who take the traditional approach to IR tend to think of power in coercive terms, as a tool associated with states and wielded largely by men. Yet, as the study and practice of global politics evolves, our attention is drawn to the power of other actors and, for that matter, to other types of power. Consider the story of Malala Yousafzai. Malala was born in 1997 in the remote Swat Valley of Pakistan. From an early age, she attended a school for girls established by her father Ziauddin, which came under attack from the Taliban, a fundamentalist religious and political movement opposed to education for girls and women.

At the age of 11, Malala spoke out against the Taliban in a lecture in Peshawar entitled "How dare the Taliban take away my basic right to education?" Over the next few years, she continued her activism, giving lectures and serving as a guest blogger for the BBC. Before long, Malala received widespread international acclaim for her efforts. As a result, at the age of 14, Malala was the target of a *fatwa* (religious edict) calling for her execution for purported crimes against Islam. Riding home on the bus from school on October 9, 2012, Malala was shot in the head and critically wounded by a man attempting to enforce this edict. She was airlifted to the United Kingdom and, after several life-threatening surgeries, returned to school in March 2013 in Birmingham, England. Later that year, as Malala recovered, she delivered a speech at the UN—on her 16th birthday—and followed this with the publication of her autobiography, *I Am Malala: The Girl Who Stood Up for Education and Was Shot by the Taliban*.

Malala Yousafzai's activism in support of the power of education for girls and women continues to make her a target of extremists. It has also won her the EU's Andrei Sakharov Prize for Freedom of Thought and made her the youngest person to win the Nobel Peace Prize (in November 2014). In congratulating the 17-year-old Malala, Pakistan's Prime Minister Nawaz Sharif said: "She is [the] pride of Pakistan, she has made her countrymen proud . . . Girls and boys of the world should take a lead from her struggle and commitment." U.N. Secretary-General Ban Ki-moon described her as "a brave and gentle advocate of peace who through the simple act of going to school became a global teacher."

On July 12, 2015—Malala's 18th birthday—she opened a school for Syrian refugee girls in Lebanon. Its expenses covered by a nonprofit fund she helped establish, the school was designed to admit nearly 200 girls from the ages of 14 to 18. At the dedication ceremony, Malala remarked, "Today on my first day as an adult, on behalf of the world's children, I demand of leaders we must invest in books instead of bullets."

A young woman from a humble background, Malala Yousafzai has confronted and overcome incredible—even life-threatening—obstacles from those who conceive of power as a way to coerce others in order to maintain the status quo. Malala's journey serves as a reminder of the power within all of us, and of our duty to use it. To learn more, check out The Malala Fund website (www.malala.org) and participate in her #BooksNot Bullets challenge. You can also follow her on Twitter (@ MalalaFund).

The Levels-of-Analysis Approach

levels-of-analysis approach A social scientific approach to the study of global politics that analyzes phenomena from different perspectives (system, state, individual).

Practically any news story dealing with world events reflects the power and influence of individuals, of states, and of the larger global political system. One way of thinking about this systematically is called the **levels-of-analysis approach**. This approach helps reveal how people, states, and the international system all "matter" in global politics, both on their own and in relationship to one another. Although the central role of nation-states in global politics makes their power and influence easy to grasp, it would be a mistake to overlook the increasing role of individual actors or the influence of the global system on states and people.

A return to the WikiLeaks saga provides a useful illustration of the independent power and influence of individuals, states, and the global system as well as the interrelationship of the three. In October 2010, WikiLeaks released almost 400,000 classified US military logs detailing its operations in Iraq. This release came shortly after publication of nearly 90,000 top-secret military records pertaining to the US and North Atlantic Treaty Organization (NATO) military strategy in Afghanistan, as well as the April

The first major "splash" made by Wikileaks was the April 2010 release of raw, authentic video footage (dubbed "Collateral Murder") of airstrikes by a U.S. Apache helicopter in the streets of Baghdad that killed at least a dozen unarmed civilians.

2010 release of a video (contentiously titled "Collateral Murder") showing a US Apache helicopter killing at least 12 people (including two Reuters journalists) during a 2007 attack in Baghdad. The continued challenge posed by WikiLeaks to the ability of states and, increasingly, private corporations and other media outlets (Twitter, Reddit, *The New York Times*) to control information flow or protect private communications led to Assange's expulsion from his diplomatic refuge in the Ecuadorian Embassy in London, and his subsequent arrest in April 2019. The WikiLeaks example illustrates that in global politics, power resides at the individual, state, and system levels—something we will consider further throughout the rest of this chapter.

Origins of the Approach

Early proponents of **behavioralism** in international relations (IR) in the mid-20th century argued that the levels-of-analysis approach offered the most sophisticated method for sorting through the complex problems that typify global politics (Singer, 1961). As such, it was considered a blueprint for a more rigorous scientific analysis, providing a greater understanding of perennial problems such as the balance of power and the outbreak of war (Waltz, 1959). And although Waltz's *Man, the State, and War* (1959) predates Singer's work (1961) and both follow a similar conceptual blueprint, J. David Singer is rightly credited with coining the term *levels of analysis* and with launching a seminal construct that is still widely taught and applied today. Subsequent challenges have exposed its limitations, but the levels-of-analysis approach continues to provide useful lenses to interpret and analyze global politics in general and the sources and use of power in particular. Among other things, the levels-of-analysis framework allows us to account for important unit-level (state and individual)

behaviorism A strand of intellectual study of global politics that focused on employing scientific methods to the study of social phenomena. Behavioral analysts believe that social science can be studied in ways similar to those employed in the biological and physical sciences.

as well as structural (system) conditions and phenomena. In doing so, this approach raises questions such as:

1. Which individuals have power in global politics? Which states? How is power distributed within the global system?

2. What are the sources of power at the individual, state, and system levels?

3. How do individuals and states use power within the global system?

Applicability of the Approach

Before moving further, it is important to understand that the levels-of-analysis framework is not a theory, but rather a useful analytic tool that cuts across the theoretical approaches discussed in Chapter 2 and throughout this book. For instance, in the context of realism, there are some realists who focus their attention on human nature and the ways social behavior is aggregated from fundamental questions about the good and evil within humans. Others are more firmly focused on the state and its capabilities, while still others (neorealists) place great weight on the impact of the system's structure upon the ways actors interact. Thus, you shouldn't consider the levels-of-analysis approach in the same context as the five theoretical approaches presented in Chapter 2, but instead as a framework that highlights the impact of different components in global politics. In many ways, when you begin by focusing on a particular level, your analysis will likely produce understanding of the relative importance of that level in explaining behavior.

The levels-of-analysis approach thus allows us to appraise power in one of three ways: (1) through individual-level analysis, in which we consider the power of individuals or small groups in global politics; (2) through state-level analysis, in which we consider how the state and/or other actors and forces within a given society influence global politics; and (3) through system-level analysis, in which we consider how the global system exerts power on states, individuals, and nonstate actors.

One prominent historical illustration of this is what the levels-of-analysis approach tells us about the role of Nazi Germany in causing World War II. From the standpoint of the individual level of analysis, there is hardly a more frightening case study than the murderous dictator Adolf Hitler. The well-known facts of Hitler's biography have generated numerous theories about the influence of his formative experiences. Factors such as Hitler's failed attempt at becoming an artist or the bitterness he felt about the outcome of World War I certainly influenced his development as a political leader. Similarly, numerous studies of Hitler's psyche and the origins and impact of his racist and anti-Semitic views have shed light on his leadership and decision-making after assuming the chancellorship of Germany in 1933.

At the same time, numerous factors related to the German state and society during the interwar period also help explain the outset of the war. The weakness of the Weimar Republic, followed by the establishment of a one-party totalitarian regime, provides insight into the consolidation of political

Levels of Analysis Meets Realism

Where do IR theory, the concept of power, and the levels-of-analysis approach meet? Understanding the interplay of these tools and concepts is not always easy. One example of the interactive relationship between the levels-of-analysis approach and IR theory is evident in the development and evolution of realist thought.

Classical realism, which we identify with great thinkers over the centuries such as Thucydides, Niccolo Machiavelli, and Thomas Hobbes, had its origins in some fundamental assumptions about human nature. Put simply, classical realism assumes that people are self-interested and willing to resort to whatever means necessary in order to ensure their survival in a state of existence that is for the most part, in Hobbes' memorable words, "solitary, poor, nasty, brutish, and short." The result of this elemental "truth" for realists when we extend and apply it to global politics is a global system comprised of states that, as mere collections of individuals, mirror these properties of humanity, albeit on a larger scale. In short, the classical realist view of how global politics works derives from its view of the human condition—namely, that states, like individuals, are prone to conflict and locked in a perpetual power struggle.

One outgrowth of the introduction of behavioralism to the field of IR in the mid-20th century was the introduction of systems theory to the field, and with that the birth of "neorealism." In this vein, scholars such as Kenneth Waltz (1979) argued that while the emphases of classical realism on power, self-interest, and conflict as driving forces in global politics are correct, deriving conclusions about how global politics works on the basis of studying individual states or their leaders is logically flawed, since these are merely units in the system. Rather, to develop generalizations and identify patterns, one must focus on the system level of analysis and examine the ways in which the prevailing anarchic structure of the global system creates and promotes the conditions by which power, self-interest, and conflict prevail.

This brief discussion of classical realism and neorealism hardly does justice to the nuances of the two main schools of realist theory. What it does show us, however, is that even a common theoretical perspective can point in different directions in terms of which level of analysis we see as most important. In the end, what this—and this entire chapter—suggests is that how we know what it is we think we know is something that is very much a by-product of the lens through which we choose to view the world.

---

power and the drive to remilitarization. In societal terms, the legacy and perception of the Versailles Treaty, which required Germans to pay impossible reparations, only worsened the crippling economic impact of the Great Depression. These and other factors, both on their own and in conjunction with Hitler's skillful manipulation, contributed to Germany's movement down the path to war.

Likewise, the structure of the global system at the time, and in particular things such as the power vacuum caused by the isolationism of the United States, the limitations of the League of Nations, and the establishment of numerous vulnerable new states on Germany's doorstep in central and eastern Europe, are important systemic considerations. This brief inventory of factors regarding Germany's role in triggering World War II demonstrates the merits of the levels-of-analysis approach as a conceptual tool for thinking about the relationship between power and discrete categories of actors in global politics.

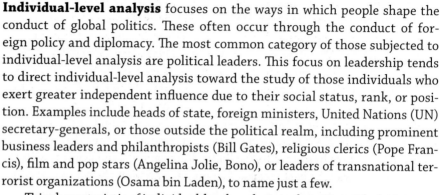 Individual-Level Analysis

individual-level analysis Emphasizes the ways in which people shape the conduct of global politics.

Individual-level analysis focuses on the ways in which people shape the conduct of global politics. These often occur through the conduct of foreign policy and diplomacy. The most common category of those subjected to individual-level analysis are political leaders. This focus on leadership tends to direct individual-level analysis toward the study of those individuals who exert greater independent influence due to their social status, rank, or position. Examples include heads of state, foreign ministers, United Nations (UN) secretary-generals, or those outside the political realm, including prominent business leaders and philanthropists (Bill Gates), religious clerics (Pope Francis), film and pop stars (Angelina Jolie, Bono), or leaders of transnational terrorist organizations (Osama bin Laden), to name just a few.

This characteristic of individual-level analysis is changing with the increasing ability of everyday individuals to influence global politics. The WikiLeaks scenario is again instructive as yet another example of the power and influence of "new media" alongside social media applications, such as Facebook, Twitter, and YouTube. Harnessing the technology we normally use on an individual-level basis, people have used these powerful social media platforms to affect global politics. To be sure, neither the WikiLeaks site nor Assange himself is going to usher in the demise of the state or the dismantling of the global system. At the same time, what the WikiLeaks story tells us is that ordinary individuals with access to information and technology—and, in Assange's case, financial capital—can significantly impact and alter the conduct of global politics. Indeed, there is no telling the impact which Assange's decision to release thousands of Hillary Clinton's personal emails on the eve of the 2016 US Presidential election may have had on the outcome of that election and, as a result, the course of US foreign policy going forward.

Governments Don't Understand Cyber Warfare.

Rationality and Its Limits

Individual-level analysis seeks to explain how the ways in which humans function, both individually and collectively, help to explain their thinking, decisions, and behavior on matters of importance to global politics. One important but often unstated assumption of those employing individual-level analysis is that humans are rational actors able to identify their interests and preferences and then order their actions accordingly. To be sure, most humans possess the faculties to make "rational" and self-serving decisions when faced with important choices. Still, human beings are complex and often act in ways that hardly seem rational. Suicide bombers probably do not seem rational to many readers of this text, in that they willingly take other lives and give up their own in service of some larger cause. On the other end of the spectrum, acts of selflessness or even altruism, such as first responders rushing into the smoking hulk of the Twin Towers on 9/11, also seem to defy rational explanation. Many of us do things that may be risky (driving a car) or self-defeating (overeating), and thus irrational, without thinking twice about it.

One way of reconciling the difference between assumed and actual human behavior is by recognizing the limitations to rational choices all of us face in every decision we make. These limits are determined by how much information is available to us, time constraints, or subconscious biases and prejudices we hold. Indeed, most individual decisions are a by-product of what the economist Herbert Simon (1957) referred to as **bounded rationality**. Our choices involve a blend of calculation and preference ordering, as well as the "guesswork" that goes along with the fact that none of us possesses all the necessary input we need to make the "best" decision at any given point in time. Such a concept helps us understand how, in the absence of a solid command of Russian strategic calculations, NATO decision-makers determined that the deployment of additional military hardware to the Baltic States and Poland beginning in the spring of 2016 was the best means of counteracting what they continue to see as Russian expansionism.

Cognitive Factors

It is similarly important to remember that individual decision-makers are influenced by cognitive, emotional, psychological, and even biological factors. Whether you are a foreign minister or a university student, it may be tough to concede that you confront real limits to your ability to "think through" a problem of consequence and come up with an effective solution. Human beings are prone to adopt one of a range of mental strategies for coping with these cognitive limits. Three examples of such coping mechanisms are cognitive consistency, optimistic bias, and heuristic devices.

COGNITIVE CONSISTENCY. Decision-makers seek **cognitive consistency** by discounting ideas and information that contradict their beliefs. The controversy over the snarl of information and misinformation about Iraq's abilities and intentions preceding the U.S.-led invasion has lasted—and will continue—for years, but it is informative to ask why in 2003 top decision-makers in London and Washington were willing to accept intelligence reports that Saddam Hussein's regime in Baghdad was attempting to buy uranium from Africa, despite insistence to the contrary from UN officials. One reason is that this finding "fit" with the existing negative images of Saddam Hussein and his intentions, whereas believing information that there was no nuclear program would have created **cognitive dissonance** among decision-makers. As some involved in the decision-making later admitted, the decision to go to war in Iraq was ultimately based on incorrect information.

OPTIMISTIC BIAS. People also justify their decisions by overestimating the likelihood that they will lead to a successful outcome (Johnson, 2004). Social psychologists refer to this

bounded rationality A concept that rational choices of individuals are bound or limited by time pressures, imperfect information, and biases that influence those choices.

cognitive consistency The tendency of individuals to hold fast to prevailing views of the world and to discount contradictory ideas and information in the process.

cognitive dissonance A discordant psychological state in which an individual attempts to process information contradicting his or her prevailing understanding of a subject.

Wishful thinking is common in human decision making. Saddam Hussein seemed to believe that he would politically survive a war with the United States in 2003, just as he had in 1991. Less than a year after this photo was taken, however, Saddam was overthrown by a US-led military invasion.

optimistic bias The pysychological tendency of individuals—particularly those in power—to overrate their own potential for success and underrate their own potential for failure.

hawk/hawkish In foreign policy, a term used to describe individuals and/or attitudes that favor a more aggressive, coercive, "hard-line" position and approach often predicated on military strength.

heuristic devices A range of psychological strategies that allow individuals to simplify complex decisions.

phenomenon as **optimistic bias**. In the view of some scholars, this bias and the "illusion of control" it fosters explain why "**hawkish**" leaders often win out in policy debates concerning the use of force (Kahneman & Renshon, 2007). For example, given the overwhelming forces that were mounted against him by the spring of 2003, it is hard to understand why Saddam Hussein chose to fight rather than retreat safely into exile.

HEURISTIC DEVICES. A third way that humans exhibit cognitive limitations is when we use **heuristic devices**. These are mental shortcuts that help us make decisions more easily by allowing us to skip the effort of information gathering and thorough analysis. Stereotypes are one type of heuristic device. For example, President Trump and others in his administration recurrently equate Islam and terrorism even though many terrorist incidents have no link to Islam at all. In fact, many argue that linking Islam to terrorism is a distortion of Islamic teaching and significantly discounts the fact that just as many terrorist incidents are perpetrated by groups with other religious ties (including Christianity) or with no religious ties at all.[2]

Analogies are another heuristic shortcut (Breuning, 2003; Dyson & Preston, 2006). We make comparisons between new situations or people and situations or people that we have earlier experienced or otherwise have learned about. One such connection that frequently figures in policy debates is the Munich analogy. This refers to the decision of France and the United Kingdom to abandon their ally Czechoslovakia and allow Nazi Germany to annex part of it in order to appease Nazi Germany in 1938. This concession failed to prevent war, and as a result, World War II signified the failure of appeasement. The "lesson" that later leaders drew from this was that compromise with dictators encourages them. The use of the Munich analogy is widespread, and it is often applied any time a politician accuses an opponent of offering too many concessions in international negotiations.

British Prime Minister Neville Chamberlain famously declared "peace in our time" after negotiating the fate of Czechoslovakia with Adolf Hitler in September 1938. Since then, Chamberlain's failed policy of appeasement at Munich has become a common analogy applied (accurately or not) to decisions to negotiate with powerful adversaries.

Sex and Gender

As discussed in Chapter 2, sex and gender are additional factors to consider when thinking about the influence of individuals on global politics. Sex is a biological variable that does not account for the ways society shapes the roles that men and women play in sociopolitical interactions. To an even greater degree, gender—a social construct rooted in idealized types of masculinity and femininity—is a crucial variable defining how individuals think about, pursue, and use power. Crucial gender analysis applications have been most prominent in feminist IR scholarship, whether in looking at the gendered nature of military and defense issues (Cohn, 1987), hegemonic power relations (Shepherd, 2015; Weber, 1999), or the structural inequalities and discrimination that require us to rethink prevailing notions of the global order and how global politics "works," including the marginalized roles and overlooked contributions of women (Enloe, 2014; Ruane, 2011; Tickner, 1992).

Social scientists are really just beginning to scratch the surface in accounting for how gender explains behavior in global politics (Ackerly & True, 2010; Caprioli, 2004; Carpenter, 2006; Tripp, 2010). For example, why it is that while half of the world's population are women, there has yet to be a woman UN Secretary-General—an outcome that also did not materialize in October 2016 despite assurances to the contrary in the selection process.[3] Also, consider things like the **gender opinion gap** on a range of issues, including war. Public opinion surveys of Americans have almost always found women less ready than men to resort to or to continue war. This outcome is true globally, with men in Australia, Canada, Great Britain, and Italy being 10% to 15% more likely to hold a favorable attitude toward war than women. These differences in attitudes persist and apply as well to military counterterrorism measures such as drone strikes (see Table 3.1).

This is not to argue that women leaders will refrain from engaging in conflict. Margaret Thatcher (former British prime minister in the 1970s and 1980s) and Golda Meir (former Israeli prime minister) rank high on any list of the most "hawkish" world leaders in the post–World War II era. But research has shown that including female voices in decision-making positively impacts the potential for conflict resolution. In addition, women overall are less prone to advocate violence as a means of conflict resolution (see Anderson, 2016; Simmons, 2011; Caprioli & Boyer, 2003). Thus, leaders like Thatcher and Meir are most likely outliers when the bigger picture is viewed.

Beyond introducing gender as a variable in global politics, feminist theory reveals critical and previously overlooked or ignored issues affecting women and girls, such as the systematic use of rape as a weapon of war or the transnational sex trade. One of the primary contributions of feminist IR scholarship is the extent to which it reveals the disproportionate—and disproportionately negative—impact that the "normal," everyday conduct of global politics has on women (Tickner, 2001). At the same time, the leading edge of contemporary feminist IR scholarship has advocated for the consideration of women as agents rather than as victims, with an increased focus on analyzing the active role of women as warriors, human traffickers, and terrorists (Cunningham, 2003; Sjoberg & Gentry, 2007). Advances in the study of gender have also exposed the fallacy of a gender binary (the notion that only two genders, male and female, exist), paving the way for greater attention to the place of transgender persons in global politics (Sjoberg, 2012).

gender opinion gap The difference in attitudes on various issues between those identifying as male and those identifying as female along any one of a number of dimensions, including foreign policy preferences.

Table 3.1 Global Gender Gap on Drone Strikes

A July 2013 Global Pew Research Center survey revealed profound differences between men and women in attitudes toward US drone strikes across a diverse range of countries. Such findings are indicative of pervasive differences by sex and gender in attitudes toward the efficacy of military force.

% APPROVE OF U.S. DRONE STRIKES			
	TOTAL	**MALE**	**FEMALE**	**MALE-FEMALE GAP**
	%	%	%	%
Japan	25	41	10	-31
Czech Rep.	32	47	17	-30
Canada	43	57	28	-29
Australia	44	58	30	-28
Germany	45	58	33	-25
Spain	21	34	9	-25
Britain	39	51	27	-24
Poland	35	45	26	-19
U.S.	61	70	53	-17
France	45	52	38	-14
S. Korea	31	38	24	-14
Uganda	43	49	36	-13

Source: Drake, Pew Research Center, 23 May 2013. Available online at: https://www.pewresearch.org/fact-tank/2013/05/23/a-majority-of-americans-still-support-use-of-drones-despite-questions/.

Tutorial: Acting As President.

Leadership

Although individual-level analysis is not and should not be solely concentrated on high-ranking leaders, they do receive most of the emphasis. This is partly due to the structure of global politics, as the conduct of foreign policy is more closely tied to a cadre of top leaders than is domestic politics. This is also partly pragmatic, in that IR scholars have more available information concerning individual leaders on which to base their analyses.

The branch of individual-level analysis focusing largely on specific individual leaders is sometimes called idiosyncratic analysis, due to the focus on each leader's unique (idiosyncratic) characteristics (Renshon & Larson, 2002). The fundamental question idiosyncratic analysis asks is how the personal traits of leaders affect their conception and use of power. Why, for example, are older leaders more likely than younger ones to initiate and escalate military confrontations (Horowitz, McDermott, & Stam, 2005)? How does the extent of an individual leader's experience impact her or his decisions (Calin & Prins, 2015)? Two possible factors to consider when employing idiosyncratic analysis are personality type and operational code.

PERSONALITY TYPE. When studying personality types, scholars examine a leader's basic orientations toward self and others, behavioral patterns, and attitudes about such politically relevant concepts as power and authority (Dyson, 2006). There are numerous categorization schemes. One of the most well-known schemes places personality along an active-passive scale and a positive-negative scale (Barber, 1985). Active leaders are policy innovators; passive leaders are reactors. Positive personalities have egos strong enough to enjoy (or at least accept) the contentious political environment; negative personalities are apt to feel burdened, even abused, by political criticism.

Ellen Johnson Sirleaf was the first woman in Africa to be a democratically elected head of state. As the president of Liberia, Johnson Sirleaf made special efforts to appoint women in her cabinet and encouraged women to take a public leadership role.

Of recent US presidents, Bill Clinton is a prime example of an active-positive personality. He reveled in the trappings of authority that came with his job and admitted that he was "almost compulsively overactive" (Renshon, 1995:59). Scholars differ on President George W. Bush. One assessment is that he was an active-positive personality who "love[d] his job and [was] very energetic and focused" (DiIulio, 2003:3). Others characterized Bush as positive-passive, in part because of perceptions of his "hands-off" delegation of authority to other top-ranking officials (Etheredge, 2001). Former President Barack Obama might fall into the active-negative category: his presidency featured an extensive number of policy initiatives, while he also frequently lamented the degree of partisan rancor in American politics and the isolation of the presidency. Canadian prime minister Justin Trudeau and French president Emmanuel Macron likely also fit into the active category, although their full stories have yet to be finalized. And soon-to-depart German Chancellor Angela Merkel became more active as a policy initiator as her time in office progressed.

OPERATIONAL CODE. An additional way of analyzing the impact of individuals on global politics is through the prism of a leader's "operational code" (George, 1969). Whatever their source, a person's perceptions create his or her worldview (Hermann & Keller, 2004). As a result, taking into account a decision-maker's **operational code**—meaning his or her philosophical beliefs (assumptions regarding the fundamental nature of politics, conflict, power, and the individual) and instrumental beliefs (specific beliefs concerning the appropriate method for attaining the ends one desires)—can be a highly effective way of explaining that person's decisions and behaviors (Schafer & Walker, 2006;

operational code How an individual acts in a given situation, based on a combination of one's fundamental worldview and understanding of the nature of politics.

Table 3.2 Alexander George and Operational Code Analysis

Alexander George was one of the first to apply the concept of "operational codes" specifically to the study of IR and foreign policy. His questions about philosophical and instrumental beliefs remain the basis for such analysis several decades later.

PHILOSOPHICAL BELIEFS	INSTRUMENTAL BELIEFS
1. What is the "essential" nature of political life? Is the political universe essentially one of harmony or conflict? What is the fundamental character of one's political opponents?	1. What is the best approach for selecting goals or objectives for political action?
2. What are the prospects for the eventual realization of one's fundamental political values and aspirations? Can one be optimistic, or must one be pessimistic on this score; and in what respects the one and/or the other?	2. How are the goals of action pursued most effectively?
3. Is the political future predictable? In what sense and to what extent?	3. How are the risks of political action calculated, controlled, and accepted?
4. How much "control" or "'mastery" can one have over historical development? What is one's role in "moving" and "shaping" history in the desired direction?	4. What is the best "timing" of action to advance one's interest?
5. What is the role of "chance" in human affairs and in historical development?	5. What is the utility and role of different means for advancing one's interests?

Source: George (1969:201–217).

Walker, Schafer, & Young, 1998). Table 3.2 provides further elaboration of the various components of the operational code.

For example, the roots of President Barack Obama's operational code were based on a philosophical belief set in which the United States operates in a complex, technology-driven, interconnected world. This led Obama to favor a multilateral, diplomatic approach. Conversely, President George W. Bush's operational code was derived from the fact that he was, in his own words, more a "gut" player than an intellectual (Daalder & Lindsay, 2003:7). This personality feature, in combination with the influence of his religious convictions, may explain why Bush tended to see the world in "black and white" terms.[4] Though still in his first term, President Donald J. Trump's operational code appears to revolve around what he has dubbed the "art of the deal" and his own unshakeable conviction in his ability to single-handedly broker favorable agreements regardless of the nature of the problem.

State-Level Analysis

For all the importance of individual-level variables, in global politics we often associate power and its use with nation-states. **State-level analysis** emphasizes the characteristics of states and how they make and implement foreign policy choices (Bueno de Mesquita, 2002; Hudson, 2005; Smith, Dunne, & Hadfield, 2016). What is important from the perspective of state-level analysis is how a sovereign state's political structure and dynamics shape decisions,

state-level analysis Emphasizes the characteristics of states and how they make and implement foreign policy choices.

behaviors, and overall use of power on the world stage (Chittick & Pingel, 2002; Kaarbo, 2015).

We can return to the WikiLeaks case to illustrate the degree to which states can and do use the power at their disposal in a changing global political environment. For obvious reasons, states oppose the widespread disclosure of sensitive information concerning the inner workings of their foreign policy process. Yet, as we discussed previously, the Internet is an extremely useful tool that allows the rapid flow of vital information across borders and boundaries (phys-

Julian Assange and Wikileaks captured the imagination of many protesters and critics of unchecked state power. Here, Russians express their support for Assange.

ical and otherwise), making it difficult for states to regulate. Practically speaking, any attempt to restrict Internet activity by states can be undermined by relocating a website to another server in another political jurisdiction, as WikiLeaks did repeatedly early on in its existence. More recently, questions persist concerning the prospect of states (notably Russia) cooperating with WikiLeaks by providing hacked emails and other sensitive documents to influence the outcomes of elections in the United States, France, the United Kingdom, and elsewhere.[5]

State-level analysis affords us the ability to look specifically at where a state's power originates. Although it is common to focus on military might and wealth, those elements of power depend on more basic factors, including the type and efficacy of the government, natural resource endowments, technological infrastructure, and demographic characteristics. The following discussion provides an accessible (if simplified) grouping of these factors under the headings of governmental and societal sources of state power.

Governmental Sources

The state has traditionally been the central actor in the global system. Accordingly, each state's pursuit of its interests through whatever sources of power are available was often considered to be the central force shaping global politics. Assessing a state's use of power in pursuit of its foreign policy goals is often referred to as **statecraft**. Scholar Michael Mastanduno defined statecraft as involving "the application and interplay of multiple instruments—military, economic, diplomatic, and informational—to achieve the multiple objectives of states, including national security, economic prosperity, and political prestige and influence" (1998:826).

When conducting state-level analysis, we should isolate and study those governmental factors that explain the power that states have available at their disposal to effectively engage in statecraft. Here, we discuss four such factors: state sovereignty, regime authority, military capability, and economic capacity.

statecraft The use of military, economic, diplomatic, and ideational tools in the pursuit of clearly defined foreign policy interests and objectives.

STATE SOVEREIGNTY.   Perhaps the most important factor to take into account when we assess governmental sources of power is state sovereignty. In an anarchic system organized around sovereign states, it is this condition that determines first and foremost whether or not a national group or political unit will have the status and "clout" necessary to engage in the conduct of global politics. State sovereignty effectively rests on the satisfaction of four conditions:

1. The existence of a clearly defined and identifiable national group, oriented around some common characteristic(s), seeking self-determination.

2. The recognized dominion of that group over a clearly demarcated territorial space.

3. The formation and successful implementation of an effective governing mechanism by that group.

4. The full recognition of all the aforementioned conditions by other states and the international community.

In some ways, it is the last—and most subjective—condition that is the most important. The recognition of a state's sovereignty by other states underscores the degree to which state sovereignty is a social construction. Following from this, it is not hard to see that sovereignty confers significant power on a national group that attains statehood and significantly limits one that does not. Sovereign states have representation at the UN and all international conferences, signatory status on international treaties, and the legal right to non-interference in their domestic affairs (according to the UN Charter). As a result, state sovereignty serves as an important platform for the exercise of power in global politics—and helps explain why stateless nations (e.g., the Palestinian nation) seek statehood and why multinational nation-states (e.g., the former Yugoslavia) sometimes fragment along national or ethnic lines.

REGIME AUTHORITY.   There is no such thing as a single foreign policy process. The way that states formulate and conduct foreign policy varies considerably. One important variable is the country's **regime type**. Regime types range along a scale that has absolute authoritarian governments on one end and unfettered democratic governments on the other. The more authoritarian a government is, the more likely that the foreign policy process will center itself in a narrow segment of the government, even in the hands of the chief executive. No government is absolutely under the thumb of any individual, however. States are too big and too complex for that, and thus secondary leaders (e.g., foreign ministers), bureaucrats, interest groups, and other domestic actors play a role even in authoritarian systems.

At the other end of the scale, the conduct of statecraft by democracies is a more open process, with additional inputs from legislators, the media, public opinion, and opposition parties. The power of the executive may be practically fragmented or constitutionally limited as well. For example, in the United States, the Senate is given the authority to formally ratify (approve) all foreign treaties—an arrangement that has often posed difficult challenges to

regime type   The type of government prevailing in a given society.

presidents engaged in complex negotiations. This was the case for President Obama in the July 2015 nuclear deal with Iran, resulting in a significant reduction in the scope of the agreement in order for it to go through.

That said, a country's top leadership tends to dominate the practice of state-craft somewhat by design, regardless of regime type. There are multiple reasons why power tends to be centralized at the "top" of the political system. For example, as public opinion and attitude surveys consistently report, foreign policy issues are generally less **salient** than domestic issues in the vast majority of countries (Holsti, 2004). Issues about which the public knows or cares little are, naturally, issues over which political leaders tend to exert more authority. For instance, President Obama spent a good portion of his second term in office promoting and negotiating the terms of one of the most ambitious trade accords ever developed—the Trans-Pacific Partnership. This agreement to reduce barriers to trade between and among the United States and 11 other countries (Japan, Malaysia, Vietnam, Singapore, Brunei, Australia, New Zealand, Canada, Mexico, Chile, and Peru) had significant economic consequences, but it drew relatively little attention from the media or the public until the 2016 presidential election campaign, when then-candidate Donald J. Trump pledged to "kill" the agreement (a pledge he made good on immediately after inauguration in January 2017).

Bureaucracy also influences every state's use of power, regardless of the strength or type of its government. Although political leaders legally command the bureaucracy, they find it difficult to control the vast understructures of their governments. President Vladimir Putin of Russia and then–US President

salient The degree to which an issue, question, or problem can be said to resonate with or "matter" to the general public.

bureaucracy The bulk of the state's administrative structure that continues to serve the public even when political leaders change.

Trans-Pacific Partnership leaders before their meeting in Manila, Philippines, on November 17, 2015.

George W. Bush candidly conceded that gap during a joint press conference. The two presidents were expounding on a new spirit of cooperation between their two countries when a reporter asked if they could "say with certainty that your teams will act in the same spirit?" Amid knowing laughter, Bush replied, "It's a very good question you ask, because sometimes the intended [policy] doesn't necessarily get translated throughout the levels of government [because of] bureaucratic intransigence." President Putin agreed. "Of course, there is always a bureaucratic threat," he asserted.[6]

MILITARY CAPABILITIES.   In an anarchic global system with no universal world government, military power is a huge determinant of a state's power. Assessing a particular state's military power objectively, however, is trickier than you might imagine. Some aspects of military power, such as defense spending, are easy to count. Others, including training, preparedness, and morale, are harder to quantify.

Defense spending is one of the largest categories in most countries' budgets, and there can be little doubt that the level of spending has some impact on military capabilities. US military expenditures ($686 billion in 2019, not including supplemental allocations for military counter-terrorism operations) far exceed those of any other country.[7] As such, there are few scenarios in which the armed forces of any other country could defeat the United States in a conventional war. Nonetheless, President Donald J. Trump submitted a budget request calling for a 5% increase for 2020.[8] Yet looking at defense spending in the aggregate or on a per capita basis (controlling for population) can be misleading because it does not account for significant differences in overall size and performance of a country's economy or the changing landscape of security threats, such as global terrorism (discussed in detail in Chapter 7).

Apart from defense spending or types of armaments, state-level analysis of military power can focus on a country's military personnel. Here too, we must account for a number of different factors. The aggregate number of troops, both total and compared to an opponent, is one facet. For example, according to the 2015 "Military Balance" report from the International Institute for Strategic Studies, China (2.84 million), India (2.8 million), Russia (1.5 million), and the United States (1.35 million), all have enough active military forces to play a major global role.[9] By contrast, Timor-Leste, one of the world's newest states and with just over 1,300 troops, has very little military muscle to use as a diplomatic asset. As for spending, governments must measure sheer numbers of troops against reasonable estimates of their potential use. For example, the large US military force becomes less dominant when we consider its numerous and extensive global commitments, leading to **overstretch** in the view of some analysts.

The quality of a state's military personnel is also important to consider. A military force comprised of intelligent, healthy, disciplined, and well-trained people is far more likely to be an effective instrument of state power than one that is undereducated, plagued by malnutrition and disease, undisciplined, or poorly trained in tactics, strategy, and weapons systems. Another related

overstretch A concept developed by historians that suggests a recurring tendency of powerful actors to overextend themselves by taking on costly foreign policy commitments that deplete their finances and generate domestic discord.

factor is whether a state's armed forces serve on an all-volunteer basis (as in the United States or India) or through conscription (as in Russia or Israel). Conventional wisdom holds that an all-volunteer armed force is likely to attract better recruits and exhibit greater morale and professionalism than a force raised by the draft.

ECONOMIC CAPACITY.   A state's influence in global politics is also a function of its economic capacity. Some determinants of a state's economic power include financial position, natural resources, industrial output, and agricultural output. The starting point for evaluating a state's economic power is its basic financial position. The overall size of the economy is one factor, and here, bigger is better. Take the United States as an example. According to World Bank and International Monetary Fund statistics, the US Gross Domestic Product (GDP)—an aggregate measure of total economic output—of $16.8 trillion is not only immense but also the world's largest, nearly double that of the next largest country (China, at $9.3 trillion), and equal to 23% of the world's combined GDP. Other important measures of financial position include the scope of a country's exports of goods and services. Here again, the US position is strong, with over $2.3 trillion in exports in 2017—slightly less than the world's leading exporter (China) and significantly more than the third largest (Germany). The extent of a state's foreign investment is also telling. In 2018, Americans had more than $25 trillion tied up in assets abroad, far more than any other country.

The aggregate size of a state's economy is only part of the story, however; financial solvency is also key to a state's economic power. This includes a country's total debt, annual budget deficits (when expenditures exceed revenues), and foreign obligations. The US example, as well as that of Greece, Spain, and Portugal, illustrates the vulnerabilities associated with large and expanding budget deficits and overall debt. The US government has run a budget deficit for all but 4 of the 35 years between Fiscal Year 1980 and Fiscal Year 2015, with banks in countries such as China holding enormous sums of resulting debt. One result of chronic deficit spending is that the US government has had to borrow more money from foreign sources to finance its debt, as Figure 3.1 shows.

Another measure of relevance here is a state's import-export ratio. The United States imports far more than it exports, and it has rung up a trade deficit during all but two years since 1971. Thus far, the immense size of the US economy has been able to absorb these negative trends, but some experts are dubious about that prospect in the future (Layne, 2012).

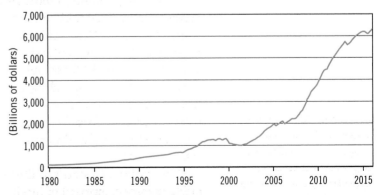

Figure 3.1   To finance its budget deficits, the US government borrows money, partly by selling bonds to foreign countries. Increasingly, such borrowing creates vulnerabilities for the US economy. In 2015, approximately 47% of US government debt was held by foreign governments. (Federal Reserve Economic Data)

Industrialization has made a state's endowment of energy, mineral, and other natural resources an increasingly important factor determining its power. Generally speaking, the greater a country's self-sufficiency in vital natural resources, the less its dependence on other actors, and vice versa. The two claims inform a third one—that possessing a surplus of a vital resource that other countries require makes a state relatively more powerful. Yet even if a country has a bounty of natural resources, its power is limited unless it can convert those assets into energy, goods, and services.

Oil is the most obvious example of these dynamics, as illustrated in Map 3.1. For countries with large reserves, high production, and low consumption, this "black gold" has historically been a major source of revenue. Oil has also increased the global political power and significance of Saudi Arabia, the Gulf States (Bahrain, Qatar, the United Arab Emirates, and others), and other oil-surplus countries. By contrast, Europe, Japan, and the United States have limited reserves and use far more petroleum than they produce. The resulting demand for petroleum has made these countries vulnerable to disruptions in the flow of oil and to fluctuations in energy prices—a vulnerability they have sought to reduce through finding new supplies or, in some cases, substitution to "greener" technologies.

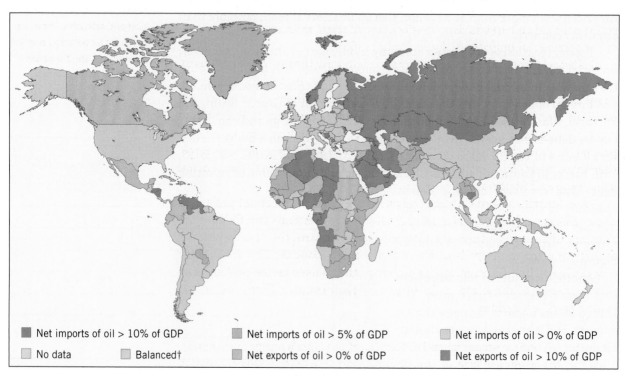

■ Net imports of oil > 10% of GDP	■ Net imports of oil > 5% of GDP	■ Net imports of oil > 0% of GDP
□ No data	■ Balanced†	■ Net exports of oil > 0% of GDP	■ Net exports of oil > 10% of GDP

Map 3.1   The persistent demand for energy ensures that many of the world's major oil producers and exporters have a source of significant financial revenue (expressed here as a percentage of GDP). This should correlate to a better performing economy and a stronger state. Similarly, high levels of oil imports should correspond with high levels of industrial activity, which is also a marker of a better performing economy and, by extension, state power. As with other data, patterns of oil exports and imports can be misleading, as a state's excessive reliance on exporting or importing a single natural resource can equate to vulnerability and weakness.

A country's agricultural capacity is also a reflection of its economic power. Self-sufficiency varies widely in the world. The United States not only meets its own needs, it also earns money from agricultural exports. In 2015, the US net agricultural trade surplus came to approximately $10 billion. Conversely, developing countries often have to use their economic resources to import food. Sub-Saharan Africa and South Asia are in particularly bad shape. Senegal, for one, needs to import machinery, fuel, and other products necessary to diversify and industrialize its economy, yet it must spend 29% of its limited import funds to buy food.[10]

Societal Factors

Assessing the power and capabilities of a state requires looking beyond those factors related or subject to governmental authorities. Undoubtedly, other societal variables can and do contribute to a state's power—both directly and indirectly. Here, we look briefly at three examples: political culture, demographics, and human development.

POLITICAL CULTURE.   Each country's foreign policy interests and orientation toward power usually reflect its **political culture**. This concept represents a society's widely held values and fundamental practices that are slow to change, particularly concerning civic affairs (Jung, 2002; Paquette, 2003). We can describe political cultures as democratic, authoritarian, militaristic, procedural, or xenophobic, among others (Pye & Verba, 1965).

> **political culture** A concept that refers to a society's long-held and fundamental practices and attitudes. These are based on a country's historical experiences and the values (norms) of its population.

Political leaders usually conduct statecraft in ways that are compatible with their society's political culture. Partly this is because the leaders themselves share many or all of those values, and partly because they wish to avoid the backlash that taking actions contrary to the dominant political culture would produce. To analyze any country's political culture, factors such as how its people feel about themselves and their country, how they view others, what role they think their country should play in the world, and what they see as moral behavior are all important.

How Americans and Chinese feel about themselves and about projecting their values to others provides an example. Both Americans and Chinese believe that their own cultures are superior. For Americans, this is called American exceptionalism. A similar sense of superiority among the Chinese is called Sinocentrism. The Chinese betray a view of themselves as the political and cultural center of the world in their word for their country, *Zhong Guó*, which means "middle kingdom."

DEMOGRAPHICS.   An additional determinant of a state's power is its population. Demographic categories of particular importance here include population size and the distribution of population by age. As is true for geography and territory, a country's population size can be a positive or a negative factor. Because a large population supplies military personnel and industrial workers, this usually correlates positively with major power status (think China, Germany, or the United States). It is unlikely, for instance, that Tonga (population 108,000 in

2019) will ever achieve great-power status. However, a large population may be disadvantageous if it is not in balance with resources. India, with 1.39 billion people in 2019, has the world's second-largest population, yet because of the country's poverty ($1,581 per capita GDP), it must spend much of its energy and resources tending to the basic needs of its massive and still primarily poor population.[11]

In considering the age distribution of a population, it is to a state's advantage to have a larger percentage of its population in the economically productive years (15–64 by international reporting standards). Some countries with booming populations have a high percentage of children who require support. In other countries with limited life expectancy, many people die before they complete their productive years. Finally, some countries are "aging," with a geriatric population segment that consumes more resources than it produces (Longman, 2004). According to the World Bank's World Development Indicators, 26% of Earth's population was less than 15 years old in 2015, 8% was 65 or over, and 66% was in the working-age years (age 15–64). Figure 3.2 shows the age distributions of several countries for comparative purposes. Many analysts would contend that South Korea is relatively advantaged by its large working-age population, whereas Uganda, with numerous children, and Italy, with a high percentage of senior citizens, are relatively disadvantaged.

Whereas growing populations and high ratios of children were once the main population worries, there is now growing worldwide concern about low birthrates, zero or even negative population growth, and population aging. A growing geriatric population challenges a country's ability to pay the cost of providing pensions as well as medical and other services to retired citizens. Population aging is already pronounced in economically developed countries and is projected to increase. By 2050, for instance, 33% of Japan's population

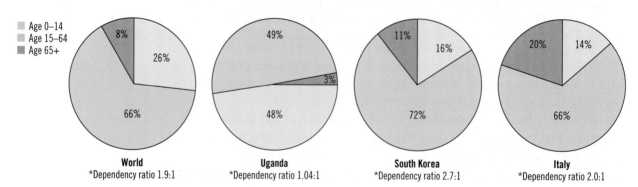

Figure 3.2 Many developing countries like Uganda have a population with a high percentage of children. These children consume resources for their education and general care that they will only begin to "repay" the system in terms of productivity and taxes when they become adults. A high percentage of senior citizens, as in Italy, is also economically suboptimal. South Korea has good age distribution, with 72% in the "working years."

*Dependency ratio is a World Bank calculation of the ratio of the working-age population (age 15–64) to the dependent population (age 14 and younger plus age 65 and older). Generally, the higher the ratio, the more economically advantaged a country is.

and 30% of Europe's will be age 65 and older. The US age distribution is still relatively well balanced, with 20% under the age of 14, 67% between the ages of 15 and 64, and 13% age 65 and older, although the US Census Bureau projects the retirement-age population to rise to 21% in 2050. Some of the social problems that occur with aging are also beginning to affect other, less affluent countries. The ramifications of China's "one-child" policy instituted to restrain population growth coupled with resulting increases in longevity, for instance, means that senior citizens will rapidly increase as a share of China's population, from 8% today to 25% by 2050. This could be part of the reason why the Chinese government recently ended this policy.[12]

HUMAN DEVELOPMENT.   As a measure of the health, well-being, and functioning of the population and society, human development (discussed at length in Chapter 11) is an important factor to consider when we analyze any state's power and capabilities. One key component of human development is education. A well-educated population is vital to a state's power.

Quantity of education is one factor. Although education has improved substantially in low-income countries as a result of its designation as a Millennium Development Goal, the primary school survival rate (the number starting school who make it to the last grade level) globally is still only 75%. In high-income countries, it is 98%.[13] Beyond primary school, the data become progressively worse. Less than half of children in low-income countries attend high school, and only about 9% receive any postsecondary technical or college education and can serve as the nucleus of the educated workforce that a modern economy needs. Moreover, in a circular problem, the lack of opportunity in many of the least developed countries (LDCs) creates a "brain drain," as those countries' professionals emigrate to seek a better life. Such problems are often compounded by other, noneconomic factors such as war and displacement, which often result in the complete collapse of the educational system or drastically restrict the ability of children to attend the schools that remain open. For example, UNICEF noted that the percentage of Syrian children attending school dropped from a pre-war total of 97% to less than half within two years—a figure which is undoubtedly much lower today.[14]

Yet another way to break down general educational statistics is to see how well a country trains various segments of its population. Most countries limit their potential by underutilizing major elements of their population. For example, sexism limits the possible contribution of women in many countries. In Bangladesh, for instance, a male teenager is almost twice as likely as a female teenager to enroll in secondary school. Racial, ethnic, and other bases of discrimination compound this failure. According to the last (2010) US Census, of the adults over age 25 in the United States, 20% of African Americans and 14% of Latinos, compared to 30% of whites, have completed a four-year college degree or beyond.

Public health also has direct implications for a state's power or weakness. Providing an example, Russian males are experiencing a health crisis largely due to widespread alcoholism and smoking. According to the World Health

Organization's Global Adult Tobacco Survey, over 60% of all adult Russian males smoke (more than three times the US rate), and the lung cancer death rate in Russia is over twice that of the United States. To make matters worse, about 60% of all Russian men are alcohol abusers, with the average Russian male drinking a quart of vodka every two days. As a result, the life span of the average Russian male has declined to less than 59 years (compared with 73 years for Russian women). If current trends continue, Russia's population could drop by a third in the next two decades. There are immense economic consequences to this decline as well, including lost productivity and the costs of providing medical treatment and supporting abandoned families.

Physical and Technical Factors

Lastly, physical and technical factors influence a state's power. The first one discussed here—technological sophistication—is at least partly in a state's control, while the second—geography—is a fixed condition with which a state must cope, adapt, and shape.

TECHNOLOGICAL SOPHISTICATION. Both in terms of availability and innovation, technology is a vital element of a state's power. Computers revolutionize business and education, robotics speed industry, new drilling techniques allow undersea oil exploration, microwaves speed information, and lasers bring the military to the edge of the future. Thus, technology is an integral influence on any state's power and capabilities. It is also worth noting, however, that technological advances have likewise created new vulnerabilities for the most advanced states, as concerns have increased about election hacking, financial vulnerability, and other cyber-crimes.

One source of American power is the considerable money that the government, corporations, and universities spend on research and development (R&D). Investment in basic research is an essential element in "the scientific balance of power."[15] According to 2016 data, the United States was the global leader in R&D investment, spending over $465 billion, ahead of the three next largest spenders on R&D: China ($333 billion), Japan ($160 billion), and Germany ($100 billion).

Transportation systems are a second and more specific part of the national infrastructure. The ability to move people, raw materials, finished products, and sometimes the military throughout its territory is another element of a country's power equation and is heavily dependent on technology. For example, faced with major demographic and environmental challenges as a function of rapid industrialization and urbanization, China has directed enormous sums toward investment in transportation—particularly in the industrial coastal cities. **Information and communications technology** is yet another part of the nation-state's technological infrastructure, one that is increasingly important to the power and influence of states. Satellites and computers have accelerated the revolution that began with radio and television. Enhanced communications technology increases efficiency and effectiveness in industry, finance, and the military.

information and communication technology An umbrella term referring to any communication device or application encompassing radio, television, cellular phones, computer and network hardware and software, satellite systems, and various services and applications.

Here again, the gaps among countries are wide. For example, US annual per capita expenditures on information and communications ($3,595) are more than 54 times that of China ($66). According to the World Bank's World Development Indicators, on a per capita basis in 2016, there were over twice as many people with "land lines" in the United States (39 out of every 100) than in China (5 of every 100) and significantly more people with access to the Internet in the United States than in China (76 of every 100, compared to 53 of every 100). For some additional context, the figures in Bangladesh were 1 of every 100 people for telephone lines and 18 of every 100 with Internet access.

GEOGRAPHY.   The territorial space over which a state exerts its sovereign authority is an important geographic factor. Many have long speculated that the British Empire was able to develop and last so long because Great Britain is a large island isolated from the rest of Europe and therefore more difficult to invade by other continental powers.

When thinking geographically, bigger is often better. As both the Napoleonic wars and World War II show, the immense expanse of Russia has repeatedly saved it from conquest. By contrast, Israel's small size gives it no room to retreat. In terms of a state's power reserves and capability, geographic location (including proximity to adversarial or friendly neighbors) can be an advantage or a disadvantage. Spain was able to avoid involvement in either world war partly because of its relative isolation from the rest of Europe. Poland, sandwiched between Germany and Russia, and Korea, stuck between China and Japan, have distinctly unfortunate locations. Location also impacts relative power. China's large conventional army has less of an influence on Beijing's relations with the United States than it does on relations with India, with whom it shares a (sometimes tense) border.

Similarly, a country's topography (mountains, rivers, and plains) is also important. The Alps form a barrier that has helped protect Switzerland from its larger European neighbors and spared the Swiss the ravages of both world wars. Throughout history, Afghanistan's rugged mountains have undermined various invaders, including the British, Soviets, and after 9/11, NATO troops trying to eliminate al-Qaeda and Taliban forces. Topography can also work against a country. For example, much of western and central Poland rests on a vast plain that has proved well suited historically to mounted cavalry and, later, to mechanized military offensives by expansionist neighbors like Germany and Russia.

Natural resource endowments can also contribute to power. Oil, minerals, and the ability to produce food in large quantities all enhance a state's power. Counterintuitively, however, resource richness is at times a source for weakness, especially when other factors of state power are weaker. **Resource curse theory** focuses on the difficulties experienced by many resource-rich countries in benefiting from their natural capital (renewable and non-renewable resource endowments). This is often paired with an inability to effectively provide for public welfare in those states, at least partly because of weak state governance capacity (Natural Resource Governance Institute, 2015; Sachs & Warner, 2001).

resource curse theory Focuses on the difficulties experienced by many resource-rich countries in benefiting from their resource wealth.

Lastly, climate also impact a state's power. Vietnam's tropical climate, with its monsoon rains and dense vegetation, made it difficult for American forces to use much of their superior weaponry during the Vietnam War. At the other extreme, the frigid Russian winter decimated Napoleon's soldiers in the winter of 1812–1813 and the German army during World War II. The formidability of the Russian winter led 19th-century Czar Nicholas I to comment that "Russia has two generals we can trust, General January and General February." One way in which climate and geography in general are likely to impact the power of all states in the years to come stems from the major dislocations we can attribute to global climate change, as we will discuss at length in Chapter 13.

🌐 System-Level Analysis

Despite the fact that states remain the central actor in the global system, they are not always able to freely convert available sources of power to achieve their interests. **System-level analysis** focuses on identifying and assessing the constraints and opportunities that the global system imposes on state and nonstate actors alike. In line with the realist and world systems approaches discussed in Chapter 2, this is a "top-down" approach to global politics that examines the system's social-economic-political-geographic characteristics and how they influence the actions of countries and other actors (Moore & Lanoue, 2003). Thus, while systems constrain state behavior, they also provide opportunities, especially to the dominant states in the system at a given point in time.

system-level analysis Focuses on identifying and assessing the constraints and opportunities that the global system imposes on state and nonstate actors alike. Also focuses analysis on how different system structures can shape behavior of actors within a system.

System-level analysis enables us to look for patterns in the interactions among all actors in the global system and to generalize about them. It also acknowledges that the conduct of statecraft requires states and their leaders to make choices in response to external constraints. These very real constraints stem largely from the structure of the global system, including factors such as the nature of authority and governance in that system and the distribution of power.

Revisiting the WikiLeaks case reminds us how a contemporary global system defined by growing interdependence among states, societies, and individuals creates new and unforeseen challenges for states and their leaders. Neither the challenge to state authority nor the challenge to individual leaders that WikiLeaks poses would exist without the Internet—which is both a product and a driver of global interdependence. The Internet and the various and innovative applications and sources of data it hosts comprise a loosely regulated but powerful medium for information distribution with a distinctly global reach. The Internet's fast, freewheeling, and "flat" nature, as well as the various and sundry applications of social media (e.g., Facebook, Twitter, Instagram, and YouTube) work hand-in-glove to enhance the impact of committed individuals (e.g., Assange) seeking to alter the dynamics of power in global politics.

System-level factors frequently limit the ability of weaker states to act in the pursuit of their interests while also limiting even the most powerful states at certain times and in certain circumstances. In the remainder of this chapter, we consider some of the primary concerns of system-level analysis in two basic groupings: structural characteristics and power relationships.

Structural Characteristics

Systemic-level analysis was introduced to the field of IR largely as a means of identifying general patterns and generating hypotheses relevant to a global political system (Boulding, 1956; Singer, 1961). Two structuring properties of particular relevance to the global system are, first, how the system organizes authority and, second, the scope and level of interdependence among actors in the system.

THE ORGANIZATION OF AUTHORITY.   The structure of authority for making and enforcing rules, allocating assets, and conducting other authoritative tasks in a political or social system can range from hierarchic (vertical) to anarchic (horizontal). Most systems, including the domestic political system in which you find yourself, tend toward the hierarchic end of the spectrum. They have a vertical authority structure in which higher levels of authority substantially regulate subordinate units.

Conversely, the global political system is a mostly horizontal authority structure. As discussed previously, it is organized around component units of sovereign states. At least theoretically, state sovereignty means that states have the legal right to noninterference in their internal affairs, and that they do not answer to any "higher" (i.e., global) governing authority. The result is a loosely organized system that is state-centric, with states existing in a self-help relationship with one another—what we know from Chapters 1 and 2 as "anarchy."

The anarchic nature of the global political system has numerous impacts on the behavior of the states and other actors that comprise it. For one, anarchy fosters militarization in many states because of the aforementioned "self-help" nature of the relationship between states. If a state is threatened, there is no global "911" to call for help. This is a stark contrast with most domestic political systems, in which the police and the courts exist to uphold a person's safety and security and the rule of law more generally. In an anarchic global political system, important and influential international organizations (e.g., the UN) and nongovernmental organizations (e.g., Amnesty International) do not possess militaries and thus can't enforce rules or laws by relying on a credible threat of punishment.

Although the structure of authority in the global political system is generally horizontal, this is changing in some issue areas. Many analysts contend that state sovereignty is declining, as even powerful states and actors are subject to a growing number of authoritative rules that international law establishes and international organizations promote. Countries still resist and often even reject global governance—as growing discord within the European Union (EU) reflects—yet in some cases they continue to comply, particularly when they view doing so as beneficial. For example, in 2010 the World Trade Organization (WTO) ruled in favor of a US and Japanese allegation that the EU was violating trade rules in policies regulating the import of flat-screen

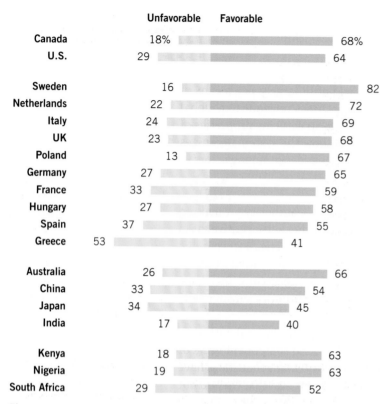

Figure 3.3 In a 2016 Pew public opinion poll, populations surveyed around the world reported varying, and sometimes surprisingly positive, attitudes toward the UN and global governance. Such attitudes are likely to vary widely not only across countries but over time, particularly in light of anecdotal evidence of mounting dissatisfaction.

transaction costs Imped-iments to commercial or other cooperative ventures stemming from a lack of trust between and among involved parties rooted in concerns about the enforceability of agreements.

televisions. This ruling came on the heels of the WTO ruling upholding an EU complaint that US tax breaks given to Boeing and other aircraft manufac-turers effectively acted as a subsidy, giving Boeing an unfair advantage over Europe's Airbus (again violating trade rules agreed to in the General Agree-ment on Tariffs and Trade).

Compliance with the constraints imposed by international institutions like the WTO often comes when states recognize that some global governing authority is necessary for beneficial interactions with other states. This ex-ample illustrates one of the primary arguments for expanding global gov-ernance and "vertical" authority in the global political system, as well as a reason for why it occurs when it does. If comprehensive and clear, interna-tional agreements have the potential to reduce what liberal IR theorists claim to be one of the primary barriers to international cooperation—namely, **transaction costs**.

Contrary to realists, liberals argue that states are not opposed to coop-eration, but are simply reluctant to cooperate because of the risks involved. In other words, states need answers to important questions (Will both or all parties uphold the agreements that they reach? Can the law adjudicate when disputes arise?) that only governance can provide. As a result, we see varying degrees of support around the world for international organizations such as the UN, with more supportive states, societies, and individuals likely pleased with the role of international organizations in reducing transaction costs and facilitating cooperation (see Figure 3.3).

INTERDEPENDENCE. A second structural characteristic of any system is the frequency, scope, and intensity of interactions among the units. In the global political system, interactions among actors have all grown extensively during the last half century. Economic interdependence provides the most obvious ex-ample, and it is often the touchstone for liberal arguments about the rise of com-plex interdependence and the resulting decline in state sovereignty (Keohane & Nye, 2001). The volume and value of goods and services traded and of foreign investment are continually expanding, and they far surpass those of even half a century ago. All but the most autarkic states (e.g., North Korea) are heavily dependent on other states for raw material inputs for goods that it produces, for finished goods and services that it needs, and/or as markets for products that it sells. Without extensive exports, the US economy would stagger because exported goods and services account for 12% of the US GDP.[16] Nevertheless, the fact of such widespread interdependence does not always correlate with support for international engagement and, in recent years, in fact seems to be triggering a backlash in the form of resurgent isolationism and nationalism (see Figure 3.4).

Data about expanding trade do not fully capture the degree to which the scope and intensity of global interactions are increasing **transnational** contacts at every level. For individuals,

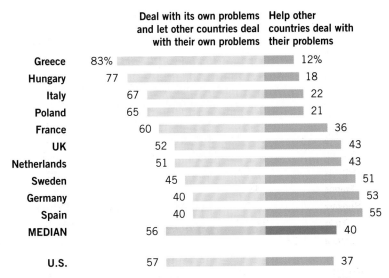

Figure 3.4 As indicated in a recent (2016) Pew Research Center survey, public attitudes in most Western countries reflects a growing sense of isolationism—a stark difference from the previous version of the same survey four years before.

the ease of travel and the expansion of modern telecommunications have made personal international interactions, once relatively rare, now commonplace. According to the US Census Bureau, between 1990 and 2010, the number of Americans traveling overseas increased 38%, from 44.6 million to 61.5 million. During the same period, the number of foreign visitors to the United States jumped 51%, from 39.4 million to 59.7 million.

Information and communications technologies such as the Internet, social media, smartphones, and satellite technology are also expanding the scope, level, and intensity of information flow between and among individuals and social groups. Trillions of phone calls, letters, and email messages add to the globalization of human interactions, and the Internet ignores borders as it connects people and organizations around the world as if they were in the next room. To cite just one example, satellite-transmitted television has revolutionized communications by providing more and different information to new and hungry audiences—as in the case of Al Jazeera, a Qatar-based global media conglomerate that first rose to prominence by offering an alternative to much of the state-controlled media in the Arab world.

The benefits of interdependence are many and often celebrated (Friedman, 2005; Keohane & Nye, 2001). Still, the absence of effective global governance means that the depth and expanse of networked interactions between and among societies and individuals can be hazardous. Most of us clearly enjoy the benefits that a smaller globe brings in terms of enhanced information flows, travel and mobility, and access to a diverse array of consumer goods and services. Yet at the same time, interdependence generates a host of densely networked and weakly governed connections in commerce, transport, energy and natural resources, migration, and information

transnational Social, political, economic, and cultural activities and processes that transcend and permeate the borders and authority of states.

technology—leaving us more sensitive and vulnerable to new security threats (Buzan, Wæver, & De Wilde, 1998).

Power Relationships

At the systemic level, considerations such as the number of powerful actors predominant in the system as well as the prevailing social context (e.g., dominant norms and ideas) heavily influence the practice of global politics. Whereas the former consideration speaks to the importance of "hard" (coercive and material) power, the latter suggests the impact that "soft" (persuasive and ideational) power can have on the wider global society of states.

POLARITY.   Historically, the number of powerful actors existing during any given time period has been used to characterize the global political system. Such power centers or "poles" (Wilkinson, 2004) are typically states or imperial powers, although one can think of nonstate actors (e.g., alliances or international organizations) in the same vein. Polarity is particularly important to the realist approach and its concern with the balance of power. Sometimes scholars use the term to describe the existing distribution of power, as in "the current balance of power greatly favors the United States." More classically, though, the theory of balance-of-power politics often associated with realism holds that (1) all states are power seeking; (2) ultimately, a state or bloc will attempt to become hegemonic (i.e., dominate the system); and (3) other states will *either* attempt to balance that dominance by increasing their own power and/or cooperating with other states *or* bandwagon with the hegemonic aspirant in order to capture the gains of allying with a dominant power (Walt, 1987).

System-level analysts concerned with polarity arrangements believe that the number of power poles in existence at any one time shapes how states (and individual leaders) are likely to act. A **unipolar system**, in which one actor is dominant, is likely to approach a vertical hierarchy such as that which exists in most domestic societies. In these systems, there is much less room for maneuver by weak states or those at odds with the dominant power. Unipolarity was arguably present in the immediate aftermath of the Cold War, with the United States the dominant actor. A **bipolar system** exists when two superpowers roughly equally split power and authority in the system, leading to the formation of blocs. The best example of bipolarity is the **Cold War** itself, with two superpowers, the United States and the USSR, representing the two "poles" in the system. A third arrangement, a **multipolar system**, prevails when power is fragmented among several great powers that can shift from rivals to allies (and back). A classic example of multipolarity is the so-called Concert of Europe, an alliance between the United Kingdom, Russia, Austria, and Prussia that prevailed from the end of the Napoleonic wars in 1815 through the outbreak of World War I in 1914. Figure 3.5 depicts these power configurations (unipolarity, bipolarity, tripolarity, and multipolarity) and ways in which interaction patterns differ across them.

unipolar system A type of international system that describes a single country with complete global hegemony or preponderant power.

bipolar system A type of international system with two roughly equal actors or coalitions of actors that divide the international system into two "poles" or power centers.

Cold War A term used to describe the relations between the United States and the Soviet Union from about 1945 to about 1990. During that period, the two countries avoided direct warfare but remained engaged in very hostile interactions.

multipolar system A world political system in which power is primarily held by four or more international actors.

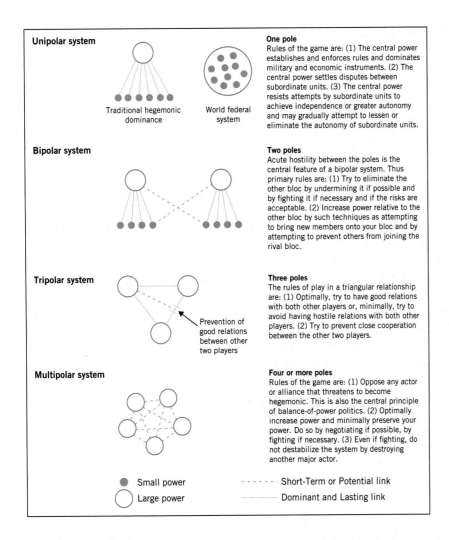

Figure 3.5 The relationships that exist among the actors in a particular type of international system structure vary because of the number of powerful actors, the relative power of each, and the permitted interactions within the system. This figure displays potential international system structures and the basic rules that govern relationships within each system. After looking at these models, which one, if any, do you think best describes the contemporary international system?

HEGEMONY. One illustration of how polarity influences global politics in practice is evident in the dynamics of a unipolar system and the related concept of **hegemony**. A hegemonic power is one that introduces and maintains control of the entire global political system. For hegemony to prevail, there must be a dominant actor in the system that possesses three distinct attributes: (1) commitment to a system governed by rules that players perceive as beneficial to most other major actors, (2) the material capability to enforce those rules, and (3) the political will to do so. From a system-level perspective, this impulse to power demonstrated by the hegemon dovetails with pressure in the system to maintain stability and order, providing "hegemonic stability" (Kindleberger, 1973).

The argument here is that "a unipolar system will be peaceful," but only as long as the hegemonic power acts like one (Wohlforth, 1999:23). This leads some scholars to worry that if a hegemon is unwilling or unable to assume

hegemony A systemic arrangement whereby one predominantly powerful actor possesses both the disproportionate material capabilities and the will to enforce a set of rules to lend order and structure to that system.

CHALLENGE YOUR ASSUMPTIONS

Toward an Era of Nonpolarity?

The concept of *polarity* introduced in this chapter assumes the existence of one to several great powers. These actors possess significant military, economic, diplomatic, technological, and natural resource advantages over the rest of the international community. But what if we live in a world in which such clear advantages no longer exist? Richard Haass, the president of the preeminent foreign policy think tank in the United States, the Council on Foreign Relations, has raised this possibility. In his forecast for the direction of global politics in the 21st century, Professor Haass has introduced the idea of *nonpolarity*. Haass accepts the premise of a decline in US power but, at the same time, sees no rising power sufficient enough to surpass (unipolarity) or even balance (bipolarity) the United States. He also rejects the more common assertion that the decline in US power is bringing the United States "back to the pack" and ushering in a new era of multipolarity.

Haass envisions a future in which power is multifaceted and spread out far beyond the narrow scope of a few great powers. Although five states (China, India, Japan, Russia, and the United States) and one regional governmental organization (the EU) currently merit that distinction, there are also multiple regional powers with extensive internal power reserves (Brazil, South Africa, Mexico, and Nigeria, to name a few). The real key to

Haass' argument is his claim that the growing importance of new types of actors and issues in global politics draws influence from a wider array of (nonmilitary) power assets. In a nonpolar system, we can reasonably consider as important centers of power international and regional organizations, nongovernmental organizations, corporations, terrorist organizations and paramilitaries, major media outlets, and even states and cities within nation-states.

Nonpolarity is the by-product of globalization and transnational networks, and of the increased volume, velocity, and importance of cross-border flows of goods, services, money, and ideas moving along those networks. Yet it is important to recognize, as Haass does, that an emerging nonpolar system is likely to be a world of great disorder. In a system where power is widely diffused, resulting in a void "at the top," the prospects for order and an effective response to important global issues, such as climate change, terrorism, and the proliferation of WMDs, may be limited. In turn, in such a "flat," nonhierarchic system, it would seem that the importance of multilateralism, cooperation, and networked responses to networked problems would be magnified.

What do you think? Does the concept of polarity still matter? Or are we entering a new, "nonpolar" era. If so, how might this affect you?

the responsibilities of maintaining order, the system could become unstable—triggering an onset of violence as well as extensive challenges to the "rules" underpinning that order which the hegemon is supposed to uphold (Ferguson, 2004; Lal, 2004).

Needless to say, there is considerable debate over such a rosy depiction. Some critics contend that hegemony is destabilizing, while others dismiss it out of hand as a destructive imperialistic impulse (Gitlin, 2003; Lobell, 2004). From the standpoint of "offensive realists," the anarchic nature of the global political system means that states constantly strive for an unattainable dominance. This striving generates a "tragedy of great power politics" in which rivalry and war are endemic (Mearsheimer, 2001). From the standpoint of power transition theory, hegemony naturally produces challengers and aspirants to the power and rules of a hegemon, with similar consequences (Organski & Kugler,

1980). The urge to resist perceived hegemonic domination may help explain why France, Germany, Russia, and China were all opposed to US action against Iraq in 2003 (Carter, 2003).

SOCIAL CONTEXT.   System-level analysts are concerned with the structure of the global political system and the distribution and deployment of power within it. Yet you will recall from the discussion earlier in this chapter that power is not something that is only coercive and material. It is not hard to imagine how social context, and in particular the dominant values or norms in the global political system, also provides a significant systemic constraint on the behavior of states and other actors.

As constructivist theorizing has helped reveal, power has persuasive and ideational (idea-based) dimensions that also help explain the system's structure and the favored behaviors, practices, and arrangements in it. As the English School theorist Hedley Bull (1977) pointed out, the very premise of a global political system and structure implies that the actors in that system comprise a loose society. Like domestic society, to the extent that a global society exists, we can say that it can turn on both coercion and persuasion. Also like domestic society, a global society exhibits certain ideas, values, and behaviors that we favor or accept (what sociologists would call "normative") and others that we do not favor or find unacceptable (which sociologists would call "deviant"). The commonplace label **rogue state(s)**, applied to regimes in places like North Korea or Sudan, reflects this very distinction.

Although the ability of powerful members of a global society to determine what is normative and what is deviant (and to reward the former and punish the latter) is nowhere near what it is in most domestic societies, some states clearly favor certain values and practices while others do not. Consider, for example, how powerful Western states and international institutions widely promote and actively support democracy as a system of government. Conversely, those same states and institutions publicly revile dictatorships and implement punitive measures, such as diplomatic and economic sanctions and threats of military invasion. Similarly, marginalized, isolated, and ultimately "illegitimate" actors carry out certain forms of behavior (acts of terrorism or genocide) that states and institutions widely, if not universally, condemn as "beyond the pale," whereas, powerful "legitimate" actors such as sovereign states may carry out acts (military intervention or trade wars) that may also have negative effects but that states and institutions accept—and even sometimes promote.

As in domestic society, those social actors with the most power and status often make the determination of what is normative and what is deviant in global politics (Checkel, 1999). In a global society, those actors are nation-states, as revealed in the fact that one of the most prominent proponents of this sociological view referred to that society as a society of states (Bull, 1977). Further to that point, it is the most materially powerful states which typically have the greatest influence on determining what is "legitimate," largely because they have the greatest capability to promote what they deem "normative" and to punish what they deem "deviant."

rogue state(s) A state that is perceived to be in noncompliance with the majority of prevailing rules, norms, and laws in the global system and therefore constituting a threat to order.

It is hard for some to accept that norms exist in a world where atrocities and injustices happen on a semi-regular basis. Moreover, it would be far too strong to say there is anything near a universally accepted standard of behavior—and certainly not one that has been or can be upheld. Yet whatever their limits or subjectivity, values do exist, and these are infused into global politics in both obvious and subtle ways. As interdependence has proceeded, so too have the prospects for greater convergence in values and norms of acceptable (and unacceptable) behavior and practices.

Consider the ever-present danger that weapons of mass destruction (WMDs) pose, whether nuclear, chemical, biological, and radiological. The widespread availability and destructive impact of WMDs would seemingly make them an attractive tool for states seeking to guarantee their security and pursue their interests in an anarchic setting where enemies and adversaries abound. Certainly, all forms of WMD have proliferated through the global political system, and states and nonstate actors have employed them. Examples of this include the United States against the Japanese cities of Hiroshima and Nagasaki in 1945, by the millennial terrorist group Aum Shinrikyo in the Japanese subway system in 1995, and by the Assad regime against civilians in the Syrian civil war in 2013 and again in 2017. Yet despite their pervasiveness, governments infrequently use WMDs. Why? Norms against the use of WMDs, translated through international treaty agreements, may provide a partial answer. The revulsion and popular backlash against the use and effects of such weapons in the "court of world opinion"—that is, in the nascent global society that does exist—have had some inhibiting effect on the behavior of states as well.

Chapter Summary

- Power shapes the conduct of global politics—requiring those engaged in the study of it to pay attention to considerations such as what power is, where it comes from, where it resides, and in what circumstances one can or cannot effectively use it.

- Power is mercurial, waxing and waning with time and by actor (or category of actor). This means that even though we most often analyze global politics at single points of time and space, we must remember that change is the only constant factor in world affairs.

- A comprehensive analysis of global politics requires us to focus on the motivations,

perceptions, and other idiosyncratic characteristics of individual leaders as well as the impact of these on decision-making and international interactions.

- An appraisal of power also requires us to take into account states and the societies that they govern—whether factors such as the government, military, or economy or the social forces that grant a state power or, conversely, limit it. Given the nature of anarchy and the structure of the global system, the state level remains the dominant focal point for many analysts.

- Lastly, students and scholars of global politics are wise to remember that both individuals and states operate within a system, one that is anarchic in nature and thus subject to definition and redefinition by its members. Power relationships between and among actors influence global politics, as do the norms, values, and ideas that help define the social structure of the global political system.

Critical Thinking Questions

1. What is power in global politics? How does it differ in the global context compared to other situations and settings?

2. Which do you think has the greatest role in shaping global politics—individuals, states, or the global system itself? Why?

3. To what extent do transnational forces and phenomena—such as the globalized media or information and financial networks like those utilized by Julian Assange and WikiLeaks—matter? How does their power compare to that of nation-states?

4. Does the levels-of-analysis framework help us understand the complex and interdependent nature of global politics today?

Key Terms

behavioralism
bipolar system
bounded rationality
bureaucracy
cognitive consistency
cognitive dissonance
Cold War
fungible
gender opinion gap

hard power
hawk/hawkish
hegemony
heuristic devices
individual-level analysis
information and
    communication
    technology

levels-of-analysis
    approach
multipolar system
operational code
optimistic bias
overstretch
political culture
regime type
resource curse theory

rogue state(s)
salient
soft power
state-level analysis
statecraft
system-level analysis
transaction costs
transnational
unipolar system

4

Nations and States: Past, Present, and Future

In January 2011, those living in the southern regions of Sudan held a referendum. Of the voting population, 98.83% chose independence, creating the world's newest state. On July 9, 2011, the Republic of South Sudan assumed membership in the United Nations (UN) and the African Union (AU) and joined the international community.

South Sudanese statehood did not occur overnight. It was the by-product of a long struggle between the poorer and largely animist (those who believe that nonhuman entities are spiritual beings) and/or Christian African population of the southern belt of Sudan and the more affluent Islamic Arab population that dominates the north, including Sudan's capital, Khartoum. This struggle played out in the two Sudanese civil wars (1955–1972; 1983–2005). South Sudanese autonomy eventually led to statehood, as the result of the Comprehensive Peace Agreement (CPA) that terminated the latter of the two conflicts. Observers hailed the CPA, the product of three years of intensive mediation, as marking the birth of a new era for Sudan.

The two civil wars that dominated over half a century of independent Sudan's history—killing, wounding, and displacing millions while disrupting and destroying much of the country's

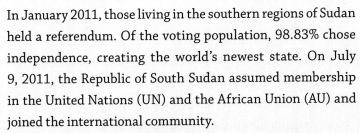

Jubilant celebrations of the independence of the world's newest sovereign state, South Sudan, in 2011 reflected the sense of triumph that often accompanies successful achievement of national self-determinaton. Unfortunately, five years later, a range of complex problems plunged South Sudan into civil war.

economy and infrastructure—reveal both the powerful appeal of national identity and the problems that can arise when a society lacks a coherent national identity. Disaffection in southern Sudan mounted throughout the 1970s in response to the dominance of the northern Arabs in the government. This disaffection was symbolized by the introduction of *shari'ah* (Islamic moral code and religious law) in various jurisdictions throughout the country. It came to a head around the same time that former army colonel John Garang, operating within Ethiopia, organized disparate elements among the southern Sudanese (including the previously adversarial Nuer and Dinka groups) into the Sudan People's Liberation Movement (SPLM) and Sudan People's Liberation Army (SPLA) on a quest for independence. Garang became South Sudan's leading pro-independence leader until his untimely death in a helicopter crash in July 2005.

South Sudanese independence and statehood, as well as its aftermath, sheds a great deal of light on the central concepts that we discuss in this chapter—nations and nationalism, statehood, and self-determination. This example has much to offer not only in reflecting the ways in which these concepts play out in the contemporary global political system, but also in revealing the complexities that can—and do—accompany the pursuit of the nation-state ideal.

Learning Objectives

Define the concepts of nations, nationalism, and the nation-state.

Discuss the historical evolution of nations and nationalism.

Evaluate the positive and negative dimensions of nationalism.

Discuss the major developments in the emergence of the sovereign state.

Nations, Nationalism, and the Nation-State Defined

The architecture of global politics rests in great part on three foundational concepts: nations, nation-states, and nationalism. Understanding both the theory and reality of what these concepts are and how they relate to one another is crucial to understanding the global political system's organization.

Building from that foundation, it is also crucial to understand the historical evolution of the global system—how it works and how it is changing—as a related concept that is difficult to separate from those in this chapter. Although we discuss the global system in various chapters, we will point out links here when and where they are relevant. In addition, as elsewhere in this book, historical material is woven into this chapter's text and the various boxed features (e.g., *Thinking Theoretically*) to highlight other important recurrent aspects of the narrative of global politics. Lastly, we also recognize that we cover much ground across nations, states, nation-states, and more throughout this chapter. All of the material focuses on how global politics is organized, but it is indeed complex and, in many places, quite nuanced in its importance when explaining global politics. We recommend that you keep the chapter's opening outline handy to remind you of the interconnections throughout the chapter and to help keep you focused on how these concepts impact everything else discussed in the book.

Nations

A **nation** refers to a group of people who:

1. Share one or more demographic and cultural traits, which all members of the group collectively recognize.

2. Possess a feeling of community or "we-feeling" (collectively identifying themselves as a group distinct from other groups).

3. Seek to control their political fate.

> **nation** A group of culturally and historically similar people who share a communal bond and desire self-government.

A nation is intangible. It exists because its members think it does. One leading scholar of nationalism has gone as far as to dub the nation an "imagined community" (Anderson, 1991). A state (country) is a tangible institution, but a nation is "a soul, a spiritual quality" (Renan, 1995:7). Another leading scholar

of nationalism, Ernest Gellner, notes: "A mere category of persons (say, occupants of a given territory, or speakers of a given language, for example) becomes a nation if and when the members of the category firmly recognize certain mutual rights and duties to each other in virtue of their shared membership of it. Their recognition of each other as fellows of this kind turns them into a nation" (1983:7).

Symbols of the nation, such as flags, are a significant component in sustaining the appeal of nationalist sentiment. Displays of national flags and symbols tend to be increasingly prominent in times of war or crisis, as well as celebrations and national holidays. Here, patriotic Americans celebrate the inauguration of President Barack Obama on the National Mall in Washington, DC, in January 2009.

DEMOGRAPHIC AND CULTURAL SIMILARITIES. The similarities that a group of people share helps make them a nation. These similarities may be demographic characteristics (e.g., language, race, and religion), or they may be a common culture or shared historical experiences. We can say that the

American nation is the outcome of Valley Forge, the Civil War, World War II, Martin Luther King, McDonald's, Silicon Valley, the Super Bowl, the 9/11 terrorist attacks, Rihanna, and many other people, events, and processes that comprise the American experience. Symbols such as the American flag, Uncle Sam, and the bald eagle reinforce that nationalism—a phenomenon that realists and liberals (as defined in Chapter 2) alike contend is important to state formation and cohesion (Geisler, 2005; Kolstø, 2006).

FEELING OF COMMUNITY.   A second element that helps define a nation is its feeling of community or a sense of "we-feeling" (Deutsch et al., 1957:5–6). Perception is the key here. Those within a group must perceive that they share similarities and are bound together by them. Constructivists point to the central role of these shared perceptions in constructing a nation around an "in-group." This in-group defines itself not only by the similarities of its members, but also in terms of how the nation's members differ from others, the "out-groups" (Stein, 2002). The group members' sense of feeling akin to one another and their sense of being different from others are highly subjective—such as the notion of *Hindutva*, which binds ardent Hindu nationalists and cements their understanding of India as (in their ideal view) a Hindu state.

DESIRE TO BE POLITICALLY SEPARATE.   The third element that defines a nation is its desire for political separateness—what political scientists and philosophers refer to as **"self-determination"** (Danspeckgruber, 2002). What distinguishes a nation from an ethnic group is that a nation, unlike an ethnic group, must seek self-governance, or at least autonomy. In the United States, there are many groups, such as Italian Americans, who share a common culture and have a sense of identification. They are ethnic groups, not nations, however, because they are not seeking to break away from the United States and form a new state. By contrast, in nationally divided states like Kosovo, with its majority Albanian and minority Serbian communities, the minority nationalities refuse to concede the legitimacy of the majority nationality governing them.

The difference between ethnic groups and nations is not always clear. In many countries, there are ethnic groups that have true nationalist (separatist) sentiments and others who do not. In Canada, for instance, there is ongoing dissatisfaction among many French Canadians in the province of Québec about their status in the Canadian state. Some Québécois favor separation. Many others do not. **Ethnonationalism** refers to a dynamic where an ethnic group's prevailing opinion is that it is a distinct political as well as cultural entity (Conversi, 2004).

Nationalism

Nationalism refers to the process of transforming the shared collective identity that we associate with the nation into a political ideology. Like all ideologies, nationalism is a set of related ideas that (1) establish values about what is good and bad, (2) direct adherents on how to act, (3) link together those who

self-determination The concept that a people should have the opportunity to follow their own political destiny through self-government.

ethnonationalism The desire of an ethnic community to have full authority over its political affairs—often marked by the pursuit of self-determination by that community.

nationalism The belief that the nation is the ultimate basis of political loyalty and that nations should have self-governing states.

adhere to the ideology, and (4) distinguish them from those who do not.

Specifically, nationalism connects individuals through links that people forge when they (1) "become sentimentally attached to the homeland," (2) "gain a sense of identity and self-esteem through their national identification," and (3) are "motivated to help their country" (Druckman, 1994:44). As an ideology, nationalism holds that the nation should serve as individuals' primary political identity. As the renowned British sociologist Anthony Smith described it, "For nationalists . . . the role of the past is clear and unproblematic. The nation was always there and it is part of the natural order, even when it was submerged in the hearts of its members" (1994:18).

Hindu nationalists believe that India belongs only to the majority Hindu population, inspiring violence and discrimination against non-Hindus. As a growing force in an officially secular political system, they reflect the persistent appeal of nationalism and identity politics in the 21st century. Here, a poster in Mumbai depicts Prime Minister Narendra Modi, the leader of the right-wing nationalist Bharatiya Janata Party, which won a sizeable majority in the most recent Indian parliamentary election in May 2019.

Although most people have more than one political identity, national identity is often their primary one. As US President Lyndon B. Johnson once said, "I am an American, a Texan, and a Democrat—in that order." As with Johnson, the persistence of nationalism suggests that many people continue to prioritize national identity. And patriotism in the United States as well as in countries around the world remains a potent unifying (and sometimes dividing) force. Whether this is natural and inevitable (as realists contend) or the product of elite manipulation (as some constructivists do) is a matter of continuing debate in international relations (IR) theory.

The Nation-State

A third element of the global political architecture is the **nation-state**—the ideal realization of self-determination in the overlap of the nation and state. States, which we will discuss in detail later in this chapter, are what we commonly refer to as "countries." They are sovereign (independent) political organizations with certain characteristics, such as territory, a population, and a government. In the "real world," many states—with examples including South Sudan, Moldova, and Afghanistan, to name just a few—fail even to approach this ideal, as we shall see. Nevertheless, the ideal of a cohesive nation-state is a powerful force for both those nations seeking to found their own states and those states seeking national unity. But as Ferguson and Mansbach (1996) argue, in the contemporary global system, very few instances of actual nation-states are left. Thus, we must be very careful in using that term because of its declining accuracy in contemporary global politics.

nation-state A politically organized territory that recognizes no higher law and whose population politically identifies with that entity.

The Historical Evolution of Nations and Nationalism

Nationalism is so widespread in the contemporary global political system that it is difficult to believe it has not always existed. The reality, of course, is that it hasn't. And most scholars contend that nationalism is not only a relatively modern phenomenon, but one with distinct roots in the Western political tradition. As we will see in this section, these roots underpin some of the contemporary challenges facing South Sudan.

In this context, it is worth pointing out several ideas before we go further. First, as discussed in Chapter 1, the Peace of Westphalia in 1648 which ended the Thirty Years War on the European continent is widely viewed as the birth of the modern nation-state. Approaching five centuries since that landmark, the contemporary global system remains tied to that peace accord, as it significantly decreased papal authority over political units in Europe and launched a world of sovereign states. Second, the development of **failed states** and weak states in the contemporary global system is fundamentally rooted in the (d) evolution of the nation-state system in the past 50 years, at least partly because of the decline of colonial empires.

failed states Countries in which the state is unable to effectively maintain order and provide public goods due to political upheaval, economic instability, crime and lawlessness, violence, ethnic and cultural divides, and other destabilizing forces.

The idea to keep in mind, then, as you read further in this chapter is that the development and evolution of nations, states and nationalism is intertwined with the history of the global system. Thus, in many ways, the history of nations, states, and nationalism is also the history of that system.

Nations Emerge: From Rome to Reformation

It is difficult to establish a precise starting point for nationalism (Smith, 2004). Its origins, however, clearly lie in modern Western experience (hence the limited and highly Eurocentric orientation of this brief historical narrative). Undoubtedly, the fall of the universalistic Roman Empire in 476 CE set the stage for the emergence of the nation. Under Roman imperial rule, a common culture, language (Latin), and law prevailed, at least among the elite in the various parts of the empire. Some semblance of universality (e.g., the authority of the pope over kings and the use of Latin) persisted in the Roman Catholic Church after the fall of Rome.

Various subsequent attempts to reestablish a centralizing empire were made in the West. For example, the king of the Franks, Charlemagne (742–814 CE) gained control over most of western and central Europe. In 800, Pope Leo III proclaimed him *Imperatori Augustus,* a symbolic title reminiscent of the Roman emperors. Such centralizing impulses were unable to prevent the Great Schism of 1054—a break that produced two competing Christian churches, one based in Rome (Catholic) and one in Constantinople (Orthodox)—but did lead to the establishment of the **Holy Roman Empire**, which lasted in one form or another until 1806 (see Map 4.1).

Holy Roman Empire The domination and unification of a political territory in western and central Europe that lasted from its inception with Charlemagne in 800 to the renunciation of the imperial title by Francis II in 1806.

The universality that had existed under Roman rule, and which the Church and the Holy Roman Empire tried for centuries to maintain, eventually

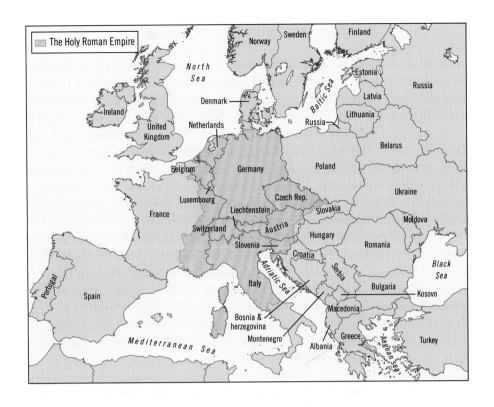

Map 4.1   Attempts to sustain central and universal authority in Europe under Christendom were typified by the establishment of the Holy Roman Empire. At its peak (pictured here), the Empire encompassed large swaths of central Europe. This arrangement still proved incapable of preventing the momentous political and social changes that led to its eventual demise in the early 19th century.

fragmented along cultural and linguistic lines. The use of Latin, a language all elites across Europe spoke, declined, and local languages that supplanted Latin divided the elites. This was the first step in a process that eventually created divergent national identities among the upper classes. Beginning in 1517, the **Protestant Reformation** divided Western Christendom and further fragmented European culture. With the Reformation and the **Thirty and Eighty Years Wars** (1618–1648 and 1568–1648, respectively) between Catholic and Protestant authorities in Central Europe and the Netherlands over political preeminence and social control that ensued, the growth of nationalism became gradually intertwined with the development of states and with their synthesis, the nation-state. And with the Peace of Westphalia signaling the resolution of these conflicts, the several hundred years since are often referred as the period of the Westphalian state system.

Nations Ascend: The Age of Enlightenment

As Benedict Anderson (1991) contends, the concept of the nation was not fully realized until the **Enlightenment** and the dynamics of popular sovereignty and revolution that it spawned combined to undermine the legitimacy of divinely ordained and hierarchic dynasties. Nationalism in its modern form first began to emerge in the early 1700s, again largely in the European context. These early stirrings of national identity had their roots in subtle shifts within—and not-so-subtle challenges to—existing authority structures, with the Protestant Reformation just one of many examples.

Protestant Reformation The religious movement initiated by Martin Luther in Germany in 1517 that rejected the Catholic Church as the necessary intermediary between people and God.

Thirty and Eighty Years Wars Two partly concurrent periods of declared and undeclared warfare during the 16th and 17th centuries throughout Europe involving the Holy Roman Empire and various opponents of its centralizing imperial rule.

Enlightenment An 18th- and 19th-century Western social and intellectual movement focused on the advancement of science, knowledge, and human rationality.

popular sovereignty A political doctrine holding that sovereign political authority ultimately resides with the citizens of a state, to whom a state's rulers are accountable.

social contract A concept associated with liberal political philosophy referring to an implicit understanding between citizens and government detailing their mutual obligations.

monarchism A political system that is organized, governed, and defined by the idea of the divine right of kings, or the notion that because a person is born into royalty, he or she is meant to rule.

Prior to the Enlightenment, the link between "the state" and its inhabitants was very different from what it is today. Most people did not identify with, and were not emotionally attached to, the political authority in the territorial space in which they lived. Instead, the vast majority were merely subjects whom a monarch, anointed by God to govern (the notion of "divine right"), ruled from afar. This point of view changed with the doctrine of **popular sovereignty**, a by-product of political liberalism. Rooted in the idea of the **social contract** (as advanced by Hobbes, Locke, Kant, and others), popular sovereignty contends that people are not subjects but rather citizens who have a stake in the affairs of the state—and whom the state must therefore serve. Moreover, rulers are to govern with the consent of the people, which subjects them to removal, at least in theory if often not in fact (Heater, 2004).

Until the late 1700s, popular sovereignty was a new phenomenon confined largely to Switzerland, England, and the Low Countries (present-day Netherlands, Belgium, and Luxembourg). This changed dramatically with the outbreak of the American Revolution (1776) and the French Revolution (1789). These violent revolutions greatly advanced popular sovereignty and the concept of nationhood by abolishing monarchs altogether. In their place, revolutionaries proclaimed, as in the words of the American Declaration of Independence, that those new governments derive their "just powers from the consent of the governed."

The idea of popular sovereignty and nationalist sentiment began to spread around the globe—first throughout Europe in the Revolutions of 1848 and 1849, and subsequently beyond. Within 200 years after the American and French Revolutions, absolute **monarchism**—previously the most common form of governance—had virtually disappeared. It is worth noting, though, that while popular sovereignty implies that nationalism percolates upward from the people, some scholars argue nationalism is more accurately portrayed as having been cultivated downward from the elites to build loyalty within their governed territories (Halperin, 1998).

Nations Consolidate: The Era of Self-Determination

The spread of popular sovereignty and nationalism also radically recast the global political landscape. An important factor was the associated concept of self-determination. Expressed in simple terms as the idea that every nation should be able to govern itself as it chooses, impulses toward self-determination propelled some nations that were divided politically to create a single state.

The most successful efforts at **state building** occur when a strong sense of cultural and political identity exists among a people, and the formation of the nation precedes that of the state. This process is called "unification nationalism" (Hechter,

US President Woodrow Wilson was known as a staunch liberal internationalist. His "Fourteen Points" proved instrumental in fashioning the League of Nations after World War I, as well as in promoting national self-determination. As a result, a number of new (and relatively weak) states were established in central and eastern Europe during the aftermath of that war—states that later became the target of Adolf Hitler's quest for *Lebensraum* (or "living space") after his rise to power in 1933.

2000:15). Europe was one place where nations generally came together first and only later coalesced into states. For example, Germans existed as a cultural people long before they established a unified German state in the 1860s and 1870s. In much the same way, the Italian peninsula was fragmented after the fall of the Roman Empire and remained that way until a resurgent sense of Italian cultural unity and its accompanying political movement unified most of the peninsula as a new country, Italy, in 1871. Similarly, on the other side of the world in Japan, increased nationalism helped end the political division of the Japanese islands among the *daimyo* (feudal nobles) during the Tokugawa Shogunate (1603–1867) and restored real power to what had been a figurehead emperor.

A major factor in the emergence and spread of nationalism was the decline and death of vast multiethnic empires. First, American colonists revolted against British colonial rule. Then, the urge for self-determination contributed to the decline and fall of the Spanish empire in the 1800s, followed by the Austro-Hungarian and Ottoman empires in the late 19th and early 20th centuries. In each case, many of the nations that had existed within these empires established states. By the mid-20th century, nearly all of Europe and the Western Hemisphere had been divided into nation-states, and the colonies of Africa and Asia were beginning to demand independence. The British and French empires were similarly doomed by nationalist pressures within them and fell apart during the three decades after World War II, with the first major global empire (Portugal) among the last to shed its colonies, in the mid-1970s (Page & Sonnenburg, 2003). Finally, the last of the huge multiethnic empires, the Russian/Soviet, collapsed in 1991, with 15 nation-states emerging in the aftermath.

Nations Expand: Colonization and Decolonization

As nations began to consolidate themselves politically in the form of states in the late 18th and 19th centuries, they began to seek to expand their power by turning outward. In the push and pull of global politics, the gradual dissolution of European multinational empires into a system of Westphalian nation-states rebounded on the majority of the non-Western world in the form of **colonialism**. As nations and nationalism introduced a competitive dynamic among larger states (mostly located in Europe) seeking to secure and advance their interests, it is not surprising that these states began to look to distant corners of the world, such as Asia, Africa, the Middle East, and Latin America, for opportunities to enrich themselves through the exploitation of human and natural resources. So it was that the impulses of popular sovereignty that led to the rise of nation-states in the Western world had the effect of suppressing liberty and political freedom in the non-Western world through the colonial arrangements introduced by those very same nation-states (Britain, France, Spain, Portugal, the Netherlands, Belgium, and later, Germany and Italy). Indeed, the industrialization of the Western world was largely dependent on the extraction of human and natural capital through colonization in the 19th and early 20th centuries (see Map 4.2).

state building The process of creating both a government and other legal structures of a country and fostering the political identification of the inhabitants of the country with the state.

colonialism The policy or practice by which a powerful and often distant state acquires political and territorial control over a weaker territory and society, creating a dependent relationship through occupying it with settlers and exploiting it economically.

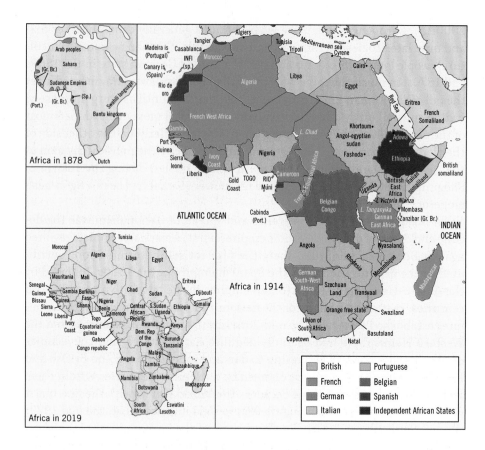

Map 4.2   This map and its insets show that Africa was largely controlled by its indigenous nations in 1878 (inset), but by 1914 (larger map) had become almost entirely subjugated and divided into colonies by the European powers. After World War II, momentum shifted toward decolonization and, ultimately, independence—with the West's influence on the continent diminished as a result. (Source: Perry et al., 1992. Adapted with permission.

decolonization The undoing of colonialism, or the unequal relation of polities in which one people or nation establishes and maintains dependent territory over another.

totalitarianism A political system in which the ruling regime recognizes no limit to its authority and seeks to regulate and control all aspects of public and private life.

In the same way that nations and nationalism helped fuel the creation and expansion of a colonial system, so too did these factors eventually contribute to the dismantling of that system through **decolonization**. By the 20th century, the same forces and dynamics that led ethnic, linguistic, religious, and tribal groups to consolidate and seek self-determination in Europe and the Americas emerged throughout the large swaths of the world under colonial rule. After the end of World War II—characterized by the Allies as a global struggle against oppression and **totalitarianism**—the perpetuation of a system of colonial oppression by some of those very same states (e.g., Britain and France) became unsustainable. This unsustainability manifested itself in the rise of national liberation movements within a number of European colonies in Asia and Africa, ushering in what political scientist Samuel Huntington (1991) called the "second wave" of democratization in the 1950s and 1960s.

Nations Collide: The Brutal and Destructive Legacy of Colonialism

The decolonization process that began in the mid-20th century accounts for the lack of national unity in many states today. As even the brief history of nationalism presented here suggests, nations, nationalism, and nation-states intersect in various patterns. Ideally, nations come together and find expression in the state. Yet in many cases, the order is different—with states preceding nations and nationalism, or nations and nationalism evolving along with states. And this inverted process is only one of many underlying factors contributing to the development of weak and failed states, as will be discussed near the end of this chapter.

NATION-STATES PRECEDE NATIONS.   In this scenario, the state is created first and then has to forge a sense of common national identity among the people and between the people and the state. This approach to state-building, which was widely employed in the decolonization of the 1950s to 1970s, is problematic. The forced coupling of populations with different tribal and ethnic backgrounds within the borders of African colonies determined by European powers remains an enduring and problematic legacy of colonialism (Larémont, 2005). When those colonies later became states, most lacked a single, cohesive nation in which to forge unity once they had achieved independence. For example, Rwanda and Burundi are neighboring states defined by colonial boundaries that indiscriminately comingled Hutu and Tutsi people. With independence, these colonial boundaries became the boundaries of independent states, as Map 4.2 depicts. The difficulty is that the primary political identification of these people has not become Rwandan or Burundian but, for most, has remained Hutu or Tutsi. The resulting mismatch between identity groups and states in such scenarios has generated enormous challenges for governance as well as occasional outbursts of devastating violence, as in the Rwandan genocide of 1994.

The difficulties of building national identities and a stable state have also beset the United States and, to a degree, other states, the UN, and regional organizations involved in the postconflict reconstruction and state-building efforts required in places such as Somalia and Bosnia-Herzegovina in the 1990s or, more recently, in Afghanistan, Iraq, and South Sudan. Outside powers can find themselves "stuck" because they are neither able to create stable political situations allowing them to withdraw nor willing to withdraw and permit a violent internal struggle for power to ensue (Etzioni, 2004; Fukuyama, 2004).

NATIONS AND NATION-STATES CO-EVOLVE. Nation-building and state-building are not always sequential; instead, they can and sometimes do evolve together. This approximates what occurred in the United States, where the idea of being American and the creation of an American state began in the 1700s and persisted despite a civil war, immigration inflows, racial and ethnic tensions, and other potentially divisive factors. Another example of this dynamic process can be seen in Germany. While consolidation of the majority of Germanic peoples into a single German state in 1871 reflects the traditional path of nation preceding state, little about the German nation-state's history since then has been traditional. Given the troubled legacy of German nationalism and World War II, the postwar period in Germany (both before and since reunification in 1990) has been one in which the German state has largely sought to limit and discredit traditional nationalist sentiments—an endeavor which most of German society has embraced.

🌐 Nationalism Reconsidered

Returning to our opening discussion of South Sudan allows for further reflection on nationalism. The aim of those seeking South Sudanese autonomy (and eventual statehood) was a unified and secular "New Sudan" in the south. Their manifesto dating to the 1980s rejected the interference of Khartoum in the region while prevailing upon the South Sudanese to unify as a separate and distinct nation (Simmons & Dixon, 2006). However, southern Sudan contains many more ethnic groups (including the Dinka, Nuer, Bari, Azande, Shilluk, and others) than the north, with corresponding linguistic differences. The divisions between these groups remain problematic and have posed serious problems for the viability of the South Sudanese state since independence. Indeed, tensions between the two largest ethnic groups (the Dinka and the Nuer), fueled by the Sudanese government in Khartoum, are part of a complicated political landscape that has plunged the country into civil war. As of the summer of 2019, armed conflict was ongoing in at least seven of South Sudan's ten states, triggered by disputes over political participation, civil rights, and the distribution of economic resources and opportunity. Forging a common South Sudanese national identity remains easier said than done.

Positive Dimensions of Nationalism

Nationalism is welcomed on numerous grounds (Conway, 2004; Wiebe, 2001). Nationalism has been a positive force in the development of the global political system, lending cohesion and order to many societies while also promoting the liberal idea that well-defined and cohesive **political communities** have the right to seek and secure self-government.

NATIONALISM PROMOTES DEMOCRACY. One arguably positive aspect of nationalism is its role in promoting ideas of popular sovereignty and liberal democracy. Liberal philosophers such as Thomas Paine in *The Rights of Man* (1791) depicted the nation and **democracy** as inherently linked in the popularly governed nation-state. By extension, nationalism was thought to promote the idea that political power legitimately resides with the people and that those in government are agents of the people. This type of democratic nationalism that helped spur the American Revolution has spread globally, especially since World War II, increasing the proportion of the world's countries that are considered "free" from 28% in 1950 to 45% in 2018 (Freedom House, 2018).

NATIONALISM DISCOURAGES IMPERIALISM. A related potentially positive feature of nationalism is the role it plays as a catalyst for dismantling empires and challenging hegemonic rule. During the past 100 years alone, as we have seen, nationalism has played a key role in the demise of the contiguous Austro-Hungarian, Ottoman, and Russian/Soviet empires while liberating the vast majority of peoples formerly colonized by the great powers of Europe.

political communities As defined by the political scientist Karl W. Deutsch (1957), social groups with a process of political communication, some machinery for establishing and enforcing collective agreements, and some popular habits of compliance with those agreements.

democracy A system of government that at minimum extends to citizens a range of political rights and a range of civil liberties that are important to free government.

Among these colonies, one of the last to gain its independence was East Timor (officially Timor-Leste). One of the final remnants of the moribund Portuguese empire, the eastern Timorese declared independence in 1975—an independence that was denied when Indonesia annexed East Timor. For the East Timorese, Indonesian overlords were no more acceptable than European ones, and their campaign for self-determination, backed by powerful outside actors such as the United States, the United Kingdom, and the UN, finally persuaded Indonesia to allow a referendum on independence. In August 1999, 78.5% of the East Timorese voted against remaining a part of Indonesia. Indonesia's military tried to keep control by supporting armed militia who killed thousands of East Timorese, necessitating the intervention of a multinational security force led by Australia and authorized by the UN. The UN then created a transitional administration for East Timor, followed by multiple UN deployments (see Table 4.1).

Table 4.1 UN Operations in East Timor, 1999–2012

The UN took on an extensive set of responsibilities after orchestrating the independence of East Timor in 1999, lasting well over a decade. The pivotal role of these various operations in administering and governing the society raises questions about the viability and sovereignty of the state.

OPERATION	INITIAL AUTHORIZATION	CHIEF MANDATE RESPONSIBILITIES	DATE INITIATED	DATE TERMINATED
United Nations Mission in East Timor (UNAMET)	UNSC Resolution 1246	Oversee and coordinate popular consultation	June 11, 1999	Oct 25, 1999
International Force for East Timor (INTERFET)	UNSC Resolution 1264	Restoration of peace and security; support UNAMET in delivery of humanitarian assistance	Sept 15, 1999	Feb 28, 2000
United Nations Transitional Administration in East Timor (UNTAET)	UNSC Resolution 1272	Provision of security; maintenance of law and order; territorial administration and governance; assistance in development and delivery of social services; coordination and delivery of humanitarian and development aid; capacity building for self-government; promotion of sustainable development	Oct 25, 1999	May 20, 2002
United Nations Mission of Support in East Timor (UNMISET)	UNSC Resolution 1410	Provision of assistance and support in post-transition independence	May 20, 2002	May 20, 2005
United Nations Office in Timor-Leste (UNOTIL)	UN Security Council Resolution 1599	Dispatch advisors to support development of critical state institutions, policing, border security, observance of human rights and democratic governance	May 20, 2005	May 20, 2006
United Nations Integrated Missions in Timor-Leste (UNMIT)	UN Security Council Resolution 1704	Support and stabilize government institutions; support parliamentary, presidential elections; restore and maintain public security; assist in security sector reform; aid in relief and recovery; aid investigation and prosecution of human rights crimes	Aug 25, 2006	Dec 31, 2012

Source: Butler (2012b).

NATIONALISM PROMOTES ECONOMIC GROWTH.   Both directly (through establishing economies of scale at the national level) and indirectly (through enhanced social cohesion), nationalism can correspond with improved prospects for economic growth within a country, even if this is not universally true. As a unifying ideology promoting self-determination, nationalism also improves the economic potential for minority nations within states and former colonial areas—two constituencies that have often been shortchanged economically.

Many countries still struggle to overcome a legacy in which the colonial power siphoned off resources for its own betterment and did little to build the colony's economic infrastructure. This pattern also occurred in multiethnic empires such as the Soviet Union. There, Russian/Soviet control neglected the six predominantly Muslim former Soviet republics (Azerbaijan, Kazakhstan, Kyrgyzstan, Tajikistan, Turkmenistan, and Uzbekistan). As a result, each state's average per capita gross domestic product (GDP) remains only one-third that of Russia's, and child mortality rates are more than four times greater than in Russia. It is certain that these new countries face years of economic hardship, but from their perspective, at least they will devote their efforts to their own betterment.

Negative Dimensions of Nationalism

For all its contributions, nationalism also has significant drawbacks. As a catalyst for war and instability, nationalism has brought great despair and destruction to the world as nations locked in a struggle for power and survival have fulfilled realist projections for the conduct of global politics. During an address to the Fiftieth UN General Assembly in 1995, Pope John Paul II acknowledged the two faces of nationalism. One was positive nationalism, which the pontiff defined as the "proper love of one's country . . . [and] the respect which is due to every [other] culture and every nation."[1] The other was negative nationalism, "an unhealthy form of nationalism which teaches contempt for other nations or cultures . . . [and] seeks to advance the well-being of one's own nation at the expense of others."[2]

After the end of the Cold War, the number of ongoing ethnonational conflicts—prominent examples being those in the former Yugoslavia and in Sri Lanka—over self-determination rose steadily from the 1950s, peaked in the 1990s, and then began to decline over the last decade. Still, whatever the number of conflicts, the intensity and magnitude of ethnonational conflicts remain high (Cederman, Wimmer, & Min, 2010). Moreover, these internal conflicts often become internationalized (Trumbore, 2003).

The troubling face of nationalism begins with how nations relate to one another. By definition, nationalism implies feeling a kinship with "like" people who comprise the nation. Differentiating ourselves from others is not intrinsically bad, but it is only a small step from positively valuing our in-group to negatively perceiving those who are even just slightly different from us. If we identify too strongly with our in-group, we may come to consider out-group(s) as alien to us (Druckman, 1994). This lack of identification with others often leads to parochialism, xenophobia and exceptionalism, nativism, discrimination and oppression and external aggression.

▲ **THINKING THEORETICALLY**

Contending Views on Nationhood

Given its central emphasis on states, realist theory considers the national interest to be a persistent and important phenomenon. In the view of realists, competing states engaged in the pursuit of interests define the conduct of global politics. Thus, those states with clearly defined interests and effective political systems are best positioned to compete. In circumstances where the state and nation are mutually reinforcing entities (e.g., a "nation-state"), the state is more likely to identify and pursue the "national interest" and effectively provide for its own security. Indirectly, realist theory treats nationhood as a crucial determinant of power in the global political system, evidenced by the fact that the nexus of nation and state tends to correlate with many of the more powerful actors in the global system, such as the United States, China, Russia, France, and the United Kingdom.

The other "grand theory" in IR—liberalism—places a direct onus on nationhood for its own sake. In its original (classical) form, liberalism treated nationhood as a natural aspiration for groups of people oriented around common defining traits (e.g., ethnicity, language, religion, or ideology). Late 19th- and early 20th-century classical liberals such as Woodrow Wilson dubbed this aspiration "self-determination," and lobbied widely for it in conjunction with democracy after World War I. Classical liberals felt that national self-determination would result in a pacific order of nation-states along the lines of what German philosopher Immanuel Kant (1795) dubbed a "league of nations" (his second definitive article of peace), an arrangement that would follow from the spread of republican forms of government (his first definitive article).

The evolution of liberal thought and the expanding globalist focus of "neoliberalism" in the late 20th century brought with it a less optimistic view of nationhood. The persistence of wars and rivalries propelled by self-determination throughout the 20th century has led neoliberals to place a greater premium on global identity and citizenship, as a by-product of cosmopolitanism (Kant's third definitive article of peace). Neoliberal thinkers tend to view nationalism and nationhood as outdated impediments to global and transnational interaction and cooperation.

More recent introductions to the theoretical conversation challenge both realist and liberal views on nationhood. Constructivist thought points to the subjective, contextual, and relational dimension of identity, raising the possibility that "the nation" is merely a social construction. Benedict Anderson introduces a definition of the nation as an "imagined political community" that is also "inherently limited" (1991:5). In Anderson's view, the nation is imagined because, while even the members of the smallest nations will never actually know or meet most of their fellow members, they still adhere to a collective "we-feeling" that breeds comradeship across the national group. Part of that we-feeling comes from the fact that nations are also limited constructs. In other words, to exist in a group's collective consciousness, we must differentiate the nation from other nations or groups of people by real "boundaries"—territorial, linguistic, ethnic, religious, or otherwise. Anderson's view, along with many leading scholars of nationalism, such as Gellner (1983) and Smith (1994), suggests that the treatment of the nation and nationhood as empirical "facts" or realities by realists and liberals alike requires reconsideration.

PAROCHIALISM.   Our nationalist sense of difference and separateness can limit our sense of responsibility or concern for the "other." Many people are quick to express concern for or assist others in their in-group, which on the national level we express through social welfare programs and other methods. Internationally, most of us feel less responsible for persons outside our national group. Horrendous conditions and events that occur in other countries often evoke little notice relative to the outraged reaction that would be forthcoming if they happened in our own.

For example, in sub-Saharan Africa, the average life expectancy at birth is 59 years, as compared to 79 years for Americans (World Bank, 2019b). Likewise, the chances of an infant in sub-Saharan Africa perishing before his or her fifth birthday are more than 12 times greater than the risk to American babies (with 81.3 African deaths per 1,000 live-births by age 5, compared to 6.5 American deaths per 1,000 live births). Even so, the US government's response to such stark realities in sub-Saharan Africa is largely limited to sending about $4 billion in total economic and humanitarian aid to the region, a figure amounting to approximately $5 per person per year.

Most Americans think this response is about right. A recent poll found that Americans were almost evenly split on the question of whether the United States should increase aid to developing nations, with 50% opposed and 48% in favor (Pew Research Center, 2016). None of the aforementioned means that Americans are uncharitable; rather, like citizens in the vast majority of countries, Americans demonstrate a much greater sense of responsibility for people in their own country than for people in others.

XENOPHOBIA AND EXCEPTIONALISM.   Valuing one's nation is a positive aspect of nationalism, but it too often leads to feeling superior to others or even fearing and hating them. **Xenophobia**, or an innate and intense fear of foreigners, is one destructive way in which some people relate to out-groups. **Exceptionalism**, or the belief that your nation is better than others and therefore "exceptional" and not limited by the rules and constraints faced by other nations, is perhaps more subtle but still problematic.

Xenophobia and exceptionalism often lead to conflict (Marx, 2003). Feelings of hatred between groups are especially powerful if there is a history of conflict or oppression. Past injuries inflicted "by another ethnic group [are] remembered mythically as though the past were the present."[3] Further to this point, a February 2017 Pew Research Center poll entitled "What It Takes to Be Truly 'One of Us'" found high levels of support in most developed countries (including the United States, Canada, Australia, Japan, and much of Europe) for the belief that speaking a country's native language and practicing and respecting its national customs and traditions is essential for individual and group acceptance into national life. These attitudes seem to be correlated with anti-immigration sentiments, which have grown in recent years, as reflected in the rise of populist movements and political parties in Europe and the United States.

Understanding the intensity that xenophobia and exceptionalism can reach helps explain some of what happened in the Balkans in the 1990s. Consider, for example, the resonance of the 1389 Battle of Kosovo, in which Ottoman Turks defeated Serbian forces led by Prince Lazar, beginning five centuries of Muslim domination. This battle, according to one commentary, is "venerated among the Serbs in the same way Texans remember the Alamo."[4] Adds Serb historian Dejan Medaković, "Our morals, ethics, mythology were created at that moment, when we were overrun by the Turks. Kosovo . . . has permeated the Serbian people."[5] The festering mythic wound of the 1389 battle was clearly a catalyst for the perpetration of ethnic cleansing attacks on Bosnian Muslims

xenophobia Fear of foreigners or other "out-groups."

exceptionalism The belief of some that their nation or group is better than others.

in the early 1990s and then on the predominantly Muslim Kosovar Albanians later in the decade.

NATIVISM. Xenophobia and exceptionalism can also manifest themselves in other problematic ways, such as intense **nativism**. Each year, millions of people are torn from their homes because of political violence, poverty, and other forces beyond their control. Intense nationalism can create resistance in many countries to the arrival of immigrants, refugees, and asylum seekers, particularly during economic downturns. Such attitudes toward immigration are linked to concerns about economic security as well as racial prejudice, leading to negative perceptions of immigrants as a "burden" and of racial and ethnic diversity more generally. The influx of migrants into Europe during recent years from the Middle East, North Africa, and other areas seems to bear this out, as nativist attitudes are highest in less affluent European Union (EU) countries, such as Hungary, Italy, and Greece (see Figure 4.1). And as the flow of refugees from Syria and other conflict-ridden areas has borne out in very recent years, the causal pressures underlying anti-immigrant sentiments in many Northern countries are unlikely to decline in the near future. It is also worth noting, however, that hate crimes and domestic terrorism have recently increased in the United States, despite rhetoric indicating significant support for diversity. Many attribute this increase to efforts to inflame anti-immigrant sentiments for political advantage, even if those sentiments are not held by a majority of those surveyed from the US population.

nativism A political attitude demanding favored treatment for established inhabitants of a nation-state and resisting the presence or claims of newer immigrants.

CNN Video: Effects of Nationalism.

CULTURAL DISCRIMINATION AND OPPRESSION. In those states with a dominant ethnonational group and one or more minority groups, the dominant group almost always has political, economic, and social advantages over the other(s). At the extreme, dominant groups sometimes violently suppress minority groups or even attempt genocide. This aptly characterizes the ethnic cleansing of Bosnian Muslims by Serbs and Croats, the genocidal attacks on the Tutsis by the Hutus in Rwanda, and the murderous campaign against non-Arab Christians, Muslims, and animists by Arab Muslims in Darfur.

The most widespread and systematic example of this dynamic occurred in Nazi Germany, where Adolf Hitler preached in *Mein Kampf* that "pure" Germans were an "Aryan nation" that epitomized the pinnacle of human civilization (Eatwell, 2006). By contrast, Hitler believed that Russians and other Slavic people were marginal humans that should exist as virtual and expendable slaves in segregated and degrading conditions. Jews and Roma were "nonpeople" and "racial vermin" to be exterminated, along with the mentally ill and homosexuals.

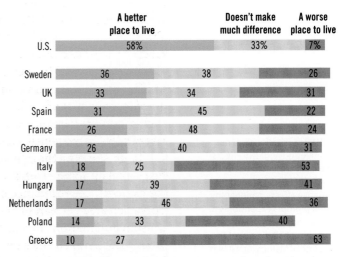

	A better place to live	Doesn't make much difference	A worse place to live
U.S.	58%	33%	7%
Sweden	36	38	26
UK	33	34	31
Spain	31	45	22
France	26	48	24
Germany	26	40	31
Italy	18	25	53
Hungary	17	39	41
Netherlands	17	46	36
Poland	14	33	40
Greece	10	27	63

Figure 4.1 Nationalism and Nativism. Despite shifts in the political rhetoric since the 2016 election, a recent Pew Global Attitudes Survey shows that a large majority of Americans express support for multiculturalism and diversity, with 58% responding that it makes a country a better place to live. Such attitudes are clearly less common in many European countries.

Even in less dire circumstances, when the oppression of minorities is limited to economic and social deprivation, conflict often occurs. Almost inevitably, the disadvantaged ethnic, racial, linguistic, or gender groups become restive. However, their complaints often receive little positive response because, as former UN Secretary-General Kofi Annan pointed out, the social and economic inequality of minority groups "tends to be reflected in unequal access to political power that too often forecloses paths to peaceful change."[6] Not surprisingly, oppressed groups then take direct action if they are unable to resolve their grievances through the legal or political process.

IMPERIALISM.   Although nationalism has contributed to the breakdown of empires, it can also lead large and powerful states to exhibit imperial tendencies of their own. Rampant nationalism can fuel the belief that it is acceptable to conquer or otherwise incorporate other nations out of a perceived superiority and/or insecurity. Russian history serves as an example. As is shown in Map 4.3, the country has long resembled a classic multiethnic empire built on territories acquired through years of czarist Russian and later Soviet expansion. From its beginning 500 years ago as the 15,000-square-mile Grand Duchy of Moscow, Russia has become the world's largest country in terms of land area.

In recent years, under the leadership of Vladimir Putin, Russian nationalism is again on the ascent. Russian neo-imperial ambitions were especially prominent during its actions in Ukraine beginning in March 2014, in the aftermath of the so-called Euromaidan Revolution that toppled Ukraine's corrupt president (and Russian ally) Viktor Yanukovych. Russia began by forcibly annexing the Crimea, a strategically vital territory ceded by treaty to the Ukrainian

Map 4.3   Nationalism has positive and negative effects, and both are illustrated by the history of Russia. Among the negative effects, nationalism often prompts expansionism. The Grand Duchy of Moscow was about half the size of the US state of Maine when it was founded around 1480. It expanded territorially under a succession of Russian czars and Soviet premiers to become the world's largest country.

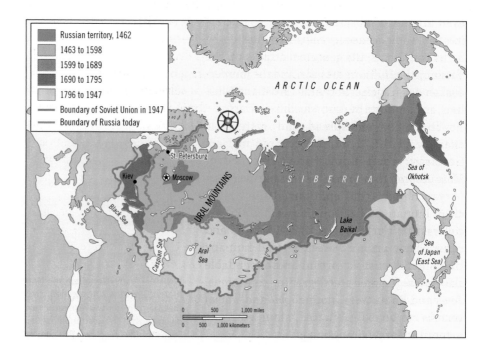

Soviet Socialist Republic by Nikita Khrushchev in 1954. Citing a duty to protect the rights of ethnic Russians within the boundaries of what some nationalists refer to as *novorossiya* (New Russia), Russia simultaneously mounted a military incursion into eastern Ukraine. Russia has also been deeply entrenched in the internal affairs of several other former Soviet republics (part of what it terms the "near abroad") over the past decade, supporting Russian nationals in the breakaway region of Transdniester in Moldova and continuing to assist separatist movements in the regions of South Ossetia and Abkhazia in Georgia. It may serve one well to remember revolutionary socialist Karl Marx's comment that "the policy of Russia is changeless. Its methods, its tactics, its maneuvers may change, but the polar star of its policy—world domination—is a fixed star."[7]

Self-Determination: Pros and Cons

An additional consideration when it comes to nationalism concerns the wisdom of self-determination as a national goal (Danspeckgruber, 2002). Consider the 2011 uprising against long-time dictator Muammar Gaddafi in Libya. Rebel forces seeking national liberation received widespread support from much of the international community, including direct military support from the North Atlantic Treaty Organization. Although ousting Gaddafi had its appeal, the competing drives for self-determination among the various factions of the opposition led to a fragmented and violent political landscape in Libya. Recent pushes for independence in Scotland and even the Brexit vote in the United Kingdom illustrate concerns about the degree of self-determination that occurs in wealthy states and produces equally complex dynamics.

POSITIVE ASPECTS OF SELF-DETERMINATION. Many observers have lauded the principle of self-determination. Perhaps the most notable was US President Woodrow Wilson (1913–1921). Wilson believed that "self-determinism is not a mere phrase. It is an imperative principle of action."[8] Moreover, the origins of many nation-states are rooted in the demand for that nation's self-determination. There are numerous reasons to support self-determination. Liberal theorists point to the potential for political self-determination to reduce or even eliminate the abuses that stem from ethnic, racial, linguistic, or gender oppression. For example, if all ethnic groups were able to peacefully establish their own sovereign units or join existing ones, the tragedies of ethnonationalist conflicts that have occurred in recent years in Bosnia, Chechnya, East Timor, Kosovo, Rwanda, Sudan, and Myanmar likely would not have occurred.

CONCERNS ABOUT SELF-DETERMINATION. The principle of self-determination becomes more problematic in practice. There are literally thousands of ethnic groups worldwide, many with the potential to develop a national consciousness and to seek independence. How could the global political system possibly accommodate all of these groups and their desire to establish sovereign states? Indeed, those of a realist perspective frequently point out the impossibility that all oppressed groups will ever be able to successfully achieve self-determination given limits to territory, resources, and opposition from existing nation-states. Realists view the quest for self-determination as a cause for violent conflict rather than a solution to it.

Disentangling groups is one dimension of the challenge posed by self-determination. Many nations are intermingled within common territorial spaces or states. Bosnia-Herzegovina was a classic example of such ethnonational heterogeneity. Prior to the ethnic conflagration in the 1990s, Bosnian Muslims, Croats, and Serbs often lived in the same cities, on the same streets, and even in the same apartment buildings. How does one disentangle these groups and assign them territory when each wants to declare its independence or to join with its ethnic kin in an existing country?

A second problem that applying self-determination raises is the prospect of dissolving existing states in order to provide statehood to national and/or ethnic groups in their midst. Examples stemming from the existence of multinational states and multistate nations include Canada (Québec), Great Britain (Scotland, Northern Ireland, and Wales), and Spain (Basque region and Catalonia), to name just a few. One has to wonder if, were he alive today, President Wilson would apply the principle of self-determination to native Hawaiians who wish to reestablish an independent Hawaii.

Yet another problem stems from the rapidly growing number of independent countries that are barely able to ensure their own survival (the primary imperative of the state, according to realists). Is it wise to allow the formation of **microstates**, countries with tiny populations, territories, and/or economies? Such countries have long existed, with Andorra, Monaco, and San Marino serving as examples. Partly as a consequence of decolonization, many more of these microstates have emerged. Roughly one-third of the world's countries have populations smaller than that of Los Angeles, California, and about 10% occupy less land than that city. Such countries often cannot defend themselves, cannot economically sustain themselves, or both. This incapacity to perform one or both of the two basic obligations of a state—to provide for its citizens' security and to allocate public goods—undermines such states' reason for existing, increases economic burdens on the rest of the world, and creates potentially unstable power vacuums (Klabbers, 2006). In the view of some observers, two of the world's newest states, East Timor and South Sudan, reflect these characteristics (Cotton, 2007; Jok, 2011).

microstates Countries with small populations that cannot survive economically without outside aid or that are so weak militarily that they are inviting targets for foreign intervention.

The Persistence of Nationalism

World War II served as a watershed moment changing the views of many people about nationalism. Liberals in particular blamed **fascism** and extreme nationalism for the war itself, and for the other horrors of the period such as the Holocaust. These critics argued that the second global war in 30 years demonstrated that the state system based on national antagonism favored by realists was not only outdated, but dangerous. The advent of weapons of mass destruction added urgency to the case, making "the nation and the nation-state . . . anachronisms in the atomic age."[9] As a counterpoint, the establishment of the UN in 1945 symbolized the desire to progress from competitive, often conflictive nationalist dynamics toward a global order founded on cosmopolitanism and cooperation.

fascism An ideology that advocates extreme nationalism, with a heightened sense of national belonging or ethnic identity and total loyalty to the leader.

Such thinking led numerous scholars—particularly liberal internationalists and critical theorists—to predict the imminent demise of the nation-state or, at least, its gradual withering away (Booth 1991; Strange, 1996; Haas, 1997). As it turned out, such obituaries proved reminiscent of the day in 1897 when an astonished Mark Twain read in the paper that he had died. Reasonably sure that he was still alive, Twain hastened to assure the world: "The reports of my death are greatly exaggerated." Similarly, one scholar notes that contrary to predictions of nationalism's impending extinction, "this infuriatingly persistent anomaly . . . refused to go away" (Wiebe, 2001:2).

The continued strength of nationalism is unquestionable. Insistence on national self-determination has almost tripled the number of states in existence since World War II. For most of this time, the primary force behind the surge of nationalism was the anti-imperialist independence movements in Africa, Asia, and elsewhere. More recently, nationalism has reasserted itself in Europe. Germany reemerged when West Germany and East Germany reunited in 1990. Czechoslovakia became two states in 1993, and Yugoslavia eventually dissolved into six countries during the 1990s. Even more momentously, another 15 countries came into existence when the last great multiethnic empire, the USSR, dissolved in December 1991. Except for Eritrea, Namibia, Palau, South Sudan, and East Timor, all of the states that have achieved independence since 1989 are in Eastern Europe or are former Soviet republics. There are also prominent nationalist movements among the Scots (who held a referendum on secession from the United Kingdom in 2014), and among the Basques and Catalans (who held a similar referendum in October 2017) in Spain, among others.

Another sign of persistent nationalism is the attachment of people to their countries. The International Social Survey Program (2013), a cross-national survey, found that a strong majority of people in over two dozen countries surveyed said that they would rather be a citizen of their own country than any other. If anything, the past several years have illustrated a resurgent wave of nationalism and national identity around the world. This rising tide is due to a wide variety of factors, and it seems to be converging in a broad form of "authoritarian populism" rooted in a rejection of globalization, resistance to immigrants and refugees, and distrust and suspicion of institutions. This resurgent nationalism explains, at least in part, a number of major political events, including the consolidation of power by authoritarian leaders in Hungary (Viktor Orbán), Russia (Vladimir Putin), and the Philippines (Rodrigo Duterte), as well as the United Kingdom's decision to leave the EU (Brexit) and the surprising Electoral College victory of Donald Trump in 2016.

The Sovereign State

Scholars are divided over the apparent resurgence of nationalism and its long-term prospects. Similar debates exist over the long-term prospects of what remains the primary unit of authority in the global political system: the sovereign state. Whereas realists contend that the state has long been—and will

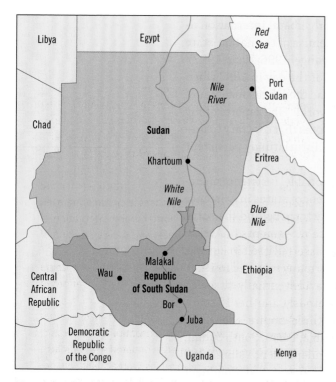

Map 4.4   South Sudan and vicinity. As depicted here, the world's newest state—South Sudan—was established in the aftermath of the second Sudanese civil war, with the conditions of autonomy first set out in the Comprehensive Peace Agreement that ended that conflict. A resource-rich but landlocked country, much of South Sudan's independence has been marked by internal conflict and uneasy relations with Sudan itself.

remain—the unquestioned centerpiece of global politics, liberals point to the rise of international institutions and nonstate actors as gaining authority relative to states. Still others, such as feminists and critical theorists, argue that suppression of the rights and representation of women and other marginalized groups by most states require direct challenges to the state and its authority.

To attain the status of a sovereign state requires meeting certain conditions. Among these are a functioning and recognized government with unchallenged authority over a territorial space and population. South Sudan provides an illustration of how these conditions can be elusive. In the shadow of the end of the second Sudanese civil war, the (now-defunct) Southern Sudan Legislative Assembly ratified a Transitional Constitution for South Sudan. This constitution established a mixed presidential system of government headed by a president, as well as a bicameral legislature and an independent judiciary, and it was signed by President Salva Kiir on Independence Day (July 9, 2011). A number of major world powers, including the United States, the United Kingdom, China, Russia, India, and perhaps most notably, Sudan itself, quickly extended diplomatic recognition to South Sudan (see Map 4.4).

Despite seeming to satisfy the conditions of statehood, the future prospects for the South Sudanese state are dubious. War has ravaged South Sudan's territory and population for decades; the result is a lack of infrastructure and major destruction and displacement. Estimates of deaths since the advent of the current civil war within South Sudan in mid-2013 exceed 300,000, on top of the more than 2 million who died in the two Sudanese civil wars (1955–1972 and 1983–2005). Furthermore, the UN Office for Coordination of Humanitarian Affairs (2019) reports over 2.3 million persons displaced as a direct result of the current conflict in South Sudan. And with a per capita annual GDP of just over US$1,500 (World Bank, 2019a), the South Sudanese economy is one of the weakest and most underdeveloped in the world. Human development is similarly problematic, as South Sudan has the fifth worst maternal mortality and the worst female literacy rates in the world (World Bank, 2019c, 2019d). With about 80% of the untapped oil in all of Sudan located in the south, the region's oil fields have been its chief source of revenue for decades.[10] Yet oil has come to reflect the so-called "resource curse" (Ross, 2015) in South Sudan, with the allocation of that revenue proving to be a major source of contention among the various ethnic groups within South Sudan and between South Sudan and

CHALLENGE YOUR ASSUMPTIONS

Women and the State

Attaining statehood is thought of in positive terms by both realists and liberals. For realists, states continue to represent the central dominant actor in global politics. As such, a national group has the greatest potential for ensuring its survival in an insecure world if it joins the international state-system. For liberals, statehood represents a boon to a national group by affording that group and its members the institutional and legal means for political expression and the pursuit and protection of civil and political rights. Simply put, for realists, the state offers protection, while for liberals, the state offers representation.

Feminist IR theory calls into question these mainstream celebrations of the state. Feminist theory reveals the state as a political entity that works to sustain a status quo defined by a highly gendered distribution of power and authority. This is true at both the domestic and the global level, with idealized types of masculinity working to undermine the supposed advantages the state confers in representation *and* protection as far as women are concerned.

In terms of representation, J. Ann Tickner (2001) notes that the historical and structural separation of most societies into "public" and "private" spheres all but ensures that the state and the political system are disproportionately populated by men—and fundamentally "male" in their dynamics. The public sphere is dominated by the state, where politics occur and men hold sway; the private sphere is dominated by the home, where domestic life occurs and women have historically

been relegated. State domination is reflected in legal restrictions on the participation of women around the world today, and not so long ago in liberal societies in which women were not granted the right to vote. Also at work are more subtle but powerful social forces that impede women's full and equal participation in political life, such as the "double shift" (in which women are more likely to be expected to handle childrearing even while working outside the home) or the celebration of so-called "masculine" attributes and the denigration of so-called "feminine" ones.

Relative to protection, Tickner (2001) and Laura Sjoberg (Sjoberg, 2010) expose the protection afforded to women by the state to be a "myth" or even a "racket." The systematic exclusion of women from civic life has resulted in a hypermasculine conception of citizenship, in which patriotic duty has been equated with practices (e.g., military service) from which women have historically been excluded (Stiehm, 1982). Thus, the state and its military force have frequently been justified and deployed on the basis of "protecting" women from harm by the predations of the society's "enemy" while at the same time excluding those very same women from civic participation! The mythology of protection is only underscored by the fact that women are disproportionately more likely to be killed or displaced in war than men, and are frequently subjected to direct harm (e.g., gender-based discrimination, sexual assault, and even murder) by the military forces (or, in recent years, peacekeepers) designated to "protect" them.

Sudan. The substantive difference between sovereignty and independence as well as the conditions which trigger state failure—two subjects to be discussed in greater detail later in this chapter—are prominent in South Sudan.

Emergence of the State

Humans have organized themselves in cities, leagues, empires, and other political units throughout history, but like nations, states have not always existed (Opello & Rosow, 2004). The gradual breakdown of the feudal system and universalistic religious authority in the West beginning in the 14th century CE created the conditions for a new form of governing entity. Although alternative forms, such as the mercantilist city-states of the Hanseatic League in the 13th through 17th centuries appeared, and older forms such as the imperial and monarchical systems of the Hapsburg, Russian, and Ottoman empires persisted, it was the state that ultimately emerged as the primary actor in the global political system.

The first major development in the emergence of the state was the move by rulers of some European nations to expand their authority by breaking away from the political domination of the Holy Roman Empire and the theological jurisdiction of the papacy. Triggering the bloody Eighty and Thirty Years Wars, these acts led to the creation of the modern state system through the Treaty of Westphalia (1648). There is more to the preeminent position of the state, however, than its recognition as a reference point for diplomacy and international law. Among other factors, the "economies of scale" associated with the state were a boon to the emerging system of capitalism in the 17th and 18th centuries. And the rise of popular sovereignty in conjunction with the Enlightenment, as embodied in the American (1776) and French (1789) revolutions, furthered the emergence of nations and nationalism.

Although political philosophers have long disagreed over why humans create societies and establish governments, individual betterment is a common theme among them (Baradat, 2003). This theme is evident in the writing of social contract theorists such as Thomas Hobbes (1588–1679) and John Locke (1632–1704). Each contended that people had once lived as individuals or in family groups in a **state of nature**. Social contract theory also argued that people eventually found this highly decentralized existence unsatisfactory, seeking to improve their lives by joining together in societies. This move in turn required people to surrender much of their sovereignty, and to create governments to conduct the society's affairs.

In this way, the modern state and the impulse toward popular sovereignty proved compatible, though explanations of that compatibility differ. As the father of modern realism, Hobbes said it was fear that caused people to create strong governments to provide protection. As one of the first liberal thinkers, Locke contended that people joined together in societies because they realized that they could improve their lives more easily through cooperation than by individual effort alone. The key point about Hobbes and Locke is they agreed that governments were instruments created for some purpose—and that the legitimacy of those governments depended on their ability to fulfill their obligations to do so under the social contract.

Ultimately, the effectiveness of the state has a great deal to do with its ability to maintain social order and stability (Mann, 1993). The prominent 19th-century German sociologist and political economist Max Weber argued that the defining feature of the modern state, and a major source of its power and authority, was the perception by a majority of those governed that it held a monopoly on the use of coercion. With the legitimacy of "the state" contingent on a widely held notion among the citizenry that the state—and only the state—possesses the right to employ violence both domestically and on the world stage, we can see (as Weber did) an important source of the sovereign state's power, coherence, and authority.

state of nature A theoretical time in human history when people lived independently or in family groups and there were no societies of nonrelated individuals or governments.

The Weberian monopoly, once asserted and (at least mostly) achieved at the domestic level, helps consolidate state power and eliminate potential challenges not just to actual states but also to the very concept of the state itself. Violence can be used to crush dissent or avert potential challenges to the government. At the same time, such a monopoly also contains an important external dimension. Possessing the sole legitimate authority to utilize organized violence permits the state to employ violence to defend national interests and advance national objectives relative to other states, or even to divert attention from domestic problems by initiating armed conflict with "enemies"—the so-called "diversionary theory" of war.

Requisites of Statehood

The modern state is a unit of governance that exercises legal authority over a specific territory and the people in it and that recognizes no legitimate external higher authority. To the extent they overlap with nations, states often take on great significance in the formation of people's political identity. Furthermore, states are the most powerful of all political actors. Some huge companies approach or even exceed the wealth of some poorer countries, but no individual, company, group, or international organization has anywhere near the coercive power that most states wield.

Having a sense of the core functions of states helps us to evaluate how well they are operating. Likewise, the ability to judge how well states are operating helps us to think about whether and why the state should remain the principal unit of governance in the global political system going forward. Judging states in terms of their performance is easier when we think about the factors that all states require in order to exist and function. Whatever their other individual differences, states share all or most of several characteristics: sovereignty, territory, population, internal organization, diplomatic recognition, and domestic support.

SOVEREIGNTY. The most important requisite for statehood is **state sovereignty**, which means that states have the exclusive legal right to govern the territory and people within their borders and do not recognize the legal legitimacy of any outside authority. Sovereignty also denotes formal legal equality among states. One important application of this principle is evident in the UN General Assembly and many other international organizations, where each member-state has one vote.

Disparities between and among states call into question this formal equality in practical terms. For example, compare the tiny republic of San Marino to the People's Republic of China (see Table 4.2). San Marino lies entirely within Italy and is the world's oldest republic, dating back to the fourth century CE. After years of self-imposed nonparticipation, in 1992 the UN granted membership to San Marino with the same representation in the General Assembly as China and every other sovereign state. "The fact of sitting around the table with the most important states in the world is a reaffirmation of sovereignty," explained the country's foreign minister.[11]

state sovereignty A central tenet of global politics established in the Treaty of Westphalia, which holds that the administrative unit of the state has the sole right to govern its territory and people, free from outside interference.

Table 4.2 San Marino and China: Sovereign Equals?

The legal concept of sovereign equality gives equal votes to San Marino and China in the UN General Assembly; as reflected here, little else about the two states is equal.

	SAN MARINO	CHINA	RATIO
Territory (sq. mi.)	24	3,705,400	1:154,392
Population	29,251	1,313,973,713	1:44,921
Gross domestic product (US$ millions)	880	2,455,900	1:2,790
Military personnel	0	2,225,000	1: ∞
Vote in UN General Assembly	1	1	1:1

Note: ∞ = infinity
Source: Boyer, Hudson, & Butler (2012:104).

Sovereignty, a legal and theoretical term, differs from independence, a political and applied term. Independence means freedom from outside control, and in an ideal, law-abiding world, sovereignty and independence would be synonymous. In the real world, however, where power is important, a state may be formally sovereign but practically dependent.

TERRITORY. A second requisite for statehood is territory. It would seem obvious that a state must have physical boundaries. On closer examination, however, the question of territory becomes more complex. Territorial boundaries can expand, contract, or shift dramatically, and they are often the source of conflict and dispute. Pakistan provides an example of the limits of a state's territorial authority. The Pashtuns, an ethnonational group that is also the largest group in neighboring Afghanistan, control northwestern Pakistan. Pakistan's Punjabi-dominated government exercises only limited authority over these so-called "tribal areas" and their Pashtun inhabitants, a reality that explains in part why the region has proven a springboard for the Taliban (Islamic fundamentalists of largely Pashtun descent) in both Pakistan and Afghanistan during recent years. Another example is the vast territory of Western Sahara, which has been the subject of dispute between Morocco and an independence movement led by the Polisario Front for decades.

Western Sahara, a vast and sparsely populated territory in North Africa formally administered by Morocco, is just one of many regions in the world in which sovereign control over a particular territorial space is disputed. Here, women demonstrate at a protest in Spain for the independence of Western Sahara.

POPULATION. People are an obvious requirement for any state, but populations vary—from the 840 inhabitants of the Holy See (Vatican City) to China's 1.5 billion people. Increasingly less clear in the shifting loyalties of the evolving global system is exactly where the population of a country begins and ends. For example, citizens of one EU country who reside in another EU country can now vote in local elections and even hold local office in the country where they reside. Also, a growing number of countries, now more than 90, recognize dual citizenship (being a citizen of two countries). For example, Spain has dual citizenship treaties with over a dozen countries in Latin America; Spaniards residing in these countries or territories do not lose their Spanish citizenship or rights even if they adopt that nationality.

INTERNAL ORGANIZATION.   Statehood requires some level of political and economic structure. Still, the condition of statehood persists even during periods of severe turmoil and unrest. Afghanistan, Sierra Leone, Somalia, Libya, and some other existing states have dissolved into chaos during the last decade or so. Yet none of these chaotic states has ceased to exist legally. Each, for instance, has continued to sit as a sovereign voting member in the UN General Assembly. Some of these disordered states have restored themselves to a modicum of order, but not all of them. For example, Somalia lacked a functioning government for over 20 years after the collapse of the state in 1990–1991, with control of Somalia divided among various warring clans. The Islamic Courts Union (ICU) sought to consolidate political authority through implementing *shari'ah* rule, but an Ethiopian-led (and US-backed) military assault in 2007 almost immediately unseated the ICU and returned Somalia to its previous semi-anarchic state. Since 2017, an internationally backed government under the leadership of President Mohamed Abdullahi Mohamed has been in power, representing the first stable governing arrangement since 1990. However, threats posed by the jihadist terrorist group *al-Shabab* underscore the continued fragility of the Somali state.

DIPLOMATIC RECOGNITION.   Another important requisite for statehood is subjective or perceptual in nature. In the end, state sovereignty rests on both a claim to that status and existing states' extension of **diplomatic recognition**. How many countries must grant recognition before a country can achieve statehood is a tricky question without an easy answer. A lack of recognition, even by a majority of other states, does not necessarily doom a state to nonexistence. For example, diplomatic recognition of the communist government of Mao Zedong in China came slowly after the communists prevailed in the Chinese civil war and consolidated power in 1949. The United States withheld diplomatic recognition until 1979. Did this lack of recognition mean that the People's Republic of China did not exist? Clearly, the answer is no, because the United States' stand that China's legitimate government was the defeated nationalists who had fled to Taiwan was obviously not credible.

Beyond the number of states extending diplomatic recognition, sometimes it matters which ones do—and which ones don't. In the former case, the quick recognition of Kosovo by the United States, the United Kingdom,

diplomatic recognition The formal recognition of one state's sovereignty by another, extended through the establishment of an embassy and/or consular relations. Diplomatic recognition is a key criterion of state sovereignty, suggesting its relational and subjective nature.

France, Germany, Turkey, and others following its declaration of independence in February 2008 went a long way toward ensuring its survival as a sovereign state. On the other side is the example of the Palestinians, who were granted the status of a nonmember observer state (a *de facto* recognition of state sovereignty) by the UN General Assembly in 2012. As of July 2019 over 70% (138 of 193) of UN member-states recognize "The Permanent Observer Mission of the State of Palestine to the United Nations" (the official legal title of the Palestinian delegation to the UN) as the sovereign government of the Palestinian nation. Yet amid all the diplomatic maneuvering, the recognition that countries extend to the Palestinian Authority clearly is largely a matter of political posturing, as full Palestinian statehood remains elusive because of opposition led by Israel and the United States. In 2012, when Palestine's "nonmember observer state status" was negotiated, 9 UN members (including the United States and Israel) voted against and 41 abstained, even though a large majority voted in favor. As a result, the Palestinians hold a seat in the UN General Assembly, can fully partake in UN business, and are bound by UN treaties, but they cannot vote within the UN bodies.

DOMESTIC SUPPORT.   Another requisite of statehood is domestic support. In its most positive form, a state's population is loyal and willing to accept the state's authority to govern. A weaker version of this is a population that grudgingly accepts the reality of a government's power to govern. For all the coercive power that states usually possess, it is difficult for any state to survive without at least this passive acquiescence. The dissolution of Czechoslovakia, the Soviet Union, and Yugoslavia are illustrations of multinational states that collapsed under the separatist impulses of disaffected nationalities. One of the continuing challenges confronting the Iraqi government, for example, is whether it will be possible to create sufficient domestic support for any government among the badly divided Shiites, Sunnis, and Kurds, all of whom in turn have their own internal divisions. In contrast, the rapid response of segments of the Turkish population to take to the streets to express support for President Recep Tayyip Erdoğan—at his urging—at the very outset of what he alleged to be an attempted military coup in July 2016 was a clear example of how domestic support underpins state authority.

Regime Types and Governance

How states are governed has a number of ramifications for global politics. Taking regime type into account raises questions as to whether some types of government are more warlike than others, whether some are more successful in their foreign policies than others, and whether it is wise to promote a specific form of governance—as United States foreign policy has been doing with democracy promotion for the past several decades.

We can begin to address these questions by dividing governance into two broad categories. The first includes authoritarian governments, those that allow little or no participation in decision-making by individuals and groups outside the upper reaches of the government. The second includes democratic

Reed Brody, "The Dictator Hunter"

Historically state sovereignty afforded legal protection to political leaders no matter what crime they might commit while in power—a concept known as "head of state immunity." In the latter part of the 20th century, this line of thinking began to be challenged, partly due to the tireless efforts of human rights lawyer Reed Brody.

Reed was born in Brooklyn, New York, shortly after his father, a Hungarian Jew who had spent three years in Nazi labor camps, emigrated to the United States. Reed graduated from Stuyvesant High School in Brooklyn and Fairleigh Dickinson University in New Jersey before obtaining a law degree from Columbia University. His work on the leading edge of human rights law began in the mid-1980s, as he exposed the atrocities committed against civilians in Nicaragua by the US-funded "Contra" rebels. With his findings used in congressional hearings and even the International Court of Justice case *Nicaragua v. United States,* Brody was publicly accused by President Ronald Reagan of being a "Sandinista sympathizer" (the Contras were backed by the United States to overthrow the democratically elected socialist government in Nicaragua during the 1980s).

Brody has worked in various capacities supporting the principle of judicial independence and training local human rights activists around the world. He was active throughout the 1990s as a legal representative to UN missions in El Salvador and Guatemala and in human rights advocacy and fact-finding roles in Sierra Leone, Haiti, the Democratic Republic of the Congo, and East Timor. In 1998, Reed joined the staff of the international nongovernmental organization Human Rights Watch (HRW), where he now serves as counsel and spokesperson, leading efforts to hold perpetrators of large-scale human rights violations accountable.

Reed has risen to prominence for his efforts to hold authoritarian leaders to account for their crimes against their citizens—earning his nickname "the Dictator Hunter." Reed directed HRW's involvement in the precedent-setting case against former Chilean dictator Augusto Pinochet in the United Kingdom during the late 1990s, and later led investigations into the crimes of autocrats such as Mengistu Haile Mariam (Ethiopia), Jean-Claude Duvalier and Raul Cedrás (Haiti), and Idi Amin (Uganda). In recent years, he has led investigations on behalf of HRW into the practices of the United States as part of the "war on terrorism"—again drawing the scorn of American conservatives.

Brody's single biggest case to date has been the 20-year effort to bring former Chadian dictator Hissène Habré to justice for the thousands of accusations of political killings and torture levied against him during his rule (1982–1990). Partly because of Brody's efforts, in 2012 the Senegalese government (where Habré fled into exile) approved creation of the "Extraordinary African Chambers," a hybrid African/international court that convicted Habré of crimes against humanity, war crimes, and torture, including sexual violence and rape, on May 30, 2016.

Although the "Dictator Hunter" has been lauded in the press, and even had a film made about his work in 2007 (*The Dictator Hunter,* directed by Klaartje Quirijns), for his part Brody views his work simply as a "wake-up call" to tyrants and a "spark of hope" for victims. In the process, he has lived out the concept of "speaking truth to power." To follow Reed on Twitter, check out @Reed Brody or his profile on the HRW website (https://www.hrw.org/about/people/reed-brody).

governments, those that allow citizens to broadly and meaningfully participate in the political process. The line between authoritarian and democratic regimes is not precise. Instead, with broad and meaningful participation as the standard, there is a scale that runs from one-person rule to full, direct democracy—or even, according to some, to anarchism (having no government).

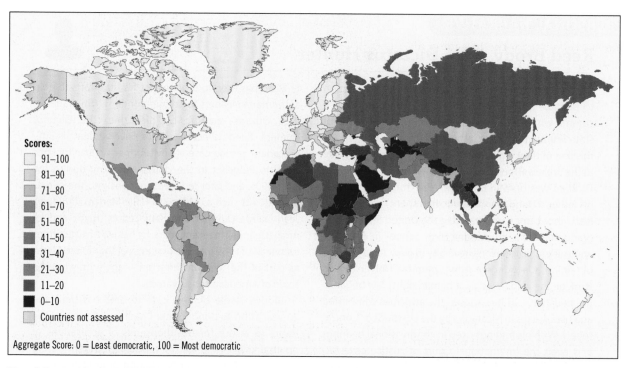

Map 4.5   Freedom in the World, 2019. The spread of democracy globally, which began symbolically with the American (1776) and French (1789) Revolutions, progressed slowly for the first 150 years, then accelerated in "waves" after the end of World War II (1945) and again after the end of the Cold War (1989). Now, as this map indicates, the majority of the world's countries are full-fledged or emerging democracies. However, in recent years there has been a resurgence of authoritarianism—particularly in key countries such as Russia, Turkey, and Egypt. (Source: http://en.actualitix.com/country/wld/democracy-index.php.)

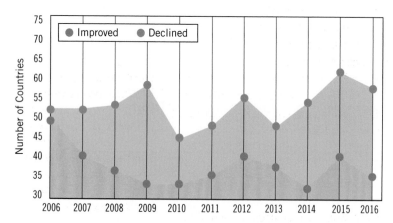

Figure 4.2   The global spread of democracy is undeniable. According to the calculations of the Freedom House Index, countries deemed "free" increased from 29% of all countries in 1973 to 44% in 2017, with an accompanying decline in those deemed "not free" over that same period. However, as this figure shows, recent years have witnessed declines in the degree of freedom in a majority of countries.

Map 4.5 provides one way to order types of government, with the countries shaded in lighter tones generally democratic and the countries in light and dark purple **authoritarian**. Recent years have been witness to what some scholars and policy-makers refer to as "The New Authoritarianism" (King, 2009), with a turn toward hardline and more restrictive forms of government in Russia, Turkey, Hungary, and elsewhere.

It is also worth noting that after the Cold War, the pace of democratization picked up considerably around the globe, but it has leveled off and even backslid over the last decade, as Figure 4.2 shows. Whether or not this most recent trend will continue is an open question.

Weak and Failed States

As is evident from the foregoing discussion of the requisites of statehood, what does or does not constitute a state is far from an absolute. Because a state's existence is more a political than a legal matter, there is a significant gray area. It is also clear that in that "gray area" are a number of political entities possessing many, but not all, of the requisites of a state. It is possible to situate these types of entities in two groups: embryonic states and failed states.

These two types of "states" are also emblematic of the evolution of the global system since the end of World War II. With the creation of many new states out of the former European colonial empires, the global community was faced with many states that did not correspond with a nation or fea-

Democracy is relative, and how democratic a country is depends on the degree to which all its citizens can participate equally in civic life. One promising development in recent years is the slow but steady advance of women to positions of political power. Here, German Chancellor Angela Merkel (at right) reviews an honor guard of Swiss federal troops with Switzerland's President Simonetta Sommaruga (at left).

ture a sense of nationalism (embryonic states), as well as those that lacked the governmental institutions and infrastructure to function as a sovereign state in real terms even if they possessed the trappings of sovereignty in political terms (failed states).

Embryonic states have many of the characteristics of a state, yet they are not generally accorded the status of a full-fledged state. No country contends that the Palestinians effectively control a sovereign state, yet many countries recognize it as such for political reasons. By the same token, Taiwan functions in most ways like a state, but China's power keeps it in a legal limbo. Regarding Tibet, no matter what the Tibetans and the Dalai Lama say, and regardless of anyone's sympathies, no government has ever recognized it, nor is Tibet a sovereign state.

Failed states are existing states, but they have lost one or more of the characteristics that define a state. They remain legally sovereign entities by default, though burdened by a lack of internal support, absent or incompetent internal organization, or lack of real independence, as distinct from legal sovereignty. Since the collapse of the Mohammad Said Barre regime in 1990, Somalia has been a failed state, while a more recent example of a state on the brink of failure is the world's newest, which we have returned to repeatedly throughout this chapter—namely, South Sudan.

One gauge of the number of failed states and states under stress is available in The Fragile States Index, a dataset compiled by the nonprofit organization The Fund for Peace. The Index's latest (2019) edition draws on over 130,000 publicly available sources to analyze 178 countries and rate them on 12 indicators of pressure on the state—from refugee flows to poverty and from public

authoritarian A type of restrictive governmental system in which people are under the rule of an individual, such as a dictator or king, or a group, such as a party or military junta.

failed states Countries in which the state is unable to effectively maintain order and provide public goods due to political upheaval, economic instability, crime and lawlessness, violence, ethnic and cultural divides, and other destabilizing forces.

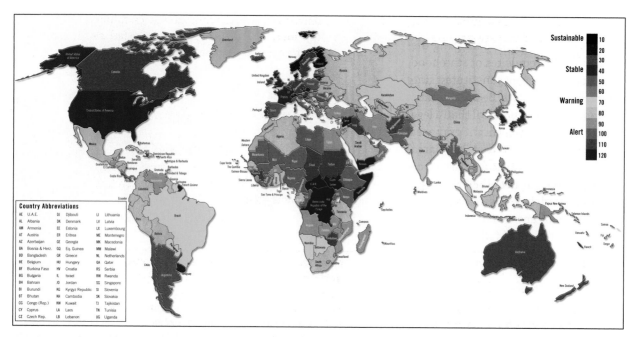

Map 4.6 **State Fragility, 2019**. One barometer of the number of failing states and states under stress is the Fragile States Index, a data set compiled by the nonprofit organization The Fund for Peace. With a possible range from 12 (absolutely stable) to 120 (absolutely chaotic), 9 countries led by Yemen (113.5) scored 100 or above in 2019 and might reasonably be considered failing states. Another 22 scored in the exceptionally stressed 90s. (Source: Foreign Policy/Fund for Peace Fragile States Index, 2019)

services to security threats (see Map 4.6). A country's performance on this battery of indicators, taken together, tells us how stable or unstable it is. For example, with a score of 16.9, the Index characterized Finland as the world's most stable country, with the United States receiving a stable score of 38.0. The map here presents categories of state rankings throughout the world. If nothing else, the plight of fragile states reminds us that states themselves, while central units in global politics, are neither permanent nor beyond challenge.

Chapter Summary

- Nations and states remain central to the organization and conduct of IR, but they are abstract and therefore contestable notions.

- The success or failure of a state depends in large part on "buy in" from citizens and identity groups within a state's borders— and on acceptance and recognition from outside actors.

- While nationalism and the state can and do provide coherence and order to both domestic and global society, they also can and do serve as sources of conflict and contention.

- The world's newest state, South Sudan, reflects all of these claims. If South Sudan can settle internal divisions between its various ethnic groups and establish a national consciousness and identity, the prospects for the South Sudanese state are likely to improve. Conversely, if a national identity remains elusive, the civil war will certainly continue, with the prospects of state failure on the not- too-distant horizon.

Critical Thinking Questions

1. What are the most important defining features of nationhood? Is it necessary to meet them all in order to consider an identity group a "nation"? Why or why not?

2. Are the concepts of popular and state sovereignty that we respectively associate with the nation and the state competing or complementary?

3. What does the reality that state sovereignty is, at least in part, a relational concept suggest about the nature and conduct of global politics?

Key Terms

authoritarian	failed states	nativism	state sovereignty
colonialism	fascism	political communities	Thirty and Eighty
decolonization	Holy Roman Empire	popular sovereignty	Years Wars
democracy	microstates	Protestant Reformation	totalitarianism
diplomatic recognition	monarchism	self-determination	xenophobia
Enlightenment	nation	social contract	
ethnonationalism	nationalism	state building	
exceptionalism	nation-state	state of nature	

5

Globalization and Transnationalism: Forces of Integration and Disintegration

In recent years, the world has witnessed a dramatic rise in anti-establishment, anti-globalization political movements. As reflected by the Brexit vote in the United Kingdom, the election of President Trump in the United States and President Duterte in the Philippines, the consolidation of power by President Erdoğan in Turkey, or the strong right-wing political movements in France, Hungary, Italy, the Netherlands, Sweden, and beyond, there is a clear trend for states to retreat from global alliances and a globalized economy in the interest of narrowly defined domestic or national politics. Along these lines, there is also a popular backlash against free trade and unrestricted movement of people, goods, and services across borders.

Media outlets abound with questions about the end or the reversal of globalization. A 2017 analysis of media for the term *globalization* across several major newspapers in the United States and the United Kingdom—*The Wall Street Journal, The New York Times, Washington Post, Times of London, The Guardian,* and *Financial Times*—reveals a marked souring of reader sentiments, with negative scores especially rising in 2016.[1]

This photo illustrates the intensity of the "Remain" supporters since the 2016 Brexit vote in the U.K. Three years after the referendum, the issue of the future status of the U.K. relative to the European Union remains as contentious as ever.

For many, globalization is to blame for economic hardships, and there is growing pressure worldwide for new protectionist and isolationist policies and politicians.

These developments and sentiments around the world require a look closer at globalization. This chapter explores the concepts of globalization and transnationalism as complex, multidimensional forces of change at work in international relations (IR). While these processes are certainly not new, they are shifting the nature of human interaction and political identification well beyond the traditional borders of the nation-state in important ways.

Learning Objectives

Identify the causes and various understandings of globalization.

Discuss the impact of globalization on the various forms of economic and cultural systems.

Discuss the various actors that constitute global civil society, how they organize themselves, and the range of transnational strategies they employ in affecting change.

Identify the various complex global and transnational forces and phenomena, and consider their place as "new" or recurring features of global politics.

Causes and Conceptions of Globalization

globalization A multifaceted concept that represents the increasing integration of economics, communications, and culture across national boundaries.

As discussed in Chapter 1, **globalization** refers to global forces, both positive and negative, operating in and transforming our daily lives. From the food we eat to the clothes we wear to the issues we care about and how we identify ourselves, we are constantly engaging in global processes from our local positions while our local realities are being impacted by global events. In this way, the world is more than just the sum of its parts; it is also a complex system with many commonalities and connections that cut across political borders, national identities, and cultural differences.

Although globalization may seem like an abstract concept, it is a phenomenon that can be seen and experienced in most everything we do and even touch on a daily basis. The computer keyboard used to type this book was made in Thailand, the mouse came from China, the monitor was produced in South Korea, and the flash drive that backed up files was manufactured in Taiwan. Just today we have all likely connected with websites in more than a half-dozen countries, and classes at our university this afternoon have students from a variety of countries beyond the United States. In short, globalization brings people and places closer together more rapidly and more cheaply than ever before. These intense exchanges of goods, services, people, and ideas disrupt our social space and can challenge our way of life in both positive and negative ways.

An Accelerating Political Force

Globalization is not new. In some ways, it has been under way since the first isolated tribes and other groups of humans began to trade, fight, and otherwise interact with one another. War and colonialization, like trade and investment, are globalizing processes that bring people into contact with one another in transformative ways. This brings us to the distinctly modern characteristics of globalization. The speed with which globalization has progressed has increased greatly over the past 200 years or so, and even more extraordinarily since World War

In late 2018, the *Gilets Jaunes* (Yellow Vests) protests broke out repeatedly over several weeks in Paris and other French cities, frequently turning violent. Representing a diverse range of anti-globalization and anti-establishment forces, the protesters directed their ire at the perceived complicity of the French government and President Emmanuel Macron with market-oriented globalization strategies.

II (Williamson, 1996). This structuring logic was further cemented with the end of the Cold War and the triumph of industrial capitalism in determining how the world was to be organized economically (Held & McGrew, 2000). This modern acceleration of globalization is the product of multiple factors, including advances in transportation and communication technology as well as shifts in government policy toward greater liberalization and internationalization of economic, political, and social transactions.

Many in the United States have misconceptions about the depth and reach of globalization. For instance, as seen in Figure 5.1 using one measure, USA total trade (exports plus imports) in 1960 was about 9% of GDP. In recent years, however, that has fluctuated between 25 and 30%. This shows the growth of trade as part of the US economy and is one reason why trade wars cause so much difficulty for the American and global economies.

Economists Steven Altman, Pankaj Ghemawat, and Phillip Bastian, from the Center for Globalization and Education and Management at New York University's Stern School of Business, utilize empirical data to see how globalization is actually evolving and how individual perceptions do not always match reality. For example, using their DHL Global Connectedness Index (Altman,

Figure 5.1   Total trade (exports plus imports) has grown steadily if sometime irregularly from 1960 to 2017. The most recent fluctuations reflect the impact of the great recession in 2008 and perhaps the impact of Trump's trade wars that past two years. This graph also illustrates how increasingly dependent even the large US economy is on world trade.

Ghemawat and Bastian, 2018), we can see that with the exception of the 2007–2008 global financial crisis, worldwide flows of trade, capital, information, and people have either stayed constant or increased annually for years. However, the reach of global interconnectedness varies.

While that has increased significantly over the past few decades, it is also among the lowest in the world today, as the global average is 28%, and the average for other high-income countries is 30% (World Bank, 2019c). And despite the American cliché that everything is made in China, less than 3% of money spent in the United States goes to Chinese imports. Ghemawat and Altman refer to this as the "Globaloney Gap"—the idea that politicians often overestimate global connections, exaggerating job losses or numbers of people crossing borders.[2] Thus, while globalization is an accelerating political force today, it is important not to overestimate the depth and reach of our interconnectedness, especially for political purposes.

TECHNOLOGICAL ADVANCES. People, money, goods, culture, and ideas have flowed across borders since ancient times. What is different, though, is the speed at which globalization is now proceeding, and the role of technology in driving it. By most estimates, the vast majority of history's significant technological advances have occurred since 1800, and the rate of discovery and invention has been accelerating during that time. Communications technologies have revolutionized our information systems, connecting humans in new and innovative ways. As Thomas Friedman argues, "Globalization 3.0 is shrinking the world from a size small to a size tiny and flattening the playing field at the same time by shifting the focus from globalizing corporations to empowering individuals to compete globally" (2005:10). Although Friedman's analysis is a bit overdrawn, he does highlight the ways more connections can actually lead to decreased inequalities around the world.

A critical aspect of the technological revolution has been the dramatic changes of global transportation. Globalization could not exist to the degree it does without the increased ability to transport products and people rapidly and in large numbers across great distances. Modern transportation carries people and their products across national borders in volume and at a speed that would have been unimaginable not very long ago. Oceangoing transport provides a good example. The most famous merchant vessel of the

CNN Video: Globalization, Healthcare, and Inequality.

The *Jahre Viking*, also named the Seawise Giant, later Happy Giant along with other names, was a supertanker and the longest ship ever. Built by a Japanese company, the ship's displacement was 657,019 tonnes fully loaded. The vessel was sold to Indian ship breakers, and renamed *Mont* for its final journey in December 2009. After clearing Indian customs it sailed to Alang, Gujarat, where it was beached for scrapping.

mid-1800s was the *Flying Cloud* (1851–1874), a 229-foot-long sailing ship. Now, modern megaships, such as the tanker *Jahre Viking*, which at 1,504 feet long were so large that crew members often used bicycles on board to travel from one point to another, dominate the oceans. This immense ship carried more than a half-million tons of cargo, 900 times the capacity of the *Flying Cloud*. Yet the *Jahre Viking* was but one of the vast world merchant fleet of almost 28,000 freighters and tankers, with a combined capacity of over 733 million tons of goods. These behemoths not only carry more cargo, but have also expanded trade by reducing seagoing transportation costs to a small fraction of what they were a century ago.

Advances in transportation have been important in moving people as well as goods. When the first English settlers traveled from the British Isles to what would be Jamestown, Virginia, in 1607, the only way to make the trip was by ship, and the voyage took nearly five months. International travel is almost routine today, with hundreds of millions of travelers moving between countries within a few hours each year. This can be seen not only in the "legitimate" travel of tourists and businesspeople, but also in the countless humans who are trafficked across borders and violently forced to work as prostitutes, domestic servants, or farmers for little to no pay under extremely exploitative conditions.

The movement of people and goods depends upon the movement of information. Technological advances that permit us to transmit images, data, and written word and sound easily and quickly all over the world are what drive globalization. Thus, it is almost impossible to overstate the impact that modern communications have had on IR. In only a century and a half, communications have made spectacular advances, beginning with the telegraph and followed by photography, radio, the ability to film events, telephones, photocopying, television, satellite communications, faxes, and now computer-based Internet contacts and information through e-mail and the World Wide Web.

The flow of these communications is too massive to calculate precisely, especially when we consider the portability of many new technologies. More than two-thirds of the world's populations now have a mobile phone, representing a dramatic jump from 11 million users in 1990 to 5 billion in 2017 globally.[3] Of course, access to such technology is not distributed equally both across and within regions, as seen in Table 5.1. What does it say that 86% of Europeans are mobile subscribers while only 44% of Africans are? What about the disparity between India and China, the two most populous countries in the world?

The technological revolution in communications has also meant that more and more people around the globe are getting their news from mobile devices and a select few media giants. The most obvious example is CNN, which now reaches virtually every country in the world and broadcasts in nine languages. And while CNN carries an American perspective to the rest of the world, non-US news networks such as Al Jazeera, France 24, and RT (formerly Russia Today) are bringing foreign news perspectives to Americans. Al Jazeera now reaches more than 310 million households in more than 100 different countries, rivaling media giants CNN and the BBC.

Table 5.1 Global Mobile Phone Subscribers

REGION	UNIQUE MOBILE SUBSCRIBERS (MILLIONS)	% OF GLOBAL SUBSCRIBER BASE	SUBSCRIBER PENETRATION (% OF POPULATION)
Asia Pacific	2,765	55%	68%
China	1,081	21%	78%
India	730	14%	54%
Europe	465	9%	86%
Latin America	459	9%	71%
Sub-Saharan Africa	436	9%	44%
Middle East & North Africa	391	8%	63%
North America	292	6%	80%
Commonwealth of Independent States	227	5%	79%
TOTAL	**5,035**	**100%***	**67%**

Source: GSMA Intelligence 2004–2019, https://www.gsmaintelligence.com/.
*Because of rounding the total is over 100%.

The instantaneous flow of news and information over the Internet is only matched by the exponential growth in the number of people around the world who are using it. Between 1995 and 2017, the share of the world population using the Internet soared from 0.4% to 54.4%, and the number of total active Internet users now stands at over 4 billion, as Figure 5.2 indicates.[4] Furthermore, today's Internet users are not only able to access the Web, but to communicate with one another via e-mail or through social media sites such as Facebook and Twitter, instantaneously sharing unfiltered information globally.

This revolution in global communications is of immense importance. It has provided citizens from different countries with the ability to espouse causes of nearly every imaginable type, to exchange views, to organize across national borders, and to undertake political actions (Schmitz, 2004). Nowhere was this more evident than the series of democratic revolutions that constituted the Arab Spring, which started in Tunisia in 2010 and quickly swept the region from Egypt to Libya to Bahrain to Yemen to Syria, and in the process demonstrated how social media can empower individuals and groups in new ways.[5] In fact, recent

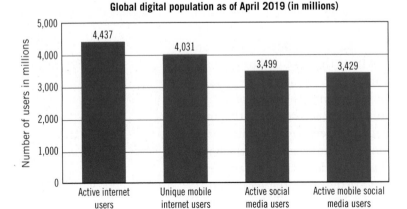

Figure 5.2   As of 2018, there are more than 4 billion people around the world using the internet. What does it mean that almost half the world still does not have access to the internet?

research on the Arab Spring suggests that "social media enabled or facilitated the protests by providing voice to people in societies with mostly government-controlled legacy media; helping people connect, mobilize and organize demonstrations; and broadcasting protests to the world at large and gaining global support" (Smidi & Shahin 2017:196).

Along these lines, global communications can undermine authoritarian governments. The rapid mass communications that are taken for granted in the industrialized democracies are still greeted with suspicion by authoritarian governments. China tries to control the Web by using technology to monitor and block dissident communications and by imposing fines and imprisonment on those the government claims endanger national security by transmitting dissident information and opinions. In 2010, Google partially pulled out of the world's largest Internet market (China) over censorship concerns and a computer hacking attempt Google claimed could be traced back to the Chinese government. This move to shut down mainland Chinese service was a major blow to the Chinese government and its international image, as it signals a major corporation's unwillingness to continue to accept such censorship. As of 2018, Google has relaunched Google Maps in a special version for Chinese users as well as Google Translate.[6] Still, China has banned Facebook, Snapchat, Pinterest, most foreign films, Apple iBooks and iTunes Movies, among other books and websites.[7]

While these media certainly provide great opportunities for enhanced information flows, the quality of the information itself can—and does—vary greatly. The impact of the well-chronicled phenomenon of "fake news" on politics around the world is largely a by-product of unregulated or poorly regulated user-driven media in which lies and conspiracy theories can be widely circulated, such as the preposterous "Pizzagate" myth perpetuated through discussion forums such as 4chan and social media outlets such as Facebook and Twitter.[8] The profit-driven motivations of platforms such as Facebook have also worked at cross-purposes to enlighten and inform political discourse and behavior.

The power of globalized communications is further reflected in the fact that the regulation of the Internet itself has become an international political issue. This has become especially prominent in the aftermath of the 2016 agreement between the U.S. government and Internet Corporation for Assigned Names and Numbers (ICANN)—the nonprofit organization responsible for assigning domains and ensuring the stable and secure operation of the internet. ICANN, whose members include myriad governments,

Flowers laid by supporters on the sign of Google's Beijing headquarters. After several years of on-again, off-again relations marked by periods of Chinese government censorship and even exclusion, as of late 2018 Google has resumed operations in the People's Republic.

corporations as well as individual internet users now officially owns and controls the Internet Assigned Numbers Authority, or IANA, the database that stores all Internet domain names.[9] And the United States no longer controls the Internet address book.

GOVERNMENT POLICY. Just as government policy can resist or seek to control globalization, it can also serve as a major catalyst in promoting globalization, especially on the economic front. After World War I, countries increasingly tried to protect their economies from foreign competition by instituting trade restrictions in the form of high tariffs and by impeding the free exchange of currencies. In hindsight, policy-makers concluded this approach had been disastrous. Much of Europe struggled economically during the 1920s, and then collapsed at the end of the decade. Between 1929 and 1932, industrial production in Europe fell by 50% and unemployment shot up to 22%. The US stock market crashed in 1929, and the American economy soon imploded, as did the economies of Japan and other countries. Global trade plummeted, and the world sank into the Great Depression. During the 1920s, fascist dictator Benito Mussolini seized power in downtrodden Italy, and during the Great Depression, Adolf Hitler and other fascists rose to power in Germany, Japan, Spain, and elsewhere. World War II soon followed, exacting a horrific price. Many observers, including the famous British economist John Maynard Keynes, argued that the restrictive economic policies after World War I had created the economic desperation that allowed fascism to take hold, which in turn led to World War II (Keynes, 2017).

Based on their analysis of the causes of World War II, policy-makers planning for the postwar period focused in part on preventing a reoccurrence of global conflict (Helleiner, 1996; Ikenberry, 2001). On the economic front, the United States led the effort to create the General Agreement on Tariffs and Trade, a treaty and an organization of the same name (later renamed the World Trade Organization [WTO]) meant to eventually eliminate the trade barriers that were blamed for World War II. Policy-makers also established the International Monetary Fund (IMF) and the World Bank (discussed in Chapter 10). Such belief in and government support for globalization continue to be powerful guides to policy choices today.

This speaks to the reality that globalization is not a natural occurrence but rather the by-product of policy choices focused on internationalizing trade, investment, and capital as well as liberalizing domestic economic systems through the dismantling of trade barriers, the deregulation of industry, and the privatization of state enterprises (Simmons & Elkins, 2004). Such organizing structures and social processes have led to the creation of new rules and institutions both formal and informal, increased human interdependence, and the expansive reach of the global market. In this way, just as Western countries largely created globalization as we understand it today, so too can countries, acting collectively, (re)shape, restrain, or even reverse many aspects of globalization by increasing economic barriers, restricting travel and interfering with transnational communications, and other policies designed to make national borders less permeable.

Interpretations of Globalization

For some, globalization is about integration and harmonization (Bhagwati, 2004), whereas for others, globalization is about systems of domination and new forms of imperialism (Veltmeyer, 2005). Globalization can simultaneously be seen as supporting democratic reform (McGrew, 1997) as well as contributing to environmental degradation (Elliott, 2004). To understand this complex and multidimensional process, it is critical to draw insights from a range of IR theory. Here, we examine neoliberal institutionalism and dependency theory, two strands of economic internationalism and economic structuralism.

NEOLIBERAL INSTITUTIONALISM.   Globalization is often about the cooperation of states and the integration of economic, social, and even political policies. Neoliberal institutionalism is one theoretical lens best situated to help explain such collaborative exchanges. As discussed in Chapter 2, neoliberal institutionalism is one of the dominant contemporary reformulations of liberal thought. Neoliberal institutionalists push us to consider why states choose to cooperate more often than not, even in the state of anarchy.

For some neoliberal institutionalists, like Robert Keohane and Joseph Nye (2001), **complex interdependence** is a useful concept for explaining the ways in which states are tied together, whether in terms of monetary policy, military alliances, trade relations, environmental policy, or something else. These ties create a mutual (although not always equal) dependence among states that are facilitated by multiple and frequent channels of communication and exchange, both in official interstate terms and less official transnational channels. Such connection and reliance can often make the use of force a nonviable tool of global politics, or at least create situations where military security does not consistently dominate the agenda (Keohane & Nye, 2001). The goals of states will vary by issue area, and international organizations play an increasingly important role in determining what issues matter by influencing the agenda-setting process, inducing coalition formation, and serving as political arenas for political action by weak states (Holsti, 2004). The political process that led to the creation of the 17 Sustainable Development Goals (discussed in greater detail in Chapter 13) is an empirical example of these theoretical commitments at work.

complex interdependence
The broad and deep dependence of issues and actors in the contemporary global political system that many scholars believe is a by-product of globalization, as evidenced by the extent to which international institutions have emerged to "govern" the multiple and complex interactions.

The SDGs are the 17 goals that set the 2030 Agenda for Sustainable Development. These goals represent a blueprint for peace and prosperity and were adopted by all United Nations Member States in 2015. Within these 17 goals are 169 measureable targets for ending poverty, improving health and education, reducing inequality, and spurring economic growth—all while tackling climate change and working to preserve the oceans and forests.

DEPENDENCY THEORY.   For other, more critically inclined theorists, global interactions are much less harmonious than neoliberal institutionalists would lead us to believe. One

dependency theory The view of global politics as an economic system in which the Global South is dependent upon and disadvantaged by the Global North as a perpetuation of the imperialist relationships established in previous centuries.

example of this perspective, as discussed in Chapter 2, is **dependency theory**. Inspired by the work of Karl Marx, dependency theory emerged in the 1950s with the efforts of leading scholars such as Raúl Prebisch, Andre Gunder Frank, and Fernando Henrique Cardoso (among others) to provide an account for contested and unequal relationships and interactions within the global system. Dependency theorists don't see harmonious relationships across borders but rather exploitative ones, with their origins in colonialism and imperialism (Larrain, 2013). From this perspective, only certain countries benefit from more connected economies and cultures, primarily because of the international division of labor that allows—and, frankly, depends upon—some countries dominating in terms of capital intensive-industries and other countries providing cheap labor, agricultural production, and resource extraction essential to a capitalist system (Wallerstein, 2004).

For dependency theorists, capitalism reinforces dominance and increasing inequality between the rich and the poor. According to Petras and Veltmeyer capitalism in the form of neoliberal globalization "provides a very poor model for changing society in the direction of social equality, participatory democratic decision-making and human welfare" (2013:148). It may be surprising to learn that the gap between rich and poor has increased in almost every region of the world over the last four decades. According to the World Inequality Report 2018, since 1980 the top 0.1% of wealth owners, about 7 million people, captured as much of the world's growth as the bottom half of the adult population—around 3.8 billion people. Further, the report estimated that 10% of the world's wealth is currently held in tax havens.[10] For dependency theorists, tax havens are a perfect of example of class division and elite cooperation across countries to ensure those at the top stay there and continue to exploit those at the bottom.

Analyzing the Impact of Globalization

Regardless of your view on the positive and negative outcomes of globalization, no one can argue with the fact that these processes have implications for economic, political, social, and cultural systems across the world. Globalization's reach is as wide as it is deep, and it has implications not only for global politics but for regional, national, and local politics as well.

Economic Globalization

Economic interchange across borders is bringing the world together and creating economic interdependence in both positive and negative ways. Goods are made more cheaply and are more widely available, but that also means we send jobs to the places where we can pay the lowest—and not necessarily livable— wages. While we will examine and evaluate how economic globalization works in later chapters, here we focus on two other critical aspects: the centrality of the informal sector and the impact of identity politics on economic exchanges.

When we look at formal sectors of the market, economic globalization has often translated into growth and prosperity. However, it is also important to consider the impact of economic globalization on informal sectors. These include both the legal and illegal profit-based exchanges that occur outside formal, market-based production. These areas of unregulated activity are rarely counted in economic studies or national assessments such as **gross domestic product** (GDP). From child care to housework to street vending to petty trade to drug dealing and the arms trade, these activities have dramatically increased in recent years and constitute more than half of all economic output. While measuring and assessing these often-invisible forms of work is controversial, this remarkable growth was documented in a special issue of the *Journal of International Affairs* entitled "The Shadow Economy" (Fleming, Roman & Farrell, 2000). The global economy as we understand it simply could not function without the informal sector and all the work, paid and not paid, legal and illegal, that it involves.

The formal sector also has personal implications. Global economic interchange is bringing people together transnationally through familiarity with one another and with one another's products. For example, some of these contacts are interpersonal; more have to do with the role of international economics in narrowing cultural differences and creating a sense of identification with trading partners. The United Nations (UN) has even been tracking the globalization of cultural trade as an economic sector emerging in recent decades to show the movement of cultural goods and services across borders and the role of that movement in conveying ideas, symbols, and ways of life. Figure 5.3 helps

gross domestic product A measure of income within a country that excludes foreign earnings and is often used as a primary indicator of a country's economic performance and standing.

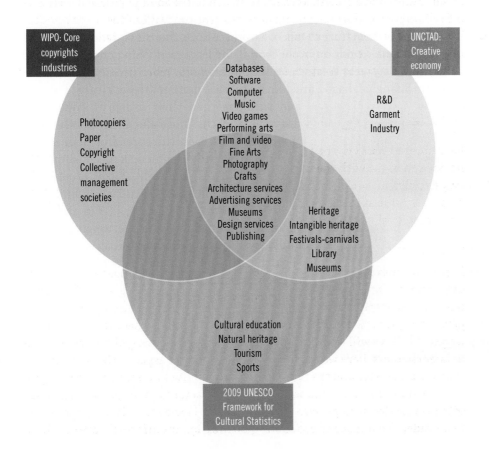

Figure 5.3 The Cultural Sector constitutes an important part of most national economies and plays a major role in globalization and the spread of ideas and values. However, culture can be difficult to define. Here you can see what industries and activities constitute the cultural sector.

us to consider the many personal implications of cultural trade. Which goods and services in the figure are most relevant to your daily life?

Cultural Globalization

Much of the early development of different languages, customs, and other diverse aspects of world cultures resulted from the isolation of groups of people from one another. It is not surprising, then, that a degree of cultural amalgamation has occurred as improved transportation and communications have brought people and societies into ever-more-frequent contact (Norris & Inglehart, 2009). Analyzing the blurring of cultural differences inevitably includes fast food, basketball, rock music, and other such aspects of pop culture, but such analysis does not trivialize the subject. Instead, a long-standing, bottom-up line of political theory argues that the world's people can build on commonplace interactions and increasing cultural commonalities that engender familiarity with—and confidence in—one another to create a global civil society where people begin to define themselves as global citizens. Some nations emerged from civil societies and, as discussed in Chapter 4, carved out their own nation-states. By the same process, if transnational civil societies develop, then regional and even global schemes of governance could conceivably form and supplement or even supplant the territorial state. Scholars who examine the bottom-up process of transnational integration look for evidence in such factors as the flow of communications and commerce between countries and the spread across borders of what people wear, eat, and do for recreation (Miller, 2007).

How Nationalism and Globalism Can Coexist.

While it is premature to talk of a world culture, there is significant evidence of cultural amalgamation in the world. The leaders of China once wore "Mao suits"; now, they wear Western-style business suits. When dressing informally, people in Shanghai, Lagos, and Mexico City are more apt to wear jeans, T-shirts, and sneakers than their country's traditional dress. One of the most alarming trends along these lines has been the spread of poor eating habits, particularly the increasing consumption of Big Macs, fries, and milk shakes around the world. The World Health Organization finds that obesity has nearly tripled since 1975 and more than 1.9 billion adults were overweight and 650 million were obese.[11] Despite the severe interpersonal, health, and economic costs of people gaining weight worldwide, the fact that it is occurring while more than 1 billion people in the world are suffering from hunger is particularly disturbing.

Before looking further at the evidence of cultural amalgamation, one caution is in order. A great deal of what is becoming "world culture" is Western, and especially American, in its origins. That does not imply that Western culture is superior; its impact is a function of the economic and

This signpost in Budapest reflects the eclectic and global mix of acts, including classic US-based hip-hop collective The Wu-Tang Clan, appearing at an upcoming open-air music festival—sponsored by MasterCard, of course.

political strength of Western Europe and the United States. Nor does the preponderance of Western culture in the integration process mean that the flow is one way. American culture, for example, is heavily influenced by many foreign imports, ranging from fajitas and sushi through soccer to acupuncture and yoga—a process scholars of cultural globalization refer to as "hybridization" (Kraidy, 2017).

LANGUAGE. One of the most important aspects of converging culture is English, which is becoming the common language of business, diplomacy, and mass communications. Many leaders of countries or international organizations converse in English, with a number of them, including former UN Secretary-General Ban Ki-moon of South Korea, learning it while enrolled at US universities. The use of English is also spreading among the world's citizens as well, especially among younger people. In Europe, for example, 9 out of 10 students in countries ranging from Italy to Spain to Austria to Norway to Greece and Croatia now receive English instruction as part of their primary education.[12]

Modern communications are one factor driving the spread of English. Notable advances, such as the ability to search in nearly 100 languages through Google, have made the Web more accessible to non-English speakers, but the vast majority of what is available on the Internet remains in English. As the webmaster at one site in Russia comments, "It is far easier for a Russian . . . to download the works of Dostoyevsky translated in English to read than it is for him to get [it] in his own language."[13] Business needs also promote the global growth of English. The status of the United States as an economic powerhouse makes it far more common for foreign business people to learn the language of Americans than for Americans to learn other languages. A report issued by the Japanese government declared that "achieving world-class excellence demands that all Japanese acquire a working knowledge of English."[14]

CONSUMER PRODUCTS. The interchange of popular consumer goods is another major factor in narrowing cultural gaps. American movies are popular throughout much of the world. In 2018, for example, three of the five top-grossing films globally were adaptations of Marvel Comics—*Avengers: Infinity War* (1), *Black Panther* (2), and *Venom* (5). Moreover, foreign distribution is vital to the US film industry, as revenues from North American box offices continued to decline in 2018 while global revenues continue to grow. For example, in 2017, China took in almost $9 billion in movie revenues—that is to say, over 20% of global box office film revenues—with the first eight months of 2018 experiencing an additional 17% increase over 2017.[15] In other industries, China, the most populous country in the world, has surpassed the United States as the largest market for new cars as well as the largest emitter of greenhouse gasses.

Evaluating Globalization

Very few would refute that globalization, as a multidimensional process, exists. At a factual level, there can be little doubt that the exchange of peoples, goods, services, and ideas across borders has increased considerably. Evidence for the extraordinarily rapid globalization of communications and transportation is beyond dispute. The economic data are also clear. Measured by trade, investment, monetary flow, and every other standard, economic globalization has advanced quickly and far. Cultural globalization is harder to measure, but anyone who has traveled internationally over the past several decades will attest to how much more frequent the use of English, Western-style dress, fast-food restaurants, and many other aspects of a spreading common culture have become. From these cursory observations, many people seem to view globalization positively; it enjoys considerable popular support around the world. Yet critics of the process are legion—and are more vehement than its supporters. Among their objections, the assumed benefits of globalization are for the few at the top, and more problematically, these benefits rely upon the exploitation and the disadvantaging for the many at the margins of global society with serious environmental costs.

Ultimately it is difficult to evaluate globalization as a purely positive or negative trend for the world. And as the discussion here demonstrates, in many ways it is both.

ARGUMENTS FOR ECONOMIC GLOBALIZATION.   As noted earlier, economic globalization accelerated after World War II because it was promoted by American and other policy-makers who believed that reducing fewer international economic restrictions would increase prosperity, thereby decreasing a source of potential conflict among countries (Ikenberry, 2001). Many policy-makers, scholars, and others continue to believe in the validity of this causal sequence and to promote globalization based on it (Russett & Oneal, 2001). They also see additional links between globalization and peace. One thought, articulated by the journalist Thomas Friedman (2012) and others, is that globalization increases prosperity and democracy is more likely in prosperous countries. Since democratic peace theory contends that democracies seldom, if ever, fight with one another, then a positive sequence is globalization → greater prosperity → more democracies → fewer wars. Yet another argument is that globalization creates interdependent economies, which make it difficult and economically self-destructive to fight wars. Thus, another positive sequence is globalization → increased interdependence → fewer wars. These sorts of rationales were certainly part of the justification behind the creation of the European Union (EU), which began as the European Coal and Steel Community following the social and economic devastation of World War II (Moravcsik, 1998).

Just as some policy-makers and scholars see positive links between economic globalization and peace, some analysts believe that as globalization creates more personal interaction, cultural interchange, and amalgamation among people, it makes others seem less alien and threatening, and the resulting familiarity enhances peace. In this positive sequence, globalization → increased cross-cultural contacts and amalgamation → a decreased sense of difference among nations and peoples → less conflict (Appiah, 2006). Whatever the precise sequence of the links, President Bill Clinton was expressing his belief in the general link between globalization and peace when he told Congress, "These are the challenges we have to meet so that we can lead the world toward peace and freedom in an era of globalization."[16] Numerous scholars also link globalization to peace, arguing that "[t]he United States and other major powers can best discourage conflict by promoting greater global economic ties" (Gartzke & Li, 2003:285).

CONCERNS ABOUT ECONOMIC GLOBALIZATION.   It is important to note that not everyone agrees that globalization promotes peace, and that even if it does, the process of getting to peace and prosperity can often be violent, repressive, and unstable (Robinson, 2006). Thus, there are serious concerns about the impact of globalizing processes in the short and long term.

One concern relates to the causal arguments linking prosperity directly to peace or indirectly, through democratization, to peace. Take Russia, for example. While Russia is certainly part of the global market in terms of oil, it is only quasi-democratic and semi-cooperative at best. According to one analyst, "The oil sector has effectively merged with the state, making Russia's deepening ties to the global economy a would-be weapon rather than an avenue of restraint. Russian economic liberalization without political liberalization is unlikely to pay the strong cooperative dividends many expect" (Goldstone, 2007). In recent years, Russia's political rights ratings by Freedom House have declined due to heavily flawed 2016 legislative elections. "With loyalist security forces, a subservient judiciary, a controlled media environment, and a legislature consisting of a ruling party and pliable opposition groups, the Kremlin is able to manipulate elections and inhibit genuine opposition" (Freedom House, 2018).

Another broad concern about economic globalization relates to how benefits are distributed. The basic arguments that critics make are that the benefits are not distributed anywhere near equally, with the wealthy benefiting but the poor gaining little or nothing—and sometimes even becoming worse off, at least relatively. The answer depends to a degree on which numbers are stressed. Since 1945, world prosperity has grown overall. The economically developed countries (EDCs) led by the United States have done exceptionally well, and conditions in the less developed countries (LDCs) have improved overall. Many of them have made great strides, and while not truly prosperous, they are not generally poor, either. Yet more than 600 million people worldwide are living in extreme poverty, defined as below $1.90 per person per day. While we are reducing poverty at considerable speeds in many Asian counties, poverty is actually rising in 30 countries, many of which are on the African continent. According to the Brookings Institute, at current rates the world will not end extreme poverty by 2030 as set out by Sustainable Development Goal 1.[17]

Similar to dependency theory, some contend that poverty persists and the wealth gap has grown because globalization is a tool used by the EDCs to exploit the LDCs by pressuring them to open their economies to penetration and domination by EDCs (Turner & Kühn, 2017). A related contention is that even within the EDCs, the wealthy are using globalization to increase their wealth by using the financial power of the multinational corporations (MNCs) they control to escape regulations protecting the environment, workers, and consumers, either by moving operations to a permissive country or by pressuring governments to ease or end regulations (Strange, 2015). Those who see globalization as a process that is making the rich richer by exploiting both poor countries and the poor within wealthy countries advocate radical change in global economic trends and policy (Shaikh, 2005). A less dire interpretation of the causes of the expanding wealth gap and other unsatisfactory trends and conditions is that many LDCs do not have an adequate economic base to compete openly in the global market. From this perspective, the solution is reform of the globalization process by giving more economic assistance to LDCs, regulating international working conditions, creating global environmental codes, and instituting a wide variety of other reforms that will create a more equitable globalization process both internationally and within countries (Rodrik, 2011).

CONCERNS ABOUT CULTURAL GLOBALIZATION. Those who object to cultural globalization condemn it for undermining the world's rich tapestry of cultural diversity and producing a monoculture that scholar Benjamin Barber has described as the "eternal yawn of McWorld" (1996:vi). For Barber, globalization imposes a culture that can threaten traditional values or sacred practices, pushing what he calls "jihad"-tribal forces to resist such homogenizing processes. The alternative perspective is, "We should not fear that globalism will lead to homogenization. Instead, it will expose us to the differences that surround us" (Nye, 2002:1).

Still, some countries try to restrict cultural imports because governments want to whip up nationalist feeling or are responding to the demands of nationalist groups. Consider the example of France. At least 90% of the French favor popular culture imports and believe their children should learn English. Yet the government of France has strongly resisted the encroachment of foreign culture. Former President Jacques Chirac warned that the spread of English poses a "major risk for humanity."[18] The government requires the exclusive use of French in teaching, business, and government, and it pressures the entertainment industry to feature French-language movies and music.

This discussion of globalization demonstrates that we are certainly at a critical point in our consideration of what global connections mean for local realities, and vice versa. We are also at a critical point in terms of thinking about how nonstate actors choose to embrace, resist, or otherwise engage with globalizing forces. It is to that consideration that we turn next.

Transnationalism: Actors and Movements

transnationalism Social, political, economic, and cultural activities and processes that transcend and permeate the borders and authority of states.

Transnationalism refers to a range of cross-border political identities and the social, economic, and political links—and related activism—among people and private organizations that transcend the sovereign state. Many of these regional or global links promote or intensify a common sense of identity among people, and these ties can form the basis of political self-identification that in some cases rivals or even supplants nationalism. Religious identity or gender roles, for example, often transcend political borders and identities. As with nationalism, however, transnationalism has both positive and negative consequences, at times simultaneously. While it can promote cooperation among some groups, it can also drive further divisions among others.

Transnationalism springs from two sources, globalization and identification. Economic interdependence, mass communications, rapid travel, and other modern factors are fostering transnationalism by intertwining the lives of people around the world and promoting a much higher level of transnational contacts. This interconnectedness and contact between and among the "average citizen" across nations, societies, and cultures is a driving engine for, as well as an outcome of, what the Enlightenment philosopher Immanuel Kant (1724–1804) referred to as "cosmopolitanism"—that is, a global citizenship or collective "we-feeling" that he considered a lynchpin to peace.

Transnationalism has both action and identification elements. Regarding action, transnationalism is the process of people working together as individuals as well as collectively in private groups across borders with other individuals and groups to accomplish a common purpose. Regarding identification, transnationalism provides alternatives to nationalism as a source of political identity. This concept refers to how we see ourselves connected as individuals to ideologies (communism), religion (Islam), demographic characteristics (ethnicity or gender), region (Europe), or virtually any other perceived common bond.

As our discussion of transnationalism proceeds, you will see that it has the potential to significantly restructure the international system and its conduct. Some aspects of transnationalism tend to undermine nationalism and, by extension, the state. For example, some citizens of the EU identify as Europeans instead of simply as French, German, Dutch, or some other nationality. In other cases, transnational identification and organization help change attitudes and policies around the world related to a specific area of concern. This chapter will explore this dynamic further by taking a closer look at the global women's movement.

As will be discussed later, transnationalism is neither an inherent force for peace nor an inherent force for conflict. Some aspects of transnationalism promote greater global interdependence and harmony and are very much in accord with the vision of the liberal school of political thought discussed in Chapter 2. Yet globalization has also spurred illegal and/or violent transnational movements, particularly in terms of transnational crime and terrorism. Those who see transnationalism in this light tend to be realists, many of whom would strengthen the nation-state as a bulwark against transnational forces, as discussed in Chapter 3. These "two faces" of transnationalism structure our considerations.

Global Civil Society

For some, the term *transnational* is a bit too narrow, or even understated in that so much as a single-border crossing would constitute a "transnational" interaction. Some scholars and practitioners instead prefer the term **global civil society** to better capture the range of common identities that emerge from various localities across the world (Castells, 2008).

global civil society The realm of ideas, values, institutions, organizations, networks, and individuals located between the society, the state, and the market and operating outside and apart from the confines of national societies, polities, and economic structures.

PERSONAL NARRATIVE

Esther Ibanga: Women Without Walls

Although the global women's movement has many unsung heroines, those working to bridge religious divides in conflict-affected areas are some of the most critical and at-risk human rights defenders in the world. Esther Ibanga, born in Nigeria in 1982, is known for her extensive work to foster cultural understanding and reconciliation between conflicting religious and tribal groups throughout Nigeria. Her work began in 2010 at the age of 18, when she protested the Jos massacres, in which more than 500 innocent civilians, mostly women and children, were brutally murdered with impunity.[19] Jos lies at Nigeria's flashpoint "middle belt," where the largely Islamic north meets the Christian south. Nigeria is deeply divided along ethnic and religious lines, and complex political, economic, and social grievances have fueled sectarian violence for decades. Most recently, Nigeria's eight-year conflict with Boko Haram has resulted in the deaths of over 20,000 civilians and a large-scale humanitarian crisis.

From this young experience, Esther joined Muslim woman leader Khadija Hawaja and founded the Women Without Walls Initiative. This is the first organization to have on its membership all the tribal women leaders, including Christian and Muslim women leaders, focused on developing "creative, nonviolent and all-inclusive approaches to conflict resolution and transformation in Nigeria through women."[20] Esther maintains, "We want to do away with the walls that divide and separate us, whether it's the walls of social class, ethnicity, or religion. We are mothers. We are life givers and we are solution bearers. And we think that we should bring solutions to the table, rather than dwell on the problem."[21]

Esther, a pastor and activist, spends her time building interfaith coalitions to create awareness, conducting research on where and how women have used unique approaches to contribute to peace-building, expanding training programs for women's empowerment, and ensuring the rights of women and girls by advocating for better laws, especially in conflict zones. Esther has been very outspoken in Nigeria, but also in Western media outlets like NPR and Western NGOs like Women in the World.

Esther's story helps us to understand the global women's movement, especially women's contribution to building peace, but her story also encourages us to think about how to overcome religious divisions in transnational ways. Esther talks about growing up in Nigeria and just "being used to" the idea that Christians and Muslims were enemies. It was the way it had always been for her, and she did not question it until the massacres hit close to her home village, Jos. Now, she knows that religion is not the problem, and that these divisions are not nature. She sees religion as a tool used by politicians trying to hold on to power. She is now using religion as a tool to mobilize women and to give them a voice. She recognizes that building bridges across religious divides takes time and trust and compromise, as it did with her Muslim counterpart, Khadija Hawaja. She believes women have the solution . . . do you? Hear more from her here at https://www.pri.org/stories/2015-01-14/its-not-about-you-being-muslim-and-me-being-christian-says-one-nigerian-activist

Global civil society goes beyond transnational linkages to include an expression of consciousness with a global reach, even if some participants do not have access to the Internet or even a telephone (Anheier, Glasius, & Kaldor, 2001:17). According to the *Global Civil Society Yearbook*, "global civil society is the sphere of ideas, values, institutions, organizations, networks, and individuals located between the family, the state, and the market and operating beyond the confines of national societies, polities, and economies" (2001). Global civil society consists of value-driven actors aiming to influence the world. While some seek global citizenship, others may seek something closer to global domination.

Global civil society can have desirable as well as harmful ambitions. This section explores the nature and scope of global civil society in terms of its membership and the ways such people often organize themselves.

INGOs: DRIVING GLOBAL CIVIL SOCIETY.   One indication of the increased strength and presence of global civil society is the phenomenal growth in number and activities of transnational organizations called **international nongovernmental organizations (INGOs)**. These are organizations that operate across national boundaries, have membership composed of private individuals and groups, and do not answer directly to any government. While INGOs may be funded in whole or in part by government agencies, their members do not include state actors (Reimann, 2006). In many ways, INGOs are legally constituted not-for-profit organizations operating across borders. For some, INGOs serve as central nodes of GCS, and many use INGOs as a proxy for evaluating trends among societal actors (Anheier, Kaldor, & Glasius, 2012). INGOs can improve state accountability, draw attention to new issues, or create better equity in global governance (Keck & Sikkink, 1998; Scholte, 2002). Of course, they are value-driven and can be politically diverse, which challenges the ideas that these global civil society actors are a wellspring of "good" intentions and progressive potential (Bob, 2012).

While there are an estimated 10 million INGOs worldwide, just over 5,000 enjoy active consultative status with the UN.[22] This is a massive increase from just 928 such groups in 1992.[23] These groups have a highly diverse range of interests that include peace, human rights, disarmament, the environment, and virtually every other public concern. A growing body of research in IR conclusively demonstrates that INGOs can be influential and, under certain conditions, can even shape policy and social practices around the globe (Lang, 2013; Stroup & Wong, 2016, 2017).

The increasing number of INGOs and their diverse range of interests and activities reflect globalizing forces in several ways. First, as noted, there is growing awareness that many issues are either partly or wholly transnational or transboundary. Second, INGOs have flourished because advances in transportation and communications have made transnational contacts easy, rapid, and inexpensive. Third, the growth of INGOs reflects disenchantment with existing political organizations based in or dominated by states in an age of globalization and transnational problems. As a result, people are seeking new ways to work with one another beyond traditional government-to-government diplomacy.

In essence, INGOs are organized interest groups that operate singly or in combination to promote their causes. Just like more domestically oriented interest groups, INGOs promote their goals by such techniques as attempting to raise public awareness and support for their causes and by providing information, argumentation, and electoral backing to policy-makers in national governments and international organizations (IGOs), in which the members are states.

INGOs often work with government agencies to accomplish goals, and sometimes even seek their help to obtain funds and other types of support. Speaking before the US Conference of Catholic Bishops in 2006, the head of

international nongovernmental organizations Organizations with an international membership, scope, and presence whose members are nonstate actors of various types drawn from the private and nonprofit sector.

Simulation: Stopping an Epidemic

INGOs such as Greenpeace International have long been a major presence at international environmental conferences and summits. Here, Greenpeace supporters make their stance on renewable energy known at the Conference of the Parties (COP-21) climate conference in Paris in December 2015.

the US Agency for International Development stressed that "the US government and NGO [nongovernmental organization] community together must use their comparative advantages . . . in combating poverty."[24] INGOs also play a role in the international policy-making processes of the UN and other IGOs, which have long sought out relationships with them; these ties have expanded greatly over time. Some scholars have found the relationship between IGOs and NGOs to be symbiotic (Reimann, 2006). For example, INGOs are active through their participation in multinational conferences convened by the UN and other IGOs to address global problems. Since the early 1990s, all such conferences have two components. One is the official conference, which includes delegates from governments. The other is the parallel NGO conference, which exists to bring nonstate actors together in an organized way to share information, mobilize, strategize, and ultimately, work to influence state actors.

One of the largest such dual conferences was the 2015 UN Sustainable Development Summit, where more than 150 world leaders adopted the new 2030 Agenda and the Sustainable Development Goals. But the creation of these goals was an unprecedented effort at inclusion and outreach to stakeholders beyond states, including global civil society and INGOs as well as the private sector.[25] "In total, 5 million people from across 88 countries in all the world's regions took part in the consultation, and shared their vision for the world in 2030."[26]

TANs: ORGANIZING GLOBAL CIVIL SOCIETY. The emergence and impact of global civil society efforts are often the result of **transnational advocacy networks** (TANs)—groups of NGOs and IGOs that seek to foster domestic and global policy change in given issue areas such as the environment or human rights through engaging in advocacy, information dissemination, and pressure campaigns of "naming and shaming," among other tactics (Betsill & Bulkeley, 2004; Park, 2005; Rodrigues, 2004). IR scholars Margaret Keck and Kathryn Sikkink (1998) were among the first to theorize and then empirically observe the nature and impact of TANs, beginning with their initial research on the human rights movement and networks organized around the issue of violence against women. While NGOs often make up the majority of a TAN, these networks also rely upon and involve media groups, foundations, churches, trade unions, consumer organizations, intellectuals, and even parts of governments. These various actors come together in voluntary ways to campaign on a

transnational advocacy networks A group of relevant actors bound together by shared values, a common discourse, and a dense exchange of information. TANs are organized around promoting principles and ideas with the goal of changing the behavior and policy of states and IGOs.

particular issue, and they multiply the channels of access for nonstate actors in a state-based political system.

TANs have been particularly influential in their ability to bring new ideas and **norms** into policy debates. According to Keck and Sikkink (1998), this activism emerges in related but distinct forms:

- Information politics, or the ability to quickly and credibly generate politically usable information.

- Symbolic politics, or the ability to call upon symbols, action, or stories that make sense of a situation for an audience that is frequently far away.

- Leverage politics, or the ability to call upon powerful actors to affect a situation where weaker members of a network are unlikely to have influence.

- Accountability politics, the effort to hold powerful actors to their previously stated policies or principles.

Take, for example, the "Madres de la Plaza de Mayo," a group of mothers that began to meet and protest every Thursday in the late 1970s in the large Plaza de Mayo in Buenos Aires, the site of Argentina's government. They walked in nonviolent demonstrations demanding the return of their children who had been disappeared during the "Dirty War" from 1976 to 1983. During this war, the military government abducted, tortured, and killed left-wing militants and anyone it claimed were political opponents of the ruling regime. Many of those disappeared were young people, college students like yourself, who expressed dissatisfaction with the regime. As mothers, these women served as a powerful moral symbol of the country, and in this way, women's political participation in Argentina has been "framed" to include them in public life as representatives of the family, defenders of morality, and defenders of the nation-as-family (Bonner 2014). They documented and disseminated the names of those missing, and they leveraged human rights organizations outside of their country as well as governments, like the United States, to put pressure on the military regime. The Madres served as the central element of a TAN that brought down the brutal ruling party and restored democracy in Argentina.

Regional and Cultural Influences

Transnationalism has in large part been determined by regional and cultural influences. Although Chapter 6

norms Ideas that come to be shared by the majority of the population in a given society, such that they become the basis for assessing and regulating social conduct and behavior.

The "Madres de la Plaza de Mayo" were a group of mothers that began to meet and protest weekly against human rights abuses and "disappearances" carried out by the Argentinian dictatorship in the 1970s and 1980s. They remain an active force and continue to fight for transitional justice and democratic transparency in Argentina today.

discusses regional organizations in greater detail, it is worth noting here that organizations like the EU are an important example of regional transnationalism. Since its genesis after World War II, the EU has evolved to the point where there is now advanced economic and social integration among European states. These changes are beginning to affect how Europeans define their political identity (Caporaso, 2005). Even if nationalism undoubtedly continues to dominate in places like Britain, we must not ignore trends in the rest of the region. In 2018, a record number of people in EU countries, approximately 68%, now personally "feel like they are a citizen of the EU" according to the Eurobarometer poll. This number has held strong and consistent since 2010, with 62% feeling this way when the poll first started asking this question of EU citizens. Further, 56% of people across the region are optimistic about the general future of the EU, which is up 6 points from the 2016 survey.[27]

Cultural transnationalism often coincides with and is driven by regionalism, but it has distinct characteristics that can be as divisive as they are unifying. While the familiarity with different cultures, and even the blending of cultures, that globalization brings holds the prospect of reducing conflict in the world, many still fear or are suspicious of difference. A darker view is that cultural transnationalism will lead to a clash of civilizations. The best-known proponent of this theory is Samuel Huntington (1993, 1996). Like many analysts, Huntington (1993:22–26) believes that nationalism will "weaken . . . as a source of identity." What will happen next is the key to his controversial thesis. He proposes that new cultural identifications will emerge to "fill this gap," and that countries will align themselves in "seven or eight cultural blocs," including "Western, Confucian, Japanese, Islamic, Hindu, Slavic-Orthodox, Latin American, and possibly African." These blocs, Huntington further predicts, will become "the fundamental source of conflict" as "different civilizations" engage in "prolonged and . . . violent conflicts."

Transnational Movements

Transnational movements of various types have emerged in the context of globalization and are challenging the state in new and critical ways. These forces from below vary in terms of strength, influence, and goals, and they increasingly operate in a complex political space that both utilizes and critiques globalization. Here, we explore various types of transnational movements and their impact on the international system.

TRANSNATIONAL RELIGIOUS MOVEMENTS.   Most of the world's major religions have a strong transnational element. This element is particularly apt to exist when a religion, which is a basis of spiritual identity, becomes a source of political identity among its members. When religion and political identities become intertwined, members of a religion may take a number of political actions (Fox & Sandler, 2004; Shah & Toft, 2006). One is to try to conform the laws and the foreign policy of their country to their religious values. Another is to provide political support for the causes of co-religionists in other countries. This sense of support is why, for example, Jews from around the world are likely to defend Israel and Muslims everywhere are apt to defend the Palestinians. Religion also helps explain why Osama bin Laden, a Saudi, was able to recruit Muslims from Egypt, Pakistan, Chechnya, and elsewhere, including the United States and Europe, to the ranks of al-Qaeda and to find a base for the organization in Afghanistan.

Although religion can be a force for peace, justice, and humanitarian concern (Johnston, 2003), it also has been and continues to be a factor in many bloody wars, conflicts, and other forms of political violence (Fox, 2004). For example, religious identity tied to politics is an element of the conflict between the mostly Jewish Israelis and the mostly Muslim Arabs, the ongoing tension dividing Pakistan and India, and the challenging efforts of nation-building in the Balkan region, especially between Orthodox Serbs and Muslim Albanians in Kosovo.

One long-standing transnational phenomenon that has gained strength in many areas of the world is religious **fundamentalism**, a form of identity rigidly committed to a return to the past and religious traditions uncorrupted by modern influences. As used here, a fundamentalist is someone who holds extreme conservative religious values that are unchangeable, external, not open to multiple interpretations, and above all secular values and rules. Most fundamentalists also have a primary political identity with their religion, not their nation-state—with membership in the religious community thereby superseding national citizenship. This perspective promotes political cooperation among co-religionists across state and territorial borders. It may also mean driving out people of another (or of no) faith or suppressing their freedoms within borders, but it does not necessarily involve violence. As Emerson and Hartman put it: "First, not all religiously based violence is done by fundamentalists . . . Second, not all fundamentalist groups are violent. In fact, most are not" (2006:136).

fundamentalism A particular, literalist interpretation of and approach to one's faith tradition that seeks a return to traditional religious attitudes and beliefs as well as the introduction of such attitudes and beliefs into the social, political, and legal realms.

Fundamentalism is especially prevalent within the three major Abrahamic religions: Judaism, Christianity, and Islam (Almond, Appleby & Sivan, 2003). However, as the sociologist Mark Juergensmeyer (2003) notes, fundamentalism is evident in all major world religions, and it has wide-ranging impact on formal political processes in places like India, as reflected in the rise of the Hindu nationalist Bharatiya Janata Party and the appeal of the concept of *Hindutva*, and Myanmar, where the government has long used religious appeals to the Buddhist majority to justify a campaign of persecution against the Muslim-minority Rohingya population (Brooten, Syed, & Akinro, 2015). What makes the

Buddhist monks in Myanmar (Burma) lead a rally denouncing the Rohingya Muslim population in the fall of 2018. The rise of Buddhist fundamentalism in Myanmar in recent years has been associated with increased attacks against the Rohingya Muslim population and allegations of a systematic campaign of ethnic cleaning by the Burmese government.

CHALLENGE YOUR ASSUMPTIONS

Islamic Fundamentalism and Legalized Discrimination in the United States

The terrorist attacks of September 11, 2001, orchestrated by the transnational terrorist organization al-Qaeda, sent shockwaves across the United States. One of the most lasting effects of the 9/11 attacks, especially in American society, has been the frequent associations of transnational terrorism with Islam, particularly Islamic fundamentalism. Current policies aimed at keeping Muslims out of the United States and in any position of influence reflect this misguided assumption. Most prominent among these is President Trump's Executive Order 13780 of March 6, 2017, entitled "Protecting the Nation from Foreign Terrorist Entry into the United States." Under the ban, nationals from eight countries, six of which are Muslim-majority, are subject to severe travel restrictions to the United States under any circumstances, including family or health-related matters.

While this "Muslim ban" has received significant criticism, it is not the first time that anti-Muslim legislation has been passed in the United States. In fact, researchers from UC Berkeley developed a United States of Islamophobia database—a comprehensive research tool providing detailed information on all anti-Sharia bills introduced in US state legislatures across the country from 2000 to 2016. They found 194 anti-Muslim bills were introduced in 39 states, with a total of 18 anti-Muslim bills enacted into law in what they see as an intentional movement increasing Islamophobia and racial anxiety in a hostile, post-9/11 political climate.

Islamic fundamentalism is little more than a transnational movement within a religious community to return to the more traditional elements of the faith. It emerged largely in response to Western interference in the Middle East during the 20th century and was led by key figures such as the Egyptian dissident Sayyid Qutb. Much of the appeal of Islamic fundamentalism in the region accelerated in the 1970s and 1980s as a direct result of the policies and practices of the United States and former colonial powers. Prescriptions for neoliberal economic reforms and Western-style electoral democracy tended to fall flat or prove counterproductive (Henry & Springborg, 2010). Compounding these failures, the United States and its Western allies used economic and military aid to prop up despotic regimes for self-serving strategic purposes. As such, large swaths of the population saw declines in their standard of living while also facing increased repression from their own regimes. The few attempts at significant reform were thwarted by the West, such as the CIA-backed coup overthrowing Iranian Prime Minister Mohammad Mossadegh in 1953.

To a population seeking meaning and justice, Islamic fundamentalism proved appealing. Many of its ideals are also espoused by Western ideology—development and industrialization, importance of education, freedom from domination, and the rule of law. Organizations like the Muslim Brotherhood in Egypt were established to promote these ideals, which were also the impetus for the overthrow of the corrupt, US-backed Shah Mohammad Reza Pahlavi in the Iranian Revolution in 1979 and explained the fleeting success of an Islamist political party (the Islamic Salvation Front) in the 1992 Algerian election. In all three cases and more, US-led resistance resulted in political repression and later, further radicalization. This raises the question: Have US and Western efforts to undermine populist transnational movements in the Middle East helped create violent extremist groups such as al-Qaeda, Islamic State, and Hamas? What is the hazard associated with equating such radical and violent groups with Islamic fundamentalism in general?

increase in fundamentalism important to global politics is that political conservatism, religious fundamentalism, and avid nationalism often become intertwined in volatile ways. For many, this is where religious fundamentalism transforms into violent extremism as many fundamentalists are committed to nonviolence, if not religious tolerance.

THE TRANSNATIONAL WOMEN'S MOVEMENT.   Women worldwide have had—and continue to have—fewer economic, political, and social opportunities than men. At the same time, there is now much more global recognition of gender equality as a priority concern. Still, pervasive inequalities exist in terms of women's health, physical security, labor rights, access to education, political participation, and environmental vulnerabilities. For some, the global women's movement has never been more important to ensure that women's human rights aren't rolled back.[28]

Women represent the most consistently marginalized group across the globe. Consider the following: Child marriage occurs in every region of the world, with one out of four girls marrying before age 18. Girls forced to marry are much more likely to drop out of school, to be illiterate, to lack economic opportunities, to suffer domestic abuse, and to die in childbirth.[29] Rape as a weapon of war is still rampant in places like Myanmar and the Central African Republic.[30] Sexual violence and harassment is alive and well in all labor industries, as the global #MeToo movement has most recently demonstrated. And the World Economic Forum's Global Gender Gap Report 2017 finds that the parity gap across health, education, politics, and the workplace is actually widening.[31]

Such economic, social, and political deprivations of women are not new. What has changed is the ability of women around the world to see their common (disadvantaged and marginalized) status through transnational communications and transportation. Also new is the increased determination of women and men who support the cause of gender equality to work together through transnational NGOs to address these issues. The global women's movement is the driving force in this political process.

Transformation toward emancipation is a notion that captures the goals of the transnational women's movement. Despite making up half the world's population, women are only a small minority of the world's heads of government, national cabinet ministers, and national legislators. International organizations are no less gendered. No woman has ever headed the UN, the WTO, or the World Bank, with the exception of Kristalina Georgieva who served as Interim President for 3 months in 2019 and its CEO since 2013 and women occupy only about 15% of the senior management positions in the leading IGOs. One exception is the 2011 appointment of former French Finance Minister Christine Lagarde as head of the IMF, becoming the first female managing director of the global lending organization. Recent research shows that women shattering the glass ceiling are not just a symbolic victory but have real implications for encouraging other women to pursue leadership roles in politics, as evident in the record numbers of women who sought elected office in 2018.[32]

As the *Thinking Theoretically* feature demonstrates, women's political advocacy can take a variety of forms. Although the end goal—gender equality—is consistent, the means to that end and the strategies that accompany this activist agenda can differ greatly. Some advocates for women want more females included in the existing power structures, while others want to remake structures and reconstruct how power is defined and used. The stakes are high for all concerned, as some scholars contend that women approach policy issues differently. For instance, countries with higher percentages of women in their national legislatures are less likely than more male-dominated countries to commit human rights abuses (Melander, 2005). Further, there is evidence that women place more emphasis on international social and economic programs than men, who are apt to stress international security programs as traditionally defined (Hicks, Hicks, & Maldonado, 2016).

The transnational women's movement extends beyond sexism's deleterious effect on women to include the effect of discrimination on the entire society. Feminists point out that keeping women illiterate impedes the entire economic and social development of a society. It is not a coincidence, for example, that the percentage of women in the paid workforce is lowest among those countries where the gap between male and female literacy is highest. Educating these illiterate women would increase the number of ways that they could contribute to their countries' economic and social growth.

Women have been and continue to be politically active in a large number of organizations that focus on these and other related issues. These organizations and their members interact transnationally at many levels, ranging from the Internet through global conferences. Over the years, these interactions have highlighted the notion that while women and women's experiences can and do vary, a substantial common theme focuses on discrimination as structurally embedded throughout the world. Collectively, women are now frequently gathering in such global forums as the UN Conference on Population and Development held in Cairo (1994), the Fourth World Conference on Women (WCW) in Beijing (1995), and the Beijing 15 Conference that convened in New York City (2000). In recent years, women have been particularly active in the UN Security Council advocating and succeeding in the passage of 9 resolutions on Women, Peace and Security (WPS)—the most recent in 2019 on sexual violence in conflict.

Such conferences and subsequent advocacy facilitate important transnational contacts among women. Parma Khastagir, a Supreme Court justice in India and a delegate to the 1995 WCW, stressed this contribution, noting that "what appealed to me most [about the WCW] was that people overcame their ethnic barriers and were able to discuss universal problems. They showed solidarity."[33] Even more important, women draw on their contacts and experiences through NGOs to promote and influence national and international policy (Jutta, 2003). A good example is Shirin Ebadi, an Iranian woman who has applied her energy and legal skills to bettering the rights of women and children in her country as well as globally. These efforts earned Ebadi the Nobel Peace Prize in 2003. Despite the Iranian government's disparagement of her award, Ebadi's work to empower Iranian women, one study concluded, has increased their "support for the international norms . . . as well as their desire to change archaic Islamic laws, [which] will nudge . . . [Iran] along the path of globalization" (Monshipouri, 2004:11).

One standard by which to judge the impact of the transnational feminist movement is the advancement of women in politics. As one scholar notes, "the growing participation and representation of women in politics is one of

Liberal and Critical Feminist Perspectives on Gender Inequality in the Workforce

The global women's movement is committed to gender equality and the emancipation of all marginalized people. The movement is made up of many different kinds of feminists and women's groups, all with varying ideologies and perspectives on what equality means and how best to achieve it. The theories and ideologies that define the different approaches to feminist activism determine what these groups value and, subsequently, what they advocate. These different theoretical approaches greatly impact the goals and strategies associated with that activism.

Liberal feminism is rooted in the liberal philosophy that emerged during the Enlightenment, utilizing an individualist approach to equality (Peterson & Runyan 2010:81). Liberal feminists believe that women possess the capacity and abilities necessary to promote and bring about equality by working within existing structures to correct prior wrongs and bring about gender equality (Tickner, 2001). Such a perspective promotes social change through a greater representation of women within existing institutions (Peoples & Vaughn-Williams, 2014).

Critical feminists consider the problem to be the privileging and promotion of a particular conception of masculinity at the expense of other attitudes, values, and dispositions. As such, the focus of advocacy and action is on changing value systems and reforming existing institutions within society that promote males and "maleness" at the expense of women and other marginalized populations (Tickner, 2001).

These theories not only differ in the way they view the world and how gender is constructed in the world, they also inform activism in significantly different ways. These varied constructs of gender and the power relations that follow from them impact the strategies feminists employ to influence global policies in order to make positive changes toward gender equality. One practical application of this theory-policy link would be the case of feminists' work toward equality of men and women in the workforce.

For their part, liberal feminists emphasize policy changes that would result in equal pay for men and women. The gender pay gap stands at 23% globally and 2% in the United States; that gap widens for women of color.[34] Liberal feminists focus on narrowing this gap, and activism for a liberal feminist might focus on promoting international legal standards requiring equal compensation for men and women in the same jobs performing the same tasks. Activists also might advocate having more women in positions of power in large corporations, particularly given that only 33 of the Fortune 500 companies are run by women.[35] In this case, liberal feminists might push for government-based incentive packages for companies that make a certain percentage of executive positions women's positions.

Conversely, critical feminists are less concerned with the wage gap and more concerned with the creation of a livable wage, as well as with the types of work available—or not available—to women. Critical feminists call attention to the fact that in many parts of the world, women are restricted to working insecure, low-paying, and unsafe jobs in the informal economy. Relatedly, women throughout the world are far more likely to undertake vital but unpaid (and, thus, economically devalued) jobs, such as caring for children and the elderly, collecting food, cooking, and maintaining the household. Critical feminists ask why this work in the "private" sphere is both unpaid and performed almost entirely by women, while work in the "public" sphere is monetarily compensated, socially valued, and—not coincidentally—disproportionately done by men.

This discussion of gender inequality in the labor market is just one example of the ways in which different schools of thought within feminism diagnose problems and, by extension, promote disparate solutions for them. Though feminist activism shares a similar concern with the elimination of gender inequality, it varies greatly on how best to work toward that goal (Sjoberg, 2017).

the most remarkable developments of the late-twentieth century" (Jaquette, 1997:23). The historic US presidential campaign run by Hillary Clinton in 2016 marked the first time a woman was the nominee for one of the two major US political parties. Several national legislative bodies have actually crossed the 50% threshold of women as elected officials; Rwanda was the first to do so, in 2008, with 56.3% women elected to seats in the lower house.[36]

It is also the case that progress is slow, however, and that women remain a political minority in both national and international governance. The changes within national governments parallel the uphill climb of women to political power in international organizations. While the UN Charter pledges equal opportunity for men and women, the reality is a half-century after the Charter was adopted women remain seriously underrepresented among the UN's professional staff positions, its top leadership posts, and the ambassadors who head their countries' delegation. In January 2018, the UN did hit a milestone: Of the 44 most senior positions in the UN system, excluding the Secretary-General himself, about half are now held by women.[37] But the UN has a long way to go. All nine Secretary-Generals have been men. Women only comprise 25% of leadership positions in peacekeeping missions. And similar to other public organizations, as women advanced through middle management to senior management roles, their numbers have thinned out.

Yet it is also the case that the progress of women almost everywhere has been facilitated by and, in turn, has contributed to the transnational feminist movement. Women have begun to think of themselves politically not simply as American, Laotian, or Zimbabwean women, but as women with a transnational identity and ties. This is a development that is both transforming national politics and weakening the hold of nationalism.

transnational crime The accelerated and illicit movement of drugs, counterfeit goods, smuggled weapons and small arms, laundered money, trafficked humans and organs, and piracy from the high seas to cyberspace.

TRANSNATIONAL CRIME.   **Transnational crime** involves the accelerated and illicit movement of drugs, counterfeit goods, smuggled weapons and small arms, laundered money, trafficked humans and organs, and piracy from the high seas to cyberspace. Just as cheaper and faster transportation and communications have encouraged the legal exchange of goods and services, so too have they assisted in numerous illegal and exploitative exchanges (Glenny, 2008). The trading routes for both are virtually the same, highlighting the dark side of globalization and transnationalism in many ways. Moreover, these illegal networks tend to overlap, as seen in Map 5.1.

In short, globalization has facilitated the growth of various forces from below, many of which present a significant challenge to the state. Rigid state bureaucracies combined with corrupt government officials have made it very difficult for the international community to respond to and "combat" the fluidity and flexibility of organized crime. In fact, many states, from Russia to China to Nigeria, actually benefit from and covertly support the existence of these illegal networks—stealing and laundering public monies in a phenomenon known as "transnational kleptocracy" (Bullough, 2018). These relationships are largely profit-driven and, through the skillful manipulation of transnational financial

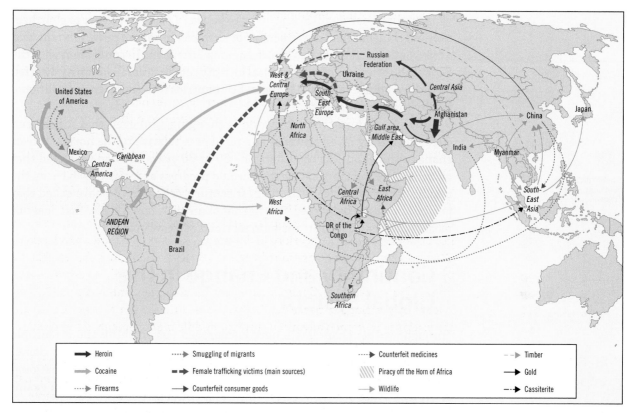

Map 5.1   This map traces the source of each illicit product through transit points and to its ultimate destination, where it is consumed or exploited. The data on which the report is based are taken from police arrests, seizures, court records, media reports, NGO reports, and experts on the ground in many different countries who have first-hand exposure to these illicit product markets.

networks and offshore banking, are often conducted in secret, allowing many transgressors to go unpunished. These criminal financial flows are quite massive and diversified, and many times translate into additional power and leverage for the state officials engaged in them, such as Russian President Vladimir Putin (Lanskoy & Myles-Primakoff, 2018). However, any effective policy response demands cooperation between national police forces at a transnational level. Considering issues of extraterritorial jurisdiction, among others, such cooperation is hard to come by.

The Future of Transnationalism

It is impossible to predict how far transnationalism will progress. It is not inconceivable that a century from now, humans will share a common culture and perhaps even a common government. That is, however, far from certain. There are those who doubt that today's trend toward transculturalism will continue into the future. Some analysts believe, for example, that English will cease to be the common language of the Internet as more and more non-English-speaking people gain access.

Moreover, nationalism is proving to be a very resilient barrier to globalization and transnational movements. For example, to some degree, it is true that a transnational identity has evolved among Europeans in connection with the EU. Yet those with that new political identity remain a small minority dwarfed by the percentage of people living in EU countries who retain their traditional loyalty to the nation-state.

Thus, we can say that the world is changing, and even that it has been changing during recent decades at a rapid pace relative to the normal rate of change throughout history. If anyone 50 or 60 years ago had predicted that globalization and transnationalism would progress as far as they have by the middle of the first decade of the 21st century, critics would have called that person hopelessly befuddled. So what has occurred is remarkable. That does not mean, however, that the transnational trend will continue.

Sweden's Bildt: Isolationism a Rising Concern

Continuity and Change in the Global System

Throughout this chapter, we have encouraged you to think about multiple actors in various spaces working to influence the way the world works. Sometimes those forces for change come from global systems and international structures imposing certain ideologies and discourses from above. For example, the logic of capitalism guiding international investment and development loans from the World Bank and the IMF demonstrates that Barber's globalizing notion of "McWorld" is alive and well, as discussed in Chapter 10. And when we look at religious fundamentalist movements, we see local forces coming together in transnational ways in search of change, for better or for worse. This sort of fragmentation and backlash from below give credence to Barber's notion of "Jihad."

The case of the global women's movement, however, raises some interesting questions for Barber's theory. While the women's movement has certainly emerged from local contexts and grassroots activism, it is not driven by hatred and does not seek to fight difference, but rather to engage with and promote difference. Women within the movement have come to embrace women's different experiences and the different forms of feminist activism and intersectional activism that have emerged. The movement has recognized that gender is just one social cleavage that marginalizes certain sects of society—as does race, class, and age. The transnational women's movement has also engaged with the globalizing forces from above in a way that respects culture difference and encourages a diversity of perspectives in global institutions. In short, the global women's movement challenges Barber's binary construction and encourages us to think about the way forces from below interact, reshape, and redefine forces from above, and vice versa. In doing so, it reminds us that globalization is an ongoing process with both contentious and constructive dimensions.

Chapter Summary

- Globalization has many and varied causes and manifestations. It is a multidimensional, complex set of processes that reflects the increasing integration of economies, polities, communication, and cultures.

- The rapid growth of technology has been a central driver in globalization and has made the movement of people, ideas, goods, and services faster, deeper, and cheaper than ever before—with profound impacts on economic and cultural systems.

- Global civil society is a useful way to understand the global and local dimensions and impact of transnational political processes and activities as well as the range of actors involved in them.

- Transnationalism emerges from both the material and the immaterial exchanges that occur with globalization and reflects the cross-border political and social identities that transcend the nation-state. These connections often shape, and are shaped by, regional and cultural influences.

Critical Thinking Questions

1. How do globalizing forces intersect with your everyday life? How do you view these engagements—positively, negatively, or some other way?

2. Are NGOs or INGOs a force for good? How might these well-intentioned organizations have unintended consequences?

3. What are the differences and similarities between fundamentalism and violent extremism? How do you see both of these forces affecting the practice of different religions—Christianity, Islam, and Judaism?

4. How can feminists be united in their commitment to gender equality but divided in how best to achieve such aims? Give an example to support your answer.

Key Terms

complex interdependence	global civil society	international nongovernmental organizations	transnational advocacy networks
dependency theory	globalization		transnational crime
fundamentalism	gross domestic product	norms	transnationalism

6

International Organization: The Evolving Quest for Global Governance

From the United Nations (UN) to the European Union (EU), the World Trade Organization (WTO) to the North American Free Trade Agreement (NAFTA), or the World Bank to the Economic Community of West African States, international organizations (IOs), more specifically intergovernmental organizations (IGOs), are important actors in global politics today. Although there is considerable diversity among IGOs, these organizations are distinct in that their membership is state-based. National governments, rather than private groups or individuals, constitute an IGO. In this way, IGOs often operate as alternatives to the traditional authority of sovereign states. These alternatives can work to supersede state sovereignty, reinforce state sovereignty, or sometimes manage both simultaneously. In this way, the relationship between IGOs, states, and even nonstate actors is complex and constantly shifting. Although the growth of formal IGOs has slowed in recent years, their reach in terms of geography, issues, and involved actors continues to play an important role in global politics.

Yu Peijie is 26-years old and the leader of the all-female peacekeeping unit deployed as part of the Chinese infantry batallion in South Sudan. Here local children are presenting a toy rifle to the young peacekeeper at a UN refugee camp. This photo was taken on April 30, 2018, marking the 70th anniversary of the UN peacekeeping operations and 28 years since China began participating in these multilateral military interventions.

This chapter chronicles both the nature and the scope of global and regional intergovernmental organizations, including why states choose to organize themselves collectively, how these organizations operate, and what influence these global governing bodies can have on international politics, national behavior, and individual lives. In particular, the chapter explores the UN in depth to illustrate the structures, policies, and controversies surrounding the world's leading intergovernmental organizations.

Increasingly, both global and regional IGOs must navigate political spaces and interactions with other organizational forms, including private-sector actors, transnational networks, and local or subnational institutions. This complex web of organizations and political actors is what contributes to global governance, the multiple structures and processes that regulate the behavior of state and nonstate actors on a wide range of global norms—from the laws of the sea to the protection of civilians in armed conflict.

Nowhere is this complex power dynamic more evident than in the case of international peacekeeping operations, one significant role that some IGOs play in global politics. Peacekeeping missions have been a defining feature of numerous IGOs, especially the UN, since the end of the Cold War. These missions continue to evolve and expand to address different types of conflict and take on different responsibilities. Further, peacekeeping is no longer under the sole purview of the UN. Numerous other organizations, like the African Union (AU) and North Atlantic Treaty Organization (NATO), now deploy peacekeepers in military and humanitarian missions. Sometimes organizations partner on missions, as is the case in Darfur, and sometimes work involves considerable overlap, as was the case in Kosovo.

Still, peacekeepers come from national armies representing their sovereign states. The UN has no standing army or peacekeeping unit ready for deployment. In most IGOs, peacekeepers are vetted not by the organization, but rather by their unique national military and government standards. In this way, peacekeeping represents the simultaneous gains and challenges that IGOs face in coordinating collective action while also preserving and respecting the sovereign rights of states—both those that are contributing troops and police units to peace missions as well as those living and fighting in the target states. Thus, throughout this chapter, we shall return to the case of peacekeeping to illustrate some key trends, achievements, and challenges of IGOs in the 21st century.

Learning Objectives

Discuss the various theoretical perspectives explaining why intergovernmental organizations form and how they function in the international system.

Identify the UN as a global IGO, and describe the key debates related to its founding principles, structure, leadership, and operations/activities.

Evaluate the relative success of intergovernmental organizations as systems of global and regional governance in constantly changing political environments.

Overview of IGOs

There is a great deal of variance among **intergovernmental organizations** (IGOs), which are organizations where membership is comprised of states. Some of them, such as the UN, have many members. As of 2019, UN membership reached 193 with the addition of South Sudan, up from the original 51 who created the organization in 1945. Other IGOs, like Africa's Economic Community of the Great Lakes Countries or NAFTA, each with only three members, are small. IGOs also differ in terms of global and regional membership as well as in function and scope. Multipurpose IGOs, such as the UN, the EU, and the Organization of American States (OAS), engage in a wide range of activities and issues. Other IGOs are more specialized; for example, the Organization of the Petroleum Exporting Countries (OPEC) focuses on coordinating and unifying petroleum policies of member-states.

> **intergovernmental organizations (IGOs)** Organizations that are global or regional in membership and scope and whose members are states.

Despite these various categorizations, IGOs are all physical entities with organizational structures that include office buildings and staff. Further, these bodies are all dependent upon member-state support for their existence and success, or lack thereof. This dynamic relationship between IGOs and states is a complex and often contentious one. Consider, for example, contributions to the UN Department of Peacekeeping Operations (DPKO). Developed states, like the United States, largely contribute financial and technical assistance to missions, leaving the contribution of actual troops to

Here is where the UN General Assembly meets at its headquarters in New York City. All 193 members of the United Nations are members of this deliberative body, with the addition of Holy See and Palestine as observer states. Each member state gets one vote regardless of population size or economic power on the world stage.

developing countries. When states don't pay their dues, the DPKO often lacks the funds and supplies to carry out UN Security Council mandates.

Military intervention, often the focus of peacekeeping, comes in different forms, including troops, treasure (financial support), and talent (Brysk, 2009). After conflicts in Yugoslavia and Somalia, Americans and Europeans found peacekeeping too risky in terms of putting actual troops on the ground. Still, states choose to intervene in conflicts all over the world and even do so collaboratively, begging the question: Why have states chosen to organize themselves collectively in the first place?

Why States Organize as Collectives

The existence of IGOs is not a modern phenomenon. Examples date far back in history. What was arguably the first rudimentary IGO was established in 478 BCE, when the Greek city-states established the Delian League to create a unified response to the threat from Persia. Although mostly an alliance, the League had two IGO precedent-setting characteristics. First, it was permanent, and second, it had an assembly of representatives appointed by the city-states to decide policy. Although Athens dominated, the assembly was a precursor of such current structures as the **UN General Assembly**, which serves as the general debate arena of the UN system.

Similarly, the intellectual roots of IGO formation include early attempts to justify IGOs as a means of promoting peace. Examples include the proposal of French official Pierre Dubois for the creation of a "league of universal peace" to settle disputes among members (1306);[1] French writer Émeric Crucé's call for creating permanent courts of arbitration to settle international disputes (1623); and German philosopher Immanuel Kant's advocacy for founding a "league of peace . . . to make an end of all wars forever" (Second Definitive Article, 1795).

Similar concepts have also prompted calls for regional organizations. In a glimmer of what would eventually become the **European Union** (EU), in 1713 the Abbé de Saint Pierre proposed establishing a league of European countries to ensure not only peace but also prosperity through economic integration (Bohas, 2003). Expanding on such ideas in 1943, French diplomat Jean Monnet, who in the 1950s was a driving force for European integration, declared, "There will be no peace in Europe if the states rebuild themselves [after World War II] on the basis of national sovereignty, with its implications of prestige politics and economic protection."[2] Furthermore, Monnet argued, "The countries of Europe are not strong enough individually to be able to guarantee prosperity and social development for their peoples. The states of Europe must . . . form a federation or a European entity that would make them into a common economic unit."[3]

Such appeals for regional unity have not been confined to Europe. To cite just one example, Simón Bolívar, the liberator of much of South America from Spanish colonialism, envisioned a South and Central American federation and initiated the first hemispheric conference, the Congress of Panama (1826), to further that goal.

Whether their proposals were global or regional, the common bond that unites these visionaries is their belief that IGOs could be a force for peace and other positive goals. Thus, for many intellectuals, the formation of IGOs—and

UN General Assembly The main representative body of the United Nations, composed of all 192 member-states and in which each state has one vote.

European Union The European regional organization established in 1993 when the Maastricht Treaty went into effect that encompasses the still legally existing European Communities, including the European Coal and Steel Community, the European Economic Community, and the European Atomic Energy Community.

the possibility for cooperation—is strongly embedded in liberalism, particularly neoliberal institutionalism. It also might be useful to review the section in Chapter 2 on liberalism and its variants to refresh your memory.

NEOLIBERAL INSTITUTIONALISM. **Neoliberal institutionalism**, a strand of liberal theory, posits that formal intergovernmental organizations as well as the less formal normative frameworks of international institutions, such as multilateralism, make cooperation easier to achieve because they provide a basis for state engagement. This regular interaction encourages habits of cooperation by facilitating transparency, monitoring state behavior, and even punishing states that defect. This is not the altruistic theoretical perspective that Chapters 1 and 2 discuss, but rather one driven by states operating according to their national interests. Neoliberal institutionalism recognizes the anarchic nature of the system and maintains that, in such a system, states will seek efficiency in managing collective action problems via institutions and organizations. These collectives reflect the general framework of international principles, rules, norms, and decision-making procedures around which states seeking to maximize interests will converge (Keohane, 1984; Krasner, 1983).

International institutions and organizations create a system of complex interdependence that both promotes and is promoted by cooperation and ties between countries. Specifically, when IGOs become the focal points for increased interaction and coordination, they make state expectations clearer and commitments more credible. In this way, IGOs become very useful for problem-solving, and at least two liberal-based international relations approaches speak directly to this understanding of IGOs.

Functionalism is rooted in the belief that global and regional governance arrangements arise from the fundamental needs of people and states. These basic common interests evolve from the bottom up, often dealing with narrow, pragmatic, and nonpolitical issues and binding "together those interests which are common, where they are common, and to the extent which they are common" (Mitrany, 1946:40). For example, functionalist theory helps us to understand why and how the Universal Postal Union developed in 1846 to resolve the issue of delivering mail internationally. Plato's description of "necessity" as "the mother of invention" in his *Republic* (ca. 380 BCE) might well serve as a motto for modern functionalists.

Functionalists support their view about how mankind is achieving global cooperation by pointing to the thousands of IGOs, multilateral treaties, nongovernmental organizations (NGOs), and other vehicles pragmatically put in place to deal with specific international concerns.

neoliberal institutionalism
Embraces and builds on the liberal school of thought that states are rational-unitary actors and that they can cooperate through international regimes and institutions. The focus is on long-term benefits instead of short-term goals.

functionalism A theoretical perspective that explains cooperation between governance structures by focusing on the necessity of people and states to interact on specific issue areas, such as communications, trade, travel, health, or environmental protection activity.

These stamps highlight the historical significance and various forms of the Universal Postal Union. Established in 1874, the Universal Postal Union (UPU), with its headquarters in the Swiss capital Berne, is the second oldest international organization worldwide. It operates as a specialized agency of the UN.

Functionalists further hold that by cooperating in specific, usually nonpolitical areas such as delivering mail, countries and people can learn to trust one another in regard to disarmament and other politically sensitive areas. Each instance of cooperation serves as a building block to achieve broader cooperation on increasingly more politically sensitive issues along the path to comprehensive cooperation or even global government.

Neofunctionalism stresses practical decision-making and incremental change in explaining the process of state integration and cooperation. Unlike functionalism, it shifts the focus to a top-down approach to solving world problems. It also rejects the idea that global cooperation and the accompanying IGOs necessarily need to evolve from cooperation through IGOs that deal with functional issues, like delivering mail, and progressively build up to cooperation and IGOs related to security and other critical political issues. Instead, neofunctionalists believe that if you create IGOs, especially regional ones, and give them the resources and the authority that they need to address central global problems, then in time countries and their people will learn to trust and govern through these IGOs—and even shift their primary sense of political identity and allegiance to them (Schmitter, 2005). Neofunctionalists thus focus on spill-over effects, where integration in one functional area tends to spill over into other areas. They challenge functionalists on what counts as technical and nonpolitical cooperation as well as political. Neofunctionalists are skeptical about the functionalist belief that nonpolitical cooperation can, by itself, eventually lead to full political cooperation and the elimination of international conflict and self-interested state action. Neofunctionalists also worry that the functionalists' evolutionary approach will not move quickly enough to head off many of the world's looming problems. Thus, they essentially focus on the top down to help spur growth from the bottom up.

Many neoliberal institutionalists focus on IGO formation around public goods, sometimes called collective goods. **Public goods** are those commodities that are "fully joint and nonexcludable"—that is, that (1) "consumption by one party does not reduce the amount available for consumption by another," and (2) "once a public good or bad is made available to one party, no other party can be barred from consuming it" (Boyer & Butler, 2006:75–76). To be sure, *pure* public goods do not exist in international politics; however, many of the global commons, such as the atmosphere and the ozone layer, constitute public goods to a significant extent. These goods are available to all groups, and consumption by one does not significantly impede the consumption by others. That said, the use of public goods involves policy choices and actions that become interdependent. States' decisions can have positive or negative—intentional or unintentional—consequences for other states.

For example, in the 20th-century manufacturers widely used chlorofluorocarbons (CFCs) as refrigerants and propellants in aerosol applications. In the 1980s, however, scientists directly linked this organic compound to the depletion of the ozone layer. The production and sale of CFCs had a dramatic and visual effect on a critical public good, prompting passage in 1989 of the **Montreal Protocol**, the international treaty that required phasing out these

neofunctionalism A theoretical perspective that explains cooperation between governance structures by focusing on the basic needs of people and states to interact on specific issue areas, such as communications, trade, travel, health, or environmental protection activity.

public goods Goods that are nonrivalrous and nonexcludable. Nonrivalrous means that consumption of the good by one individual does not reduce availability of the good for consumption by others; nonexcludable means that no one can be excluded effectively from using the good.

Montreal Protocol on Substances that Deplete the Ozone Layer A 1987 treaty designed to protect the ozone layer by phasing out the production of numerous substances that scientists have proved are responsible for ozone depletion.

dangerous substances. According to public good theorists, international organizations and the international laws that follow exist to govern such problems that we associate with public goods, like the ozone layer.

REALIST RESPONSES.   As Chapters 1 and 2 discuss, realism and its many variants have little broad use for intergovernmental organizations and international institutions. Realists remain skeptical about the power and influence that these collectives have, particularly for major power states. For realists, IGOs are marginal actors because they lack enforcement powers and do not have the capacity to engage as autonomous actors in the international political arena. Like liberals, realists also see a system of anarchy, where states act in their own self-interest in self-help sorts of ways; however, realists see IGOs as convenient tools for the most powerful to seek out such interests. States comply when the IGOs serve their interests. For example, it is in the self-interest of most states to have their shipping vessels freely and safely navigate international waters. When IGOs do not fulfill those narrow interests, states can override IGOs, as the United States did in 2003 when the Bush administration decided to invade Iraq without UN Security Council approval. However, even here the Bush administration felt the need, or maybe simply the desire, to attempt to obtain Security Council approval first. Unilateralism was not the first choice, even in this case.

Trends in IGO Formation

Although theories about the need for intergovernmental organizations—or zones of peace, as Immanuel Kant called them in the 18th century—have a long history, IGOs as we know them today are primarily a modern phenomenon. By the 1800s, a few IGOs began to come into existence to deal with specific transnational matters. The six-member Central Commission for the Navigation of the Rhine, established in 1815, is the oldest surviving IGO, and the International Telegraph Union (now the International Telecommunications Union), established in 1865, is the oldest surviving IGO with global membership. However, only six IGOs were established during the 1800s.

The IGO creation rate began to grow slowly during the first part of the 1900s, which saw the formation of the **Hague Convention**, the first IGO dedicated to curbing, or even preventing, warfare. Participant organizers, which included major powers like the United States, Russia, Germany, France, and Great Britain, named it for two conferences held at The Hague, the Netherlands, in 1899 and 1907. The goals were to limit weapons, establish procedures to arbitrate and mediate international disputes, and otherwise avoid or mitigate warfare. The second conference was more comprehensive, with 44 European, North American, and Latin American states participating. Organizationally, it included a limited general assembly and a judicial system. A third Hague Conference was supposed to meet in 1915, but it never took place because of the outbreak of World War I (1914–1918).

After the war, the Versailles Peace Conference (1919) sought to establish postwar order by, among other things, creating the **League of Nations**. It had

Hague Convention Name given to the peace conferences held in the Netherlands in 1899 and 1907 where the global community issued the first formal statements of the laws of war and war crimes.

League of Nations The first attempt to establish an intergovernmental organization with global reach in terms of membership and issue areas. It existed between the end of World War I and the beginning of World War II and was the immediate predecessor of the United Nations.

a more developed organizational structure than that of the Hague Convention. Although intended mainly as a peacekeeping organization, the League had some elements aimed at social and economic cooperation. Again, unfortunately, peace did not prevail, and the League died in the rubble of World War II.

The core idea behind the Hague system and the League of Nations did not perish, however. More than 50 countries met after the war and established the **United Nations** (UN) in October 1945. Like the League, the UN was founded "to save succeeding generations from the scourge of war . . . to unite our strength to maintain international peace and security . . . to employ international machinery for the promotion of the economic and social advancement of all peoples" (Preamble, UN Charter). Abiding by this mandate, the UN has increasingly become involved in a broad range of issues that encompasses almost all the world's concerns.

The years surrounding the formation of the UN also saw a rapid growth in the number of all types of IGOs. The pace was especially fast in the 1960s and 1970s, a time of rapid decolonization. The many new countries of Africa, Asia, and other regions, joined by already independent countries seeking to improve conditions and their leverage in the international system, created an array of new, most commonly regional IGOs. Since then, the rate at which new IGOs are emerging has declined, although it is still faster than at any time since before the 1960s. Almost all of the IGOs that disbanded or fell into disuse were regional and were duplicates of other existing or new IGOs. The overall number of IGOs peaked at 365 in 1984, after the growth spurt in the 1960s and 1970s, and then declined to 276 by 2016 (although the number varies every year).[4]

REASONS FOR GROWTH.   Both functionalist and neofunctionalist concepts help us to understand these patterns of growth and expansion. Whatever the immediate impetus for founding an IGO, their creation results because states realize that through IGOs they "are able to achieve goals that they cannot accomplish [alone]" (Abbot & Snidal, 1998:29). At least five causes explain this expansion:

1. *Increased international contact*. As discussed in Chapter 5, the revolutions in communications and transportation technologies have brought the states of the world into much closer contact. These interchanges need organizational structures in order to become routine and regulated. The International Telegraphic Union, founded over a century ago, has been joined in more modern times by the International Mobile Satellite Organization (1979) and many others.

2. *Increased interdependence*. The International Monetary Fund (IMF) and the World Bank are just two IGOs that address international economic issues beyond the control of individual countries. Regional trade and monetary organizations, cartels, and to a degree, multinational corporations are others. (The interdependent global economic system is discussed in detail in Chapter 9.)

United Nations A global intergovernmental organization with near universal membership of the world's sovereign states; established in 1945 after WWII.

3. *The expansion of transnational problems.* Some issues that affect many states require solutions that are increasingly beyond the resources of any single state to address. One such issue (and its associated IGO) is transnational crime (International Criminal Police Organization, more commonly known as Interpol). As Chapters 12 and 13 explore, global problems in health, food, human rights, and environmental degradation have also spurred collective responses from states through various IGOs.

4. *The failure of the current state-centered system to provide security.* This factor in IGO expansion is not only about the failure to prevent recurrent wars, including World Wars I and II, but also about its general failure to restrain the development and use of weapons capable of killing more people more quickly. The first Hague Convention worried about such horrors as explosive projectiles dropped from balloons. World War I introduced the use of machine guns, tanks, warplanes, and poison gas, leaving almost 9 million dead. World War II left 58 million soldiers and civilians dead from military action and another 10 million or more civilians dead from the Holocaust and other atrocities. Then, in 1945 with the dawn of the atomic age, the prospect of a death toll reaching into the millions within minutes rather than years now loomed. The twin realities of continued warfare and ever more lethal weapons have convinced many people that peace is not safe in the hands of nation-states. The UN is the latest attempt to organize globally for the preservation of peace, but many regional organizations also are involved in mediation and other forms of crisis intervention.

5. *The efforts of small states to gain strength through joint action.* The concentration of military and economic power in a handful of countries has led less powerful actors to cooperate in an attempt to influence events. For example, less developed countries (LDCs) have formed such IGOs as the 118-member-country Nonaligned Movement and the Group of 77, now with 132 member-countries, to promote economic development.

Operation Lionfish III
Disrupting transnational drug networks   INTERPOL

5,000 law enforcement officers

357 suspects arrested

13 COUNTRIES
Argentina
Bolivia
Brazil
Cape-Verde
Chile
Colombia
Dominican Republic
Ecuador
Ghana
Guinea-Bissau
Nigeria
Panama
Peru

55 TONNES drugs seized

CANNABIS
COCAINE
HEROIN
OTHERS
PRECURSOR CHEMICALS

20 clandestine drug laboratories

This Interpol program targets drug trafficking along air, land, and maritime routes, resulting in significant seizures and new intelligence. Operation Lionfish III involved 13 countries across Latin America and West Africa, and the seizure of drugs including cocaine, cannabis, and heroin. The operation also highlighted how precursor chemicals are being diverted from legitimate to illicit purposes, with 20 clandestine laboratories dismantled and three tonnes of precursor chemicals seized.

These reasons, combined with some successful cooperative experiences between states and IGOs, have led to IGOs' consistent presence and credibility as significant actors on the world stage. Literally thousands of international organizations exist today, many global in scope and power and some much less so. However, all these actors play an important role in global politics, some

Table 6.1 Sample Types and Numbers of International Organizations

The data in this table illustrate some of the ways we can categorize international organizations and provide a better sense of the roles they play. Literally thousands of international organizations exist today, and these categories are only some of the various types. Many are global in scope and power, and some much less so. However, all of these actors play an important role in global politics, some primarily as independent actors and others through their relationships with states.

TYPE	INTERGOVERNMENTAL (IGO)	NONGOVERNMENTAL (NGO)
Conventional International Bodies		
1. Federations of IOs	1	38
2. Universal membership organizations (e.g., UN)	37	548
3. Intercontinental membership organizations (e.g., NATO)	37	1,805
4. Regionally oriented membership organizations (e.g., EU)	210	7,012
Some Special Types		
1. Recently created bodies (not yet categorized)	55	1,168
2. Religious orders and secular institutes		906
3. Multilateral treaties; intergovernmental agreements (organizations that monitor and administer agreements)	2,454	
4. Dissolved or apparently inactive bodies	879	5,199

Source: Union of International Associations (2018: xxxii).

primarily as independent actors and others through their relationships with states. As testimony to the diversity and pervasiveness of organizations in global politics, Table 6.1 illustrates one set of criteria that help to categorize international organizations and provide a better sense of the roles they play.

How IGOs Function

Given the breadth and depth of IGOs, we should consider what they do as well as what we want them to do (Cogan, Hurd, & Johnstone, 2016). It is possible to arrange the current and potential future roles of IGOs on a scale that measures how close each is along the continuum ranging from the traditional approach that keeps state sovereignty central to approaches that supplement—and even attempt to supplant—the primacy of the sovereign state. The four possible roles, starting at the traditional end of the scale and moving toward the alternative end, are arena for interaction, facilitator of cooperation, independent international actor, and supranational organization.

ARENA FOR INTERACTION. The most common role of IGOs is to provide an interactive arena in which member-states pursue their individual national interests. IGO members rarely openly state this intention but it is obvious in the struggles within the UN and other IGOs, where individual countries and blocs of countries vigorously wage political struggles (Foot, MacFarlane, & Mastanudo, 2003; Thompson, 2006). In this way, states use IGOs as instruments of foreign policy. Small states use IGOs as a venue to gather information about other states and as a place to make their foreign policy goals known. IGOs have become valuable informational forums where data are gathered, analyzed, and disseminated among state and even nonstate actors. Further, IGOs provide small states with networking opportunities those states might not otherwise have.

Such interaction does not always necessitate a cooperative outcome, however (Voeten, 2004). For example, during the maneuvering in the UN Security Council in 2003 over Iraq, France and Russia (both of which have a veto in the Security Council), along with Germany, were at the forefront of resisting US efforts to win UN support for military action. In addition to their views on Iraq, these countries used the crisis to demonstrate their diplomatic independence and to try to rein in what they saw as an arrogant, overly aggressive United States. Forums can be a place of exchanging views, both those that are supportive and those that are contentious.

The use of IGOs as an interactive arena does have advantages. A first advantage is that international integration can advance even when IGOs are the arena for self-interested national interaction. The reasoning is that even when **realpolitik** is the starting point, the process that occurs in an IGO fosters a certain level of socialization that can bring states together in the adoption of more progressive policies (Greenhill, 2010).

realpolitik A realist interpretation of "power politics" where material and practical factors matter and ethical or moral values do not.

A second advantage is that it is sometimes politically easier to take action if an IGO has authorized it. For example, there was considerable consensus behind international efforts to bring an end to Colonel Muammar Gaddafi's 42-year rule of Libya. In March 2011, the UN Security Council passed a resolution authorizing a no-fly zone over Libya and NATO-led air strikes to protect civilians until rebels took over the capital city and ended the brutal dictatorship in August of that year.

In a third advantage, debate and diplomatic maneuvering may even provide a forum for diplomatic struggle, which, as an alternative to the battlefield, helps promote the resolution of disputes without violence. As Winston Churchill put it once, "To jaw-jaw is better than to war-war."[5]

FACILITATOR OF COOPERATION.   Another IGO role is to promote and facilitate cooperation among states and other international actors. Secretary-General Kofi Annan observed correctly that the UN's "member-states face a wide range of new and unprecedented threats and challenges. Many of these transcend borders and are beyond the power of any single nation to address on its own."[6] Therefore, countries have found it increasingly necessary to cooperate to address physical security, the environment, the economy, and a range of other concerns. The Council of the Baltic Sea States, the International Civil Aviation Organization, and a host of other IGOs all came about

Kofi Annan, the first UN Secretary-General from sub-Saharan Africa, was a charismatic diplomat, a masterful mediator, and often a force for good in the world. Here, Annan is overseeing President Mwai Kibaki and Prime Minister Raila Odinga (opposing Kenyan leaders) signing the National Accord in the presence of African Union Chairman President Jakaya Kikwete at the entrance of Harambee House on February 28, 2008.

to address specific needs and, through their operations and sharing of information, to promote further cooperation.

regime theory Regime theory argues that international institutions or regimes affect the behavior of states or other international actors on a specific issue, such as nuclear weapons or human rights, by promoting and upholding norms and rules governing behavior.

international regime Sets of implicit or explicit principles, norms, rules, and decision-making procedures around which actors' expectations converge in a given area of international relations.

When cooperation develops in a number of related areas, then **regime theory** argues that the specific points of cooperation become connected with one another in more complex forms of interdependence called an **international regime**. This term does not refer to a single organization. Instead, *regime* is a collective noun that designates a complex of norms, rules, processes, and organizations that, in sum, have evolved to help govern the behavior of states and other international actors in an area of international concern. Central to international regimes is their association with a specific issue, such as nuclear weapons proliferation or food aid. In addition, although some critics would argue that international regimes fall short of formal institutions, they still help govern, or at least condition, the behavior of states.

One such area is the use and protection of international bodies of water and the corresponding regime that has evolved for oceans and seas (Heasley, 2003). Figure 6.1 depicts this regime's array of organizations, rules, and norms that promote international cooperation in a broad area of maritime regulation, including navigation, pollution, seabed mining, and fisheries. The 1994 UN Convention on the Law of the Sea proclaims that the oceans and seabed are a "common heritage of mankind," to be shared according to "a just and an equitable economic order."[7] To that end, the treaty provides increased international regulation of mining and other uses of the oceans' floors and empowers the International Seabed Authority to help advance the treaty's goals.

NGOs such as Greenpeace have also pressed to protect the world's seas. Dolphins are killed less frequently because many consumers now buy only those cans of tuna that display the dolphin-safe logo. In combination, multilateral law-making treaties, IGOs, NGOs, national efforts, and other programs that regulate the use of the seas are part of an expanding network that constitutes a developing regime that governs behavior and sets standards for states and other actors using the oceans and seas.

INDEPENDENT INTERNATIONAL ACTOR. Given that states form IGOs and grant them the authority to act, IGOs often function as agents of states. There are times, however, when IGOs, like other large bureaucracies, do much more than their member-states originally intended. Some even take on the role of independent international actors (Barnett & Finnemore, 2004; Haftel & Thompson, 2006), as we will discuss in detail later in this chapter

International laws and norms
Concept of international waters
Freedom of the seas
Maritime rules of the road
Fisheries conservation
Pollution prevention
Endangered species protection

International organizations
International Seabed Authority
International Whaling Commission
Commission for the Conservation of Antarctic Marine Living Resources
International Maritime Organization
International Court of Justice (deciding cases)
International Maritime Satellite Organization
Greenpeace

Treaties
Convention on the Law of the Sea
Convention on Fishing and Conservation
Convention on the Continental Shelf
Anti-Dumping Convention
Convention on the Preservation and Protection of Fur Seals
Convention for the Prevention of Pollution from Ships

Other regime contributors
Consumers demanding dolphin-safe tuna
Public outrage at the killing of whales, baby seals, and other marine life
National laws to prevent pollution
National courts enforcing established international law

Figure 6.1 The concept of an international regime represents the nexus of rules, actors, and other contributors that regulate a particular area of concern. This figure shows some of the elements of the expanding regime for oceans and seas. These entries are only a sample of all possibilities. (Source: Union of International Associations, 2018, https://uia.org/sites/uia.org/files/misc_pdfs/pubs/yb_2018_vol4_lookinside.pdf, p. xxxii.)

when we focus on the EU. This role is most evident for some of the strong, relatively permanent administrative staffs, known as the **IGO secretariats**, that have evolved in the 20th century. These international civil servants act to set the international agenda, persuade states to act, draft international legislation, facilitate diplomatic exchanges, and monitor state compliance. From inspectors determining whether uranium enrichment in Iran is a peaceful operation to health experts maintaining surveillance on a possible bird flu epidemic, international secretariats are important and often autonomous actors in global and regional governance (Mathiason, 2007).

IGO secretariat
The executive body that manages the organization.

These individuals often identify with the organization and try to increase its authority and role. As a result, some IGOs have a "strong measure of autonomy from their member-states" and are "especially likely to act on their own initiative if states are indifferent to a situation." Indeed, IGOs "may act, at least obliquely, against the perceived interests of member-states, even against the interests of important states" (Ferguson, 2005:332). Thus, an IGO may be a force unto itself, more than the sum of its (member-country) parts. Sometimes this independence is controversial, as we shall see in the discussions of the UN and EU that follow. In other cases, a degree of organizational independence is intended and established in the charters of various IGOs, such as in the International Criminal Court, particularly in the role of its chief prosecutor (Schiff, 2008).

SUPRANATIONAL ORGANIZATION.   Some analysts believe that the world is moving toward—and should continue to move toward—a more established form of international government (Falk & Strauss, 2011; Tabb, 2004). "The very complexity of the current international scene," one scholar writes, "makes a fair and effective system of world governance more necessary than ever" (Hoffmann, 2003:27). This model envisions a role for IGOs as **supranational organizations**, in which legal authority transfers from the sovereign members to the IGO to the point where the IGO can override decision-making at the national level.

supranational organization
An organization that is founded and operates, at least in part, on the idea that intergovernmental organizations can or should have authority higher than individual states and that those states should be subordinate to the supranational organization.

Some IGOs already possess a degree of limited supranationalism in specialized areas because many states in practice accept some IGO authority in the realm of "everyday global governance" (Slaughter, 2003). For example, countries now regularly give way when the World Trade Organization (WTO) rules that one of their laws or policies contravenes the WTO's underlying treaty, the General Agreement on Tariffs and Trade. According to the WTO, its international dispute settlement mechanism is one of the most active in the world with over 500 disputes brought to the WTO and over 350 rulings issued since 1995.[8] Although it resolved close to half of these before proceeding to the adversarial panel process, "with a few exceptions, the remaining disputes that did go to full-fledged panel proceedings were resolved by Members who brought themselves into compliance with the rulings and recommendations of the Dispute Settlement Body" (Agah, 2012:1).

The EU exercises even greater supranational authority on a regional level. It not only has most of the structure of a full-scale government, but also makes policy, has courts, receives taxes, holds international popular elections, and in many other, if still limited ways functions like a government of Europe. A major question for the future is whether and how far to extend the supranational authority of IGOs and how to structure such powerful new actors.

Ultimately, limited supranationalism might evolve into regional governments or a world government. The powers of any such global or regional government also range along a scale based on the degree of power sharing between the central government and the subordinate units, as Figure 6.2 depicts. Unitary government is at the end of the scale, where the central government has all or most of the power and the subordinate units have little or none. In such a system, countries would be nonsovereign subordinate units that serve only administrative purposes. A less centralized alternative is a federation, or federal government, in which the central authority and the member-units each have substantial authority. The United States and Canada are both federal structures, in which the 10 Canadian provinces have greater authority than the 50 US states. A confederation is the least centralized of the three main arrangements. In a confederal government, the central government has quite limited powers while the members retain all or most of their sovereign authority. In many respects, the UN system is confederal in nature. The least centralized model of all, though, and one that borders on not being a government at all, is a league, an arrangement in which the centralized government is mostly symbolic and has little, if any, functional authority.

The arguments for greater global government begin with the criticism of the current state-based system approach to security, which Chapter 7 details (Volgy & Bailin, 2002; Wendt, 2004). The World Federalist Movement (WFM), for one, argues, "Ours is a planet in crisis, suffering grave problems unable to be managed by nations acting separately in an ungoverned world." Given this perspective, the WFM calls for founding "world institutions . . . [with] actual and sufficient authority to make and enforce law in their given jurisdictions."[9] However, the WFM and most others who favor greater **global governance**

global governance The multiple structures and processes that regulate the behavior of state and nonstate actors on a wide range of global norms, from the laws of the sea to the protection of civilians in armed conflict.

do not advocate the abolition of state sovereignty and the creation of an all-powerful world government. More common are calls for a federal structure, with countries retaining sovereignty over their internal affairs.

Critics of greater global governance raise numerous objections (Coates, 2005):

1. They argue that there are practical barriers. The assumption here is that nationalism has too strong a hold and that neither political leaders nor their constituents would be willing to surrender substantial sovereignty to a universal body.

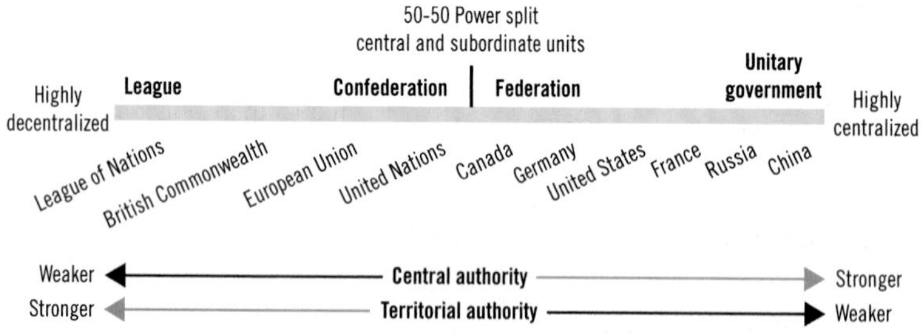

Figure 6.2   Whether at the national, regional, or global level, power is shared between the central government and territorial governments in a variety of ways. In countries, territorial units are commonly termed *states* or *provinces*. In a global or regional government, countries would be the territorial unit. This figure shows the scale of possible power-sharing relationships. At one end of the scale, a league, the central government has little more than symbolic authority, and most power remains with the territorial units. At the other end, a unitary government, the central government monopolizes power, and the territorial units perform only administrative functions. The most centralized international government organization today, the EU, is a confederation.

2. They pose political objections. Critics worry about the concentration of power that would be necessary to enforce international law and to address the world's monumental economic and social problems.

3. They doubt whether any such government, even given unprecedented power, could succeed in solving world problems any better than states can.

4. Some skeptics further argue that centralization would inevitably diminish desirable cultural diversity and political experimentation in the world.

5. Other critics worry about preserving democracy. With power concentrated in a central international government and little countervailing power left to countries, the seizure of the world government by authoritative forces might, in a stroke, roll back hundreds of years of democratic evolution.

The idea of regional government does respond to some of these concerns. Regions would still have to bring heterogeneous peoples together and overcome nationalism, but that would be an easier task than addressing even greater global heterogeneity. Moreover, regional governments would allow greater cultural diversity and political experimentation than a global government would. To this approach, skeptics reply that regional government is at best the lesser of two evils compared to global government. Opponents also contend that creating regional governments would simply shift the axis of conflict from among states to among regions.

Indeed, in his novel *1984*, George Orwell predicted in 1949 that the future would find world political control exercised by three regional governments (Oceania, Eurasia, and Eastasia) all perpetually at war with one another. Making matters worse, democracy was a memory. Oceania was ruled by the totalitarian iron hand of "Big Brother," and the other two mega-regions were presumably also subject to authoritarian discipline. It is not difficult to project the EU as the core of Eurasia, a US-centered Oceania, and an Eastasia built around China. So, although Orwell's vision did not come to pass by 1984, opponents of regional or global government might contend that he should have entitled the book *2084*.

Global IGOs: Focus on the UN

Of the growing range and importance of activities of IGOs at the global level, those of the UN are by far the most notable. As Mingst, Karns, and Lyon argue, "more than 70 years after its creation, the UN continues to be the only . . . IGO of global scope and nearly universal membership that has an agenda encompassing the broadest range of governance issues . . . serv[ing] as the central cite for multilateral diplomacy" (2016:2). Therefore, this section focuses on the UN both as a generalized study of the operation of IGOs and as a specific study of that key institution. Discussion includes issues related to UN membership, voting procedures, executive leadership, administration and finance, and—most important—core functions and activities.

Figure 6.3 provides an overview of the UN's structure, beginning with the six major bodies established by the **UN Charter**, the organization's principal

UN Charter Signed on June 26, 1945, the Charter serves as the foundational treaty of the United Nations. All members are bound by its articles. The Charter also states that obligations to the United Nations prevail over all other treaty obligations.

Figure 6.3 The UN System is a massive, complex bureaucracy that consists of the six core charter-based bodies and numerous subsidiary bodies, such as the separately administered funds and programmes, research and training institutes, specialized agencies, and affiliate organizations. For the fuller visual of the many organizations, agencies and other bodies part of the UN system, see https://www.ungm.org/Shared/KnowledgeCenter/Pages/VBS_UNSystem (Source: https://www.unsystem.org/organizationchart.)

General Assembly
All 193 UN members, one vote per member
The main policy-making and representative organ
Meets in regular sessions

Security Council
15 members
5 permanent, 10 serve 2-year terms
Veto power for permanent members
Responsible for maintenance of international peace and security
Establishes peacekeeping operations and international sanctions
Able to authorize military action under Chapter VII

International Court of Justice
15 judges, serving 9-year terms
Seated in The Hague
Settles legal disputes submitted by individual states according to noncompulsory jurisdiction
Gives advisory opinions on questions referred by other UN bodies

Secretariat
Headed by the Secretary-General, who can serve up to two 5-year terms
Carries out day-to-day operations of UN, ranging from dispute mediation to writing reports documenting and monitoring global problems

UNITED NATIONS

Trusteeship Council
Tasked to govern United Nations trust territories during decolonization
Task completed
Suspended operation in 1994

Economic and Social Council (ECOSOC)
54 members, serving 3-year terms
One vote per member
Coordinates activities of 14 specialized agencies, functional commissions, and regional commissions
Examines and recommends economic and social policies for member-states and the General Assembly

constituent agreement. The figure also includes some of the specialized agencies and global conferences that have come to define the UN system's work and international capacity.

IGO Membership: Procedures and Challenges

Fundamentally, every IGO is an intergovernmental organization whose membership comprises two or more states. Therefore, one key element of how an IGO operates is how it structures its membership, who it includes and excludes, and why. Membership matters in terms of the overall organization as well as within the various substructures within the organizations. It is impossible to grasp the politics of the UN without awareness that the Security Council has seats for only 15 out of a body made up of 193 members-states, and that 5 of the 15, known as the **Permanent Five (P5)** are permanent seats reserved for the China, France, Russia, the United Kingdom, and the United States. Thus, the other 188 UN member-states must rotate on the Security Council and thus have a very limited say on Council matters including the deployment of peacekeepers around the world.

GENERAL MEMBERSHIP ISSUES. Theoretically, membership in the UN and most other IGOs is open to any state that is within the geographic and functional scope of that organization and also subscribes to its principles and practices. In reality, politics is sometimes an additional standard. Today, with the exception of the Holy See (the Vatican), the UN has near universal membership, but that was not always the case.

Permanent Five (P5) Refers to the five permanent members of the UN Security Council who have the power to veto resolutions. These include China, France, Russia, the United Kingdom, and the United States.

Standards for admitting new members to the UN are a point of occasional political controversy. One instance occurred in 1998, when the General Assembly voted overwhelmingly to give Palestinians what amounts to an informal associate membership. In 2012, Palestine was granted observer status to the UN, meaning that while they cannot vote, they can take part in debates and can perform other functions that states undertake. In 2018, the Palestinian Authority officially sought to upgrade its status from observer-state to full member-state in conjunction with its effort to be recognized as a sovereign state. As of August 2018, a majority of UN member-states (137 out of 193) recognized Palestine as a state with a nonmember observer status at the UN, but this support did not come from major world powers, especially the United Sates. In 2019, Palestine announced that it will launch a bid for to become a full member, despite US opposition.

For the Palestinians to receive full admittance, they would need the UN Security Council's approval—that is, 9 out of 15 votes and no veto from any one of the P5. Any Council recommendation for membership would then require a two-thirds majority vote in the General Assembly. However, the United States has made clear that it will wield its veto power in the Security Council before such a vote ever reaches the General Assembly. Most recently, the United States has unilaterally declared Jerusalem the capital of Israel, making the potential for a two-state solution even less likely.

In addition to adding new members, the UN has a very political process of dealing with successor status states. For example, when the UN recognized Russia as the successor state to the Soviet Union, it meant, among other things, that Russia inherited the USSR's permanent seat and veto on the Security Council. Taking the opposite approach, the UN in 1992 refused to recognize the Serbian-dominated government in Belgrade as the successor to Yugoslavia once that country broke apart. Instead, the General Assembly required Yugoslavia to (re)apply for admission, which it finally (re)granted in 2000 not as Yugoslavia but as seven distinct states: Bosnia-Herzegovina, Croatia, Macedonia, Montenegro, Serbia, Slovenia, and most recently, Kosovo. The refusal to recognize Yugoslavia as a successor state began an expulsion that lasted eight years until a less oppressive government gained power.

Withdrawal, suspension, or expulsion is another issue. Nationalist China (Taiwan) was, in effect, ejected from the UN when the "China seat" was transferred to mainland China. Between 1974 and 1991, in a move close to expulsion, the General Assembly refused to seat South Africa's delegate because that country's apartheid policies violated the UN Charter.

MEMBERSHIP IN AN IGO SUBSTRUCTURE.   Not every internal decision-making structure in an IGO necessarily has representatives from each member-country. At the core of the UN and other IGOs is usually a comprehensive representative body (often called a plenary) that includes all members. The UN General Assembly is the UN's **plenary body**. Such assemblies normally have broad authority within their organizations and are supposedly the most powerful elements of their organizations. In practice, however, the

plenary body A session that is fully attended by all qualified members.

limited membership council
A representative organizational body of the United Nations that grants special status to members who have a greater stake, responsibility, or capacity in a particular area of concern (e.g., the Security Council).

UN Security Council The main organ of the United Nations charged with the maintenance and promotion of international peace and security. The Security Council has 15 members, including 5 permanent members.

P5 Refers to the five permanent members of the UN Security Council who have the power to veto resolutions. These include China, France, Russia, the United Kingdom, and the United States.

assembly may be secondary to the administrative structure or some other part of the organization.

Another type of representative body is a **limited membership council**. Based on the theory that smaller groups can operate more efficiently than large assemblies, many councils have representatives only from some parent organization's membership. For example, the UN's Economic and Social Council (ECOSOC) has representatives from 54 members, elected by the General Assembly for three-year terms based on a plan of geographic representation. Sometimes membership is limited on the theory that some members have a greater concern or capacity in a particular area. The **UN Security Council** has five permanent members who were the leading victorious powers at the end of World War II; thus, the founders thought they would have a special role to play in matters of security. Additionally, with the idea of keeping membership limited to improve efficiency, the Security Council set total membership at 15, with the General Assembly choosing 10 nonpermanent members for two-year terms.

The P5's powerful role on the Security Council should not indicate that the other 10 seats have little consequence. Although secondary to the P5, the rotating seats are much sought after by members. Not only do these nonpermanent members share the limelight in a key decision-making body, but some receive increased foreign aid and other incentives from the United States, China, and other big powers in order to win their cooperation (Kuziemko & Werker, 2006).

CONTROVERSY OVER MEMBERSHIP ON THE UN SECURITY COUNCIL. The P5's permanent status and veto power reflects the distribution of military power in 1945; as such, it has always been controversial, particularly among small- and middle-power states. Given the many changes in the international system since the end of World War II and the fact that other states actually contribute more to the UN than some of the P5 members, many have raised legitimate and serious criticisms of the Security Council. Lack of democracy is one line of questioning: How many representatives should sit around the table? Should permanent status be extended? Should the veto power be modified or eliminated? Geographic and demographic imbalance is another source of frustration. Geographically, Europe and North America have four of the five permanent seats, and those four permanent members are also countries of predominantly Eurowhite and Christian heritage.

Other criticism charges that the permanent members are an inaccurate reflection of power realities. As the German mission to the UN puts it, "The Security Council as it stands does not reflect today's world, which has changed dramatically since 1945."[10] From this perspective, Germany, India, Japan, Brazil, and some other powerful countries are leading efforts for reform. Given the stalled nature of these efforts, one scholar has proposed not tackling the permanent seat or veto issues but rather expanding the Council to 20 members, of whom 15 would be nonpermanent, would serve three-year terms, and would be eligible for reelection. Council decisions would require the formative votes of twelve members, including the concurring votes of the P5 (Luck, 2016).

Most countries in the UN favor reform, yet none has been possible because of the two nearly insurmountable hurdles to amending the UN Charter and altering the Security Council's composition. First, Charter amendments require the approval of two-thirds of the Security Council, and the P5 are not especially open to diluting their influence by adding more permanent or even nonpermanent members, by giving new members a veto, or least of all, by eliminating the veto altogether. Specific rivalries also influence the P5. China, for instance, would be reluctant to see either of its two great Asian power rivals, Japan or India, get a permanent seat. Beijing also complains that Japan has not apologized adequately for its aggression and atrocities during World War II. Second, another hurdle for a Charter revision is to get a two-thirds vote of the General Assembly. There, agreement on any new voting formula would be difficult, given the specific sensitivities of the 193 countries.

Voting Formulas and Debates

One of the difficult issues that any IGO faces is its formula for allocating votes. Most of the major IGOs use one of three formulas: majority voting, weighted voting, or unanimity voting. The implications of the various voting formulas are evident in Figure 6.4.

Majority voting is the most common formula that IGOs use. This system has two main components: (1) Each member casts one equal vote based on the concept of sovereign equality, and (2) the issue is carried by a simple majority (50% plus one vote), reflecting the democratic notion that the will of the majority should prevail. The UN General Assembly and most other UN bodies operate on this principle. A variation to majority voting is **supermajority voting**. This requires more than a simple majority to pass measures. A two-thirds vote is most common, and some of the supermajority formulas, like the one the Council of the European Union uses, can be complex.

The objection to equal voting power is that it does not reflect some standards of reality. Should Costa Rica, with no army, cast an equal vote with the powerful United States? Should San Marino, with a population of thousands, cast the same vote as China, with its more than 1.3 billion people? In the UN General Assembly, for example, 128 states whose combined populations are less than 15% of the world's population can wield about 67 of the votes. In contrast, the 11 countries with populations over 100 million combine for 61% of the world's population yet have just 6% of the available votes in the General Assembly.

Weighted voting allocates unequal voting power on the basis of

majority voting A system used to determine how votes should count. This system has two main components: (1) each member casts one equal vote, and (2) the issue is carried by either a simple majority or, in some cases, an extraordinary majority (commonly two-thirds).

supermajority voting A majority (such as two-thirds or three-fifths) that is greater than a simple majority.

weighted voting A voting formula that counts votes depending on what criterion is deemed to be the most significant, such as population or wealth.

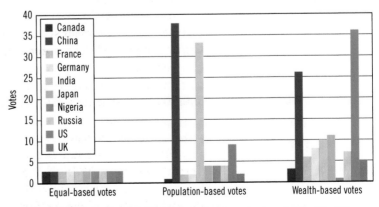

Figure 6.4 To see the impact of various voting formulas, imagine that the UN allocated the 193 votes in the General Assembly based on one-state-one-vote, population, or wealth. Voting power would vary widely depending on which formula was used. Which formula is the most fair? Which is the most equitable? Should other factors be taken into consideration, such as a country's geographic territory or level of democracy domestically?

a formula. Two possible criteria are population and wealth. As detailed in Chapter 9, the European Parliament provides an example of power in an international representative body based in part on population. Power in the World Bank and the IMF is based on member contributions. The United States alone commands about 17% of the votes in the IMF. It and a handful of other top economically developed countries have majority control, yet combined, these countries have little more than 10% of the world population. In contrast, China and India combined have 37% of the world's population yet combined have less than 6% of the IMF votes.[11] This wealth-weighted voting is especially offensive to LDCs, which contend that it perpetuates the system of imperial domination by the industrialized countries.

unanimity voting A system used to determine how votes should count. In this system, in order for a vote to be valid, all members must agree to the proposed measure. Abstention from a vote may or may not block an agreement.

Unanimity voting requires unanimous consent, although sometimes an abstention does not block agreement. The Organization for Economic Cooperation and Development (OECD) and some other IGOs operate on that formula. Unanimity preserves the concept of sovereignty but can easily lead to stalemate. In a related formula, the rules of the UN Security Council allow any of the five permanent members to veto proposals. For many, this is an anti-democratic practice not in accordance with the principle of the sovereign equality of states. Vetoes were cast frequently during the Cold War, mostly by the Soviet Union. During the Cold War, the veto power was employed over 200 times; however, since the end of the Cold War, the veto power has been used in only about 50 instances. As Figure 6.5 makes clear, the United States and Russia have used their veto power the most.

Although use of the veto has declined dramatically, its power remains important. First, vetoes are still sometimes cast in critical cases. In 2006, for example, the United States vetoed a resolution calling on Israeli forces to withdraw from Gaza on the grounds that the resolution ignored the provocation—the kidnapping of two Israeli soldiers. Second, and more commonly, a veto threat can persuade countries not to press an initiative. Over the past seven years, many efforts to intervene in Syria's civil and internationalized war have been thwarted before even making it to the Security Council agenda because member-states know that Russia and China will veto any intervention given their complex interests and allies in the Middle East. The veto can also serve as a diplomatic tool. The United States, for instance, has successfully pressured the UN to exempt American troops serving as UN peacekeepers from the jurisdiction of the International Criminal Court by threatening to veto all UN peacekeeping operations.

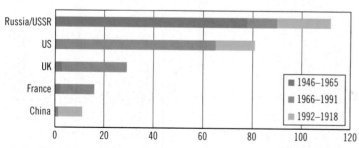

Figure 6.5 The veto power of the P5 make the Security Council a highly political and often inept principal organ of the UN. The veto power is clearly used by some states more than other, and can often reflect broader geopolitical and economic tensions between states. (Source: www.securitycouncilreport.org.)

Leadership

Intergovernmental organizations rely upon its member-states, executive heads, and even nonstate actors to exercise initiative and leadership. Administrative structures, or secretariats, are critical to guiding and directing these large, multilateral organizations and often wield a significant amount of power in the process. The **UN Secretariat** employs approximately 55,000 professional and support staff based in UN offices all over the world. The **UN Secretary-General** (SG) is the chief executive officer of this complex UN system, serving as both the managing administrator of the Secretariat as well as the diplomatic leader of the entire global institution. Virtually all IGOs have some type of chief administrative officer with varying degrees of authority, legitimacy, and power.

The SG, a highly political position with complex responsibilities, works primarily with two constituencies: the Secretariat and the member-states. In this balancing act, the SG is responsible for managing the Secretariat, preparing the UN's budget, submitting an annual report to the General Assembly, overseeing studies conducted at the request of other major organizations, and bringing any issues that may threaten international peace and security to the Security Council. This is a tall order that at times grants the SG the authority to act independently—and increasingly as a political actor. Such leadership has become largely dependent on the individual SG's personality. Leaders like Dag Hammarskjöld and more recently Boutros Boutros-Ghali and Kofi A. Annan have been particularly instrumental in putting forth a neoliberal institutionalist agenda and pushing the UN forward as a driver of ideas and new norms (see *Thinking Theoretically: The Neoliberal Legacy of Dag Hammarskjöld*).

One indication that IGOs are important players on the world stage is the often intense struggle among member-countries over who will head various IGOs. Seemingly, the selection process would not engender such sound and fury if it were not important. In the formal process of selecting the UN SG, the Security Council nominates one or more candidates for the post, and the General Assembly then elects one candidate for a five-year term. Reality is less democratic than theory, however. In practice, the Security Council controls the choice by submitting only one name to the General Assembly. Moreover, each of the permanent members, the P5, can veto candidates. Other possible contenders do not even bother to seek the office because of known opposition from one or more of the P5. The 2006 selection of Ban Ki-moon from the Republic of Korea (South Korea) seemed somewhat less contentious than that of his immediate predecessors, but there was still considerable maneuvering, most of it behind tightly

UN Secretariat The administrative organ of the United Nations, headed by the Secretary-General.

UN Secretary-General The head of the Secretariat of the United Nations and who also serves as the UN spokesperson. Many other intergovernmental organizations also use the term secretary-general to designate their organizational leader.

Dag Hammarskjöld, former UN Secretary-General, was known for his heroic conflict mediation efforts during the Cold War, particularly over the Suez Canal and in the Congo, until his untimely death.

▲ THINKING THEORETICALLY

The Neoliberal Legacy of Dag Hammarskjöld

Intergovernmental organizations are often the products of collaboration between diverse people and groups. The UN is a product of many individuals, each with his or her own unique theoretical ideologies. Perhaps Dag Hammarskjöld, the second Secretary-General of the UN, best exemplifies this collaboration. His actions as Secretary-General reinforced his neoliberal institutionalist identity and expanded the role of the Secretary-General as a more active leader in the international community. He is one individual among many who have demonstrated not only how theoretical worldviews matter, but also how individuals can play a critical role in the development of IGOs.

Dag Hammarskjöld was relatively unknown outside Sweden when the Security Council recommended his appointment as UN Secretary-General. He had earlier served as a Swedish delegate to the UN and as Secretary-General of the Swedish Foreign Office. In April 1953, the General Assembly unanimously appointed Hammarskjöld the second Secretary-General of the UN. He served from 1953 to 1961, a time threatened by the tensions of the Cold War and constant threat of nuclear war.

Both as an individual and as Secretary-General, Hammarskjöld embodied the ideals and principles of neoliberal institutionalism. He believed that despite the anarchic nature of the system and states with narrow self-interests, common goals could lead to cooperation, and that such collaboration would be mutually beneficial to all nations over the long run (Boehmer, 2006). Thus, Hammarskjöld maintained that the international community needed a set of rules and regulations to promote cooperation and create an environment in which all would benefit.

Shortly after taking office, Hammarskjöld put neoliberal institutional theory into practice. In an unprecedented move, the General Assembly asked Hammarskjöld to intervene on behalf of 11 American airmen imprisoned by the People's Republic of China, which was then not represented in the UN (Dag Hammarskjöld Library, 2012). His success in negotiating their release demonstrated his strong diplomatic skills and the role the UN can take in interstate relations, even with nonmember-states. Both the United States and China benefited from these negotiations. The airmen were released, and the negotiations established the groundwork for admission of the People's Republic to the UN. Hammarskjöld's mediation enabled both sides to cooperate for mutual gain. Many credit him with "inventing the idea of preventive diplomacy" (Karns & Mingst, 2012:85).

With the creation of the United Nations Emergency Force (UNEF), Hammarskjöld also initiated the first UN peacekeeping operation. Its goal was to quell the violence that had erupted over the Suez Canal crisis of 1956. Importantly, UNEF reported to the General Assembly and was not responsible to any singular nation. This was the first solely international military force and the predecessor to modern peacekeeping operations. UNEF met with great success in a short time, proof that Hammarskjöld's innovative diplomatic skills were working.

Hammarskjöld was an extremely active Secretary-General. His world travel included visits to 21 African nations as part of UN efforts to foster more inclusion and cooperation with African states. He spent the last year and a half of his time working to resolve violence in the Congo. The Soviet Union, extremely displeased with the actions of the Secretary-General, called for his resignation. Hammarskjöld stood firm in his beliefs and publicly dismissed the call for his resignation. Even if leaders and individual nations were not entirely in agreement, the goal was the greatest good for the most people. Hammarskjöld stayed loyal to this belief until his untimely death in 1961.

Hammarskjöld was often quoted as saying, "The United Nations was not created to bring us to heaven but to save us from hell" (Urquhart, 2011). Structures like the UN cannot create a perfect world where each country gets exactly what it wants. What it can do, however, is save the world from another devastating world war. Hammarskjöld's actions at the UN paved the way for collaborations among many diverse nations. Through his expanded role of Secretary-General, Hammarskjöld embedded neoliberal institutionalist ideals in the UN and created the system that exists today.

shut diplomatic doors. Not surprisingly, Ban Ki-moon, like those elected before him, comes from a relatively small and noncontroversial state.

Succeeding Ban Ki-moon, António Guterres, the former Prime Minister of Portugal and UN High Commissioner for Refugees, became the ninth man to serve as SG. Working in a world where some world powers, most notably the United States, are pulling back from multilateral agreements and collective organizations, Guterres finds himself leading a global organization when much of the world is fracturing into ever-smaller pieces and allegiances. As Guterres says, "[I]t's not just dysfunctional democracies and xenophobic nationalism that made it this way. The culprits also include shifting power dynamics and resurgent great-power conflict in a world organized neither by the bipolar competition of the Cold War nor by the singular leadership that the United States exercised after the collapse of the Soviet Union."[12]

As Guterres' leadership at the UN develops, however, the debate over the proper role of top officials in other IGOs will continue. Traditionally, nation-states have sought to control IGOs and their leaders. As IGOs and their leaders have grown stronger, however, they have more often struck out independently and even in opposition to certain powerful states. As former SG Kofi Annan commented, all the Secretaries-General have carried out their traditional role as chief administrative officer, but each has also, to one degree or another, assumed an alternative role, one that Annan described as "an instrument of the larger interest, beyond national rivalries and regional concerns."[13]

Administration and Finance

Related to challenges of leadership, no organization can be successful unless it is well organized and efficient and also receives the staffing and budget resources needed to accomplish its missions. Matters such as staff and finances are critical to the UN, as for other IGOs, even though they do not often capture headlines.

ADMINISTRATIVE CHALLENGES. The SG appoints the other principal officials of the Secretariat. However, in doing so, the SG must be sensitive to the desires of the dominant powers and must pay attention to the geographic and, increasingly, the gender composition of the Secretariat staff. For example, the UN has a relatively good record compared to most countries for increasing the percentage of management positions held by women. As of 2018, the gender breakdown in the Secretariat was 61% men and 39% women. However, these numbers are lower when you look at more senior positions in the UN system. As part of the Sustainable Development Goals, the UN established a Gender Parity Task Force in 2017 to create a clear roadmap, with benchmarks and

Major General Kristin Lund, the Head of Mission and Chief of Staff of the UN Truce Supervision Organization, pins a medal on New Zealand Army Captain Luke Greenaway, who served as a Military Observer in Israel.

Major General Kristin Lund

Major General Kristin Lund has always owned her unique and important position in both military and human history. Her impressive military career with the Norwegian Army and with the UN demonstrates her dedication to empowering women and "shattering several glass ceilings."[14] By achieving tremendous success in a male-dominated field, she has opened the door for future generations of women striving for equality and appreciation in environments traditionally reserved for men.

Born on May 16, 1958, in Norway, General Lund began her military career with the Norwegian army in 1979 at the age of 21. She became involved with the UN after joining the UN Interim Force in Lebanon (UNIFIL) in 1986, where she worked to uphold the Lebanese government and restore peace and security to the region. In 1991, she was deployed to Saudi Arabia as a part of Operation Desert Storm. She continued with the UN as a part of the UN Protection Force (UNPROFOR) and from 2003 to 2004 served at the NATO Headquarters for the International Security Assistance Force in Afghanistan. General Lund attended the Norwegian Defence Command and Staff College, the Norwegian Defence University College, and the US Army War College, where she received a Master's Degree in Strategic Studies in 2007.

In 2009, she became the first female officer to become a Major General. Soon after, she became the Chief of Staff of the Norwegian Home Guard, with responsibilities equivalent to those of the US Chairman of the Joint Chiefs of Staff. Since rising in the ranks, General Lund has made a conscious effort to reach out to other women in the military. She reflects that "it has been crucial for me to meet women in similar situations . . . . I believe it contributes to show other women that you can climb to the top, including in the military."[15]

On May 12, 2014, General Lund, placed in charge of the UN peacekeeping force in Cyprus, became the UN's first female commander of such a mission. Out of the 900 soldiers present in Cyprus, only 6% were women. Despite those low numbers, General Lund is proud of her appointment and the other women in her ranks. She expresses that there is a need for women in the military, and especially in the UN:

> In certain cultures being a woman means I have access to 100% of the population, while a man has only access to 50%. That is an important difference. Since we represent the UN, it is also fairly important to reflect what the UN stands for when it comes to issues like gender equality.[16]

General Lund believes the UN, as an intergovernmental organization that represents the world's nations and addresses global human rights issues, should be held to its own standards.

In 2017, Major General Lund was named a UNWOMEN champion. One of twelve champions, she "will advise UN Women on emerging issues for peace and security, and advocate for gender equality and women's human rights in conflict affected settings."[17] Advocating for gender equality has given her life enormous fulfillment. Though she had to "work hard and fight to be accepted as equal to [her] male colleagues,"[18] she believes that she "has paved the way for many."[19]

time frames, to achieve parity across the system.[20] In 2014, the UN appointed its first female commander of a UN peacekeeping force, as discussed in the *Personal Narrative* feature.

Controversies have occasionally arisen over these distributions, but in recent years, the focus of criticism has been the size and effectiveness of the UN headquarters staff in New York and its regional offices in Geneva, Nairobi, and Vienna. As Mingst and Karns relate, studies have identified a "lack of coordination, the expansion of programs with little consideration of financial commitments, and weak to nonexistent program evaluation" (2012:58). In this way, the UN is like many other IGOs and, indeed, national governments, with allegedly bloated, inefficient, and unresponsive bureaucracies that have made them a lightning rod for discontent.

Over its existence, critics of the UN, especially those in the United States, have regularly charged that it costs too much, employs too many people, and manages its affairs poorly. There is an element of truth to this accusation, but even UN defenders, who reply that many of these charges reflect animus toward the UN rather than a balanced evaluation, have agreed that the organization's operation needs improvement. To address these issues, the UN has instituted many administrative changes. Budget increases have been modest, and the number of staff members has remained static despite significantly increased peacekeeping operations.

As with almost any government bureaucracy, it is possible to find horror stories about the size and activities of IGO staffs. The UN oil-for-food program scandal and the evidence of sexual abuse of supposedly protected persons by UN peacekeeping troops and personnel that swept over the UN like a tsunami in 2004 are particularly disturbing examples (Pilch, 2005). However, we should put into perspective the charges that the UN and its associated agencies are corrupt and a bureaucratic swamp. These problems also occur in national governments, including the US government, and the standards that one applies to the leaders of countries and those of IGOs should not differ, nor should reactions to bureaucratic blundering. Within countries, problems may lead to the abolition of a particular agency, but the thrust is reform, not destruction of the entire endeavor. From this perspective, it is more reasonable to address problems at the UN through reform rather than by disbanding it.

FINANCIAL REALITIES IN CONTEXT.   All IGOs face the problem of obtaining sufficient funds to conduct their operations. Most do not have independent sources of money and depend almost entirely on member-states for financial support. National contributions, while often assessed, are still voluntary, and IGOs have very little authority to compel member-countries to support them.

The UN budget system is complex. In its narrowest organizational sense, the UN has two budgets: (1) the regular budget for operating the UN's headquarters, its organs, and its major administrative units ($5.4 billion for 2017), and (2) the peacekeeping budget to meet the expenses of operations conducted by the Security Council ($7.8 billion for 2017).[21] In a broader sense, the UN system also includes the specialized agencies budgets and the voluntary contributions budgets of the agencies and other UN associated programs. The agencies raise some funds based on assessments on members, but they and some other UN programs rely for most of their funding on voluntary contributions from countries, private groups, and individuals. UN spending through these budgets has increased considerably, but the lion's share of that increase has been caused by a sharp rise in funds for peacekeeping operations and for various UN socioeconomic programs rather than in funds for the central administration, as critics sometimes charge.

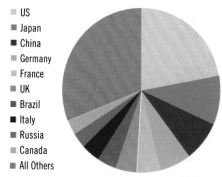

- US
- Japan
- China
- Germany
- France
- UK
- Brazil
- Italy
- Russia
- Canada
- All Others

Figure 6.6   The United States is responsible for a significant portion of many UN agencies' budgets. For many of them, especially those that depend on voluntary funding, cuts in U.S. contributions could be quite painful. For example, the UN agency for Palestinian refugees, UNRWA, which previously depended on the United States for about a third of its budget, said it would be forced to cut 250 jobs in 2018 after the Trump administration eliminated over $300 million in funding. For more, see https://www.cfr.org/article/funding-united-nations-what-impact-do-us-contributions-have-un-agencies-and-programs. (Source: https://factly.in/united-nations-budget-contributions-by-member-countries/.)

arrearages   The state of being behind in the discharge of obligations, often an unpaid or overdue debt.

To pay for its regular and peacekeeping operations, the UN depends almost entirely on the assessments that it levies on member-countries. By ratifying the UN Charter and joining the UN, members accept a legal obligation to pay these assessments and may have their voting privilege in the General Assembly suspended if they fall behind by more than a year. A complicated equation that the General Assembly formulates based on national wealth determines the amount each country is supposed to pay. The UN recommends assessment levels based on gross national income and other economic data, with a minimum assessment of 0.001% and a maximum assessment of 22%. The United States is currently assessed at 22% of the regular budget; other top contributors include Japan, China, Germany, and France.[22] As a result, the top-10 contributors provide about 70% of the UN's regular budget (see Figure 6.6). Because of their special responsibility (and their special privilege, the veto), permanent Security Council members pay a somewhat higher assessment for peacekeeping, with the US share at 25%.

These numbers are something of a fiction, however, because some countries do not pay their assessment. In 2014, **arrearages** (unpaid assessments or debts) to the UN's regular budget totaled $3.5 billion, with the United States alone owing a significant portion of that debt (Mingst et al., 2017:63). As a result, the UN's financial situation is always precarious because of the increasing demands to provide protection and help meet other humanitarian and social needs.

Activities and Behaviors

The most important aspects of any intergovernmental organization are what it does, how well this corresponds to the functions it should perform, and how well it is performing these functions. Here, we explore these aspects by examining the scope of IGO activity, with emphasis on the UN. Much of this discussion only briefly touches on these activities, however, as they receive more attention in other chapters.

PEACE AND SECURITY GOALS.   The opening words of the UN Charter dedicate the organization to saving "succeeding generations from the scourge of war, which . . . has brought untold sorrow to mankind." The UN attempts to fulfill this goal in numerous ways.

Creating norms against violence is one way. Countries that sign the charter pledge to accept the principle "that armed force shall not be used, save in the common interest" and further agree to "refrain in their international relations from the threat or the use of force except in self-defense."[23] Reaffirming the charter's ideas, the UN (and other IGOs) condemned Iraq's invasion of Kuwait in 1990, Serbian aggression against its neighbors (the Croatian War of Independence from 1991 to 1995), and other such actions. These denunciations and the slowly developing norm against aggression have not halted violence, but they have created an increasing onus on countries that strike the first blow. When, for example, the United States acted unilaterally in 1989 to depose the regime of Panama's strongman General Manuel Noriega, the UN and the OAS condemned Washington's action. Five years later, when the United States toppled the regime in Haiti, Washington took care to win UN support for its action. Norms, however, do not always restrain countries, as the US-led invasion of Iraq in 2003 demonstrates. Yet, the efforts of US and British diplomats to obtain a supportive UN resolution underlined the existence of the norm. Moreover, the angry reaction in many parts of the globe to the Anglo-American preemptive action and the postwar difficulties during the occupation may, in the long run, actually serve to reinforce the norm.

Providing a debate alternative is a peace-enhancing role for the UN and some other IGOs. Research shows that membership in IGOs tends to lessen interstate military conflict (Chan, 2004). One reason is that IGOs serve as a forum in which members publicly air their points of view and privately negotiate their differences. Thus, the UN acts like a safety valve, or perhaps a soundstage, where players can carry out the world drama without the dire consequences that could occur if they were to choose another method or locale. This grand-debate approach to peace involves denouncing your opponents, defending your actions, trying to influence world opinion, and winning symbolic victories.

Intervening diplomatically to assist and encourage countries to settle their disputes peacefully is another role that IGOs play. IGOs engage in such steps as providing a neutral setting for opposing parties to negotiate, brokering a settlement between opposing parties, and even deciding issues between disputants in forums like the International Court of Justice.

Promoting arms control and disarmament is still another IGO function. The International Atomic Energy Agency, a specialized agency, focuses on the nonproliferation of nuclear weapons. The UN also sponsors numerous conferences on weapons and conflict and has played an important role in the genesis of the Chemical Weapons Convention and other arms control agreements.

Imposing **sanctions** is a more forceful way to pressure countries that have attacked their neighbors or otherwise violated international law. As discussed in Chapter 10, sanctions are controversial and often do not work, but sometimes they are effective and can serve as an important symbol of the views of the international community.

sanctions Economic, diplomatic, or military actions put in place to punish a state in an attempt to coercively force states to comply with legal obligations.

Peacekeeping is the best-known way that the UN and some other IGOs promote peace and security. Peacekeeping is extensively covered in Chapter 8, but a few preliminary facts are appropriate here. Through 2018, the UN had mounted 71 peacekeeping operations and utilized military and police personnel from most of the world's countries. These operations ranged from lightly armed observer missions to police forces to full-fledged military forces.[24] Never, however, have international forces been as active as they are now. The number of UN peacekeeping operations has risen markedly. As of 2018, there were 15 UN peacekeeping forces of varying sizes in the field, with about 90,000 troops

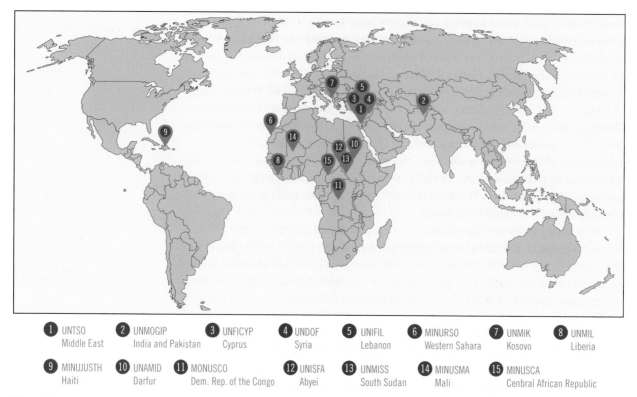

1 UNTSO	2 UNMOGIP	3 UNFICYP	4 UNDOF	5 UNIFIL	6 MINURSO	7 UNMIK	8 UNMIL
Middle East	India and Pakistan	Cyprus	Syria	Lebanon	Western Sahara	Kosovo	Liberia

9 MINUJUSTH	10 UNAMID	11 MONUSCO	12 UNISFA	13 UNMISS	14 MINUSMA	15 MINUSCA
Haiti	Darfur	Dem. Rep. of the Congo	Abyei	South Sudan	Mali	Cenbral African Republic

Map 6.1   Here you can see where UN peacekeeping missions are operating around the world, from some of the oldest missions like those in Cyprus or along the India/Pakistan border to the more recently established missions like the one in Haiti. (Source: https://peacekeeping .un.org/en/where-we-operate.)

and police from 123 countries deployed throughout the world.[25] As Map 6.1 shows, the operations are clustered on the African continent and the Middle East, which are recurrent conflict hot spots.

Fortunately, UN peacekeeping forces have suffered relatively few casualties, although about 3,644 have died in world service since 1948. For these sacrifices and contributions to world order, the UN peacekeeping forces were awarded the 1988 Nobel Peace Prize. Peacekeeping has had successes, such as the Namibia mission from 1989 to 1990, as well as many failures, including the UN's inability to prevent genocide in Rwanda in 1994 and, more recently, ethnic cleansing in South Sudan. Many individuals have criticized even the most successful cases. For example, Sandra Whitworth (2004) raised critical questions about soldiers trained to kill in traditional military organizations who are now deployed as *peacekeepers* tasked with maintaining law and order, rebuilding infrastructure, monitoring democratic elections, documenting gross human rights abuses, and providing humanitarian aid, among other tasks that are the functions of **complex peacekeeping**. Further, numerous reports of sexual exploitation and abuse since the early 2000s have raised serious concerns about the conduct of peacekeepers. Recent research has even found that

complex peacekeeping

International, multidimensional operations comprising a mix of military, police, and civilian components to lay the foundations of a sustainable peace. Tasks include monitoring and ceasefire enforcement as well as the monitoring of democratic elections, disarmament programs, and human rights documentation.

the presence of UN peacekeeping forces correlates positively with a state's being cited as a destination for forced prostitution and sex trafficking (Bell, Flynn, & Machain, 2018).

SOCIAL, ECONOMIC, AND OTHER AREAS OF INTEREST.   In addition to maintaining and restoring the peace, IGOs engage in a wide variety of other activities. During its early years, the UN's emphasis was on security, a concern that has not abated but has been joined by social, economic, environmental, and other nonmilitary security issues. This shift has been a result of the ebb and eventual end of the Cold War, the increasing number of LDCs since the 1960s, growing realization that the environment is in danger, and changing global values that have brought an increased focus on human and political rights.

Although peacekeeping operations often claim the headlines, much of the UN's budget and personnel are devoted to the lower-profile work of helping countries to create jobs and raise standards of living; to deliver relief aid to victims of famine, war, and natural disasters; to protect refugees; to promote literacy; and to fight disease. To most people around the world, this effort is the face of the UN, and is most clearly apparent in the UN's goal to promote and implement the Sustainable Development Goals (see Chapter 11).

Simulation: Building
the USS Relief

It is impossible to list here, much less fully describe, the broad range of endeavors involving the UN and other IGOs. Indeed, they cover most of the issues that humans address at all levels of government. Because we will highlight many of these endeavors in subsequent chapters, the discussion here is limited to a few of the programs and successes of the UN and other IGOs.

Promoting economic development is an important role of the UN. The United Nations Development Programme (UNDP), the World Bank, and a significant number of other global and regional IGOs work to improve the economic well-being of those who are deprived because of their location in the global south, their gender, or some other cause. For instance, the UNDP reports that from 2014 to 2017 it assisted in creating 3 million jobs in 101 countries, improving access to energy for 6.7 million people living in 55 countries, and delivering anti-retroviral treatment to some 2 million people in 22 countries.[26]

Advocating human rights is a closely related IGO role. Beginning with the **Universal Declaration of Human Rights** in 1948, the UN has actively promoted dozens of agreements on political, civil, economic, social, and cultural rights. The UN Commission on Human Rights has used its power of investigation and its ability to issue reports to expose abuses of human rights and to create pressure on the abusers by highlighting and condemning their transgressions. In an associated area, the International Labour Organization leads the global effort to free the estimated 250 million children who are forced to work instead of attending school, to end the sexual predation of children that is big business in some parts of the world, and to eliminate other abuses that debase the meaning of childhood. (Chapter 12 discusses this critical human rights work in detail.)

Advancing international law and norms is another important UN and IGO role (Coate & Fomerand, 2004). For example, international courts associated

Universal Declaration of Human Rights Adopted by the UN General Assembly in 1948, it is the most fundamental internationally proclaimed statement of human rights in existence.

with IGOs help establish legal precedent. IGOs also sponsor multinational treaties, which may establish the assumption of law. UN auspices have negotiated over 300 such treaties. As one scholar sees the norm-building function of IGOs, "The procedures and rules of international institutions create information structures. They determine what principles are acceptable as a basis for reducing conflicts and whether governmental actions are legitimate or illegitimate. Consequently, they help shape actors' expectations" (Keohane, 1998b:91). This topic is discussed in greater detail in Chapter 9.

Improving the quality of human existence is a role that has many aspects. The Office of the UN High Commissioner for Refugees has provided shelter, fed, and assisted more than 34.4 million refugees suffering from war, famine, and other dangers. A wide variety of IGOs also devote their energies to such concerns as health, nutrition, and literacy. For example, the United Nations Children's Fund, the World Health Organization, and other agencies have undertaken a $150 million program to develop a multi-immunization vaccine. This vaccine program is designed to double the estimated 2 million children who now annually survive because of such international medical assistance.

The Food and Agriculture Organization (FAO) has launched a program to identify, preserve, and strengthen through new genetic techniques those domestic animals that might prove especially beneficial to LDCs. Western breeds of pigs, for example, usually produce only about 10 piglets per litter. The Taihu pig of China, however, produces 15 to 20. The FAO hopes to use the latter and other appropriate animals to increase protein availability in the LDCs.

Guarding the environment is one of the new IGO roles. Beginning in 1992 with the UN Conference on Environment and Development (dubbed the Earth Summit), the UN has sponsored several global meetings on the environment. These have resulted in the initiation of programs that will slow down, stop, or begin to reverse the degradation of the environment. As Chapter 13 discusses, IGOs increasingly also require that environmental impact statements accompany requests for economic development aid. In some cases, they are even refusing to finance projects that have unacceptable negative impacts on the biosphere.

Encouraging independence through self-determination has long been a role of IGOs. The **UN Trusteeship Council** once monitored numerous colonial dependencies, but the wave of independence in recent decades steadily lessened its number of charges. When Palau, an island nation in the Pacific Ocean that is 500 miles east of the Philippines, gained its independence from the United States in October 1994, the last trust territory in the world was free. Therefore, the Trusteeship Council had fulfilled its mission, and although it technically continues to exist, it no longer meets.

▷

How China Is (and Isn't) Fighting Pollution and Climate Change

UN Trusteeship Council
Suspending operation on November 1, 1994, with the independence of Palau, its major goals were to promote the advancement of the inhabitants of Trust Territories and their progressive development toward self-government or independence.

As a direct result of immunization, the world is closer than ever to eradicating polio, with only three remaining polio-endemic countries: Afghanistan, Nigeria, and Pakistan. Deaths of children under age 5 from measles, a major child killer, declined by 85% worldwide and by 89% in sub-Saharan Africa between 2000 and 2016. And as of March 2018, all but 14 countries have eliminated maternal and neonatal tetanus, a disease with a fatality rate of 70% to 100% among newborns.

CHALLENGE YOUR ASSUMPTIONS

Do IGOs Matter?

Although it may be difficult to envision a world without IGOs, many critics have raised serious questions about the authority, legitimacy, and power of such organizations, particularly the UN. Many see a world where state sovereignty triumphs and IGOs like the UN system remain fundamentally weak, consistently underfunded, poorly managed, and overtly politicized. Thus, the UN is associated with the inability to stop genocide in places like Rwanda or Myanmar, to curb weapons proliferation in places like Iran or North Korea, or to respond to outbreaks of disease, like the Ebola epidemic of 2014 that resurfaced in the Democratic Republic of the Congo in 2018.

Recent research, however, facilitated by the UN Intellectual History Project (http://www.unhistory.org/) challenges these assumption on at least two fronts. First, the Project has documented the UN's role in the development of certain ideas that drive human progress and make substantial contributions to the evolution of international society. From redefining security as human security and development as human development, the UN generates ideas, gives ideas legitimacy, and ultimately transforms ideas into policy and practice. Ideas such as the notion that states have a responsibility to protect their own citizens from war crimes and crimes against humanity, or the notion that human rights are universal, inalienable, and indivisible protections guaranteed for all, have proved critical signs of our times. Such ideas do not always translate into action, but oftentimes they do. Most important, they will continue to influence change in the centuries to come.

Second, the Project challenges us to add the concept of a "third UN" to our analytical toolkit. Thomas Weiss, Tatiana Carayannis, and Richard Jolly (2009) argue that there are in reality three UNs: (1) the intergovernmental arena; (2) the Secretariat and staff members; and (3) the scholars, experts, and NGOs that work closely with the actors and staff that constitute the first and second UNs. They posit:

> The third UN's roles include advocacy, research, policy analysis, and idea mongering. Its elements often combine forces to put forward new information and ideas, push for new policies, and mobilize public opinion around UN deliberations and operations . . . [I]n our view, informed scholars, practitioners, and activists have a value-added and comparative advantage within intergovernmental contexts to push intellectual and policy envelopes. These circles—a third UN—are independent of and provide essential inputs into the other two UNs. Such "outside-insiders" are an integral part of today's United Nations. What once seemed marginal for international relations now is central to multilateralism. (2009:23)

In this way, the third UN not only serves as an additional driver of ideas but also collects and disseminates data, influences the international agenda, and even promotes and monitors targets related to human development, human security, and human rights. These functions are significant, as this research provides information for decision-making around the world. At a minimum, it illustrates the soft power of IGOs as they fill gaps of global governance.

Considering the UN as three constituent parts allows us to reevaluate the UN system as an actor on the international stage. But are you convinced? *What do you think?* Do ideas matter as much as the UN Intellectual History Project claims they do? If so, what ideas coming from the UN system do you find most significant? In what other ways has the UN made a difference, particularly in terms of actions within the third UN? In what ways is the UN currently under attack?

Evaluating IGOs

The UN has existed for only about 70 years. Most other IGOs are even younger. Despite their relatively short history, many critics are quick to pass judgments on whether or not an IGO, and especially the UN, is successful.

Some start by looking at whether or not the organization has fulfilled its ultimate goals. Article 1 of the UN Charter establishes lofty goals. These include maintaining peace and security and solving economic, social, cultural, and humanitarian problems. Clearly, the world is still beset by violent conflicts and by ongoing economic and social misery. Thus, from the perspective of meeting ultimate goals, it is easy to be skeptical about what the UN and other IGOs have accomplished. One has to ask, however, whether the meeting of ultimate goals is a reasonable standard. In fact, are the expectations placed on IGOs, especially the UN, implausible? Others point to the UN's conflicting goals to promote international peace and security while also maintaining and respecting the sovereign equality of states.

A better standard by which to evaluate the UN and other IGOs might be to assess what is possible as to their goals. Insofar as the UN does not meet expectations, for example, is it an organizational flaw, or is it the product of the unwillingness of member-states to live up to the standards that countries accept when they ratify the Charter?

Just as President George W. Bush and others castigated the UN for not supporting the war with Iraq in 2003, others berated the UN for not stopping the US invasion. Reflecting on his decade as SG, Kofi Annan told an audience, "The worst moment, of course, was the Iraq War, which, as an organization, we couldn't stop. I really did everything I could to try to see if we could stop it."[27] Given UN resources, however, there was nothing he could do. At a less dramatic level, simply paying their assessments regularly and on time is another thing more countries could do. Ultimately, the UN would also work better if countries try to make it effective. What states want of the UN does not always align with—and can even be in direct opposition to—what they actually allow it to be.

Progress is also a good standard by which to evaluate the UN and other IGOs. Is the world better off for their presence? That is the standard for which Kofi Annan appealed when he urged, "Judge us rightly . . . by the relief and refuge that we provide to the poor, to the hungry, the sick and threatened: the peoples of the world whom the United Nations exists to serve."[28] Between its 50th and 60th anniversaries, the UN surpassed all previous marks in terms of numbers of simultaneous peacekeeping missions, deployed peacekeeping troops, and other international security efforts. The **Millennium Development Goals** that the members of the UN unanimously adopted in 2000 for attainment by 2015 "have become the principal global scorecard for development."[29] The record shows that, although much remains to be done, much has also been accomplished by the UN to address the world's social, economic, and environmental problems.

Millennium Development Goals In 2000, 189 nations made and committed to eight global goals aimed at poverty reduction, education, public health, and human rights. This pledge encompassed eight specific goals to achieve by 2015.

The UN kicked off the 21st century by sponsoring a series of global conferences on issues such as racism (2001), aging (2002), sustainable development (2002, 2012, and 2015), indigenous peoples (2014), financing for development (2002, 2008, and 2015), and wildlife (2017). Such conferences and other planning efforts have not been all talk and no action. The Sustainable Development Goals are now the global goals to watch for as we assess the value and impact of IGOs, especially the UN.

World opinion is another good standard. An old saying suggests not being able to fool all of the people all of the time, and the UN earns good marks from the average person around the world. One survey of 19 different counties found that 17 had, on average, positive views of the UN, ranging from a high of 82% in Sweden to 40% in India. In the United States, 64% had favorable views of the UN, which is up from 48% in 2007.[30]

Whether alternatives exist is yet another good standard by which to evaluate the UN and other IGOs. John Bolton, former US ambassador to the UN (2005–2006) and currently the US National Security Advisor, is of the opinion that "there's no such thing" as a well-functioning UN.[31] If this is correct, one must ask, "If not the UN then what?" Can the warring, uncaring world continue unchanged in the face of nuclear weapons, persistent poverty, an exploding population, periodic mass starvation, continued widespread human rights violations, resource depletion, and environmental degradation? Somehow the world has survived these plagues, but one of the realities this book hopes to make clear is that we humans are hurtling toward our destiny at an ever-increasing speed. In a rapidly changing system, doing things the old way may be not only inadequate, but may even take us down a road that, although familiar, will lead the world to cataclysm.

At the very least, former US Secretary of State Madeleine Albright, who served under President Bill Clinton, noted, "The United Nations gives the good guys—the peace-makers, the freedom fighters, the people who believe in human rights, those committed to human development—an organized vehicle for achieving gains."[32] Thus, we must return to the question, "If not the UN, then what?"

Regional IGOs

Even more striking than the growth of global IGOs has been the growth of regional IGOs. Prior to World War II, there were no prominent regional IGOs. Now there are many, and they constitute the majority of all IGOs. Most are specialized, with regional economic IGOs like the Arab Cooperation Council the most numerous. Other regional IGOs are general purpose and deal with a range of issues, such as the African Union (formerly the Organization of African Unity) and the OAS.

Another noteworthy development regarding regional IGOs is that some of them are transitioning from specialized to general-purpose organizations. The Association of Southeast Asian Nations (ASEAN) was founded in 1967 to promote regional economic cooperation (see Figure 6.7). More recently, though, ASEAN has begun to take on a greater political position, and in particular may serve as a political and defensive counterweight to China in the region. The Economic Community of West African States (ECOWAS) has also expanded its roles. Created in 1975 to facilitate economic interchange, it has since established a parliament and a human rights court. ECOWAS has also taken on regional security responsibilities and intervened in civil wars raging in Ivory Coast, Liberia, and Sierra Leone.

Beyond any of these examples of regional IGOs, the most visible and copied is in Europe. There, the EU, with its 28 member-countries, has not only moved toward full economic integration, it has also achieved considerable political cooperation. Chapter 10 discusses the EU in much greater detail.

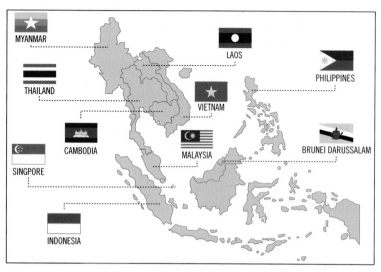

Figure 6.7 ASEAN is an IGO made up of many small states in terms of land mass; however, it is not to be underestimated. If ASEAN were a country, it would be the seventh-largest economy in the world, and by 2050 it's projected to rank as the fourth-largest economy. It is home to more than 622 million people, a larger population than the European Union or North America, and it has the third-largest labor force in the world, behind China and India.

Simulation: Intervening in Bhutan

Both regional and global IGOs face the serious challenges of accountability, enforcement, coordination of actors and activities, management of long-term projects, and quick reaction in a crisis. The issues in need of global governance defy easy categorization. Whether the global community addresses older problems like piracy and slavery or newer dynamics like those associated with climate change and cybersecurity, global governance is a complex, but critically important, set of processes. In addition, global governance must take into account the proliferation of nonstate actors—both those considered legitimate, like NGOs and multinational corporations, and those that are not, like terrorist organizations and drug traffickers.

Global governance is indeed a multilayered and multifaceted set of processes, interactions, and actors all working to shape the behavior of states and individuals in meaningful ways. And although global governance is certainly limited, global governance actors, especially organizations like the UN, can and do contribute to the development of norms and ideas, fill knowledge gaps, set and monitor goals, and shape the agenda from the global to the local. What we must continue to evaluate is the ability of IGOs to adapt, reform, and innovate as political movements continue to create obstacles in international cooperation, collective action, and multilateralism as a means to peace and prosperity.

Chapter Summary

- Current IGOs are the product of three widely accepted ideas: that humans should live in peace and mutual support, that the big powers have a special responsibility for maintaining order, and that the growth of specialized intergovernmental organizations to regulate interaction should be based on less political and more functional issues.

- The rapid growth of all types of international organizations stems from increased international contact among states and people, increased economic interdependence, the growing importance of transnational issues and political movements, the inadequacy of the state-centered system for dealing with world problems, the need for small states to gain strength by joining together, and the role model that successful IGOs provide for new organizations.

- As the number and scope of IGOs expand, they serve as increasingly important actors in global politics today, particularly in challenging as well as reinforcing the sovereign state.

- IGOs can potentially function as an interactive arena, a center for cooperation among states, an independent national actor, and at times, a supranational organization. Some observers argue that IGOs are best suited to promoting cooperation among states rather than to replacing the state-centered system. Others argue that IGOs should concentrate on performing limited functional activities in order to build a habit of cooperation and trust that later can grow. Still others claim that IGOs are vehicles of manipulation to gain national political goals.

- The UN provides an example of the development, structure, and roles of a global IGO, including peacekeeping, intervening diplomatically, imposing sanctions, promoting arms control, and supporting international law.

- Fundamentally, every IGO is an intergovernmental organization whose membership comprises two or more states. Therefore, one key element of how an IGO operates is how it structures its membership, who it includes and excludes, and why.

- In regard to voting power, IGOs use a range of voting formulas, from majority-based to weighted to unanimity voting in order to give voices to its member-states. No voting formula is more consequential and controversial than the veto power of the P5.

- Whatever the definition of the best purpose of an international organization, there must be realistic standards of evaluation. The most fruitful standard is judging an organization by what is possible rather than setting inevitably frustrating ideal goals.

Critical Thinking Questions

1. Why do states choose to organize as collectives? How does international relations theory help us to understand international cooperation and multilateralism?

2. How do IGOs function? In other words, what roles do they play in global politics? Give three specific examples, including that of the UN, in your response.

3. What are three major criticisms of the UN system? Do you find these criticisms convincing? Why or why not?

4. How do peacekeeping operations serve as an example of global governance, both its promise and its perils?

5. What advantages do regional IGOs have over global ones?

Key Terms

arrearages	international regime	P5	UN Secretariat
complex peacekeeping	League of Nations	plenary body	UN Secretary-General
European Union	limited membership	public goods	UN Security
functionalism	council	realpolitik	Council
global governance	majority voting	regime theory	UN Trusteeship
Hague Convention	Millennium Develop-	sanctions	Council
IGO secretariat	ment Goals	supermajority voting	unanimity voting
International Atomic	Montreal Protocol	supranational	United Nations
Energy Agency	neofunctionalism	organizations	Universal Declaration
intergovernmental	neoliberal	UN Charter	of Human Rights
organizations	institutionalism	UN General Assembly	weighted voting

7

War and Terrorism

The decisive and persistent role that violence continues to play in global politics is evident in the Syrian civil war, which has the dubious distinction of being the deadliest conflict of the 21st century. Conservative estimates point to over 450,000 deaths, over 1 million wounded, and over 12 million Syrians—fully half of the country's pre-war population—now displaced from their homes.[1] Sparked initially by protests against the autocratic regime of Bashir al-Assad in conjunction with the so-called "Arab Spring" in 2011, the conflict quickly escalated and intensified. Various rebel factions opposed to the Assad regime engaged in prolonged and fierce clashes with Syrian government loyalists over the course of several years, with civilians caught in the middle. Perhaps the most prominent of the anti-Assad factions was Islamic State or ISIS, which succeeded in securing a significant amount of territory within Syria at the height of the war before losing its grip on that territory in the face of counterattacks by Kurdish forces. Compounding this war has been the involvement of various external actors, such as the United States, Russia, Turkey, Iran, Saudi Arabia, and others—as well as the documented use of chemical weapons against civilian-populated rebel strongholds by the Assad regime. Ultimately, the sheer horror of this war is a stark reminder of the persistent appeal of armed conflict in global politics, and an illustration of the variable dimensions that war has taken on in the 21st century.

A Russian military police officer stands guard in the courtyard of Aleppo's oldest mosque in late 2017. As of the summer of 2019, largely due to Russian military support, Syrian President Bashar al-Assad's forces had regained control of the country after eight years of a devastating civil war that has claimed hundreds of thousands of lives and displaced roughly half of Syria's population while destroying much of the country's infrastructure.

War as a Concept

The famous Prussian military strategist Carl von Clausewitz is best known for his statement that "war is the continuation of political intercourse, with the addition of other means" (Clausewitz, 1976:605). Like politics, war is as old as humanity itself. There is an element of truth to the classic observation of sociologist Max Weber in "Politics as a Vocation" (1918): "The decisive means for politics is violence."

Given the regrettable but regular role that violence continues to play in global politics, we have no choice but to examine war and political violence. Doing so requires starting with how we define and measure war.

Defining and Measuring War

Like other aspects of global politics, war lacks a single widely accepted definition. Definitions vary in relation to how one chooses to answer questions such as what defines a "combatant" and what actions "count" as war. One of the most common definitions stems from J. David Singer and Melvin Small's Correlates of War project, originating at the University of Michigan in the early 1960s. Singer and Small focused on interstate wars, which they defined as "conflicts involving at least one member of the interstate system on each side of the war . . . [and] resulting in a total of 1,000 or more battle deaths" (1972:35). Those with fewer casualties fell under the heading of "armed conflict." Their contemporary, Lewis Richardson, took the opposite approach, building his data set around the unit of "deadly quarrels," defined as "anything which caused death to humans, including murder, banditry, mutiny, insurrection, and wars small and large" (1960).

More recent endeavors have sought to strike a middle ground. The Militarized Interstate Dispute data set (an extension of the Correlates of War project) examines interstate conflicts with fewer than 1,000 deaths and featuring some use of military force (Ghosn, Palmer, & Bremer, 2004). Sweden's University of Uppsala Conflict Data Project (UCDP), in collaboration with the Centre for the

Study of Civil War at the International Peace Research Institute in Oslo, Norway (PRIO), focuses on the unit of "armed conflict." This refers to prolonged combat between the military forces of two or more governments, or of one government and at least one organized armed group. This definition includes both interstate (war between two or more sovereign states) and intrastate (internal or civil) wars.

Additional examples of efforts to systematically study war and armed conflict exist. Some, like the International Crisis Behavior Project, avoid these definitional problems by focusing on a distinct unit of analysis: crisis rather than war (Brecher & Wilkenfeld, 2000). Others, such as the Minorities at Risk Project (housed at the Center for International Development and Conflict Management), incorporate a concern with violence including terrorism and guerrilla war as forms of political behavior used by political minorities around the world.

Classifying Warfare

There are as many ways to classify war as there are to define it. One important consideration concerns the causes of war and the intentions of those launching it. Wars of **aggression** are those that do not meet the standards embedded within the norms and laws of war (Butler, 2012a; Sagan and Valentino, 2018). In global politics, aggression is reflected in the tensions between states that produce arms races, militarized interstate disputes, and war. While there is no universally accepted definition of aggression in international law, an unprovoked military attack by one state on another is a commonly understood act of aggression.

Conversely, wars of **self-defense** involve defending oneself, one's property, or the well-being of another from harm. It can include individual self-defense, such as Kuwait's short-lived resistance to Iraq's invasion in the 1990–1991 Gulf War, or collective self-defense (coming to the defense of a country victimized by aggression), such as the United Nations (UN)–authorized, US-led military coalition that came to Kuwait's aid. One example of collective self-defense is when all members of the North Atlantic Treaty Organization (NATO) alliance responded to the 9/11 attacks on the United States by invoking Chapter V of the NATO Charter, thereby designating the attack as an attack on all of NATO's members. This was not just a symbolic act; subsequently, several NATO members (Canada, the United Kingdom, and Germany, among others) deployed significant troop contingents to Afghanistan as part of

aggression Tensions between states that produce arms races, militarized interstate disputes, and war. An unprovoked military attack by one state on another is a commonly understood act of aggression.

self-defense A measure that involves defending oneself, one's property, or the well-being of another from harm. The right of self-defense is available in many jurisdictions as a legal justification for the use of force in times of danger, but the interpretation varies widely.

Following their unprovoked invasion in September 1939, German forces sought to systematically destroy all existing symbols of the Polish state and nation. Here, German soldiers in Krakow in 1940 stand by the toppled Battle of Grunwald memorial, a monument commemorating the defeat of the Teutonic Knights by the combined forces of Poland and Lithuania in the 15th century.

a coalition force targeting the Taliban and al-Qaeda. Oftentimes in war, who is the aggressor and who is the victim is unclear, with each side claiming to act in self-defense. Indeed, Nazi Germany's brutal attack on Poland in September 1939 was presented by Adolf Hitler as an act of self-defense in response to Polish provocations!

preemption A strategy of warfare predicated on the legitimacy and desirability of using military force against an evident security threat from an adversary prior to one's own state or interests being attacked.

Wars of **preemption** illustrate the difficulties in simply categorizing a war as offensive or defensive. Preemptive policies use military force against a security threat prior to that threat fully materializing. Scholars have hotly debated whether preemptive war was justified in the aftermath of President George W. Bush's declaration in 2002 that "[t]o forestall or prevent hostile acts by our adversaries, the United States will, if necessary, act preemptively"—a key tenet of what became the "Bush Doctrine" used to justify the US invasion of Iraq in 2003. Countries have long undertaken first strikes to preempt what they believed to be an impending attack. The line between preemption as aggression (which violates international law) and preemption as self-defense (which does not) is unclear (Beard & Strayhorn, 2018). You should also note that preemptive war is different from **preventive war**, an offensive approach aimed at destroying a potential threat long before it emerges. Preventive war contrasts with preemption, which is undertaken in anticipation of an imminent attack from an adversary.

preventive war The use of offensive military force against a potential adversary in order to eliminate a perceived threat before it ever materializes.

Persistence Versus Obsolescence

The use of organized armed violence in the pursuit of interests has been a recurring feature of global politics since the dawn of time. The codification of the rules and practices of a state-based system in the Treaties of Westphalia (1648) has done little to change that. To once again paraphrase the great American writer Mark Twain, the reports of war's death are greatly exaggerated. Possibly because war is so horrific, such reports are also quite frequent. War has been declared obsolete as a result of the rise of popular sovereignty during the so-called "Age of Enlightenment" in the late 18th century, with the founding of the **Concert of Europe** (a consensual balance-of-power arrangement among the European great powers) in the aftermath of Napoleon's defeat in 1815, and amidst the convening of a series of peace conferences in the late 19th and early 20th centuries (the Hague Conferences of 1899 and 1907). The founding powers of the Concert of Europe included Austria, Prussia, the Russian Empire, and the United Kingdom—the "Quadruple Alliance" responsible for the downfall of the First French Empire. The chief function of the Concert of Europe was maintaining stability and averting major wars between and among the great powers of the Continent, while also policing skirmishes and disputes along its periphery.

Concert of Europe The balance of power arrangement in Europe from the end of the Napoleonic Wars (1815) to the outbreak of World War I (1914). The chief function was maintaining stability and averting major wars between the powers of the Continent while also policing skirmishes and disputes.

Declarations of war's obsolescence have persisted, and even expanded, during the 20th century (Mueller, 1989). The formation of not one but two international organizations (the League of Nations in 1919 and the UN in 1946) as well as numerous nongovernmental organizations dedicated to the pursuit of peace have been used to support the claim. Further supporting evidence includes the European integration process, beginning in the early 1950s, as well as multiple successive "waves" of democratization expanding the liberal

CHALLENGE YOUR ASSUMPTIONS

Are International Courts the Key to Limiting War?

International law is limited by the fact that there is no world court with full compulsory jurisdiction over states. Even so, the number and use of international tribunals and courts to adjudicate disputes has grown dramatically over the last century, especially since the end of the Cold War. As one study found, 63% of all international judicial activity (5,598 out of 8,895 cases) has occurred since 1989. The 1990s witnessed the creation of more international courts than any other decade, and the trend continues. All of this suggests an expansion of international legal authority intended to limit some of the more damaging behavior conducted by states and other actors in the global political system—especially the use of armed violence.

As an approach to limiting war, the adjudication of disputes through international courts has some advantages. The rulings of courts and tribunals impose a detailed, fixed, and final decision that the parties to the conflict may be obligated to accept—if they have expressed their willingness to do so. Submitting disputes to legal judgment by a standing international court with jurisdiction over matters related to war (e.g., the International Criminal Court) or to an ad hoc tribunal established to mete out justice in relation to a particular conflict (e.g., the Special Court for Sierra Leone or the International Criminal Tribunal for the former Yugoslavia) also provides all parties with "due process" (established, consistent, and fair legal rules, principles, precedents, and procedures). This shift also reaffirms the idea of the rule of law, which is a key to restoring order in postconflict societies and building order in global society more generally.

At the same time, a legalist approach has its disadvantages. Arbitrators and judges are typically concerned with resolving the immediate dispute. They also often are bound by a particular set of rules and processes. As a result, the immediate and major impact of most rulings and judgments extends only to the parties in the dispute rather than establishing a legal precedent that can be applied to other conflict situations. Also, adjudication is an adversarial process. Legal arguments can in some cases lead courts or arbitrators to issue "zero-sum" rulings, creating further dissatisfaction in one or more parties to the conflict.

Adjudication also clearly shifts a great deal of control to the court or arbitrator(s). While they are pledged to principles of fairness and equity, the parties to the conflict could interpret this enhanced authority as threatening. Compounding this problem is the fact that one or more of the concerned parties may not accept a relevant international court's jurisdiction (e.g., the International Court of Justice or International Criminal Court). Even in the event that the parties overcome these problems, international courts and tribunals are slow-moving, with significant delays between petition of the court and the case appearing on the docket—delays that may prompt a return to violence in heated and protracted international or intrastate conflicts.

What do you think? Are international courts and tribunals an effective tool to restrain war and conflict? Or are they, as critics claim, the epitome of utopian idealism?

"zone of peace" and supporting assertions of the "iron law" of the **democratic peace**—the notion, supported to some degree empirically, that democracies do not go to war with one another (Doyle, 1983; Levy, 1988). Those who accept this proposition view democracy promotion as the key to containing war and expanding the zone of peace. And for many, the end of the Cold War signified the dawn of a **new world order** defined by a heightened emphasis on maintaining and promoting peace, democracy, and human rights. A concept with long historical roots, the new world order here referred to a Western-led international

democratic peace The proposition, supported empirically to some degree, that democracies do not engage in war with one another. Those who accept this proposition view democracy promotion as the key to containing war and expanding the "zone of peace."

new world order An emphasis on maintaining and promoting peace, democracy, and human rights. The "new world order" referred to a Western-led international system in which particular norms and laws favored liberal democracy, civil and political rights, and market-led economic globalization.

Simulation: Preventing World War

system in which particular norms and laws favoring liberal democracy, civil and political rights, and market-led economic globalization would prevail.

Despite these apparent harbingers of peace, warfare has endured. The sudden and extensive proliferation of armed conflict unleashed in the aftermath of the Cold War quickly exposed the fallacy of triumphal proclamations of the "end of history" (Fukuyama, 1989). Though precise counts are impossible, most estimates agree that since 1990, roughly 4 million people (90% of them civilians) have died in wars, with tens of millions of people worldwide forced from their homes as a direct result of conflict (Sheehan, 2005).

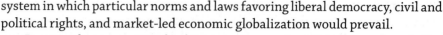

Armed Conflict: Causes and Objectives

Why war? This question has defied an easy answer for centuries (Caplow & Hicks, 2002). Philosophers, world leaders, and social scientists have advanced many different theories about the root cause of war, but there is no one single explanation. As a result, we can better understand the various causes of war by classifying them according to individual-level, state-level, and system-level analysis. It was precisely this concern with classification that motivated one of the earliest applications of the levels-of-analysis approach, in Kenneth Waltz' landmark work *Man, the State, and War* (1959). We apply that approach here in the service of answering that difficult and important question.

Individual Level

Waltz began his analysis with what he called the "first image." This explanation considers war to be a form of behavior resulting from an individual's choice. The choice to go to war is very much a by-product of human nature and the capacity, and sometimes favorable attitudes, that humans have toward violence against others in self-defense or for personal gain.

HUMAN CHARACTERISTICS. One version of this perspective is that a penchant for violence is something that political leaders, soldiers, and citizens alike share since it is intrinsic to human beings. Proponents of this view agree that while human behavior may be predominantly learned, there are also behavioral links to our primal origins (Rosen, 2004). Territoriality is one such possible instinct, and the fact that territorial disputes are frequent causes of war may point to some instinctual territoriality in humans (Vasquez, 1995). Another possibility is that human aggression, individually or collectively, can stem from stress, anxiety, or frustration (Senese, 2005). The backlash of German society during the 1930s to its defeat and humiliation after World War I in the 1920s is an example.

INDIVIDUAL LEADERS. The personality traits of leaders are also an individual level factor that can help explain the continued appeal of war (Bennett & Stam, 2004). A leader may have a personality that favors taking risks or might have a psychological need for power. Despite the many brutal atrocities carried out on his orders during the Syrian civil war, Bashar al-Assad is generally considered quite pragmatic, rational, and largely motivated by maintaining and expanding his power—hardly traits unique among world leaders. Individual experiences and emotions also play a role, and so one could ask what impact Iraq's attempt to assassinate former President George H. W. Bush in 1993 had on his son's view of and approach to that country and its leader, Saddam Hussein, once George W. Bush became president in 2001.

State Level

Not satisfied with an explanation for war resting entirely on individual factors, Waltz introduced an alternative explanation pointing to the state and the society it governs—what he referred to as the "second image." This explanation rests on the premise that nation-states are the dominant actors in global politics, with their interests and associated policies often accounting for the outbreak of war.

STATECRAFT.   The use and threatened use of military force has long been and remains the ultimate tool for states to use in the pursuit of their interests known as the practice of statecraft. It is a tool that the leaders of nearly all states have and employ regardless of regime type, level of economic development, geographic location, population size, and various other factors that might otherwise set them apart (Hewitt, Wilkenfeld, & Gurr, 2010; Huff & Schub, 2018; Rosato, 2003). The ability and willingness of states to initiate armed conflict of their own choosing, with few obstacles to restrain them, is a long-standing feature of the anarchy defining the international system.

MILITARISM.   The internal processes and conditions of countries may lead to war (Finnemore, 2004). This is particularly true when a country promotes **militarism**, the belief that a country should maintain a strong military capability and be prepared to use it to defend its national interests. The argument here is that as the persistence and expansion of warfare requires more soldiers, as well as more sophisticated and increasingly more expensive weapons, it creates a need for political units with larger populations and economies. This in turn creates a further need for professional standing armies and sophisticated military arsenals. In this view, militarism and the state are two sides of the same coin, and they have been since the emergence of the state as a dominant political unit and actor (Mann, 1993).

> **militarism** The belief or desire of a government or people that a country should maintain a strong military capability and be prepared to use it aggressively to defend or promote national interests.

DIVERSION.   The **diversionary theory of war** holds that a faltering government may attempt to stay in power by instigating a foreign crisis in order to rally the populace and divert its attention (Foster & Palmer, 2006; Kellett, 2006; Meernik & Ault, 2005; Pickering & Kisangani, 2005; Tir & Jasinski, 2008). This scenario is sometimes referred to as "wagging the dog," a phrase borrowed from the 1997 Hollywood film of the same name depicting the efforts of political spin-doctors to drum up the case for war with Albania in order to distract the US public from a presidential sex scandal (a scenario not unlike

> **diversionary theory of war** A thesis that a war is instigated by a country's leadership in order to distract its population from their own domestic strife.

Argentine military officers pay tribute to that nation's soldiers who died in the 1982 Falklands/Malvinas War with the United Kingdom on the 33rd anniversary of the war in April 2015. The war remains a source of contention between the two states as well as a prominent example of "diversionary war" for both sides.

what occurred a year later with President Bill Clinton and Kosovo). Systematic studies offer fuller support for this idea. For instance, transitional democracies or revolutionary regimes frequently consolidate their power by inciting tension with other countries (Andrade, 2003; Mansfield & Snyder, 1995; Mitchell & Prins, 2004). Countries are also more likely to go to war while they are experiencing times of economic distress. Political analysts believed, for example, that Argentina's decision to seize the nearby Falkland (Malvinas) Islands in 1982 was an attempt by Argentina's faltering military regime to divert the attention of its people away from a sagging economy (Oakes, 2006).

offensive realism An explanation of war and armed conflict in international relations rooted in the realist appreciation of states, power, and anarchy. Offensive realists contend that war is a result of the inherently aggressive tendencies of states and their leaders, who capitalize on the condition of anarchy and purposefully choose war as a tool of advancing their interests and amassing greater power.

defensive realism An explanation of war and conflict in international relations rooted in the realist appreciation of states, power, and anarchy. Defensive realists contend that war is a by-product of the anarchic nature of the international system: States and their leaders typically do not choose war, but the mutual and sometimes incompatible quest for security by states inherently produces armed conflict.

System Level

Waltz also pointed out that a number of factors related to the world's political system may also cause wars. In the "third image," or what we call the systemic level of analysis, war is the by-product of the global system's structure and the ways in which that structure binds, shapes, and limits states and other actors subsumed within it. We can view this structure, which the prevailing distribution of power at a given point in time largely determines, as providing aggressive states with opportunities for wars of discretion in the pursuit of interests and expansion (**offensive realism**). From this perspective, anarchy rewards the inherently aggressive tendencies of states and their leaders, who capitalize on it and purposefully choose war as a tool for advancing their interests and amassing greater power. Likewise, the anarchic structure of the system can be seen as creating an environment in which war is endemic and extremely difficult to avoid even for states who do not seek it and merely wish to ensure their own survival (**defensive realism**). From this perspective, states and their leaders typically do not choose war, but the mutual and sometimes incompatible quest for security by states inherently produces armed conflict (Bartelson, 2016). To illustrate some of the ways in which the structure of the global political system produces war, we touch on three system-level variables here.

THE DISTRIBUTION OF POWER.   As discussed in Chapter 3, some scholars believe that factors such as the system's number of poles (big powers), their relative power, and whether the poles and their power are stable or in flux influence the system's stability (Powell, 2006). Conflict is likely to occur when a system is experiencing a significant power transition because some powers are rising and others are declining. The onset of World War I was in part about the attempt of the declining Austro-Hungarian Empire to defend its fading status as a big power. Similarly, the outbreak of World War II can be explained by rapidly rising powers—Nazi Germany and Imperial Japan—challenging the status quo in the international balance of power. The Cold War between the United States and the USSR (and their allies) following World War II proved to be a relatively stable order, in that it didn't produce direct conflict between the two superpowers.

THE ANARCHIC NATURE OF THE SYSTEM.   In some sense, wars occur because there is nothing to prevent them. Unlike the case in most domestic societies, the global system has no regularized and effective process of law creation, enforcement, or adjudication. Thus, when Russia sought to extend its influence in eastern Ukraine during the spring and summer of 2014, it did so by introducing irregular military forces (militias and paramilitaries) despite the warnings of the United States and the European Union (EU) against it. Not surprisingly, a low-level conflict not only erupted in the region but persists. The "self-help" nature of this anarchic system, in which states are ultimately responsible for their own security and survival, also causes insecurity through escalating arms races and heightened tensions and rivalries that sometimes produce war—a dynamic known as the "security dilemma," which Chapter 8 discusses in detail.

This famous photo of Winston Churchill (left), Harry Truman (middle), and Josef Stalin (right) from the Potsdam Conference represents the last major summit of the "Big Three" Allied powers (the United Kingdom, United States, and USSR, respectively) in the waning days of World War II. This wartime alliance quickly fractured along ideological lines, ushering in a half-century of tense confrontation known as the Cold War.

SYSTEM-LEVEL RESOURCE AND ECONOMIC FACTORS.   The global pattern of production and use of natural resources is another system-level factor that can cause conflict. For example, when Iraq endangered the world's oil supply by attacking Kuwait and threatening Saudi Arabia in 1990, a US-led coalition of countries that were dependent on that resource rushed to defend the Saudis and to liberate the Kuwaitis and secure access to their oil.

The gap between wealthy and poor countries is another system-level factor, playing out through both absolute and **relative deprivation**. Whereas absolute deprivation can be understood as an objective condition, relative deprivation is exactly that—a relative condition wherein one gauges what they do not have by comparing themselves with others who are better off. Relative deprivation is enhanced in scenarios where information about disparities in wealth and standards of living becomes more widely available to those who are relatively worse off. Some analysts believe that this extensive economic inequality is one reason that a great deal of terrorism is rooted among states and societies in

relative deprivation A condition wherein one gauges what they do not have by comparing themselves with others who are materially better off.

which the negative impacts of that inequality are evident and profoundly felt (Piazza, 2006).

WAR'S CONTINUED APPEAL.   Before leaving our discussion of the causes of war, it is important to note that whatever its root cause(s), war continues as a political instrument at least in part because it works. Countries that threaten or attack another country sometimes get their way. Big powers win more often than not, whether they begin a war or another country attacks them. Moreover, states, especially more powerful ones, confront few if any meaningful obstacles to employing force in the pursuit of interests. Thus, to some degree, the decision to go to war is a rational process, one in which countries decide that the ever-present risks of war are worth the potential gains that victory will bring (Langlois & Langlois, 2006).

There are also many armed conflicts around the world that fall short of what most people would generally define as "war." These conflicts are often waged by nonstate actors, sometimes against states but also against other nonstate actors. It is important to keep the distinction between war and lower-level armed conflicts and episodes of political violence in mind as we discuss the material in this chapter and the next.

🌐 Global Trends in Armed Conflict

Major changes in the structure and conduct of global politics since the end of World War II, and especially the end of the Cold War, have brought about equally major changes in armed conflict. These changes are reflected in the incidence, distribution, types, and intensity of contemporary armed conflict.

These changes are evident in current examples of armed conflict such as the Syrian civil war. Like the vast majority of contemporary conflicts, the Syrian civil war is an intrastate conflict fought over political authority by largely irregular military forces and defined by frequent egregious atrocities committed against civilians. Though it is an outlier in terms of its scope, the Syrian civil war is strongly representative of many of the trends in armed conflict (see Jones 2017; Uzonyi & Hanania, 2017).

Incidence

Although difficult to quantify, some estimates point to the occurrence of at least 14,000 wars throughout recorded history, killing over 3 billion people (Sheehan, 2008). As Map 7.1 demonstrates, armed conflicts remain prominent in the global system.

TIME (HISTORICAL TRAJECTORY).   Armed conflict of all types increased by a factor of three during the period 1960–1992 (Human Security Centre, 2010). However, this increase can be largely attributed to colonialism (wars of national liberation) and the Cold War rivalry (proxy wars), neither of which is relevant today. In some cases, the end of the bipolar rivalry of the Cold War helped bring

CNN Video: Syrian
Civil War

Map 7.1   This map from the Uppsala Conflict Data Program (UCDP) depicts the status of armed conflict for the year 2016, during which there were over 50 ongoing armed conflicts, as compared to 30 in 2010. An "armed conflict" is defined by the UCDP as a contested incompatibility featuring the use of armed force between two parties resulting in at least 25 battle-related deaths in one calendar year. If more than 1,000 battle-related deaths are recorded in one calendar year, the conflict is considered to have reached the intensity of "war."

about resolution of numerous long-standing civil conflicts around the world, such as those in Namibia, Angola, and Cambodia. Democratic transitions in the former Soviet bloc, while often difficult, helped dampen some of the conflicts involving these states and republics.

The end of the Cold War had a restraining effect on armed conflict. Empirical data suggest that the outbreak of new armed conflicts each year, either between or within states, is in steep decline, as Figure 7.1 depicts. Since 1990, there have been only six instances of direct wars between states: the Persian Gulf War (1990–1991) and its aftermath, Eritrea–Ethiopia (1998–2000), India–Pakistan (1997–2003 and 2014), Iraq versus the United States and its allies (2003), Djibouti–Eritrea (2008), and Russia-Ukraine (2014–2017). The diminishing likelihood of interstate war since the end of the Cold War is an historical trend. This trend is not only evident in the UCDP/PRIO armed conflict data set, but is also reflected in other research on political violence (Center for Systemic

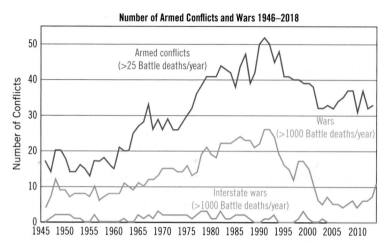

Figure 7.1 There has been a steady decline in the number of international conflicts, especially wars of greater intensity in terms of battle-deaths per year and wars between states (interstate wars), since the end of the Cold War. (Source: Data from Uppsala Conflict Data Programme/Peace Research Institute Oslo.)

Peace, 2017; Goldstein, 2011; Holsti, 1996; Marshall & Gurr, 2005; Mueller, 2004). This decline is magnified by the fact that the total number of states have significantly increased during the same time period.

SPACE (REGIONAL DISPERSION). The geographic distribution of armed conflicts (see Figure 7.2) shows great consistency over time. Asia and sub-Saharan Africa have long been and remain by far the most war-torn regions, followed by the Middle East and North Africa, Europe, and the Americas. Still, conflict in general across all regions is in decline.

The enduring legacy of colonialism in both Asia and Africa can explain greater conflict in these regions. Throughout the 1950s, 1960s, and early 1970s, colonial powers waged wars to try to retain their colonial holdings (sometimes referred to as "extrastate" wars). Though colonialism no longer formally exists, numerous wars persist today both between and within states as a consequence of the political instability and economic underdevelopment that are often the legacy of colonialism.

Type

While interstate wars are in steep decline, armed conflict is increasingly likely to take place within a state's boundaries, as Figure 7.3 shows.

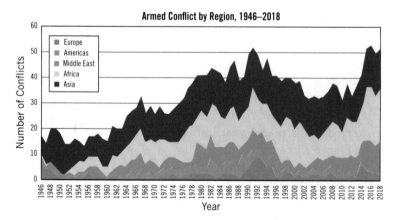

Figure 7.2 Armed conflicts since the end of World War II have been heavily concentrated in Asia, Africa, and the Middle East, while Europe and the Americas have been (relatively) more peaceful regions. (Source: Data from Uppsala Conflict Data Programme/Peace Research Institute Oslo.)

INTERSTATE AND INTRASTATE. According to the UCDP, the overwhelming number of wars since the end of the Cold War have been intrastate in nature, as have the associated deaths associated with war (Melander, Pettersson, & Themnér, 2016). However, two qualifications are in order. First, it is important to recognize that an increasing number of intrastate wars are internationalized—meaning that they also feature the involvement of one or more external actors (state or nonstate). Thus, we can loosely categorize the dominant mode of armed conflict today as "globalized civil war."

The involvement of global powers (the United States and Russia), regional powers (Saudi Arabia and Iran), and nonstate actors (jihadists and humanitarian nongovernmental organizations alike) in the Syrian civil war is a perfect example. Likewise, the majority of intrastate or civil conflicts are protracted. The outbreak of new internal conflicts has been and remains low.

Intensity

Assessing the intensity of contemporary armed conflict again returns us to the question of how one defines war. One of the prevailing standards for distinguishing war revolves around the occurrence of 1,000 (or more) battle deaths as a direct result of the

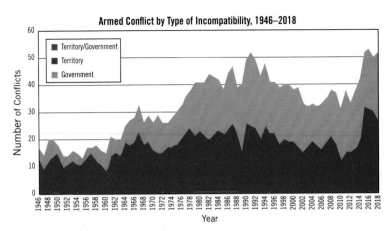

Figure 7.3   The vast majority of armed conflicts since the end of World War II have been intrastate (internal to a state). While some of these conflicts feature the involvement of outside states or nonstate actors (being "internationalized"), over time the number of wars occurring between states (interstate) has been and remains in steep decline. (Source: Data from Uppsala Conflict Data Programme/Peace Research Institute Oslo.)

conflict, either in general or annually. Though problematic, this remains a predominant benchmark in the field, with those falling short of that target earning alternative designations such as "armed conflict," "low-intensity conflict," "militarized interstate dispute," and the like. If we accept this definitional starting point, the track record since 1945 shows that armed conflicts falling short of war—in this case, conflicts resulting in fewer than 1,000 battle deaths within a given calendar year—have been and remain much more frequent occurrences than those meeting or surpassing that criterion.

Measuring intensity when studying armed conflict is a tricky business. One would be hard-pressed to imagine any armed conflict that is not intense. Still, one would not likely equate the intensity of the US invasion of Grenada in 1983 with that of World War II or the Vietnam War. Assessing aggregate patterns of armed conflict requires one to introduce ways of gauging the intensity of the violence. One proxy measure for this is the number of people directly killed in and by armed conflicts. As Figure 7.4 shows, state-based conflict continues to account for the vast majority of fatalities in armed conflict, compared to much more modest death tolls resulting from violence by governments against

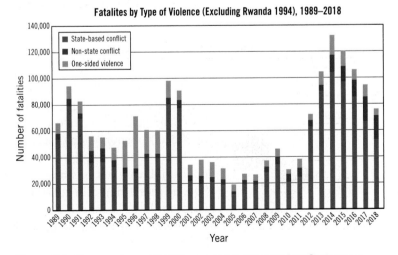

Figure 7.4   The resurgence of fatalities associated with armed conflict in recent years is explained largely by the outbreak of major state-based conflicts, including in eastern Ukraine and especially Syria. (Source: Data from Uppsala Conflict Data Programme/Peace Research Institute Oslo.)

civilians (one-sided violence) or violence waged by nonstate actors such as terrorist groups (Melander et al., 2016). Yet from the standpoint of intensity, by virtue of the fact that they usually do not involve the mass mobilization of the entire society or the employment of the technologically sophisticated military arsenal of the world's great powers, the aggregate level of sustained violence tends to be less.

Other Patterns and Trends

The preceding reveals a mixed picture of warfare as something generally in decline yet still vitally important to global politics. These aggregate patterns and trends aside, it is also the case that warfare has changed in qualitative terms over the centuries. Technological advances, the infusion of nationalism, the changing scope and costs of war, and innovations in strategy are each areas in which the very nature of war itself has changed.

Technology has rapidly escalated the ability to kill. There have been "advances" in the ability to manufacture weapons with a staggering capacity to destroy, as well as in the ability to deliver those weapons at increasing distances and speed. These advances impact the delivery and development of weapons-related products that do not attract notice, such as gunpowder and the internal combustion engine, as well as those that occupy a prominent position in global political discourse, such as nuclear fission/fusion and intercontinental ballistic missiles. More recently, the infusion of cutting-edge scientific and technological advances in the areas of robotics and artificial intelligence into warfare has resulted in new classes and categories of weaponry, such as unmanned aerial vehicles (drones) featuring highly destructive capabilities but involving little risk to those employing them.

Nationalism has also qualitatively changed warfare. Before the 19th century, the houses of nobles generally fought wars with limited armies. The American (1776) and French (1789) Revolutions, along with the era of popular sovereignty and mass politics that followed, changed that. The revolutionary French state declared that military service was a patriotic duty and instituted the first comprehensive military draft in 1793. The idea of patriotic military service, coupled with the draft, allowed France's army to be the first to number more than a million persons. Subsequently, in the 19th and 20th centuries, nation-states mostly fought each other in interstate wars, with increases in intensity and in numbers involved as entire societies mobilized in service of the war effort (a phenomenon that we sometimes refer to as "total war").

The scope and cost of war have expanded as a result of technology and nationalism. Entire nations have become increasingly involved in wars. Before 1800, no more than 3 in 1,000 people of a country participated in a war. By World War I, the European powers called 1 of every 7 people to arms. Technology increased the need to mobilize the population for industrial production and also increased the capacity for—and the rationality of—striking at civilians. Nationalism made war a movement of the masses, increasing their stake and also providing justification for attacking the enemy nation (Mann, 1993). One result is the blurred distinction between military and civilian targets. Modern technology has also reversed the connection between war effort and the nation, largely separating the war effort from the daily lives of citizens (Wood, 2016).

War as an endeavor has always been and remains costly, both in terms of blood and treasure. Preparations, waging war, and repairing the damage have always been expensive, but the increasing technological sophistication of war and military arsenals has in some ways escalated these costs. This is true not only with respect to the staggering financial costs of waging and preparing for war but also in human terms, given the potentially high death and casualty tolls that high-tech weaponry can inflict. While proponents of such innovations in weaponry argue that they are likely to correspond with greater precision and therefore reduced deaths and casualties (especially for the state employing them), their destructive capacity remains great.

The Changing Context of War

The changing context of war is illustrated in Syria, a conflict with deep roots dating to the contentious rule of Hafez al-Assad (the father of the country's current President, Bashar al-Assad) from 1971 until his death in 2000. Social and economic tensions related to and fostered by identity group politics were used by Assad's Syrian Ba'athist Party as a means of attracting popular support and consolidating power (Yassin-Kassab & Al-Shami, 2016). These underlying grievances propelled the country over the brink into full-on civil war in the spring and summer of 2011. They also explained the numerous competing factions among the opposition to the Assad regime throughout the war, especially during its peak years. (see Map 7.2).

The unraveling of state control over warfare, as seen in the Syrian civil war (among others), has prompted scholars to question the utility of "standard theoretical devices of international politics" for explaining contemporary warfare (Holsti, 1996:25; see also Henderson & Singer, 2002). Most wars today reflect a "new pattern of conflict" defined by "challenges to existing state authority" rather than territory or other conventional national interests (Wallensteen & Axell, 1994:345). The defining theme is the lack of centralized state control over the prosecution of war.

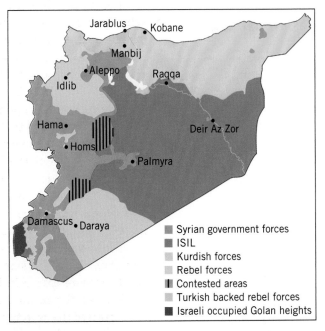

Map 7.2 Factionalism in Syrian civil war, 2017. Map 7.2 depicts the entrenched divisions among the various factions of the Syrian civil war—arrayed around identity and ideological divisions exacerbated by political elites, supported by outside parties, and distributed in a patchwork territorial quilt around the country.

"Old" Wars: Origins and Logic

By the late 1990s, a number of scholars of conflict and security studies responded to perceived changes in the nature of global politics by

"new" wars Identity-fueled, intrastate conflicts that are waged by a wide range of official and irregular combatants and are sustained and fueled by remittances, organized crime, and transnational networks moving money, arms, and people.

"old" wars Wars fought by and through the state and its organized, professional, standing armies in pursuit of the national interest. Key distinctions typifying the "modern" state (disaggregated civil and military authority, distinctions between combatants and noncombatants, etc.) shaped the conduct of such wars.

introducing the conceptual device of **"new" wars**—intrastate or intrasocietal conflicts often fought by irregular armed forces, in an absence of state authority, caused and sustained by global and transnational forces. Assertions of "new" wars implicitly assume that contemporary conflict is somehow different than before. In the view of proponents of this thesis, **"old" wars**—those fought by states, between standing professional armed forces loyal to the state, often over territory or other material gain—originated in a specific place and era (Western Europe in the 18th and 19th centuries). "Old" wars were the by-product of a metamorphosis that transformed war from a feudal endeavor to a thoroughly modern one (Kaldor, 1999). Whereas armed conflict was once a contest of honor and skill as well as a display of power that vassals launched at the behest of monarchs and waged through the proxy of knights and mercenaries (think *Game of Thrones*), modernity brought armed conflict under the control of the state.

The state's centrality in the global political system is closely tied to this "old" form of warfare. Consider the formation of professional standing armies to wage war, the establishment of permanent taxation systems to fund those armies and their military campaigns, the introduction of the convention of *raison d'etat* ("reason of state") as a justification for war, or the promulgation of rules attempting to govern the conduct of war. These are all characteristics of "old" warfare (evident in such widely chronicled conflicts as World War I) that we take for granted today, but which did not exist prior to consolidation of the modern state (Mann, 1992).

The historical association between the state and war has been so extensive (and mutually reinforcing) that "old" wars were considered mere exercises in statecraft, along the lines of that which the famous 19th-century Prussian

Postcard from a series on the "Armies of the European War of 1914." As depicted here, the French Army included not only various units from France itself but also contingents drawn (willingly or otherwise) from France's African colonies in Morocco and Senegal as well as the Administrative Department of Algeria—all enlisted to fight on behalf of the French state in World War I.

Clausewitz, War, and Realism

The noted war theorist Bernard Brodie once said that *On War,* written between 1816 and 1830 by 19th-century Prussian military strategist Carl von Clausewitz and published posthumously in 1832, was "not simply the greatest, but the only truly great book on war" (in Clausewitz, 1976:53). Clausewitz's belief that war is nothing more than a continuation of policy by other means is a vital illustration of, and contribution to, realist thought.

On War contains two essential and related themes concerning the political character of war and the very nature of warfare itself. These themes are enduring reflections of political realism in light of their emphasis on states, interests, and power. Concerning the political character of war, Clausewitz insisted that war only originates in politics, and that consequently, policy will determine the character of war. This means that the calculation of interests by statespersons, along with their determination that war is the best option for securing those interests, are what determines whether and when war happens or does not. The onus on the state, the pursuit of interests, and the assumption of states as rational actors in Clausewitz's logic are clearly consistent with, and reflective of, realist thinking.

With respect to the nature of war, Clausewitz insisted that while the particular objectives of wars vary by situation, the purpose of war is always to impose one's will on the adversary—in other words, to compel the enemy to submit. Accordingly, he contended that war has both objective ("abstract war") and subjective ("real war") facets. While war as a form of social behavior possesses some qualities that are common across time and space,

Clausewitz was quick to point out that the actual prosecution of any war depends on the political aims it seeks and the calculations of the political leaders seeking those aims. Again, the emphasis on power and coercion as well as the guiding hand of the state—all central to the realist worldview—are quite clear.

Clausewitz tied these two insights about the purpose and nature of war together in the concept of the "remarkable trinity" (see figure below). In thinking about when, how, and whether states opt for war in pursuit of their interests, he argued that "real war"—that is, war as it is actually fought—is always governed by the volatile mix of passion, chance, creativity, and reason. Clausewitz and the many scholars that he influenced have extended the remarkable trinity to provide an account for war as a phenomenon produced by the aligned (and sometimes competing) impulses of the people, the armed forces, and the government. This triangular relationship remains one of Clausewitz most oft-cited contributions to the study of war and statecraft.

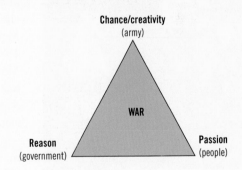

strategist Carl von Clausewitz described (see the *Thinking Theoretically* feature). Cleverly inverting Clausewitz's view, China's Premier Zhou Enlai in 1954 referred to diplomacy as "a continuation of war by other means."[2]

"New" Wars: Origins and Logic

The archetype of the "old" war held that wars were the product of rational calculation. Political leaders used the machinery of the state to deploy military force against similarly organized opponents in a contest over competing national interests (Rice, 1988). By contrast, "new" wars are identity-fueled and chaotically disorganized conflicts waged by a range of combatants. Such conflicts are likely to be carried out by actors other than states, to have root causes other than traditional national interests, and to feature tactics other than those associated with regular, professionalized armies (Harding, 1994; Kaldor, 1999). They are sustained by **remittances** (monetary transfers abroad from a foreign worker to an individual in their home country), organized crime, and transnational networks moving money, arms, and people (Shaw, 1999). In "new" wars such as those in Bosnia-Herzegovina, Nagorno-Karabakh, Sierra Leone, Afghanistan, and Syria (to name a few), armed conflict is advanced without much regard for separation between internal and external political and social realms, public and private goods and activities, civilian and military authority, or even between states of "war" and "peace" (Azar, 1990; Brown, 1996; Münkler, 2004).

remittances A transfer of money by an expatriate to persons in his or her home country.

So-called "new" wars feature clashes between identity groups fueled by transnational flows of money, weapons, and combatants. One of the best examples of a "new" war occurred in Bosnia-Herzegovina amidst the breakup of Yugoslavia in the 1990s. This photo shows members of perhaps the most infamous of many paramilitaries and militias active in that conflict—the 'Serb Volunteer Guard.' Also known as 'Arkan's Tigers,', the SVG were led by Željko Ražnatović (a.k.a. 'Arkan', pictured holding a tiger), a career criminal who led the Tigers through a ruinous campaign of murder and plunder in Bosnia and Croatia.

GLOBALIZATION AS CATALYST. Why are "new" wars happening now? They are at least partly a result of the way that globalization has transformed society. While globalization obviously did not begin with the end of the Cold War, the intensity of the current wave of globalization has proven a catalyst for "new" wars. The increasingly easy and unregulated flow of goods, services, capital, people, and ideas has proven destabilizing to patterns of life in some societies. This has unleashed a backlash in some quarters against globalization's perceived beneficiaries. Scholars have characterized this backlash as "Jihad vs. McWorld" (Barber, 1996), a "clash of civilizations" (Huntington, 1996), or "globalization and its discontents" (Stiglitz, 2002). More recently, vehement and vocal opposition to globalization has become a rallying cry for the alt-right. But how, specifically, does globalization create the conditions for "new" wars? Theorists make the link through two closely related "crises."

The first crisis stems from states' increasing inability to maintain control over domestic affairs. This diminished control leaves the state (and especially weak states) struggling to contend with the effects of globalization and transnationalism on commerce, health, migration, the environment, and even military affairs, to name a few. The inability of an increasing number of states to cope with the disruptive and seemingly haphazard processes of globalization only supports the perception of millions of individuals that globalization is threatening—leaving them feeling insecure. At the very point when state capacity is most pivotal, the inefficacy of many states has become more apparent.

At the same time, some scholars believe that "new" wars produce a second "crisis"—one fueled by a **particularistic identity politics**, in which one's political identity becomes totalizing and exclusionary, thereby turning politics into a zero-sum contest between different identity groups (Kaldor, 1999). The manipulation of group identity by elites has always been an important consideration with respect to war, but it has become especially prominent in the midst of the chaotic violence and lawlessness of "new" wars. In such circumstances, extreme group loyalties become crucial factors in promoting the use of violence in relation to real or perceived grievances.

"New" wars are violent reactions to the perceived destabilization of globalization in which the social-psychological distinctions of "in-group" and "out-group" take over a society and trigger and sustain intercommunal violence (Druckman, 1994). This happens between and among ethnic, religious, linguistic, and other groups. These distinctions are often rooted in deep-seated historical and cultural grievances (real or imagined) sustained through a mix of exaltation (of the in-group's honor, past, and traditions), demonization (of the out-group's motives and actions), and the manufacturing of a sense of perpetual threat (Stein, 2001).

We should not overlook the extent to which the twin crises of the state and identity are mutually reinforcing, at least in the view of "new" war theorists. With the capacity of all states (and particularly weak states) exposed by globalization, the decline of personal loyalty to the nation-state further undermines state capacity and, by extension, national cohesion. In such a context, it is natural that individuals look to other sources for both security and identity reinforcement—or, perhaps more accurately, are encouraged to do so by opportunistic political and social elites. In this way, ethnic, religious, or other so-called **primordial identities** (identities thought to be "hard wired" and intrinsic to a person, and thus permanent and unchanging) serve as appealing replacements for national identity.

WAGING AND SUSTAINING "NEW" WARS.   In "new" wars, the basic calculus of warfare in terms of strategy and tactics is also transformed. That is not to say that "new" wars lack a political dimension. We often associate "new" wars with an effort by substate groups (with transnational support networks) to contest, hijack, or weaken the state's authority. In strategic terms, however, the employment of violence in "new" wars veers drastically from the pursuit of traditional political or military objectives. Instead, "new" wars are advanced and shaped by the desire of combatants to sow and reap the gains of fear and hatred associated with radical identity politics. Combatants engaged in "new" wars are unified in the pursuit of political power and economic gain, and they are roundly dismissive of unifying ideologies, restraints on the use of force, or concerns with perceived political legitimacy. Rather than a tool to advance the national interest, violence in "new" wars is both the means to an end and an end unto itself.

particularistic identity politics A zero-sum conception of political identity that tends to generate fragmentation and intercommunal violence along national, ethnic, religious, or linguistic lines. Identity politics employed by elites to consolidate power through zealous appeals to one identity group and derogation of the "other."

primordial identities The view of some political and social theorists that a given identity may be deeply embedded or "hardwired" in a person's consciousness. Such identities override other possible sources of identity, which can produce extreme intolerance and violence toward members of other identity groups.

Targeting civilians, systematic campaigns of rape and sexual violence, profiteering and mercenary activity, and forced population displacement (depicted here) are all features of the long-running internal conflict in the Democratic Republic of the Congo. This conflict, which began with the fall of long-time dictator Mobutu Sese Seko in 1997, is often referred to as "Africa's World War" due to the involvement of a multitude of other states and nonstate actors.

The chief point of departure for "new" wars is that the combatants' interests and the source of mobilization are one and the same: the defense and advancement of one's own group and the weakening, if not destruction, of the much-demonized "'other." In "new" wars, population displacement, massacres, widespread and systematic human rights violations, and organized criminal activity transform from ancillary outcomes to deliberate war strategies.

A combination of paramilitaries, mercenaries, organized crime syndicates, and various other irregular forces substitute for standing, professionalized, hierarchically organized state armies. These irregular forces straddle and intentionally blur the distinction between combatants and noncombatants, both because they don't neatly fit into such categories and because they wish to actively target members of both categories in the "out-group(s)." The object of "new" war violence is typically not the corresponding irregular forces of other competing groups, but civilians (Snow, 1996). As a result, rules governing the conduct of war embodied in various international treaties and conventions (e.g., the Geneva Conventions) are routinely and grossly violated. In the process, core distinctions at the heart of "modern" society and "old" wars—such as that between combatants and noncombatants—are stretched to the point of irrelevance (Berdal, 2003).

"New" wars are sustained by the globalization of arms production and trade, transnational organized criminal activity, and financial remittances drawn from transnational communities of exiles and other supporters. The (often illegal) movement of weapons and money into conflict zones is relatively easy in a deregulated system of global trade and finance. At the same time, the basis of "new" wars in clashing identities serves as a natural animus for recruiting, fundraising, and propagandizing along such networks, wherever émigré and refugee communities with strong kin loyalties flourish. Combatants are drawn from all quarters of the globe and are relatively easy to recruit and move into and out of conflict zones using the channels of transnational (oftentimes diaspora) networks (Jung, 2003). Some of these defining characteristics of "new" wars are also evident features of another important type of political violence: terrorism.

Video: The Intricate Economics of Terrorism.

Asymmetric Warfare: Terrorism

Despite the low odds for the vast majority of the world's population of being directly impacted by terrorism, it remains an important instrument of political violence. And the huge gap between the likelihood of experiencing terrorism and the fear of experiencing it is precisely what makes terrorism so important. The spectacle of carnage associated with terrorist activities, filtered through the lens of a 24-hour news cycle and various forms of social media, is a major part of terrorism's impact, explaining why the most prominent terrorist organizations in recent years, such as ISIS and al-Qaeda, have focused so extensively on communications and publicity.

Terrorism Is a Failed Brand.

As the Nobel Prize–winning psychologist Daniel Kahneman (2011) notes, the extreme—and extremely vivid—images of death and destruction associated with terrorist attacks, reinforced by media attention and frequent conversation, cause individuals to exaggerate the probability of such events. In fact, most scholars of terrorism agree that by definition, terrorism is an act of political violence designed to instill fear in a large target population far beyond and apart from those individuals who are directly wounded or killed in any attack (Hoffman, 2006). In this way, terrorism is a highly effective example of **asymmetric warfare**, a specific and targeted use of organized violence by a weaker actor against a stronger one. This aspect of terrorism is a crucial component of any current or historical example of terrorism.

asymmetric warfare A strategy of conflict employed by a weaker actor in contending with a stronger one, in an attempt to "level the playing field." Terrorism is the most commonly cited example of asymmetric warfare.

The overall prominence of terrorism is reflected, in part, by the overlap between the transnational terrorist group ISIS and the Syrian civil war. Certainly, the start of the conflict had nothing to do with ISIS, which did not exist as such at the time, and everything to do with the Assad regime's brutal crackdown on protests in early 2011 as part of the Arab Spring. Yet like other transnational terrorist groups such as al-Qaeda and its affiliates, ISIS thrives on identifying and operating in what some scholars call "ungoverned spaces" (Clunan & Trinkunas, 2010). As such, given the void of authority created by the initial revolt against the Assad government by largely secular opponents, the leaders of what would become ISIS saw an

One of the deadliest terrorist attacks in the United States since September 11, 2001 took place in June 2016, when an assailant armed with an assault rifle and handgun opened fire at Pulse, a nightclub in Orlando, Florida. Forty-nine people were killed and more than 50 injured before law enforcement officers shot and killed the assailant, identified as Omar Mateen. During the course of the attack, Mateen pledged allegiance to ISIS and claimed the attack was in retaliation for US airstrikes in Iraq and Syria.

opportunity to build a stronghold in Syria from which it could advance its radical and violent agenda.

Definition and Scope

One of the main challenges of examining terrorism is that it defies efforts to define it. The failure of the international community to come up with a single agreed-upon definition of terrorism has impeded treaty development and other collaborative efforts to combat it—all while the scope and impact of terrorism have grown.

terrorism A form of political violence carried out by individuals, nongovernmental organizations, or covert government agents or units that specifically targets civilians using clandestine methods.

SEEKING A DEFINITION. Comprehensive efforts to combat terrorism by the UN and other international and national actors have failed, in part, because of disagreements over what defines a terrorist group or its activities. These differences occur across states (US and UK government definitions vary widely, for instance) and even between and among governmental agencies within states (various agencies of the US government employ different definitions). On the global stage, many non-Western states argue that violent struggles for national liberation against occupation should be considered legitimate activity, not terrorism. Such differences of opinion help explain disagreements over how to categorize groups such as the Palestinian Liberation Organization or the African National Congress in the past, or groups such as the Kurdistan Workers Party or Hezbollah more recently (Law, 2009). Terrorism is certainly in the eye of the beholder.

Despite this lack of consensus on which groups "count," the activity of terrorism itself is a bit clearer. **Terrorism** is best understood as a form of political violence, carried out by individuals, nongovernmental organizations, or covert government agents or units, that specifically targets civilians using clandestine methods. This definition stresses that terrorism focuses on harming some people in order to create fear in others by targeting civilians and facilities or systems on which civilians rely (Kydd & Walter, 2006). The terrorists' objective is not just killing and wounding people or destroying infrastructure. Equally important are the emotions of those who see or read about the act of violence and become afraid or dispirited (Hoffman, 2006).

Although the tactics are similar, it is useful to distinguish between domestic terrorism,

Though definitional debates persist, terrorism tends to embody the spirit of former US Supreme Court Justice Potter Stewart's comment regarding the definition of pornography: We know it when we see it. Without a doubt, the 9/11 attacks, by targeting civilians in a spectacular fashion designed to elicit major worldwide attention to a cause, meet any conceivable definition of terrorism.

international terrorism, and transnational terrorism. Domestic terrorism includes attacks by nationals of a country against a purely domestic target for domestic reasons. International terrorism involves terrorists attacking a foreign target, either within their own country or outside of it. And **transnational terrorism** consists of terrorist activities carried out by globally networked actors operating covertly across multiple national borders simultaneously. The attack on the Oklahoma City federal building in 1995 that killed 168 people and injured 800 more was an example of domestic terrorism. The kidnapping and murder of 11 Israeli athletes and one West German police officer by the

transnational terrorism
Terrorism carried out either across national borders or by groups that operate in more than one country.

PERSONAL NARRATIVE

Mairead (Corrigan) Maguire

Mairead (Corrigan) Maguire, the second of eight children, was born in 1944 in Belfast, Northern Ireland, to Andrew and Margaret Corrigan. Her childhood was relatively typical of the Catholic community in Belfast at the time. She attended St. Vincent's Primary School until age 14, at which point financial burdens forced her to leave school for the workforce—as a babysitter, as an accountant at a local factory, and later, as a secretary at the Guinness brewery.

Mairead's life took a dramatic turn in August 1976, when three of her sister's children were killed by a car driven by Danny Lennon, a fugitive member of the Provisional Irish Republican Army, a terrorist organization in Northern Ireland. Lennon was shot by British troops while operating the vehicle, which then careened out of control, killing Joanne (age 8), John (age 2), and Andrew (age 6 weeks) Maguire. A witness to this tragedy, Betty Williams, turned her outrage into action, obtaining over 200 signatures (Protestant and Catholic alike) and organizing a women's march for peace across Belfast. As the march passed her home, Mairead joined—in the process establishing, with Williams, the foundation for what would become a mass movement in Northern Ireland, the "Women for Peace" (later, "Community of Peace People").

Throughout the late 1970s, the two women continued to lead increasingly larger marches for peace, numbering in the thousands in Belfast and persisting even as militants on both sides harassed and threatened them. Beyond marches and petitions, Mairead was convinced that re-education was crucial to breaking the cycle of violence and terror. She created a biweekly peace newspaper, as well as peace education among the scores of imprisoned Republican and Unionist militants. In recognition of the efforts of these two extraordinary women to combat "The Troubles," Maguire and Williams received the Nobel Peace Prize in 1976.

Mairead Maguire remains active in the leadership of the Community of Peace People. She and the organization have taken on a global focus, extending their attention beyond Northern Ireland. She has been involved in activism on behalf of political prisoners in Myanmar, Turkey, China, and elsewhere, and she was selected to spearhead the UN's "International Decade for the Promotion of a Culture of Peace and Non-Violence for the Children of the World" in 2003. She was also instrumental in starting the Nobel Women's Initiative in 2006, to strengthen support of women's rights around the world.

Beginning in the 1990s, Mairead became a vocal critic of US and British foreign policy, particularly the military campaigns in Iraq and Afghanistan. In a 2015 interview with the US public radio program *Democracy Now*, Maguire explained her stance as one motivated by nothing more than "the desire to end militarism and war, and to build peace and international law and human rights and democracy."[3] When presenting Mairead with the Nobel Prize, the committee's vice-chair, Egil Aarvik, lauded the two women for "showing what ordinary people can do to promote peace. They had the courage to take the first step, and they did so in the name of humanity and love of their neighbor . . . theirs was a courageous unselfish act that proved an inspiration to thousands, that lit a light in the darkness."[4]

Palestinian terrorist organization Black September at the 1972 Summer Olympics in Munich is an example of international terrorism. And al-Qaeda's 9/11 attack on the World Trade Center in New York and the Pentagon in Arlington, Virginia, is an example of transnational terrorism.

The definition of terrorism provided here reflects the prevailing view in global politics that it is a form of political violence used by nonstate actors. This perspective does not mean that all military actions that states undertake are acceptable or permissible, nor does it mean that states cannot and do not engage with terrorism as supporters, sponsors, or beneficiaries. However, acts of violence carried out by states that resemble terrorist activities—especially when targeting civilians—are better understood as war crimes or crimes against humanity, as stipulated in various international conventions concerning the use of violence by states.

The intentional targeting of civilians is a distinguishing feature of terrorism. This aspect of terrorism negates the claim many terrorist organizations and their sympathizers make that the "ends" (political objectives) necessarily justify the "means" (targeting of civilians). An example of this logic was evident in a message entitled "Where are the lions of war?" issued by ISIS spokesperson Abul Hasan al-Muhajir in the May 2017 issue of that group's *Rumiyah* magazine. He stated:

> Do not despise the work. Your targeting of the so-called innocents and civilians is beloved by us and the most effective, so go forth and may you get a great reward or martyrdom.

FREQUENCY AND EXTENT.   For the vast majority of people around the world, the likelihood of being injured or killed in a terrorist attack is infinitesimal (see Map 7.3). For example, the odds of an American dying in a terrorist attack since 9/11 are equivalent to being crushed to death by a piece of furniture (Zenko, 2012). According to the US Department of State, the number of US citizens killed overseas as a result of incidents of terrorism from 2001 to 2017 was 181.

During that same time period, 3,081 Americans were killed in terrorist attacks on US soil, a number largely attributable to the 2,996 Americans who died in the 9/11 attacks.[5] By contrast, during that time frame, 440,095 Americans died by firearms on US soil,[6] and using the average of 100 fatalities per year, over 500,000 Americans died in auto accidents (Gigerenzer, 2004). Despite these statistics, in the 2016 US presidential election, 80% of those surveyed indicated terrorism was their top issue of concern (Pew Research Center, 2016).

It is worth noting that domestic terrorism is more common and claims more lives than international or transnational terrorism. Since 2004, domestic terrorist attacks have far exceeded international attacks in both number and lethality.[7] In the United States, violent attacks by right-wing groups including white supremacists, neo-Nazis, and anti-federal militias have averaged more than 300 per year since 9/11, according to the Combating Terrorism Center at the US Military Academy at West Point.[8] A 2015 survey by the Police Executive Research Forum found US law enforcement groups considered anti-government

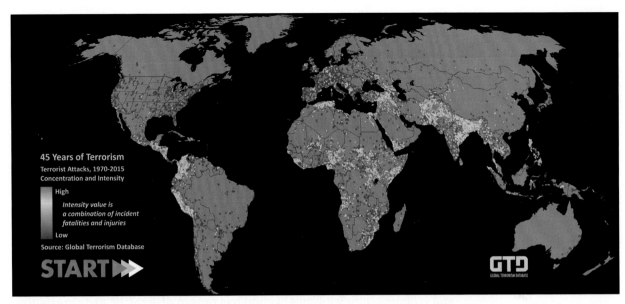

Map 7.3   As this map reflects, terrorist attacks—especially those of moderate or high intensity—have been highly concentrated in particular regions of the world over the past four decades. The vast majority of attacks have occurred in the Middle East and North Africa, South Asia, sub-Saharan Africa, and parts of Latin America. Most are correlated with insurgencies and civil wars. (Source: Data from Global Terrorism Database, START.)

violent extremism a more severe security threat than Islamist terrorism.[9] This trend is also evident in Europe, with the rise of various far-right xenophobic and anti-Islamic groups such as the AfD (Alliance for Deutschland) in Germany or Golden Dawn in Greece. These and other similar groups preach—and sometimes use—violence against targeted populations, as in attacks on refugee facilities throughout Germany by AfD sympathizers or in the murder of anti-fascist rapper Pavlos Fyssas by members of Golden Dawn in 2013.

In some ways, the distinction between domestic and international terrorism is a false one. We can attribute this to transnationalism, which links groups, issues, and ideologies across national borders. The two dominant trends in terrorism during recent years, the upwelling of radical religious terrorism exemplified by groups such as ISIS as well as the resurgence of right-wing extremism, are both reactions to larger global political and social forces, and both manipulate globalization and transnationalism to carry out their attacks. For instance, ISIS as well as various al-Qaeda affiliates have turned in recent years to recruiting citizens of countries where they wish to stage attacks (especially in Western Europe and the United States), an approach sometimes referred

The neofascist political party Golden Dawn has risen to prominence during recent years in Greece. Its growing popularity can largely be explained by the country's crippling economic problems, resentment toward the major influx of refugees from Syria and the Middle East, and dissatisfaction with national and European politics.

"homegrown" terrorism A thesis that contends the most recent wave of transnational terrorism is being advanced by "homegrown" actors living in, and citizens of, Western countries with only loose ties to groups such as ISIS and al-Qaeda.

to as **"homegrown" terrorism** (Bergen, 2016). ISIS-inspired attacks in Paris, Berlin, Brussels, Nice, London, and Barcelona between 2015 and 2017 were all planned and/or perpetrated by such individuals.

Causes of Terrorism

Although the September 11, 2001 attacks brought it to the fore front of the global agenda, terrorism has long existed. Understanding the causes of terrorism and its recent record are important parts of combating it (Laqueur, 2004; Sinclair, 2004).

Untangling the causes of terrorism is much like trying to understand why war occurs. At the systemic level of analysis, it is possible to argue that such political violence is in part a product of unequal global distribution of wealth (Ehrlich & Liu, 2005; Piazza, 2006). This inequality is hardly new, but globalization has brought the wealth gap into sharper focus. That reality points to another frequently articulated system level explanation for terrorism—the profound clash between Western liberalism and other views of politics, society, and economic activity. Globalization has proven dislocating and threatening not only in its impact but also for what it represents, inspiring a sociocultural backlash in many states and societies (Mousseau, 2003).

State- or societal-level analysis often points to the emergence of terrorism in political systems with few (or no) available nonviolent options for the expression of political views or when political violence is an attractive alternative that will call attention to the group and its agenda (Gurr, 1998; Weinberg, 1991). States' actions also clearly elicit terrorism, as we see with the foreign policy behavior of Israel and the United States in the Middle East, which provides constant fodder for jihadi terrorism that ISIS, al-Qaeda, and its affiliates perpetuate.

On the individual level, one can seek to analyze the psychology and motivation of terrorists themselves. We can extend this inquiry to leaders such as Abu Bakr al-Baghdadi, Osama bin Laden, Ulrike Meinhof (leader of the left-wing Red Army Faction in Germany during the 1970s and 1980s), and Shoko Asahara (leader of the Japanese millennial group Aum Shinrikyo), or to the scores of suicide bombers who have blown themselves up in Israel, Sri Lanka, Iraq, and elsewhere (Post, 2008).

Terrorism occurs because, like war, it can be effective (Abrahms, 2006). As one expert puts it, "Terrorism has proved a low-cost, low-risk, cost-effective and potentially high-yield means of winning useful tactical objectives for its perpetrators" (Wilkinson, 2005:4). From this perspective, terrorism is not the irrational act of crazed fanatics (Bueno de Mesquita, 2005; Hoffman, 2006). Instead, it is usually carried out by those who consider it a necessary, legitimate, effective, and available tool for advancing and pursuing political aims (Crenshaw, 1988).

Moreover, prevailing global conditions are ripe for terrorist operations. First, technology and mobility combine to make attacks easier to carry out with relatively low "barriers to entry." As we have seen in recent years, ISIS has relied heavily on the rather rudimentary (if effective) tactic of driving cars and trucks

Inside the Mind of a Former Radical Jihadist.

into large crowds in major urban areas such as London or Barcelona. Second, and relatedly, increased urbanization has brought people together so that they are easier targets, especially when gathered in everyday places such as cafes, shopping malls, and sports stadiums. Third, modern communications have also made terrorism more attractive because the terrorist's goal is not just to kill or injure. Instead, the aim is to gain attention for a cause or to create widespread anxiety that will, in turn, create pressure on authorities to cave to their demands or allow them to pursue their agenda without interference. Without some form of media to transmit the news of their acts, terrorist attacks would affect only their immediate victims, which would not accomplish the goal of "propaganda of the deed" (Nacos, 2007).

Sources of Terrorism

Two sources of political terrorism concern us here. One is state-sponsored terrorism. The second comprises transnational terrorist groups. They can be, and sometimes are, closely linked.

STATE-SPONSORED TERRORISM.   To argue that uniformed military personnel serving in the armed forces of a state are not proper terrorists does not mean it is impossible for states to engage in terrorist activity. For one, states can participate in **state-sponsored terrorism**, in which an established government's clandestine operatives or nonstate actors who a country has specifically encouraged, funded, trained, equipped, and/or granted sanctuary carry out terrorist activities and operations.

In recent years, the US Department of State has listed Cuba, Iran, Iraq, Libya, North Korea, Sudan, and Syria among state sponsors of terrorism. For their part, each of these countries has vehemently denied involvement in terrorism, and some of the US allegations would fall outside the definition of terrorism that we use here. Not all would, though. For example, Syria's involvement in the 2005 assassination of former Lebanese Prime Minister Rafiq Hariri, a strong opponent of Syria's long-time infiltration of Lebanon, would certainly qualify.

Likewise, some have accused the United States of engaging in state terrorism. "We consider the United States and its current administration as a first-class sponsor of international terrorism, and it along with Israel form an axis of terrorism and evil in the world," a group of 126 Saudi scholars wrote in a joint 2002 statement.[10] Supporting examples include Washington's complicity in political assassinations and other forms of state terrorism practiced internally by some countries in Latin America and elsewhere during the Cold War.

TRANSNATIONAL TERRORIST GROUPS.   The global changes that have given rise to a rapid increase in the number of international nongovernmental organizations have also expanded the number of transnational terrorist groups that are organized and operate internationally and that commit transnational terrorism. The US Department of State identifies 40 such groups, including ISIS and its various regional and local affiliates, and has also accused dozens of other

state-sponsored terrorism
Terrorism sponsored by nation-states. In general, state-sponsored terrorism is associated with providing material support and/or sanctuary to terrorist or paramilitary organizations.

such organizations of terrorist activity or support. Transnational terrorist organizations are notable both for the global and transboundary reach, scope, and targeting of their activities and planning, as well as for their ability to utilize the networked structure of global society to draw upon materiel (weapons and money) and people (recruits) and promote their message (ideas and objectives) to sustain that global and transboundary scope and reach. In many ways, they are among the most skillful manipulators of globalization, utilizing things like financial deregulation, relaxed border standards, and social media to sustain and expand their activities and support.

SPOTLIGHT: ISIS. ISIS is surely the most prominent transnational terrorist organization in recent years, although it did not exactly start that way. The earliest precursor to ISIS was al-Qaeda in Iraq (AQI), led by the fanatic Jordanian terrorist Abu Musab al-Zarqawi. Established amidst the upheaval caused by the US invasion of Iraq in 2003, AQI initially worked closely with al-Qaeda leadership, including Osama bin Laden (McCants, 2015). Over time, however, Zarqawi became too extreme even for al-Qaeda, largely because of his indiscriminate attacks on Muslim civilians such as the bombing of three hotels in Amman, Jordan, in November 2005. The so-called "Anbar Awakening" in the Anbar province of western Iraq, which proved critical to the eventual containment of the Iraqi insurgency in 2007–2008, was prompted by widespread revulsion among Iraq's Sunni Muslim minority to the methods used by Zarqawi, a Sunni himself (McCants, 2015).

The domination of the elected government in Iraq by the Shiite Muslim majority alienated some elements of the Sunni population. Motivated by centuries of theological divisions between the two groups, more extreme elements among the Sunnis in Iraq sought to return to the path blazed by Zarqawi in the early 2010s. These remnants of AQI, various Sunni militia, and some former Ba'athist supporters of Saddam Hussein came together under the banner of the Islamic State of Iraq (ISI) with the goal of avenging the Sunni population against the Shia-led Iraqi government and its American and Iranian backers (McCants, 2015). Emboldened by initial success on the ground, the group expanded its scope of operations, forging a partnership with the Syrian jihadist group Jabhat al-Nusra.

In April 2013, the ISI leader Abu Bakr al-Baghdadi proposed a formal merger in which Jabhat al-Nusra would subordinate itself to his authority. Al-Baghdadi declared himself the caliph of the "Islamic State of Iraq and al-Sham"—"al-Sham" being an antiquated term referring to the Levant, used to convey the group's rejection of the territorial borders and designations assigned to

The secretive leader of ISIS, Abu Bakr al-Baghdadi, went over five years without making a public appearance between his declaration of a restored caliphate across segments of Syrian and Iraqi territory from Mosul's grand mosque in July 2014 and an April 2019 video in which he vowed revenge for the group's loss of a territorial base in Syria and Iraq. He was rumored to have been killed in counterterrorism strikes on numerous occasions, but his whereabouts remain unknown.

Syria, Iraq, and Lebanon by the British and French imperialists through the Sykes-Picot Agreement in 1916. However, the al-Nusra leadership rejected this proposal and renewed its allegiance to al-Qaeda, creating a split between the two groups in July 2013 which played out, often violently, in the Syrian civil war.

ISIS made dramatic gains throughout 2014, quickly capturing Iraq's second-largest city (Mosul) and a wide swath of territory not only in Iraq but also in war-torn Syria. In this first iteration, Baghdadi and other ISIS leaders were chiefly concerned with controlling and expanding a territorial base of operations in order to establish an Islamic state. Using a mix of coercion and service provision, ISIS introduced an austere version of Islamic law and taxation to control the local population and began building institutions and infrastructure (funded largely through stolen oil reserves) while also using violence against moderates and opponents in the region (al-Tamimi, 2014). At the same time, ISIS undertook a major communications offensive, largely through social media, to attract and recruit combatants and supporters to Syria and Iraq in order to wage jihad and contribute to restoration of the caliphate, a move reflecting the increasingly transnational orientation of the group (Gulmohamad, 2014).

These ventures—and the increasing prominence they brought ISIS—drew the group into clashes with the Iraqi military, Kurdish security forces, the Assad regime in Syria, various rival jihadist groups, and eventually, the United States, Russia, and other foreign powers active in the region. Through a mix of airstrikes and ground engagements with its many enemies in Iraq and Syria, ISIS suffered a number of critical if gradual defeats in Iraq and Syria beginning in late 2015, seriously weakening its territorial base (see Map 7.4). These assaults against ISIS continued full-scale into 2018, though with less precision and

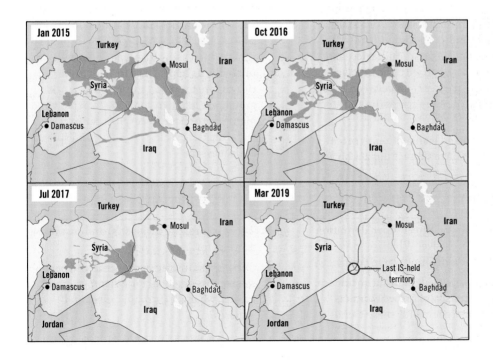

Map 7.4 While at its peak in January 2015 ISIS controlled large swaths of territory in northwest Iraq and eastern Syria, as this map shows. By early 2019 its base of operations was greatly reduced through clashes with various military adversaries in the region, as well as with the U.S. and some of its European allies, Russia, and Iran.

discrimination, leading both to the group's unseating from Syria and Iraq as well as to a proportional increase in civilian casualties resulting from US and Russian attacks.[11]

As ISIS began to experience increased dislocation, the group undertook a clear tactical shift, turning its attention away from its immediate vicinity and from the goal of restoring the caliphate in Syria and Iraq (Bergen, 2016). Capitalizing on its extensive and effective social media presence and recruiting networks, ISIS began to rally support for jihadist operations "in place" by "homegrown" operatives living in and often born in Western states (Sageman, 2008). This marked an almost total reversal of course for ISIS, spawning a wave of attacks in Europe and the United States, beginning with the Charlie Hebdo assault in Paris in January 2015 and continuing through the Christmas market attack in Strasbourg, France in December 2018. By turning its focus to what Osama bin Laden referred to in a 1998 fatwa as the "far enemy," ISIS managed to increase its notoriety as a terrorist group at the expense of establishing its version of an Islamic State. In that way, ISIS offers a pointed reminder of the ever-evolving tactics, strategies, and objectives of terrorism as well as war.

Chapter Summary

- War remains very much the by-product of a combination of factors and conditions at the individual, societal, and systemic levels.
- Armed conflict today is far more likely to take place within the bounds of a state (intrastate conflict), between "irregular" forces (e.g., militias, paramilitaries, and nonstate actors), and with the involvement of third parties than between regular armies of two or more states (interstate conflict).
- Globalization and transnational forces and processes have a direct impact on war

and armed conflict, especially intrastate conflicts. The ease of movement of people, goods, money, weapons, and ideas can and does trigger and sustain armed conflict.

- Globalization and transnational forces and processes also have a direct impact on terrorism, increasing its scope and profile and, relatedly, its appeal as a form of asymmetric warfare for nonstate actors. Terrorist groups are likely to continue to exploit and manipulate these forces in order to carry out attacks, recruit, fundraise, and spread their message.

Critical Thinking Questions

1. Why does a single, agreed-upon definition of war remain elusive? What are some of the central features defining war in your view?

2. What trends are evident in the incidence, type, and intensity of armed conflicts today? What accounts for these trends?

3. What is (are) the catalyst(s) and sustaining force(s) for "new" wars?

4. What explains the persistence and pervasiveness of global terrorism? In other words, what are its main causes and sources?

Key Terms

aggression
asymmetric warfare
Concert of Europe
defensive realism
democratic peace
diversionary theory of
  war

"homegrown" terrorism
militarism
"new" wars
new world order
offensive realism
"old" wars

particularistic identity
  politics
preemption
preventive war
primordial identities
relative deprivation
remittances

self-defense
state-sponsored
  terrorism
terrorism
transnational terrorism

Pursuing Security

Many of the dilemmas involving security are evident in the foreign policy behavior and governing strategy of the Democratic People's Republic of Korea (DPRK), more commonly known as North Korea. Since its invasion of South Korea in June 1950, the DPRK has been at the forefront of numerous efforts to destabilize the Asia-Pacific security theater. Currently led by Kim Jong-Un—the grandson of the country's founder, Kim Il-Sung—the DPRK continues to expand its nuclear weapons capability while also possessing the fifth-largest conventional army in the world. As a result, the North Korean regime poses a persistent challenge to the security of its people, its neighbors, and the international community, as does the uncertain and volatile relationship between the North Korean regime and the Trump administration in the United States. We will return to the topic of North Korea repeatedly throughout this chapter to emphasize key points concerning the evolving role of security in contemporary global politics.

This chapter seeks an understanding of security that moves us beyond the more traditional aspects of conflict and war and toward a broader conception of security and its impact on a wide swath of daily life. As a result, this chapter covers much more varied ground, and with a wider focus, than Chapter 7. The thread tying it all together, however, is the idea that security takes various forms across time, location, and sociopolitical context. Thus, we need to be sensitive to the particular

Missiles are paraded In the North Korean capital, Pyongyang, in April 2017 during celebrations of the 105th anniversary of the birth of Kim Il-Sung, the country's founder. North Korea's escalating rhetoric and expanding missile capability have further heightened insecurity in the Asia-Pacific security theater and beyond.

circumstances facing individuals and governments as they pursue security in the contemporary world. This implies that security is not a constant, unchangeable concept, but rather one that is constructed and evolves in different ways from the individual through the systemic level. It also means that all five theoretical perspectives laid out in Chapter 2 bring valuable insights to our understanding of security. We recommend that you keep each of the five perspectives in mind as you make your way through this chapter.

Learning Objectives

Identify and explain the defining features of security in the traditional (realist) view, including the concept of anarchy.

Explain the basis for and main examples of efforts to "broaden" and "deepen" the concept of security over the past quarter-century.

Compare, contrast, and assess different approaches to the provision of security, especially those concerned with limiting arms races and international conflict.

Discuss how broader transformations in the structure of the global political system have revealed a "new" security environment featuring different rules, actors, and threats.

Describe different types of weapons of mass destruction, the global security threats they pose, and efforts to limit and contain those threats.

 The Traditional Approach

It is impossible to make sense of global politics without understanding the concept of security. The term saturates the speeches of politicians, activists, and journalists, all of whom attach it to a range of issues. From energy security to food security, from the individual level to the global level, security is one of the most important concepts of our time. It is also the epitome of what social theorist W. B. Gallie referred to as an "essentially contested concept" (Gallie, 1956). Accordingly, one must accept that security necessarily means different things to different people, though at its core, the concept of security begs four fundamental questions (Williams, 2008:5):

1. What is security?
2. Whose security are we talking about?
3. What counts as a security issue?
4. How can we achieve security?

The traditional approach to security emphasizes the primacy of the nation-state (see Chapter 4) and the need for material capabilities to defend the security of the state. This typically translates into states cultivating military power in order to preserve their sovereignty and territorial integrity at all costs. Accordingly, **national security** has become synonymous with attaining and amassing military force sufficient to deter aggression.

This traditional approach to security has drawbacks, however. In revisiting the current security situation with North Korea, such an approach places primary, if not sole, emphasis on the security of each individual state. In theory, this gives each state "carte blanche" to preserve and protect itself by any and all means necessary. So from this perspective, the North Korean regime would be well within its rights, and indeed would be expected, to assemble and deploy any and all resources necessary to ensure its own survival in the face of real or perceived threats from South Korea, Japan, or the United States—including the development and even use of nuclear weapons.

The appeal of the traditional approach to security and the ideas on which it rests remains great. One need look no further than how the world spends its money in the pursuit of security (Figure 8.1). According to the Stockholm International Peace Research Institute (SIPRI; 2019), the world spent about $1.8 trillion on military arms in 2018. Of these expenditures, the United States allocated roughly $610 billion to its national defense budget, accounting for 36% of total global defense spending. With this enormous amount of military spending in the name of national security, it is worth asking whether or not such policies actually make the world a more secure place. Perhaps Trygve Lie, the first Secretary-General of the United Nations (UN), was onto something when he suggested that "wars occur because people prepare for conflict, rather than for peace."[1]

national security The goal of maintaining the survival of the state through all available means. Originally (and still largely) focused on amassing military strength to forestall the threat of military invasion, national security now also encompasses a broad range of factors related to a nation's nonmilitary or economic security, material interests, and values.

Anarchy and Self-Help

The Treaty of Westphalia (1648) marked the emergence of the state as the dominant unit of governance in the global system. The establishment of sovereign states as the primary actors in the system has had profound consequences for the way the world works, as well as for the way we study global politics. The emergence of the security studies field in the 20th century was defined by an overriding concern with preserving sovereign states through the concept of national security. As one leading scholar of international security, Michael Sheehan, puts it, "During the long domination of international relations by realism [approximately from the late 1930s to the late 1970s], the working definition of security was a strictly limited one, which saw its nature as being concerned with military power, and the subject of these concerns as being the state . . ." (2005:5).

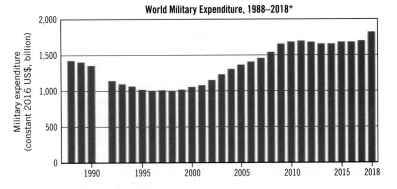

Figure 8.1 Global military spending peaked in the late 1980s, at the end of the Cold War, and then declined into the mid-1990s, reaching a low point in 1996 and being fairly steady for the rest of that decade. Beginning in 2000, arms spending began to accelerate more rapidly, increasing about 22% in constant dollars (adjusted for inflation) to just over $1 trillion in 2005, and crossing the $1.8 trillion mark in 2018.
* 1991 total cannot be calculated as no Soviet Union data is available. (Source: SIPRI, 2019.)

A central assumption of a Westphalian (state-based) system is that no central global authority exists to maintain order and ensure justice. From this perspective, the conduct of global politics is largely shaped by the anarchy in which states are embedded. Absent any central governing authority in the global system, states are locked in a self-help relationship with one another (Herz, 1950). As such, realists contend that states will do whatever they must to survive—up to, and frequently including, engaging in armed conflict, as discussed in Chapter 7.

This does not mean that the global system is a scene of unchecked chaos. An informal hierarchy exists where more powerful states seek to maintain some semblance of order, and most countries find it in their interests to act predictably and seek to conform (Hobson, 2005). For instance, while in recent years Japanese foreign policy has shifted toward self-reliance and "normal nationalism" (Samuels, 2006), that country's foreign policy rhetoric has attempted to reassure the United States that Japan intends to remain a close and dependable ally, so that the terms of that partnership remain clear to each partner. Conversely, when a state decides that breaking the largely informal rules of the system is in its own interests, as Iraq did when it invaded Kuwait in 1990, there is little to stop it except countervailing power.

security dilemma Given anarchy, the tendency of states and other actors to undertake actions to enhance their own security in a "self-help" system may result in posing a threat to other states or actors who are uncertain of the original state's intentions. This is a dilemma in that the original action, intended to make the state or actor more secure, has the opposite effect.

A Security Dilemma for States

The logic of self-help anarchy produces a global political system that is inherently competitive, volatile, and insecure. One by-product is the **security dilemma**—a situation in which states misinterpret largely defensive actions and capabilities by other states as threats (Booth & Wheeler, 2008; Herz, 1950). This dilemma is often illustrated in bilateral interactions between states, particularly those locked in arms races or protracted conflicts, and it centers on the idea that actions intended to enhance security only breed greater insecurity for all involved—as shown in Figure 8.2. Ultimately, the overarching condition of anarchy that defines the international system puts states in a position to undertake measures for the protection and advancement of their own security that in turn make other states insecure.

The absence of reliable information flowing between states means that decision-makers are often unsure of one another's intentions—and, therefore, often threatened by one another's actions. The degree to which security depends on the perception of one's actions by other actors reminds us that security as a condition can be difficult to obtain (Jervis, 1976, 1978). The prominent realist theorist John Mearsheimer (2001) argues that

Security Dilemma Spiral

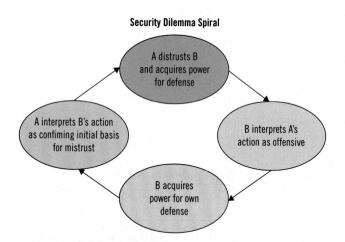

Figure 8.2   The logic of the security dilemma. Given the structuring condition of anarchy (lack of central governing authority) in the international system, State A decides to undertake an action intended largely to ensure its own security and survival. This action (say, the procuring of a new weapons system, or the crafting of a bilateral defense accord) may be a response to some specific action or behavior of another state or states, or it may be entirely self-regarding. Regardless of the actual intent, State B necessarily *perceives* the action of State A to be a threat to its own security and survival. Therefore, in responding to the perceived threat out of a desire to protect itself, State B undertakes a response to the action of State A. Then, reacting to the reaction, State A retaliates to its own heightened sense of threat, at which point the dynamic escalates, leaving both states (and their neighbors, and the world) less secure in the long run.

states must assume and act according to "worst-case scenario" possibilities because states can never be certain about others intentions, leading to frequent and recurring "offensive" postures of destabilizing threats and occasional military attacks. From this perspective, ultimate safety comes only from being the most powerful state in the system. This means that by extension all states not only can but must pursue that lofty position, which only one can conceivably attain, if they desire security. Undoubtedly, the escalating rhetoric—and possibility for direct conflict—between North Korea and the United States serves as a clear, if frightening, example of the security dilemma and its real-world implications.

Balance-of-Power Politics

In an anarchic global system, states engage in a number of strategies to balance against rivals and/or threats to their security. In the words of the modern architect of classical realism, Hans Morgenthau, the concept of the **balance of power** refers to:

> [t]he aspiration for power on the part of several nations, each trying to maintain or overthrow the status quo, [which] leads . . . to a configuration [of] policies that aim at preserving [the status quo]. (1948:173)

This concept assumes that unbalanced power alone represents a threat to the survival of less powerful states. Therefore, when a more powerful state confronts two or more relatively weak states, the weaker states will seek to counter the source of that threat, often through the formation of alliances, thus balancing against the larger, more powerful state. The relationships between European countries in the 19th century (especially Britain, France, Germany, and Russia) are often cited as the consummate example of balance of power.

Alliances are a primary tool that states can use in their pursuit of security, and they are a frequent response to potential aggression or threats from adversaries and provide opportunities for enhancing a state's power position in the system (Walt, 1987). Alliances form not only through the efforts of weaker states working together in a **balancing** strategy against a stronger actor, but also as a product of weaker states joining with stronger actors in a strategy known as **bandwagoning**.

The larger point about the realist approach to security is that realists view armed conflict as a valid and useful instrument for achieving and defending a favorable balance of power. It is important to remember that the goal of the balance of power is not peace, but rather maintenance of the status quo and prevention of the system being dominated by any one state or alliance (Walt, 1985). In this way, states seek to balance and bandwagon in a search for power or in response to common threats.

Security Re-Envisioned

Because the emphasis on military defense has not made the world secure, it is worth considering whether we can supplement—or even replace—traditional conceptions of security with alternative ways of thinking that are not similarly

balance of power A concept that describes the degree of equilibrium (balance) or disequilibrium (imbalance) of power between and among powerful actors in the global or regional system.

alliances Formal political associations between two or more parties, made in order to advance common goals and to secure common interests.

balancing The act of states responding to the threat of an emergent (international) power or coalition of powers by banding together to balance against that emergent state or states.

bandwagoning The act of a weaker sovereign state or states joining a stronger (international) power or coalition as a subordinate partner with the expectation of deriving gains by riding on the "coattails" of that rising power.

bound to the state and militarism. The origins of such alternatives require one to take seriously a range of diverse threats, "new" actors, and shifting global rules and norms.

During the 1980s, international relations scholars and policy-makers began to challenge traditional assumptions about security and the centrality of the state. Scholar Ken Booth has described this period as one of "growing unease with the traditional concept of security, which privileges the state and emphasizes military power" together with a "frequent call for the broadening or updating of the concept of security" (1991:317). Along these lines, Richard Ullman published a well-known article in 1983 entitled "Redefining Security." Ullman challenged the dominant militaristic paradigm by calling attention to issues such as environmental security. Similarly, Jessica Tuchman Mathews argued a few years later that we needed to rethink the concept of security as "global developments now suggest the need . . . to include resource, environmental, and demographic issues," thereby challenging the use of national borders as a determinant of national security threats (1989:162). While these ideas may seem logical to you today, they were quite revolutionary at the time and helped launch a more serious consideration of the traditional, "realist" approach to security—in the process generating challenges to it as well.

One can see an obvious manifestation of the state-centric and militarized approach to security reflected in the behavior of the North Korean regime toward not only its external adversaries but also its own people. The extent of militarization in North Korea is evident in the ubiquitous military parades and inflammatory propaganda focusing on the legacy of the Korean War as well as the existential threat posed by the United States. Three successive generations of North Korean leaders have viewed amassing military power as the most vital priority of the state, even in the midst of catastrophic famine or economic stagnation. The diversion of much of the country's meager resources to building up and maintaining the world's fifth-largest conventional army (1.2 million persons in uniform), as well as an expanding nuclear arsenal and missile development program has had little objective effect on its security, apart from contributing to the regime's ability to maintain strict control over North Korean society.

This image is representative of not only the highly militarized and provocative nature of much of the propaganda created and distributed by the North Korean regime, but also the intense focus on the United States that typifies most of it. Here, we see a depiction of North Korean missiles striking the US Capitol building in Washington, DC. The caption, loosely translated, states, "When a war of aggression is provoked, we will hit back—beginning with the United States." (Source: Heather & De Ceuster, 2008.)

Limits to the Realist Approach?

Following the end of the Cold War, the traditional realist conceptualization of security became increasingly unsatisfactory because it failed to account for important aspects of global politics. The proliferation of ethnic conflict, humanitarian disaster, and general social disorder in a number of high profile cases (Somalia, Bosnia, Rwanda, and the Democratic Republic of the Congo, to name a few) further challenged traditional definitions of security.

The recognition that security equals the absence of insecurity points to the conclusion that we can define the latter in many different ways (Bobrow, 1996). The use or threatened use of military force could produce insecurity, but it might also be an outcome produced by human action (e.g., a suicide bomber), natural phenomena, economic recession, or various other factors that may make people feel insecure. In this sense, history, culture, and identity all interact to determine the meaning of security and the objectives and policies that follow from it.

From the critics' vantage point, realism's emphasis on state sovereignty makes it unable to account for emerging security challenges that do not directly pertain to or impact the state (Brown, 1998). For example, we might consider Haiti a relatively "secure" state in that it does not confront a major military challenge from any of its neighbors. Such a conclusion seems foolish in light of the crippling poverty and devastated infrastructure plaguing the country and leaving the vast majority of Haitians vulnerable and insecure. As a result, critics have called for a "post-Westphalian" approach in which state sovereignty would no longer occupy a position of primacy in security thinking.

Broadening and Deepening the Security Agenda

While attempts to redefine security in the post–Cold War era proved controversial, consensus did emerge on two fronts. First, it was impossible to ignore how the speed, enormity, and complexity of globalization impacted the security agenda at the local, national, and international levels (Held & McGrew, 2000). The political scientist James Rosenau argued at the time that "more than ever, security is elusive; more than ever, it is embedded in the interaction of localizing and globalizing forces" (1994:255). The increasing relevance and intensity of these processes and interactions raised the specter that a **global security** approach might include concerns other than narrow, state-focused military ones and point to responses beyond those associated with military capacity (Rothschild, 1995).

Scholars associated with the Copenhagen Peace Research Institute in Denmark were among those heeding this call for a broadening of security. Often referred to as the Copenhagen School, this group developed a theory of **securitization**, which critically evaluates how security threats are identified and prioritized across various dimensions (military, political, social, economic, and environmental) through political discourse and other mechanisms (Butler, 2019). Taken together, the process of securitization as well as the sectoral approach often associated with it suggest that "security"—and the threats associated with it—are subjective matters rooted in one's perception, ideology, and politics. In this way, security is best understood as a social construct rooted in collective political discourse (Wæver, 1995). Adherents to the Copenhagen School look at why some issues (e.g., terrorism) get securitized and receive priority treatment by states and international organizations while others with crucial security implications for individuals, groups, and even nations (e.g., economic inequality) do not (Baele and Thomson, 2017; Mortensgaard, 2018).

global security The efforts taken by a community of states to protect against threats that are transnational in nature. The responses to these threats are usually multilateral, often involving regional and/or international organizations.

securitization A highly politicized process by which policy issues across various sectors and domains (military, political, social, economic, environmental, etc.) are identified and prioritized as "security threats." This process tends to result in the devotion of greater attention and resources to the securitized issue or problem.

◄ **THINKING THEORETICALLY**

The Drug War in Mexico

What is the best reference point for security—the nation-state, the global system, or the individual person? This question harkens back to the levels of analysis introduced in Chapter 3. One example that illustrates the importance of this question is the ongoing drug-related turmoil in Mexico. According to the US Congressional Research Service, over 80,000 people have died in drug-related violence since the initiation of a major crackdown on Mexico's powerful and competing drug cartels in December 2006.[2]

From the traditional reference point of the state, Mexico's security situation is hardly dire. Realists focus on the security of the state as something determined by the state's ability to guarantee its own survival. In other words, the state should seek to protect itself from attack by other states. Although worthy of governmental attention, the cartels are not a major security threat to Mexico because the threat emanates from nonstate actors operating largely within the domestic arena. These violent actors do not directly threaten Mexico's sovereignty and survival. The Mexican state is not likely to collapse, nor do any of its neighbors compromise Mexico's sovereignty. In addition, the world's preeminent military superpower, the United States, has worked in close collaboration with and support of the Mexican government's crackdown.

Viewing the same situation through different security lenses, however, suggests that the security implications of Mexico's "war on drugs" are massive. If one considers the security of individuals a prime concern, as some feminists and critical theorists advocate, then the violent clashes between the cartels and the security forces clearly compromise the security of ordinary Mexicans. The discovery of mass graves is commonplace, as are kidnappings, public beheadings, and other human rights atrocities. On the other hand, the security forces' broad leeway has led to intimidation, violence, and violations of the rights and liberties of those Mexicans the government suspects of working with the cartels. The degree of corruption among the police further compromises the security of individuals, as the police are prone to bribery and infiltration by the well-funded cartels, making threatened individuals reluctant to trust such unreliable sources of authority.

Another view of the drug war in Mexico comes from those concerned with the security of the global system. The security implications of transnational activities involving nonstate actors has become a hot button issue for liberal theorists, who emphasize the need for institutionalized cooperation in order to define and respond to security threats collectively. The Mexican cartels' domination of trafficking routes from South America to the United States suggests the regional, if not global, ramifications of these events. These are especially great for the United States, which is the final destination for 90% of the cocaine trafficked through Mexico, a business enterprise estimated at $13 billion a year. The Mexican war on drugs is intertwined with the United States, not only because of the insatiable demand from Americans for illicit drugs but also through the potential for violent attacks on US Border Patrol agents and citizens by drug traffickers. At the same time, the connection between drug trafficking and other transboundary phenomena, such as migration, money laundering, gang violence, and arms transfers, poses security problems not only for Mexico and the United States but for all states in the region. This regional dimension is reflected in the Mérida Initiative, a multiyear commitment (currently totaling $1.6 billion) of equipment and training by the United States to law enforcement officials in Mexico as well as in Central America, Haiti, and the Dominican Republic. Whether such initiatives have contributed to an overall increase in security is debatable.

One useful illustration here is what some have referred to as the securitization of climate change (Brown, Hammill, & McLeman, 2007). Climatologists and security scholars alike have long warned that climate change threatens the security of food and water supplies, the allocation of important natural resources, and the very existence of coastal populations. These threats are likely to increase forced migration, raise tensions over scarce resources, and trigger armed conflicts. Such warnings went more or less unheeded in the United States until the Department of Defense began considering the implications of climate change on national security.[3]

In a textbook example of securitization, the Pentagon's first such report (in 2003) sparked a flurry of media stories, including a *Fortune* magazine article famously labeling climate change the "mother of all security problems" (Stipp, 2004). With respect to securitization, this example highlights the reality that securitization is a political act with real-world implications, leading to the allocation of a substantial proportion of a state's resources to address an issue. Using security talk as a political framework for action elevates a particular issue or a vulnerable population to the forefront of the policy agenda.

In addition to the widespread agreement that security issues were not limited to the military domain, a second point of consensus among scholars and policy-makers centered on the need to focus on the security of the individual as well as the state. This focus on the individual had much to do with the global political context of the 1990s, when the explosion of intrastate violence, rampant civilian casualties and displacement, as well as gross and systematic human rights violations all challenged the credibility of the state and the idea that states were the only means to provide for societal and individual security. In response, political scientists helped coin the term **human security** to direct attention toward a wider spectrum of security threats both inside and outside the state. This new conceptualization argued that unlike under traditional approaches, people can be insecure inside a secure state, and that security threats are not always connected to identifiable enemies (Hamill, 1998). You should also note that the Copenhagen School's focus on securitization and the human security framework more specifically underlie many feminist and gender-focused approaches to security studies. Gender's impact on conflict resolution is a focus of the *Challenge Your Assumptions* feature later in this chapter.

As the scholarly debates demonstrate, human security remains a controversial concept, and even some of its proponents acknowledge that it may lack clear definition and even logical consistency (King & Murray, 2001).[4] Even for those who do find validity in it, human security comes up short, as in the eyes of

Human security is predicated on a priority concern for the safety and well-being of individuals, especially civilians and noncombatants. Many contemporary peace operations are at least loosely predicated on this notion, and the interaction of peacekeepers with the affected communities they seek to secure is vital to ensure the success of such operations.

human security An emerging paradigm for understanding security vulnerabilities that challenges the traditional notion of national security by arguing the proper referent for security should be the individual rather than the state. Human security holds that a people-centered view of security is necessary for national, regional, and global stability.

critical security scholars in the Aberystwyth School, named for the Welsh university home to many of them, who have issued a call to recast security studies and policies around human emancipation (Booth, 1991, 2005; Krause & Williams, 1996, 1997; Sheehan, 2005; Wyn Jones, 1996, 2001). Even more critical of this approach are those scholars associated with the Paris School, who reject the inherently hegemonic concepts and practices of security and freedom more generally (Bigo, 2014).

If nothing else, a primary value of the human security concept is that it illustrates where realist notions of security seemingly fall short. The Indian scholar and policy analyst Kanti Bajpai observed that "[r]ealism's appropriation of the term security rests on the assumption that interstate war is the greatest threat to personal safety and freedom. This may or may not be the case at any given time" (2000:51). Human security provides a direct remedy to this problem. As Lloyd Axworthy, a prominent Canadian politician, explains, human security "puts people first and recognizes that their safety is integral to the promotion and maintenance of international peace and security" (2001:19). From here, the international community has gone on to link human security concerns and provision to the concept of a **Responsibility to Protect (R2P)**.

Responsibility to Protect (R2P)
A global policy doctrine, endorsed by the United Nations in 2005, based on the idea that sovereignty confers responsibilities on states and their leaders—first and foremost, to ensure the well-being of their citizens. Among other things, R2P seeks to afford the international community the authority to address threats to human security in the event that a given state and its leaders are unwilling to do so themselves or are responsible for them.

One of the earliest statements concerning human security appeared in the UN's 1994 Human Development Report. The politics of security, the report made clear, must include not only "the security of borders [but] also . . . the security of people's lives" (United Nations Development Programme, 1994:23). The final report from the UN Commission on Human Security further defined human security to mean "protecting fundamental freedoms . . . protecting people from critical (severe) and pervasive (widespread) threats and situations" (2003:4). The report further connects different types of freedoms (freedom from want, freedom from fear, and freedom to take action on one's own behalf) and offers two general strategies to address these fears: protection and empowerment. Expanding this notion, the report identified seven specific elements that comprise human security: economic security, food security, health security, environmental security, personal security, community security, and political security.

Again, the security situation concerning North Korea provides an instructive tool for thinking about the redefinition of security and the notion of human security. Whereas a narrow, state-centric conception of security might suggest that maintaining the regional political order in East Asia takes precedence, a broader reformulation of the concept points in a different direction. If we think beyond secure borders and stable regimes to consider the rights of actual human beings and the security of the environment they inhabit, then the plight of North Koreans living under the repressive rule of Kim Jong-Un (and his father and grandfather before him) would point to massive insecurity within the state. From a human security perspective, the extensive network of political prisons, well-documented human rights violations, abject poverty, and chronic food shortages that typify North Korean society are more directly threatening to the security of the vast majority of North Koreans than any external actor. Of course, the same can be said for those coping with similar direct threats to their existence among the populace of any of North Korea's adversaries.

CNN Video: Life in
Korea's DMZ

🌐 Seeking Security: Illustrations

As the concept of security has evolved, so too have efforts to respond to widely recognized security threats. Among the most widely recognized and persistent threats to the security of nation-states, individuals, and the global system are the spread of armaments and the outbreak and persistence of armed conflict. This section examines efforts to respond to these pressing security challenges through arms control and conflict management.

Arms Control

The international arms trade is a booming industry. The estimated value of transfer agreements in major arms worldwide in 2018 was approximately $90 billion, with global arms transfers reaching their highest point since the end of the Cold War. Three quarters of those arms exports came from the world's five leading arms exporters—the United States, Russia, France, Germany, and China (in that order)—with close to 60% of those countries' exports going to developing nations and a significant proportion to rebel groups and nonstate actors (SIPRI, 2019). For realists, arms sales can help create stabilizing balances of power among states. However, other perspectives consider the flow of arms, ranging from heavy weaponry such as aircraft and tanks to small arms and light weapons, to be destabilizing, particularly in the hands of repressive states and insurgent groups. Either way, it is clear that the global arms trade is one of the most significant security issues of the 21st century.

A range of geopolitical factors drive the global arms trade, including the role of arms exports in maintaining strategic alliances as well as in subsidizing the industrial bases of arms-exporting countries. As Figure 8.3 shows, the United States was once again easily the world leader in the export of arms for the period from 2014 to 2018, accounting for 36% of the arms trade (SIPRI, 2019). Russia (21%) and France (6.8%) rounded out the top three global arms exporting nations (SIPRI, 2019). These numbers largely speak to the trade in major conventional arms and weapons systems, which is the best known and most lucrative aspect of the global arms business.

arms control Ranges from restricting the future growth in the number, types, or deployment of weapons to the reduction of weapons to the elimination of some types (or even all) weapons on a global or regional basis.

ATTEMPTING ARMS CONTROL. To enhance security, states and international organizations have long sought to monitor and limit the international exchange and production of weapons. **Arms control** involves limiting the numbers and types of weapons that countries possess. This approach aims at reducing military (especially offensive) capabilities and lessening the damage even if war begins. Additionally, arms control advocates believe that the decline in the number and power of weapons systems will ease political tensions, thereby making further arms agreements possible.

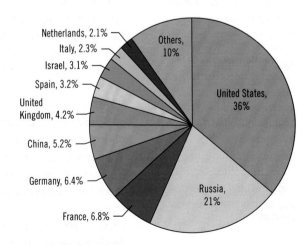

Figure 8.3 World arms sales during the years 2014 to 2018 were the highest of any five-year period since the end of the Cold War. A few countries dominated sales, as the pie chart indicates. (Source: SIPRI, 2019.)

There are many methods to control arms in order to limit or even reduce their number and to prevent their spread. These methods include numeric restrictions; categorical restrictions; development, testing, and deployment restrictions; geographic restrictions; and transfer restrictions.

Numeric Restrictions

Placing numeric limits above, at, or below the current level of existing weapons is the most common approach to arms control. This approach specifies the number or capacity of weapons and/or troops that each side may possess. In some cases, the numerical limits may be at or higher than current levels. By contrast, the US and Russian governments structured two bilateral **Strategic Arms Reduction Treaties (START I and II)** to significantly reduce the number of American and Russian nuclear weapons.

Categorical Restrictions

This approach to arms control involves limiting or eliminating certain types of weapons. The **Intermediate-Range Nuclear Forces Treaty (INF)** eliminated an entire class of weapons—intermediate-range nuclear missiles. The **Anti-Personnel Mine Ban Convention (aka the Ottawa Treaty)** and the **Convention on Cluster Munitions** outlawed weapons that often affect innocent civilians given their indiscriminate use and their ability to long outlast armed conflict.

Development, Testing, and Deployment Restrictions

This method of limiting arms seeks to ensure that weapons systems are limited in their development and testing phase as a means of preventing their deployment. The advantage of this approach is that it stops a specific area of arms building before it starts. For instance, the countries that have ratified the nuclear **Treaty on the Nonproliferation of Nuclear Weapons (NPT)** and that do not have such weapons agree not to develop them. Similarly, the **Comprehensive Test Ban Treaty (CTBT)** establishes restrictions on various forms of nuclear testing, with the overall goal of constraining the utility and effectiveness of nuclear weapons by limiting their research and development.

Geographic Restrictions

This method of arms control prohibits the deployment of any weapons of war in certain geographic areas. An example are the bans on deployment of military weapons in Antarctica, the seabed, and space. There can be geographic restrictions on specific types of weapons, such as the Treaty for the Prohibition of Nuclear Weapons in Latin America (1989).

Transfer Restrictions

This method of arms control prohibits or limits the flow of weapons and weapons technology across international borders. Under the NPT, for example, countries that have nuclear weapons or nuclear weapons technology pledge not to supply either to non-nuclear states.

MONITORING AND REPORTING.   In 2001, at the UN Conference on Curbing Illicit Trafficking of Small Arms and Light Weapons in All Its Aspects, states committed to voluntarily instituting better controls to mark and track weapons so that they could trace arms involved in conflict and human rights abuses to their source countries. From a human rights and humanitarian law perspective, this is critical for addressing civilian deaths as small arms and light weapons account for an estimated 60% to 90% of the conflict deaths each year (Small Arms Survey, 2012) and tens of thousands of additional deaths outside of war zones.

OBSTACLES TO ARMS CONTROL.   Despite support for limiting or reducing arms, arms control has proceeded slowly—and sometimes not at all (Figure 8.4). None of the factors discussed here is insurmountable, but together, they help explain the challenges of arms control. Each has their origins in the insecurity caused by an anarchic global system as well as the widespread acceptance of that condition.

Anxieties about the possibility of future conflict are probably the single greatest obstacle to arms control, with some analysts convinced that countries cannot maintain adequate security if they disarm totally or substantially. Whereas this mindset during the Cold War led to a huge arms buildup between and among the superpowers (the United States and USSR) and their allies, the expansion and spread of arms since 9/11 has been largely triggered by fears about the threat of terrorists and **rogue state(s)**. The security dilemma is again helpful here. One can see India's drive to acquire nuclear weapons in the 1970s, for instance, in part as a reaction to the nuclear arms of China to the north.

Convention on Cluster Munitions Adopted by 107 states in Dublin, Ireland, on May 30, 2008, this treaty prohibits all use, stockpiling, production, and transfer of cluster munitions (a form of air-dropped or ground-launched explosive weapon that releases or ejects smaller munitions).

Treaty on the Nonproliferation of Nuclear Weapons A multilateral treaty concluded in 1968, then renewed and made permanent in 1995. The parties to the treaty agree not to transfer nuclear weapons or to "assist, encourage, or induce any nonnuclear state to manufacture or otherwise acquire nuclear weapons" in any way. Non-nuclear signatories of the NPT also agree not to build or accept nuclear weapons.

Comprehensive Test Ban Treaty Bans all nuclear explosions in all environments for military or civilian purposes. Adopted by the United Nations General Assembly on September 10, 1996, but has yet to enter into force.

rogue state(s) A state that is perceived to be in noncompliance with the majority of prevailing rules, norms, and laws in the global system and therefore constituting a threat to order.

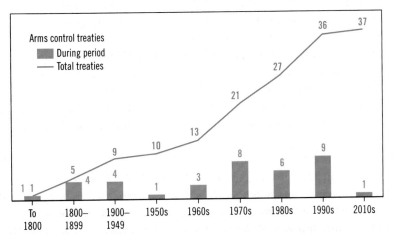

Figure 8.4 The development and use of increasingly devastating weapons has spurred greater efforts to limit them. This graph shows the number of treaties negotiated during various periods and the cumulative total of those treaties. The real acceleration of arms control began in the 1960s in an effort to restrain nuclear weapons. Of the 37 treaties covered here, 26 (70%) were concluded between 1960 and 1999. Note that treaties counted here are limited to those entered into force and dealing with specific weapons and verification only. (Source: Data from the Federation of American Scientists, the UN Department for Disarmament Affairs, the US Department of State, and various historical sources.)

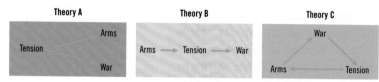

Figure 8.5 Theory A approximates the realist view, and Theory B fits the liberal view of the causal relationship between arms, tension, and use. Theory C suggests that a complex causal interrelationship exists between arms, tension, and war in which each of the three factors affects the other two.

India's program to defend itself against China then raised anxieties in Pakistan, which had fought several wars with India, so the Pakistanis began their program. "Today we have evened the score with India," Pakistan's prime minister exulted, after his country's first test.[5] Similarly, North Korea has repeatedly maintained that it needs nuclear weapons to act as a deterrent against foreign aggression, particularly what it perceives as aggression from the world's largest nuclear weapons state, the United States.

Doubts about the value of arms control, also rooted in the widespread acceptance of anarchy, work to impede arms control. Those who are skeptical about arms control begin with the belief that humans arm themselves and fight because the world is dangerous. Such skeptics believe that tensions are endemic in global politics (see Theory A in Figure 8.5) and, as a result, that states should achieve political settlements before they negotiate arms reductions. Those holding this view (mostly realists) reject the idea that arms control agreements necessarily represent progress; in fact, from this perspective one may argue that more, not fewer, weapons increase security by establishing a hierarchy of power that makes stable interactions between states more likely.

In contrast, other analysts agree with Homer's observation in the *Odyssey* (ca. 700 BCE) that "the blade itself incites to violence."[6] Theory B in Figure 8.5 demonstrates the belief that insecurity leads countries to have arms races, which lead to more insecurity and conflict in a hard-to-break cycle (Gibler, Rider, & Hutchison, 2005). From this perspective, the way for states to increase security is by reducing arms, not increasing them.

It is not always clear whether decreases in arms cause, or are caused by, periods of improved global cooperation. Instead, a host of domestic and systemic factors influence a country's level of armaments. What this means is that the most probable answer to the chicken-and-egg debate about which should come first, political agreements or arms control, lies in a combination of these theories. That is, arms, tension, and wars all interact, as Theory C in Figure 8.5 depicts.

Concerns about verification and cheating constitute an additional barrier to arms control, again rooted in anarchy. The problem here is simple: Countries suspect that others will cheat, a suspicion embodied in one of President Ronald Reagan's favorite maxims when discussing arms control negotiations with the Soviet Union—"Trust, but verify." This suspicion persists despite great advances in verification procedures and technologies. For example, many arms control treaties provide for on-site inspections by an agency such as the **International Atomic Energy Agency** in the case of nuclear materials. National technical means of verification using satellites, seismic measuring devices, and other equipment have also advanced rapidly. These have been substantially offset, however, by other technologies that make verification more difficult.

International Atomic Energy Agency The world's center of cooperation in the nuclear field. Established in 1957 as the world's "Atoms for Peace" organization within the United Nations family. The Agency works with its member-states and multiple partners worldwide to promote safe, secure, and peaceful nuclear technologies.

Domestic political factors also can work against arms control. Arms—conventional or otherwise—signal prestige as well as confer material power. For many countries, acquiring or developing arms represents a tangible symbol of strength and sovereign equality. "EXPLOSION OF SELF-ESTEEM" read one newspaper headline in India after that country's nuclear tests in 1998.[7] "LONG LIVE NUCLEAR PAKISTAN" read a Pakistani newspaper headline soon thereafter.[8] In addition, the importance of the global arms trade to the economies of many of the world's leading arms exporters should not be overlooked. Supplying the military is big business, and economic interest groups pressure their governments to build and sell weapons and associated technology. Additionally, bureaucratic elements, such as ministries of defense, often ally with the defense industry and its workers. Finally, both interest groups and bureaucratic actors receive support from legislators who represent the districts and states that benefit from military spending. This alliance between interest groups, bureaucracies, and legislators forms an **iron triangle** at the heart of the **military-industrial complex**, an arrangement that often generates strong domestic opposition to arms control.

Arms control, particularly with respect to nuclear arms, is at the heart of the current security challenges posed by North Korea. Once a signatory to the NPT—which binds non-nuclear weapons states to a pledge not to pursue or acquire them—North Korea withdrew from this agreement in 2003, announcing its nuclear weapons capability two years later. To some degree, the expansion of North Korea's nuclear weapons program is a response to the flaws of the NPT and the breakdown in nuclear arms control talks with North Korea over the years. In 1994, for instance, the Clinton administration was on the verge of a breakthrough with Kim Jong-Il—the "Framework Agreement"—that would have bound North Korea to abandon its weapons program. However, the US Senate rejected the agreement. The North Korean regime viewed this as treachery on the part of the Americans, which played a part in undermining the so-called "Six Party Talks" (United States, Russia, China, North Korea, South Korea, and Japan) on nuclear weapons that began in 2003. Following the election of President Donald Trump in 2016, North Korea's nuclear weapons program and capacity vaulted to the top of the international security agenda—first because of incendiary remarks threatening nuclear war by both Trump and North Korean leader Kim Jong-Un, and later as a result of two unprecedented bilateral

iron triangle A close, mutually beneficial arrangement between interest groups, the bureaucracy, and legislators within a given political system that forms the basis for the military-industrial complex.

military-industrial complex A term coined by President Dwight Eisenhower that refers to political and economic relationships between legislators, national armed forces, and the defense industrial base that supports them. These relationships include political contributions, political approval for defense spending, lobbying to support bureaucracies, and beneficial legislation and oversight of the industry.

Characterized both as a precedent-setting breakthrough as well as a pointless debacle, this photo from the second face-to-face summit between President Donald Trump and North Korean leader Kim Jong-Un in Hanoi, Vietnam, in February 2019 suggests at a minimum the paramount importance of nuclear weapons to the security of both countries—and the entire world.

summits featuring direct talks between both men. While neither summit has produced a concrete breakthrough, the issue remains on the front-burner as North Korea has continued to expand and improve its nuclear weapons delivery capabilities.

Conflict Management

Another prominent challenge to individual, national, and global security is the continuing prevalence of armed conflict around the world. Here, we look at some of the more common efforts to promote security by limiting the outbreak of war and armed conflict and reducing its damaging consequences—efforts that we lump under the broad heading of "conflict management." In the field of international relations, **conflict management** is understood as any effort to control or contain an ongoing conflict between politically motivated actors operating at the state or substate level (Burton & Dukes, 1990). You should also note that many forms of conflict management are not mentioned here. These include mediation, dual-track (informal) diplomacy, and many more. We encourage you to study these further if you wish to delve deeper into this important aspect of security provision.

Conflict management seeks to contain a conflict's damaging and destabilizing effects to other parties ("horizontal escalation") as well as the conflict's escalation of violence ("vertical escalation"). The goal of conflict management is to deny "victory" to the aggressor(s)—or, perhaps more accurately, to deny the utility of aggression. Conflict management approaches are utilized when the prospects for full resolution of the conflict seem far-off but the dynamics of the conflict demand that something be done to contain it (Von Hippel & Clarke, 1999). Over the past three decades, much greater attention has been paid to a wider array of issues in conflict management, including conflict's impact on noncombatants, the unique impacts on women and children, and much more. One recent study argues that conflict management and postconflict peace-building can be significantly enhanced by drawing on the insights from the subfield of women, peace, and security studies (Thomson, 2018). We look at several approaches here, but also note that this discussion is far from exhaustive given the wide array of methods that exist to pursue conflict management.

COLLECTIVE SECURITY. The idea of **collective security** is based on three core ideas:

1. Armed aggression is an unacceptable form of international political behavior.

2. An act of aggression directed against any one member in good standing in the international community is a breach of security and an act of aggression against all parties.

3. The provision of security (including the prevention and reversal of acts of aggression) is the duty of all actors in the global political system.

---

conflict management An approach to security provision that focuses on containing the use of violence in interstate and intrastate conflicts and disputes. Conflict management efforts, which often take the form of third-party mediation or peace operations, are best understood as a necessary prelude to conflict resolution.

collective security Holds that an act of aggression against one state constitutes an act of aggression against all members in good standing of the international community and therefore is deserving of a collective response. Underpins the peace and security strategies and operations of the United Nations, other international organizations, and some states.

To this end, as Baylis (2001:264) points out, collective security involves a recognition by states of the following:

1. They must renounce the use of military force to alter the status quo and agree to settle disputes peacefully.

2. They must broaden their conception of the national interest to take account of the interests of the international community.

3. They must overcome the fear which dominates world politics and learn to trust one another.

The emphasis on the security of the entire international community, combined with the obligation of all to join in a shared, collective response to aggression, is what distinguishes collective security systems. Examples of regional or global institutionalized collective security arrangements include the North Atlantic Treaty Organization (NATO) and, in part, the UN as well as various other organizations, including the Organization of American States, the Organization for African Unity (now the African Union), the Association of Southeast Asian Nations, and the Organization for Security and Cooperation in Europe (OSCE; established as the Conference on Security and Cooperation in Europe).

PEACEKEEPING.   **Peacekeeping** operations involve the introduction of armed military (as well as civilian police) personnel into conflict zones to support the cessation of hostilities. This is a very different use of military force, which traditionally is employed to defeat adversaries, hold or acquire territory, capture valuable resources, and the like through offensive actions. As Figure 8.6 indicates, since the end of the Cold War the UN has carried out the bulk of peacekeeping operations, although regional organizations and other arrangements can and have provided peacekeeping. Typically, peacekeeping forces carry out mandated responsibilities (specified in multilateral agreements, peace agreements, or resolutions passed by the UN or regional organizations) to monitor ceasefires, maintain buffer zones, and otherwise facilitate security.

We can plausibly characterize a wide variety of activities as peacekeeping tasks, including but not limited to observation, fact-finding, monitoring ceasefires, and interposition (Bellamy, Williams, & Griffin, 2010). In more recent years, peacekeeping operations have expanded to include various tasks related to political administration, infrastructure rebuilding, and the promotion of civil society (sometimes called "wider" or multidimensional peacekeeping).

In whatever form they take or wherever place they occur, peacekeeping features three distinctive emphases. These are a limited reliance on coercive force, impartiality, and consent from the combatants.

With respect to limited force, peacekeeping deployments can be numerous in terms of personnel but are always lightly armed. The typical peacekeeper possesses no more than a rifle or small arms, and the typical peacekeeping deployment is arrayed around the use of transport and logistics equipment (e.g., helicopters and armored personnel carriers) rather than those better suited for

peacekeeping The use of military means in a noncoercive posture by an international organization such as the United Nations to prevent a recurrence of military hostilities, usually by acting as a buffer between combatants in a suspended conflict. The international force is neutral and must have been invited by the combatants before deployment.

Simulation:
Keeping the Peace in
Gineau-Bissau

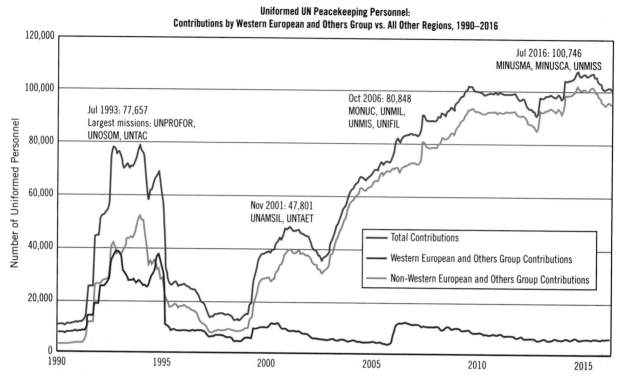

Figure 8.6   UN peacekeeping deployments between 1990 and 2016, both in terms of total personnel and major operations. As is evident here, though not without some variation, peacekeeping operations since the end of the Cold War have been on a steady upward trajectory, partly as a result of the many and varied armed conflicts and related security challenges confronting the international community. As is also evident, the vast majority of peacekeepers are drawn from non-Western countries. (Source: Data from Peace and Security Section, Department of Public Information / Department of Peacekeeping Operations [DPKO] Office of Military Affairs.)

offensive action (e.g., tanks, fighter planes, and aircraft carriers). The extent to which peacekeepers are armed and equipped is consistent with their need to exercise their right to self-defense and to possess a visible and credible deterrent capability, but it does not go beyond that.

Peacekeeping operations are also defined by their impartiality. The neutral nature of the character, activities, and composition of peacekeeping operations has both strategic and political dimensions. Within any peacekeeping deployment, the peacekeepers' behavior must be impartial in order to avoid lending strategic or tactical advantage to any one party to the conflict. From a political standpoint, the practice of peacekeeping is wholly dependent on maintaining the view that peacekeepers (especially when provided the auspices of the UN or some other international organization) are neutral. Since the resources committed to peacekeeping come from nation-states, impartiality is crucial (See Figure 8.6).

Another crucial aspect of peacekeeping operations is that they obtain the consent (permission) of the combatants—typically, the governmental authorities operating where they will be deployed. This means that peacekeepers require the consent of warring parties before they can enter into a conflict zone. For both political and legal reasons, peacekeeping has been and remains fundamentally oriented around upholding state sovereignty and defending the principle of noninterference, making consent from the warring parties an essential condition.

Ultimately, peacekeeping is a frequently misused term that has been applied to very dissimilar operations. Operations ranging from observer missions monitoring contested borders (e.g., the UN Military Observer Group in India/Pakistan in 1949) to multifaceted missions effectively administering an entire country (e.g., the UN Transitional Administration in East Timor in 1999)—and everything in between—have been lumped under the heading of "peacekeeping." It is important to stress that peacekeeping is always a reactive activity that occurs after conflicts abate. It is also a military operation with highly limited rules of engagement using low levels of force with the consent of the warring parties. Peacekeeping does not seek to alter the direction of a conflict, but rather to secure sometimes fragile peace agreements and processes.

PEACE ENFORCEMENT. Another tool of conflict management is **peace enforcement**. This refers to a concerted initiative organized under international auspices to impose the conditions for peace where they do not exist (Johnston, 2001). As such, it is a very different form of peace operation, born from recognizing the limitations of peacekeeping for the effective management of certain types and forms of conflict. Former UN Secretary-General Boutros Boutros-Ghali popularized the term peace enforcement, as we conventionally understand it, in his 1992 policy proposal "An Agenda for Peace." Since that time, prominent peace enforcement operations have included the Australian-led International Force for East Timor in 1999–2000, NATO's Operation Allied Force in Kosovo beginning in 1999, and the United Nations Organization Mission in the Democratic Republic of the Congo, initiated in 1999.

Peace enforcement is in many ways a reaction to, if not a rejection of, peacekeeping. In many contemporary conflicts, the interposition of impartial and lightly armed forces as a buffer between the warring parties is unlikely to provide a sufficient deterrent. By contrast, peace enforcement operations are intended to forcefully impose a cessation in hostilities to provide the conditions amenable to the crafting of a long-term peaceful settlement. The first and most distinguishing feature of peace enforcement is its **rules of engagement**. Unlike peacekeeping, peace enforcement operations possess the authority to use armed force not only in self-defense but in other circumstances as well. Chief among these circumstances are the imperatives of defending noncombatants who are under attack or threat of attack and to engage on a military basis with armed combatants. In this sense, peace enforcers may use coercive force along the lines of what might occur in a conventional military operation.

In some cases, the parties to the conflict may not want to stop warring. Peace operations in this sort of conflict environment require the infusion of force by a third party. This contributes to another key distinguishing feature of peace enforcement operations—namely, that they do not rely on the consent

peace enforcement The use of military means in a semi-coercive posture by an international organization such as the United Nations to introduce and enforce peace in an ongoing conflict setting. Peace enforcement operations relax some of the restrictions on peacekeeping, allowing more expansive rules of engagement and deployment without full consent of the warring parties.

rules of engagement Rules defining acceptable conduct by members of the armed forces engaged in a theater of conflict during operations or in carrying out the course of their duties. Typically, the rules of engagement are clearly stipulated by political leaders and military commanders and are formulated to advance strategic goals while ensuring compliance with the laws of war.

CHALLENGE YOUR ASSUMPTIONS

Gender, Conflict, and UN Security Council Resolution 1325

United Nations Security Council Resolution (UNSCR) 1325, passed in October 2010, represents a landmark in the arena of gender and international security. This resolution was the first time the Security Council directly addressed the subject of women and armed conflict, not simply as vulnerable victims but as agents, with the right to participate in decision-making at all levels and during all phases of conflict and conflict resolution. Adopted unanimously, UNSCR 1325 calls for all participants in peace negotiations "to adopt a gender perspective" and "expresses its willingness to incorporate a gender perspective into peacekeeping operations" (S/1325/2000).[9] In short, this resolution recognizes the importance of women in international peace and security policy, making women's needs and gender equality relevant to negotiating peace agreements; planning refugee camps and peacekeeping operations; designing disarmament, demobilization, and reintegration programs; generally reconstructing war-torn societies; and ultimately, making gender equality relevant to every single Security Council action (Rehn & Sirleaf, 2002).

UNSCR 1325 represents the first time that gender mainstreaming has become official policy in the context of the UN's peace and security work, setting a new threshold of action for the Security Council, the UN system, and for all member states in the "new" security environment. On the ground, this resolution has translated into important procedural changes for UN country missions as well as a new focus on the individual security needs, particularly those of women, in conflict situations across the globe.

One UN entity that has perhaps advanced furthest in implementing USCR 1325 is the Department of UN Peacekeeping Operations (DPKO). The DPKO has implemented significant organizational changes after adoption of an internal action plan on UNSCR 1325, ranging from the establishment of a Gender Team at its UN headquarters to institutionalization of gender advisors or Gender Units in all peacekeeping missions established after 2000 (Tryggestad, 2009). With some select support from member-states, the DPKO has also overseen deployment of the first all-female unit of peacekeepers, which the UN first sent to Liberia in 2007. In 2011, the United Nations–African Union Mission in Darfur began training the first all-female police contingent in Sudan. The establishment of these units is important, as they seek to empower local women and further institutionalize consideration of gender-based violence as a serious threat relevant to rebuilding security sectors in post-conflict societies.

Possibly one of the greatest achievements of UNSCR 1325 has been its ability to frame gender equality and women's rights as issues relevant, if not central, to security provision. This has meant not only recognition of women's unique security needs during and after conflict, but also acceptance of the notion that women's security is essential to the fundamental goal of the Security Council—namely, the promotion and protection of international peace and security. This represents a significant expansion of what constitutes a security issue and how countries transitioning from armed conflict have the opportunity to redefine state security (Hudson, 2009).

of the combatants, and even may proceed without securing consent at all. Although this differs sharply from peacekeeping, peace enforcement does share an operational emphasis on impartiality. The main "enemy" of any peace enforcement operation, therefore, is the persistence of organized aggression, not any of the warring parties. By design, peace enforcement operations usually strive to implement their mandate in an even-handed fashion that sustains and enhances the conditions for peace but does not target or assist any party to the conflict.

Peace enforcement operations require (and sometimes receive) a different form of legal authorization than do peacekeeping missions. One way of understanding the difference comes through reference to the UN Charter, which is the source of legal authority for all UN peace operations (and which influences decisions about non-UN peace operations as well). Because they are noncoercive, peacekeeping operations can be seen as extensions of Chapter VI (subtitled "Pacific Settlement of Disputes"). On the other hand, peace enforcement operations more closely resemble the impulse of Chapter VII (subtitled "Action with Respect to Threats to the Peace, Breaches of the Peace and Acts of Aggression"). It was this chapter that the UN Security Council invoked in September 2003 to authorize the UN Mission in Liberia (UNMIL)– a multidimensional peace enforcement operation that continued until March 2018.

Peace enforcement is a controversial method of security provision in a global political system that continues to emphasize the normative and legal authority of state sovereignty. This is because peace enforcement operations permit actors other than states (e.g., the UN and various Regional Governmental Organizations, or RGOs) to employ coercive military force and to determine why, when, and how to do so. In this way, peace enforcement offends the sensibilities of realists and others who point to the state as the central and most legitimate security actor. Peace enforcement also clashes with the norm of noninterference derived from the concept of state sovereignty and articulated in international law through the UN Charter—making peace enforcement not only an affront to realists, but to some liberals as well. These factors make peace enforcement difficult to implement, even when it might enhance individual, national, regional, or global security.

🌐 The "New" Security Environment

The "broadening" and "deepening" of security as a concept referenced above is both a cause and an effect of apparent changes in the global security landscape. Here, we highlight the origins of what some scholars and policy-makers refer to as the "new" security environment, as well as the rules, actors, problems, and threats that define it.

Origins: The End of the Cold War

Most contemporary scholars and practitioners concerned with security have come to accept the changing nature of security threats and responses. This characterization is difficult to dispute given the prominence of the **new security environment** as a point of reference in such disparate pockets of officialdom as United Nations Educational, Scientific, and Cultural Organization (UNESCO) policy reports (UNESCO, 2001), position papers produced by the various US war colleges (Yarger, 2010), and even keynote addresses by NATO military commanders (de Hoop Scheffer, 2005). Those changes, and the recognition of them, are undoubtedly tied to the seismic geopolitical shift brought about by the collapse of the Soviet Union and the end of the Cold War. Differing interpretations about the significance of the end of the Cold War for global security ranged from proclamations of a utopian "end of history" (Fukuyama, 1989) to predictions of a multipolar balance of power arrayed across the United States,

new security environment
A catch-all term referring to the emergence of a multiplicity of "new" (or perhaps newly recognized) threats to the security of states, individuals, and the global system in the contemporary (post–Cold War) world.

Europe, and Japan (Mearsheimer, 1990) to dire forecasts of an impending and all-encompassing "clash of civilizations" (Huntington, 1993).

The common theme in attempts at forecasting the post–Cold War landscape was that dramatic changes were afoot. One leading scholar referred to the post–Cold War period as one of new world disorder (Zartman, 2008). In this view of the contemporary security landscape, the end of the Cold War triggered or revealed a plethora of new or previously overlooked security threats and challenges. Included among these were the increasing frequency of intrastate conflicts; the rampant spread of small arms and light weapons; the simultaneous increase in failed and failing states, environmental degradation, and population displacement; and the blossoming of transnational terrorism and crime.

Many observers have equated the new security environment with the rise to the fore of transnational terrorism in the aftermath of the 9/11 attacks. Certainly, 9/11 has had an appreciable effect on the ways that states define and pursue security. Perhaps most important from the standpoint of considerations of a new security environment, 9/11 illuminated for the first time, for a mass audience and particularly in the United States, the importance of nonstate actors and transnational forces and processes within the security realm. The importance of transnational terrorism notwithstanding, the concept of a new security environment speaks to something much more fundamental and far-reaching. While terrorism is certainly a prominent feature of the contemporary security landscape, so too are ethnic conflict, state failure, climate change, genocide, and numerous other security threats and challenges (C.A.S.E. Collective, 2006; Mathews, 1989).

Defining Features: New Rules, Actors, and Threats

The new security environment is defined by shifting rules, emerging actors, and intensifying threats.

SHIFTING RULES: STATE SOVEREIGNTY IN DECLINE. Sovereign states were the centerpiece of traditional approaches to security. In seeking to understand the complex dynamics of contemporary security, one must acknowledge that while state sovereignty remains important, it is no longer the only or even the most important consideration. Critical approaches to security studies share a concern with defining security as something beyond militarized interactions between competing sovereign states (Baldwin, 1997). Empirical data suggest that states are increasingly unlikely to even engage in such behavior anyway. According to the estimates of the Uppsala Conflict Data Programme, of the 49 active armed conflicts in 2017, only two (Ethiopia-Eritrea, and India-Pakistan) were wholly interstate (Pettersson & Eck, 2018).

The emphasis of realism on states, power, order, and competing interests made it a highly useful theory for describing security threats and proscribing security responses in an era when states were dominant. However, given the central importance of social inequality, gender inequity, poverty and relative deprivation, resource scarcity and environmental degradation, organized crime, public health, external and internal migration, and the like, the utility of realist accounts for thinking about security—not to mention for providing

CNN Video: What After Bin Laden?

it—is an open question in a world where the source and/or target of a security threat may have nothing to do with the state. This thinking has led to a growing focus on the study of security governance and the transformed nature of security in the contemporary global system (Hameiri, Jones, & Sandor, 2018). In line with this argument, one scholar even argued that China, long viewed as a classic Westphalian state, is much less unitary, coherent, and strategic than many scholars have long believed (Jones, 2018).

EMERGING ACTORS: THE IMPACT OF NONSTATE ACTORS.   The rise to prominence of nonstate actors underscores the state's diminished role in the contemporary security arena. One should be careful not to underestimate the impact of multinational corporations, nongovernmental organizations, transnational terrorist networks, paramilitaries, private military contractors, policy think tanks, peace advocates, and even individuals. This "party-crashing" by nonstate actors altered the status quo in the global system, with direct ramifications for security thinking and action. Consider, for instance, the implications of the far-reaching appeal (both ideationally and spatially) of ISIS, and before that al-Qaeda, on the security agendas and policies of much of the international community; the role of nongovernmental organizations, such as the Coalition for an International Criminal Court in shaping international law and institutions; or the impacts of remittances from migratory workers on the economies of many developing countries. These and many other similar examples point to two crucial dimensions of structural change in the contemporary security environment: the rise to the fore of nonstate actors as sources of both collective security threats and responses, and the potential that nonstate actors in either capacity may foster and perpetuate a weakening of state capacity in the security realm.

INTENSIFYING THREATS: THE "DARK SIDE" OF INTERDEPENDENCE.   Characterizations of a new security environment recognize new or previously overlooked sources of insecurity. We can understand these in many ways as by-products of the complex interdependence that defines global politics today. The benefits of interdependence are many, and they are often celebrated (Friedman, 2007; Keohane & Nye, 2001). Yet at the same time, networked interactions between and among societies and individuals is not without its hazards. Most notable among these is the increased sensitivity and vulnerability of an ever-greater number of actors, including states, to an increasingly wide range of security threats (Baldwin, 1980).

The dramatic response of public officials to threats of Avian flu (the H5N1 virus) symbolizes the rising impact of "nontraditional" security threats (e.g., the spread of disease) and the ways in which increasingly dense and expansive transnational linkages exacerbate these problems and their security implications. In this photo, public health professionals in China inoculate citizens against the virus in order to prevent the type of crippling epidemic that could undermine national, regional, and global security.

Without a doubt, the political, social, economic, cultural, and intellectual processes of globalization, as well as the backlash against these processes, pose a very real security challenge. Just as we enjoy the benefits that a smaller globe brings in terms of communications and access to a diverse array of consumer goods and services, globalization has also produced violent protests and conflict rooted in frustrations about those transformations and the unequal benefits they yield. Yet it is not just opposition from globalization's discontents that is important here. The increasing intensity and penetration of interdependence has created a degree of densely networked but weakly governed connections in commerce, transport, energy and natural resources, migration, and information technology. Whether in the rise of transnational terrorism, potential global epidemics such as HIV/AIDS or the Avian flu, the activities of multiple and competing organized crime networks, the proliferation of weapons of mass destruction as well as the easy exchange of conventional arms, or a variety of other developments, the new security environment provides an account of what we might consider the "dark side" of interdependence.

⊕ Threat Assessment: Weapons of Mass Destruction

The new security environment has changed the way citizens and decision-makers perceive security and respond to security threats. This section discusses one example of a pressing contemporary security challenge: weapons of mass destruction (WMDs), their proliferation (spread), and efforts to control them. The security threat posed by WMDs serves as a useful illustration of the ways in which a somewhat traditional military security issue has evolved in light of the changing rules, actors, and threats associated with the new security environment.

weapons of mass destruction
Often referring to nuclear weapons, but also including biological and chemical weapons. Weapons of mass destruction warfare refers to the application of force between countries using biological, chemical, and/or nuclear weapons.

Weapons of mass destruction are the most lethal and destructive in the world and are grouped into three categories: biological, chemical, and nuclear. The security threat associated with WMDs is heightened by the fact that such weapons kill and wound indiscriminately, with widespread impact on civilians as well as combatants. The dropping of the atomic bombs over Hiroshima and Nagasaki in 1945 clearly illustrates this dramatic and devastating impact. Here, we deal briefly with biological and chemical weapons, then turn to a more extensive examination of nuclear weapons and their strategic and security implications.

Biological Weapons

Biological warfare—defined as the use of pathogens such as viruses, bacteria, or other disease-causing biological agents or toxins as weapons—is hardly new. As early as the sixth century BCE, the Assyrians poisoned enemy wells with a parasitic fungus called rye ergot that caused gangrene and convulsions. More catastrophically, the Tartar army besieging Kaffa, a Genoese trading outpost in the Crimea in 1346, catapulted plague-infected corpses and heads over the walls to spread the disease among the defenders. Many of those who fled back to Italy carried the disease with them and, according to some historians, set off the Black Death that killed millions of Europeans. North America first experienced biological warfare in 1763 when the British commander in North

PERSONAL NARRATIVE

Security and Self: An Exercise

In 1994, the security studies scholar Ken Booth published a paper entitled "Security and Self: Confessions of a Fallen Realist" (Booth, 1994). The primary intention of Booth's paper was to document the shift in his thinking about security from his early days as a classically trained realist to his emergence as a leading voice in critical security studies. More broadly, however, Booth sought to engage in a bout of self-reflection, as a way of underscoring that "the personal, the political, and the international are a seamless web." In Booth's view, such an exercise was especially radical in the field of security studies—yet at the same time absolutely critical in order to reveal the factors that influence our thinking and perception about the very nature of security itself.

Other chapters present stories of the impact that "normal," everyday people have had on global politics. Now it is *your* turn. In the spirit of Booth, here is an exercise in self-assessment. Whether you complete this on your own, with your classmates, or in class, the question is the same: What shapes your view of global politics, and especially security? We have already discussed the contested nature of security as a concept. So how do *you* understand it, and what explains why you see it that way?

Self-Assessment

Evaluate the following statements on the following basis: 1 = Strongly Disagree; 2= Moderately Disagree; 3= Neutral/No Opinion; 4= Moderately Agree; 5 = Strongly Agree

STATEMENT	EVALUATION (1 TO 5)
1. Conflict in the international system is inevitable.	
2. The state is the most important actor in the international system.	
3. The state is likely to remain the most important actor in the international system for the rest of my lifetime.	
4. Human rights are something best determined by individual societies.	
5. Structural forces largely determine and constrain the actions of individuals.	
6. Academics and academia have relatively little impact on the actual conduct of international relations.	
7. Security in any given society is best provided by and through the state.	
8. In international relations, material interests and power are more important than ideas and identities.	
9. Global governance is problematic, if not impossible.	
10. Acquiring knowledge through analyzing the "real world," looking for recurrent patterns, and formulating and testing theories is the best way to study international relations/security.	

America, Sir Jeffrey Amherst, wrote to subordinates at Fort Pitt, "Could it not be contrived to send the smallpox among those disaffected tribes of Indians?"[10] As it turns out, soldiers at the fort had already given disease-infected blankets to members of the Shawnee and Delaware tribes.

Although the 1972 Biological Weapons Convention bans the production, possession, and use of germ-based **biological weapons**, some states are thought to possess stocks of them or to have an interest in acquiring them. These states include North Korea, Iran, Russia, and Syria. Relatively recent evidence of bioweapons activity gives credence to such possibilities. The UN-led inspections

biological weapons Living organisms or replicating entities (viruses and other pathogens) that reproduce or replicate within their host victims. Employed in various ways to gain a strategic or tactical advantage over an adversary, either by threats or by actual deployments.

Chemical weapons attacks have occurred repeatedly during the Syrian civil war, which began in early 2011. Here, aid workers remove infants from the rubble of Aleppo, where the United Nations contends the ruling Assad regime has employed chemical weapons, including chlorine bombs, on multiple occasions.

of Iraq after the 1991 Persian Gulf War indicated that the country also had a germ warfare program that had produced, at minimum, 132,000 gallons of anthrax and botulism toxins. Anthrax has also become a security threat to the United States, particularly in 2001 when someone sent a small amount of anthrax spores through the US Postal Service to government and media offices, killing several and significantly disrupting the mail service. Although the US government ultimately blamed the anthrax attacks on an American scientist with access to military bioweapons programs, there are ongoing fears about the potential use of this biological agent.

Although a large-scale biological attack has not happened to date, many scientists and policy-makers continue to see a significant security risk with no regard for state borders or national boundaries. Considering ongoing advances in the field of biotechnology, both the expertise and the materials necessary to mount a biological attack are becoming more accessible, as are the tools and facilities for doing so. In this way, many fear that terrorists could also find it easier to produce and weaponize various pathogens. Thus, bioterrorism has emerged as a potential security threat and an area of policy activity.

Chemical Weapons

chemical weapons Devices that use chemical agents to inflict death or harm to human beings. They are classified as weapons of mass destruction.

Chemical weapons have earned the nickname "the poor man's atomic bomb" because they are relatively easy and inexpensive to produce. As one former CIA director told Congress over two decades ago, "Chemicals used to make nerve agents are also used to make plastics and [to] process foodstuff. Any modern pharmaceutical facility can produce biological warfare agents as easily as vaccines or antibiotics."[11] Again, there is a much longer backstory here. Both sides used mustard gas widely during World War I, and to horrific effect. As a result, the international community adopted the 1925 Geneva Protocol banning the use (though not the production or possession) of chemical weapons. This treaty, which is still in effect today, has been supplemented by the Chemical Weapons Convention, a multilateral treaty that entered into force in 1997. The Chemical Weapons Convention bans the use and the production of chemical weapons and provides a timetable for the eventual destruction of existing stockpiles.

Despite these international agreements, states continue to use chemical weapons both in interstate and civil wars. The United States used Agent Orange, a highly toxic herbicide, extensively to defoliate the jungle during the Vietnam War. Both Iran and Iraq used chemical weapons during their grueling war (1980–1988), and Iraq used them to attack rebelling Kurdish and Shiite populations after the Gulf War in 1991. Throughout the 1990s, UN inspectors uncovered stores of chemical weapons in Iraq, revealing a systematic chemical weapons program administered by Iraqi President Saddam Hussein's first cousin, Ali Hassan al-Majid (aka "Chemical Ali"), who directly ordered numerous attacks against civilians, including one in 1988 that killed approximately 5,000 people in the Kurdish city of Halabja. More recently, in April 2017, the embattled Syrian regime headed by Bashar al-Assad used the nerve agent sarin against the rebel-held town Khan Sheikhoun in Idlib province, killing nearly 100 people and leaving many more sick and wounded (Organization for the Prohibition of Chemical Weapons, 2017). This was the second internationally verified use of chemical weapons by the Assad regime against opposition forces during the Syrian civil war, the first occurring in an opposition-controlled area outside the capital of Damascus during August 2013 and killing over 1,000 people.[12]

Nuclear Weapons

As made horrifyingly clear during World War II, nuclear weapons are by far the world's most destructive weapons. **Nuclear weapons** include both fission weapons, like the atomic bomb, as well as fusion weapons, like the hydrogen bomb. The latter tend to be smaller and less expensive to produce. Of course, either category is potentially lethal to large numbers of people, making the proliferation of nuclear weapons states in recent years one of, if not the most, serious sources of insecurity at the global, national, and local levels.

Roughly as old as nuclear weapons themselves are efforts to limit their spread, or to disarm those states that have acquired nuclear weapons capabilities. As reflected in the two primary multilateral treaty instruments dedicated to nuclear arms control—the NPT and the CTBT—the twin strategies of **nonproliferation** and **disarmament** are the primary avenues by which the international community has sought to control nuclear weapons. The NPT restricts lawful possession of nuclear weapons to the initial five members of the so-called nuclear club (the United States, USSR/Russia, United Kingdom, France, and China), with all other signatories to the treaty agreeing to renounce nuclear weapons aspirations. In return, these five states pledged to make meaningful progress toward nuclear disarmament—progress that the limits on testing and research stipulated by the Partial Test Ban Treaty, which entered into force in 1963, and later the CTBT, (which was adopted in 1996 but has yet to enter into force), further advanced. The continued pursuit of disarmament, as well as the perceived inequities in the NPT, have limited the effectiveness of multilateral efforts to control nuclear weapons.

NUCLEAR WEAPONS ARSENALS.   With the end of the Cold War, concern over the threat of nuclear war virtually disappeared from the media and from general political discussion. Unfortunately, the perception of great advances in safety and security is not borne out by facts. It is true that the number of strategic nuclear weapons has declined. Nevertheless, many extremely powerful nuclear weapons remain in the arsenals of several states, and the interest in acquiring nuclear weapons by non–nuclear weapons states has seemingly intensified, as reflected by the addition of India, Pakistan, and North Korea to the ranks of nuclear weapons states in recent years (Map 8.1).

nuclear weapons Explosive devices that derive their destructive force from nuclear reactions, either fission or a combination of fission and fusion.

nonproliferation Limitation of the production or spread of any form of weaponry. Higher-profile nonproliferation efforts concern nuclear, chemical, and biological weapons.

disarmament The act of reducing, limiting, or abolishing a category of weapons.

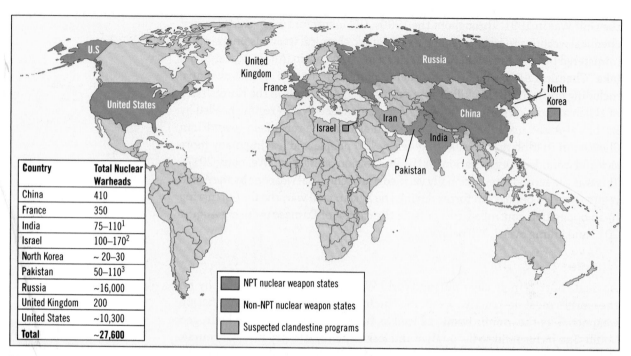

Country	Total Nuclear Warheads
China	410
France	350
India	75–110[1]
Israel	100–170[2]
North Korea	~ 20–30
Pakistan	50–110[3]
Russia	~16,000
United Kingdom	200
United States	~10,300
Total	**~27,600**

■ NPT nuclear weapon states

■ Non-NPT nuclear weapon states

■ Suspected clandestine programs

Map 8.1 The possession and spread of nuclear weapons remains a front-burner global security issue due to the destructive power of the weapons, the size of existing arsenals, and the clandestine nature of some nuclear weapons programs. (Data Source: Carnegie Endowment for International Peace, Deadly Arsenals, http://www.carnegieendowment.org/files/DeadlyII.)

strategic-range delivery vehicles Delivery vehicles for nuclear weapons, such as land- or submarine-based ballistic missiles and long-range heavy bombers, capable of attacking targets at distances greater than 5,500 kilometers. These delivery systems confer tremendous strategic advantage to states possessing them and have often been a great source of instability as well as a target of arms control efforts, such as those between the United States and USSR/Russia.

deterrence Persuading an opponent not to carry out an undesirable action by combining both sufficient capabilities and credible threats so as to forestall that action.

With enormous stockpiles inherited from the Cold War, the United States and Russia remain the nuclear Goliaths. In 2018, each of these two countries deployed a strategic-range (5,550 kilometers/3,416.8 miles) arsenal of approximately 1,600 warheads (Federation of American Scientists, 2018). Each country's **strategic-range delivery vehicles** also remain numerous, with the United States currently having nearly 700 nuclear-ready, long-range missiles and heavy bombers operational and Russia about 800 such delivery vehicles. Both countries also keep a substantial number of nuclear warheads and bombs in reserve. In 2018, Russia had a total nuclear inventory of approximately 6,850 warheads and the United States 6,450, together accounting for an overwhelming majority of the roughly 15,000 nuclear weapons known to be stockpiled worldwide (Federation of American Scientists, 2018).

China, France, India, North Korea, Pakistan, and the United Kingdom all openly possess nuclear weapons, with Israel possessing an undeclared nuclear weapons arsenal. All told, these states add another 1,185 nuclear devices to the volatile mix of deployed tactical and strategic nuclear devices (Federation of American Scientists, 2018). Additionally, other countries, most notably Iran, have or are suspected of having nuclear weapons development programs, and another 30 countries have the necessary technology base to build nuclear weapons (Map 8.2).

NUCLEAR DETERRENCE AND STRATEGY. The concept of deterrence remains at the center of the strategy of all the nuclear powers. **Deterrence** is persuading an enemy that attacking you will not be worth the cost, and it relies on two

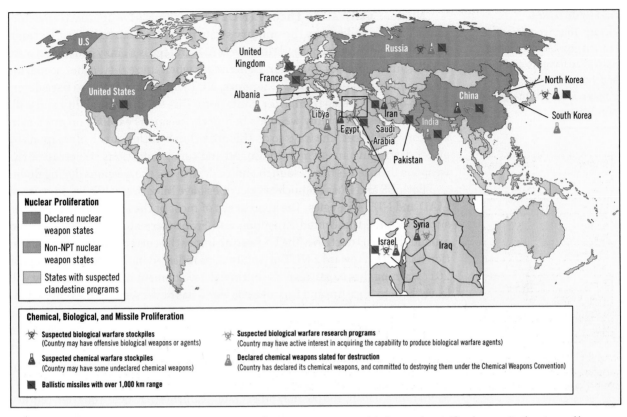

Map 8.2   Folding in the status of chemical and biological weapons programs and their spread magnifies the security threat posed by weapons of mass destruction. (Data Source: Carnegie Endowment for International Peace, Deadly Arsenals, http://www.carnegieendowment.org/files/DeadlyII.)

factors. Capability is one. Effective deterrence requires that even if you are attacked, you must be able to preserve enough strength to retaliate powerfully. Of all current strategic weapons systems, submarine-launched ballistic missiles are least vulnerable to attack and, therefore, the most important element of deterrence. Fixed-silo intercontinental ballistic missiles (aka ICBMs) are the most vulnerable to destruction in an attack. Credibility is another factor of deterrence. An opponent must also believe that you can and will use your weapons if attacked, or perhaps even use them in a first strike.

The strategy of **mutually assured destruction (aka MAD)** bases deterrence exclusively on having the ability and will to deliver a devastating counterstrike. Proponents of MAD believe that nuclear weapons have a deterrent effect if each nuclear power's capabilities include a sufficient number of weapons that are capable of surviving a nuclear attack by an opponent, which can then deliver a retaliatory attack that will destroy that opponent. In essence, this approach is deterrence through punishment. The result, MAD theory holds, is that no power will start a nuclear war because doing so will lead to its own destruction—even if it destroys its enemy. This was a key presumption at the heart of the **containment doctrine** advanced by US foreign policy strategist George Kennan in the early Cold War period.

mutually assured destruction (aka MAD) A situation in which each nuclear superpower has the capability of launching a devastating nuclear second strike even after an enemy has attacked it. The crux of the MAD doctrine is that possessing an overwhelming second-strike capacity prevents nuclear war due to the rational aversion of the other side to invite massive retaliation.

containment doctrine A cornerstone of US foreign policy during the Cold War, devised by George Kennan, that sought to prevent the spread of communism through a mix of coercive diplomacy, strong alliances, and military strength.

Nuclear Utilization Theory This theory asserts that it is possible for a limited nuclear exchange to occur and that nuclear weapons are simply one rung on the ladder of escalation.

Nuclear utilization theory (NUT) is an alternative approach to deterrence. First articulated by the military strategist and systems theorist Herman Kahn, NUT advocates contend that the MAD strategy is a crazy gamble because it relies on rationality and clear-sightedness when, in reality, other scenarios also could lead to nuclear war. Therefore, NUT supporters prefer to base deterrence partly on damage denial (or limitation). This requires the ability and willingness to destroy enemy weapons before the weapons explode on one's own territory and forces. The ways to do this are to prevent the launch of weapons by either destroying an enemy's command and communications structure or the weapons themselves before launch and/or destroying the weapons during flight.

Both US and Russian nuclear doctrines have historically been a mixture of MAD and NUT strategies. The approaches of most of the lesser nuclear powers, such as China, the United Kingdom, and France, are almost purely oriented around the MAD doctrine. The US posture under the current Trump administration has shifted toward a NUT orientation, as reflected in the President's August 2017 warning that North Korea's continued development of missile capacity will leave them to "face fire and fury like the world has never seen."[13] The renewed interest in nuclear disarmament expressed by the Obama administration, and the March 2010 bilateral agreement between the United States and Russia ("Measures to Further Reduction and Limitation of Strategic Offensive Arms"), seem almost a relic of a bygone era with respect to nuclear weapons and international security.

The prospect of a showdown with North Korea involving the United States, South Korea, Japan, and possibly other states reaffirms that, over a quarter-century after the end of the nuclear standoff that was the Cold War, nuclear weapons remain a deadly and dangerous source of global, regional, and human insecurity. Though reliable information is hard to come by, most estimates contend that North Korea currently possesses at least 20 nuclear warheads, with the capability to produce up to 20 more per year at its Yongbyon facility. This number is of course tiny compared to the massive US nuclear arsenal. More troubling from a security standpoint is the extent to which the North Korean regime is seeking to negate that difference by improving the range and reliability of its nuclear weapons delivery vehicles, with an ultimate goal of long-range missiles that can reach the US heartland. The occasionally ominous rhetoric from both sides threatens to significantly worsen an already problematic security dilemma between North Korea, the United States, and its allies—with nuclear brinkmanship a very real possibility.

Chapter Summary

- Anarchy—the absence of any effective central governing authority in the global system—is just as relevant for consideration in the new security environment as it was in the old. The lack of such governing authority, along with the violent contests it spawns both between and within states, has long been and remains a catalyst for insecurity in our world.

- Increased recognition of the importance of environmental, economic, political, and social factors and forces, as well as the security of human beings themselves, has transformed the security studies field both by "broadening" considerations of what a security issue or threat is and by "deepening" the focus on individuals and other nonstate and substate actors.

- Military threats remain vital security concerns, both alone and in their interactions with other types of security threats. Accordingly, widespread efforts at arms control, directed at conventional as well unconventional weapons, and the tools and practices of conflict management remain central to efforts at promoting enhanced global security.

- The end of the Cold War, and with it the organizing principle of bipolarity, revealed the security implications of a wide range of actors and problems as well as the need for new rules and practices to promote security. In this way, changes in the nature and structure of the international system have produced what some scholars of security studies characterize as a "new" security environment for the 21st century.

- Despite long-standing efforts to control and even eliminate them, weapons of mass destruction continue to pose a dangerous challenge to global and human security. These challenges have been magnified in recent years by the seeming resurgence of nuclear weapons in the strategic thinking of states that possess them.

Critical Thinking Questions

1. What is the basis for the traditional approach to security studies? On what key concepts and core assumptions does it rest?

2. What precipitated the move to "broaden" and "deepen" security studies beginning in the 1980s? What are some of the leading examples of these efforts?

3. What are the major approaches to conflict management? What distinguishes them from one another? Which, in your view, is or could be the most effective and why?

4. What were the origins of the "new" security environment? What are its crucial defining features?

5. What are the major obstacles to efforts at controlling the development and spread of weapons of mass destruction? Do you think that such dangerous and destructive weapons can ever be eliminated?

Key Terms

alliances
Anti-Personnel Mine Ban Convention (aka the Ottawa Treaty)
arms control
balance of power
balancing
bandwagoning
biological weapons
chemical weapons
collective security
Comprehensive Test Ban Treaty
conflict management

containment doctrine
Convention on Cluster Munitions
deterrence
disarmament
global security
human security
Intermediate-Range Nuclear Forces Treaty
International Atomic Energy Agency
iron triangle
military-industrial complex

mutually assured destruction (aka MAD)
national security
new security environment
nonproliferation
Nuclear Utilization Theory
nuclear weapons
peace enforcement
peacekeeping
Responsibility to Protect (aka R2P)

rogue state(s)
rules of engagement
securitization
security dilemma
Strategic Arms Reduction Treaties (START I and II)
strategic-range delivery vehicles
Treaty on the Nonproliferation of Nuclear Weapons
weapons of mass destruction

International Law and the Search for Justice

9

In April 2012, the world witnessed an international court convict a head of state for war crimes and crimes against humanity for the first time since the Nuremburg trials following World War II. An international tribunal, called the **Special Tribunal for Sierra Leone**, found Charles Taylor, the former president of Liberia and a once-powerful warlord, guilty of arming, supporting, and guiding a brutal rebel movement that committed mass atrocities in Sierra Leone during its civil war in the 1990s. The rebel groups in Sierra Leone were notorious for gruesome tactics, including the systematic and widespread mutilation of thousands of civilians, in order to terrorize the country as they captured diamond mines to fund their insurgency.

The prosecution proved to a panel of three judges, from Ireland, Samoa, and Uganda, that Taylor was guilty of "aiding and abetting" (direct forms of responsibility) these crimes, including murder, rape, slavery, and the use of child soldiers. In fact, it was the first time an international criminal court convicted a former head of state for gender-based crimes. While it is widely accepted that Taylor committed much more violence in Liberia,

Charles Taylor was indicted on direct and indirect forms of criminal responsibility. Forms of criminal responsibility are crucial, as they enable prosecutions against high-ranking civilian or military superiors. Such charges ensure that superiors who formulate or implement overarching strategies and policies, for instance, are not exculpated on the grounds that they did not physically perpetrate crimes.

particularly during his dictatorial rule as president from 1997 to 2003, the tribunal's mandate only covered crimes committed in Sierra Leone from 1996 to 2002.

Throughout this chapter, we will employ the case of Charles Taylor to explore both the progress and the ongoing challenges in establishing binding and effective international legal standards. The case raises critically important questions about what it means to pursue justice, particularly in regions emerging from armed conflict and extreme violence. You might also note that many of the examples we discuss come from relatively recent conflicts, even if from your own possibly distant memories of the 1990s and early 2000s. The international legal issues raised by these conflicts have become archetypes in our understanding of power and limitations of international law in our global society, and we thus consciously choose to continue discussing them here. Particularly with these cases, understanding history matters.

Learning Objectives

Discuss the principles, customs, and practices of international law.

Explain the philosophical roots and historical evolution of international law, and how international laws are made, obeyed, and decided.

Discuss legal standards and justice amid differing cultural values and ideals, as well as the application and enforcement of international legal rights and responsibilities to states and individuals.

Identify and evaluate the underlying sources of and continuing debates concerning international humanitarian law.

The Fundamentals of International Law

With the example of Charles Taylor in mind, it is useful to begin considering how international law differs from domestic law. The difference between global and domestic systems is not so much a difference across the motives of the actors as the fact that domestic systems place greater constraints on the pursuit of self-interest than the international system does (Joyner, 2005). Legal systems are one constraint on the power-based pursuit of self-interest in a domestic system. Hierarchic structures exist for making law (legislatures), for enforcing law (police and military), and for interpreting law (judiciaries). These bind individuals and groups to domestic legal systems. Ideas about justice also restrain the pursuit of power in domestic systems. In other words, what is just and what is legal are not always the same. Justice involves what is "right" in a particular situation, not only what is "legal."

Whether we use the term *just, moral, ethical,* or *fair,* there is a greater sense in domestic systems that justice should prevail, that the ends do not always justify the means, and that those who violate the norms should suffer penalties. Surely, there is no domestic system in which everyone acts justly (Amstutz, 2005). Yet the sense of justice that citizens possess in stable domestic (mostly democratic) systems does influence their behavior.

At the global level, such authoritative structures are largely absent. There is no international executive, legislature, or judiciary. **Compulsory jurisdiction** does not exist, and anarchy often enables chaos and violence. Further, differences in culture and historical experiences lead people and nations to develop very different conceptions of what is right and just. Yet despite these significant obstacles, international law not only exists but increasingly functions in impactful ways across the globe.

The Charles Taylor case focuses on the role of international law and justice in communities emerging from war and mass atrocities. International law is not, however, limited to criminal and humanitarian law; it is just as important in times of peace. Workers' rights, environmental policy, political asylum, diplomatic immunity, and maritime borders all constitute matters that demand international regulation and cooperation among a range of global actors and therefore fit squarely into the realm of international law. **International law** refers to the body of principles, customs, and rules recognized as regulating interactions among and between states, international organizations, individuals, and in more limited cases, multinational organizations. These binding legal obligations can serve multiple purposes, from establishing expectations and order to protecting the status quo and legitimizing the use of force or humanitarian intervention. Laws are often those mechanisms put into place to settle disputes and regulate interactions between global actors. They also serve as moral guidelines determining what is right, wrong, and just. In short, international law seeks to govern behavior. We will explore the fundamentals of these legal systems and moral codes by looking first at the primitive nature, growth, and current status of international law.

compulsory jurisdiction
A state's acceptance of the authority of an international tribunal, thereby creating an obligation for that state to abide by tribunal decisions.

international law The body of principles, customs, and rules regulating interactions among and between states, international organizations, individuals, and in more limited cases, multinational organizations.

Evolutionary Nature of International Law

All legal systems, domestic or international, evolve. Each advances from primitive practices to more sophisticated interactions. As such, any legal system exists on an evolutionary scale ranging from primitive to modern. Modern does not mean finished, permanent, or necessarily better, however. People in the future may consider our current legal systems to be rudimentary, and regressions happen easily. Still, this concept of a primitive but evolving legal system is important to understand the constantly changing nature of international law in terms of scope, interpretation, and implementation.

In a broad sense, the current international legal system falls toward the primitive end of the evolutionary scale of legal systems. First, it does not have a formal rule-making (legislative) process as more sophisticated systems do. The United Nations (UN) General Assembly, for instance, is the world's most general debate arena, where each state is represented with one vote. There, states can (and do) pass resolutions, but these resolutions are not legally binding for states (see Chapter 6). Instead, codes of behavior and legal obligations derive from custom or from explicit agreements among specific actors.

Second, there is little established authority to judge or punish violations of law. Ancient societies, domestic or international, did not have formal police or courts. They relied on self-help techniques ranging from negotiation to violence, and occasionally on mediation to resolve disputes. While the prosecution and conviction of war criminals like Charles Taylor may signal that this self-help system is slowly changing, the reality is that most war criminals still go unpunished. Viewing international law as a legal system in its early stages helps us to understand that international law does exist, even if it is not fully developed. Such an historical perspective also leaves open the possibility that international actors, and the legal systems they put into place, are likely to continue evolving into a higher order similar to that of many domestic systems.

The Growth of International Law

International law has its beginnings in the origin of states and their need to regulate their relationships. Gradually, elements of ancient Jewish, Greek, and Roman custom and practice combined with newer Christian concepts to form the beginning of an international system of law. International law as we know it today primarily developed from the ideas and practices of Western civilization (Nussbaum, 2001). Many theorists were also important to the genesis of international law. The most famous of these was Holland's Hugo Grotius (1583–1645), who wrote *On the Law of War and Peace* and was the first scholar of international law. Grotius and others advanced ideas about the sources of international law, its role in regulating the relations of states, and its application to war and other specific circumstances. From this base, international law evolved slowly over the intervening centuries, as the interactions between the states grew and as the needs and expectations of the international community became more sophisticated.

During the last century or so, the global focus on international law has grown rapidly. Globalization has significantly expanded the need for rules to govern functional areas such as trade, finance, travel, and communications (see, e.g., Davis & Morse, 2018). The UN Global Compact is just one instance of norm-building around global business practices (see Chapter 11). Similarly, humanity's awareness of our ability to destroy ourselves and our environment, and of the suffering of victims of human rights abuses, has led to law-making treaties on such subjects as genocide, nuclear testing, use of the oceans, and human rights. There is even a treaty on the laws of treaties, known as the **Vienna Convention on the Law of Treaties**, drafted in 1969 and entered into force in 1980. And the most political activities of all—war and other

Vienna Convention of the Law of Treaties Defines a treaty as "an international agreement concluded between states in written form and governed by international law," and affirms that every state possesses the capacity and right to conclude treaties.

Both Hugo Grotius and Christopher Joyner (d. 2011) were leading scholars of their times in the field of international law, and they are cited throughout this chapter. While both were brilliant thinkers, each brought a particular experience and perspective to what constitutes justice. How could one's educational, national, gender, or class experience be influential here?

aspects of national security—have increasingly become the subject of international law. There is a widespread belief and practice that aggressive war is not acceptable. The UN's authorization of sanctions and then the use of force against Iraq after that country invaded Kuwait in 1990 reflected that. So did the UN's refusal to support what most countries saw as an unjustified US-led invasion of Iraq in 2003.

The Practice of International Law

Those who discount international law contend that it exists only in theory, not in practice. As evidence, they cite war, human rights violations, and other largely unpunished examples of "lawlessness." What this argument ignores is that international law is effective in many areas despite its limitations. There is substantial evidence about the behavior of states and how they "do accept international law as law, and, even more significant, in the vast majority of instances they . . . obey it" (Joyner, 2000:243). Further, the fact that parties do not always follow the law does not disprove its existence. There is, after all, a substantial crime rate in the United States and many other countries, but that does not mean they are lawless. We must consider perceptions about legal obligations as well as the frequency and significance of violations of the law. Thus, an evaluation of the existence of international law must not only account for the degree to which the relevant actors have accepted the legitimacy of the rule, but also assess the general practice by all relevant actors over time (Arend, 2003).

International law is most effective in governing the rapidly expanding range of transnational functional relations. These involve "low politics," which

Across the globe, huge protests occurred both in 1991 and in 2003 when the United States sent forces into Iraq.

traditionally (even if questionably) designates such things as trade, diplomatic rules, and communications. International law is least effective when applied to "high politics," which designates issues such as national security and conflict. When vital interests are at stake, governments still regularly bend or even ignore international law. Yet the law and standards of justice sometimes do influence strategic political decisions. Both international law and world values, for instance, are strongly opposed to states resorting unilaterally to war except for their immediate self-defense. Now, even countries as powerful as the United States regularly seek UN authorization to act in cases such as Afghanistan in 2001 and Iraq in 2003, when not long ago they would have acted on their own initiative. The United States and United Kingdom ultimately did go ahead in 2003 without UN support, but the widespread condemnation of the US-UK invasion shows that a norm does exist. The ability of the United States to ignore the norm, however, demonstrates that state power continues to override international law and justice in some instances.

🌐 The International Legal System

International law, like any legal system, is based on four critical considerations: the philosophical roots of law, how international laws are made, when and why these laws are obeyed (adherence), and how legal disputes are decided, or adjudicated. In the case of Charles Taylor, we should consider how the international community is challenging the sovereign rights of states and increasingly questioning and objecting to certain actions of state leaders. A norm seems to be emerging that argues for state leaders to be held at least to minimal standards when it comes to the treatment of people within their sovereign borders.

It was the UN Security Council that established a special tribunal in the Taylor case. As we know, the Security Council is a political body within the UN often beholden to the power dynamics between the P5. The origins of the tribunal's mandate obviously shaped what was under the court's jurisdiction and, just as important, what did not fall under the court's mandate, such as anything occurring in Liberia. Lastly, the case highlights some of the procedural challenges of international prosecutions, not the least of which is incredibly slow procedures.

The Philosophical Roots of Law

There are three major schools of thought on where laws originate. Two of these are rooted in sources external to the practices of human society; the third holds that law reflects the internal desires and conduct of each society. A key implication of law that is external to society is that a standard of law exists that governs all human beings, whether or not they accept or abide by it. By contrast, if law is derived from society and, indeed, there are many human societies (countries), then there is (1) no single law and (2) no basis for asserting the moral superiority of one system of law and values over another.

Specifically, the three schools of law can be broken down as follows:

1. The first external law perspective is the **ideological/theological school of law**, which holds that law derives from an overarching set of beliefs rooted in political, religious, ethnic, or cultural identity.

2. The second set of ideas about an external source, the **naturalist school of law**, contends that humans, by nature, have certain rights and obligations, in what English philosopher John Locke argued in *Two Treatises of Government* (1690) is "a law of nature" that underpins law in any form.

3. The third view, focusing on the customs and practices of society, is the **positivist school of law**, which advocates that law reflects society and the way people want that society to operate. Therefore, according to positivist principles, law is and ought to be the product of the codification or formalization of a society's standards.

Each of these schools has detractors as well as advocates. Those who reject the idea of external sources of law contend that standards based on ideology or theology are undemocratic because the law is decided and interpreted by non-governmental authorities. As for natural law, critics charge that it is vague and puts so much emphasis on individualism that it almost precludes any sense of communitarian welfare. Critics condemn the positivist approach as amoral and sometimes immoral, in that it may legitimize immoral, albeit common, beliefs and behavior of a society as a whole or of its dominant class. These critics would say, for instance, that slavery was once widespread and widely accepted, but that it was never moral or lawful by the standards of either divine principle or natural law. The pervasiveness of the Atlantic slave trade is illustrated in Map 9.1.

ideological/theological school of law A set of related ideas in secular or religious thought, usually founded on identifiable thinkers and their works, that provides a coherent legal framework.

naturalist school of law A system of law that is purportedly determined by nature, and thus is universal. Classically, natural law refers to the use of reason to analyze human nature—both social and personal—and to deduce binding rules of moral behavior.

positivist school of law Social and cultural contexts necessitate a legal standard and set of rights and obligations that are consistent with the norms and values of the people living in those states and societies.

How International Law Is Made

Countries usually make domestic law through a constitution (constitutional law), through a legislative body (statutory law), or through legally authorized rule made by government agencies and officials (decrees or regulations). In practice, they also establish law through judicial decisions (interpretation), which set guidelines known as precedents for later decisions by the courts. Less influential sources of law are custom (common law) and what is fair (equity law). Compared to its domestic equivalent, modern international law-making is

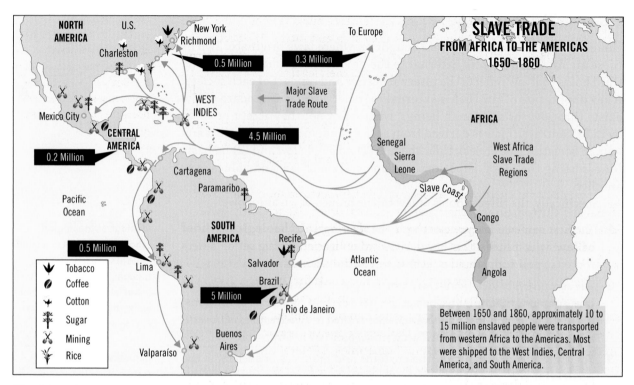

Map 9.1 The TransAtlantic Slave Trade. The trade of slaves, mainly from Africa, was legal for centuries, occurring from the late 15th to the mid-19th century. Despite the abolition of slave trading by Britain and other countries from 1807 onward, illegal trading continued for a further 60 years. Often, a change in laws does not mean a change in practice as is today the case with many prohibitions of trade in animal parts like ivory from elephant tusks. For more, see https://www.youtube.com/watch?v=3NXC4Q_4JVg.

International Court of Justice Serves as the primary judicial organ of the UN and is headquartered in The Hague (Netherlands). Consisting of 15 judges serving rotating nine-year terms, its main function is to settle international legal disputes and to provide advisory opinions on legal matters.

much more decentralized and fragmented. Still, there are some specific sources of law that the international legal community officially recognizes. Article 38(1) of the Statute of the **International Court of Justice (ICJ)** explicitly recognizes the following:

- International conventions or treaties, whether general or particular.
- International custom, as evidence of general practice accepted as law.
- General principles of laws, recognized by civilized nations.
- Judicial decisions.
- The teaching of the most highly qualified writers and scholars.

These five sources rely heavily on the positivist approach but, like domestic law; include elements of both external and internal sources of law.

International treaties are the primary source of international law (Simmons & Hopkins, 2005). A primary advantage of treaties is that they codify, or put in writing, the rules that states officially and publicly recognize by signing the document. Such agreements, often seen as "hard" law, between states are explicit, deliberative, and therefore binding according to the doctrine of ***pacta sunt servanda*** ("agreements must be kept"), the norm that states must carry out the treaties they sign and ratify. All treaties are binding on those countries that are "party to them"—that is, those countries that have signed and ratified or otherwise given their legal consent. Moreover, some treaties may also be applicable to nonsignatories. When a large number of states agree to a principle, it begins to take on system-wide legitimacy. For example, 140 countries have ratified the Convention on the Prevention and Punishment of the Crime of Genocide (1948). Therefore, genocide is arguably a crime under international law, and such a standard is binding on all states whether or not they are party to the treaty.

International custom is the second most important source of international law. Custom is more than merely habitual or regular action, however. A legal custom represents a practice that not only is habitual but is also attached to a belief or perspective that there is a legal obligation to interact in such a way. The old, now supplanted rule that territorial waters extend three miles from the shore grew from the distance a cannon could fire. If you were outside the range of land-based artillery, then you were in international waters. International law extended this territory as technology changed, and states now have a 12-mile territorial extension. Diplomatic practice is another important area of law that grew out of custom. Sometimes, bilateral and multilateral treaties codify long-standing custom. An example is the Vienna Convention on Diplomatic Relations (1961), which codified many existing rules of diplomatic standing and practice such as **diplomatic immunity,** the doctrine that grants most diplomats freedom from prosecution for certain crimes while working abroad.

International custom also exists in domestic legal practices and standards that are common to most states. Such commonalities help determine international law, and sometimes a country's courts apply these to cases involving domestic as well as international law. In one well-known example, the US Supreme Court ruled in *Roper v. Simmons* (2005) that executing individuals for crimes committed as a juvenile violated the Constitution's ban on "cruel and unusual punishments." To demonstrate that such punishment was "unusual," the Court pointed to "the stark reality that the United States is the only country in the world" to execute people for crimes committed as a child and also noted "the overwhelming weight of international opinion against the juvenile death penalty."[1] Some hailed the Court's decision as an advance for human rights. Others condemned it as a violation of US sovereignty. One such critique charged that "globalization has [spawned] a variety of 'global networks,' including . . . a transnational class of judicial . . . elites who are increasingly freed from the constraints of territoriality, national sovereignty, and domestic political constituencies, and whose judicial . . . decisions reflect a deterritorialized, 'cosmopolitan' moral sensibility" (Delahunty & Yoo, 2005:329). President Trump's rejection of "global governance" in his speech to the UN in September 2018 fits closely with critiques rejecting the value and power of international law.[2]

pacta sunt servanda From the Latin as "treaties are to be served/carried out"; an important international norm that treaty agreements between states should be considered to have binding legal force.

diplomatic immunity The notion that official diplomatic emissaries of a sovereign state are to be largely immune from prosecution under the laws and procedures of the foreign country to which they are dispatched.

General principles of law are a third source of international law. The ancient Roman concept of *jus gentium* ("the law of peoples") is the basis of these principles, and the ICJ depicts them as "the general principles of law recognized by civilized nations." Such language serves to incorporate "external" sources of law into international law, by making freedom from unprovoked attack an inherent human right.

More than any other standard, it is the violation of basic principles of human rights that was the focus during the arraignment in 2002 of former Liberian President Charles Taylor before the international tribunal in The Hague. Some charges against Taylor were for violating specific treaties, such as the Geneva Conventions. But the indictment was also based on *jus gentium,* including such "crimes against humanity" as abetting "sexual slavery and other inhumane acts," and including enslavement and "conscripting or enlisting children under the age of 15" into armed forces or groups.[3]

Judicial decisions also add to the law. In many domestic systems, legal interpretations by courts set precedent according to the doctrine of *stare decisis* ("let the decision stand"). Article 59 of the Statute of the International Court of Justice specifically rejects this doctrine, but in practice, judges on both domestic and international courts cite other legal decisions in justifying their own rulings (Slaughter, 2003). Judicial review, deciding whether a government law or action is constitutional, is another possible role of international judicial bodies. Many domestic courts have this authority, and a few international courts also have it. The European Union (EU) Court of Justice, commonly called the **European Court of Justice**, can review decisions of EU political and bureaucratic decision-makers for compliance with EU law and, to a degree, can also review EU member-state decisions by the same standard. Such arguable breaches of national sovereignty were one root argument underlying the Brexit debate in the United Kingdom (see Chapter 10).

Writings of scholars and publicists represent a fifth, albeit subsidiary source of international law. These individual, private commentators often provide international judicial bodies with critical historical analyses, speculation on future development, and/or scientific or technological implications—all for determining varying implications of the law.

While each of these sources is distinct, the strongest foundation for international law emerges in cases where multiple and reinforcing sources are apparent. The prohibition of torture provides a useful example (Wallace, 2014). Numerous multilateral treaties bar torture. Among them, approximately 75% of the world's countries have ratified the Convention Against Torture and Other Cruel, Inhuman, or Degrading Treatment or Punishment (1984). Various judicial decisions, including recent US Supreme Court decisions, have found that torture violates the specific treaties and the general principles of law, and some individuals have been jailed for ordering or tolerating torture. The UN General Assembly has repeatedly—and by lopsided margins—condemned torture, and as Figure 9.1 indicates, many individual countries oppose torture. Thus, it is obvious that torture constitutes a violation of international law.

European Court of Justice Supranational court that serves as the "high court" in the European Union and is responsible for the enforcement of European Union "community law" and ensuring its application across and within all 27 current EU member-states.

Adherence to the Law

Adherence to the law is a third essential element of any legal system. Although the international system lacks impartial third-party mechanisms to enforce international law, international lawyers routinely argue that "states comply with most international law most of the time" (Glahn & Taulbee, 2007:14), a statement first made by Louis Henkin (1979). This raises important questions about why states do comply, which states are most likely to comply, under what conditions compliance is most likely, and even why law is developed when great powers are not involved in the process (Bower, 2015). We now turn to these issues of compliance and enforcement and what such processes reveal about the overall accountability and legitimacy of international law today.

COMPLIANCE WITH THE LAW. Obedience to the law in any legal system—whether international or domestic,

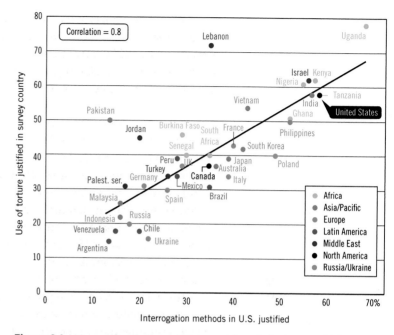

Figure 9.1 The wording for the questions used above is: "In the period following the September 11, 2001, terrorist attacks on the United States, the US government used interrogation methods that many considered to be torture on people suspected of terrorism. In your opinion, were these interrogation methods justified, or not justified?" "If the [survey country] government used torture against people suspected of terrorism to try to gain information about possible attacks in our country, do you think this could be justified or could not be justified?"

primitive or sophisticated—is based on a mix of voluntary compliance and coercion. Voluntary compliance occurs when the subjects obey the law because they accept its legitimacy; that is, people abide by rules because they accept the political authority that made the rules and/or agree with the rules themselves. *Coercion* is the process of gaining compliance through threats of violence, imprisonment, economic sanction, or other punishment.

Compliance with international law is mostly voluntary rather than based on coercion. States comply when it is cost-effective and thus in their interests to do so (Chayes & Chayes, 1995). Pragmatic legitimacy is the key to international voluntary compliance. States recognize the need for a system that is made predictable by adherence to laws. Desire for general order and reciprocal behavior encourages states to abide by the rule of law. In other words, states follow the law because it is in their interest for other countries to follow it as well (Goldsmith & Posner, 2005; von Stein, 2005). For this reason, functional international law governing day-to-day relations between states has expanded. Legitimacy based on norms is less well-established, but also has grown. Aggression, violation of human rights, and other unacceptable practices still occur, but they increasingly meet with widespread condemnation. Unilateral military action, for example, is becoming ever more difficult for a country to launch without meeting severe criticism.

Such cases highlight the fact that extralegal factors, such as reputation, credibility, and socialization, tend to promote state compliance with international law. Peer pressure matters, as do well-ordered domestic systems that promote the utmost respect for the rule of law. Further, as states increasingly create, join, and remain parties to international organizations that promote participation in international legal processes, interests and norms change as states and their leaders internalize the general habit of law (Koh, 1997).

ENFORCEMENT OF THE LAW. In all legal systems, enforcement relies on a combination of self-help and central authorities. Primitive societies begin by relying primarily on self-help to enforce laws and norms. They then gradually develop central enforcement authorities. Advanced legal systems, like those in stable countries, rely mostly on formal law enforcement organizations, such as the police, and sanctioning mechanisms, ranging from fines to prison terms in order to compel compliance with the law. Still, even advanced legal systems recognize the legitimacy of such self-help doctrines as self-defense.

The global community, as an underdeveloped legal society, continues to focus on self-help for enforcement, and neither law enforcement organizations nor sanctioning mechanisms are well developed at the international level. Yet there is observable movement along the evolutionary path toward a more centralized system. For example, in the area of international criminal law, the victors of World War II tried and convicted a select number of German and Japanese military leaders at the Nuremberg and Tokyo tribunals. More recently, international ad hoc tribunals and even the permanent **International Criminal Court** (ICC) have handed down indictments for war crimes in Bosnia, Rwanda, and the Democratic Republic of the Congo, and the courts have tried, convicted, and imprisoned some of the accused. We will discuss the details of these cases later in the chapter.

In addition to tribunals and courts, centralized enforcement of international law is also evident in the increasing use of economic and diplomatic sanctions. In some ways, many argue they are increasingly effective (Lopez, 2004). We discuss sanctions as tools of economic statecraft in Chapter 11.

Of course, enforcement also occurs through armed intervention, but armed enforcement by central authorities is notably less common and harder to justify. Consider the time and effort the Obama administration put in to justifying the limited humanitarian intervention in Libya in 2011. Similarly, the UN-authorized military action against Iraq in 1991 and the North Atlantic Treaty Organization intervention in Kosovo in 1999 were hardly true police actions, but they did represent a step toward enforcement of international law by central authorities.

International Criminal Court The first permanent global tribunal established to try individuals for war crimes, genocide, crimes against humanity, and crimes of aggression.

Adjudication of the Law

How a political system resolves disputes between its actors is a fourth element along the primitive-to-modern evolutionary scale. As primitive legal systems develop, the method of settling disputes evolves from (1) primary reliance on bargaining between adversaries through (2) mediation/conciliation by neutral parties to (3) **adjudication** and the closely related process of arbitration by neutral parties. International adjudication is distinguishable by the essential condition that it involves a formally binding decision that the parties reach according to a legal rule, principle, or precedent (Gray & Kingsbury, 1993).

Whether through the use of arbitrators (a "dependent" form of adjudicatory tribunal that is formed by and linked to the parties to a dispute) or more independent standing courts, international adjudication has taken on particular importance since the end of the Cold War, with international judicial activity increasing significantly. There are currently more than 20 different international legal bodies issuing binding decisions in clashes over trade policy, enforcing rules pertaining to the law of the sea, and rendering judgments designed to promote and protect the rights of citizens, refugees, and civilians during wartime. Whether adjudication involves arbitration or judicial procedure, the parties to the dispute agree in advance to comply with the tribunal's ruling or award. Under international law, an international court or arbitration panel can render a binding decision only when the states or other parties in question have explicitly or implicitly consented to the court or arbitrator exercising jurisdiction over the particular dispute, or to the area of the law in which that dispute resides (Bilder, 2007:198).

adjudication Referral of an ongoing dispute to an impartial third-party tribunal (either a board of arbitrators or a standing court) for a binding legal decision.

INTERNATIONAL COURTS.   The genesis of international courts extends back more than a century to the Permanent Court of International Arbitration established by the Hague Conference at the turn of the 20th century. In 1922, the Permanent Court of International Justice (PCIJ) was created as part of the League of Nations, and in 1946, the current ICJ, which serves as the UN's judicial arm, evolved from the PCIJ. The ICJ sits in The Hague, the Netherlands, and consists of 15 judges who the UN elects to nine-year terms through a complex voting system. By tradition, each of the five permanent members of the UN Security Council has one judge on the ICJ, and the UN members elect others to provide regional representation, as evident in Map 9.2. The ICJ settles disputes among UN member-states and gives advisory opinions on legal questions that the General Assembly or the Security Council refers to it.

In addition to the ICJ are a few regional courts of varying authority and levels of activity: the European Court of Justice and the European Court of Human Rights, the Inter-American Court of Human Rights, the Central American Court of Justice, and the Community Tribunal of the Economic Community of West African States. None of these regional courts has the authority of domestic courts, but like the ICJ, they are gaining more credibility, rendering more decisions, and often ruling against states in favor of individuals. Some scholars argue that the rise of regional courts is a game changer for how international law can go beyond just settling economic disputes to actually upholding specific regional values around human rights and good governance. (Alter & Hooghe, 2016).

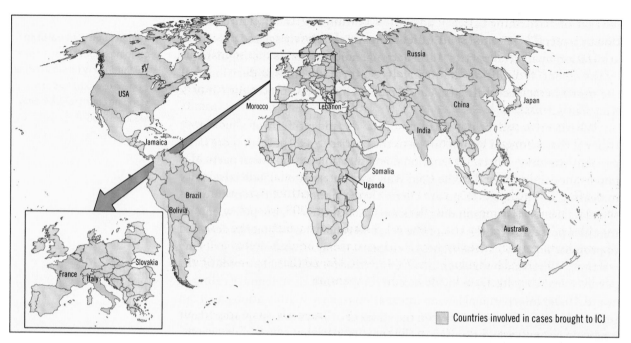

Map 9.2 The International Court of Justice (ICJ), which sits in The Hague, the Netherlands, draws both its judges and its cases from around the world. The map shows the home countries of the ICJ's 15 judges in 2012, and the 92 countries that have been a part in cases heard before the ICJ between 1947 and 2012.

JURISDICTION OF INTERNATIONAL COURTS. Although the creation of international tribunals over the past century indicates progress, the concept of sovereignty remains a potent barrier to adjudication. The ICJ's authority extends, in theory, to all international legal disputes. Cases come before the ICJ in two ways. The first is when states submit legal disputes that arise between them and other states. The second is when one of the UN's organs or agencies asks the ICJ for an advisory opinion.

From 1946 through 2005, the court averaged only about two new cases annually. Although this number has increased to an average of 3.3 cases per year from 2006 to 2018,[4] it remains relatively low given the ICJ's broad jurisdiction and the number of issues facing the world and its countries. More than any other factor, the gap between the court's theoretical and actual roles is a matter of the willingness of states to submit to its jurisdiction, to litigate cases before it, and to abide by its decisions. Although all UN member-countries are technically parties to the ICJ statute, they must also sign the so-called **optional clause,** agreeing to be subject to the ICJ's compulsory jurisdiction. About two-thirds of all countries have not done so, and others that once were adherents to the optional clause have withdrawn their consent. For example, in a very well-known case from 1984, when Nicaragua filed a case with the ICJ charging that US support of the Contra rebels and its mining of Nicaraguan harbors violated international law, the United States argued that the charges were political and, therefore, that the court had no jurisdiction. When the ICJ ruled that it did

optional clause All United Nations member-countries must sign the *optional clause,* agreeing to be subject to the International Court of Justice's compulsory jurisdiction. About two-thirds of all countries have not done so, and others that once were adherents have withdrawn their consent.

have jurisdiction in the case, the United States withdrew its consent to the optional clause. US National Security Advisor John Bolton's pronouncements in late 2018, including alleging "Iran's abuse of the ICJ," show that these concerns remain for the United States when on the losing side of ICJ rulings.[5]

Nonadherence to the optional clause does not entirely exempt a country from ICJ jurisdiction. It is common for treaties to have a clause that commits the signatories to submit disputes arising under the treaty to the ICJ. One such treaty that has brought two suits against the United States in the ICJ in recent years is the Vienna Convention on Consular Relations (1963). In it, the signatories, including the United States, agree to settle disputes arising from the treaty in the ICJ. The treaty permits countries to assist their citizens who have been accused of serious crimes in another country, and in 2003, Mexico brought a case to the ICJ contending that various US states were violating the treaty in several death penalty cases by not allowing consular officials access to 54 accused or condemned individuals. In 2004, the ICJ found that the United States had breached its obligations to the Vienna Convention.

EFFECTIVENESS OF INTERNATIONAL COURTS.   There are some important limits on the success of the ICJ and other international courts. The *jurisdictional* limits that we just discussed are one restraint. Lack of enforcement is a second impediment to the effectiveness of international courts. All courts rely heavily on the willingness of those within their jurisdiction to comply voluntarily or, when that fails, on a powerful executive branch to enforce court decrees. Effective domestic courts have these supports. By contrast, countries are often reluctant to follow the decisions of international courts, which, unlike the courts in most countries, are not backed up by an executive branch with powerful enforcement authority. Therefore, the ICJ has only limited effectiveness, as the UN Secretariat, which is the ICJ executive branch, does not have the authority or power to enforce ICJ rulings. This allows countries to sometimes ignore ICJ rulings.

Fortunately for global peace and justice, not all ICJ cases end this way, and the ICJ sometimes does play a valuable role. Its rulings help define and advance international law. Further, the court can contribute by giving countries a way, short of war, to settle a dispute once diplomacy has failed. The ICJ case filed in 2004 by Bulgaria against Ukraine over their maritime border in the Black Sea provides a good example. More important than

As might be expected in a world governed by states, boundary issues on land and sea are often the subject of international legal disputes. The case being judged here is one between Bulgaria and Ukraine over their "border" in the Black Sea.

the details of the dispute is the fact that unlike many other disputes through-out history centering on land and maritime borders that have resulted in war, the existence of the ICJ provided Bulgaria and Ukraine with a way to come to a peaceful resolution.

ICJ advisory opinions also help resolve issues between intergovernmental organizations (IGOs), and may even help establish general international law. In separate actions, the UN General Assembly and the World Health Organization each asked the ICJ to rule on the legality of using nuclear weapons. The court ruled in 1996 that "the threat or use of nuclear weapons would generally be contrary to the rules of international law applicable in armed conflict," except arguably "in an extreme circumstance of self-defense, in which the very survival of a state would be at stake."[6] Among other consequences, the ICJ's ruling puts any leader considering the use of nuclear weapons, except in extreme circumstances, on notice that he or she could wind up the defendant in some future war crimes trial.

Given the limitations on the effectiveness of the ICJ and most regional courts, it is tempting to write them off as having little more than symbolic value. Such a judgment would be in error. Whatever the outcome of a specific case, countries are gradually becoming more willing to utilize the ICJ, the European Court of Justice, and other international courts—and to accept their decisions. Map 9.2 of the ICJ's justices shows that countries around the world have justices on the court and that almost half are or have been a party to its cases. Now more than 60 countries, including Canada, India, and the United Kingdom, but not the United States, adhere to the optional clause giving the ICJ compulsory jurisdiction over their international legal disputes. In sum, the international judicial system may still be primitive, but each of the over 165 opinions issued by the PCIJ and the ICJ since 1922 is one more than the zero instances of international adjudication in previous centuries.

🌐 Applying International Law and Justice

Perhaps the major challenge in applying international law stems from the vast disparities in national legal systems and even legal cultures across the globe. Whereas most people around the world undoubtedly value justice and the rule of law, the social norms and cultural values that inform a given society's conception of justice or shape a society's system of laws and preferences for how to enforce those laws can and do differ drastically. Laws are in many ways a reflection of dominant social norms concerning acceptable and unacceptable or deviant behavior. Obviously, creating and enforcing a unified body of international law to encompass nearly 200 nation-states and the societies and social preferences that they govern—not to mention untold additional numbers of substate and nonstate actors—is difficult.

Among other challenges facing the effective translation of international law, we will discuss two here: the promotion of legal standards and justice amid differing cultural values and ideals, and the application and enforcement of international legal rights and responsibilities to states and individuals. These two major challenges confronting development of a robust system of international law have produced highly politicized debates concerning the nature and scope of international jurisprudence, particularly surrounding accusations from some in the non-Western world that contemporary international law bears too much of the West's imprint. The ongoing "story" of Charles Taylor unfolding throughout this chapter is clearly applicable in this regard.

Few people around the world would defend the brutal methods that the Liberian strongman employed in his rise to power, or in fomenting civil war in neighboring Sierra Leone, but significant debates persist concerning the nature of the charges that prosecutors brought against him and even the legal authority of the court that convicted him, the **Special Tribunal for Sierra Leone (STSL)**, in 2012. Taylor's conviction for **war crimes** including murder, enslavement, and the promotion of widespread and systematic rape, is in many ways a landmark for international justice, both in advancing the continuing challenge to the notion of **head-of-state immunity** and in the successful exercise of jurisprudence by a "hybrid" (national/international) court. At the same time, in claiming that the court largely served a political function, critics have noted that Western powers such as the United States and the United Kingdom (along with Canada and the Netherlands) exclusively funded the STSL, as well as supported the court's role in ensuring Taylor's ouster and isolation from power (Cheng, 2012).

Law and Justice in a Multicultural World

As the international legal system evolves to better recognize and respect the rights and preferences of a diverse range and number of peoples, the challenge to reconcile differing conceptions of "justice" and differing translations of that concept into law are magnified. Most of international law and many of the prevailing ideas about justice that influence world politics are based on the concepts and practices of the West. This reality is a reflection of a disproportionately Eurocentric influence in constructing and advancing international law in conjunction with the Westphalian state system, and obviously not a reflection of the innate superiority or intrinsic appeal of Western conceptions of justice and law or definitions of legal rights (Cutler, 2001). The Western orientation that prevails in international law has come under increasing scrutiny and criticism by scholars and practitioners, particularly from the Global South, both as the international system has evolved to include greater attempts at global governance and as non-Western states and societies have amassed greater power and influence over global politics (Acharya, 2014).

LAW AND CULTURAL PERSPECTIVES.   Western and non-Western translations and applications of law and justice differ on numerous points, with these differences at the domestic level having significant bearing on international law

Special Tribunal for Sierra Leone A judicial body established by the government of Sierra Leone and the United Nations with the authority to prosecute persons bearing responsibility for violations of international humanitarian law and/or Sierra Leonean law during the civil war in Sierra Leone.

war crimes Violations of the laws of war (e.g., international humanitarian law), including the murder or mistreatment of prisoners of war; wanton destruction of cities, towns, villages, or other civilian areas; the murder or mistreatment of civilians; and the forced deportation of civilian residents of an occupied territory to internment camps.

head-of-state immunity The notion that a person's conduct as the head of state or a high-ranking political official renders that person "above the law" and not culpable for any criminal activity carried out in the dispatch of his or her responsibilities.

▲ THINKING THEORETICALLY

When Is Justice Really Served?

Despite the relative newness of international courts, political theorists have had much to say about their responsibilities, legitimacy, and jurisdiction. Some argue that their role should be merely to address transboundary conflicts and wrongs that are brought to them, by arresting and punishing criminals and expunging the evildoers from public life. Others see the courts as serving a much wider, sociological purpose of holding perpetrators accountable for crimes in the eyes of their victims and their communities. Such public recognition and punishment not only serve criminal justice goals but promote reconciliation, a human rights culture, and respect for the rule of law. Recent cases dealing with some of the world's worst criminals, such as Saddam Hussein, Osama bin Laden, and Moammar Gaddafi, outside international courts, raise fundamental questions about the capacity of such judicial bodies to deal with contemporary armed conflict and violence.

For example, Saddam Hussein, captured by US military forces in 2003, faced his charges in the specially created Iraqi High Criminal Court and Iraqi Special Tribunal. The court gave the illusion of domestic jurisdiction while actually being presided over by the United States. The court prosecuted Hussein for war crimes, crimes against humanity, and genocide, among other wrongdoings—crimes recognized as being under the jurisdiction of the ICC. What, then, are the implications of not trying this case in the ICC? The court ultimately convicted Hussein, sentenced him to death, and executed him for his crimes. Had the ICC tried the case, the death penalty would not have been an option. Some critics argue that Hussein's death is the only true justice that could have emerged, and thus it was necessary that he was tried in this court. But doing so undermined the ICC's jurisdiction and subsequent hope for this institution to be a powerful actor in bringing global justice.

Hussein's case went through some form of judicial process. Bin Laden and Gaddafi were both killed extrajudicially—bin Laden by US military forces and Gaddafi by Libyan rebel forces. At the news of bin Laden's death, President Barack Obama declared, "Justice has been done."[7] But should national military or rebel forces have determined their crimes, their punishment, and taken their lives? Indeed, simply killing these individuals does not make them convicted war criminals. Such acts actually preclude the possibility of conviction. Moreover, such killings often undermine the social-psychological benefits of bringing perpetrators to justice for the victims, their families, and their communities.

From this perspective, the killings of these men undermined the development and developing power of international courts and the pursuit of transitional justice more broadly. Surely, trying them in international courts would have been incredibly complex and challenging, but might it have been worth the effort?

Sources: Barash, D. 2011. "Why We Needed Bin Laden Dead," *Chronicle of Higher Education,* 57.37, B14–B15.
Bassiouni, C. 2007. "Ceding the High Ground: The Iraqi High Criminal Court Statute and the Trial of Saddam Hussein," *Case Western Reserve Journal of International Law,* 39.1, 21–97.
Caron, D. 2006. "Towards a Political Theory of International Courts and Tribunals," *Berkeley Journal of International Law,* 24.2, 401–422.
Robertson, G. 2011. "Why It's Absurd to Claim That Justice Has Been Done?," *The Independent*

and the debates surrounding it. Although somewhat of an oversimplification, we can say that the Western view of law is based on a shared Judeo-Christian tradition and set of legal principles that society has incorporated into international law in ways that reflect the norms and values of Western liberal societies (Berman, 1985). The domestic legal norms in most, if not all, Western societies place great emphasis on the rights of individuals and seek to afford these rights particular attention and protection. This onus on the individual has translations in the political sphere as well as in the economic sphere. In the former, Western legal systems prioritize civil or political rights—which often translate through legal rights that guarantee free expression, including rights to dissent and protest—as a function of this individualistic ethos (Joseph & Castan, 2013). Similarly, Western legal systems tend to place great emphasis on the right of individuals and firms to acquire and accumulate private property and the enforceability of contracts, and to construct laws with the goal of protecting those rights in mind (Commons, 2017).

Western legal traditions also place a great deal of emphasis on **due process** and the idea that a rule of law must rest on formal, extensive, and detailed—if sometimes complex and confusing—procedures and precedents that funnel through standing courts and professional jurists (Bottke, 1989). These have led some to criticize the legal system in the West as privileging process over fairness.

due process The legal principle that the state must respect in full the rights of the individual within the legal system, allowing judges to define matters of fundamental fairness and justice.

One current international legal controversy that touches on both the sanctity of property rights and the critique of the Western legal tradition as prioritizing process over equity concerns the protection of patents held by largely Western (German, Swiss, and American) pharmaceutical firms and the desire of firms in some emerging economic powers (e.g., Brazil and India) to produce low-cost generic equivalents (Elms, 2007). Again, although an oversimplification, it is possible to talk about a non-Western view of international law shaped largely by the different cultural heritage of non-Western states, the recent independence of those states, and the history of exploitative practices (e.g., slavery, colonialism, and imperialism) that non-Western states and societies have often experienced at the hands of Western powers (Anghie, 2006; Strang, 1996). This view is, not surprisingly, critical of the preponderant influence of Western conceptions of rights and law and, in particular, of the Western focus on individual liberties, private property, and due process over social cohesion; social, cultural, and economic rights; and fairness.

The most basic source of the "non-Western" criticisms stems from the claim that since non-Western states had little or no role in determining the rules that govern the international system, they are not necessarily bound by commonplace sources of international law, such as preexisting agreements, principles, or practices. By extension, non-Western states tend to strongly emphasize the inviolability of state sovereignty while rejecting aspects of international law that they claim violate that principle (Jackson, 1993).

STANDARDS OF LAW FOR STATES AND INDIVIDUALS.   Yet another issue related to the application of international law is whether we should judge states and individuals by the same standards—or even what the appropriate standards for individuals and states (as well as other actors like nongovernmental organizations or multinational corporations) might be (Erskine, 2003). States and official representatives of states generally have not been held accountable

This poster shows the individuals wanted for war crimes by the International Tribunal for the Former Yugoslavia. The issue of fugitives and how to ensure that they are brought to justice has been one of the Tribunal's greatest challenges throughout much of its existence. In the Tribunal's early years, the large number of fugitives compared to the small number of persons in custody threatened to undermine much of its work. Since 2011, however, none of the fugitives remains at large.

for assassination, massive attacks on noncombatant civilians, and other acts that would be criminal actions in domestic law if individuals carried them out. Some critics have argued that the dictates of governing mean that we cannot hold states and leaders to the same moral or legal standards as individuals.

Italian realist philosopher and statesman Niccolo Machiavelli wrote in *The Prince* (1513) that a ruler "cannot observe all those things which are considered good in men, being often obliged, in order to maintain the state, to act against faith and charity, against humanity, and against religion."[8] Taking the opposite view, then–US Secretary of State Thomas Jefferson argued in 1793 that since a society is but a collection of individuals, "the moral duties which exist between individual and individual" also form "the duties of that society toward any other; so that between society and society the same moral duties exist as between the individuals composing them."[9]

Debates concerning the applicability of legal rights and responsibilities in international law have become more common as international law and jurisprudence have evolved to extend those rights—and those responsibilities—to parties other than states and, by extension, to hold states to greater account in legal terms for their behavior (Bieler, Higgott, & Underhill, 2004). Sovereignty, while still a powerful concept, is no longer a legal absolute. A growing number of international conventions and doctrines that challenge the inviolability of state sovereignty are eroding it (Simmons, 2009). So too is the increasing tendency of international, regional, and national courts to hear the claims of individuals and other nonstate actors against states (Trindade, 2011). These legal developments are both causes of and responses to changing attitudes that no longer see state sovereignty or head-of-state immunity as an airtight defense for acts constituting war crimes or **crimes against humanity** (Akande & Shah, 2010).

There are numerous policy areas where the reach and the authority of international law have expanded in ways that encroach upon state sovereignty. For example, Chapter 12 examines the interface of human rights and international law, and Chapter 13 discusses international legal conventions concerning the global environment.

crimes against humanity Can include murder, extermination, torture, rape, and other inhumane acts. These are not isolated events but rather official government policy or a systematic practice tolerated or condoned by a government or *de facto* political authority.

States, War, and International Law

Efforts to advance and codify a law of war dominated much of the early development of international law. These continue to be a primary concern of international legal scholarship and jurisprudence, but in addition to issues of traditional state-versus-state warfare, international law now also attempts to regulate revolutionary and internal warfare and terrorism.

At the heart of the long-standing debate over the merits and terms of the "laws of war" is the social, legal, ethical, and moral debate over when (if ever) we can justify war and how a nation, groups, or individuals can wage it. In the Western tradition, much of this debate has been advanced and shaped by, or has been in response to, the centuries-old just war tradition and just war theory (Johnson, 1999; Sagan & Valentino, 2018). Just war theory has three components, respectively concerned with the decision to go to war (***jus ad bellum***), conduct during war (***jus in bello***), and more recently, the justice of outcomes after war (***jus post bellum***). We primarily focus on the first two components in what follows, although the third will be touched upon in this chapter and in Chapter 12.

Both classical and modern just war theorists have worked to elaborate specific and minimally necessary criteria that decision-makers, combatants, and citizens alike can employ to evaluate the "justice," legitimacy, and in some sense legality of any war or potential war on all three accounts (Walzer, 2006). These criteria have evolved over the centuries, gradually informed, and in some cases melded into international legal conventions concerning the resort to war (including, but not limited to, the UN Charter itself) as well as proper legal conduct during wartime (again including, but not limited to, the Geneva Conventions).

INTERNATIONAL LAW ON DECISIONS TO GO TO WAR. The main criteria around which the *jus ad bellum* was established remain both central to that convention and largely unchanged over the centuries. Within the context of the just war tradition, evidence of these criteria enhances the "just" nature of any war, thereby increasing the moral permissibility and perceived legitimacy of the resort to war. As rudimentarily established by Saint Augustine and later and more definitively characterized by Thomas Aquinas, the main *jus ad bellum* criteria are:

1. *Just cause:* discernment and possession of a "just cause" for war.

2. *Competent authority:* the sanctioning of war by what Aquinas would term a "legitimate authority," or an authority possessing a right to rule on such a question on the basis of its sovereignty.

3. *Right intention:* the actor's motivation for war as stemming from a just motivation.

4. *Reasonable hope for success: a priori* evidence of at least a reasonable hope for a successful outcome to the war.

5. *Proportionality (of ends desired):* the end goal(s) of war should be relatively comparable to the means used to achieve the goal(s).

6. *Last resort:* military force can only be employed after all other peaceful alternatives have been exhausted.

jus ad bellum From the Latin as "just right to wage war"; the primary decision-law of just war theory that is intended to provide the minimal moral and legal criteria necessary to justify a resort to war.

jus in bello From the Latin as "justice in war"; theory that is intended to provide the minimal moral and legal criteria necessary to govern proper conduct in war.

jus post bellum From the Latin as "justice after war"; the third and least developed component of just war theory that is intended to provide the minimal moral and legal criteria necessary to define and assess just outcomes after war.

This photo shows leading Nazis and their fates from the Nuremberg war crimes tribunal shortly after World War II. This tribunal remains a landmark in the prosecution of war crimes to this day.

Because gauging the justice of a particular war is difficult in a real-world situation, it is worthwhile to examine a specific case, such as the US-led invasion of Iraq in 2003, to explore the intricacies of *jus ad bellum* (Rodin, 2005). Given that the *jus ad bellum* convention provides only a minimum necessary standard to establish the legitimacy of a resort to war, a strict interpretation of the theory would require us to satisfy all of the associated criteria in relation to the following questions, among others:

Was the war the last resort? President George W. Bush argued that it was. He told Americans, "For more than a decade, the United States and other nations have pursued patient and honorable efforts to disarm the Iraqi regime without war."[10] President Jacques Chirac of France disagreed. He told reporters that he believed the "disarmament" of Iraq could "be done in a peaceful way."[11]

Was the US action taken under legitimate authority? The United States made a legal argument that the authority from the UN to act existed under earlier Security Council Resolutions 678 and 687. Taking an opposing view, Secretary-General Kofi Annan declared just before the war that if "action is taken without the authority of the Security Council, the legitimacy and support for any such action will be seriously impaired."[12]

Was the war waged in self-defense or to promote justice? Bush argued that the United States was threatened by the possibility that Iraq might give weapons of mass destruction to terrorists or someday use them itself. By contrast, Episcopal Bishop John B. Shane argued that "I don't see the threat from Iraq to the United States as an imminent threat, so . . . military action against Iraq is inappropriate."[13] The underlying conceptual argument here has been explored more fully by Subitic and Steele (2018).

Was the war fought to bring about peace? Here again, President Bush argued "yes." He told Americans, "The cause of peace requires all free nations . . . to work to advance liberty and peace" in the Persian Gulf region. Taking a very different view of US motives, one Middle East analyst contended that the US invasion of Iraq "has to do with oil and to do with empire—getting control of Iraq's enormous oil resources."[14]

INTERNATIONAL LAW ON THE CONDUCT OF WAR. In the realm of *jus in bello*, or conduct during war, there are clear guidelines stipulating the tactics and strategies of waging war that are acceptable (or unacceptable) that have persisted over the centuries. These guidelines include, but are not limited to:

1. *Discrimination:* The conduct of war must be directed solely toward enemy combatants and not toward noncombatants, who should be immune from attack, injury, or reprisal.

2. *Proportionality (of means):* Conduct in war should be governed by consideration of incidental injury and harm to noncombatants, with the benefits of such an attack considered in relation (proportion) to such harm and weighed accordingly.

3. *Military necessity:* At all times, minimum necessary force should be employed with the overriding goal of advancing the military defeat of the enemy. Attacks should be on military targets with military objectives in order to contribute to direct military advantage while limiting excessive death and destruction.

The Hague Conferences (1899, 1907) and the Geneva Conventions (1949) have established rules regarding impermissible weapons, the treatment of prisoners, and other matters. Other treaties have banned the possession and use of biological and chemical weapons, and the ICJ has ruled that in most circumstances, the use of nuclear weapons would be illegal. The Rome Statute establishing the ICC in 2002 articulated an extensive list of war crimes. It is worth noting that new technologies, like drones, are also creating new challenges to the law of war (Gregory, 2015).

As is the case with *jus ad bellum*, many uncertainties exist about *jus in bello*. The treatment of prisoners provides one example relative to the notion of discrimination in general and the definition of combatants in particular. American military personnel and CIA operatives violated just war standards in their egregious abuse of Iraqi prisoners of war at Abu Ghraib prison and elsewhere in Iraq. However, there is greater debate about whether the provision of the Geneva Conventions regarding the status of irregular forces applies to al-Qaeda fighters captured by the United States in Afghanistan and held at the US naval base at Guantánamo Bay, Cuba. In a convoluted exercise in legalism, the US government eventually took the position that suspected al-Qaeda members were "enemy combatants" by virtue of their lack of association with a state, and thus were not deserving of the legal protections associated with the Geneva Conventions. These included prohibitions against torture, or what the Bush administration referred to as "enhanced interrogation" methods, as well as restrictions against trials by special military courts (commissions) rather than civilian ones (de Nevers, 2006a and 2006b; Forsythe, 2006).

Another uncertainty concerning attempts at applying *jus in bello* principles involves how to gauge proportionality of means. Almost everyone would agree, for instance, that France, Great Britain, and the United States would not have been justified in using their nuclear weapons against Yugoslavia in 1999 to force it to withdraw from Kosovo, or against Afghanistan in 2001 for refusing

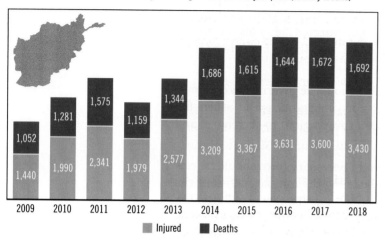

Civilian Deaths In Afghanistan Reach Record Levels
Number of civilians killed and injured in Afghanistan at mid-year point (January to June)

Figure 9.2 Soldiers and other combatants aren't the only casualities of war. This figure shows the civilians injured and killed in Afghanistan in the last decade. (Source: https://www.statista.com/chart/14703/civilian-deaths-in-afghanistan-reach-record-levels/.)

CNN Video:
Afghanistan: Mission
Re-evaluated.

to surrender the al-Qaeda terrorists. However, what if Iraq had used chemical weapons against the forces of those three countries during the Persian Gulf War in 1991, or against US and British forces in 2003? Would such actions alter the proportionality of means calculus, or does the awesome and total destructive power of nuclear weapons invalidate any consideration of proportionality?

The *jus in bello* standard of military necessity also raises questions concerning an appropriate (discriminant) level of force. There was heavy bombing, some of it in urban areas, during the invasion of Iraq in 2003. American officials went to great lengths to give assurances that they were making all efforts to avoid unnecessary civilian casualties. For example, Secretary of Defense Donald H. Rumsfeld told reporters, "The targeting capabilities and the care that goes into targeting, to see that the precise targets are struck and other targets are not struck is as impressive as anything anyone could see—the care that goes into it, the humanity that goes into it."[15] Yet as Figure 9.2 illustrates, civilian deaths in Afghanistan are significant and remain ongoing, in the US-led invasion and the conflict that followed it. These staggering numbers are more than simply "collateral damage." They represent individual people who died and countless families destroyed—all complicating our understanding of when military intervention is justified and when the costs of the means may outweigh the potential benefits of the end.

Applying International Law and Justice to Individuals

Particularly in the case of Charles Taylor, international law has begun to deal with the actions of individuals, at last holding people in positions of power accountable for their roles in committing and ordering mass atrocity. At least three key institutional benchmarks have marked this development, beginning with the post–World War II tribunals, then followed by the ad hoc tribunals of the 1990s, and finally culminating with the establishment of the ICC in 2002.

TWENTIETH-CENTURY WAR CRIMES TRIBUNALS. The first modern instances of individuals charged with crimes under international law came in the aftermath of the horrors of World War II. In the Nuremberg and Tokyo war crimes trials, German and Japanese military and civilian leaders were tried for waging aggressive war, for war crimes, and for crimes against humanity. Twelve Germans and seven Japanese were sentenced to death. Many Germans and Japanese also went to prison.

These tribunals established three important precedents:

1. Leaders can be criminally responsible for war crimes that they ordered.

2. Leaders are responsible for war crimes committed by their subordinates unless such leaders tried to prevent the crimes or punish perpetrators.

3. Obeying orders is not a valid defense for having committed atrocities.

The power behind these precedents, however, has always been compromised given that the tribunals clearly reflected a narrow pursuit of justice. Nuremberg and Tokyo were cases of victor's justice and punishment for the vanquished; thus, they lacked lasting legitimacy.

After an absence of nearly 50 years, international tribunals reemerged in the 1990s. The atrocities that occurred in Bosnia-Herzegovina and in Rwanda during that time were a driving force in this process. In both places, innocent civilians on all sides were abused, injured, and killed. In Bosnia-Herzegovina, the Bosniak population were disproportionately victimized, with Serbian and, to a lesser degree, Croatian militia forces predominantly responsible for inflicting mass atrocities during the period from 1992 to 1995. In the Rwandan genocide, which took place over a period of roughly 100 days in the spring of 1994, Hutu extremists both within and external to the Rwandan government were responsible for waging a campaign of murder and aggression against the Tutsi, the Twa, and even moderate Hutus. In both instances, violence was horrific, widespread, and systematically employed. In Bosnia, for example, Serbian forces executed more than 8,000 Bosnian Muslim men and boys over a matter of days in Srebrenica in 1995. In Rwanda, close to 800,000 Tutsis and any Hutu sympathizers were killed in about three months' time.

Beyond the mass murders, in both conflicts rape and forced impregnation emerged as a strategic weapon of war. In the context of the conflicts in Bosnia and Rwanda, the perpetrators predominantly targeted women, with the goal not only of harming the victims themselves but of destabilizing social and familial relationships within the targeted population. This strategic objective was pursued by damaging relationships between the victims and their spouses and partners, and in the process seizing on and manipulating existing (and highly gendered) conceptions of honor and protection in order to emasculate the fathers, husbands, brothers, and sons of the rape victims (Skjelsbaek, 2001). Apart from these social and gendered dimensions of the strategy, the direct physical and health impacts on the victims were staggering, and these impacts were magnified by the fact that the victims of rape and forced impregnation all too often were shunned by the males within their own communities (Kirby, 2013). Compounding the atrocity was the connection of rape with the practice of ethnic cleansing, in a strategy intended to further one ethnonational group at the expense of another through forced impregnation (MacKinnon, 2017).

The atrocities in Bosnia and Rwanda shocked the conscience of the world, particularly as the media brought images from these regions to our newspapers and televisions. This jarring reality led the UN Security Council to establish an

Fatuo Bom Bensouda: A Calling to Justice

Born to a Muslim family in Gambia in 1961, Fatuo Bom Bensouda felt called at a very young age to work for justice. "The issue of justice and accountability seems to be . . . in my DNA. . . . As soon as I was able to know and analyze certain injustices in society around me, I wanted to do something about it."[16] In 1986, she graduated from the University of Ife with a Bachelor of Laws (Hons) degree, obtained her Barrister-at-Law (BL) professional qualification from the Nigerian Law School, and later became Gambia's first expert in international maritime law after earning a Master of Laws from the International Maritime Law Institute in Malta.

Bensouda's international career as a civil servant formally began with her work as a Legal Advisor and Trial Attorney at the International Criminal Tribunal for Rwanda. Her efforts contributed to the enormous task of prosecuting war criminals for the genocide in Rwanda in 1994; one notable case was that of Jean-Paul Akayesu—the first conviction of sexual violence and rape as crimes of genocide. Bensouda was then elected as Deputy Prosecutor of the International Criminal Court (ICC) in 2004, and by 2011, she was chosen to succeed Luis Moreno-Ocampo as the court's second Chief Prosecutor. Bensouda is the first woman and the first African to head the ICC, and in 2012, *Time* magazine named her one of the most influential people in the world. She recognizes her power and position, vowing to work for justice for Africans. "I am working for the victims of Africa, they are African like me. That's where I get my inspiration and my pride."[17]

In her work, she has also focused specifically on how international and national laws do and don't work for women. She maintains, "I have sent very loud and clear messages that we will do whatever is in our power and in our mandate to address sexual violence in conflict. Because as you know, in these conflicts, unfortunately the most vulnerable groups are women and children. Whether they are taken as sexual slaves, or forced labor, or the children are recruited to fight wars that they shouldn't be fighting—this happens."[18]

Bensouda will serve as the ICC's Chief Prosecutor until 2021, and she acknowledges the mental and emotional challenges of investigating such horrific acts of violence across the world. The job takes a toll, but she recognizes her position of power and privilege to hold individuals accountable for war crimes, crimes against humanity, genocide, and crimes of aggression. In a recent article, she tells the story of interviewing a woman who was a survivor of the Rwanda genocide and who had been held as a sex slave throughout most of the conflict. Bensouda remembers:

> She was crying, so I said: "I am so sorry, it's just that we have to ask these questions . . . She said, 'No, no no. I am not crying because you are asking these questions. I am crying because somebody is listening. Finally someone is listening to me.'"[19]

Bensouda recognizes the power of listening and the value of truth and believes that justice is possible even in an unjust world. And that is what she has committed her life to.

International Criminal Tribunal for the Former Yugoslavia (ICTY) in 1993 and another for Rwanda (ICTR) in 1994. The ICTY was established in The Hague, the Netherlands, while the ICTR was located in Arusha, Tanzania. The *Personal Narrative* feature relates one person's story and involvement in the ICTR and subsequent work at the ICC.

Before drawing to a close in 2017, the ICTY (which was expanded to include crimes related to the conflict in Kosovo in 1998–1999) indicted 161 individuals as war criminals and convicted 90 of them, with most transferred to other countries in Europe to serve their time (ICTY, 2017). The most important of the trials conducted by the ICTY was that of Slobodan Milošević, given his prominence and stature as the former president of Yugoslavia. However, he died in 2006 of heart failure before his trial was complete. Milošević was the first head of state to be indicted since Nuremburg; Taylor was the first to be convicted. The ICTY's activities were not without controversy, of course, given the overwhelming focus on Serbian criminals as well as the highly politicized nature of its existence and proceedings, which sometimes ran at cross-purposes with the goal of **transitional justice** and reconciliation (Subotic, 2009). The ICTY, however, did convict a significant number of prominent perpetrators and orchestrators of war crimes and crimes against humanity—including, in its last major trial, the so-called "Butcher of Bosnia," the Bosnian Serb commander Ratko Mladić.

The International Criminal Tribunal for Rwanda (ICTR) made headway more slowly than its counterpart in The Hague. Still, it became the first international tribunal since the Tokyo war crimes trials after World War II to punish a head of government when, in 1998, former Rwandan Prime Minister Jean Kambanda pleaded guilty to genocide and was sentenced to life in prison. As of its termination on December 31, 2015, the ICTR had indicted 96 individuals of crimes related to genocide and convicted 61. As with the ICTY, Hutu civilian and military leaders comprised most, but not all, of the convicted and accused, leading some critics to accuse both courts of being biased instruments of victor's justice (Waldorf, 2009). For instance, a Belgian-born Italian citizen, Georges Henry Joseph Ruggiu, who was a radio journalist in Rwanda, was sentenced to 12 years in prison for inciting genocide, a verdict that arguably was set by victorious parties. Among the many other chilling calls to mayhem he broadcast in 1994: "You [Tutsi] cockroaches must know you are made of flesh. . . . We will kill you."[20] The ICTR set another critical precedent when it found Jean-Paul Akayesu guilty of acts of genocide, including rape, as a strategy against Tutsi women.

Following a somewhat different pattern, a joint UN–Sierra Leonean tribunal (the Special Tribunal for Sierra Leone) was established in 2002 in Freetown, the capital of Liberia. Comprised of international and domestic justices and drawing from both legal traditions, the Tribunal was tasked with investigating and prosecuting war crimes that occurred during the civil war in Sierra Leone (1996–2002), which also spilled over into Liberia. There, three main rebel groups killed and mutilated thousands of noncombatants in an attempt to terrorize the population. Prior to its termination in December 2013, the Tribunal indicted 23 individuals, with 17 convicted (and three more dying prior to trial). This, of course, includes the trial, conviction, and sentencing of Charles Taylor in April 2012. Taylor's trial was so explosive that it had to be moved to The Hague, where a special session of the court tried him.

Though each of these courts represented significant developments in the effort to extend international law—particularly with respect to crimes committed during wartime or by political authorities—these and other ad hoc tribunals were not without their problems. Among other issues, each was only able

CNN Video: Arrest of Ratko Mladić.

transitional justice Judicial and nonjudicial processes and mechanisms associated with a society's attempts to redress the legacies of massive human rights abuses and work toward accountability, justice, and reconciliation.

(or perhaps only willing) to prosecute a select few individuals, leaving many perpetrators unpunished. More problematic is the fact that many alleged war criminals can and do become part of the peace processes and therefore negotiate positions of power in the newly emerging government. These challenges raise serious questions about the ability of such ad hoc courts to justly punish perpetrators, combat cultures of impunity, and restore the rule of law in ways that are both timely and victim-focused.

THE INTERNATIONAL CRIMINAL COURT.   In 1998, in light of the many limitations of the ad hoc tribunals since the end of the Cold War and in the context of a long-standing movement within the UN to create a permanent international criminal court, member-states convened a global conference in Rome to create such a court (Leonard, 2007). During the conference, most countries favored establishing a court with broad and independent jurisdiction. A smaller number of countries, including the United States, wanted a much weaker ICC. The crux of US opposition to a strong ICC was the fear that US leaders and military personnel might become targets of politically motivated prosecutions. The US stand drew strong criticism. For one, an Italian diplomat expressed disbelief "that a major democracy . . . would want to have an image of insisting that its soldiers be given license never to be investigated."[21]

Although some of the US reservations were met, such as preventing the ICC from having universal jurisdiction even over nonparty states, more than 80% of the 148 countries attending ultimately voted to create a relatively strong court. Only seven states rejected the statute in Rome; notably, the United States, Israel, India, and China were among them. The statute entered into force on July 1, 2002, and currently, 122 states have ratified the treaty.

The ICC has jurisdiction over four crimes and can only prosecute crimes committed since the treaty was ratified in April 2002. The crimes include genocide (according to the Genocide Convention of 1948), crimes against humanity, war crimes (according to the Geneva Conventions), and crimes of aggression (addressed for the first time at the 10-year review conference in June 2010). According to the statute, crimes against humanity refer to widespread and systematic crimes, including murder, enslavement, forcible transfer, torture, rape, enforced prostitution, and enforced disappearance committed during times of civil strife and even peace. In this way, the court focuses on crimes that represent a policy or a plan rather than just random acts of violence.

The ICC does not have universal jurisdiction. Three "trigger mechanisms" exist for bringing a case under the jurisdiction of the court. The initiation of an ICC investigation can be triggered by a state that is party to the statute, by the UN Security Council, or by the prosecutor, as long as the crime occurred in the territory of a state that is party to the statute, on a vessel or aircraft that is registered to that state, or the perpetrator is a national of a state that is party to the statute. The only other time the ICC can act in a nonparty situation is if that nonparty state consents or if the Security Council refers it to the court, as it did in referring the recently ousted president of Sudan, President Omar Hassan Ahmed al-Bashir, through UN Security Council Resolution 1593 in 2005. If the Security Council refers a situation to the court, then and only then does the ICC have universal jurisdiction. ICC jurisdiction is also limited by the principle of complementarity codified in the statute. Thus, the ICC can consider a case if, and only if, the domestic judicial system is "unwilling or unable to genuinely" investigate or prosecute the alleged crime. Such a situation would most likely occur because of a lack of national infrastructure or a collapse of the state's domestic judicial system. Of course, unwillingness to investigate or prosecute is not as easy to identify or define.

The countries party to the ICC treaty met in 2003 and elected the court's 18 judges and its other top officials, including its chief prosecutor. The court began to operate the following year. Several African countries soon filed complaints with the ICC in 2005 alleging atrocities by various forces involved with the long and gruesome fighting in the central African area that encompasses parts of the Democratic Republic of the Congo, Uganda, Sudan, and the Central African Republic, and the ICC prosecutor has launched investigations and issued indictments in these areas. As of 2019, there are 11 official investigations opened by the ICC, which have culminated thus far in 44 individual indictments. Included among these are indictments—and in some cases arrest warrants—issued for such prominent figures as Ugandan rebel leader Joseph Kony, President Omar al-Bashir of Sudan, President Uhuru Kenyatta of Kenya, (deceased) Libyan leader Moammar Gaddafi, President Laurent Gbagbo of Côte d'Ivoire, and Vice-President Jean-Pierre Bemba of the Democratic Republic of the Congo.

There is little doubt that creation of the ICC represents an important step in the advance of international law. However, French President Jacques Chirac was guilty of overstatement when he proclaimed, "Starting now, all those who might be inclined to engage in the madness of genocide or crimes against humanity will know that nothing will be able to prevent justice."[22] One issue is that the Rome Statute remains either unsigned or unratified by a number of the world's major powers, including such notable countries as the United States, China, Russia, and India. Compounding this is the ratification withdrawal of Burundi, Gambia, and South Africa in 2016, and the withdrawal of the Philippines in 2018.

In light of its prominent role in the international system, the US opposition to the ICC remains an important obstacle to the court's success (Johansen, 2006; Ralph, 2005). Given the Trump administration's open disdain for international treaty obligations in general, little change should be expected. Indeed, the administration's current National Security Adviser, John Bolton, is on the record saying that the "ICC should be strangled in its cradle"[23] (CFR, 2018). The Trump administration has subsequently followed this by threatening ICC justices with sanctions[24] (Telegraph, 2018). The hardline, unilateral turn of the United States under President Trump defies the hopeful prediction of the ICC's first President, Philippe Kirsch of Canada, that "[i]n the end, this court is going to become universal. It will not happen overnight. I think it may take a few decades to reach universality, but I believe it is only a question of time."[25]

Perhaps Judge Kirsch is correct and American attitudes will eventually change. Even the Bush administration relented a bit when in 2005 it abstained rather than vetoed the Security Council resolution that referred the situation in Darfur to the ICC for investigation and possible prosecution. The Obama administration followed by showing support through its backing of the Security Council resolution that referred Sudanese President al-Bashir to the ICC.

In addition to the ICC's complex relationship with major powers like the United States and Russia, the emerging caseload and initial trials raise important questions about the pursuit of justice and the many ways that justice is incomplete and imperfect. That many people in Sierra Leone and Liberia were not even aware of Charles Taylor's conviction begs the question, "Justice for whom?"[26] Such concerns are only magnified by the fact that the overwhelming majority of ICC cases involve accused parties from African nations—a fact cited by Burundi's government in its withdrawal, and by South Africa in its deliberation over the same prospect. The *Challenge Your Assumptions* feature takes this critical question one step further—asking "Justice for what end?"—and encourages us to consider seriously the cost and *benefit* of pursuing justice across the globe.

The Pragmatic Application of Law and Justice

As this chapter demonstrates, the pursuit of law and justice is complicated, and at times it can compete with and even contradict other international goals related to reconciliation, peace, security, and order. Within and across cultures, people differ on what counts as just and moral. The line between victim and perpetrator is not always clear. Of course, resources are always limited. However, we raise these critiques not out of pessimism or fatalism, but rather to challenge you to consider several critical questions regarding the prudence of pursuing standards of law, justice, and morality in the global system.

Can ends justify means? One conundrum is whether we can justify an act that by itself is evil if it is done for a good cause. Some believe that ends never justify means. The German philosopher Immanuel Kant took a position of **moral absolutism,** the idea that absolute standards can be used to judge ethical and moral questions, in his *Groundwork on the Metaphysics of Morals* (1785), in which he argued that ends never justify means. He therefore urged us to "do what is right though the world should perish."

Others disagree and argue that when faced with complex choices, lofty goals sometimes do justify acts that most people consider morally abhorrent in the abstract. Terrorism is a case in point. For example, the Middle East terrorist group Hamas justifies suicide bombings against Israeli civilians on the grounds that the "heroic martyrdom operations . . . represent the sole weapon" available to the Palestinian people. The statement goes on to argue that "denying the Palestinian people the right of self-defense and describing this as terrorism,

moral absolutism A philosophical viewpoint that contends that the ends alone cannot and should not justify the means, or that morality should be the absolute guide for human decisions and actions.

CHALLENGE YOUR ASSUMPTIONS

Why Pursue Justice?

The idea that states can and should deal with perpetrators of violent crimes committed during armed conflict or repressive rule is relatively new. Only since the end of the Cold War has the international community pursued the prosecution of perpetrators of mass atrocities. From Rwanda to the former Yugoslavia to the Democratic Republic of the Congo, the world is holding political and military leaders responsible for war crimes, crimes against humanity, and genocide, and transitional justice has become a growth industry for scholars and policy makers alike. From prosecuting criminals to deterring future atrocities to bringing psychological closure for victims and facilitating reconciliation among war-torn communities, transitional justice institutions can serve a wide range of interests and goals. These varied interests and goals do not always go hand-in-hand, however, and at times can even be contradictory.

The ICC is attempting to resolve these tensions by defining the "interests of justice" with three elements: enforcing justice on behalf of the international community, ending impunity for the most serious criminals, and emphasizing the interests of the victims. Many questions of interpretation and implementation remain. For example, are each of these elements equal? Is it acceptable to sacrifice one of the elements in the pursuit of another?

The issuance of an arrest warrant for Omar al-Bashir, the former president of Sudan (ousted and arrested in 2019), brings to light this tension. The indictment initially incited more violence and local unrest as the international community pursued "justice" for the war crimes and the crimes against humanity that al-Bashir and the government-supported Janjaweed committed in Darfur. Since 2002, two rebel groups have been at war with the Sudanese government through the Janjaweed counterinsurgency movement, with fighting primarily occurring within Darfur. One third of the population in Darfur has been displaced; tens of thousands have been killed. As a result of his actions and despite the urgings of the Citizens Organizations of Sudan, the ICC issued a warrant for the arrest of then President al-Bashir in March 2009. The ICC claimed that al-Bashir's crimes were too heinous to go unpunished and that his arrest was in the interest of justice.

On March 5, 2009—the day after the ICC issued the warrant—al-Bashir expelled 13 humanitarian aid agencies from Sudan and ordered all other aid organizations to leave within the year. The effect was immediate. About 60% of the population was without access to any kind of medical or humanitarian aid. Al-Bashir claimed that these organizations were passing erroneous information on his activities to the ICC, but the rest of the world could see the truth. He was punishing the people of Sudan for the actions of the international community. These same people who were now without aid were those who had already been displaced or affected by the military conflict—they were the "victims" whose interests were to be a priority in the pursuit of justice.

Could this situation have been handled differently? President al-Bashir was responsible for ordering the murder, rape, torture, and forced displacement of hundreds of thousands of his own people. The international community demanded attention and action for the genocide in Darfur, and the ICC indictment and arrest warrant was just that. Yet the justice the international community sought only brought with it greater abuses and suffering. Did the ICC make a mistake in handling al-Bashir's case? Is the pursuit of justice worth the risk of violent backlash? And how do we balance or prioritize this tension between justice and peace moving forward?

Sources: Jones, S. 2010. "In the Pursuit of Justice: A Comment on the Arrest Warrant for President Al-Bashir of Sudan. Eyes on the ICC," [https://eds.b.ebscohost.com/eds/detail/detail?vid=0&sid=24dd5453-fc9b-4c0b-80a2-db673c8fef97%40sessionmgr101&bdata= JkF1dGhUeXBlPWNvb2tpZSxpcCxjcGlkJmN1c3RpZD1zODk4NjY1OSZzaXRlPWVkcy1saXZl#AN=48002538&db=mfi]. 6.1, 13–42.

Wakabi, W. 2009. "Aid Expulsions Leave Huge Gap in Darfur's Health Services," *The Lancet* [Online]. 373.9669, 1068–1069.

Everyday life goes on even in conflict zones, as shown by these youths on bikes near a bombed building. While not a war in a legal sense, the Palestinian-Israeli conflict remains disputed ground in international law and likely will be for some time to come.

CNN Video: Upheaval in Mali

which should have been linked with the occupation [of Palestinian lands by Israel], violates all laws and norms which granted the people the right of self-defense" and that "considering the Palestinian resistance as a terrorist act and an outlaw legitimizes occupation because it delegitimizes its resistance."[27] This complex and protracted conflict raises critical questions about who is really violating international law, which violations are more problematic than others, and how do we approach situations where all sides are committing various war crimes, crimes against humanity, or fundamental human rights abuses?

In practice, what some view as a weak international legal system still provides for the application of strong moral principles, adherence to international law, and other problematic actions unwise and even dangerous. Clearly, most of us tend toward moral relativism rather than assuming a position of either complete moral certainty—or amorality. In essence, this requires us to evaluate actions in context. Consider the example of child soldiers. Insurgent groups and governments alike often forcibly recruit or abduct children to serve in their armed forces; for instance, thousands of children currently are engaged in armed conflict in South Sudan (Human Rights Watch, 2018), while Islamist groups in Mali such as Ansar Dine have resorted to forced conscription of hundreds of children. These children often witness their families and villages perish at the hands of such violent groups, which then become the only "family" they know, giving them food, drugs, and most important, a sense of belonging. International efforts to assist these children must take into account this complex scenario, where children are both victims and perpetrators, considering children's agency as such efforts address the psychological, social, and practical needs of reintegrating these children back into society, especially when it comes to the different experiences and needs of girl and boy soldiers (MacKenzie, 2009).

Should we judge others by our own standards? The issue about whether to judge others rests on two controversies. The first, which we have already addressed, is whether one should apply generalized standards of international law and justice uniformly given the divergent values of a multicultural world. Some claim that doing so is cultural imperialism, whereas others believe that at least some universal standards exist (Le, 2016).

A second controversy, whether any country or even the UN should impose sanctions or take other action against a country for committing supposedly illegal, unjust, or immoral acts, asks whether it violates the sovereignty of the target country. Americans overwhelmingly supported sanctions and even war against Iraq for its invasion of Kuwait in 1990. Most Americans would have been outraged over the violation of US sovereignty, however, had the UN imposed sanctions on the United States for what many, and perhaps even most, people around the world considered the illegal US invasion of Iraq in 2003.

A third concern stems from what one might call "selective interventions." The United States intervened in Haiti and Iraq at least partly in the name of democracy, yet in 1990, it sent its forces to defend Saudi Arabia and liberate Kuwait, both of which are ruled by distinctly undemocratic monarchies. In turn, such selective interventions lead to a fourth concern: the suspicion that the invocation of international law and justice is often a smokescreen to cover old-fashioned imperialist intentions (Orford, 2003; Welsh, 2004).

Is it pragmatic to apply standards of legality and justice? Another objection to trying to apply moral principles is based on self-interest. Realists maintain that national interest sometimes precludes the application of otherwise laudable moral principles. They further contend that trying to uphold abstract standards of justice casts a leader as a perpetual Don Quixote, a pseudo knight-errant whose wish "[t]o dream the impossible dream; to fight the unbeatable foe; . . . [and] to right the unrightable wrong," while appealing romantically, is delusional and perhaps dangerous.[28] From this perspective, states abide by international law only when it is in their national interest to do so, but they are skeptical about the long-term gains of giving up any sovereign control in the global interest of law and order. Thus, international law applies to different states differently, depending on the state's position in the system.

This theoretical perspective, however, fails to account for all the middle-power states that contribute significantly to the development and implementation of international law and justice. Alison Brysk (2009) refers to these states as "Global Good Samaritans"—those who courageously stand up for what is right, pursuing global norms committed to justice, human dignity, and the rule of law. They might even recall the remonstration of President John F. Kennedy, who, evoking Dante Alighieri's *The Divine Comedy* (1321), commented, "Dante once said that the hottest places in hell are reserved for those who in a period of moral crisis maintain their neutrality."[29] More pragmatically, advocates of applying principles of law and justice contend that greater justice is necessary for world survival. This argument deals, for example, with resource distribution. It contends that supporting a system in which a large part of the world remains both impoverished and without self-development possibilities is unjust. The inevitable result, according to this view, is a future world crisis that will destroy order as countries fight for every declining resource.

One way out of the dilemma about when and to what degree law, justice, and other principles should apply to foreign policy may be to begin with the

moral relativism A philosophical viewpoint that contends ascertaining the morality of human actions or decisions requires careful appreciation of the context in which said actions or decisions take place.

moral pragmatism The idea that a middle ground exists between amorality and moral absolutism that acts as a guide to human actions, particularly in regard to international law.

observation that it is not necessary to choose between moral absolutism and amorality. Instead, there is a middle ground of **moral relativism** that relies on **moral pragmatism** as a guiding principle. From this perspective, a decision-maker must ask, first, whether any tangible good is likely to result from a course of action and, second, whether the good will outweigh any negative collateral consequences. By the first standard, taking high-flown principled stands when it is impossible or unlikely that you will affect the situation is quixotic. By the second standard, applying standards of justice when the overall consequences will be vastly more negative also fails the test of prudence. However, not taking action when change is possible and when the good consequences will outweigh the bad fails the test of just behavior.

The Future of International Law and Justice

The often anarchic and inequitable world makes it easy to dismiss idealistic talk of conducting international relations according to standards of international law and justice. This view was probably never valid, however, and it certainly is not true now. A clear trend in world affairs during recent decades is the rapid growth of transnational interaction among states and people. As these interactions have grown, so too has the need for regularized behavior and for rules to prescribe that behavior.

Thus, for very pragmatic reasons, many people have come to believe that, as one analyst notes, "most issues of transnational concern are best addressed through legal frameworks that render the behavior of global actors more predictable and induce compliance from potential or actual violators" (Ratner, 1998:78). The growth of these rules in functional international interactions has been on the leading edge of the development of international law. Advances in political and military areas have been slower, but here too progress has occurred. As with the UN, the pessimist may decry the glass as less than half-full; however, in reality, it is encouraging that there is more and more water in the previously almost empty glass.

Most signs point to increasing respect for international law and a greater emphasis on adhering to at least rudimentary standards of justice. Violations of international standards are now more likely to draw criticism from the world community. It is probable, therefore, that international law will continue to develop and to expand its areas of application. So too will moral discourse have an increasing impact on the actions of international actors. There will certainly be areas where growth is painfully slow. There will also be those who violate the principles of law and justice and who sometimes get away with their unlawful and unjust acts. However, there will be prosecutions and convictions, and there will be progress.

Chapter Summary

- We can best understand international law as weak and underdeveloped in comparison to domestic law, particularly if we take into account the relatively limited capacity for enforcement and adjudication. At the same time, the international legal system has evolved rapidly and expanded significantly in recent decades, with important implications for the conduct of global politics.

- Competing legal philosophies (e.g., natural and positive law) as well as differing legal norms and systems and cultural values all pose fundamental challenges to the development and implementation of a coherent body of international law.

- International law is derived from multiple sources, including norms and principles, customs, and treaties. Adjudication in general and the creation and use of standing international and regional courts and tribunals in particular have been leading factors in the growth and development of international law since the end of the Cold War.

- The push for an expanded concept of legal personhood in international law—to include individuals as well as other nonstate actors—represents a shift in legal practice with the potential to expand dramatically the scope of legal rights and responsibilities subsumed within the international legal system.

Critical Thinking Questions

1. What do you think are the major obstacles to effective implementation and enforcement of international law? Are these obstacles unique to global politics? If so, how and why?

2. In the view of some international legal scholars, international law has progressed the furthest on matters of so-called functional politics. Do you agree with this assessment? What examples from this chapter do (or do not) support this claim?

3. How and in what ways has international law influenced state sovereignty and related concepts such as head-of-state immunity and crimes against humanity in recent years? What examples from this chapter stand out in this regard?

4. Is a robust system of international law possible given the extensive political, social, and cultural diversity that defines our world? What are the arguments for and against such a system?

Key Terms

adjudication	head-of-state immunity	*jus ad bellum*	*pacta sunt servanda*
compulsory jurisdiction	ideological/theological	*jus in bello*	positivist school of law
crimes against	school of law	*jus post bellum*	Special Tribunal for
humanity	International Court of	moral absolutism	Sierra Leone
diplomatic immunity	Justice	moral pragmatism	transitional justice
due process	International Criminal	moral relativism	Vienna Convention on
European Court of	Court	naturalist school of law	the Law of Treaties
Justice	international law	optional clause	war crimes

Global Political Economy: Protecting Wealth in the Global North

"The Broken Bargain" that Jack Snyder discusses in a 2019 *Foreign Affairs* article raises critical questions about the future of the post–World War II liberal order designed to balance the needs of internationalism and national autonomy. The populist, anti-globalist uprisings that have occurred in the United States, Italy, the United Kingdom, Hungary, and elsewhere have shaken the global consensus centering on free markets and liberal economic policies guided by international institutions. It is unclear, however, whether these nationalistic economic impulses will persist and define global policy for years to come or merely reshape globalization in the world economy.

The economic crisis that engulfed the globe in 2008 became the longest recession since the Great Depression of the 1930s. In the United States, the recession and its impact on unemployment, federal spending, and a host of other economic indicators became a signature set of events for many people. The recession forced college students, as emerging contributors to the global economy, to confront the realities of a shrinking job market, declining federal financial aid, rising educational costs, and likely lower earning potential after graduation.

The World Economic Forum, held annually in Davos, Switzerland, has become a focal point for global collaboration. Attesting to the pomp of this forum, these Alphorn players launched the meeting with a traditional Swiss performance.

Moreover, the global recession demonstrated the level of global interdependence that every person and every country experiences daily. The European crisis emerging from the Brexit decision of 2016 illustrates this point directly, and has recurrently highlighted the degree to which the European Union (EU) countries are interdependent not only among themselves but also with the United States, Canada, and beyond. President Barack Obama put the issue of economic interdependence this way: "The biggest headwind the American economy [can face] . . . is uncertainty about Europe, because it is affect[s] global markets. . . . If Europe is weak, if Europe is not growing . . . that's going to have an impact on our businesses and our ability to create jobs here in the United States."[1] President Obama's recognition of interdependence stands in stark contrast to the "America First" economic policies that have since emerged from the Trump administration. From tariffs on steel and aluminum imposed on Canada and Europe to the administration's on-again, off-again confrontation with China over trade, the Trump approach directly questions the value of the liberal economic order and challenges the core of the global economic system that has been in place for over 70 years.

This chapter primarily focuses on the dominant global economic system that links economically developed countries in the group often referred to as the Global North. It is also worth noting that the dominant focus on economic interdependence and liberal economics often ignores, or at least downplays, the plight of the less developed countries and the ways in which the Global South is dependent on the Global North for its prosperity. The countries of the Global North are relatively wealthy and can essentially live on their savings and other resources when times get tough. However, the countries of the Global South generally are poor and have little in the way of savings and other easily convertible financial resources on which to live in tight times. As a result, the Global South and its citizens are truly at risk when the global economy declines, as it did dramatically after 2008. The Global South is the primary focus in Chapter 11.

The world remains in a period of unprecedented economic turmoil. As a result, we authors do not know what the next year will bring, or whether pushback from other countries will nudge "American First" back toward "America First Among Equals." The many economic statistics we cite in this chapter and the next are approximate examples rather than hard, unchangeable figures. Thus, let us begin by discussing theoretical perspectives on global political economy, which are more constant in their constructs.

Learning Objectives

Discuss the three theories relevant to understanding global political economy: economic nationalism, internationalism, and world systems.

Explain the concepts of globalization and interdependence.

Identify the dominant global economic institutions.

Describe efforts to promote regional and bilateral economic cooperation.

Theories of Global Political Economy

Many scholars and analysts believe that economic forces and conditions are the key determinants of the course of global politics (see Chapters 1 and 2). The various theories these scholars have advanced to explain the interaction between politics and economics roughly divide into three approaches: economic nationalist, internationalist, and world system approaches. Each of these three approaches purports to describe how and why conditions occur and offers prescriptions for policy.

Although the three approaches correspond to the theoretical perspectives discussed at length in Chapter 2, the fit is not as precise as you might think. Yes, the world systems approach is indeed world systems theory. But as to other specific theoretical correlations, things get muddier, both theoretically and politically. Economic nationalists equate roughly with realist perspectives, as they emphasize the need to protect state power and wealth. But there are economic nationalists in both the Republican and Democratic parties in the United States, including (arguably) both Donald Trump and Bernie Sanders, as is discussed in the Thinking Theoretically feature.

Internationalism equates largely with liberalism, and it includes a large swath of the center of American politics as well as probably most other countries in the **Global North**. This approach is also the dominant economic school underlying the Bretton Woods system and the overall prosperity that has ensued since the end of World War II, as Table 10.1 summarizes. These three approaches are the theoretical drivers for analysis in this chapter and in Chapter 11, as both focus on global political economy but through different lenses: dominance and dependence.

Economic Nationalism

The core of **economic nationalism** is the realpolitik belief that the state should use its economic strength to further national interests. By extension, economic nationalists also advocate using state power to build that nation's economic strength. To accomplish their ends, economic nationalists rely on a number of political-economic strategies that often result in the exploitation of weaker countries. Colonialism, or **imperialism**, seeks national economic gain

Global North Refers to the countries with high economic and human development. Most, but not all, of these countries are located in the Northern Hemisphere.

economic nationalism The realpolitik theory that the state should use its economic strength to further national interests.

imperialism A term synonymous with colonialism, recalling the empire building of the European powers in the 19th century. The empires were built by conquering and subjugating Southern countries.

Table 10.1 Analysts Take Very Different Approaches in Describing How the International Political Economy Works and in Prescribing How It Should Work

	ECONOMIC NATIONALISM	INTERNATIONALISM	WORLD SYSTEMS
Associated terms	Mercantilism, economic statecraft	Liberalism, free trade, free economic interchange, capitalism, laissez-faire	Marxism, dependency, neo-Marxism, neoimperialism, neocolonialism
Primary economic actors	States, alliances	Individuals, multinational corporations, intergovernmental organizations	Economic classes (domestic and state)
Current economic relations	Competition and conflict based on narrow national interest; zero-sum game	National competition but cooperation increasing; non-zero-sum game	Conflict based on classes of countries; wealthy states exploit poor ones; zero-sum game
Goal for future	Preserve/expand state power; secure national interests	Increase global prosperity	Eliminate internal and international classes
Prescription for future	Follow economic policies that build national power; use power to build national economy	Eliminate/minimize role of politics in economics	Radically reform system to end divisions in wealth and power between classes of countries
Desired relationship of politics and economics	Politics controls economic policy	Politics used only to promote domestic free markets and international free economic interchange	Politics should be eliminated by destruction of class system
View of states	Favorable; augment state power	Mixed; eliminate states as primary economic policy makers	Negative; radically reform states; perhaps eliminate states
Estimation of possibility of cooperation	Impossible; humans and states inherently seek advantage and dominance	Possible through reforms within a modified state-based system	Only possible through radical reform; revolution may be necessary
Views on development of Global South countries	No responsibility to help; also could lose national advantages by creating more competition, higher resource prices	Can be achieved through aid, loans, investment, trade, and other assistance within current system; will ultimately benefit all countries	Exploitation of countries must be ended by fundamentally restructuring the distribution of political and economic power

Conception sources: Isaak (2000), Balaam & Veseth (2007), Gipin (2001), authors.

by directly controlling another land, its people, and its resources. This motive propelled Europeans outward to conquer and build the great colonial empires. Classic colonialism has largely died out, but many observers charge that neocolonialism (neo-imperialism) continues to exist with the powerful Global North exploiting and extracting resources from the **Global South**.

Economic nationalists also advocate furthering their country's policy goals by using economic incentives, such as foreign aid and favorable trade terms, as well as economic disincentives, such as sanctions, **tariffs** (or taxes on goods coming into a country), and other economic tools. Attempting to lever favorable trade outcomes for the United States is inherently the logic behind the steel and

Global South Countries that have medium or low economic and human development. The Global South is made up of some 133 countries out of a total of 197. Most of them are in South and Central America, Asia, and Africa.

What Do Donald Trump and Bernie Sanders Have in Common?

Both Donald Trump and Bernie Sanders have played central roles in recent American politics. On the surface, these two might appear politically opposed, as Trump has led a successful populist, conservative campaign for president while Sanders calls himself a democratic socialist and advocates a larger role for government in many policy areas. When you take a look at what they stand for on trade, however, you might come to a different conclusion, as both could be placed into the economic nationalist camp.

Although each of the three theories in this chapter is distinct, they all share some commonalities and cut across perspectives in interesting, and sometimes, confusing, ways. These ways make it possible to understand why odd political bedfellows (like Trump and Sanders) at times agree. For instance:

- Like realists, economic nationalists focus on the competitive nature of global economic relations and emphasize that states must protect and expand their economic power to be successful.
- Like liberals, internationalists focus on the value of global institutions in enhancing and preserving free economic exchange. Both also emphasize the idea that enhancing free trade (or "fair" trade, in Trump's view) ultimately benefits all players in the world community.
- Like world systems analysts, economic nationalists agree on the competitive nature of the economic system. Yet they also agree with the internationalists about the need to reform the global trading system, even if they might differ on the type and extent of reform. Along these lines, world systems analysts also differ from the internationalists in that they advocate much more widespread and fundamental reforms than would be supported by the internationalists.

Given the perspectives listed in Table 10.1, how can Trump (most closely associated with an economic nationalist perspective) agree with anything espoused by Sanders (most closely associated with the neo-Marxist views of the world systems approach)? Specifically, one poll of Republicans in early 2018 found that 65% supported the imposition of a wide range of tariffs against Canada, Europe, and China.[2] For that 65% of respondents, they likely view free trade through a national security lens that argues for market protection and safeguarding of American jobs.

For Sanders supporters, opposition to free trade comes from a different direction: that free trade helps corporations and does not provide jobs at home for the "99%" of Americans that the once-popular Occupy Wall Street movement purported to represent. Thus, many Sanders supporters oppose the expansion and ratification of free trade pacts. In fact, Sanders' opposition to the creation of a Trans-Pacific Partnership on trade is "well documented" and focuses on the damage it would do to working people, and somewhat oddly also on the "loss of sovereignty" it would bring for the United States.[3] That last point sounds a lot like a national security argument put forth by Trump and his supporters, even though Sanders' primary focus is anti-corporate and takes aim at enhancing personal prosperity, social equity, and US jobs.

Regardless of why they take these stands about free trade, Trump and Sanders supporters both end up at basically the same place. They may be strange bedfellows, but the important idea to take away from this discussion is that political and theoretical categories are not always so neat when we apply them to reality.

---

aluminum tariffs imposed on Canada and the EU by the Trump administration in early 2018. Economic nationalists are suspicious of free trade and many other aspects of economic globalization on the grounds that these take away important national economic levers and thus reduce their state's sovereignty and power.

tariffs A tax, usually based on a percentage of value, that importers must pay on items purchased abroad. Also known as an import tax or import duty.

Internationalism

internationalism
A theoretical approach holding that entities should and can conduct international economic relations cooperatively.

Internationalism, commonly called liberal internationalism, is another theoretical and policy approach to global political economy. Economic internationalists believe that international economic relations can and should be conducted cooperatively because, in their view, the international economy is not a zero-sum game and prosperity is available to all. At the core here is the liberal belief that states should engage in trade according to their comparative advantage. In other words, countries specialize in the production of commodities and services where they can be most efficient. Economic internationalists favor freeing trade to spread prosperity and allowing states to produce and export those products they can make most efficiently. Therefore, economic internationalists (in contrast to economic nationalists) generally oppose tariff barriers, domestic subsidies, sanctions, and any other economic tools that distort the free flow of trade, investments, and currencies.

capitalism An economic system based on the private ownership of the means of production and distribution of goods, competition, and profit incentives.

The origins of economic liberalism lie in the roots of **capitalism**. One early proponent of capitalist theory, Adam Smith, wrote in *The Wealth of Nations* (1776) that people seek prosperity "from their regard to their own interest" and that this self-interest constituted an "invisible hand" of competition that created the most efficient economies. Therefore, he opposed most political interference in trade. Smith argued that "if a foreign country can supply us with a commodity cheaper than we ourselves can make it, better buy it of them with some part of the produce of our own industry, employed in a way in which we have some advantage."

In sum, modern economic liberals generally believe in the capitalist approach of eliminating political interference in the international economy—that is, *laissez-faire* economic policies. They are modified capitalists, though, because they also sometimes favor using international governmental organizations (IGOs) and national government programs for two ends: (1) to ensure that countries adopt capitalism and free trade; and (2) to ease the worst injustices within the system so that future competition can be fairer and current members of the Global South can have a chance to achieve prosperity. Political scientist John Ruggie (1983) referred to this as "embedded liberalism"—one that embraces free markets while subjecting them to institutionalized political regulation at the national and international levels.

World Systems

Advocates of a world systems approach believe that economic structure is a primary factor shaping political relationships and the power they engender. World systems adherents contend that the world is divided between *have* and *have-not* countries, where the haves (the Global North) work to keep the have-nots (the Global South) weak and poor in order to exploit them. To change this, world systems analysts generally favor a restructuring of the economic system to end the uneven distribution of wealth and power. As discussed at some length in Chapter 2, the world systems approach has its roots in Marxist political economy.

Dependency theory, a strand of world systems theory, holds that under-development and poverty in the Global South are the result of exploitation by the Global North. However, dependency theorists focus on nationalist effort, and unlike purer Marxists, they do not believe that the workers of the world will unite if freed of their respective bourgeoisie masters. Dependency theorists contend that the Global North's exploitation of the Global South is driven by the North's need for cheap **primary goods** (e.g., oil), large external markets for the North's expensive **manufactured goods** (e.g., automobiles), profitable investment opportunities, and low-wage labor. Because this economic system enriches the North and impoverishes the South, dependency theories argue that the North follows policies designed to keep the South dependent. For this reason, world systems theorists term the system *neocolonialism* because it op-erates without colonies but is still imperialistic.

The Global North maintains the dependency of the Global South in a number of ways. Some are subtle, such as giving rich countries much greater voting power in the International Monetary Fund (IMF), thereby allowing the North to manipulate the world economy to its advantage. Other techniques are less subtle. These include corrupting and coopting the local elites in the South by allowing them personal wealth in return for governing their countries to the benefit of the North or, if the local elites are defiant, using military force to overthrow them and replace them with a friendlier regime.

At a systemic level, **world systems theory** contends that the evolution of the Western-dominated capitalist system over the last several centuries has dis-torted development, leaving vast economic, social, and political disparities be-tween the core (the Global North) of the international system and the periphery (the Global South). As for countries that have achieved a high level of North-ern style development and prosperity, like South Korea and even increasingly China, world system theorists are apt to argue that these semi-peripheral states have achieved success only by dutifully serving the interests of the North.

A Note on Statistics

Before further discussing the Global North, it is important to familiarize yourself briefly with the distinctions between some economic terms that you will encounter frequently. **Gross national product** (GNP) is the value of all domestic and international economic activity by a country's citizens and busi-ness. **Gross domestic product** (GDP) is the value of all economic activity within

dependency theory The belief that the industrialized Global North has created a neocolonial relationship with the Global South in which the less developed countries are dependent on and disadvantaged by their economic relations with the capitalist industrial countries.

primary goods Agricultural products and raw materials, such as minerals. Distinct from manufactured goods, which require substantial processing or assembly to become usable.

manufactured goods Items that require substantial processing or assembly to become usable. Distinct from primary goods, such as agricultural and forestry products, that need little or no processing.

Wealth inequality is a long-term problem within both the Global North and the Global South, but is no more striking than across that North-South divide.

world systems theory The view that the world is something of an economic society brought about by the spread of capitalism and characterized by a hierarchy of countries and regions based on a gap in economic circumstance and by the domination of lower tier countries and regions by upper tier ones.

gross national product
A measure of the sum of all goods and services produced by a country's nationals, whether they are in the country or abroad.

gross domestic product
A measure of economic activity within a countries territory that includes both domestic and foreign enterprises.

purchasing power parity
A measure of the relative purchasing power of different currencies. Measured by the price of the same goods in different countries, translated by the exchange rate of that country's currency against a base currency, usually the US dollar.

real dollars Dollars that have been adjusted for inflation.

merchandise trade The import and export of tangible manufactured goods and raw materials.

a country by its own and foreign individuals and companies. Some sources use raw numbers to report GNP and GDP; others adjust these two measures for **purchasing power parity** (PPP), as in GNP/PPP or GDP/PPP, so that the figures can be compared across country values. This process adjusts the GNP and the GDP to a relative value against the US dollar based on differentiations in the cost of food, housing, and other local purchases.

It is also important to understand the difference between current dollars and real dollars. Current dollars (including inflated values) report values in terms of the worth of the currency in the year being reported. **Real dollars** (or constant dollars, adjusted for inflation) express value in terms of a base year adjusted for inflation. For example, if your current dollar earnings were $50,000 a year in 2017 and you got a raise to $60,000 in 2019, but annual inflation was 10%, then using 2017 as the base year, your real-dollar earnings in 2019 would be just $55,000, with the other half of your $10,000 raise being offset by inflation.

A final technical note is about sources and statistics. The data used here for any given indicator may vary somewhat from another source because the methodology used to calculate data varies among reporting organizations, such as the World Bank, IMF, World Trade Organization (WTO), United Nations, and US government. Also, the data are imperfect. Economic data for poorer countries is especially imperfect, given the limited resources those countries' governments have to collect statistics and the larger portions of those countries that may exist in an "informal" or nonrecorded portion of the economy. Thus, it is best to concentrate on trends, such as the rapid growth of international trade, and on major differences, such as the per capita income gap between the wealthy and poor countries.

The World Economy: Globalization and Interdependence

Theories allow us to take a set of events and understand how those events fit together into a pattern of relationships. Often, theories allow us to develop models of causality so that we can then formulate policies to solve political and social problems. As a result, we now consider some basic data about the global political economy so that we can combine these theories with real-world information. We thus examine trade, investment, and monetary affairs to understand the patterns of relationships in each policy area.

Trade

The international flow of goods and services is a vital concern to all world states in the quest for prosperity. **Merchandise trade** is most frequently associated with imports and exports. These tangible goods are subdivided into two main categories: primary goods and manufactured goods. **Services trade** is less well known but is also important. Services include things that you do for others. When US insurance companies earn premiums for insuring foreign assets or people, when American movies earn royalties abroad, or when US trucks carry goods in Mexico or Canada, the revenue they generate constitutes the export of services. Note that exported services do not have to be performed overseas. American colleges and universities, for example, are one of the country's largest exporters of services. During 2018, about 1.1 million foreign students studying in US colleges spent billions of dollars for tuition, room, board, and the other aspects of college life ranging from textbooks to pizzas. Notably, the US share of globally mobile students has declined in the past two decades in relative terms as more countries send their students abroad, but American students continue to study elsewhere in increasing absolute numbers.[4]

Steel cargo containers are a ubiquitous sight in world trade. They carry legitimate goods around the world and are easily transferable, but also can be at times used to conceal illegal commodities as well.

services trade Trade based on the purchase (import) or the sale (export) to another country of intangibles, such as architectural fees; insurance premiums; royalties on movies, books, patents, and other intellectual properties; shipping services; advertising fees; and educational programs.

Whether merchandise or services, trade is booming. For the US economy, trade amounted to just over $2 billion in 1900 but had grown to almost $4.5 trillion in 2017.[5] Trade expanded similarly for other industrialized countries. Even considering inflation, these figures represent a tremendous jump in world commerce. Trade growth has been especially rapid during the post–World War II era of significant tariff reductions. During the 1913–1948 period of world wars, depression, and trade protectionism, trade increased at an average annual rate of only 0.8%. The postwar period has seen trade increase at an average annual rate of over 5%.

The rapid growth of trade has been caused by a number of supply and demand factors and the implementation of a free trade philosophy. Improved production technology is one factor that has increased the supply of goods. The Industrial Revolution, beginning in 18th-century Europe, led to mass manufacturing. As production rates sped up, manufacturers increasingly had to seek markets for their burgeoning supply of goods farther away and even across national borders. In turn, these changes created an increased demand for resources to supply the factories. Trade in raw materials imported by the industrialized European countries peaked during the 19th century and through World War II as demand outstripped domestic resource availability. In the past 75 years, this demand has decreased for several reasons, such as the use of synthetic materials in the manufacturing process. Today, primary products account for only about one-fifth of all goods in international trade.

Materialism has also helped to account for increased trade. The rise in the world's standard of living, especially in the industrialized countries, has contributed to demand pressure on international trade as people have sought more material goods and improved services. Improved transportation has increased our ability to carry the growing supply of materials and manufactured goods and to meet the demand for them. Modern developments in transportation technology have also greatly decreased per-unit transportation costs.

Wide acceptance of a free trade philosophy has promoted trade as well, which is very much in line with an internationalist approach to global political economy. The early advocacy of free trade by Adam Smith and others came into vogue after the global trauma of the Great Depression of the 1930s and World War II in the early 1940s. One cause for these miseries, critics believed, was the high tariffs that had restricted trade and divided nations. As a result, countries accounting for 80% of world commerce began in 1947 to cooperate to reduce international trade barriers through the General Agreement on Tariffs and Trade (discussed in detail later). This and a series of related efforts have dramatically decreased world tariff barriers.

Tariffs are not the only trade barrier, but their sharp decreases have greatly reduced the cost of imported goods and have strongly stimulated trade. This dramatic and progressive ratcheting down of tariffs since 1947 is a primary reason why the aggressively nationalist policies of the Trump administration have been received so negatively by many world leaders. In fact, at the conclusion of the Group of Eight summit in June 2018, Canadian Foreign Minister Chrystia Freeland told reporters that "the national security pretext is absurd and frankly insulting to Canadians, the closest and strongest ally the United States has had. That is where the insult lies."[6]

International Investment

Trade has not been the only form of growing international economic activity; international investment has also created increased financial interdependence among countries. For example, Americans had just over $6 trillion in direct investment abroad in 2017,[7] making not only individual investors but also the health of the entire US economy dependent to some degree on the state of the world economy. Conversely, foreigners had just about $4.4 trillion directly invested in the United States,[8] and the ebb and flow of those funds into the country are also central factors in Americans' prosperity—or lack of it.

The world's multinational corporations (MNCs), also called transnational corporations, account for the lion's share of global foreign investment. MNCs are businesses that operate in more than one country. These operations can involve sales outlets, mines, and other natural resource–extraction processes, farms and ranches, manufacturing plants, or offices that supply banking and other services. MNCs date back at least to the Dutch East India Company in 1602, but it was not until after World War II that they began to expand rapidly in both number and size. Now over 60,000 MNCs exist, and they pack enormous economic muscle. Their annual revenues (gross corporate product) provide one good measure (Figure 10.1).

The immense wealth of the largest MNCs gives them considerable influence and impact on many aspects of daily life (Hertel, 2019), and in ways that run counter to the national interest of the parent company. For instance,

Facebook has data-sharing agreements with several Chinese companies. One of those companies is Huawei, "a telecommunications equipment company that has been flagged by American intelligence officials as a national security threat."[9] As we know from other data-sharing concerns regarding Facebook and other technology firms, user information is perhaps the "new gold" in the world economy, as firms operate independently at times from the interests of their parent or host country. The exact threats posed by companies like Huawei remain in dispute, however, with many European countries largely ignoring the warnings from Washington. At this writing, Huawei filed a lawsuit in US courts in late May 2019 against the Trump administration policy, which will likely persist for some months to come. As Huawei's chief legal counsel put it "The U.S. government has provided no evidence to show that Huawei is a security threat…There is no gun, no smoke. Only speculation."[10]

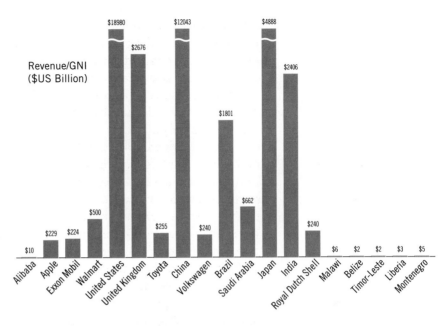

Figure 10.1   Many global corporations rival and sometimes dwarf the size of some countries in the global system. This raises questions about who actually wields power in world affairs: states or corporate entities? (Sources: fortune.com; CIA World Factbook: https://www.cia.gov/library/publications/the-world-factbook/; Alibaba source: fiscal year 2017 [ended March 2018]. Other company source: fiscal year 2017 [ended March 2018]. Country GNI source: 2017.)

Monetary Relations

As a result of the globalization of trade and investments, **monetary relations**, the management of currencies cross-nationally, have become an increasingly significant factor in both international and domestic economic health. The globalization of money is one aspect to consider, as a torrent of money amounting to an estimated $1.2 quadrillion in 2017 flowed through the world economy.[11] Much of this flow involves exchanging one country's currency for another's, greatly increasing the importance of **exchange rates**, the values of currencies in relation to each other. Exchange rates and their stability (or lack thereof) are important because they strongly influence the flow of trade and investment. Map 10.1 shows the range of country approaches to exchange-rate management.

There are various exchange rate systems, depending on the degree to which governments control rates. In a fixed exchange rate system, like that in Saudi Arabia, rates are held constant or allowed to fluctuate within very narrow bands. Freely floating exchange rate systems allow the market alone to determine rates; most of the world's currencies are floating or fluctuating. Managed float exchange rate systems allow rates to move freely on a daily basis, but

monetary relations The entire scope of international money issues, such as exchange rates, interest rates, loan policies, balance of payments, and regulating institutions.

exchange rates The values of two currencies relative to each other (e.g., how many yen equal a dollar or how many yuan equal a euro).

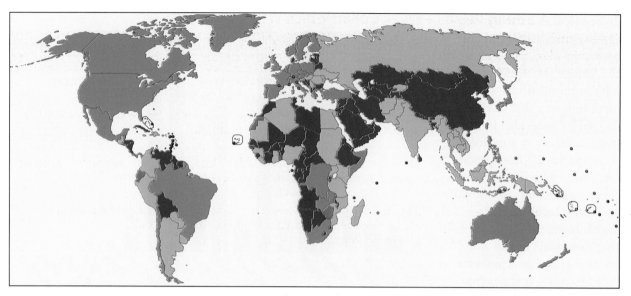

Map 10.1   Roughly equating the more committedly capitalist countries with green (the darker the green, the more committed to free currency markets), this map identifies which countries are most adherent to liberal free market principles and shows which countries have adopted which exchange rate regime. Dark green is for free float, light green is for managed float, blue is for currency peg, and red is for countries that use another country's currency. (Source: http://oer2go. org/mods/en-boundless/www.boundless.com/economics/textbooks/boundless-economics-textbook/open-economy-macroeconomics-32/exchange-rates-130/exchange-rate-systems-518-12614/images/foreign-exchange-regimes/index.html.)

governments may intervene to prevent rates from moving too much in a certain direction. The Chinese yuan used to be a fixed currency, but the government is transitioning slowly to a managed floating system. In a pegged exchange rate system, the home currency's value is pegged to a foreign currency, as in Mexico in 1994 when the peso was pegged to the US dollar, or to some unit of account, as European countries did in 1979 to the European Currency Unit.

Trade in currencies happens 24 hours a day, 7 days a week—a market that trades over $5 trillion a day. What are the advantages and disadvantages to each of these systems? Who benefits from weak versus strong currencies? As Table 10.2 demonstrates, weak and strong currency should not be equated with good and bad because exchange rates are a two-edged sword. There are advantages and disadvantages for Americans both when the dollar is strengthening (and can buy more units of a foreign currency) and when the dollar is weakening (and can buy fewer units of a foreign currency).

There has been a parallel globalization of financial services such as banking to accommodate the globalization of money. In recent decades, banks have grown from hometown to national to multinational enterprises that operate in many countries and whose power to lend money—or not—gives them immense financial clout. To illustrate the banking industry's immense financial power in the global economy, they can influence the flow of loans, investment capital, and other financial transactions across borders. It is also worth noting that in the past decade, the top three largest banks as defined by assets are all based in China, although such rankings can change quickly with mergers and

Table 10.2 A Strong Versus a Weak Dollar: Which Would You Choose?

STRONG DOLLAR		WEAK DOLLAR	
ADVANTAGES	**DISADVANTAGES**	**ADVANTAGES**	**DISADVANTAGES**
Lower prices for foreign goods/services	US exports more costly in foreign markets	Easier for US firms to sell goods and services abroad	Higher prices for foreign goods/services
Lower prices on foreign goods/services restrain inflation	US firms forced to compete with lower-priced imports	Less pressure on US firms to keep wages/benefits low	Higher prices on imports add to higher cost of living
Less costly to travel to foreign countries	More costly for foreigners to visit/study in the United States	More affordable for foreign tourists to visit the United States	More costly to travel to foreign countries
Less costly foreign stocks/ bonds	US stocks/bonds more costly abroad, restricting flow of capital to the United States	US investments more attractive to foreign investors	Foreign investments more costly

acquisitions. Only three American banks were among the top 10 globally in 2019: JPMorgan Chase (6th), Bank of America (9th), and Wells Fargo (10th).[12]

Another aspect of monetary relations is the international regulation of money. As trade, transnational investing, and other forms of international economic interchange increased during the 20th century, some mechanisms were clearly needed to help regulate the rapidly expanding flow of currencies across borders. The most pressing problem was—and still is—how to stabilize the values of currencies against one another. To that end, there have been a number of regional and global efforts to keep exchange rates stable and to ensure that currency issues do not impede economic activity. Globally, the IMF (detailed later in this chapter) has the primary responsibility for attempting to maintain monetary stability. Regionally, the most advanced efforts have been in the EU, which has the European Central Bank and now a common currency, the **euro** (€).

euro The official currency of the Euro zone, used by 17 of the 27 member-states of the EU.

The Dominant Global Economic Institutions

It is helpful to keep the three perspectives introduced earlier in this chapter—economic nationalism, internationalism, and world systems—in mind as we discuss the primary global economic institutions. One can argue that the primary global economic institutions were created with internationalist goals in mind, but analysts view their roles and policies in the contemporary global political economy in very different ways. In the following sections, we discuss the IMF, the World Bank, and the WTO, along with several of the regional economic organizations. Chapter 11, where we examine the dependent economic system, includes a discussion of the United Nations' role in global economic issues. Here, however, we first take a brief historical tour of the Bretton Woods system and then examine some of the economic challenges facing the Northern countries and how they relate to one another economically.

Bretton Woods: Institutions for Peace or Oppression?

The Great Depression engulfed the world in the most severe economic crisis of the 20th century. Scholars and policy-makers blame the emergence of the Great Depression at least partly on the prevalence of economic nationalist policies in the 1920s and early 1930s that significantly reduced international trade. The US **Smoot-Hawley Tariff Act** of 1930 imposed an effective average tariff rate of 53% on imports. Although the act aimed to protect American industry and to promote jobs at home, it spurred economic nationalism worldwide. Protectionism may not have caused the Great Depression, but it certainly made it worse.

Smoot-Hawley Tariff Act
Senator Reed Smoot and Representative Willis C. Hawley proposed this act on June 17, 1930. The act raised U.S. tariffs on over 20,000 imported goods to record levels.

These experiences led many leaders to look toward more liberal economic policies as the world sought to recover its prosperity after World War II. Cordell Hull, US Secretary of State to President Franklin Roosevelt, expressed his liberal ideals in this way: "unhampered trade dovetail[s] with peace; high tariffs, trade barriers, and unfair economic competition, with war."[13]

These ideals were the foundation of the economic architecture that emerged from the Bretton Woods conference of 1944. Attended by 44 countries, the conference set up a system of institutions to regulate finance, trade, and postwar reconstruction. The three institutions created were the IMF; the International Bank for Reconstruction and Development (IBRD), which evolved into the World Bank; and the International Trade Organization, which never formally came to be but laid the groundwork for what we know today as the WTO. Each had a unique mission:

- *International Monetary Fund:* Founded to assure currency convertibility and manage short-term balance of payments problems. The IMF was set up to help countries with cash flow issues and provide short-term loans to bridge those financial problems. Currencies under the original IMF structure had fixed values and were pegged to gold. This fixed exchange rate system fell apart in the early 1970s, giving way to the floating currency system we have today in which relative monetary values are variable over time.

- *International Bank for Reconstruction and Development:* Founded to provide longer-term loans to countries rebuilding their economies after World War II. Eventually, that mission gave way to one focused primarily on providing financing to the developing world. The IBRD became one of the main organizations within the World Bank.

- *International Trade Organization:* Supposed to be created in the late 1940s to reduce tariff levels on world markets in an effort to reestablish higher levels of trade. Republican opposition in the United States prevented approval of this Bretton Woods' component. Instead, a series of multilateral negotiations called the General Agreements on Tariffs and Trade (GATT) emerged. These negotiations were extraordinarily successful at reducing tariff rates worldwide, even if less effective in controlling nontariff trade barriers or in dealing with trade-related development issues for the Global South. In 1995, the GATT became the WTO (discussed later), finally creating the global trading institution as originally envisioned. The growing liberalization of trade worldwide is also seen as a motivating force behind the evolution of regional trading arrangements, like those engendered by the EU and the recently revised North American Free Trade Agreement.

Much more might be said about the three legs of this institutional triad, and we will return to these structures recurrently in various ways. For now, we encourage you to think about which perspective best allows you to understand the institutions created by the dominant global economic powers at Bretton Woods. Was the institutionalism launched at Bretton Woods aimed at promoting peace and prosperity or at preserving Northern wealth at the expense of greater global equity and social justice? That distinction underpins the remaining discussion of this chapter and all of Chapter 11.[14] And although we will focus on global political economy in this chapter and in Chapter 11, much of the material and the arguments that are presented apply broadly to issues of the future of global governance in an evolving global system (Kahler, 2018; Larson, 2018).

Economic Relations Among the Global North

Although the Global North is extraordinarily advantaged compared to the Global South, these dominant countries also face many economic challenges, even if those challenges focus more on preserving prosperity than on providing for basic human needs and economic survival. In addition to the normal competitive tensions of the economic system, economic and political changes are creating strong competitive pressures on the North. The global economic downturn that began in 2008 only heightened those pressures and created further tension among the dominant global economies as they struggle to pursue prosperity and preservation of their wealth.

CHANGES IN THE NORTH'S ECONOMIC CLIMATE.   One factor accounting for increasing economic tensions within the North is that its economic growth rate has slowed. The average annual real GDP growth rate of the North during the 1980s was 3.4%; during the 1990s, that declined to 2.3%; and between 2000 and 2006, it rebounded only marginally, to 2.6%. Europe and Japan, in particular, have been in the doldrums since the early 1990s. From 2000 to 2006, Japan's economy had a lackadaisical 1.5% annual growth rate, and the EU's was barely better at 1.8%. Although the reasonably healthy US growth rate of 3% for the period was much better than its main economic rivals, US GDP growth was below its even more robust levels of the 1980s and 1990s. The most recent economic growth figures have shown some signs of hope, especially in the United States, where the 2017 growth rate was again over 3%. But the most recent threats of rising tension and trade wars have prompted the US Federal Reserve to downgrade the growth projections to just under 2% over the longer term.[15]

The North's slowing economies and trade tensions have sharpened the competition among them not only to export their products to one another and to the South, but also to protect their domestic economies against imports. Adding to this pressure is significantly increasing competition from China, India, and other Southern countries in the manufacturing and service sectors (see Figure 10.2). Companies in the North have tried to deal with the competition

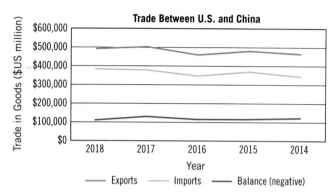

Figure 10.2   The United States has been running a significant trade deficit with China in recent years, which increases tension between the two countries and at times leads to accusations against the Chinese of unfair trading practices.

in some cases by reducing their workforces and using robotics and other high-tech manufacturing processes to replace workers. In other cases, companies have eliminated entire plants, laid off their employees, and moved operations overseas to take advantage of cheaper labor. Many of the workers displaced by the shift of manufacturing jobs abroad either remain unemployed or find jobs in the usually lower-paying service sector. Now, however, even service sector jobs are increasingly subject to foreign competition. In what is called outsourcing, companies in the United States and elsewhere in the North are hiring workers abroad to do data entry work, to respond to service telephone calls and email inquiries, to write software, and to do many other service jobs. The economic impact of outsourcing has created mounting domestic pressures on Northern governments to protect jobs. The policy dilemma centering on how to manage the free trade/jobs at home priorities is the central point of the *Challenge Your Assumptions* feature.

CHANGES IN THE NORTH'S POLITICAL CLIMATE.   Declining political accord is also increasing the sense of rivalry within the Global North, as witnessed at the June 2018 Group of Eight Summit (discussed later). The end of the Cold War, and with it the looming threat of the Soviet Union, lessened the need for strategic cooperation among the industrialized Western allies. As a result, long-standing economic disputes among the trilateral countries (Japan, the United States/Canada, and Western Europe) that had once been suppressed in the name of allied unity have become more acrimonious.

This political context provides the background for an examination of the major global economic institutions and emphasizes the tension between collective "Northern" economic goals and the more nationalistic views held by leaders in some Northern countries, like the United States, Hungary, and Poland. Even though tensions exist across the North and within individual countries, the liberal economic institutions briefly discussed earlier remain the foundation of Northern economic health and the preservation of those economies' dominant place within the global system. Further straining Northern relationships are the long-running conflicts in Iraq and Afghanistan and the fracturing of solidarity of the Northern industrialized countries over the wisdom of continued involvement in those places. In fact, one US government study found that roughly 10% of the $2.2 trillion in factory output in the United States "goes into the production of weapons sold mainly to the Defense Department for use by the armed forces."[16] As a result, war remains a powerful economic engine for some Northern countries, and especially for the United States (see Figure 10.3).

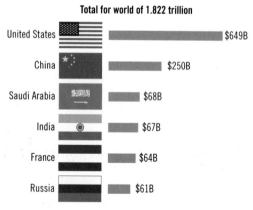

Figure 10.3   Global military spending remains a powerful economic engine for many countries around the world, including the United States and China. (Source: Stockholm International Peace Research Institute, 2018.)

CHALLENGE YOUR ASSUMPTIONS

How Would You Handle the Chinese Economic Challenge?

China and the United States are seemingly on an economic collision course, especially under the Trump regime. The path to conflict begins with the US trade deficit with China, as shown in Table 10.3. It has been steadily mounting and reached $376 billion in 2017. US officials put part of the blame for the deficit on China's halfhearted effort to deal with the illegal production of everything from music to movies and software to machinery. The US entertainment and software industries alone estimate that they have lost $2.6 billion to such piracy. US officials also claimed that Beijing is maintaining an artificially high yuan-to-dollar exchange value after the dollar weakened against most currencies. Repeated demands by US officials that China mend its ways have been backed by Congress, which recurrently threatened to enact stringent US tariffs on Chinese goods unless Beijing gave way.

A third US allegation is that China provides economic subsidies to many industries, which gives them an unfair advantage. Until recently, the history of US action was not one of swift or hardline policy stances. Under President Trump, however, policy has taken a much more bellicose line. After months of hostile rhetoric and initial policy forays on trade with China, Trump further escalated the dispute over trade in spring 2019 by imposing even more tariffs on Chinese exports to the United States. When he imposed the first wave of tariffs on China, he argued that "China apparently has no intention of changing its unfair practices related to the acquisition of American intellectual property and technology. Rather than altering those practices, it is now threatening United States companies, workers, and farmers who have done nothing wrong."[37] Thus far, most of Trump's trade sanctions have been undertaken from the Office of the President under a relatively obscure law allowing him to undertake action to protect national security; they have not been supported by legislative action by Congress. Rather ironically, it is the US farmers and workers who have borne the brunt of these sanctions, not the Chinese companies targeted.

What do you think? Imagine you are a US senator deciding on whether to vote on three competing measures:

- The first is a resolution urging the White House to follow quiet diplomacy and persuade China to continue its economic reforms.
- The second is a resolution supporting the continuation of limited sanctions.
- The third is a bill to impose a 25% tariff on all US imports from China until the president certifies that China is fulfilling its obligations.

Which would you choose and why? What are the advantages and disadvantages of each policy? It is worth considering the relative economic power of each country, their level of interdependence with each other, what might be the longer term implications of US action in this policy area, and even who might benefit domestically from each approach.

Table 10.3 US–China Trade

This table shows two clear trends. First, after growing moderately in the 1980s, US-China trade began to rise more quickly in the 1990s and then increased dramatically after 2000. Second, the US trade deficit with China (exports minus imports) followed a similar course, changing from a relative balance in 1985 to a $84 billion deficit in 2000 to a $376 billion deficit in 2017. These lopsided numbers have created increasing tensions and been a recurrent focus of diatribes against China by President Trump.
All figures in billions of U.S. dollars.

	1985	1990	1995	2000	2011	2014	2017
US exports to China	$4	$5	$12	$16	$103	**$123**	**$129**
US imports from China	$4	$15	$52	$100	$399	**$468**	**$505**
US trade deficit with China	$0	$10	$40	$84	$295	**$344**	**$376**

Source: Data from https://www.census.gov/foreign-trade/balance/c5700.html.

Trade Cooperation Under the WTO

World Trade Organization
Implements and enforces the General Agreement on Tariffs and Trade (GATT) and mediates trade-related disputes between and among parties to the GATT.

General Agreement on Tariffs and Trade A series of multilateral trade negotiations that reduced tariffs after World War II and continued into the early 1990s. Became enforced by the World Trade Organization beginning in 1993.

Doha Round The ninth and latest round of global trade negotiations to reduce barriers to international free economic interchange.

We begin our examination of trade cooperation with the institution that arguably has the greatest daily impact on global commerce: the **World Trade Organization** (WTO). As discussed earlier, the WTO grew out of its underlying series of international agreements, the **General Agreement on Tariffs and Trade** (GATT). The organization's initial membership of 23 countries has expanded to 164 members, and most of the nonmember countries are seeking to join. In keeping with the GATT's original mission—the reduction of trade barriers—the WTO has sponsored a series of trade negotiations, called rounds, that have greatly enhanced the free flow of trade and capital. The most recent of these rounds, the **Doha Round**, began in Qatar in 2001. Perhaps the most significant achievement for Doha was the focus on the Global South, where effort was made "to place developing countries' needs and interests at the heart of the Work Programme" of the negotiation round.[17] A world systems analyst might argue that this focus on development is a major reason so little tangible Doha progress was achieved, as the process is less Northern-centric than previous rounds. The Doha Round was suspended in 2006 without any significant achievements. Attempts to revive it have yielded little of substance to date.

With its headquarters in Geneva, Switzerland, the WTO holds regular ministerial meetings that give it a political prominence that the GATT did not have. Another important procedural change is its Dispute Settlement Body, which is designed to hear and settle trade disputes between countries. Countries can file complaints against one another for alleged violations of the GATT. This body uses three-judge panels to hear the complaints, and if a panel finds a violation, the WTO may authorize injured countries to levy sanctions on the offending country. Despite grumbling by critics about countries losing their sovereignty, the WTO judicial process has been busy, with an average of about 50 cases filed annually in recent years.[18] The pattern since this process began in 1995, as Figure 10.4 shows, indicates that Northern countries are the most common complainants, with the United States leading in both categories shown in the table.

The workload for the WTO dispute settlement body increased significantly in 2018, with seven complaints filed by Mexico, Canada, the EU, and others disputing US tariffs on steel and aluminum and complaints against China filed by the United States. Currently, however, the WTO appellate body is stuck in legal limbo as the Trump administration is withholding appointments to the seven-member panel. This panel is at present operating with only three members, but that

Figure 10.4 The two most frequent parties to WTO trade disputes are the United States and the EU, long-time economic powers who are increasingly challenged by up-and-comers like China, India, and Brazil. Figures here do not include stats for when a country is a third party in a dispute.

is the minimum number required to hear an appeal. If no new judges are appointed by December 10, 2019, to replace those with expiring terms, the dispute settlement body will not be able to function legally.

Monetary Cooperation in Support of Development: The IMF

As trade and the level of other international financial transactions have increased, the need to cooperate internationally in order to facilitate and stabilize the flow of dollars, euros, yen, pounds, and other currencies has become vital. To meet this need, a number of organizations, of which the **International Monetary Fund** is the most important, have been established. Western powers created the IMF as one of the Bretton Woods organizations committed to the liberalization of economic interchange. World leaders recognized the importance of monetary stability and the easy convertibility from one currency to another and felt that a global structure was needed to facilitate financial stability. The IMF began financial operations in 1947, with 44 member-countries. Early in its history, the IMF followed a pegged exchange rate system under which currencies were exchanged at a fixed rate tied to the price of gold. In 1971, a new system evolved that relied on free-floating currency relations and it now has 189 members.

> **International Monetary Fund** The world's primary organization devoted to maintaining monetary stability by helping countries to fund balance-of-payment deficits.

To fund its operations, the IMF utilizes hard currency reserves placed at its disposal by the Global North and from interest on loans it has made to countries that draw on those reserves. On rare occasions, the IMF also sells part of its gold reserve, weighing in at over 2,800 metric tons in 2016, to support its operations. The agency can also borrow up to about $25 billion to meet emergency needs. Whatever their source, the value of IMF resources is expressed in terms of **special drawing rights** (SDRs), a virtual currency whose value is based on an average, or market basket, value of the EU euro, Japanese yen, British pound, and US dollar. In June 2018, the exchange rate was 1 SDR = $1.41.

> **special drawing rights** Reserves held by the International Monetary Fund that the central banks of member-countries can draw upon to help manage the values of their currencies.

ROLE OF THE IMF. The IMF's primary function is to help maintain exchange rate stability by making short-term loans to countries with international balance-of-payments problems because of trade deficits, heavy loan payments, or other factors. In such times, a country can use the IMF's loan to help meet debt payments, to buy back its own currency (thus maintaining exchange rate stability by balancing supply and demand), or to take other financial steps.

Currency trading has long been a potential source of global economic uncertainty. In theory, governments control their currencies, but traders (like the one shown here) try to predict currency fluctuations for profit that at times run counter to national and global economic goals.

As with many other aspects of international economic cooperation, the focus of the IMF has turned largely to the Global South with the challenges of dealing with the increased demands brought on by loan repayment and financial crises in Mexico (1995), Asia (late 1990s), Argentina (2001–2002), and Greece over the past decade. As recently as 1980, IMF loans were under $15 billion. Committed funds stood at $189 billion in 2018, however, with almost $700 billion available for lending.[19]

In addition to responding to monetary crises, the IMF tries to prevent financial difficulties by encouraging member-countries to follow sound fiscal policies and by providing them with technical support to achieve that goal. Under its surveillance program, the IMF regularly conducts detailed analyses of each country's economic situation and discusses the findings of their appraisal with the country's financial officials. The IMF also offers countries technical assistance in developing monetary and exchange rate policy, regulating banks and other financial institutions, and gathering and interpreting statistics.

CRITICISMS OF THE IMF.   Although states are not required to accept IMF loans, the IMF is often the best option. Nevertheless, many states, particularly from the Global South, are critical of the IMF, especially for the conditions that are part of IMF loan packages and the decision-making process within the organization, which is entirely controlled by the Global North.

conditionality The policy of the International Monetary Fund, the World Bank, and others to attach conditions to their loans and grants. These conditions may require recipient countries to devalue their currencies, lift various controls, and cut their budgets.

Critics accuse the IMF of imposing unfair and unwise conditions on countries that borrow from it. Most IMF loans are subject to **conditionality**, or restructuring. This refers to requirements that the borrowing country take steps to remedy (restructure) the practices and policies that, according to the IMF, either caused the recipient's financial problems or will retard its recovery. The IMF also often requires borrowing governments to make significant changes in domestic policy, such as reducing their budget deficits by cutting domestic programs and/or by raising taxes. Although such requirements, also known as austerity measures, may seem reasonable, critics take exception. One objection is that IMF conditions violate sovereignty by interfering in the recipients' policy-making processes. When the IMF provided Greece with its first bailout loan in 2010 for 110 billion euros over three years, it required the Greek government to raise taxes, cut pensions, and decrease public service pay. Since then, the IMF, the EU, and Greece have agreed to two more bailouts under renegotiated terms.[20]

Critics also charge that IMF conditions often harm economies in the Global South by requiring fiscal austerity and other stringent conditions that are counterproductive. In January 2019, for instance, Egyptian authorities announced that they would suspend government-funded subsidies for most energy products. That decision, while in line with IMF guidance about fiscal austerity, will result in higher energy prices for Egyptian consumers. The Egyptian decision will allow further access to IMF loans, but will be unpopular among its citizens.[21] Another related charge is that IMF conditions often destabilize governments by forcing them to institute policies that cause a domestic backlash and political protest. And yet another contention is that IMF conditions undermine social welfare by pushing countries to cut their budget, thereby reducing social services, laying off government workers, and taking other steps that harm the quality of life of their citizens.

A closely related charge is that as part of its conditions, the IMF generally promotes the capitalist model by pressing the South to move toward easing restrictions on their economies and adopting free international economic exchange. It advocates such steps as privatizing state-run enterprises, reducing barriers to trade and investment, and devaluing currencies to increase exports and decrease imports. According to one of the IMF's detractors, Walden Bello, such policies as the "liberalization and deregulation of trade and finance" only serve to "bring about crises, widen inequalities within and across countries, and increase global poverty."[22]

Another criticism focuses on the North's control of IMF policy and the ways conditionality promotes a neocolonial relationship. The voting formula for the IMF board of directors is based on how much each member-country contributes to the IMF's resources. On this basis, the United States has over 16.5% of the votes—or 550 times the voting strength of Palau's 0.03%. Moreover, many IMF decisions must be decided by special majorities, further skewing voting power toward the wealthy. For instance, changes to financial quotas for members must be decided by an 85% majority. Thus, with 16.5% of the votes, the United States could veto any amendments to quota changes if it so desired.[23] This record and the voting apportionment lead critics to charge that the IMF is undemocratically controlled by the United States and other Northern countries, and that these countries use it as a tool to dominate the South now and into the future.

DEFENSE OF THE IMF.   Those who defend the IMF reject these charges. With respect to the voting formula, defenders argue that since it is the Global North countries that provide the funds, they should have a proportionate share of the say in how they are invested. As for conditionality, the IMF acknowledges that its demands often cause hardship, but it argues that the required reforms and restructuring are necessary to correct the problems that led the borrower-country into financial difficulty in the first place. Certainly, that is the logic behind the Egyptian energy subsidy decision mentioned earlier.

The IMF has responded to the criticism of its conditionality standards and eased them during the second bailout for Greece. In 2012, the Eurozone joined the IMF to offer lower interest rates on loans and a debt buy-back program as well as to ease its 2020 debt reduction goals. Greece received a third rescue package in 2015 from the EU; in exchange for the 86 billion euro bailout, Greece agreed to cut public spending, privatize state assets, implement tax reforms, and reform labor laws among other measures. The IMF did not contribute additional funds to this third bailout because the organization did not find it realistic for Greece to repay all of its debt without some sort of relief, like longer payment schedules, from creditors. As of 2018, Greece owed roughly 290 billion euros ($330 billion), part of a public debt that had climbed to 180% of GDP.

To the charge of promoting capitalism and economic internationalism, those who defend the IMF argue that it is doing just what it should do to promote global prosperity. From this perspective, Johan Norberg argues, "Free markets and free trade and free choices transfer power to individuals at the expense of political institutions," and, "[p]eople who have acquired a taste of economic liberty and expanded horizons will not consent to be shut in again by walls or fences. They will work to create a better existence for themselves. The aim of our politics should be to give them that freedom."[24]

Development Cooperation: The World Bank Group

World Bank Group Four associated agencies that grant loans to less developed Countries for economic development and other financial needs.

Another type of multilateral economic cooperation involves granting economic development loans and aid to the Global South. The most significant development agency today is the **World Bank Group**, commonly referred to as just the World Bank. The designator "Group" reflects that the World Bank consists of several distinct agencies. The IBRD still exists as part of the World Bank Group, but the World Bank is now focused away from postwar reconstruction and deals almost exclusively with development financing in the Global South.

WORLD BANK OPERATIONS. Like the IMF, the World Bank was established in the World War II era to promote the postwar economic prosperity of the United States and its allies, and in recent decades, priorities have shifted to assisting the development of the Global South. While several agencies are within the World Bank Group, this text highlights two.

Almost every country is a member of each agency of the World Bank Group. The IBRD has lending policies that resemble those of a commercial bank in that the IBRD analyzes the financial worth of projects it funds and charges some interest. In 2017, the IBRD had commitments of almost $23 billion to 133 projects around the world.[25] Since its founding in 1944, the IBRD has disbursed just over $681 billion.

The International Development Association (IDA), created in 1960, focuses on making loans at no interest to the very poorest countries to help them provide better basic human services (e.g., education, health care, safe water, and sanitation), to improve economic productivity, and to create employment. All of the IDA's loans are on a concessional basis, with no interest, no repayment for 10 years, then a 15- to 30-year repayment schedule. During 2017, the IDA disbursed over $19 billion in loans, many in sub-Saharan Africa.[26] Most loans are for small amounts, especially compared to those of the IBRD. Credits and grants from the IDA have totaled over $345 billion since 1960. Some of the IDA's funding comes from the income of the IBRD, but most comes from member-country contributions.

The regional distribution of funds from the World Bank is shown in Figure 10.5. This pie chart shows aggregate figures for the Bank, but each organization has a somewhat different regional focus. The IDA provides over half of its lending to Africa countries (55%), while the IBRD distribution is spread more evenly across global regions, with Latin America being the largest regional recipient at 24% of the total IBRD funds.

CONTROVERSY ABOUT THE WORLD BANK.
Like the IMF, the World Bank has done a great deal of good, but it also receives recurrent criticism. Many object that the World Bank, like the IMF, is dominated by the Global North. It also uses a wealth-based voting formula. This gives the United States 16.88% of the votes and, along with other Global North countries, majority control of the Bank's board of directors. Thus, at least for the foreseeable future, the leadership of the World Bank will remain in the *de facto* hands of the North. From the South's perspective, the North's ongoing domination of the World Bank limits its ability to understand the views and problems of the Global South.

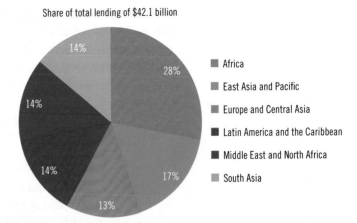

Share of total lending of $42.1 billion

- ■ Africa
- ■ East Asia and Pacific
- ■ Europe and Central Asia
- ■ Latin America and the Caribbean
- ■ Middle East and North Africa
- ■ South Asia

Figure 10.5 This chart gives you a sense of the primary destinations for the World Bank's development financing with Africa receiving the most, while also likely needing the most.

A harsher interpretation in line with world systems theory is that the Global North uses the World Bank and other IGOs to maintain neo-imperialist control of the South. This view has gained added weight under Jim Yong Kim's leadership of the Bank (2012–2019), as one analyst argues that Kim has undertaken an "embrace Wall Street" approach to the Bank's management and role in the world not seen under previous leaders.[27] These moves further fuel the argument that global finance remains a club-centric, elite model of governance (Tsingou, 2014).

Critics also grumble that the World Bank provides too little funding. Figures such as those discussed earlier for the IBRD and IDA pale in comparison to Northern national budgets, and progress has been slow in cultivating development, as Chapter 11 discusses. Further criticism charges that the World Bank is too conservative in the distribution of loans and is thus more inclined to provide funding to "safer" countries than to those that perhaps need it more. For instance, China was the largest IBRD recipient in 2017.

For many analysts, there is a growing question of whether the Bank should be loaning money to countries like China that can get loans on the world's commercial credit markets, that have large foreign reserves, or that spend huge sums on nuclear weapons and other military programs. Economic nationalist critics suggest that the Bank is no longer needed at all, whereas liberal critics urge the Bank to devote most or all of its resources to giving grants, not loans, to the poorest countries. Finally, liberal critics also charge that the World Bank's conservatism causes it, like the IMF, to use its financial power to impose the capitalist economic model on recipient countries. We discuss economic development concerns of the Global South in detail in Chapter 11.

Cooperation Among the Dominant

As globalization progressed in the latter half of the 20th century, the Global North created several organizations to help ensure their continued economic health. Although these IGOs still pursue this goal to some degree, they, like the IMF and other economic IGOs, have expanded their focus to include development.

ORGANIZATION FOR ECONOMIC COOPERATION AND DEVELOPMENT.   Of the two major Northern organizations focused broadly on economic development, the first to be created was the **Organization for Economic Cooperation and Development** (OECD), which was launched in 1961 by the United States, Canada, and 18 European countries. It has subsequently admitted several Southern countries that have close economic ties to the North, such as Mexico, or that are increasingly prosperous, such as South Korea. Still, the bulk of the OECD's 36 member-states are Northern countries, making the organization something of a club for rich countries. The OECD serves as a forum for member-countries to discuss economic issues, and it generates copious statistics and numerous studies and offers economic advice and technical assistance. It has also become increasingly involved with the Global South and such issues as globalization and sustainable development, and has established links with some 70 Southern countries, ranging from Brazil, China, and Russia to the low-income, least developed countries in sub-Saharan Africa and elsewhere.

These photos provide some insight into the intense negotiations by world leaders during the G-7 Summit in 2018. Pictured here is German Chancellor Angela Merkel; US President Donald Trump; Japanese Prime Minister Shinzo Abe; John Bolton, the US National Security Adviser; British Prime Minister Theresa May; French President Emmanuel Macron; and Prime Minister of Canada Justin Trudeau. It doesn't look like a happy exchange.

THE GROUP OF SEVEN/EIGHT AND THE GROUP OF 20.   If the OECD is a reasonably exclusive club of prosperous member-countries, the **Group of Seven/Eight** (G-8) is equivalent to the executive board. The G-8 does not have a formal connection to the OECD, but it does represent the pinnacle of economic power, with its members generating well over half of the world's GDP. The G-8 began in 1975 as the Group of Five to coordinate economic policy among the most economically powerful noncommunist countries (France, Germany, Great Britain, Japan, and the United States). Canada and Italy were eventually added shortly thereafter to create the Group of Seven (G-7).

In 1997, the G-7 became the G-8 when it added Russia, in recognition of its economic potential and geostrategic importance, but it reverted back to the G-7 in 2014 after Russia's invasion of Crimea and the expulsion of Russia from the group.

The apex of G-7 activity comes at its annual summit meeting. The yearly agenda varies greatly, ranging from development to timely matters of importance to the Global North. One indication of the focus on development is that since 2000 a number of countries of the South have been invited as participating nonmembers to each summit. The leaders of Brazil, China, India, Mexico, and South Africa now regularly attend, as does the president of the European Commission.

The agenda of individual meetings is also driven by events, as was the case during 2017 in the face of increasingly hostile relations between the United States and the other members. At the end of that meeting, President Trump was widely criticized for storming out without even signing the collective communique. That abrupt departure was at least partly based on Trump's demand that Russia be included once again in the G-7 deliberations, something opposed by others.

As for the importance of the G-7 and its resolutions, one analyst depicts it as an emergent "shadow world government."[28] Such a role, of course, could be a positive or a negative force. A less expansive view, according to another scholar, is that G-7 members "do comply modestly with the decisions and consensus generated [at their summit meetings]."[29] Similar arguments can apply to the larger body, the **Group of 20** (G-20). This more inclusive group brings China, India, Indonesia, Brazil, and Argentina to the table, as well as the usual "suspects" from the Global North. The G-20 has played an increasingly higher profile role since its creation in 1999, largely in response to the global financial crises of the late 1990s. Its potential role as a global coordinating body was well shown at the July 2017 Bonn G-20 summit, where the growing fractures between the United States and its long-time allies were on full display regarding differences of opinion about economic and environmental issues.

In the shadow of the Trump–Kim Jung-Un summit meeting, in June 2018, US President Trump did not even attend the full summit in Québec that year. In the end, the tensions between Trump and the other leaders were again on full display. As French President Emmanuel Macron put it, "The American president may not mind being isolated, but neither do we mind signing a six-country agreement if need be . . . because these six countries represent values, they represent an economic market which has the weight of history behind it and which is now a true international force."[30] Sentiments like these may well be setting the stage for greater "G-6" independence from the United States as well as further isolation of the United States in the world community, breaking with the long-standing US leadership tradition in the world economy. (See the *Personal Narrative* feature, which focuses on Canadian Prime Minister Justin Trudeau's struggle to maintain liberal internationalist views given a changing relationship with the United States.)

Organization for Economic Cooperation and Development An organization that has existed since 1948 (and since 1960 under its present name) to facilitate the exchange of information and otherwise promote cooperation among the economically developed countries.

Group of Seven/Eight The seven economically largest free market countries (Canada, France, Germany, Great Britain, Italy, Japan, and the United States) plus Russia (a participant since 1998, suspended in 2014).

Group of 20 A standing forum for economic summitry amongst sectoral policy officials (finance, environment, etc.) and heads-of-state from the world's largest and fastest growing economies.

Justin Trudeau: The New Generation of Old-School Internationalism?

Canadian Prime Minister Justin Trudeau is not new to political life. The son of former Prime Minister Pierre Trudeau, the current Canadian leader was long viewed as avoiding the life he was destined to lead. A window on his re-emergence into public life came in 2000 when he delivered a stirring eulogy at his father's funeral, but it wasn't until 2008 that his swift rise to leadership began in earnest, with his election to the House of Commons. By 2013, he had assumed leadership of the Liberal Party and, through national elections, became Prime Minister in 2015.

From the start, his smooth working relationship with President Barack Obama showed a commonality of global philosophy grounded in the liberal internationalist consensus that has long defined the global economic system. Trudeau is committed to a "progressive approach to global affairs, [but also that] global trade has to benefit everyone, not just the rich and powerful." And in January 2018, Trudeau was still insisting that he "must find common ground with Trump on creating jobs and achieving a successful outcome to the North American Free Trade Agreement renegotiation."[31] He again showed his commitment to working toward positive negotiated outcomes, especially with Canada's largest trading partner and southern neighbor.

Trudeau's views and his commitment to liberal internationalism were severely tested, however, at the G-7 summit he hosted in Québec in June 2018. Standing physically and metaphorically with another member of the new generation of internationalist leader, President Emmanuel Macron of France, Trudeau took Trump to task for his aggressive unilateralism. "We are going to defend our industries and our workers" and "show the US president that his unacceptable actions are hurting his own citizens."[32] But as one analyst of Canadian foreign policy argued, "Trudeau is in a very difficult place because the G-7 summit signals the approach the Trudeau government took to deal with the Trump administration has failed . . . the charm offensive has produced little of what the prime minister hoped."[33]

The question that will remain unanswered for some time is: Will Trump's unilateralism force other long-time adherents to internationalism to abandon that approach for unilateral approaches of their own? Or will it serve to isolate the United States from its long-time allies and foreign policy collaborators and force them to develop their own collaborations, thus sidelining the United States? Or will it, as Trump indeed assumes, force those allies to capitulate to American demands?

Canadian Prime Minister Justin Trudeau remains a stalwart of the liberal internationalist view of Northern economic collaboration. Only time will tell if his approach or the rising tide of economic nationalists will win the day.

🌐 Regional and Bilateral Economic Cooperation

In addition to activity promoting economic cooperation and development from a global perspective, important efforts are underway at the regional and bilateral levels to reduce barriers to economic interchange. This activity does not exclusively involve the Global North. Still, similar to global cooperation, regional and bilateral ties have become extensively intertwined with the development of the South. We discuss development cooperation more fully in Chapter 11. A brief discussion is appropriate here, however, as regional cooperation has been a linchpin of Northern efforts to solidify global prosperity.

One area of cooperation is financing through several regional development banks. In terms of loan commitments, the largest of these (and their loans in 2016) are the African Development Bank ($4.33 billion), the Asian Development ment Bank ($9.76 billion), the Inter-American Development Bank ($9.6 billion), and the European Bank for Reconstruction and Development ($8.63 billion),[34] which focuses on projects in the weaker economies in Eastern Europe, Russia, and the former Soviet republics. There are other regional banks, but those are not as well funded, as exemplified by the Caribbean Development Bank, which despite that region's pressing needs had disbursements of only about $261 million in loans in 2017. In addition to the development banks, numerous IGOs are dedicated to promoting economic cooperation and development among groups of countries based on their geographic region (e.g., the 12-member Black Sea Economic Cooperation Zone), culture or religion (e.g., the 57-member Islamic Development Bank), or some other link tying the group together (e.g., the 21-member Arab Monetary Fund).

An even more common type of international effort involves a free trade agreement (FTA). This is a treaty between two (or more) countries to reduce or eliminate tariffs and other trade barriers and to otherwise promote freer economic exchange. First, we should note that different IGOs, governments, and studies designate these agreements with different names and accompanying acronyms. Here, we use **regional trade agreement (RTA)** to designate an FTA among three or more countries within a region.

There is no precise count of FTAs, but the WTO estimates that there are about 30 RTAs and perhaps another 270 bilateral trade agreements. There is also a wide variety of structures among FTAs—some with developed institutions, others less so; some with formal dispute resolution practices; and many more differences that influence the way they operate and interface with other organizations (Gomez-Mera & Molinari, 2014). The EU is almost certainly the best known and most successful regional economic cooperation organization, even if it has become much more than a simple free trade area. Nonetheless, like other organizations, it has experienced some serious cleavages in recent years, most notably the UK Brexit vote in June 2016. At this writing, it is yet unclear what path will be the final one for Brexit.

regional trade agreement
A broad term the World Trade Organization uses to define bilateral and cross-regional agreements as well as multilateral regional ones.

A Look at the EU

The European Union, with its 27 member-countries, has not only moved toward full economic integration but also achieved considerable political cooperation. As a result, this regional institution could easily be discussed in Chapter 6 focusing on international organization. We discuss it here, however, as its roots were unquestionably economic in nature. Thus, it fits well with the discussion of Northern efforts to preserve and enhance wealth after World War II.

European Union The European regional organization established in 1993 when the Maastricht Treaty went into effect. The EU encompasses the still legally existing European Communities (EC).

ORIGINS AND EVOLUTION OF THE EU. The **European Union** (EU) has evolved through several stages and names in the 60-plus years of its existence, expanding its role in the world and its ambitions as an organization (Bengtsson and Elgström, 2012; Blagden, 2018; Walker et al., 2018). The initial agreement involved only six Western European states and was focused on the security and economic needs of a devastated post–World War II Europe. Since then, this agreement has expanded along economic and political lines, exemplifying functional needs along the way. It operates through a hybrid system marked by both supranationalism and intergovernmentalism. In short, the EU represents a unique regional organization in that it has become deeply institutionalized, transforming governance in Europe in significant and lasting ways. Ironically, the very institutionalization that gives the EU its uniqueness and strength as a political-economic global actor is what a majority of UK voters rallied against in 2016. When the dust settles, it will be interesting to see what forces win out.

The EU's genesis occurred in 1952, when Belgium, France, (West) Germany, Italy, Luxembourg, and the Netherlands created a common market for coal, iron, and steel products, called the European Coal and Steel Community. Europeans were motivated by their common experience of war and the security and economic threats they faced because of their shared history. The success of this functional agreement prompted the six countries to sign the Treaty of Rome on March 25, 1957, which established the European Economic Community to facilitate trade in many additional areas and the European Atomic Energy Community to coordinate matters in that realm (Dinan, 2004).

Continued economic success led the six countries to found an overarching organization, the European Community, in 1967. Each of the three pre-existing organizations became subordinate parts of the EC. As the financial transactions among the EU's countries rapidly grew, it became clear that continually converting currencies from one to another made little sense. Therefore, in the early 1990s, the EC agreed to move toward a common currency. Thus, in 1992 the Maastricht Treaty was signed, and the European Community became the EU. This shift signaled member commitment to greater political and economic integration, including common foreign and security policies as well as a common currency. Map 10.2 shows a temporal map of EU entry.

Once the new currency was ready for launch, only those countries that met certain criteria for sound governmental financial management (e.g., limited inflation and budget deficits) could adopt the euro. With a few exceptions, all member countries are required to meet that criteria and to adopt the euro. In 2002, the euro went into general circulation in those countries, while their traditional currencies ceased to be legal tender (Martin & Ross, 2004).

As of 2017, 19 of the EU countries were using the euro, and three other smaller, non-EU countries (Montenegro, Vatican City, and Monaco) have also adopted it. Of the older EU members, the United Kingdom, Denmark, and Sweden still do not use the euro for various reasons. Of the countries that have joined the EU since 2004, Slovenia and the Baltic countries (Estonia, Latvia, and Lithuania) already use the euro, and the rest of the newer members are

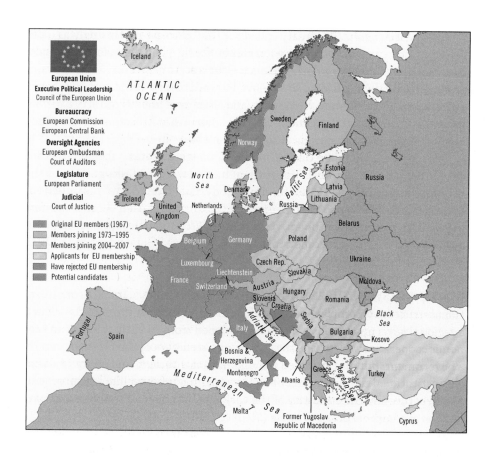

Map 10.2 At this writing, the United Kingdom remains part of the EU. Whether or not that continues remains to be seen with Brexit as yet uncertain in summer 2019.

slated to transition to the euro once they achieve the required benchmarks of financial stability.

Creating the euro was important both economically and politically. Economically, it has tied the EU members even closer together by eliminating one of the hallmarks of an independent economy, a national currency. Adding to the economic importance of adopting a common currency that may well one day spread across an entire continent, there is great political symbolism in the replacement of Germany's deutschemark, France's franc, Italy's lira, and other countries' national currencies with the euro. Increased economic integration, however, has not been without its opponents. For example, the United Kingdom first rejected use of the euro, and then in June 2016 narrowly voted to withdraw from the EU entirely and began its halting journey to do so (perhaps).

That vote for **Brexit** shook the EU politically and economically. Missing the original exit date of March 29, 2019, the details of EU-UK divorce have yet to be finalized. Only time will tell what outcome ultimately is implemented and what types of consequences for economic prosperity will occur throughout Europe (Kugler, Fisunoglu, & Yesilada, 2015).

There comes a point where economic integration cannot continue without also taking steps toward political integration. The Maastricht Treaty was significant not only for establishing a common currency, but also for expanding

Brexit Refers to the 2016 UK referendum and follow-on negotiations with the EU so that the UK can leave EU membership. Literally, a combination of BRitish EXIT.

European citizenship. The treaty called for the EU to act increasingly as a political unit by eventually creating a common foreign and defense policy and a common internal policy relating to such issues as crime, terrorism, and immigration. Gradually, such ideas have moved toward reality. People can now travel on either an EU or a national passport, and citizens of any EU country can vote in local and European Parliament elections in another EU country where they live rather than in the country of their citizenship.

The EU has also taken on the symbols of a state. It has a flag and has adopted the *European Anthem*. The anthem has no words, in recognition of the EU's linguistic diversity. However, its melody, the "Ode to Joy" movement of Ludwig van Beethoven's Ninth Symphony (1823), was chosen because it refers to Friedrich von Schiller's poem, "Ode to Joy" (1785), which expresses hope for a time when "All men become brothers." This view is also evident in the EU's motto, "United in diversity."

GOVERNING STRUCTURES AND AUTHORITY OF THE EU.   The EU's organizational structure is complex, but a brief look helps illustrate the extent to which a regional government exists and has developed from its early times as an economic cooperative. As an IGO, the governance structure of the EU is not exactly a government, but it is arguably moving in that direction and shares most of the institutional characteristics of a government. Moreover, like a government, the structure and the authority of the various EU units play an important part in determining how policy is made (Meunier, 2000; Raunio, 2011; Ugur, 2013). The EU's government can be divided for analysis into its political leadership, bureaucracy, legislature, and judiciary.

Political decision-making is centered in the European Council, formerly called the Council of Ministers. It came into existence in 1974 when heads of state and heads of government decided to hold regular summit meetings to decide, along with the European Parliament, on the most important policy directions for the region, including enlargement, the single market, foreign policy, and constitutional reform. Assisting the Council is an administrative staff called the General Secretariat headed by the Secretary-General of the Council.

The European Council meets twice a year as a gathering of the prime ministers, national presidents, and key ministerial (e.g., finance) leaders. Most Council sessions are held in Brussels, Belgium, the principal site of the EU administration. With the Lisbon Treaty, the European Council moved to double majority voting, a form of qualified majority voting, in almost all policy areas starting in 2014. Any decision taken under this scheme will require the support of at least 55% of the Council who must in turn represent at least 65% of the EU's citizens. Thus, the majority must reflect the majority of countries as well as the majority of the population. The advantage of the voting rules is that the qualified majority plans require a high degree of consensus in Europe before the EU can adopt policies that one or more of its members oppose. This check has made moving forward along the economic and political integration tracks easier because the sense of sovereignty that EU members retain seems less threatened. Even so, the Brexit vote illustrates the degree to which national sovereignty and identity remains a powerful force within the EU.

The EU's bureaucracy is organized under the **European Commission,** which has the power to propose legislation to the Council and the European Parliament (discussed later) and to execute the policies adopted by those branches. As the "engine for integration in keeping with neofunctionalist theory," the Commission has the "exclusive responsibility for initiating new community laws and for advancing the goals of the treaty" (Karns & Mingst 2009:167). There are 27 commissioners, one from each country, who serve five-year terms and act as a cabinet for the EU; they are expected to act in the interests of the EU rather than their respective national governments. Each oversees a particularly functional area. This practice of having a minister from each country has arguably led to an overly large commission and a fragmented bureaucratic structure, including a ministry of multilingualism, as the number of EU members has grown.

> **European Commission**
> A 27-member commission with shared executive power that serves as the bureaucratic organ of the European Union.

Counterbalancing the commission's fragmentation, the post of president has evolved into one of the most significant in the EU. One of the commissioners is selected by the Council of the European Union to be President of the Commission. This official serves as the EU's administrative head and is the overall director of the EU bureaucracy headquartered in Brussels.

The **European Parliament** serves as the EU's legislative branch and meets in Strasbourg, France. With the 2019 elections, there are 751 MEPs, with each member-state having at least 6 and at most 96. Members are elected to five-year terms, apportioned among the EU's 27 countries on a modified population basis according to the voting system within each state. The most populous country (Germany) has 96 seats; the least populous country (Malta) has 6 seats. What is yet to be known is the degree to which populist and pro-withdrawal wins in a variety of EU countries will impact EU decision-making, especially as the UK stumbles to some sort of Brexit resolution. Delegates to the assemblies of most IGOs are appointed by their government, but members of the European Parliament are elected by voters in their respective countries. Furthermore, instead of organizing themselves within the European Parliament by country, the representatives have tended to group themselves by political persuasion. The European Parliament's role began as a mostly advisory authority, but it has grown and now has "co-decision" legislative authority with the Council of the European Union on the EU budget and a significant range of other policy matters. Parliamentarians also confirm the members of the European Commission and its president.

> **European Parliament** The 751-member legislative branch of the European Union. Representation is determined by population of member-countries and is based on 5-year terms.

The **European Court of Justice** is the main element of the judicial branch of the EU. The 28-judge court—one justice from each EU country—sits in Luxembourg and hears cases brought by member-states or other EU institutions and sometimes acts as a court of appeals for decisions of lower EU courts. Only rarely does the full court hear a case. Instead, almost 90% of the cases are heard by

> **European Court of Justice** A supranational court that serves as the "high court" in the European Union (astride the Court of First Instance and Court of Auditors) and is responsible for the enforcement of European Union "community law" and ensuring its application across and within all 27 current EU member-states.

three- or five-judge panels. This arrangement allows the court to deal with a much higher number of cases (400–500 a year) than the US Supreme Court (about 75 cases a year). As of now a British judge sits on the court but that will likely change.

Like other EU institutions, the power of the court has expanded over time, and its responsibilities now include interpreting and enforcing EU law. Further, the court can strike down both EU laws and regulations and those of member-countries that violate the basic EU treaties. In 2006, for example, the court invalidated an EU-US agreement made soon after 9/11 by which the EU was giving American officials 34 items of personal information about any passenger leaving on a flight to the United States. The European Parliament had objected that the EU Commission lacked a legal basis to make such an agreement, and the court agreed. This ruling has obvious continuing implications for information sharing in the world of social media and the extensive flow of information across boundaries.

FUTURE CHALLENGES FOR THE EU.   Part of the story of the EU is its rapid evolution, beginning with the formation of the European Coal and Steel Community in 1952. Within just a few decades, much of Europe was transformed from a continent marked by perpetual rivalry and frequent war to a continent largely at peace, with a high degree of economic integration and with the beginning of significant political integration as well. In the grand sweep of human history, the approximately 60 years in which all this happened was a proverbial blink of the eye. Yet despite this overall success, Europeans are currently facing a number of significant challenges that will ultimately determine just how far the economic and political integration can go in the region. Brexit and elections of anti-EU governments in Italy, Poland, Hungary, and other countries may further complicate the future of EU integration, although others have witnessed the Brexit debacle and seem more content now to remain within the EU.

At a much more general level, the questions, issues, and factors regarding the future of the EU are either the same or similar to those that relate to how we will govern the international system at large in the decades and centuries to come. In this way, the evolution of the EU is noteworthy beyond the immediate issue of Europe's future. The EU also serves as a test case to see if humans, who have found that the way they had been conducting themselves politically for centuries is not working well, can overcome tradition and inertia and establish a new form of governance at a regional or perhaps even global level.

NAFTA, USMCA, and Beyond?

Proposals for regional economic cooperation date back to a US effort in 1889 to create a hemispheric free trade zone that would reduce trade barriers among the countries and adopt common external tariff and nontariff barriers. The notion of RTAs in the Western Hemisphere then lay dormant for almost a century until the further press of globalization began to convert the idea into reality.

The largest RTA in the Western Hemisphere, measured in trade volume, is the **North American Free Trade Agreement** (NAFTA) among Canada,

North American Free Trade Agreement An economic agreement among Canada, Mexico, and the United States that went into effect on January 1, 1994.

Mexico, and the United States. The 2,000-page agreement, which took effect in 1994, established schedules for reducing tariff and nontariff barriers to trade by 2004 in all but a few hundred of some 20,000 product categories and by 2009 for all products. NAFTA also reduced or eliminated many restrictions on foreign investments and other financial transactions, and it facilitated transportation by allowing trucking largely unimpeded access across borders. There is a standing commission with representatives from all three countries to deal with disputes that arise under the NAFTA agreement.

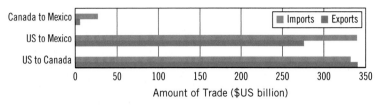

Figure 10.6 These trade figures show that the United States remains the pivotal player in the Canada-Mexico-US economic relationship. The Canada-Mexico bilateral relationship is dwarfed in comparison.

NAFTA has had an important impact on the three trading partners. Intra-NAFTA trade is a key component of the exports of all three partners, as can be seen in the data on merchandise trade in Figure 10.6. Mexico and Canada are especially dependent on intra-NAFTA trade, with each sending between 80% and 90% of their exports to the United States and to one another. The United States is the least dependent among the three members, albeit still heavily so, with NAFTA trade accounting for 26% of US exports.

Issue Navigator: Free Trade

A vigorous debate continues in each of the three countries about the pros and cons of NAFTA. Canada is the least affected, both because it has relatively little interchange with Mexico and because preexisting US-Canada trade was already quite high. For Americans, there certainly have been losses. Many American businesses have relocated their facilities to Mexico, establishing *maquiladoras* (manufacturing plants just south of the border) to produce goods for export to the United States. According to a US Department of Labor study, American job losses from this shift of production and from Mexican imports total more than a million since NAFTA's signing.[35] Yet economists point out that those jobs, even if they had not been shifted to Mexico, would have probably gone to other Southern countries anyway. Further, American consumers benefited from lower prices for goods imported from Mexico. Such gains often are less noticed, however, than are losses. As one economist explains, "The gains are so thinly spread across the country that people don't thank NAFTA when they buy a mango or inexpensive auto parts."[36]

Who loses in the US-Mexico trade tensions? Texas is the number-one state trading partner with Mexico, making it particularly vulnerable to changes in US-Mexican relations and the trilateral trading agreement including Canada. Roughly 37.7% of all exports from Texas—the biggest percentage among all 50 states—go to Mexico. That percentage represents 5.8% of the state's gross domestic product, also the biggest among all the states.

NAFTA has had the greatest effect on Mexico, in large part because both the size and the strength of its economy are so much smaller than those of the United States and Canada. Some aspects have been clearly positive. NAFTA has diversified Mexico's economic base by increasing the percentage of its exports that are manufactured goods. The country's *maquiladora* program, dating back long before NAFTA, was set up to promote industrialization by giving special tax and other advantages to industries in a zone near the US border. After NAFTA went into effect, however, the *maquiladora* zone boomed, doubling its production and tripling its workers by 2000.

These apparent asymmetries negatively influencing the United States have been a recurrent aspect of the Trump administration's "America First" trade efforts. As of this writing, the three countries signed the **United States–Mexico–Canada Agreement** (USMCA) in 2018, but it has yet to be ratified and put into force. Regardless of the outcome, the high level of uncertainty that remains regarding this nascent agreement is making it difficult for American businesses to plan for the short to medium term. An official at the US Council for International Business implored the Trump administration for "an urgent meeting with you and your team before you head to Mexico for Round 2. . . . I cannot emphasize enough the degree of concern in the business community based on the press reports we have seen of major changes in US policy."[37] The reality, however, is that the new agreement mostly tinkers at the edges of the original NAFTA arrangements and is far from the breakthrough change promised by President Trump. Canada had to loosen dairy production restrictions to allow American farmers to compete; there must be more domestic auto parts in cars sold in member countries; and some intellectual property rules have been tightened.[38] All this said, at this writing, it is unclear what impact Trump's sanctions against Mexico that are linked to immigration will have on Congressional approval of the deal.

United States–Mexico–Canada Agreement The follow-on trade agreement to NAFTA signed in 2018, but not yet approved by the US Congress.

Cultivating Free Trade in Latin America and Asia

As we discussed regarding the WTO and the suspension of the Doha Round of trade talks, the future of the dominant liberal internationalist view of global trade seems to be at a crossroads with many of the populist elections in Europe and the United States. From Brexit to Trump's rejection of the Obama-era Trans-Pacific Partnership trade initiative, it is currently difficult to see a path of significant expanding regional and global trading organizations in the near future. Nonetheless, we highlight a number of significant agreements and prospects for the future in the remainder of this chapter.

Southern Common Market (aka Mercosur) A regional organization established in 1995 that emphasizes trade relations among countries in South America.

MERCOSUR. Whatever the future of free trade in the global economy or in the United States, a number of countries have undertaken or continued efforts to establish or expand their own trade treaties. The **Southern Common Market (aka Mercosur)** is of particular note. Mercosur was established in 1995 by Argentina, Brazil, Paraguay, and Uruguay. Venezuela later joined as a full member, and Bolivia, Chile, Colombia, Ecuador, and Peru have become associate members. A number of issues, including recurrent economic and political crises in the region and some countries' concerns about the powerful role played by Brazil, have slowed the negotiations to expand and strengthen Mercosur, but other factors push for its enlargement and invigoration.

Taking a step in that direction, the South American leaders agreed at summits in 2004 and again in 2007 to seek to merge Mercosur and the Andean Community (Bolivia, Colombia, Ecuador, and Peru) into a Union of South American Nations that would eventually emulate the EU, with its own currency, a continental parliament, and a common passport. Mercosur itself also continues to develop, and all the countries of the Andean Community of Nations are now either full or associate members—although Venezuela was suspended from membership in 2016. Additionally, Mercosur has allowed Mexico and New Zealand observer status. Mercosur also established a parliament that convened for the first time in 2007. In sum, Mercosur remains a work in progress.

ASIA AND THE PACIFIC.   In Asia, the first RTA was the Association of Southeast Asian Nations (ASEAN) established in 1967. It now includes Brunei, Cambodia, Indonesia, Laos, Malaysia, Myanmar (Burma), the Philippines, Singapore, Thailand, and Vietnam. The ASEAN countries have a combined population of over 600 million, a GNP of about $2.4 trillion, and total exports of about $2.3 trillion. Like the EU and some other RTAs, ASEAN is also expanding its responsibilities to include development, health, and other matters. ASEAN is working to forge greater political cooperation among its members and to bargain as a group with external countries and other trade organizations. Some observers view this RTA as a counterbalance to China in the region. Many ASEAN countries are responding to China's multibillion-dollar Belt and Road Initiative, which has been described as a 21st century Silk Road. This initiative funds massive investment in China is investing in massive construction across both land and sea as a means to dominate infrastructure and shipping "lanes" starting in Asia and moving westward.

The **Asia-Pacific Economic Cooperation (APEC)** was founded in 1989. Its website declares that it is the "only intergovernmental grouping in the world operating on the basis of nonbinding commitments . . . [with] no treaty obligations required of its participants . . . decisions made by consensus, and commitments . . . undertaken on a voluntary basis."[39] Despite its amorphous nature, APEC is important because among its 21 members are most of the countries of the greater Pacific Ocean region, including China, Japan, Russia, and the United States. Additionally, APEC members account for over 40% of the world population, about 50% of the global GDP, and over 40% of world trade. There is a small APEC secretariat based in Singapore, but it is symbolic of APEC's still-tentative status that it has not added a word such as "organization" or "community" to the end of its name.

Asia-Pacific Economic Cooperation A regional trade organization founded in 1989 that now includes 21 countries.

Can you pick out US Vice President Mike Pence in the photograph? One might argue that his placement close to the far left of the group speaks to how marginalized the United States has become in global forums in recent years.

Somewhat like the G-7, APEC facilitates numerous routine economic consultations among members. Its focus, however, is the annual APEC summit meeting, which serves as a forum for discussions among the United States, Japan, China, South Korea, and other leading members. Although APEC does not claim to be moving toward RTA status, there have been agreements in principle—for example, to achieve free and open trade and investment in the Asia-Pacific region. Beyond this goal, few specific agreements have resulted from these summits, but they are part of a process of dialogue that helps keep lines of communication open.

This region has also seen significant economic cooperation through the 2016 Trans-Pacific Partnership. Although this initiative was central to President Obama's strategic pivot to the Asia-Pacific region, President Trump withdrew the United States from the agreement in 2017. The remaining 11 states revised the treaty, which covers tariffs on goods and services, intellectual property rights, e-commerce rules, labor and environmental standards, dispute resolution mechanisms, and other aspects of global trade. This ambitious megaregional deal spans several continents and covers some 40 percent of world trade. For Obama, the pact was a means to ensure that "the United States—and not countries like China—is the one writing this century's rules for the world's economy."[40]

BILATERAL TRADE AGREEMENTS.   Countries have long concluded bilateral trade agreements (BTAs) with one another, but as with RTAs, recent years have seen a rapid expansion of BTAs between countries and between RTAs and individual countries. The WTO estimates that at least 270 (and probably many more) BTAs are currently in effect. The United States, for example, has concluded BTAs with over 20 individual countries, including Australia, Chile, Israel, Morocco, and South Korea, and with one RTA, the five-member Southern African Customs Union (Botswana, Lesotho, Namibia, South Africa, and Swaziland).

Among the US BTAs is the confusingly named Central American Free Trade Association—Dominican Republic (CAFTA-DR). In addition to the United States and the Dominican Republic, it includes Costa Rica, El Salvador, Guatemala, Honduras, and Nicaragua. Despite its RTA-like name, CAFTA-DR is actually a series of similar BTAs between the United States and the other countries, and between those countries with each other.

What has been the overall effect of RTAs and BTAs? They have the advantages of opening trade, investment, and other forms of economic interchange among countries. These are good insofar as they generally improve the economic circumstances of most people in all of the countries party to any FTA. Such agreements also can potentially create commonalities and ease tensions among nations and lead to greater regional cooperation on many fronts. The current EU serves as an example of what can evolve from a very limited RTA.

Yet there are also downsides to RTAs and BTAs. One is that their proliferation has created a patchwork of agreements that undermine global trade liberalization (Haftel, 2004; Kahler, 2018). This may harm, rather than advance, the Global South's economic development. According to one former director-general of the WTO, RTAs are an unsatisfactory substitute for global trade liberalization because "they are by their very nature discriminatory. None has really succeeded in opening markets in sensitive areas like agriculture. They add to the complexities of doing business by creating a multiplicity of rules. And the poorest countries tend to get left out in the cold."[41] This sentiment remains valid for many looking toward greater global liberalization.

Chapter Summary

- Economics and politics are closely intertwined aspects of global politics. This interrelationship has become even more important in recent history. Economics has become more important internationally because of dramatically increased trade levels, tightening economic interdependence between countries, and the growing impact of global economics on domestic economics. The study of the global political economy examines the interaction between politics and economics.

- There are many technical aspects to explaining and understanding the international political economy, and it is important to understand such concepts as GDP, GNP, as well as current and real dollars, among other concepts mentioned early in this chapter.

- The approaches to understanding the global political economy roughly comprise three groups: economic nationalism, internationalism, and world systems.

- Globalization and interdependence have increased at an exponential rate since the beginning of the second half of the 20th century, with a rapid rise in the level of economic interchange (trade, investments and other capital flows, and monetary exchange) in the international political economy.

- Numerous IGOs and international programs focus on economic cooperation, and many give the development of the Global South top priority, at least rhetorically.

- The IMF is the primary IGO dedicated to stabilizing the world's monetary system. The IMF's primary role in recent years has been to assist countries of the Global South by stabilizing their currencies and reducing their foreign debt. There is, however, considerable controversy over how the IMF is run and the conditions it attaches to its loans.

- The World Bank Group is the best known of the IGOs that provide developmental loans and grants to Global South. As with the IMF, there is controversy about the governance of the World Bank and its policies.

- Two other economic organizations associated with the Global North are the OECD and the G-7, although they also devote considerable attention to development in the Global South.

- In addition to promoting economic cooperation and development at the global level, important efforts are underway at the regional level. The most important of these is the expansion in the number and size of regional trade organizations.

- Receiving particular attention in the chapter are the EU; NAFTA and Mercosur in the Western Hemisphere; and ASEAN and APEC in the Asia-Pacific Region.

Critical Thinking Questions

1. Which theoretical perspective best characterizes how you think the global political economy really works?

2. What are the primary goals for creating, maintaining, and expanding the dominant global economic institutions? Have they been successful in achieving those goals? Why or why not?

3. Does global economic interaction yield increased welfare for all or only for a select few? Explain your thinking.

4. Will regional economic integration lead to political integration? Give some examples to support your answer, and think back to Chapter 6 on international organization as well.

Key Terms

Asia-Pacific Economic
  Cooperation
Brexit
capitalism
conditionality
dependency theory
Doha Round
economic nationalism
euro
European Commission
European Court of Justice
European Parliament
European Union
exchange rates

General Agreement on
  Tariffs and Trade
Global North
Global South
gross domestic product
gross national product
Group of Seven/Eight
  (G-7/8)
Group of 20 (G-20)
imperialism
International Monetary
  Fund
internationalism
manufactured goods

merchandise trade
monetary relations
North American Free
  Trade Agreement
Organization for
  Economic
  Cooperation and
  Development
primary goods
purchasing power parity
real dollars
regional trade
  agreement
services trade

Smoot-Hawley Tariff Act
Southern Common
  Market (aka Mercosur)
special drawing rights
tariffs
United States–
  Mexico–Canada
  Agreement
World Bank Group
world systems theory
World Trade
  Organization

11

Global Political Economy: Searching for Equity in the Global South

Many people on the Global North have preconceived notions of what conditions are like in the countries of the Global South. Most people in the North know relatively little about the economic and daily life challenges that face a large majority of the world's population. These misconceptions about the quality of life in the Global South often ignore the fact that the living conditions and prospects for personal economic viability in much of the Global South are very, very low. And this at least partly frames the immigration debate in ways that obscure why people wish to move to the Global North. Immigrating to the Global North is seen as a path to a better life. For the most part, people in the Global North do not seek immigration to other countries in the North because their economic prospects are on a par with, and in some cases even better than, those in other Northern countries. As a result, immigration is at its core a global political economy issue.

Global political economy focuses on the ways political forces interact with economic forces in the global economy. In this chapter, we first sample the overall economic conditions and

Economic disparities between the Global North and Global South remain a powerful rationale for migration to the North. These mostly Central American migrants wait in a holding pen in El Paso, Texas, in 2019 to gain entry to the United States.

trends in the Global South. We then focus on the dominance and dependence relationships that exist within the Global South and between the South and the North. We conclude with a broad discussion of the tools of economic policy and how they can serve national goals in the global political economy.

Learning Objectives

Discuss the economic circumstances that define the developing world.

Describe the relationships between the Global North and the Global South.

Explain the tools of economy policy.

Evaluate different visions of our global economic future.

The World Economy: Diverse Circumstances

Every country, whatever its domestic economic system, has citizens whose circumstances range from wealthy to poor. Similarly, the countries of the world range from wealthy to destitute. Traditionally, analysts have divided the world's countries into two spheres: the Global North, which consists of the generally prosperous and economically developed countries, and the Global South, which consists of the relatively—and in many cases unquestionably—poor developing countries. It is also noteworthy that most countries of the Global South were also colonial holdings of the European imperial powers. The poorest Southern countries are financially destitute (as is often measured by gross domestic product [GDP] per capita), and many of their people live on the equivalent of pennies per day.

The North and South designations are based on the fact that most developed countries lie to the north of the equator, in North America and Europe, and most underdeveloped countries lie near or south of the equator, in Africa, Asia, and South America. These geographic locations are not perfect, but they are widely accepted and reflective in general of global location.

Using a closely parallel categorization, Table 11.1 summarizes categories of world countries using four income levels (high, upper middle, lower middle, and low) established by the World Bank. The Global North and Global South categories are somewhat fluid and do not exactly match the dichotomy between the high-income countries and the low- and middle-income countries. Five oil-producing countries—Brunei, Kuwait, Qatar, Saudi Arabia, and the United Arab Emirates, which are usually classified as part of the South—fall into the high-income group. Two **newly industrializing countries** once considered part of

newly industrializing countries (NICs) Less developed countries whose economies and whose trade now include significant amounts of manufactured products. As a result, these countries have a per capita GDP significantly higher than the average per capita GDP for the Global South.

Table 11.1 Country Economic Classification

	INCOME RANGE PER CAPITA GDP	NUMBER OF COUNTRIES IN GROUP	% OF WORLD POPULATION	GDP PER CAPITA (CURRENT US DOLLARS)
High Income	>$12,055	81	17%	$41,214.30
Upper Middle Income	$3,896 to $12,055	56	35%	$8,610.70
Lower Middle Income	$996 to $3,895	47	38%	$2,192.30
Low Income	<$996	34	10%	$785.60

Source: http://datatopics.worldbank.org/world-development-indicators/stories/the-classification-of-countries-by-income.html; https://data.worldbank.org/indicator/NY.GDP.PCAP.CD?name_desc=false.

the Global South—Singapore and South Korea—have joined the high-income group. A few high-income countries, however, like Israel, Malta, and Cyprus (with a well-off Greek Cypriot majority and a much poorer Turkish Cypriot minority) cannot be easily categorized as either North or South.

Also noteworthy is the status of the **former Soviet republics (FSRs)**, particularly Russia and the former communist countries of Eastern Europe. Some of these countries have a reasonably strong industrial base, but only one—Slovenia—falls into the high-income group. Russia and most of the other European FSRs are middle-income countries (either upper or lower), and Tajikistan and most of the other Asian FSRs are low-income countries. One relatively new term in this topical discussion is **BRIC**, which stands for Brazil, Russia, India, and China, all of which exhibit increasingly strong economic sectors but the characteristics of many developing countries as well, as we will discuss later.

former Soviet republics (FSRs) These are 15 independent states that seceded from the Union of Soviet Socialist Republics in its dissolution in December 1991. They include Armenia, Azerbaijan, Belarus, Estonia, Georgia, Kazakhstan, Kyrgyzstan, Latvia, Lithuania, Moldova, Russia, Tajikistan, Turkmenistan, Ukraine, and Uzbekistan.

North-South Patterns

Despite some imprecision, we use the North-South dichotomy throughout this book because it captures the reality of the great divide that exists in the global pattern of economic and social circumstances. In addition to their economic circumstances, most countries of the Global South share a history of colonialism or neocolonial domination by one or another Northern country, often within living memory. In fact, most sovereign countries did not exist in the Global South immediately after World War II, gaining their independence largely through struggles in the 1950s and 1960s. According to world systems analysts (and even many liberal internationalists), this dependence relationship continues to a large

Bulgaria may have gained entry into the European Union, but enormous wealth disparities remain within its borders. These ethnic Pomaks struggle to earn a living in a region known for charcoal production, which is tied to respiratory and other health problems.

BRIC   This term indicates the group of countries including Brazil, Russia, India, and China that all exhibit a somewhat higher level of development than many in the Global South, but also continue to face large development-related challenges.

The BRIC Countries

degree today and shapes global interactions transnationally. Thus, it is useful to keep the concept of neocolonialism in mind, as it provides one lens into the circumstances that continue to challenge the countries of the Global South.

NORTH-SOUTH ECONOMIC PATTERNS.   *Significantly poorer* is an apt phrase to begin any analysis of the economies of the Global South compared to those of the Global North. The most common measure of any country's, or group of countries', economic prosperity is per capita gross domestic product or GDP. By this measure, as Figure 11.1 illustrates, a huge wealth gap exists between the high-income countries and the middle- and low-income countries. Further, although the wealth gap has narrowed a bit in recent decades, the improvement is so slight that it would take centuries at the current rate to approach anywhere near equal prosperity for all countries.

There are many reasons why the Global South fares so poorly compared to the Global North. One reason is that the South takes in considerably less capital through exports and inflows of investment money, both of which are major sources of income for the North. Thus, trade differences leave the North advantaged. Overall, the upper-income countries of the Global North, which account for 16% of the world population, exported almost 70% of all goods and services in 2016.[1] Thus, about 30% of all exports come from the vast majority of countries and people that comprise the South. Moreover, China, which indeed holds a unique place in the Global South, accounted for 46% of all exports from upper-middle-income countries, showing its growing dominance as a world economic player.

The products that a country exports also make a difference. A diverse range of services (e.g., telecommunications or air transport) and manufactured goods accounts for more than 90% of Global North exports. By contrast, over the past decade, services and manufactured goods have comprised about 70% of exports from high- and upper-middle-income countries and around 50% of exports for low-income countries. Southern countries rely more than Northern countries on the export of primary products, such as food, fibers, fuels, and minerals. This disadvantages the South because primary product prices are less stable even over short time frames and also generally have not risen as fast as the price of manufactured goods.

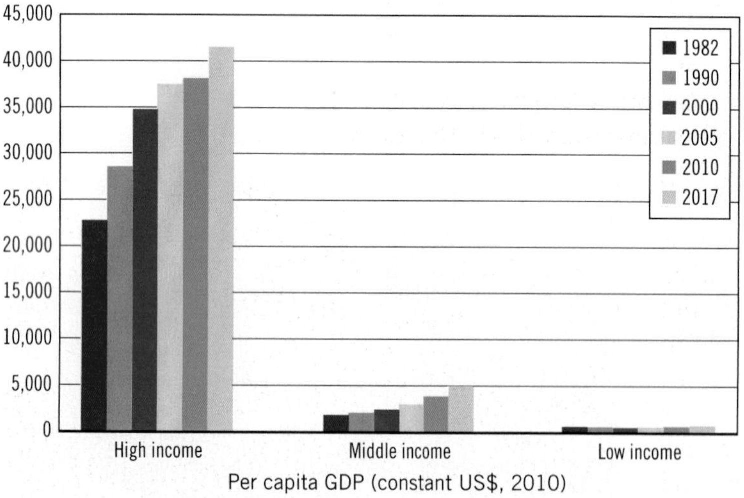

Similarly, investment differences also favor the Global North, although China's rise as a global economic power may be changing that fact. First, the North is the recipient of large flows

Per capita GDP (constant US$, 2010)

Legend: 1982, 1990, 2000, 2005, 2010, 2017

Figure 11.1   This figure shows the per capita GDPs between 1982 and 2017 of the high-, middle-, and low-income countries calculated in constant dollars. Note the huge gap between the high-income countries and the middle- and low-income countries. Also notice that while the per capita income of all three groups has increased, the income gap has remained relatively stable and significant. (Source: Data from World Bank, Development Indicators. 2016–2017.)

Table 11.2 World's 10 Largest Corporations

RANK	COMPANY	HOME COUNTRY	INDUSTRY	REVENUE IN US DOLLARS
1	Walmart	United States	Retail	$486 billion
2	State Grid	China	Power	$315 billion
3	Sinopec Group	China	Petroleum	$268 billion
4	China National Petroleum	China	Petroleum	$263 billion
5	Toyota Motor	Japan	Automobiles	$255 billion
6	Volkswagen	Germany	Automobiles	$240 billion
7	Royal Dutch Shell	Netherlands	Petroleum	$240 billion
8	Berkshire Hathaway	United States	Diversified products	$242 billion
9	Apple	United States	Technology	$216 billion
10	ExxonMobil	United States	Petroleum	$205 billion

Source: Fortune Global 500, 2017, http://fortune.com/global500/.

of investment capital. Of the 500 largest multinational corporations (MNCs), about 90% are based in the North, with US firms making up about a third of the Fortune Global 500. Moreover, of the 10 largest companies in the world, as shown in Table 11.2, the global number-one is Walmart, but numbers two through four are Chinese-based, emblematic of China's rise. Still, US companies occupy nine of the positions in the global top 20. As these data suggest, the flow of profits from the world's largest MNCs mostly generate benefits to the North, even if China may change this.

Second, about two-thirds of all global investment flows from one Northern country to another, not to the South where the need is greatest. Economically, this means that Northern economies are helping each other much more than they are helping the South develop. This may not be surprising, but it doesn't bode well for Southern development trajectories.

Third, China, newly industrialized countries, and a few privileged others receive most of the investment capital, whereas most countries in the Global South receive little or none. Any tourist visiting China in the past few years can testify to the pervasiveness of Western culture and investment in all of the major cities, from Hong Kong to Shanghai to Beijing. This corporate growth and concentration of wealth has also accelerated in recent years. As one analysis put it, "If it seems like big business is getting bigger, it is. Over the last two decades, the largest US companies have grown faster than the economy as a whole. And it's the biggest of big businesses that are making up a larger and larger share of the growth."[2] As you might suspect, this trend in the largest corporations isn't positive for development concerns in the Global South.

Starbucks and other symbols of American global dominance are ubiquitous around the world, as shown by this franchise in Shanghai, China.

NORTH-SOUTH SOCIETAL PATTERNS.   Economic data can seem dry until you realize the social implications of differences in per capita GDP and similar statistics. Consider what it means for their comparative quality of life: On a per capita basis, the people who live in the Global North produce more than $60 for every $1 produced by people who live in the poorest parts of the Global South. In these countries, about 1 billion people live in extreme poverty, which the World Bank defines as less than $1 a day. Almost half of the world's population lives on less the $2.50 per day.[3] In societal terms, these numbers translate into poor health care, limited education, lack of safe drinking water, inadequate nutrition, and other grim realities of daily life. For example, about a quarter of the world's population is illiterate; in contrast, less than 1% of adults living in the Global North are.

Medical facilities in the South are overwhelmed. There are about 0.3 doctors per 1,000 people in the poorest countries, with 10 times as many physicians (3 per 1,000) in the North.[4] These data mean that hundreds of millions of people in the South have no access to any kind of health care. These conditions lead to disease, malnutrition, and death on a large scale. A child born in one of the poorest countries is 17 times more likely to die before age 5 than a child born in the Global North. Having children is also risky, with the maternal mortality rate in the poorest countries being 37 times greater than the rate in the Global North.[5] And overall, the average person in the poorest areas of the Global South dies almost 20 years earlier than a person living in the Global North.[6]

Evaluating the North-South Gap

Although annual data about economic and societal factors are important in evaluating the indisputable economic and well-being gaps between North and South, such statistics do not tell the whole story. Trends are at least of equal importance. As to the trends, however, data are mixed and somewhat subject to interpretation. There is also a highly uneven pattern of development both regionally and across time.

MIXED DATA ON DEVELOPMENT. Statistics measuring development progress throughout the Global South do not tell a consistent story. This fact is further complicated by the reality that "objective" numbers are often open to interpretation and variance in reporting, and that they also do not necessarily reflect the nuances of authority and power in the global system (Rocha de Siqueira, 2017). Analyses of conditions in the Global South tend to be gloomy, but these countries are

This classroom in Tanzania makes the crowding in Global North classrooms pale in comparison. By the educational standards of the Global North, it is hard to imagine the quality of learning that emerges from this and classrooms like it throughout the Global South.

indeed making significant advances. Table 11.3 shows that by many health, education, and economic measures, overall circumstances throughout the Global South are improving. A greater percentage of the population in the South has access to safe water and adequate sanitation facilities. There has been a marked decrease in child mortality and a substantial increase in overall longevity. Literacy has also improved. As a whole, the countries of the Global South now account for a greater share of the world's collective GNP, its trade, and its inflow of investment capital. These are not the only signs of progress. For example, although a distressing 19% of the population still lives in extreme poverty in the Global South, this is a distinct improvement over the 28% who lived in that condition in 1990.

Although such statistics are a cause for some optimism, unfortunately they are not an indication that conditions are good, or that the Global South no longer requires substantial help both financially and technologically. The stark contrast between conditions in the South and North endures. For example, it is positive that the child mortality rate in the Global South has plummeted,

Table 11.3 Development Indicators for Global South Countries

TYPE	INCOME LEVEL	INDICATOR NAME	1960	1980	1990	2000	2010	2017 (EXCEPT WHERE NOTED)
Economic	Middle income	Exports (% of world)		20.0%	16.6%	19.9%	30.6%	25%
	Low income			0.7%	0.5%	0.4%	0.5%	N/A_
	Middle income	FDI net inflows (% of world)		14.5%	10.3%	10.4%	35.0%	28%
	Low income			0.8%	0.3%	0.2%	0.9%	.1%_
	Middle income	GDP (% of world)	24.0%	21.5%	16.2%	17.7%	31.1%	35%
	Low income		1.7%	1.0%	0.7%	0.5%	0.7%	.6%
Health	Middle income	Improved sanitation facilities (% of population with access)			39%	50%	59%	66% (2015)
	Low income				21%	31%	37%	29% (2015)
	Middle income	Improved water source (% of population with access)			73%	82%	90%	90% (2015)
	Low income				54%	58%	65%	56% (2015)
	Middle income	Life expectancy at birth, total (years)	48	61	64	67	69	71 (2016)
	Low income		42	50	53	55	59	63 (2015)
	Middle income	Mortality rate, under 5 (per 1,000 live births)		110	85	68	51	36
	Low income			200	165	137	108	69
Education	Middle income	Literacy rate, adult total			72	80	83*	86 (2016)
	Low income				51	57	61*	61 (2016)
Population	Middle income	% of world	68%	71%	72%	72%	72%	73%
	Low income		8%	9%	10%	11%	12%	10%

*Note: 2009 data.
DataSource: World Bank, World Development Indicators.
Source: Data from World Bank, World Development Indicators.

but even in the middle-income countries, it remains six times the rate in the high-income countries. Further, the progress is often quite slow.

Also, statistics can sometimes tell almost contradictory stories. Extreme poverty provides an illustration. The percentage of people in the Global South who live in extreme poverty has indeed decreased. But because populations continue to rise rapidly, especially in the poorest parts of the Global South, there are still more than 1 billion people in these countries trying to survive on the equivalent of less than $1 a day. This poses a significant and long-term challenge not only to the economic and political stability throughout the Global South but also, by extension, to the Global North (Acemoglu & Robinson, 2013; Collier, 2008).

UNEVEN PATTERNS OF DEVELOPMENT.   Uneven patterns of development also temper the optimism about economic growth within the Global South and any potential improvements in their socioeconomic conditions. Disparity between countries is one anomaly in the overall picture of economic growth in the South. As noted previously, the middle-income countries have advanced more quickly than the low-income countries. There are also regional differences. Some regions, such as East Asia, have made major economic strides, but at the other end of the regional spectrum, sub-Saharan Africa has struggled and in some cases even lost ground economically. Its per capita GNP is less than half that of the average in the Global South. The region's merchandise exports are only 24% manufactured goods and services, compared to 64% for the Global South overall.

Although the level of investment flowing into the region is comparable to that in the rest of the Global South when measured in terms of the percentage of GDP, it is dwarfed in volume when we note the disparity in GDP between sub-Saharan Africa and the Global South more generally. Hence, the region that arguably needs investment more intensively gets much less than it really needs to make progress. Life expectancy in the region has actually slowly increased over the past 50 years, but people living in sub-Saharan Africa still lag far behind the rest of the Global South nutritionally. Thus, the overall data about socioeconomic conditions in the Global South do not always reflect the wide range of circumstances within this large and diverse category of countries.

Disparity within countries is another characteristic of socioeconomic development in the Global South that can make both aggregate and average data deceiving. All countries, including those in the Global North, have disparities in income and other measures of wealth across their population, but unequal distribution is particularly strong in much of the Global South. More than in the Global North, the countries of the Global South tend to have a quite small, very wealthy upper class and an enormous, very poor lower class. Figure 11.2 shows the percentage of

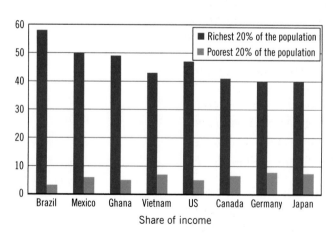

Figure 11.2   Great attention has been given to the wealthiest 1% in the United States during recent years. This figure shows that the US distribution of wealth is more similar to countries like Ghana and Mexico than it is to other industrialized countries like Japan and Germany. (Source: Data from World Bank, Development Indicators, 2016–2017.)

income possessed by the wealthiest and poorest 20% of each population in countries from the Global South and the Global North.

Negative by-products of development have also partially offset some of the South's advances. Explosive population growth has occurred as a result of medical and other advances, which have decreased infant mortality and increased longevity. The population of sub-Saharan Africa, for instance, rose from 210 million in 1960 to 1.061 billion in 2017—an increase of 405%. And even though statisticians predicted that the region would reach almost 900 million people by 2015, the billion level was reached that year.[7] Obviously, the growth in those numbers is staggering and creates even further stress on the fragile socioeconomic systems in the Global South.

Rapid urbanization has also beset the South, as the hope of finding jobs and better health, sanitation, and other social services has set off a mass migration from rural areas to cities. Between 1965 and 2008, the share of the South's population living in urban areas doubled, from 22% to 44%, and statisticians project it to reach more than 50% by 2020. There are now approximately 175 cities in the Global South with populations over 1 million, and of the world's 20 most populous cities, all but three (Tokyo, New York, and London) are in the Global South.

This rapid urbanization has created a host of problems. One is the weakening of the social order. This is destroying older tribal, village, and extended-family loyalties, with newer offsetting values and other social support systems yet to emerge. Another problem is that the hope of employment is often unfulfilled, and unemployment and poverty in many cities are staggering and often the roots of unrest. Finally, struggling governments in the Global South are often unable to meet the sanitary, housing, and other needs of the flood of people moving to or being born in the cities. About a quarter of the South's urban population is living in conditions below minimum health standards. In Nigeria, for example, less than half the urban households are connected to a sewer. Only about half the urban population in Haiti have access to safe drinking water, and more than half of Bangladesh's urban population live in dwellings without a "durable structure"—that is, they live in makeshift shacks.

Industrial and environmental dangers have also been undesirable by-products of development. Chapter 13 details the impact of development on the environment, but a brief note of the dangers is appropriate here. One problem is rapid deforestation due to demands for wood, expanding farm and ranch acreage, and general urban growth. Loss of these forests increases soil erosion and has numerous other deleterious effects. Industrial development in the Global South also adds to air, water, and soil pollution, and most major cities in the Global South are now far more polluted than are major cities in the Global North.

As a case in point, during the 2008 Beijing Summer Olympics, air pollution became a serious concern for athletic performance and health (for both athletes and attendees). The Chinese government took drastic measures to control the pollution—and the growing public relations problem—by shutting down many manufacturing sites, banning the use of nearly 300,000 high-polluting vehicles during the games, and halting major construction projects. The results were mixed, but the Chinese were able to reduce the air quality index rating to 88, below the 101 level deemed unsafe by Chinese authorities. However, the "safe" limit set by World Health Organization standards is 50.[8] China is not alone in this regard, as other rapidly industrializing countries like India, Thailand, and others have similar pollution challenges.

🌍 Dependency in the Global Economy

official development assistance (ODA) Often referred to as foreign aid, ODA refers to concessional financial flows from the Global North to the Global South. It can take the form of grants or loans with interest rates below normal market rates (thus, it is considered concessional and not commercially driven).

An important change in governance practices since the end of the 1800s has been the expansion of governmental regulation of national economies. Even countries like the United States that see themselves as bastions of capitalism and individual liberty have many laws that constrain private economic interaction and seek to prevent some of the undesirable aspects of capitalism. For instance, laws about labor practices (e.g., abolishing child labor and creating a 40-hour workweek) are outgrowths of the national regulation of economic affairs. Further, most countries have accepted that they must balance the economic interests of individual citizens to some degree with the collective welfare of the national society.

In contrast to domestic economic systems, however, the global political economy is still a largely unregulated arena. Countries pursue their national economic interest in competition with other countries, and shared responsibility for the welfare of the global society is held to be less valuable. Two factors, however, have increasingly constrained the maneuvering for economic advantage among states.

First, globalization—and its often-attendant economic theory, liberal internationalism—has generally made countries much less likely to use tariffs and other forms of barriers to manipulate the free exchange of trade, investment capital, and currencies. Clearly, President Trump fails to comprehend the economic logic of this approach, as we discussed in Chapter 10 and will mention again later. Second, in the past half-century, a greater awareness that the Global North *should* help the Global South has emerged, partly because of a sense of postcolonial obligation and partly because of a growing sense of shared economic fate. The South often bristles, however, at the paternalism of that normative global view.

A manifestation of this sentiment is development assistance, commonly referred to as foreign aid. This development funding mechanism did not exist before World War II. In 2017, however, $146 billion in aid— more formally called **official development assistance**—flowed from North to South, representing a slow but steady increase from recent years.[9] Thus, the dog-eat-dog image of the global political economy is not quite as stark as it once was, especially during the colonial era that largely ended (at least in explicit forms) shortly following World War II.

As children in the Global North, most of us complained about our chores at home. But very few of us reading this book ever had to carry bricks on our heads as part of our assigned chores, like these Burmese children are doing.

Nevertheless, competition and self-reliance, not cooperation and mutual assistance, remain the prevailing realities of the global political economy. This struggle for advantage and prosperity exists both between and within the North and South, and it perpetuates the sense of dependence of the South on the North.

North-South Economic Relations

In this dependency context, one can identify several ways that economic relations between the North and South remain strained:

Resentment in the Global South over its past and present treatment by the Global North. Most of the countries of the South were once colonies of, or were otherwise dominated and exploited economically by, one or another country in the North. Moreover, remnants of the exploitive relationship continue to exist. During the colonial period, the dominant country typically imported fuels, agricultural produce, mineral ore, and other raw materials from the colony and exported manufactured goods to it. Although formal colonialism has almost entirely disappeared, the same flow of goods continues to a degree. Rooted in colonialism, the trading relationship remains asymmetric, with greater value added in production continuing to favor the Europeans and others in the North. For instance, according to the European Union (EU), Europeans receive mostly raw or transformed goods from Africa, such as fuels, agricultural products, and textiles. And although there is indeed some reciprocal trade, Africa receives large quantities of more refined products, like machinery, chemicals, and pharmaceuticals.[10] This ongoing asymmetry in trading relationships is often referred to as neocolonialism, and it suggests to many critics that even though the formal political control of colonialism is gone, the informal, structural relationships remain, as world systems analysts argue.

Continued assertiveness by countries in the Global South that they have a right to a much greater share in the world's economic wealth (especially given the colonial legacy). This argument underlies, for instance, the rationale for development assistance and the target of 0.7% of GDP from Northern countries, as recommended in the Millennium Development Goals (MDGs). Unfortunately, for the South, very few Northern countries approach this level of aid-giving, with the average at just over 0.3% in 2016 and the US share at a meager 0.18% of GDP.[11] To put this in comparative budgeting perspective, the United States spent about 3% (not "point" 3%) of GDP on the military in the same year. Comparisons like this are often identified as representing a lack of priority placed on alleviating global poverty by the Global North.

The Global North's general and recurrent rejection of the Global South's demands for unilateral and compensatory economic reforms by the North. Instead, the North is apt to demand reciprocal concessions from the South. The South most often rejects such reciprocity on the grounds that the Southern plight is largely the North's fault and, furthermore, that it is unfair to ask relatively poor countries of the South to swap concessions with the richer countries of the North. As Chapter 13 discusses, the North's efforts to control greenhouse gases, all the while asking the South to help cope with a problem that was caused by the industrializing Northern countries, is a case in point.

An increase in the number of countries in the Global South that are major exporters of manufactured goods and, to a lesser degree, services. Such efforts directly compete with the North's products and services; thus, they challenge the North's dominance in those economic areas. This is especially true of the newly industrializing countries and their unique position in the world economy between developed and underdeveloped. The rankings of global corporations listed in Table 11.2 showing the rise of Chinese firms into the top 10 hint at the reality of this type of global challenge for the North. These and other factors shape North-South relations and perpetuate the mixture of cooperation and competition among the developed and developing worlds.

The United Nations and Global Political Economy

The United Nations (UN) is one of the primary forums for the Global South to bring their most important issues to the global agenda. Among its many functions, the UN serves as a global umbrella organization for numerous agencies and programs that deal with economic issues. The UN's economic duties focus roughly on two broad, though imperfect, categories: global economic regulation and the economic development for the South.

THE UN AND GLOBAL ECONOMIC REGULATION.   The UN is involved in a number of areas related to global economic cooperation, such as the regulation of transnational or multinational corporations. Many observers argue that IGOs must regulate MNCs because globalization has allowed businesses to escape a great deal of domestic regulation. By the mid-1990s, there were increasing calls for greater global regulation of commerce, especially when MNCs were operating in the Global South. These calls sometimes took the form of anti-globalization protests in cities around the world, like the ones that turned violent in Seattle in 1999 coinciding with the timing of World Trade Organization meetings held there.

In response to such concerns, the UN established the Center for Transnational Corporations as part of the effort to create global standards and regulations to constrain capitalist corporations' inherently self-serving practices. And in 2000, the **UN Global Compact** was launched, articulating 10 principles to guide corporate behavior globally. The *Personal Narrative* feature discusses the Global Compact in detail, and Chapter 12 covers issues of corporate social responsibility as they pertain to human rights.

UN Global Compact A UN initiative launched in 2000 to guide corporate behavior globally in ethical and sustainable ways.

Millennium Summit
A meeting among many world leaders at the UN headquarters in New York City in 2000 to discuss the role of the UN at the turn of the 21st century. World leaders ratified the United Nations Millennium Declaration.

THE UN AND ECONOMIC DEVELOPMENT.   A second major focus of UN economic activity has been development of the Global South. One role that the UN has played since 1981 is sponsorship of North-South economic summit conferences that have helped increase international awareness among Northern policy-makers about the need for development. This has elicited expressions of concern and even brought some financial support. For example, in 2000 the UN's **Millennium Summit** brought together 150 national leaders who established eight development goals to achieve by 2015 in such areas as reducing extreme poverty, increasing education, and improving health. Those goals

Kofi Annan and the UN Global Compact

August 18, 2018, marked the passing of Kofi Annan, the seventh Secretary-General of the United Nations and the first black African to serve in that role. A recipient of the Nobel Peace Prize in 2001, Annan served as Secretary-General for 10 years, starting in 1997, and was widely "credited with revitalizing the United Nations' institutions, shaping what he called a new 'norm of humanitarian intervention.'"[12] A native of the West African country of Ghana, the first country to win independence from the British after World War II, Annan worked to push the UN's global role beyond that of his predecessors. As he stated, "[A]t the end of the 20th century, one thing is clear: A United Nations that will not stand up for human rights is a United Nations that cannot stand up for itself."[13]

Although his time in office was not without controversy, particularly as the UN was accused of being too slow to respond to African genocide, he is widely viewed as a path-breaking global leader. From UN institutional reform to the development of the Millennium Development Goals (MDGs), his leadership reflected an activist period.

Perhaps his most significant accomplishment was the creation of the UN Global Compact in 2000. First proposing this in a speech to the World Economic Forum in 1999, Annan anticipated that the "goals of the United Nations and those of business can, indeed, be mutually supportive [through] a global compact of shared values and principles, which will give a human face to the global market."[14]

The UN Global Compact is built on 10 principles. By focus area, they are:

Human Rights

- *Principle 1:* Businesses should support and respect the protection of internationally proclaimed human rights; and
- *Principle 2:* Make sure that [businesses] are not complicit in human rights abuses.

Labor

- *Principle 3:* Businesses should uphold the freedom of association and the effective recognition of the right to collective bargaining;

Former UN Secretary General Kofi Annan, a native of Ghana, remains one of the most prominent global leaders to rise to influence from Africa. His passing in 2018 was seen as a great loss for collaborative approaches to solving global problems.

continued

- *Principle 4:* The elimination of all forms of forced and compulsory labor;
- *Principle 5:* The effective abolition of child labor; and
- *Principle 6:* The elimination of discrimination in respect of employment and occupation.

Environment

- *Principle 7:* Businesses should support a precautionary approach to environmental challenges;
- *Principle 8:* Undertake initiatives to promote greater environmental responsibility; and
- *Principle 9:* Encourage the development and diffusion of environmentally friendly technologies.

Anti-Corruption

- *Principle 10:* Businesses should work against corruption in all its forms, including extortion and bribery.

The business practices of MNCs have long been a significant focus of attention in global policy and academic research, especially where they have run counter to the interests of parent countries in the Global North (see Chapter 10). Initiatives like the UN Global Compact, however, aim to refocus attention on the sometimes predatory practices of MNCs in the Global South. These practices have spurred the development of ethical business norms, such as those discussed further in Chapter 12. Annan and those around him endeavored to press MNCs for more socially responsible policies and

practices. From college campuses to retail consumer outlets, corporate social responsibility has become a real force for personal purchasing preferences and a marketing tool for those companies wishing to tout their achievements in ethical production. Even *Fortune* magazine, a bastion of corporate promotion, has developed its "Change the World" list of companies focused on social responsibility.[15] Although this may seem like a largely semantic, public relations effort to promote the best of a "questionable" group of global actors, the mere fact that *Fortune* has created such a list of companies (including well-known brands like Hilton, Kroger, and Merck) shows that many people are keeping track of social progress in the commercial sector.

Whether Kofi Annan was the primary force behind the development of corporate social responsibility or not, his roots in the Global South and use of his office to promote such concerns were integral to moving the efforts beyond conversation and to ward action. In a memorial to his passing in August 2018, Lise Kingo, Chief Executive Officer and Executive Director of the UN Global Compact, summed up Annan's influence: "As a result of Mr. Annan's vision, the UN Global Compact is attracting new participants on a daily basis and providing corporate executives around the world with the inspiration and tools needed to drive a more sustainable and responsible business culture which can create prosperity while respecting people and the planet."[16]

Millennium Development Goals (MDGs) In 2000, 189 nations made and committed to eight global goals aimed at poverty reduction, education, public health, and human rights. This pledge encompasses eight specific goals to achieve by 2015.

were not met by the target date, but setting standards for measuring progress was an important step. How theory might inform analysis of the **Millennium Development Goals** (MDGs) is the focus of the Thinking Theoretically feature.

Although UN members didn't meet the MDG goals by 2015, member-states launched the **Sustainable Development Goals** (SDGs) that year as a follow-up with even more ambitious targets. Focusing attention on people, planet, prosperity, peace, and partnership, the 17 SDGs "seek to realize the human rights of all and to achieve gender equality and the empowerment of all women and girls. They are integrated and indivisible and balance the three dimensions of sustainable development: the economic, social and environmental."[17] Member-states set a new target of 2030 for the realization of progress toward the 17 goals and their 169 measurable targets on sustainable development.

Whether this new agenda will be more successful than the MDGs is a question that only time can answer. But adoption of the SDGs is one signal that

Three Views of the Millennium Development Goals

"We can end poverty by 2015" says the UN website dedicated to the Millennium Development Goals (http://www.un.org/millenniumgoals/). In September 2000, at the UN's Millennium Summit, world leaders from over 150 countries pledged to eliminate extreme poverty by 2015. The eight specific goals were:

1. Eradicate extreme poverty and hunger.
2. Achieve universal primary education.
3. Promote gender equality and empower women.
4. Reduce child mortality.
5. Improve maternal health.
6. Combat HIV/AIDS, malaria, and other diseases.
7. Ensure environmental sustainability.
8. Develop a global partnership for development.

These were indeed noble goals for the leaders of the global community to espouse. But given the level of tension that exists between the North and the South, why would the developed countries endorse such an aggressive agenda for development in the South? We can glean some answers to this question by considering our theoretical perspectives.

For internationalists, signing on to the MDGs is based on the assumption that everyone wins from improving the lives of the world's poor. As economic prosperity takes hold in the developing world, opportunities to sell Northern goods in Southern consumer markets will increase. It can also create greater availability of cheaper imports for Northern markets from Southern production facilities. Thus, in the long run, the North also helps itself by helping the global poor.

For economic nationalists, the MDGs represent an opportunity. Assuming that Northern governments have the funds to spend on development assistance and Northern corporations have the capital to invest in developing economies, economic nationalists see opportunities for the taking. As economies move up the development ladder, they will need capital, finished products for industrial processes, and the expertise that exists only in the North—and the Global South will have to pay for those things, now or later. Either way, the Northern countries will gain from Southern economic development. Certainly, the tendency of Northern countries to provide much of their assistance in the form of government loans or private investment at market rates of interest is indicative of this perspective. Although a subtle difference, internationalists are more likely to advocate for concessionary rates for financial flows to the South.

World systems analysts take a more cynical and less economically focused view of why the North would endorse the MDGs. For these analysts, the North's primary goal is to continue the subjugation of the South. Even though colonialism is mostly over, why not pursue it in a different structural way, as we discussed regarding neocolonialism? Thus, the North endorsed the MDGs as a way to placate the South, at least for the time being. In fact, the repeated failure of the North to meet the relatively meager 0.7% of GDP development assistance pledge is evidence that the North is not really serious about the needs of the South.

As you contemplate these three different interpretations of the North's motives for signing on to the MDGs, what evidence would you cite to support your own view? Would analysis of the most recent wave of UN development goals, the Sustainable Development Goals, be different for each of the three theoretical perspectives?

---

development issues have made a turn toward including concepts of resilience and sustainability as fundamentals in the developmental policy project (Reid, 2013). Clearly, however, these goals cannot be achieved without explicit and concentrated cooperation across the Global North and Global South. And what role US leadership will play in the coming years will also be a crucial variable in the SDGs' prospects for success.

Sustainable Development Goals (SDGs) Adopted by the UN in 2015 as a roadmap for peace and prosperity for humanity and the global ecosystem now and into the future.

Focusing more specifically on economic development and illustrative of the South's ongoing frustration with the North on development issues, UN Secretary-General Kofi Annan in 2002 called on the Global North to increase annual economic foreign aid from the current 0.3% of GDP to the long-pledged target of 0.7%. Meeting that standard by 2011 (Annan's target date) would have required an increase in aid that year from $133 billion to $309 billion. Some leaders supported that goal, but President George W. Bush and most other Northern leaders were more cautious. Still, the pressure to respond to the South's needs had an effect, with Bush, for example, pledging late in his presidency to ask Congress to increase US economic aid by 50% within three years.

Such an increase never came to pass. Congressional appropriations fell short of that mark, but US international assistance did increase by about 30%. This was still far below the 0.7% target, however, which continues to be unmet by most countries in the Global North and remains a point of tension between the North and South, especially relative to other expenditures that dwarf aid as a budget item. Moreover, analyses of the "payoffs" from aid for both donors and recipients remain unclear. Thus, the value of aid is an ongoing question (see Bueno de Mesquita and Smith, 2016; Dreher et al., 2018; Hook & Rumsey, 2016).

The UN also has numerous development programs. For example, established in 1965, the **UN Development Programme (UNDP)** provides technical assistance (e.g., urban and regional planning) and development funds to **least developed countries (LDCs)** and is the focal point in the UN for implementation of the SDGs. It spends about $5 billion annually, has offices in most countries of the Global South, and focuses on grassroots economic development, such as promoting entrepreneurship, supporting the Development Fund for Women, and transferring technology and management skills from the North to the South. There remains continued dominance by the North, however, in an organization focused on providing resources and organizational capacity in the South.

Table 11.4 shows the membership of the UNDP Executive Board. Of the 36 countries with representation on the board, one-third are Northern. One argument for this proportion is that the countries funding development should have a significant voice in how those monies get used and what programs are created. But the 12 countries holding the largest regional share have great power among a diverse and impoverished group. Moreover, several others with representation on the board (China, South Korea, Saudi Arabia, Russia, and Brazil) do not exhibit the same development challenges faced by countries like Burkina Faso, Chad, and Laos. Although the UNDP does indeed do good work in the South, this dichotomy points out the continuing structures that maintain the North's power and influence in world affairs.

Another important UN organization, the **UN Conference on Trade and Development (UNCTAD)**, was founded in 1964 to promote the positive integration of the Global South into the world economy. Virtually all countries of the UN are members of UNCTAD, although the organization primarily gives voice to the South. The most recent UNCTAD quadrennial conference, held in

---

UN Development Programme (UNDP) An agency of the UN established in 1965 to provide technical assistance to stimulate economic and social development in the Global South. The UNDP has 48 members selected on a rotating basis from the world's regions.

least developed countries (LDCs) Those countries in the poorest of economic circumstances. In this book, this includes those countries with a per capita GNP of less that $400 in 1985 dollars.

UN Conference on Trade and Development (UNCTAD) A UN organization established in 1964 and currently consisting of all UN members plus the Holy See, Switzerland, and Tonga that holds quadrennial meetings aimed at promoting international trade and economic development.

Table 11.4 Country Membership of the UNDP Executive Board

REGIONAL GROUPS	2019
African states (8 members)	Botswana (2021)***
	Burkina Faso (2020)
	Cameroon (2021)*
	Egypt (2020)
	Gambia (2021)***
	Mauritius (2019)
	Rwanda (2021)***
	South Africa (2021)***
Asia-Pacific states (7 members)	Cambodia (2020)
	China (2019)
	India (2021)***
	Irán, Islamic Republic of (2019)
	Republic of Korea (2021)*
	Saudi Arabia (2020)
	Vanuatu (2021)***
Eastern European states (4 members)	Albania (2019)
	Republic of Moldova (2019)
	Russian Federatlon (2020)
	Ukraine (2021)***
Latín America and Caribbean states (5 members)	Antigua and Barbuda (2020)
	Brazil (2020)
	Cuba (2019)
	Mexico (2021)***
	Panama (2019)
Western European and other states (12 members)**	Australia
	Belgium
	Canada
	Ireland
	Italy
	Monaco
	Norway
	Sweden
	The Netherlands
	Kingdom of Turkey
	United Kingdom
	United States

NOTE: *Term expires on last day of the year indicated.* *Re-elected **Own rotation scheme ***Newly elected for 2019-2021
(Source: https://www.undp.org/content/undp/en/home/executive-board/membership.html)

Nairobi, Kenya, in 2016, emphasized UNCTAD "as the focal point within the United Nations system for the integrated treatment of trade and development and interrelated issues in the areas of finance, technology, investment and sustainable development reflecting our common conviction that, by enhancing its developmental role, impact and institutional effectiveness, UNCTAD will help turn a new page in international economic relations, in support of the new consensus for development."[18] Following from that mission statement, the overlap between UNCTAD and the UNDP within the UN system is also apparent.

Group of 77 (G-77) The group of 77 countries of the South that cosponsored the Joint Declaration of Developing Countries in 1963 calling for greater equity in North–South trade. This group has now come to include 134 members and represents the interests of the less developed countries of the South.

An organization related to UNCTAD is the **Group of 77** (G-77). Its name derived from the Joint Declaration of the Seventy-Seven Countries that some in the Global South issued at the end of the first UNCTAD conference in 1964. Since then, membership of the G-77 has expanded to 134 members and represents an institution for Southern collective action.

We should remember that World War II was a turning point for many structures and relationships in the global system. The decline of the traditional European world powers and their global colonial empires was critical to the trend that produced a tremendous influx of poor, corrupt, and often unstable countries in the Global South. As decolonization progressed, these newly independent countries recurrently sought global roles commensurate with their status as sovereign states and UN members, and UNCTAD serves as one of the primary forums for Global South influence in global affairs. As described on its web site, UNCTAD "promotes the development-friendly integration of developing countries into the world economy. UNCTAD has progressively evolved into an authoritative knowledge-based institution whose work aims to help shape current policy debates and thinking on development, with a particular focus on ensuring that domestic policies and international action are mutually supportive in bringing about sustainable development."[19]

Although it is difficult to name many tangible successes of UNCTAD in global development policy, the collective action pushed by the G-77 has given voice to issues that would otherwise have received little attention. Some landmark UNCTAD achievements include:

- Adoption of the Generalized System of Preferences (GSP) in 1968 under the General Agreement on Tariffs and Trade. The GSP provided for improved access for LDCs into EDC markets.

- Passage of the New International Economic Order (NIEO) in 1974 by the UN General Assembly. The NIEO requested changes to the global terms of trade, greater development assistance flowing from EDCs to LDCs, and a restructuring of global economic institutions. Although the NIEO was never implemented as global policy, it established these issues as ongoing concerns in the global economic system.

- Creation of commodity agreements to stabilize supply and demand on global markets for some primary products. Commodity agreements provide for greater price stability for countries that rely heavily on the sale of primary products for export revenues.

UNCTAD has also worked to highlight how economic downturns and periodic crises actually affect the South much more significantly than they do the North, because the countries of the South are much more vulnerable to disruption in both the short and the long term. Thus, from the emergence of debt crises of the 1980s, the global recession starting in 2008, and the economic uncertainty of the past decade, UNCTAD has remained a voice for the poor in global forums. Even though it is difficult to call UNCTAD a global development success story, development concerns would not occupy their current place on the global policy agenda if it were not for the collective power of the G-77 within UNCTAD and, more broadly, within the UN.

THE SOUTH'S REFORM AGENDA.   A basic point we must realize in understanding the Global South's perspective is that many people living there agree with much of the world systems argument that, whether by design or by happenstance, the global political economy works to the advantage of the Global North and serves to keep the Global South relatively poor and dependent. However, the South has worked recurrently, although not always successfully, to promote a collective front to the North regarding an agenda for global economic reform.

One of the most notable of these proposals is the Declaration on the Establishment of a **New International Economic Order** (NIEO), which UNCTAD drafted and the UN General Assembly approved in 1974. UNCTAD and the G-77 have regularly reiterated, refined, and expanded these largely unmet demands. A reassertion of these principles occurred at the 2005 G-77 summit meeting of the South's leaders in Doha, Qatar. The leaders adopted the Doha Plan of Action, which reiterated a number of earlier declarations and pledged its signatories to "continue strengthening the unity and solidarity among countries of the South, as an indispensable element in the defense of our right to development and for the creation of a more just and equitable international order."[20] The most recent G-77 summits have continued to argue for policy change in the following areas:

New International Economic Order (NIEO) A term that refers to the goals and demands of the South for basic reforms in the global economic system.

- *Trade reforms*, such as lowering Northern barriers to agricultural imports, that will expand and stabilize markets for Southern exports.
- *Monetary reforms* that will create greater stability in the exchange rates of Southern currencies and moderate the sometimes sudden and significant ebb and flow of investment into and out of the South.
- *Institutional reforms* that will increase the South's influence over policies of the International Monetary Fund (IMF), the World Bank, and other such international financial agencies. Currently, wealthy countries dominate decision-making in these institutions (see Chapter 10).
- *Economic modernization* in the Global South with significant assistance from the North through such methods as relaxing patent rights to permit easier technology transfers to the South.
- *Greater labor migration* for Southern workers seeking employment in more prosperous Northern countries.
- *Elimination of economic coercion*, including the use of sanctions, which the South tends to see as a tool of the North to punish and control the South.
- *Economic aid* to the South by the North that steadily increases to meet the UN's target of 0.7% of each Northern country's GDP.

- *Debt relief* granted by the Northern countries, the World Bank, and the IMF to reduce the money owed to them by many Southern debtors and eliminate the debt for the poorest in the South. Currently, countries in the Global South owe more than $4 trillion, and payments have increased by 85% in the past decade[21] to Global North creditors, including the IMF, the World Bank, and creditor countries.

THE NORTH'S RESPONSE TO THE SOUTH'S REFORM AGENDA.   To say that the North has ignored the South's plight is inaccurate, but it is also misleading to assert that the North has gone very far to meet the South's demands. One reason for the North's limited response is the view of many that the main barriers to the South's development are internal issues, including political instability, inefficient market controls, and corruption. Taking that view, President George W. Bush told one international development conference in 2012 that LDCs had not done enough to reform themselves.

Under the Trump administration thus far, there are few direct indications of how the United States will interact with Southern interests, except where the administration's focus on immigration intersects with Southern concerns. Building on the America First ethos, it seems unlikely that progressive development of the Global South will figure significantly in overall policy priorities. Certainly, the president's openly hostile stance on immigration has soured many relationships with Southern countries.

One recent example, however, illustrates that some forms of North-South collaboration remain in play. In August 2018, Argentina asked the IMF to release $50 billion earlier than originally planned in their agreement regarding economic restructuring. Facing the prospect of default on its debt, the Argentinian government needed the additional cash to repay heavy governmental borrowing. IMF President Christine Lagarde stressed her "support for Argentina's policy efforts and our readiness to assist the government in developing its revised policy plans." Argentinian President Mauricio Macri says that the action was taken to address "new expressions of lack of confidence in the markets, specifically over our financing capacity in 2019. . . . We have agreed with the International Monetary Fund to advance all the necessary funds to guarantee compliance with the financial program next year. This decision aims to eliminate any uncertainty" in domestic and global markets about Argentinian economic stability moving forward.[22]

Domestic resistance within the Global North has also limited progressive responses to the plight of the Global South. Many of the changes that Southern countries want are unpopular in the North. Greater labor migration is part of a larger flashpoint issue in the United States and Europe during recent years. This issue also influences the debates about immigration more generally that have been waging in Europe, centering on the Syrian crisis, and in the United States, centering on immigration from Latin America and Muslim countries.

Foreign aid also faces stiff opposition in much of the Global North, especially in the United States (Hurst, Tidwell, & Hawkins, 2017). A 2019 poll of Americans found more than two-thirds think that US foreign aid is too high and less than 10% thinking it is too low.[23] These response percentages are quite consistent over time regarding the low priority given to foreign aid by most Americans. The result of this attitude in the United States and elsewhere is, as Figure 11.3 shows, that foreign aid, as a percentage of the Global North's GDP, has decreased instead of rising toward the 0.7% standard that the Southern countries and the UN advocate.

As we will discuss later regarding barriers to trade, various powerful interest groups in the Global North oppose other steps that would help the South. For instance, numerous Southern countries have large sugar crops, yet their exports to the United States are limited by an array of strict quotas and high tariffs that the US sugar lobby has persuaded the American government to impose. These are a sweet deal for domestic sugar producers, as the price of US sugar is more than three times the world market price. However, such protectionist measures are a bitter pill for both American consumers of sugar, soda, and other products and for poor Southern countries, which cannot export their crop freely to the United States.

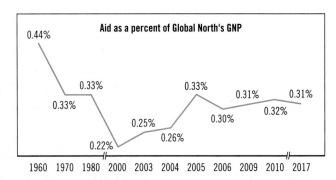

Figure 11.3   The foreign aid effort of the economically developed countries (EDCs), measured as the share of their annual combined GNPs that they give in foreign aid, has declined since the 1960s. As you can see, the effort dropped sharply until 2000, before recovering somewhat in recent years. (Source: Data from Organization of Economic Cooperation and Development, https://www.oecd.org; *Development Cooperation*.)

NEW DEVELOPMENTS IN NORTH-SOUTH COMPETITION.   A relatively recent and growing development in North-South relations is that some Southern countries are increasingly competing with the North for markets, resources, and other economic assets, creating global repercussions. China is the prime example, as some earlier examples suggest. With a 2016 per capita GNP of $8,123, China cannot yet be considered part of the Global North by that measure. Yet by 2012 China's aggregate GNP earned it the title of the world's second-largest economy, behind only the United States and now ahead of Japan and Germany. Thus, China is an economic giant on an overall basis and is expected to possess the world's largest economy in the not-so-distant future.

Among many effects, China's large economy has increased its needs for energy imports, which the North also needs. China consumed over 23% of the world's energy consumption in 2017,[24] surpassing the United States, which consumed about 18% of global energy.[25] Because China produces increasingly less petroleum than it needs, its oil imports have risen steadily, making the country more dependent on oil exporters. Continually high global oil prices are one outcome of the sharply increased demand for petroleum. There have also been diplomatic ramifications. China has lent support to the long-time, anti-American government in Venezuela led by late President Hugo Chávez and his successor, Nicolás Maduro, by agreeing to invest billions of dollars to modernize the country's oil production facilities. As this relationship unfolded, Chávez argued that "[t]he United States as a power is on the way down. China is on the way up. China is the market of the future."[26]

The Coca Codo Sinclair Hydrodam in the Ecuadoran highlands on the edge of the Amazon rainforest aims to provide electricity to remote areas. Some have raised concern, however, over the fact that Export-Import Bank of China is financing 85% of the project, perhaps giving China greater influence in the region.

Trade is another source of tension between China and the North. A major factor has been the mounting US trade deficit with China. The US trade deficit in 2017 of $376 billion set yet another record for any single trading partner. The EU also has an escalating trade deficit with China that stood at $374 billion in 2017. Economic factors such as China's vastly lower labor costs explain some of the trade imbalance. Some of the deficit also reflects Americans' nearly insatiable appetite for consumer goods.

US officials and others, however, blame part of the problem on what they term illegal or unfair practices by China. One US charge is that China does far too little to suppress the rampant piracy of intellectual property—that is, reproducing and selling patented goods and copyrighted music, software, and other material. Northern countries also have long alleged that China heavily subsidizes its industries, enabling them to compete unfairly with foreign companies. In addition, US officials charge that China has manipulated the yuan to keep it artificially low relative to the dollar in order to promote Chinese exports and discourage foreign imports.

Chinese leaders have long argued "that they can outlast Mr. Trump in a trade standoff. Their authoritarian system can stifle dissent and quickly redirect resources, and they expect Washington to be gridlocked and come under pressure from voters feeling the pain of trade disruptions. . . . And as [one Chinese high-tech worker put it], 'If we are going to fight a trade war . . . even if my job may be affected, I will still support our country.'"[27] It's unclear if worker patriotic sentiments are that strong in Northern countries.

South-South Economic Relations

Although the South generally shows a united front in calling on the North for economic reform, Southern countries also compete with one another. One contentious example is the price of oil. Increased prices benefit those few in the South that export oil, like Nigeria, Venezuela, and many Middle Eastern countries, but higher prices restrict the economies of oil-importing Southern countries, which are much less able to afford price increases than those in the North. And because global oil prices are valued in US dollars, both exporters and importers are captive to the variance of the dollar on international financial markets.

Additionally, Southern countries compete among themselves for investment capital from the North and for export markets. For example, Chinese goods may be flooding the United States, the EU, and other countries of the

North, but the Chinese rely on investment in those industries and do not own all their production facilities making those export goods. MNCs from the North own large shares of those industries. At one time these factories may have been in the United States and other countries of the North and employed those countries' workers. But in most cases, the plants had long ago left the North and gone to countries like Mexico.

In the past few years, however, China has undercut substantially Mexico's role as a provider of low-cost exports to the United States; an average factory worker's wages in China are less than half those of the average Mexican worker. As a result, production in Mexico's *maquiladora* manufacturing zone near the US border dropped about 30% in the early 2000s. Since then, the economic fortunes of the *maquiladoras* and their Mexican workers have seen some improvement, but that has come in part at the cost of wage restraints for low-paid workers and tax breaks to lure MNCs back to the border. Again, the waging of a trade war by the Trump administration will, no doubt, bring associated economic difficulties for Mexico, China, and others trading with the United States. What remains unclear even at the latest editing of this text is which trading partners have more economic leverage with the others.

Another question that remains is whether Northern consumers will pressure companies to take action through purchase decisions based on knowledge of worker conditions. Concerns about corporate social responsibility have become a more visible part of the global economic discussion (see further discussion in Chapters 10 and 12), but action in the form of consumer choices has yet to change production patterns dramatically.

Another point regarding China's changing role in global finance is that Chinese entities are increasingly becoming a source of investment capital and not just a recipient of it from the "traditional" Northern countries. In recent years, China's role as a financier for projects in Africa, Latin America, and elsewhere has made its global reach a point of concern for some countries, especially given the long-term leverage China might now have in those economies. This story, however, is far from completely written.

Simulation:
Negotiating with
China

🌏 Applied Economic Policy

As any national election cycle illustrates, decisions about how best to pursue economic growth and prosperity are a matter of perspective. And those perspectives can vary greatly, especially as they relate to the appropriate role of government in directing economic policy nationally and globally. There is a large degree of consensus, however, that economic policy is not just a matter of theoretical models but rather is the subject of important political decisions. Whether political partisans like it or not, actors in the political process make economic decisions and ultimately serve both economic and political goals. As a part of our discussion of the relationship between the Global North and the Global South, we focus here on the tools available and the ways that countries use those tools both economically and politically.

We are indeed at a fork in the figurative road of global economic relations. Liberal internationalist views on the value of free trade and the ease of economic interchange among countries of the world have dominated world affairs since the end of World War II. But the Trump administration has ushered in an aggressively nationalist view in most economic policy areas that may or may not take hold in the United States and around the world in the coming years. The verdict on that possibility will be made clear only by time and the degree to which the interdependence borne of globalization will win the day because it has—or has not—made us all too intertwined to risk nationalist economic warfare and its unknown long-term consequences for prosperity.

Using Economic Means to Achieve Economic Ends

Globalization is increasingly linking the economies of all countries. Nonetheless, all countries to a degree still attempt to shape their economic policies primarily to promote their own prosperity. When national leaders must answer to domestic constituents who are demanding jobs, higher wages, and stable and rising economic prospects, the welfare of the world is a secondary issue. To accomplish their self-interested goals, all states practice **protectionism** to some degree by using a variety of tools to manipulate the flow of trade, investments, and other forms of economic interchange into and out of the country. Each of these protectionist measures has benefits and costs, both in the short and the long term.

protectionism Using tariffs or nontariff barriers, such as quotas or subsidies, to protect a domestic economic sector from competition from imported goods or services.

TRADE AND INVESTMENT BARRIERS.   Countries can erect a range of barriers to limit imports or foreign investment. These include:

- Tariffs
- Nontariff barriers.
- Monetary barriers.
- Investment restrictions.

Restrictions on trade and investments are the most familiar form of protectionism. Of the tools available, tariffs, or taxes imposed on foreign goods imported into a country, are the most widespread. Currently, tariff rates are quite low relative to what they once were, but two qualifications are important. First, tariff rates in the Global North are generally much lower than those in the Global South. The logic of this differential is that states in the Global South need higher tariff rates to protect their "infant industries" from overpowering foreign competition. For example, the average tariff is 3.4% in the United States, 4.5% in Japan, and 5% in the EU, compared to 10% for China, 31.4% for Brazil, and 48.5% for India. Second, globally and for almost every country individually, the average tariff on agricultural products is much higher than it is on manufactured products. US tariffs on agricultural goods average 4.9%, in contrast to 3.2% on manufactured goods.[28]

A lesser-known, but more common way, that countries restrict trade is by using **nontariff barriers (NTBs)**. Health and safety standards are one type

nontariff barriers (NTBs) A nonmonetary restriction on trade, such as quotas, technical specifications, or lengthy quarantine and inspection procedures.

of NTB. These are sometimes reasonable regulations to protect the well-being of the importing country's citizens. At other times, health and safety standards are simply an excuse for protectionism, and trade disputes over whether the restriction is legitimate or protectionist are common. Not long ago, the EU had a "banana war" with some banana-producing countries, when the EU put in place guidelines that allowed EU imports only from former EU colonial countries.[29]

Quotas limiting the number of units that a country can ship is another form of NTB. The EU has long had quotas on textile imports from China that limit the annual growth rate on imports, which are aimed at preventing China from gaining dominance in the European market too quickly.

> **quotas** Quotas are used to create balanced (e.g., gender, race, ethnicity, region, etc.) representation within legislative bodies of national governments and can be mandated by the constitution or electoral laws

The United States sets quotas on imported raw and refined sugar by estimating US sugar production. As one analyst puts it, "US import quotas kept prices here several times above world levels. The benefits of that policy [go] to a few thousand sugar growers, for each of whom it [is] worth tens or hundreds of thousands a year. The costs were thinly spread among tens of millions of consumers, the vast majority of whom had no idea there even was an import quota."[30]

Administrative requirements are yet another type of NTB. These are particularly important in limiting service imports. For example, many countries license architects, engineers, insurance agents, stock and bond traders, and other professionals, and they can use these licensing requirements to make it difficult for foreign professionals and companies to provide services in another country.

Another way that a country protects its domestic producers by constraining imports and promoting exports is by manipulating the exchange rate so that its currency is weaker against other currencies than it would be if it were allowed to float—that is, to trade freely on financial markets. The United States has long alleged that China is keeping the value of the yuan artificially low versus the US dollar, a claim that has been denied by the Chinese government. Through mid-2005, as Figure 11.4 shows, China managed to keep the value of its currency at a steady 8.3 yuan/$1, but the dollar declined further through 2012 against the yuan, to about 6.3 yuan/$1, with a slight rebound in the most recent years. This monetary manipulation is one reason that US imports from China and the trade deficit with it rose so quickly.

Most countries want to attract international investment because it brings outside capital into their national economy. Yet countries are also wary of outside control of their companies and real estate. The most common form of

Food import inspections, like the ones being done by these Chinese meat inspectors, are one form of nontariff barrier to trade that can impede the free flow of goods across borders. But what is seen as health and safety for an importing country is often viewed as unfair trade practices by the exporting country.

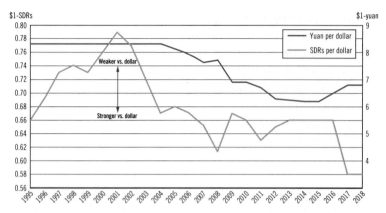

Figure 11.4 Countries sometimes try to manipulate their currencies to achieve certain economic goals. To stimulate its exports and to attract foreign investment capital, China kept the yuan at a weak rate of 8.3 yuan to the dollar until 2005. The artificiality of that rate is evident when compared with the exchange rate of the dollar with SDRs (special drawing rights), a market basket of currencies designated by the International Monetary Fund. Since 2005, China has allowed the yuan to trade with somewhat more freedom, and it has strengthened against the dollar, just as SDRs have. The yuan still does not vary like the SDR relative to the dollar, however, indicating a continued effort to control the currency by China. (Source: Data from the IMF; https://www.imf.org/external/np/fin/data/param_rms_mth.aspx)

investment restriction limits foreign ownership of companies. All countries have some limits. For example, foreigners are barred from controlling airlines in the EU, Canada, and the United States. Japan does not allow foreign ownership of its telecommunications companies. Only citizens may own fishing and energy enterprises in Iceland. And some countries directly control companies, such as Mexico's state-owned oil monopoly Petróleos Mexicanos (better known as Pemex). Each of these national policies shows the limits of liberal internationalism and supports the validity of arguments made by economic nationalists and world systems analysts who focus on nationalistic manipulation of economic policy for narrower nationalistic economic gains.

TRADE AND INVESTMENT SUPPORTS. In addition to erecting protectionist barriers to foreign trade and investment, countries also try to increase the economic prospects of their domestic products and producers through a variety of support techniques. Subsidies, dumping, and cartels are three of these.

Countries give tax breaks, provide low-cost services (e.g., energy and transportation), and offer various other forms of financial support to subsidize domestic producers, which then can lower the price that they charge for their product. Less direct supports include such techniques as funding research for product development and undertaking government trade promotion campaigns (advertising).

Agriculture is the most heavily subsidized economic sector, with large-scale agribusiness rather than small family farms generally being the primary recipient of subsidy funds. In the United States, for instance, the 2013 Farm Bill (the name for the subsidy package) cost $940 billion for its duration. In the EU, the Common Agricultural Policy costs about $69 billion annually to help maintain agricultural production within those countries and to keep prices low in those markets.[31] Many Southern countries also give subsidies to their producers, sometimes to promote the production of goods for export to the North rather than food for their own citizens. Potato production in Ecuador provides an example, with the revival of "specialty" potatoes for consumption as high-end produce in the United States and Canada.

subsidies Assistance paid to a business or economic sector. Most subsidies are made by the government to producers or distributed as subventions in an industry to prevent the decline of that industry or an increase in the prices of its products or simply to encourage it to hire more labor.

Also, like other forms of economic intervention, agricultural **subsidies** benefit one segment of a country's economy through taxation to maintain the cost of subsidies and price increases for the country's citizenry. The subsidies also suppress the competition from cheaper foreign sources of agricultural products. And trade is indeed a political tool, even at a domestic level. In President Trump's trade war with China, Canada, Mexico, and the EU, the response from many of those countries has been to impose retaliatory tariffs on American agricultural products from soybeans, pork, sugar, and orange juice, to cherries. In an effort to ease the burden on mid-Western farmers in the run-up to the fall 2018 mid-term elections, the Trump administration announced $12 billion (that is, subsidies) to go to farmers trying to weather Trump's trade storm. Another $18 billion was announced in the May 2019 as the conflict with China escalated.[32] The final outcome is yet to be told.

Another trade tactic is **dumping**. This occurs when a company, often with the support of its national government, violates trade laws by selling its products abroad at very low cost, sometimes even below the cost of production. The difficulty, however, is in determining whether the dumping is predatory dumping or distress dumping. Predatory dumping occurs when a foreign manufacturer sells below cost abroad with the intent of driving other competitors out of business (or at least out of a specific foreign market). Distress dumping happens when a foreign corporation possesses an oversupply of its product because of market or production miscalculations. During the 1980s and 1990s, for instance, US officials recurrently accused Japanese and Korean steel manufacturers of predatory dumping on American markets. For their part, the Asian companies continually argued that they had simply overproduced. The only definitive outcome to note is that American steel companies are now nearly extinct.

Countries, especially those in the Global North, have also occasionally tried to control trade by establishing **cartels**. A cartel is an international trading agreement among producers who hope to control a primary product's supply and price. The International Tea Agreement of 1933 introduced the first successful cartel, which was effective in increasing tea prices globally. During the 1960s, a total of 18 cartels had come into existence, resulting in the apex of cartel formation. They ranged in importance from the Organization of Petroleum Exporting Countries (OPEC) to the Asian and Pacific Coconut Community.

Cartels, however, have not always been successful. Even OPEC has had to struggle to maintain prices in the face of internal economic and political disputes (e.g., the Iraq-Iran War in the 1980s), the production of about 60% of the world's petroleum by non-OPEC countries, and other factors. Over the years, price increases, including sharp ones beginning in 2004, have had less to do with OPEC's efforts to increase prices by manipulating supply than with uncertainty in the oil markets caused by the Iraq War, tensions with Iran and other events, and the increasing demand for oil in an energy-addicted world. The rise of China as an oil importer and the development of

dumping Predatory pricing, especially in the context of international trade, where manufacturers export a product to another country at a price either below the price charged in its home market, or in quantities normal market competition cannot explain.

cartels An international agreement among producers of a commodity that attempts to control the production and pricing of that commodity.

From left to right, Alexander Novak, the Russian energy minister, sits alongside Khalid al-Falih, the Saudi energy minister, and Suhail Mohamed Faraj Al Mazrouei, UAE minister of energy and industry at a press conference held by energy producing countries in 2018. Even though Russia and some others are not OPEC members, members and non-members regularly collaborate to control production and thus prices.

oil sand technology in the United States and Canada have also changed patterns of consumption.

Using Economic Means to Achieve Political Ends

Countries primarily use tariffs, quotas, and other tools of economic nationalist policy to achieve economic ends, such as the protection of domestic producers. It is not uncommon, however, for countries also to use a range of economic techniques to support noneconomic political goals.

Along those lines, national security restrictions are one aspect of such policy. All countries that produce major military weaponry require government approval of foreign sales. In many cases, there are blanket prohibitions of sales to countries that are considered either current or potential enemies. As circumstances change, such bans can prove controversial. In recent years, for instance, Chinese émigrés to the United States have come under increasing scrutiny for their work and what they might be sharing with colleagues (or the government) in China. The degree to which this issue is a concern for Chinese-American academics and business people was the focus of a CBS *60 Minutes* investigation in August 2018.[33] Although the national security threat in some cases may be legitimate, seminars are now being held to teach Chinese-Americans how to better handle their own business and research dealings to avoid such accusations.

Governments also sometimes use economic incentives or economic sanctions to try to convince one or more other countries to commence, continue, or cease acting in a certain way (see Grauvogel, Light, & von Soust, 2017; Morgan & Reyes, 2018). For example, incentives have played a prominent role in recent efforts to stem nuclear proliferation. Both multinational diplomatic efforts to persuade Iran to halt its alleged nuclear weapons development program and similar efforts to convince North Korea to stop building nuclear weapons and to dismantle its ability to do so include offers of energy aid, food aid, and other important economic incentives—as well as economic disincentives like trade embargoes on those countries.

Countries can apply their economic power in a negative way by imposing sanctions (Lektzian and Patterson, 2015; Peksen, 2017). Sanctions that they apply for political reasons most often occur when there has been a major event, such as Iraq's 1990 invasion of Kuwait, or amid a long-term hostile relationship, such as the US sanctions on Cuba. Most often, though, countries use incentives and sanctions simultaneously—in other words, a well-worn carrot-and-stick approach to behavior modification.

Global Economic Development Futures

Undoubtedly, the expansion of world trade, investment, and currency exchange has profoundly affected numerous countries and their citizens. Economic interdependence has inexorably intertwined personal, national, and global prosperity. The local and the global are now forever linked, no matter whether national policy-makers wish otherwise. Domestic economics, employment, inflation, and overall growth are heavily dependent on foreign markets, imports of resources, currency exchange rates, capital flows, and other international economic factors. Economic globalization is a reality.

The process of globalization has also brought the issue of global economic development and the attendant disparities in wealth and living conditions much more to center stage than in the past. Globalization has had advantages and disadvantages for all countries. But there is widespread agreement that, both within and among countries, those with the greatest wealth have benefited the most and those with the least wealth have gained the least—and in some cases have been harmed. This reality has brought increasing resistance to globalization in the South and sympathy from those in agreement with its stance.

Globalization, and the attendant tension between cooperation and conflict that it entails, are also beginning to have a significant influence on the way that we organize our world politically. Globalization and sovereignty are not mutually exclusive, but cooperation sometimes requires that countries surrender some of their sovereign rights regarding unilateral policy decisions and be more willing to accept international rules that benefit the collective. The World Trade Organization's authority to find a country's trade practices legal or illegal serves as an example. Some analysts see this diminution of sovereignty as acceptable, or even as a positive development. Others are distressed and see it as a direct affront to their own sense of nationalism, which has fed the so-called "populist" uprisings in the United Kingdom around Brexit, in the United States during the 2016 election cycle, and in other places like Hungary, Poland, and France.

Other arguments exist both for and against globalization, and they spring in many ways from the three theoretical perspectives that we have discussed throughout this chapter and in Chapter 10. Thus, the discussion of alternative views of our global economic future starts with internationalism, moves to economic nationalism, and closes with comments from the world systems perspective. To begin, ponder the *Challenge Your Assumptions* feature on page 362; it should help you determine which perspective best characterizes your own views on the global political economy.

Internationalism: Benefits for All?

Internationalists make a number of arguments in favor of furthering free economic interchange and increasing support for development. They advance both economic and noneconomic reasons to support their case (Bhagwati, 2004) and explain why this trajectory is the most likely (and the most desirable) one to develop in the coming decades.

ECONOMIC ADVANTAGES.   According to internationalists, there are several economic advantages to globalization and to assisting LDCs as part of that process. These positive results include:

- General prosperity.
- Benefits of specialization.
- Avoiding the cost of protectionism.

CHALLENGE YOUR ASSUMPTIONS

Internationalism, Economic Nationalism, or World Systems?

Internationalists favor few restrictions on free trade and investment. They believe that a mostly unfettered flow of goods, services, and capital will, in the long term, advance the prosperity of all countries. Economic nationalists disagree. They generally see the global economy as a zero-sum game where the prosperity of some comes at the expense of others. Therefore, economic nationalists believe that restrictions are often warranted to protect their country's economy and to advance its political interests. Like economic nationalists, world systems analysts view the global economy as zero sum, but instead focus on how the powerful take from the weak (or at least keep the weak from getting their due). Thus, you might interpret world systems theory as viewing economic nationalism as an accurate analysis of global economic relations, but world systems supporters would emphasize the degree to which the economically powerful collude to prevent gains by the least developed countries. Economic nationalists would defend their perspective as the best method to protect national interests rather than as a concerted effort of the strong to oppress the weak.

Test your own economic worldview by deciding on several policy issues listed here. Although some are expressed in generic terms, each is related to a current or recent US policy decision.

- Should the United States repeal its long-standing economic embargo on Cuba?
- Do you think the United States and other Northern countries should make sufficient concessions on agricultural subsidies in global trade negotiations to provide more (and perhaps more equitable) export opportunities for Global South producers?
- Would you approve acquisition of a controlling interest in a major US corporation by a Chinese company?

- Would you maintain the US president's authority to negotiate trade agreements? Current law limits congressional power to only approving or disapproving the agreements (the so-called "fast-track" approach to negotiating trade deals). Further, Congress cannot amend such agreements, as any amendment would require their renegotiation.
- Should the United States tax imports of foreign products to protect jobs of workers at home?
- Should countries abide by rulings made by the World Trade Organization regarding trading practices even if they mean high prices on consumer goods?

For each question, a Yes vote casts you as a supporter of economic internationalism, and a No vote aligns you more with economic nationalism.

	YES	NO
Repeal the embargo on Cuba		
Make concessions on agricultural subsidies		
Permit Chinese acquisition of a US energy company		
Renew the president's fast-track trade authority		
Reject tariffs on imports		
Abide by World Trade Organization rulings		

A final question: Do you think that any decisions on these policy questions simply reinforce a global system in which the wealthy get more and the poor, at best, muddle along? If your answer is Yes to this question, maybe your worldview reflects a world systems perspective.

- Advantages of competition.
- Advancement of the Global South through the provision of development capital.

Internationalists argue that unhindered trade and other forms of free economic exchange promote prosperity. Especially since the mid-20th century, trade has accounted for a rapidly growing share of the world's economic activity. Exports have grown from 11% of the world's collective GDP in 1955 to 28% in 2015. Thus, more and more of what countries and their workers produce goes abroad. Without trade—or with a marked decline in trade—national economies will slow, perhaps stall, or might even decline. By comparing the annual growth of exports and the world's collective GDP, it is evident that trade growth helps drive economic expansion, as Figure 11.5 shows. More specifically, for example, the US government calculates that because of trade liberalization since the founding of the General Agreement on Tariffs and Trade in 1947, the income of the average American household is more than $10,000 higher than it otherwise would have been.

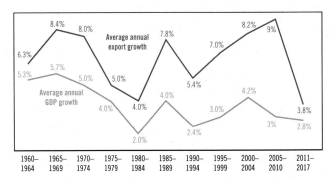

Figure 11.5   World trade measured in exports, which generate GDP, has grown faster in each period between 1960 and 2010 than did the collective GDPs of the world's countries. This means that exports have played an important role in driving overall economic growth. Globalization supporters point to such data to show that freer trade is having an overall positive impact on world economic circumstances. (Source: Data from the IMF, https://www.Imf.org.)

A corollary of this argument, according to internationalists, is that development of the Global South will increase the prosperity of the Global North. Assisting the South will require a substantial short-to-medium-term cost for the North in foreign aid, debt reductions, and other assistance. Many analysts argue, however, that in the long run, this investment would create a world in which many more of the 1.4 billion Chinese, 1.3 billion Indians, and the other 3 billion people living in Global South (or what was the Global South) could buy products labeled "Made in America" or at least made in the Global North, visit the North as tourists, and otherwise benefit Northern economies.

Another advantage of globalization according to internationalists is based on the long-standing theory that all countries benefit when each sells what it can produce most efficiently. Among those who have propounded this idea are English economists David Ricardo in *On the Principles of Political Economy and Taxation* (1817) and John Stuart Mill in *Principles of Political Economy* (1848). Ricardo developed the theory of "comparative advantage," which held that everyone would benefit if each country produced and exported its most cost-efficient products. Based on this view, Mill argued that trade's "advantage consists in a more efficient employment of the productive forces of the world." These views have dominated liberal economic practices at least since the end of World War II.

Protecting jobs from foreign imports has a tremendous emotional appeal, but most economists argue that trade barriers result in higher prices for consumers, either because tariff costs are passed on to those consumers or because consumers are forced to buy more expensive goods produced domestically. The US Federal Reserve has long argued that "protectionism is pure poison for an economy" and estimates that each American job that is saved by protectionism costs over $200,000, with an overall cost of nearly $100 billion annually to US consumers.[34] How does a protected job cost over $200,000? The cost includes not just the higher price of the protected items but also the higher prices of downstream products. Protecting domestic sugar production, for instance, increases the cost paid for candy, soft drinks, and other sweet items that many of us enjoy.

Internationalists also argue that free economic interchange promotes beneficial competition. Without foreign competition, the argument goes, domestic manufacturers have a captive market, which can have a variety of ill effects, such as price fixing and lack of innovation. For example, during the 1980s and 1990s, American automakers did not begin to offer US consumers well-built, inexpensive, fuel-efficient small cars until pressure from foreign competition forced them to reshape their products and modernize their production techniques. Somewhat surprisingly, US automakers did not seem to learn this lesson very well, as they had to restructure massively again when the recession hit in 2008. They have again recovered, although without the market dominance they held globally through the 1960s and 1970s.

NONECONOMIC ADVANTAGES.   Arguably, there are also several noneconomic advantages to internationalism. These include advancing global cooperation, decreasing violence, and promoting democracy.

First, internationalists argue that free economic interchange enhances cooperation around the globe. The logic is that if countries can trade together in peace, their interactions will bring greater contact and understanding. Cooperation will then become the rule rather than the exception, and this will lead to political interaction and political cooperation. The move toward the political integration of Europe, which began with economic cooperation, is the most frequently cited example. This was also the logic of the Marshall Plan aid package to Europe and the economic package for Japan after World War II—that is, help your former enemies recover and rebuild, and they will more likely be cooperative trading and political partners in the future.

Second, internationalists argue that free economic interchange decreases violence by promoting interdependence. In the words of one foundational study, "Higher levels of economically important trade . . . are associated with lower incidences of militarized interstate disputes and war" (Oneal & Russett, 1997:288). For example, if oil and metals are necessary to fight, and if Country A supplies Country B's oil and Country B supplies Country A's metals, then they are too enmeshed to go to war. A related argument is that the North will be more secure as the South achieves prosperity and greater interdependence.

A third argument some economic internationalists advance is that the openness required for free economic exchange promotes democracy. The idea is that it is difficult to simultaneously have a free enterprise system and an authoritarian political system. Gradually, the habits of independent decision-making inherent in a capitalist system, the flow of ideas within the country as well as between it and the outside world, and the growth of powerful financial interests all work to undercut authoritarian political regimes. For example, during the past two decades, such newly industrializing countries as Mexico, South Korea, and Taiwan have had their first truly democratic elections either ever or in many decades. One well-known study has argued that trade agreements have also helped to protect human rights in countries where human rights compliance had been more challenging (Hafner-Burton, 2005).

In summary, the promises of liberal internationalist approaches to global economic development have never quite been fulfilled, and certainly not at the speed with which they were promised by the proponents of this world order in the mid-twentieth century. While we can state that the absolute conditions have improved in many parts of the Global South, the gap between the North and South has largely widened. Thus, the relative conditions of the South have worsened. This reality lends general credence to the world systems arguments.

Economic Nationalism: A Competitive Future

Several political and economic arguments suggest that economic nationalists also accurately portray at least portions of the reality of global economic interactions.

It is a long-held Western belief that economic liberalization, development, and democracy are mutually reinforcing. That is one reason why so much time and energy is spent assuring that fair and free elections are held in the Global South, like one shown here in Sierra Leone in 2018.

ECONOMIC ADVANTAGES.   Economic nationalists advance a number of arguments to support their position about why nationalistic policies are, and should be, the structuring approach for our economic future. These include the following benefits:

- Protecting the domestic economy.
- Diversification.
- Compensating for existing distortions.
- Putting domestic needs first.

The need for economic barriers to protect domestic industries and workers from foreign competition is a favorite theme of economic nationalists. "I'm not a free trader," one former U.S. trade negotiator confessed. "The goal," he said, "is to nurture American workers and industry. It is not to adhere to some kind of strict ideology."[35] This type of nationalist protectionism has taken on new urgency and form in the Trump administration, which sees foreign economic villains around every corner threatening American enterprises.

An associated argument seeks protection for new or still small, so-called infant industries. This is an especially common contention as the Global South works to industrialize, but the argument is voiced in the Global North as well. Many economists give the idea of such protection some credibility, at least in the short term. Economic nationalists also argue that the loss of jobs when MNCs move operations to another country, or when MNCs create new jobs in another country rather than in their home country, offsets the positive impact of creation or preservation of jobs at home, thus further justifying protectionism. American

MNCs, for example, employ about several million more workers in other countries than foreign MNCs employ American workers in the United States. Further, these opponents say, forcing well-paid workers in the United States and elsewhere to compete with poorly paid workers in the Global South depresses the wages and living conditions in the Global North in what some call "a race to the bottom."

The US clothing industry, for example, has been devastated, with its workforce dropping between 1990 and 2017 from 929,000 to 81,000. Some of this loss is the result of robotics and other forms of mechanization, but most is the result of foreign competition. The tags on your own clothing can give you a picture of where your wardrobe is made.

We can also measure lost jobs and wages in terms of the ripple effect that multiplies each dollar several times. A worker without a job cannot buy from the local merchant, who in turn cannot buy from the building contractor, who in turn cannot buy from the department store, and so on, rippling out through the economy. Displaced workers also collect unemployment benefits and may even wind up on public assistance programs. These substantial costs diminish the gains that we derive from free trade. Finally, there is the psychological damage from being laid off and from other forms of economic dislocation that we cannot measure in dollars and cents but that still take a toll.

Economic nationalists also argue that countries should encourage economic diversification. Specialization will make a country too dependent on a few resources or products (Honke, 2018). If demand for those products falls, economic catastrophe will result. In reality, no modern, complex economy will become that specialized, but the argument does have a simplistic appeal. As we will discuss later, this idea is integral to arguments about the national security value of maintaining production in a wide array of economic sectors.

Another economic nationalist argument is that protectionism and other trade distortions continue, and so "nice-guy" free traders will finish last. This logic is at the heart of the President Trump's push for trade agreements that are "fairer" to American workers. In essence, when faced with such realities as cartels that set petroleum prices and governments that use tariffs, subsidies, currency manipulation, and other techniques to benefit themselves, domestic industries in countries committed to freer trade will lose ground to others that play unfairly. An example is China's recurring refusal to substantially revalue its artificially low currency, the yuan, against the dollar. The economic nationalist argument is that the United States should retaliate against China by raising tariffs and setting quotas or even embargoes on Chinese goods. This argument regarding Chinese competition has been put forward for at least two decades. Similar arguments were made against the Japanese in the 1980s and 1990s, when Japan was America's primary economic competitor. In these ways, the economic nationalists are fundamentally skeptical that global institutions can effect change on any of these issues, thus requiring more unilateral approaches to trade management.

Further, according to economic nationalists, citizens create and authorize their government to look after national welfare and safety, not to lead idealistic quests to solve other people's problems. From this perspective, the amounts of funding that the UN recommends and other development organizations advocate are prohibitive. Based on 2016 data, it would cost the Global North another $123 billion each year to increase aid to the recommended level of 0.7% of their GDPs.[36] Debt forgiveness, trade concessions, and other financial measures would further add to the annual expenses that yield ambiguous results at best. With most of the Global North already running annual budget deficits, the added funds would mean higher taxes for their people, fewer domestic social programs, and/or larger deficits.

NONECONOMIC ADVANTAGES.   Economic nationalists also argue that their view protects national sovereignty, enhances national security, and permits the beneficial use of their country's economic power as a policy tool. Another argument claims that globalization is harming the welfare of many individuals and also increasing damage to the environment.

One of the fastest-growing sources of sentiment against globalization is the belief held by many people that the process is eroding their country's national sovereignty. Many people are shocked to find that their country's laws and regulations must sometimes give way when they clash with the rules of the World Trade Organization or some other international organization or agreement. This concern in the United Kingdom relative to the EU was a primary force behind the Brexit vote in 2016. But as the Brexit process has unfolded, the world has seen that negotiating to regain perceived sovereignty is easier said than done, and that interdependence inside the EU has been difficult to unravel in ways that will satisfy enough officials to pass a negotiated outcome.

A closely related sentiment is the fear that foreign investors will gain control of a country's economy and be able to influence its political processes and its culture. American sensitivities are now primarily focused on the level of Chinese acquisitions of American companies and the possible loss of intellectual property from those Chinese overtures, just as they have been in the past regarding Japanese acquisitions of real estate, manufacturing interests, and even a controlling interest in the Seattle Mariners baseball team in the 1990s.

A related economic nationalist argument advocating protectionism involves national security. The contention is more or less the reverse of the conflict-inhibition, free-trade argument made earlier. Protectionists stress that the country must not become so dependent on foreign sources that it will be unable to defend itself. In recent years, the US government has acted to protect industries ranging from specialty steels to basic textiles, partly in response to warnings that the country was losing its ability to produce weapons systems and uniforms.

Economic nationalists also warn of the dangers of unchecked acquisitions by foreign investors. A Chinese company's bid to take control of the major US oil company Unocal in 2005 sparked the warning from one analyst that "in today's China, we are up against a country that has a strategy to acquire US critical technology companies. If we continue to ignore it—let alone enable it by acquiescing to the sale of companies like Unocal—we will do so at our peril."[37] Many Americans agreed, and the ensuing uproar in the United States ultimately persuaded the Chinese company to withdraw its bid.

Also under the rubric of national security is the issue of strategic trade. How far should a country go in restricting trade and other forms of economic interchange with countries that are or may become hostile in the future? Currently, the primary focus of the strategic trade debate is on dual-use technology, which has peaceful uses as well as military applications. Here, China is again the cause of the greatest current concern. In this vein, since the spring of 2018, the Trump administration has been waging a trade war partly focused on high-tech goods. To date, the United States has imposed tariffs of more than $200 billion of Chinese goods, and is threatening to impose over $300 billion more. China for its part imposed retaliatory tariffs of American goods.[38] How these actions will play out in the longer term remains unclear, but free trade voices are also emerging. James Zimmerman, former chairman of the American Chamber of Commerce in China, put it this way: "We really need to find a way to embrace China, and encourage the moderate voices here."[39] Such sentiments tend to focus on the interdependencies that exist between the two economic giants rather than the threats they pose to one another.

Another economic nationalist argument maintains that trade "follows the flag" (Keshk, Pollins, & Reuveny, 2004)—that is, that politics can and should determine economic relations, more than the other way around, and that trade is a powerful political tool that countries can and should use to further their interests. The extension or withdrawal of trade and other economic benefits also has an important—albeit hard-to-measure—symbolic value. Clearly, a country can use economic tools to promote its political goals, and free economic interchange necessarily limits the availability of economic tools to pursue policy. One example is the US embargo on most trade with and travel to Cuba, which has existed since 1960. Although these policies were eased late in the Obama administration, the Trump administration reconstituted the extensive restrictions on relations between the United States and Cuba. As former UN ambassador Nikki Haley (2017–2018) put it, the United States wishes to continue to demonstrate America's "continued solidarity with the Cuban people . . . in the hope that they will one day be free to choose their own destiny."[40]

The chairman of Dow Chemical Company once confessed, "I have long dreamed of buying an island owned by no nation and establishing the world headquarters of the Dow company on . . . such an island, beholden to no nation or society" (Gruenberg, 1996:339). Critics of MNCs claim such statements confirm their suspicions that these global enterprises use their ability to move operations around the world to undercut protections relating to child labor, minimum wages, and many other socioeconomic standards, and also to escape environmental regulations, many of which we discussed earlier regarding the UN Global Compact. This competition could set off "a 'race to the bottom' in which wages and social and environmental conditions tend to fall to the level of the most desperate" (Brecher, 1993:685).

This type of competition over corporate headquarters even happens within the Global North—and even inside specific countries in the Global North. The relocation of General Electric's headquarters from Fairfield, Connecticut, to Boston, Massachusetts, in 2017 occurred largely because Massachusetts offered more in the way of tax breaks than Connecticut was willing or able to do at the time. British energy company En+ considered moving from Jersey in the United

Kingdom to Russia after it was hit by sanctions imposed by the United States in April 2018. This move would have allowed for less regulation and more protection from US sanctions than it had with its UK headquarters. But the Trump administration lifted the sanctions in January 2019 easing the tension.[41]

Critics of globalization also charge that the race to the bottom will mean, among other evils, gutting desirable social programs and other focal points enumerated in the UN Global Compact. Europe has built an extensive social welfare support system through government programs and mandates on industries (e.g., health insurance for workers, paid vacations, and maternity and other benefits). Such programs and benefits are costly and partly funded by relatively higher tax rates, however, and European economies struggle to meet them while also keeping the price of their products low enough to be competitive in world markets—or even competitive at home compared to often cheaper imported goods and services. Similarly, critics worry that countries attempting to maintain high standards of environmental protection or institute new safeguards will see companies move their production facilities and jobs elsewhere.

A World Systems Postscript

The clash between internationalism and economic nationalism likely is fundamental to an understanding of the political economic trajectory of the coming decades (Helleiner & Pickel, 2005; Kahler, 2018). The rapid globalization process that began after World War II has brought the world much closer to a truly global economy than seemed possible not long ago. The Global North has generally prospered, and even much of the Global South has improved its health, education, and many other social conditions.

These two dominant perspectives nevertheless fail to captivate the thinking of many policy-makers and citizens, especially in the developing world. To them, an alternative future based on global restructuring, economic redistribution, and the establishment of equity and human rights as guiding principles in North-South relations is the only path to long-term peace, stability, and prosperity. Such a future could build on the constructs put forth in the NIEO, in the MDGs, and most recently, in the SDGs. Success, however, would require a substantial change in policy attitudes from Northern political elites who buy into one of the two more dominant perspectives discussed in this chapter.

World systems views fit rather closely with those espoused by Vermont Senator Bernie Sanders and his wing of the US Democratic Party. Those at the center of both the Democratic and the Republican parties are most closely aligned with the internationalist approach to economics and trade. Thus, if we think about a future more in line with a world systems view, we would start with some of the following fundamental principles:

- **Fair trade:** This approach to global exchange refocuses attention away from profit as the first goal of commerce. Promoting worker rights and acceptable living standards is the starting place for a more people-centric form of prosperity.

- **Human rights:** Those in the Global South have long argued for greater emphasis on economic rights relative to the civil and political rights that historically have taken center stage for the North.

- **Social justice:** The legacy of colonialism persists in the South and will not soon disappear. Will the global community accept a policy project that begins from the assumption that some degree of global wealth redistribution is essential to global peace and security?

The interesting dilemma, from both policy and scholarly perspectives, is whether the collective (and, some of us would argue, moral) power that the Global South possesses in pursuit of greater economic equity can overcome the wealth and structurally entrenched interests of the Global North. For now, and also for the foreseeable future, it is more likely that the internationalists or the economic nationalists will have more to say about the shape of our global economic future. Still, the economic crises of the early 21st century have given many of us pause to reconsider the older models. Just as few of us expected the aggressive nationalism of President Trump, it is quite difficult to predict the direction or intensity of economic pressures in the global political economy.

Chapter Summary

- The world is generally divided into two economic spheres: a wealthy Global North and a much less wealthy Global South. There are some overlaps between the two spheres, but in general, the vast majority of the people and countries of the South are much less wealthy and less industrialized than the people and countries of the North. The South also has a history of direct and indirect colonial (neocolonial) control by countries of the North.

- The wealth gap persists between North and South. By some measures, economic and social conditions in the South have improved over recent decades. But those improvements mask the reality of ongoing poverty and desperate living conditions in many locations in the South.

- Economic competition occurs across a number of different classes of countries: North-North competition, North-South competition, and South-South competition.

- Numerous intergovernmental organizations (IGOs) and international programs focus on economic cooperation, and many give the development of the South some priority. The largest general IGO, the UN, maintains a number of efforts aimed at general economic development, with an emphasis on the Global South.

- Countries attempt to advance their economic policy and prosperity by using their economic power through a mixture of protectionist barriers and incentives in the areas of trade and investment. Although each approach is sometimes successful, both incentives and, particularly, sanctions are difficult to apply consistently and successfully. Such policies have costs and benefits for both sender and recipient countries.

- Although globalization and interdependence constrain economic nationalism, national approaches to economic policy remain a driving force behind global political economy. Moreover, persistent state sovereignty, nationalism, and problems with globalization are all helping to maintain the central role of the state in global political economy.

- There are significant arguments on both sides as to whether or not to continue expanding economic globalization, including advancing both free international economic interchange and development in the Global South. Internationalists make a number of economic and noneconomic arguments in support of their view, most notably the reality of growing interdependence among countries in the global system. Nationalists continue to focus on demands to protect sovereignty.

- The world systems perspective provides an alternative future focusing on such policy themes as fair trade, human rights, and social justice. Such a future would entail a dramatic reorientation of global political economy, but it would also arguably be more focused on human welfare than either of the two other dominant perspectives.

Critical Thinking Questions

1. What signs of economic progress are apparent for developing world countries?

2. What are the primary roadblocks to development for countries in the Global South?

3. How effective are current global economic institutions in promoting development?

4. To what extent do you view global political economy as a product of global politics?

5. Which of the three theoretical perspectives best describes the current state of the global political economy?

6. Which of the three theoretical perspectives might best provide a framework or roadmap for coping with global political economic development in the future?

Key Terms

BRIC
cartels
dumping
former Soviet
    republics
Group of 77
least developed
    countries

Millennium
    Development Goals
Millennium Summit
New International
    Economic Order
newly industrializing
    countries
nontariff barriers

official development
    assistance
protectionism
quotas
subsidies
Sustainable
    Development Goals

UN Conference
    on Trade and
    Development
UN Development
    Programme
UN Global Compact

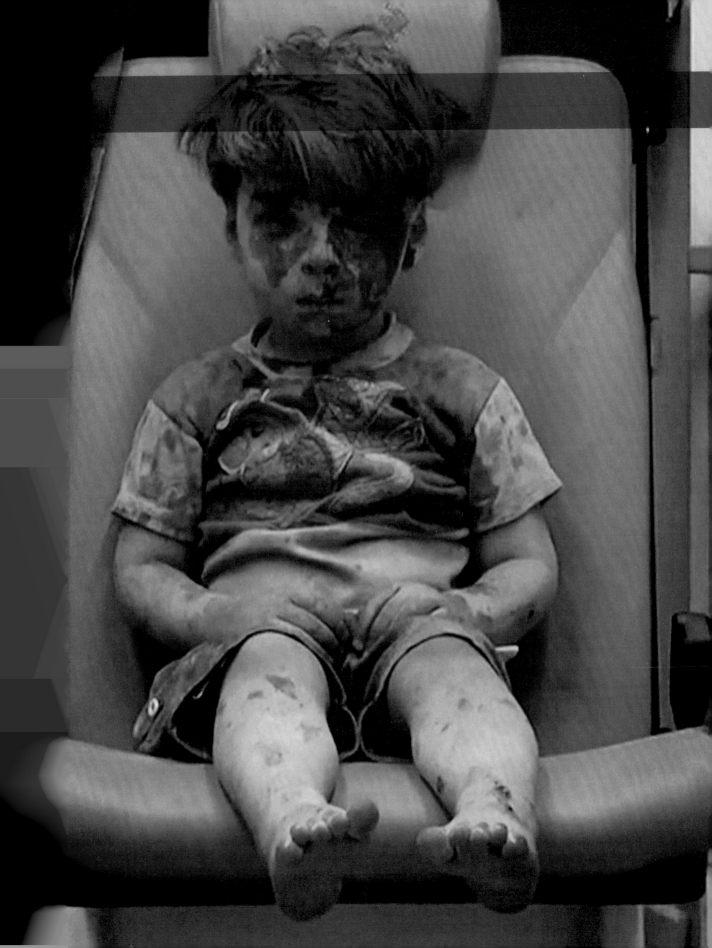

Human Rights: A Tool for Preserving and Enhancing Human Dignity

Human rights abuses of individuals, groups, and whole segments of humanity have existed throughout history. What is new today, however, is a rising global consciousness and condemnation of such treatment and a resolve (albeit far from perfect) to help the oppressed and the marginalized. This chapter examines the evolving language and framework for action that centers on the notion of human rights. We begin by exploring the nature of human rights, then turn to the critical human rights challenges of the 21st century, and finally consider what human rights advocacy looks like from global to local levels.

One of the greatest human rights challenges of our time is the record number of migrants and forcibly displaced individuals and communities across the globe. The extreme vulnerability of individuals and families who seek refuge and security across borders is a critical issue challenging many countries and leaders. According to the **United Nations High Commissioner for Refugees** (UNHCR) 2018 report, the number of displaced

The hauntingly stoic face of Omran Daqneesh, a Syrian boy, following the August 17, 2016, airstrike in Aleppo, has come to represent the country's devastation during an unrelenting civil war. Omran's older brother died from injuries he sustained during the bombing. Losing their home to bombs and fearing retaliation from the Assad regime for an image that unintentionally served as rebel propaganda, the Daqneesh family retreated from the world stage. As of June 2017, images of a healthy Omran and his family appeared on news channels supportive of President Bashar al-Assad, apparently as part of a calculated public relations campaign by the Syrian government.

people is now over 68.5 million—an increase of nearly 3 million over the previous year.[1] This staggering number of human beings forced from their homes certainly includes those coming from the war zones of Syria, Iraq, and Afghanistan, but they are also being displaced in Colombia, Ukraine, Somalia, South Sudan, the Democratic Republic of the Congo, and other countries. This disturbing number includes refugees, asylum seekers, internally displaced persons, returnees, and stateless persons, and a troubling trend within many of these categories is an increasing number of children.

This vulnerable population confronts countless threats to their rights, including the right to security, the right to a nationality, the right to food, the right to an education, and even the right to life itself. Another critical challenge for refugees, if they do survive their journey, is the right to work. Many of the states hosting the highest numbers of refugees—for example, Lebanon and Jordan—have laws that prohibit or strictly limit refugees from obtaining work permits even if those refugees are in the recipient country for many years. This denial of the right to work has a ripple effect on the ability of individuals and families to meet their basic needs, often forcing them to work in the informal sector where labor exploitation and abuse are rampant, particularly when it comes to human trafficking—that is, modern day slavery. The cascading effects of displaced people who are being denied the right to work is difficult to overestimate.

Further, the majority of the world's 19.9 million refugees are not ending their journeys in rich countries. (These numbers do not include asylum seekers, internationally displaced persons, or stateless persons.[2]) With Western Europe taking in close to 2.4 million, the United States accepting only approximately 287,000, and Japan accepting only about 2,000 (UNHCR Population Reference Database 2017), the rest of the world is left to share the remaining 17.3 million refugees.[3] The burden for some poor countries—for example, Ethiopia, a recipient of large numbers—is simply unmanageable given limited state resources, corruption in government, and fragile national economies.

This global crisis of displaced people is critical to any discussion of international human rights. We will return to this situation throughout the chapter, as it highlights not only the many actors involved in human rights abuses but, more importantly, our shared responsibility as global citizens to promote and protect the basic rights of individuals forced to flee their homeland. Individual consumers, major corporations, states, and intergovernmental organizations (IGOs) alike all bear responsibility in promoting and upholding the dignity of all humans.

United Nations High Commissioner for Refugees
Established December 14, 1950, by the United Nations General Assembly and mandated to lead and coordinate action to protect refugees and resolve refugee problems worldwide. Its primary purpose is to safeguard the rights and well-being of refugees.

Identify core human rights principles as outlined by the Universal Declaration of Human Rights, and understand various theoretical perspectives on how human rights standards have emerged since World War II.

Describe the complex international legal system, as well as the range of state and nonstate actors within the system, working to monitor, implement, and enforce human rights norms.

Discuss some of the greatest human rights violations of the 21st century, and consider the ways in which advocacy from local to global levels seeks to respond to these contemporary social, political, and economic challenges.

The Emergence of Human Rights

Consider the following events that have (so far) defined the 21st century:

- Democratic movements challenging and overthrowing authoritarian governments in the context of the "Arab Spring."

- Prisoner abuse of suspected terrorists at Guantanamo Bay in the context of the "War on Terror."

- Multinational corporations moving manufacturing jobs to low-wage countries with lax labor laws.

- Native Americans on reservations; the urban poor in Flint, Michigan; and rural villagers in developing countries dying from preventable diseases because of a lack of clean water and access to basic medicine.

- Men and women organizing to establish the right to marry and start a family regardless of sexual orientation while some homosexuals are still facing death for their relationship choices.

- Increased trafficking of men, women, girls, and boys across national borders, where they are forced into prostitution, domestic servitude, agricultural work, and other forms of forced labor.

All of these have something in common, for it is difficult to talk about them—and, more importantly, to act on them—without invoking the language of human rights. This language is not inconsequential because "to assert a human right is to make a fundamentally political claim: that one is entitled to equal moral respect and to the social status, support, and protection necessary to achieve that respect" (Goodhart, 2009:4).

Human rights have become part of mainstream politics, giving rise to an emerging body of human rights norms and laws. The term *human rights* refers to the normative principles that each person needs in order to live a life with dignity. According to the Universal Declaration of Human Rights,

human rights Inalienable fundamental rights to which a person is inherently entitled simply because he or she is a human being. Conceived as universal and egalitarian, these rights may exist as natural rights or as legal rights in both national and international law.

(UDHR), adopted by the UN in 1948, "All human beings are born free and equal in dignity and rights. They are endowed with reason and conscience and should act towards one another in a spirit of brotherhood."[4] As human beings, individuals can claim certain rights as inalienable and universal. Humans make these fundamentally moral claims in the context of some social structure—ranging from local communities to the state to international organizations—that has the (assumed) duty to protect and fulfill these rights. In this way, human rights are social constructions that have become codified in national, regional, and international legal systems of governance (Donnelly, 2013; Sikkink, 2018).

Human Rights Language

Political theorists have long written about the rights of humanity. Prior to the 20th century, this language emerged gradually, notably with (but not exclusive to) development of the European Enlightenment. Political philosopher John Locke articulated this reasoning by focusing on the fundamental freedoms (natural rights) that individuals possess simply by being human. From this perspective, these rights of individuals predate national and international law, and no state can usurp them. Individuals should not be "deprived of life, liberty, or property without due process of law."[5]

This first group of human rights is often referred to as **first-generation rights**,—or rights that focus on civil liberties and political freedoms and that, for many states, serve as the core to a rights system based on equality and non-discrimination.[6] Some international relations scholars have classified these rights as **proscriptive rights,** or policies and actions that governments cannot do to groups. Discrimination based on race, ethnicity, gender, or sexual orientation is a good example of a breach of such rights. The obligation to respect these proscriptive rights extends to private individuals, organizations, and corporations, and protections include freedom of speech, of religion, and of association as well as rights to receive a fair trial and to vote. These rights can also be termed *negative rights*; akin to the concept of negative liberty ("freedom from"), they focus on refraining from intervening in or interfering with people's rights.

Human rights also include positive rights ensuring that people have equal access to basic needs and goods, similar to the concept of positive liberty ("freedom to"). These **second-generation rights** are largely centered on economic and social rights, such as economic subsistence, education, nutrition, sanitation, work, housing, and health care. For some international relations scholars, these **prescriptive rights** include the essentials that a society and its government are arguably prescribed (obligated) to provide in order to assure certain qualitative standards of life for everyone in the community (see Hertel & Minkler, 2007). Indeed, such rights are mandated to be provided to refugees by signatories of the international Convention Relating to the Status of Refugees. Many people disagree, however, about the role of governments in preserving rights, and about which rights are most essential.

One source of differing views about proscriptive and prescriptive rights is linked to a society's conceptions of individual success or failure: Is it based on

---

first-generation rights Based on the principles of individualism and noninterference, these are "negative" rights based on the Anglo-American principles of liberty. Developed under a strong mistrust of government, they have evolved into "civil" or "political" rights.

proscriptive rights Obligations on a society and its government to try to provide a certain qualitative standard of life that, at a minimum, meets basic needs.

second-generation rights Based on the principles of social justice and public obligation, these tend to be "positive" rights associated with continental European conceptions of liberty as equality. The notion has evolved into what is now called "social" or "economic" rights.

prescriptive rights A right that has existed for so long that it is as effective as a law.

each person's effort or on outside forces, such as government programs and policies? What responsibility does government have to ensure that basic needs are met? Differences in these views about the appropriate role of the state in "promoting" individual human rights have substantial implications on state policy and programming at local, national, and even international levels. They particularly apply in the case of resettling refugees and the questions that the state and its citizens must address in determining the state's responsibility in providing basic needs for the world's most vulnerable.

Not everyone, however, is comfortable with distinctions between categories of rights. Henry Shue (1980) was among the first to criticize the negative and positive categories of rights as an artificial and even problematic division because it often leads to the prioritization of one set of rights over the other. Shue maintained that it is irrelevant whether torture tactics or food deprivation leads to an individual's death. Both are sources of fundamental human rights violations and therefore equally important and indivisible. In other words, people cannot live a life of dignity without *both* security and subsistence; those rights are intertwined. Rights providers are obligated *to avoid depriving* people of necessary rights, *to protect* people from deprivation of those rights, and *to aid* people when they are deprived. All three of these actions require state commitment, political will, and of course, resources. Shue argued that negative and positive rights require state action and substantial investment. A person's physical security requires state resources, such as police forces and criminal courts, just as personal health and education rights demand state resource investment. All rights require social institutions to secure them.

The international community has acknowledged that the abilities of developing countries to fully realize rights, especially social and economic rights, will differ, but shortage of resources does not exempt a state from taking action on these issues. States must "take steps . . . to the maximum of [their] available resources with the view of achieving progressively the full realizations of rights recognized in the present Covenant" (UN General Assembly, 1966, Art. 2). Recent attempts to measure this achievement capacity—that is, what states are able to provide in terms of social and economic rights—finds a mixed picture. A global study demonstrates that while there is "serious underperformance by most of the world's government . . . overall, across the world there has been steady improvement" (Fukuda-Parr, Lawson-Remer, & Randolph, 2015:198).

This more holistic approach to human rights brings us to **third-generation rights**, or those rights focused on the communal aspects of being human. These rights, labeled group or solidarity rights, can only be realized collectively. Group rights demand that we implement them jointly, based upon the agreement and will of the collective. Such rights include the right to a clean environment, the right to economic development, the right to natural resources, and the right to self-determination. Because the rights-holders and duty-holders in this category of rights are not easily identifiable, these rights are some of the most controversial and least institutionalized (Hiskes, 2009; Knox and Pejan 2018).[7]

Whatever the focus, though, the prominent Norwegian sociologist, mathematician, and peace studies advocate Johan Galtung (1994) suggested that

third-generation rights
Remaining largely unofficial, this broad spectrum of rights includes group and collective rights, rights to self-determination, rights to economic and social development, rights to a healthy environment, rights to natural resources, rights to communicate, rights to participation in cultural heritage, and rights to intergenerational equity and sustainability.

the most fruitful way to think about human rights is that ultimately they are supposed to serve basic human needs. These basic human needs, which generate corresponding rights, include:

- *Survival needs—to avoid violence*: the right of individuals and groups to be free from violence.

- *Well-being needs—to avoid misery*: the rights to adequate nutrition and water; to movement, sleep, sex, and other biological wants; to protection from diseases and from adverse climatological and environmental impacts.

- *Identity needs—to avoid alienation*: the rights to establish and maintain emotional bonds with others; to preserve cultural heritage and association; to contribute through work and other activity; and to receive information about and maintain contact with nature, global humanity, and other aspects of the biosphere.

- *Freedom needs—to avoid repression*: the rights to receive and express opinions, to assemble with others, to have a say in common policy, and to choose in such wide-ranging matters as jobs, spouses, where to live, and lifestyle.

natural law A system of law that is purportedly determined by nature and thus universal.

legal positivism A philosophy of law that emphasizes the conventional nature of law—that it is socially constructed and even codified. According to legal positivism, law is synonymous with positive norms, that is, norms made by the legislator or considered as common law or case law.

Unfortunately, people do not recognize many rights until individuals or groups are denied or deprived of them. Human rights scholar Jack Donnelly (1989) referred to this irony as the "possession paradox." Much like their need for oxygen, people are unaware they even possess certain rights—until those rights are denied. Then, it quickly becomes obvious that these rights are essential and necessary to live a life of dignity. Some of the new "emerging" rights include technology-related human rights (access to information, as explored in the WikiLeaks case study in Chapter 3) and environmental human rights to clean water, air, and soil (Hiskes, 2009). For example, the right to clean air is a defining issue in the world's most populous country.

Air pollution is a major environmental health threat, especially for young and developing respiratory systems. Exposure to fine particles in both the ambient environment and in the household causes about seven million premature deaths each year for Chinese children. The economic costs are significant too. For more information, see https://www.who.int/ceh/publications/air-pollution-child-health/en/.

China is home to 16 of the world's 20 most polluted cities, and the average life expectancy of Chinese inhabitants has decreased by 5.5 years largely because of air pollution (Xu, 2014). China's rapid growth over the past 30 years has resulted in serious pollution problems, most notably in the thick smog that settles over cities like Beijing and Shanghai. In January 2017, Chinese human rights lawyers sued the government over air quality, saying that although laws do exist to protect air quality, these laws must be enforced by authorities if China hopes to reduce air pollution to levels considered safe by the World Health Organization.

Explaining Where Human Rights Come From

The idea of human rights as a global norm is relatively new, but moral and philosophical justifications date back centuries before the establishment of the Universal Declaration of Human Rights (UDHR) in 1948. How we justify the existence of human rights determines what we define as "rights," as well as how those rights are best achieved and protected. Two justifications framing the opposite ends of the spectrum are **natural law** and **legal positivism**—the former maintaining that human rights are inherent protections that all people can claim, and the latter asserting that human rights exist only when there are legal guarantees for them.

Perhaps the most widely accepted justification for human rights is embedded in the notion of natural law and rights, particularly as the classical liberal John Locke conceived of them. Proponents of natural rights claim that natural law is the only way to establish the universality of rights. There are certain rights that all people are entitled to, and no government, culture, or civilization is morally allowed to take those rights from them. In his *Second Treatise of Government,* Locke (1689) argued that even in a state of nature (where there is no government or societal norms to govern behavior), all men are free and equal to pursue their own interests. They are limited, however, to only those actions that do not impose on the freedom of others. Thus, Locke's argument states that just by being human, all people have a natural right to their lives, property, and liberty that predates national and international law. Liberalism, grounded in equality and freedom, espouses a belief in these same natural rights. From this perspective, human rights are moral demands that become translated into laws and protected by organizations.

Other theorists start with laws in explaining human rights and why they are what they are. Such theorists, known as legal positivists, might accept that humans possess inherent rights like those listed earlier; however, the task of justifying human rights has been superseded by the establishment of legal documents and the creation of an international human rights regime. The UDHR, written more than 60 years ago, created the framework for today's human rights. Although natural law theorists argue that rights existed before the UDHR and subsequent conventions, legal positivists would argue that they were neither acknowledged nor enforced. From this perspective, then, the task of defining human rights should be undertaken not by philosophers but by legal scholars and through the application of legal institutions, for it is only after the signing of the human rights conventions that there is any global consensus on the legitimacy of these rights. This approach to rights essentially holds that universal human rights exist because they are codified under international law with near-global recognition. Critics of legal positivism argue that this approach to human rights puts them in jeopardy of being seen only as a legal guarantee—if these treaties did not exist, then neither would basic human rights.

From these two examples, we can see how distinct theoretical perspectives derive unique understandings of where human rights come from and how human rights should be defined and respected worldwide. Part of the difficulty, however, lies in identifying "new" or "emerging" rights. These rights are those that have never been codified into legal documents or debated in moral arguments because we assumed they were not under threat or had only recently been denied. In essence, people do not recognize most rights as being rights until they are denied or deprived; once denied, however, it is obvious how essential and necessary they are to living a life of dignity, as set forth in the UDHR. Some of the new "emerging" rights include environmental human rights (clean water, air, and soil) and technology-related human rights (access to information). Do you see these issues as matters of human rights? More deeply, how do you justify the existence of human rights? Where do they come from and how do you know they exist?

As you continue to read this chapter, consider how you would conceptualize and categorize rights. Do you tend to prioritize certain rights over others? Does the international community need to ensure certain rights, such as basic education and nutrition, in order for people to enjoy other rights, such as the right to vote, or vice versa? Do you agree with Shue's view that human rights are indivisible? If so, which rights do you believe constitute the fundamental ones? These and other questions are further explored in the *Thinking Theoretically* feature.

Human Rights Laws and Norms

The horrific human rights violations that defined the 20th century—the killing of over 20 million by Stalin in the USSR, approximately 6 million Jews in Nazi-occupied Europe, and the mass torture and execution of an estimated 70 million Chinese and Tibetans—catalyzed the modern human rights movement. The Holocaust in particular united the international community in groundbreaking ways in an effort to prevent genocide from ever occurring again. All proved to be critical motivators in galvanizing the United Nations (UN) to create laws and institutions and in mobilizing individuals and organizations to raise global consciousness about systematic abuses of human rights by the state.

Nelson Rolihlahla Mandela (1918–2013), born in South Africa, served as the first democratically elected president of South Africa from 1994 to 1999. Before his election, he was a leader in the anti-apartheid movement and cofounder of the armed wing of the African National Congress. During the country's long struggle against the repressive white minority, Mandela was imprisoned for 27 years for his role in the anti-apartheid movement. After leaving office in 1999, Mandela was a global leader in promoting reconciliation, combating poverty, and eliminating inequality throughout Africa. During his lifetime, he received more than 250 honors, including the Nobel Peace Prize in 1993.

The power of people, from elite actors like South Africa's Nelson Mandela to ordinary people like the Madres de la Plaza de Mayo (an association of Argentinean mothers whose children were "disappeared" by the military dictatorship between 1976 and 1983), continue to drive the movement and shape the development of organizations (Bonner, 2007). As nongovernmental organizations (NGOs) became increasingly influential in "naming and shaming" major human rights violations and in sharing information and utilizing technology in innovative ways, these nonstate actors also emerged as critical components of the movement. For example, Human Rights Watch, one of the leading human rights NGOs, talks about their advocacy work as beginning with framing, naming, and shaming in order to publicize, motivate, and mobilize individuals and groups to act. For more, check out these Human Rights Watch videos at https://www.hrw.org/students-and-educators.

THE UN AND INTERNATIONAL LAW.   Under the auspices of the UN, international human rights law began to take shape and set standards of conduct for states soon after World War II. The UN Charter gave the first formal and authoritative expression to the concept of human rights and defined the UN's central role in driving the movement. The most far-reaching and foundational legal expression of human rights, however, is the **Universal Declaration of Human Rights** (UDHR), which the UN General Assembly overwhelmingly adopted on December 10, 1948. Drafted as a "common standard of achievement for all peoples and nations," the Declaration spells out basic economic, social, cultural, civil, and political rights for all. In this way, the UDHR promotes a universal approach to human rights by declaring in Article 1, "All human beings are born free and equal in dignity and rights," and by further proclaiming in Article 2, "Everyone is entitled to all the rights and freedoms set forth in this Declaration, without distinction of any kind."

The UDHR is one of the most comprehensive, yet simple, international human rights agreements to date. Overall, it consists of a preamble and 30 principles that provide the cornerstone of international human rights law. Table 12.1 is a shortened version of the rights articulated in the UDHR, which has become the normative standard in this field. However, as this chapter highlights, the devil is in the details, and how these principled aspirations translate into law, policy, and most important, practice is anything but simple.

Universal Declaration of Human Rights Adopted by the United Nations General Assembly in 1948, it is the most fundamental internationally proclaimed statement of human rights in existence.

Table 12.1 Basic Principles of Human Rights as Codified in the UDHR (Abbreviated Version)

1. All human beings are born free and equal in dignity and rights.
2. Everyone is entitled to all rights and freedoms without distinction of any kind, such as race, color, sex, language, religion, political or other opinion, national or social origin, property, birth, or other status.
3. Everyone has the right to life, liberty, and security of person.
4. No one shall be held in slavery or servitude.
5. No one shall be subjected to torture or to cruel, inhuman, or degrading treatment or punishment.
6. Everyone is equal before the law and entitled to equal protection of the law.
7. No one shall be subjected to arbitrary arrest, detention, or exile.
8. Everyone is entitled in full equality to a fair and public hearing by an independent and impartial tribunal.
9. Everyone charged with a penal offense has the right to be presumed innocent until proved guilty.
10. No one shall be subjected to arbitrary interference with his privacy, family, home, or correspondence, nor to attacks upon his honor and reputation.
11. Everyone has the right to freedom of movement and residence within the borders of each state; the right to leave any country, including his own; and to return to his country.
12. Everyone has the right to seek and to enjoy in other countries asylum from persecution.
13. Men and women of full age, without any limitation due to race, nationality, or religion, have the right to marry and to found a family. They are entitled to equal rights as to consent to marriage, during marriage, and at its dissolution.
14. Everyone has the right to own property alone as well as in association with others.

(Continued)

Table 12.1 *(Continued)*

15. Everyone has the right to freedom of thought, conscience, and religion and to express their beliefs in public and in private.

16. Everyone has the right to freedom of opinion and expression to seek, receive, and impart information and ideas through any media.

17. Everyone has the right to freedom of peaceful assembly and association. No one may be compelled to belong to an association.

18. Everyone has the right to take part in their country's government directly or through freely chosen representatives.

19. Everyone has the right to equal access to public services in his country.

20. The will of the people shall be the basis of the authority of government expressed in periodic elections, which shall be by universal and equal suffrage and shall be held by secret vote or by equivalent free voting procedures.

21. Everyone has the right to work, to choose their work, to reasonable work conditions, and to protection against unemployment.

22. Everyone has the right to equal pay for equal work.

23. Everyone has the right to form and to join trade unions.

24. Everyone has the right to an adequate standard of living, including food, clothing, housing, medical care, and other necessary social services regardless of age, health, or any other circumstance beyond their control.

25. Mothers and children are entitled to special assistance and to equal help, regardless of marital or any other circumstance.

26. Everyone has the right to education. It shall be compulsory and free, at least at the elementary level. Parents have a prior right to choose the kind of education given to their children.

27. Everyone has the right to participate freely in the cultural life of the community, to enjoy the arts, and to share in scientific advancement and its benefits.

28. Everyone has the right to the protection of the moral and material interests resulting from any scientific, literary, or artistic production of which he is the author.

29. Everyone must uphold these rights, except as determined by law to be necessary to meet the just requirements of morality, public order, and the general welfare in a democratic society.

30. Nothing in this Declaration may be interpreted as implying for any State, group, or person any right to engage in any activity or to perform any act aimed at the destruction of any of the rights and freedoms set forth herein.

Notably, the UDHR is a declaration and is not binding in the way a treaty, convention, or covenant is. Still, its overwhelming passage, perceived legal authority, and ongoing influence in practice makes it an important influence on global norms and state behavior (Simmons, 2009). It is the most widely translated document in the world, existing in nearly 360 languages (http://www.un-ngls.org/spip.php?article614). For legal scholars, this is a clear example of **customary law**.

customary law In international law, a reference to the Law of Nations or the legal norms that have developed through the customary exchanges between states over time, whether based on diplomacy or aggression.

Following passage of the UDHR, UN member-states took steps to further elaborate basic rights in the context of two multilateral treaties: the **International Covenant on Civil and Political Rights** (ICCPR; 1966) and the **International Covenant on Economic, Social, and Cultural Rights** (ICESCR; 1966). Together, these three agreements constitute the **International Bill of Human Rights**. More than 80% of countries in the UN have ratified each pact; as Maps 12.1 and 12.2 reflect, a large majority of states have committed to undertake and put into place domestic legislation and other policy measures compatible with and supportive of these treaty obligations and duties. There are, however, some major exceptions. For example, China has not become a party of the ICCPR, and the United States has not ratified the ICESCR. Further, many states have ratified these treaties but have laws, policies, and customs in place that directly violate the standards set forth in the two covenants.

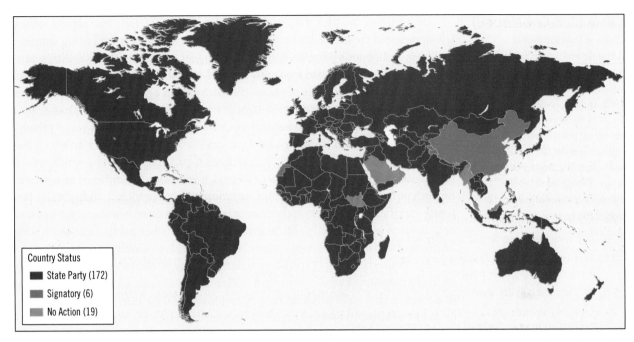

Map 12.1   According the UN High Commission for Human Rights, most countries in the world (172 as of 2018) have signed and ratified the International Covenant on Civil and Political Rights. While this certainly represents global acceptance of particular human rights norms, how this treaty is enforced at the national level and what reservations states have attached to their adoption are important questions.

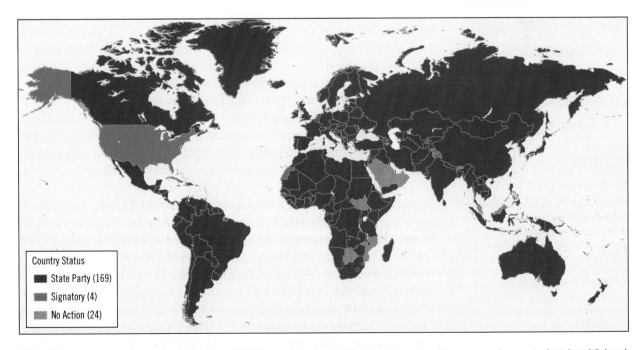

Map 12.2   Most countries in the world (169 as of 2018) have signed and ratified the International Covenant on Economic, Social, and Cultural Rights. Notably, the United States has signed, but has not fully adopted, this foundational human rights treaty. Why might the United States not ratify this human rights treaty but do so with the International Covenant on Civil and Political Rights?

International Covenant on Civil and Political Rights

A multilateral treaty the United Nations General Assembly adopted on December 16, 1966, and in force from March 23, 1976. It commits the parties to respect the civil and political rights of individuals, including the right to life, freedom of religion, freedom of speech, freedom of assembly, electoral rights, and right to due process and a fair trial.

In addition to the two covenants and the UDHR, numerous other UN-sponsored treaties address the rights of specific groups, including women, children, indigenous peoples, migrants, refugees, people with disabilities, and ethnic, racial, and religious groups. Several multilateral treaties also address specific types of abuse. One of these, the Convention against Torture and Other Cruel, Inhuman, or Degrading Treatment or Punishment (UNCAT), has drawn considerable recent attention because of confirmed and alleged abuses of prisoners by US personnel in Iraq, Afghanistan, and elsewhere. The treaty, to which the United States became a party in 1994, defines torture as "any act by which severe pain or suffering, whether physical or mental, is intentionally inflicted on a person for such purposes as obtaining . . . information [or a confession]." Additionally, the treaty specifies: "No exceptional circumstances whatsoever, whether a state of war or a threat of war, internal political instability or any other public emergency, may be invoked as a justification of torture" (UN General Assembly, 1984).

At a domestic level, US military tribunals have punished some low-ranking military personnel who committed indisputable abuses. But it is now widely understood that interrogation tactics employed and authorized by the US government against suspected terrorists beginning with the George W. Bush administration violate international treaty obligations. Since 1984, a total of 155 states have ratified the UNCAT, yet today, 35 years after its creation, many states, including the United States, say that torture can be justified, especially in the case of counterterrorism (see Figure 12.1). As important as it is to ask about public opinion in relation to torture, it is just as important—if not more important—to look at research about the efficiency of torture tactics. For example, some research finds that torture is ineffective for reducing insurgent-perpetrated killings (Sullivan, 2014), and others find respect for human rights of physical integrity—freedom from murder, torture, disappearance, or political imprisonment—is statistically associated with fewer terrorist attacks and conclude that abuse of these rights therefore promotes terrorism (Walsh & Piazza 2010).

We will discuss numerous other treaties and agreements throughout this chapter, including two in particular detail: the Convention on the Rights of the Child (1989) and the Convention on the Elimination of All Forms of Discrimination Against Women (CEDAW, 1979).

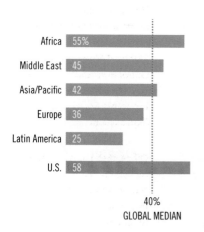

Africa	55%
Middle East	45
Asia/Pacific	42
Europe	36
Latin America	25
U.S.	58

40%
GLOBAL MEDIAN

Figure 12.1   Recent public opinion poll data from the Pew Research Center shows that people in the United States are more likely to say that torture is justified against people suspected of terrorism than those in most of the rest of the world. While China and Ethiopia were not included in this study, it is still striking how differently many Americans view the morality of torture when compared to the rest of the world. Do you believe torture is ever justified? (Source: https://www.pewresearch.org/fact-tank/2016/02/09/global-opinion-use-of-torture/.)

OTHER INTERNATIONAL HUMAN RIGHTS CONVENTIONS.   In addition to UN-sponsored treaties, a number of regional conventions and judicial arms of IGOs supplement the global community's effort to protect and promote human rights. Perhaps the most robust is the European Convention on Human Rights, developed by the Council of Europe, which entered into force in 1953 and is enforced by the European Court on Human Rights. Another example is the American Convention on Human Rights, which was introduced by the Organization of American States, entered into force in 1969, and is upheld by the Inter-American Court of Human Rights. Domestic courts also increasingly apply human rights law (Jayawickrama, 2003; Roht-Arriaza 2015).[8] Additionally, many

NGOs, such as Amnesty International and Human Rights Watch, are concerned with a broad range of human rights and work toward their protection and enforcement. These groups work independently but also in cooperation with the UN, regional organizations, and state actors. They add to the swell of information about and criticisms of abuses and help to promote the adoption of international norms that support human rights (Sikkink, 2011).

Human Rights Enforcement

It would be naïve to argue that the world has even come close to resolving its numerous human rights issues. But we can say that since World War II, a normatively robust global human rights regime has developed where "international human rights norms have been fully internationalized [but] implementation of international human rights obligations remain almost entirely national" (Donnelly, 2013:14). In this way, all states have accepted that human rights are a legitimate subject of contemporary global politics, and most states have adopted a majority of the 18 international human rights treaties.[9] The challenge is in the enforcement of this normative agenda at the regional, national, and local levels. Such enforcement relies on constant advocacy from states, IGOs, NGOs, and private individuals, but it is also furthered by institutional monitoring mechanisms that focus on reporting, agenda-setting, evaluation, and information-sharing. In this vein, it is important to examine human rights enforcement mechanisms and their goals, and then to evaluate them in the context that the modern human rights movement is still relatively young. For example, the United Nations Human Rights Council (UNHCR) was created in 1950 to help European refugees, and now the agency is not only working on major refugee crises in Africa, the Middle East, and Asia but at magnitudes the world has never seen before.

UN Monitoring Mechanisms

The UN sponsors numerous human rights treaties monitored by the **Office of the UN High Commissioner on Human Rights**. From 1946 through early 2006, the UN Commission on Human Rights (UNCHR) was also a leading UN organization on human rights. It consisted of 53 member-countries elected by the UN Economic and Social Council (ECOSOC) for three-year terms. During its annual meetings, the UNCHR was often the site of controversy. One example was a penchant for regularly condemning Israel as violating the rights of Palestinians while at the same time ignoring the human rights violations of other countries. Adding to the dismay about the commission from some sources, ECOSOC regularly named countries with poor human rights records as members. In 2003, the commission elected authoritarian Libya, which had a deplorable human rights record, to its chairmanship. Then, making matters worse, ECOSOC elected Sudan to the commission at nearly the same time that the Security Council was calling on its leaders in Khartoum to cease its genocidal policies in Darfur.

Responding to these recurrent conflicts of interest, the UN General Assembly in 2006 replaced the UNCHR with a new organization,

International Covenant on Economic, Social, and Cultural Rights A multilateral treaty the United Nations General Assembly adopted on December 16, 1966, and in force from January 3, 1976. It commits the parties to work toward the granting of economic, social, and cultural rights to individuals, including labor rights, the right to health, the right to education, and the right to an adequate standard of living.

International Bill of Human Rights An informal name given to one United Nations General Assembly resolution and two international treaties, including the Universal Declaration of Human Rights (adopted in 1948), the International Covenant on Civil and Political Rights (1966) with its two Optional Protocols, and the International Covenant on Economic, Social, and Cultural Rights (1966).

Office of the United Nations High Commissioner on Human Rights Established by a United Nations General Assembly resolution in 1993 and mandated to promote and protect the enjoyment and full realization, by all people, of all rights established in the United Nations Charter and in international human rights laws and treaties.

United Nations Human Rights Council (UNHRC) An intergovernmental body within the United Nations system responsible for strengthening the promotion and protection of human rights around the globe and for addressing situations of human rights violations and making recommendations.

the **UN Human Rights Council (UNHRC)**. A 47-member body elected by the General Assembly, its members are supposed to uphold the highest human rights standards. Nevertheless, the United States was one of the few countries that voted against creating the UNHRC, arguing that there was little to keep it from repeating the mistakes of the UNCHR. More than 10 years after its adoption, UNHRC membership has improved. "In fact, from 2007 to 2015, over 74 percent of the Council's members met Freedom House standards of free or partly free . . . [and] other states with notorious human rights records—Iran, Sudan, Syria, Azerbaijan and Belarus, for example—have either failed in the campaign to win a seat or have withdrawn in the face of heavy opposition" (Piccone, 2016).

Additionally, under the Obama administration in 2009, the United States joined the UNHRC, supporting a number of actions by the Council to move human rights forward regarding both country situations like North Korea and Iran and thematic priorities like **lesbian, gay, bisexual, transgender, queer, asexual and ally** (LGBTQA) rights and albinism rights. For example, the United States led the effort to establish a special rapporteur on the human rights situation in Iran. The approach was to seek reform from within, by being at the table. However, this approach was dramatically reversed by the Trump administration, which withdrew completely from the UNHRC in June 2018, with then US Ambassador to the UN Nikki Haley calling the UNHRC a "cesspool of political bias," largely as a result of the UN body's criticism of the administration's policy of separating children from their parents at the US-Mexico border as well as of Israel's attacks on unarmed civilians in Gaza.[10]

lesbian, gay, bisexual, transgender, queer, asexual and ally In use since the 1990s, and then amended, the term is intended to emphasize diversity of sexuality and gender identity–based cultures and sometimes refers to anyone who is nonheterosexual instead of exclusively to people who are homosexual, bisexual, or transgender.

Despite the US withdrawal, the UNHRC continues to focus on advancing human rights norms via regular dialogue and engagement as well as monitoring of implementation under the auspices of the **Universal Periodic Review** and High Commissioner.[11] The Universal Periodic Review process subjects all states to public discussion of their human rights record every four years. This repeated engagement with the global community on all human rights issues contributes to honest and open discussion about how states can improve human rights within their borders.

Universal Periodic Review A unique process that involves a review of the human rights records of all 192 United Nations member-states once every four years.

This mechanism assumes, however, that states will submit their reports to the Universal Periodic Review, that the reports will be honest reflections of reality on the ground, and that the input from the Council and High Commissioner will be strong and influential in state policy going forward. But as human rights scholar David Forsythe has found, "[T]he change from the Commission to the Council [has] amounted to a repackaging of old wine in a new bottle, although some [still] hold out hope for progress over time" (2012:96). Still, the UNHRC plays a key role in providing the global community with up-to-date information on some of the most serious human rights abuses, and it uses that information to help set the global agenda. On this latter point, it is worth noting how proactive the Council was in 2011 and 2012 in sending independent investigators to Syria early in the current civil war, documenting and condemning human rights abuses occurring on all sides, and calling upon the international community to intervene. More recently, the UNHRC played a vital role in conducting independent inquiries into the use of chemical weapons attacks against civilians by the Assad regime, as well as the deliberate targeting of medical facilities.

Role of NGOs

The Vienna World Conference on Human Rights in 1993 officially recognized the role of NGOs in the promotion of human rights when it noted "their contribution to increasing public awareness of human rights issues, to the conduct of education, training and research in this field, and to the promotion and protection of all human rights and fundamental freedoms" (para 38). NGOs have been advocating for human rights since long before the 1990s, and the insertion of various human rights provisions in the UN Charter can be attributed to the work of NGOs (Glasius, 2013). NGOs engage in a

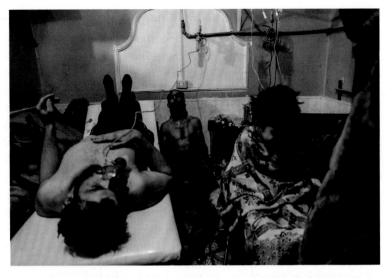

A 2019 study by the Berlin-based Global Public Policy Institute finds evidence of over 300 chemical weapons attacks over the course of the Syrian civil war, which has left hundreds of thousands dead. According to authors Tobias Schneider and Theresa Lütkefend, of the at least 336 attacks that have occurred, Syrian President Bashar al-Assad's regime carried out 98% of them, while the other 2% can be attributed to the Islamic State. These attacks primarily involve dropping chlorine gas, sarin, and sulfur mustard gas on Syrian civilians. For more see, https://www.gppi.net/media/GPPi_Schneider_Luetkefend_2019_Nowhere_to_Hide_Web.pdf.

range of political strategies in their advocacy efforts. From information-sharing to mobilizing activists to delivering humanitarian services, NGOs focus on the prevention, protection, and promotion of human rights laws and norms (Keck & Sikkink, 1998; Lake 2018). One of the most widely used tactics for NGOs is the "naming and shaming" of major human rights violators, in which NGOs publicize countries' violations and urge reform. These efforts can sometimes have a positive impact on holding states accountable to their international commitments (Hafner-Burton, 2008; Neier, 2018).[12]

NGOs have been critical in providing information and distributing life-saving services in Syria and to Syrian refugees. These include large organizations like Save the Children, Mercy Corps, Doctors Without Borders, and Oxfam, as well as much smaller ones like Questscope (a US-based organization that works with Syrians living in Jordan as refugees), Refugees Welcome (a German nonprofit that functions like an "Airbnb for refugees"), and the Karam Foundation (a US-based charity working in Turkey focused on educational opportunities for Syrian children). Lastly, NGOs have been savvy in using symbolic politics by calling upon stories, actions, and images to help the public and those in power make sense of a situation and feel connected to it. From the white scarfs worn by the Madres de la Plaza de Mayo to the rainbows in the LGBTQA rights movement to the red cross and crescent of the International Federation of the Red Cross and Red Crescent Societies, symbols serve as powerful markers of identity—and as marketing tools—for social movements advocating the enforcement of international human rights laws and norms.

CNN The Haitian Cholera Epidemic, Part 1.

CNN The Haitian Cholera Epidemic, Part 2.

State Sovereignty and Enforcement

Since the Treaty of Westphalia in 1648 and the emergence of the modern state, the state's right to sovereign control within its borders has often run counter to efforts to promote and uphold human rights. Until the end of World War II (1945), when human rights were officially recognized under international law, human rights essentially remained a national matter, for states to accept, reject, or simply ignore. Relations between a state and its people were largely the state's concern. The French and American revolutions of the 18th century ushered in some human rights–centric polities, but they still focused on rights for certain advantaged individuals within the state, like white males of European descent. The US Constitution focused quite directly on white males and paid little attention to the idea of women and African Americans as fully human and deserving of rights as citizens.

The international community did begin to chip away at this sovereign control prior to 1945. Of historical note was the 1890 treaty among major European powers effectively obligating all states to abolish the global slave trade, as well as the 1926 Convention to Suppress the Slave Trade and Slavery under the auspices of the League of Nations. Still, the rights of people have until recently been strictly a matter of domestic control. As discussed in earlier chapters, the UN Charter stipulates that foreign intervention in the internal affairs of a sovereign state constitutes a violation of state sovereignty. Many states, like China and Russia, frequently refer to this provision in their vocal support for the primacy of state sovereignty as a global organizing principle. For instance, both states have frequently used their UN Security Council veto power to stop resolutions condemning the violence in Syria, demanding an end to human rights violations by the Syrian government, and threatening nonmilitary sanctions. The two states also vetoed an attempt to refer the Syrian conflict to the International Criminal Court, despite a consensus that all parties in the conflict are committing war crimes and crimes against humanity, including widespread and targeted attacks on civilians resulting in torture, rape, murder, and enforced disappearances.

Russian and Chinese opposition to a collective response to the conflict in Syria has only exacerbated the massive flow of men, women, and children into neighboring countries, Europe, and beyond. Although the military interventions of several countries in the Syrian war has highlighted the continued power and influence of states, the Syrian human rights crisis also demonstrates how state borders quickly become obsolete. Slavery and refugees are interconnected issues that raise critical questions about the movement of people, the porous nature and power of national borders, and the sovereign rights *and* duties of the state. The movement of people across borders as slaves, refugees, or migrants highlights the ways in which the recipient state can function as protector, promoter, and even perpetrator of human rights—sometimes simultaneously.

ILLUSION AND REALITY OF GEOGRAPHIC BORDERS.   One of the most significant challenges in turning human rights rhetoric and laws into reality is the power of state sovereignty and state borders in determining what is right and just. Given the multifaceted processes of globalization discussed in Chapter 5, borders between states are becoming more porous and, in some ways, less relevant. At the same time, many states are increasingly focusing on strengthening and further militarizing geographic borders. The complicated and often contradictory nature of state borders only intensifies when we consider regions with open border policies, like the European Union (EU). For example, coastal countries, such as Italy and Greece and other countries bordering the EU, have been receiving an influx of refugees who hope to gain entry to EU countries and then be able to move to their desired destination. In 2015, the EU was forced to develop a quota plan to deal with the more than 1.2 million refugees and asylum seekers arriving on its shore that year. As of December 2018, despite previously declaring it a "moral duty," the EU essentially abandoned its promise to relocate 160,000 refugees from temporary camps in Greece and Italy to other permanent homes in EU countries. In sum, fewer than 40,000 refugees were resettled, with most EU countries accepting only a fraction of what they had agreed to—and some accepting no refugees at all.[13]

Some EU members, such as Hungary and Poland, believe that being required to accept refugees infringes on their sovereignty, with vocal critiques of resettlement arguing that refugees will not be able to integrate into their country's culture and traditions. Others have resorted to more extreme actions. For example, Slovakia decided that it would comply with the EU quota by allowing admittance only to Christians. In 2015, the Slovakian Interior Ministry spokesman claimed, "We could take 800 Muslims but we don't have any mosques in Slovakia so how can Muslims be integrated if they are not going to like it here?"[14] He later added, "We only want to choose the Christians."[15] These flagrant rejections of EU asylum policy and the European Convention on Human Rights reflect a reassertion of claims to the sanctity of national borders within the EU, as well as a challenge to European integration more generally.

RESPONSIBILITY TO PROTECT (AKA R2P).   One prominent challenge to state sovereignty in the realm of human rights has been the 2005 UN **Responsibility to Protect (aka R2P)** initiative that sets forth a set of principles based on the idea that sovereignty is not a privilege but a responsibility. This provides a framework that obligates states to intervene in cases where massive human rights abuses are occurring and a justification for using tools that already exist, including mediation, early warning mechanisms, economic sanctions, and UN Charter **Chapter VII** powers to prevent and stop mass atrocities. It is this framework that drove the international community to act in the case of Libya in 2011 with a North Atlantic Treaty Organization–led humanitarian intervention to aid the Libyan people in bringing down long-ruling autocrat Muammar Gaddafi. Challenging the sovereign authority of the state is not just happening in the context of war, famine, and migration; indeed, the international community is increasingly intervening in the name of human rights.

Responsibility to Protect (aka R2P) A global United Nations initiative doctrine, endorsed by the United Nations in 2005, which is based on the idea that sovereignty is not a privilege but instead confers responsibilities on states and their leaders—first and foremost, to ensure the well-being of their citizens.

Chapter VII Part of the Charter of the United Nations that deals with action regarding threats to peace, breaches of the peace, and acts of aggression.

According to the UN, the Rohingya genocide is the "world's fastest-growing refugee crisis." UNICEF estimates 687,000 have sought refuge dangerously by boat, primarily in neighboring Bangladesh, and over half of them are child refugees. Beyond Bangladesh, the U.N estimates that there are at least 420,000 Rohingya refugees in Southeast Asia in 2017. This does not account for the over half a million Rohingya still in Myanmar facing oppression, torture, and death.

The KONY 2012 campaign by Invisible Children was one of the most prominent human rights advocacy efforts in recent years, and still one of the top 10 viral videos of all time. This nonprofit effort goes against all best practices for going viral: it's long, serious, and tragic. The symbol of the campaign is an upside-down triangle, illustrating how the masses—ordinary people like you and me—can effect change throughout the world. It is an effort to make "the many" more powerful, through the use of social media, than the few in top decision-making roles. The symbol raises important questions about power: who has it, who doesn't, and how it can best be utilized.

THE INFORMATION TECHNOLOGY REVOLUTION. Cases such as Libya and Syria, or more recently the ethnic cleansing of tens of thousands of Rohingya Muslims in Myanmar, highlight how human rights continue to be a defining feature of the 21st century. Human rights challenges are enormous in terms of the issues at stake, the varied strategies of activism, and the ethical choices behind these activities. Not surprisingly, technology has played a significant factor by providing a much more extensive and graphic detailing of human rights atrocities through television, the Internet, and social media. Reading about human rights abuses does not have anywhere near the emotional impact of seeing images of violence, torture, and other abuses in vivid color on television screens and computer monitors in the intimate surroundings of our own homes. Such images are harder to ignore and have added to slowly changing attitudes about human rights abuses. The impact of technology, and of social media in particular, on the human rights movement is abundantly clear in the Invisible Children campaign aimed at finding, arresting, and trying Joseph Kony, the leader of the Lord's Resistance Army operating in Northern Uganda, the Central African Republic, the Democratic Republic of the Congo, and South Sudan, for war crimes and crimes against humanity.

Invisible Children, a US-based NGO, started the KONY 2012 campaign with a 30-minute video that went viral, receiving over 100 million views in six days.[16] The video received significant criticism and backlash for its oversimplification of the Uganda conflict, its lack of Ugandan voice or perspective, and its emphasis on punitive justice for Kony over all other basic needs in Uganda. Nonetheless, it garnered media attention from all major international and US-based news sources, as well as an increased US military presence. Yet despite the viral success of making Kony a household name, the war criminal remains at large. Further, Invisible Children was unable to capitalize on its viral success and eventually had to substantially downsize its operations. To be sure, the awareness-raising campaign was incredible, but only time will tell whether or not Kony will face justice.

Human rights success stories are obviously complex; although positive change is happening, new challenges and setbacks are also evident. In the sections that follow, we will discuss how real changes have started to take hold and where human rights groups have made progress to translate rhetoric into reality, and we will consider the problems and barriers that human rights advocates face.

Barriers to Progress on Human Rights

Unfortunately, a state's signature and ratification of a treaty do not mean that it always complies with a treaty's precepts. For instance, in 1971 Iraq ratified both the ICCPR and the ICESCR, yet throughout the 33 years of its reign of terror, Saddam Hussein's regime egregiously violated many—if not most—of the rights set forth in both covenants. As we have noted, the impact of human rights treaties, the efforts of IGOs and NGOs, and the general advancement of human rights norms have all been mixed. Enforcement is often lacking, and in some ways, human rights laws challenge the international community to rethink what it means to hold states accountable to their normative and legal commitments. Related to, but also beyond, states' claims to sovereignty are a number of other significant challenges to the full realization of international human rights, particularly when it comes to the rights of refugees.

A DIFFERENCE IN CULTURAL STANDARDS.   Cultural beliefs and practices remain a serious obstacle in the promotion and protection of human rights. What constitutes a human rights violation in one country may be culturally acceptable in another (Dahre 2017; De Bary, 2004). **Cultural relativism** rejects **universalism** and the idea that people and their rights can (or should) be separate from or precede the societies in which they live. Cultural relativists argue that human rights are normative values appropriate to the cultures out of which they emerge. They frequently criticize the mainstream international human rights movement for lacking respect for different cultural, religious, and philosophical traditions. Relativists therefore assert that in a world of diverse cultures, no single standard of human rights exists—or is likely to exist. Cultural relativist arguments can emerge as a reaction to the argument that universal human rights are a new form of imperialism, or as scholar Nicholas Rengger described, "a mask for Western interests" (2011:1173). This debate is highlighted in the *Challenge Your Assumptions* feature.

cultural relativism The principle that an individual human's beliefs and activities are understood by others in terms of that individual's own culture.

universalism A belief that human rights are derived from sources external to society, such as from a theological, ideological, or natural rights basis.

POLITICAL SELECTIVITY.   A second problem is political selectivity, which disposes all countries to feel shock when their opponents transgress human rights but ignore abuses they, their allies, or their potential allies commit. The United States regularly proclaims its commitment to the global spread of democracy, yet it continues to support the governments of Saudi Arabia, the Philippines, and several other unabashedly authoritarian regimes. Making

CHALLENGE YOUR ASSUMPTIONS

Is Human Rights Advocacy a Form of Modern-Day Imperialism?

Discussions of imperialism often imply historical narratives about European dominance and expansion through violent colonial conquest. Many see this as a problem of the past, when powerful states would claim land as their colonies, ruling with an iron fist for nationalistic and economic gains. Anthropologist Laura Agustín, however, argues that imperialist values run rampant in modern society, particularly in the context of the global human rights movement.

Consider human rights "activists" today who often combine celebrity status with their charity. For example, Hollywood went through a phase where the best "accessory" was a child from an underdeveloped country, and now everyone wants a pair of shoes from TOMS, a for-profit company that matches every pair of purchased shoes with a new pair of shoes for a child in need. Critics like Agustín argue that the promotion of human rights has become an industry in the United States, a tool to force American culture and ideology onto other countries and peoples in the name of human rights—in other words, another imperialist venture.

Agustín uses *New York Times* columnist and reporter Nicholas Kristof as an example of this Western, imperial approach. Kristof has investigated and written many reports on human trafficking in foreign countries, looking at prostitution and brothels as the enemy of freedom. He has participated in police raids on brothels and has even purchased a slave to give her back her freedom. In the media's eyes (and his 2.06 million Twitter followers), Kristof is a hero. They believe that by closing these brothels or buying these slaves, he is improving lives, giving young girls a "second chance."

The reality, however, is that the "rescued victims" often "choose" to return to oppressive situations. They are poor, uneducated, and—perhaps most importantly—unloved, with no social safety nets; thus, they often find freedom more problematic than enslavement. They are ideal prey for traffickers. When a brothel closes, desperation ensues, and they are willing to search for any job. Traffickers exploit this weakness, and through fraud, force, or coercion, they lure them into sex trafficking. From Agustín's vantage point, Kristof's stories revolve around the thrilling tale of their rescue, where good triumphs evil. But there is little interest in their reintegration to society, where the real work begins. This less exciting story requires a much longer-term attention span and much greater investment from the human rights movement and society in general.

Kristof's dedicated readers might argue that at least he is doing *something* in trying to prevent human rights violations. Agustín considers such rhetoric again to be reminiscent of colonial paternalism, where any signs of development served to quell the doubters. If Kristof's efforts save one woman from sex trafficking but create an environment where more women will be trafficked, do we count that as a victory? If he saves one but does nothing about the increasing demand for cheap labor, whether in the sex industry or in agribusiness, is this really working toward the common good? This situation is challenging and requires that you consider both the intended and unintended consequences of the human rights movement.

Source: Some of this discussion draw on posts at http://www.lauraagustin.com/.

matters worse, even though the United States is the self-proclaimed champion of human rights and innocent civilian protection, it continues to carry out targeted killings, often with the use of aerial drones, against alleged militants outside conventional war zones, including strikes in Yemen, Pakistan, Libya, and Somalia. In July 2016, the director of national intelligence claimed that the United States had killed between 64 and 116 "noncombatants" in such strikes since 2009, a figure that advocacy groups argue undercounts the civilian lives lost. Some human rights groups estimate closer to 1,100 civilians killed.[17]

A LACK OF SUPPORT.   A third challenge is that concern about human rights remains a low priority for most countries. In the abstract, most people support advancing human rights, but in actual application, it becomes clear that support is shallow. For example, a recent survey by the Pew Research Center in the United States that asked respondents about important foreign policy goals for their country found that promoting human rights ranked 19th of 26 possible goals.[18] Consider, for a moment, where human rights rank for you as a foreign policy goal amid such others as physical security, economic prosperity, or even environmental quality.

LEGAL BIAS.   Lastly, many activists find the legal emphasis of human rights to be state-centric, narrow, and even patriarchal in its understanding of who counts as humans, where rights violations actually occur, and which institutions are best situated to address abuses. Take, for example, women' rights. Historically, the "rights of man," and even the rights originally codified in the US Constitution, denied rights to women, among other nondominant groups. Although the modern human rights movement has recognized rights of gender equality in the International Bill of Rights, and women's rights specifically in the Convention on the Elimination of All Forms of Discrimination Against Women (1979), there is still a long way to go to reach full equality. For example, feminists are very critical of the emphasis on law and top-down approaches to human rights protection. This legalist bias focuses attention on rights violated in the public sphere by state actors, which largely ignores the majority of human rights abuses that women in the world suffer (Richards & Haglund, 2015). Human rights violations for many women occur in "private" contexts of family and community and are generally perpetrated by nonstate actors, such as spouses and family members (Bunch & Reilly, 1994).[19] In this way, some feminists question why domestic violence is not treated with the same seriousness and commitment as are acts of torture, when in reality the suffering caused by domestic violence is very much the same and perhaps much more pervasive (Swaine, 2018). Clearly, there are differences in how the reach of law and the hierarchy of violence and victims play out in human rights practice.

Human Rights Issues and Advocacy

Advocacy efforts and media coverage around the issue of displaced people peaked in 2014 and 2015, when reports, photographs, and video footage emerged documenting the plight of the thousands of mostly Syrian and Iraqi refugees fleeing their homes and attempting to seek refuge in Europe on boats

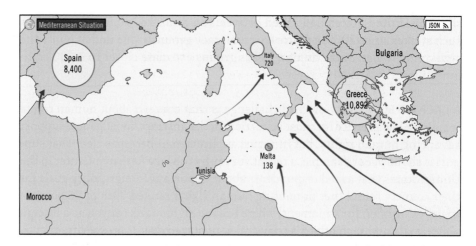

Map 12.3   Increasing numbers of refugees and migrants take their chances aboard unseaworthy boats and dinghies in a desperate bid to reach Europe. The vast majority of those attempting this dangerous crossing are in need of international protection as they flee war, violence, and persecution in their country of origin. Every year, these movements continue to exact a devastating toll on human life. According to UNHCR, 2,275 lives were lost crossing the Mediterranean in 2018 alone.

across the Mediterranean (see Map 12.3). By 2015, close to 1.5 million had survived the dangerous voyage, while over 10,000 were reported dead or missing. Although the number of refugees and migrants crossing the Mediterranean dropped significantly in 2016, the death toll was the highest ever recorded with an average of 14 people dying every day in the sea.[20]

Advocacy efforts changed the conversation on the global refugee crisis when images went viral of a three-year old Syrian boy, Alan Kurdi, dead on a Turkish beach. This event shocked the global conscience and highlighted our collective failure to protect the world's most vulnerable. The image not only roused the world to the massive number of desperate people fleeing their homes, but also energized activist outreach and government policy in Europe and Canada. For example, 2016 surveys conducted by the Environics Institute in Canada found that public opinion toward immigration is the most favorable it has been in decades and has become noticeably more positive since 2015.[21] In a 2018 public opinion survey, Canada topped the list of countries that found immigrants to be a strength, as seen in Figure 12.2.[22]

In many ways, Canada is seen to be a world leader in terms of its immigration policies, with the UNHCR, Filippo Grandi, praising the country for its "extraordinary generosity, openness and willingness" to help displaced people.[23] In 2019, Canada announced that it planned to take more than 1 million new immigrants by 2021. Canada relies on both public and private partnerships for this work. For example, Canada's Refugee and Humanitarian Resettlement Program along with private sponsors help resettle refugees once they have been identified by the UNHCR. Allowing private sponsorship of refugees for up to one year is distinctive to Canadian immigration policy and reflects the degree of personal responsibility thousands of Canadians feel toward Syrian families. As we will see in this section, it is critical to understand both the cause and global responses to human rights violations from all levels of analysis—individual, state, and system. To put a specific human face on the plight of displaced persons, consider the experiences of poet Warsan Shire in the Personal Narrative feature.

Critical Human Rights Violations

Despite the development of international human rights norms and laws, human rights violations continue to occur in every country in the world, often in horrific and systematic ways. For example, the **Convention on the Rights of the Child** (1989) is one of the most widely ratified international treaties. Somalia, South Sudan, and the United States are the only three states not to have ratified the treaty. Still, the world's children suffer tremendously; millions have no access to education, work long hours under hazardous conditions, and are subject to forced marriage before the age of 18.[24] Two ongoing issues facing the most vulnerable of the world's children today include forced military conscription and unaccompanied child refugees fleeing armed conflict zones.

CHILD SOLDIERS. The UN's Special Representative for Children and Armed Conflict estimates there are at least 250,000 child soldiers worldwide, which is likely an underestimation given the difficulty in collecting accurate data from war-torn regions. Of these, an estimated 40% of all child soldiers are girls, who serve not only as soldiers but also as "wives" or sex slaves to the male combatants.[25] Child soldiers are often forced to kill their own parents, accept their abductors as their new families, and become addicted to drugs and/or alcohol. Although many children are forcibly recruited, others join government forces or armed opposition groups out of social and/or economic desperation in a belief that belonging to such groups offers their best chance for survival. A recent report from Human Rights Watch found that child soldiers are pervasive among armed groups in Iraq, Syria, South Sudan, and the Philippines.[26] Although these may be the most glaring examples, there are at least 10 others on the "list of shame" for recruiting and using child soldiers, according to the UN Special Representative of the Secretary-General

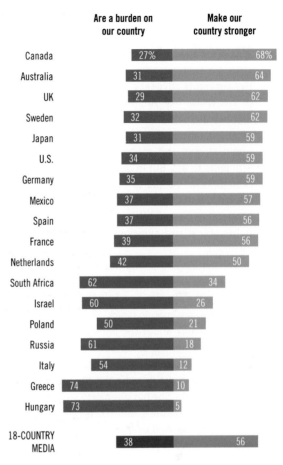

Are a burden on our country / **Make our country stronger**

	Are a burden on our country	Make our country stronger
Canada	27%	68%
Australia	31	64
UK	29	62
Sweden	32	62
Japan	31	59
U.S.	34	59
Germany	35	59
Mexico	37	57
Spain	37	56
France	39	56
Netherlands	42	50
South Africa	62	34
Israel	60	26
Poland	50	21
Russia	61	18
Italy	54	12
Greece	74	10
Hungary	73	5
18-COUNTRY MEDIA	38	56

Figure 12.2 In a 2018 survey of the top migrant destination countries, majorities of publics say immigrants strengthen their countries. By contrast, majorities in five countries surveyed—Hungary, Greece, South Africa, Russia, and Israel—see immigrants as a burden to their countries. With the exception of Russia, these countries each have fewer than 5 million immigrants.

Convention on the Rights of the Child A human rights treaty setting out the civil, political, economic, social, health, and cultural rights of children.

Powerful Words, Pop Culture, and Poetry

Human rights advocacy often leads us to think about global NGOs like Amnesty International or Human Rights Watch. We focus on the ways these large organizations raise awareness about situations of human rights abuses and mobilize people and their governments to act. But in order for human rights advocacy to move people to act, stories must be told and human connections made. Advocacy work requires connecting people to the actual survivors of human rights abuse and allowing the stories of victims to be heard.

Warsan Shire, a young poet, educator, and African feminist, has a tremendous capacity to capture in words and verse the human experience, particularly for those who suffer, are marginalized, or are oppressed. Shire writes primarily about the immigrant experience and speaks from her life as an outsider, as an immigrant. Born in Kenya to Somali parents, Shire grew up in London, where she became the city's first Young Poet Laureate in 2014. She has given new understanding and feeling to how we think about belonging, displacement, love, and home. And although she doesn't use the language of human rights specifically, her talent takes her readers there.

She has written several collections of poems, including her first book, *Teaching My Mother How to Give Birth*, published in 2011 with flipped eye publishing. One of the poems in this book, entitled "Home," captures the

stark reality of some of the horrifying decisions refugee parents must make. Shire writes:

> you only run for the border when you see the whole city running as well . . .
> you have to understand, no one puts their children in a boat unless the water is safer than the land . . .
> I want to go home, but home is the mouth of a shark home is the barrel of the gun, and no one would leave home unless home chased you to the shore . . .

This reading gives deep meaning and understanding to this chapter's discussion of the millions of people displaced across the globe. You can listen to a full reading of this hauntingly powerful piece, at https://www.youtube.com/watch?v=p50wrd2JiX4.

With over 78,000 Twitter followers (@warsan_shire), Shire represents a new genre of poets who can capture empathy and power, often in under 280 characters. Her quiet charisma and poignant lines have particular resonance in the digital age. Her international reach and capacity to cross into pop culture are impressive. Her poetry has been translated into Italian, Spanish, Portuguese, Danish, Estonian, and Swedish, and it was adapted for Beyoncé's album *Lemonade*. Check out her work, and consider how she uses words to explore memory, voice, trauma, healing, and belonging. How do those experiences relate to our understanding of those people forced to leave their homes?

for Children and Armed Conflict. Map 12.4 illustrates several hotspots for the use of child soldiers.

REFUGEES AND INTERNALLY DISPLACED PERSONS.   Children also suffer as refugees and internally displaced persons resulting from armed conflict. Syrian children have endured tremendous rights violations since the civil war began in 2011, and NGOs have found increased rates of suicide, human trafficking, and sexual slavery.[27] From physical security to meeting basic human needs, children forced to flee their homes are particularly vulnerable, and their painful experiences have significant long-term consequences. For example, a recent UNICEF report found that across the Middle East, a total of 2.7 million Syrian children are not attending school. Most of those young people are still inside war-torn Syria, but about 380,000 in Turkey alone cannot enjoy their basic human rights

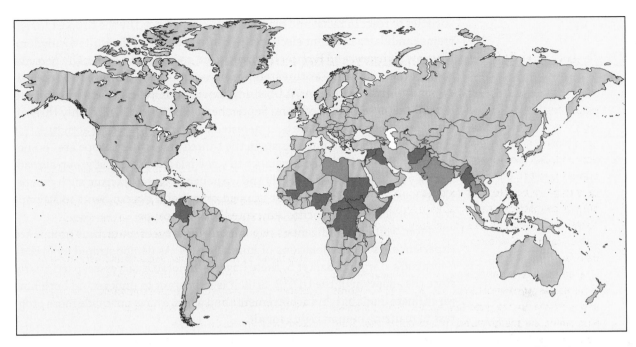

Map 12.4   The map shows (in red) the countries where armed forces or groups recruit children, according to the UN's "list of shame" in 2017. These countries are Afghanistan, Central Africa Republic, Colombia, Democratic Republic of Congo, Iraq, Mali, Myanmar, Nigeria, Philippines, Somalia, South Sudan, Syria, and Yemen. In addition to countries on the UN list, nonstate armed groups also recruit children in India, Pakistan, Israel/State of Palestine, Libya, Philippines, and Thailand (shown in orange).

to education.[28] It is difficult to overestimate the serious damage done to a community when its children have no access to education and know only violence, war, and life in refugee camps.

Refugees, asylum seekers, **internally displaced persons**, and economic migrants suffer the full range of human rights abuses as they are forced to leave their homes, livelihoods, and communities. For the old and the young, rights abuses occur during and after the migration, sometimes for decades in exile. Although no continent is immune from mass displacement, most of the world's refugees are located in the Global South.

According to the 1951 Convention Relating to the Status of Refugees, states are required to protect the basic rights of those granted refugee status as well as to accept the right of resettlement and legal protection from deportation, or forcible return to their country of origin. The fundamental principle here is that people should never be forced into harm's way. Unfortunately, this definition covers only about one-third of the world's displaced; thus, the legal status protects only a percentage of the affected population. Further, the human rights challenges for these groups have only intensified in the wake of globalization and the "War on Terror," as states are increasingly concerned about terrorism, illegal migration, organized crime, and even jobs.

Unfortunately, as mentioned, many Americans and Europeans have become fearful of certain immigrant populations, even though the causal links to terrorism simply do not exist. These fears have led even the most liberal

refugees People who are outside their country of origin or habitual residence because they have suffered persecution on account of race, religion, nationality, or political opinion or because they are a member of a persecuted "social group."

internally displaced persons People who are forced to flee their homes but who remain within that countries borders.

societies to react in racist and bigoted ways, as evidenced by the support for extreme candidates in recent elections in the United States, the United Kingdom, Norway, Hungary, and France. In many cases, societies automatically perceive some of these "victims" as threatening, or even criminal. However, the empirical reality is much different. A US study, for example, found that of the close to 800,000 refugees resettled from September 11, 2001 until 2017, only three of those resettled refugees have been arrested for planning terrorist activities.[29] It is much more likely that terrorists in the United States and Europe are "homegrown."[30] They may pledge allegiance to some Islamic extremist group abroad, but they are acting independently and without any direction from such groups. Nonetheless, this reality has not stopped xenophobic governments to attempt travel restrictions for specific "unwanted" ethnic groups.

From women to indigenous populations to refugees, numerous groups are experiencing serious violations of human rights. As demonstrated by Malala Yousafzai's story in Chapter 3, there have been notable successes, particularly since the adoption of the UDHR. Still, it is important to understand both how we evaluate human rights achievements and why we have not made more progress to realizing human rights for all.

Measuring Human Rights

Increasingly, human rights scholars and practitioners are recognizing the critical need for, as well as the challenges of, systematically measuring and reporting on compliance with global human rights standards. Measurement is important not only for advocates attempting to make their case to state actors, but also for human rights research aimed at improving accountability mechanisms for such standards. We measure human rights to describe and document situations and events, using the raw information to serve a number of important functions. Human rights scholar Todd Landman (2004, 2006) has argued that measurement enables us to:

- *Classify* different rights violations and abusers.
- *Monitor* the degree to which states promote and protect human rights.
- *Recognize patterns* of the causes and consequences of human rights violations.
- *Advocate* for necessary rights improvements at local, national, and global levels.

Human rights measurement can focus on events, like the disappearances in Latin America; on surveys, which examine individual perceptions of protected or abused rights; on socioeconomic statistics, such as the Human Development Index or measures of gross domestic product; and on standards, such as the democratic principles coded into the Freedom House scales. In 2018, Freedom House data found democracy to be its most serious crisis in decades (see Figure 12.3). Basic tenets including guarantees of free and fair elections, the rights of minorities, freedom of the press, and the rule of law came under attack around the world.

Although policy-makers usually look for these kinds of "hard" data sources, collecting the necessary qualitative and quantitative information to make such concrete assessments presents a number of significant challenges. To begin, when measuring human rights, we are assuming that everyone agrees on what exactly constitutes a particular right and its fulfillment. Data collectors often deal with information that is biased and incomplete as well. Even government reports frequently are suspect in terms of reliability; these can intentionally be vague or lack information. Further, sometimes there are incentives for nongovernmental organizations to underreport or exaggerate human rights violations, as a means of politicizing certain rights issues. What makes a particular measurement a good indicator (if there can be such a thing)? The next sections illustrate a number of the challenges inherent in measuring human rights in objective and defensible ways.

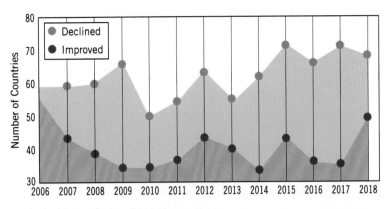

Figure 12.3   According to the 2018 Freedom House report, democracy is in crisis globally. Seventy-one countries suffered net declines in political rights and civil liberties, including guarantees of free and fair elections, rights of minorities, freedom of the press, and the rule of law, with only 35 countries showing gains. This marked the 12th consecutive year of decline in global freedom.

WOMEN'S RIGHTS.   Let's consider, for example, the concept of women's rights. When trying to gauge the development of women's rights in Afghanistan or Iraq, for example, we often look at whether or not women are voting in democratic elections. Although the right to vote is certainly important, just because a woman has the right to vote does not mean that she feels safe enough to actually travel to the election polls, or that she is literate enough to read the ballot. Similarly, regarding women's right to work, many optimists point to the increasing number of women in the workforce worldwide. But does access to jobs necessarily translate into empowerment and dignity for women? This measure of women's rights does not, for instance, take into account the disparity between women's and men's wages—even in the United States, where women on average across all industries make approximately $0.80 for every dollar a man earns in a similar position, amounting to significant income differences over one's lifetime.[31] Measuring women's rights by looking at the increasing percentages of women in the workforce also assumes that women's working conditions are healthy and that, at the end of the week, they actually have control over how they spend their earned income. These illustrations raise questions about what it is we are measuring and how we interpret these measures of women's rights.

HUMAN TRAFFICKING.   From labor trafficking in agriculture, brick-making, and textile factories to sex-trafficking in countries like the United States or Thailand and at sporting events like the World Cup, **human trafficking** is a modern-day form of slavery that affects most supply chains in the global economy. The International Labor Organization estimates that there are 40.3 million victims of human trafficking globally, amounting to a $150 billion industry worldwide.[32]

There are many obstacles to measuring human rights—both in terms of problems and progress. Although these obstacles are not insurmountable, the fact the most human trafficking exists in a black market setting makes

human trafficking The illegal trade of human beings for the purposes of reproductive slavery, commercial sexual exploitation, forced labor, or a modern-day form of slavery.

Lana H. Haroun
@lana_hago

Follow

Taken by me
@lana_hago
#8aprile

2:01 PM - 8 Apr 2019

20,196 Retweets   68,863 Likes

1.0K   20K   69K

Alaa Salah, the iconic female student in Sudan, reflects the many women who have peacefully fought for decades against Khartoum's militarism and have laid the foundations for bringing an end to President Bashir's oppressive dictatorship and the country's ongoing revolution against military rule. That day she chanted, "They imprisoned us in the name of religion, burned us in the name of religion . . . killed us in the name of religion…But Islam is innocent. Islam tells us to speak up and fight against tyrants . . . the bullet doesn't kill. What kills is the silence of the people," quoting a poem by Sudanese poet Azhari Mohamed Ali. For more, see https://www.aljazeera.com/indepth/opinion/alaa-salah-sudanese-mothers-190501175500137.html.

CNN Video The Millennium Seed Bank, Part 1 and Part 2

measurement in this area particularly difficult. The international community needs more comprehensive—as well as disaggregated—data that it can cross-check from a variety of sources in order for the human rights movement to maintain its momentum in this long-enduring venue for human rights violations. You might want to review yet again the *Challenge Your Assumptions* feature presented earlier.

Student-Led Human Rights Campaigns

As the preceding sections argue, reliable information is crucial to human rights advocacy. Because the logic of human rights relies on the simple premise of inherent equality, these rights embody revolutionary justifications insomuch as they undermine assumed authority and subjection. From the Greensboro, North Carolina, sit-ins in 1960 to apartheid divestment in the 1970s and 1980s to Tiananmen Square in 1989 to the Iran protests in 1999, student resistance and protest are not new.[33] We have, however, seen an increase in student advocacy on rights issues ranging from race to immigration to guns in the United States, as elsewhere, during recent years. Many of these revolutionary rights-based campaigns have emerged in the context of society's young people, particularly those in colleges and universities around the world.

As a center of academic discussion and debate, college students are some of the first to bring attention to pressing human rights abuses. Look at your own university's student activities and organizations catalogue. More than likely, multiple groups on campus are dedicated to one or more rights-based issues. Some focus on domestic concerns, like poverty, homelessness, or LGBTQA issues. Others may focus on international causes, like preventing or punishing genocide or ensuring environmental rights. Students are key to human rights advocacy, as they are capable of creating media attention, mobilizing support for their cause, and bringing about subsequent change in policies and regulations worldwide.

As we emphasize throughout this book, you should not discount the power of individuals (and their collective voices) to effect change in our world. As the vignettes in the *Personal Narrative* features highlight, individuals indeed have influenced their communities and the world. Each of us can find ways to effect change, but one interesting entry point is the NGO, the Harry Potter Alliance (www.thehpalliance.org), which is "changing the world by making activism accessible through the power of story. Since 2005, we've engaged millions of fans through our work for equality, human rights, and literacy."[34] Take a few minutes to check out what this one group is doing to enhance individual action and empower global change in the human rights arena. Beyond that NGO example, two recent movements of student agency include the anti-sweatshop campaign and anti-trafficking movement.

THE ANTI-SWEATSHOP MOVEMENT.   We can trace the anti-sweatshop movement back to the early 1990s. After President Bill Clinton's election to office, Secretary of Labor Robert Reich wanted to make anti-sweatshop legislation a key policy point for the administration. Unfortunately, there was little awareness of the issue, and even less media interest in covering it. This policy environment changed in 1996, however, following the high-profile exposé of a **sweatshop** producing a clothing line for celebrity Kathie Lee Gifford. The NGO National Labor Committee in Support of Human and Worker Rights researched and found evidence that her endorsed line, which Walmart sold, was manufactured in Central American sweatshops rampant with human rights abuses, including the use of child labor. The media frenzy around the investigation catapulted the issue of sweatshops into the mainstream consciousness and proved a rallying point for the anti-sweatshop campaign.

> **sweatshop** A negative term for any working environment that is unacceptably difficult or dangerous. Employees often work long hours for very low pay, regardless of laws mandating overtime pay or a minimum wage.

Probably closer to home for each of you, the collegiate apparel industry is a $4.5 billion a year industry, licensing and selling everything from caps to sweatshirts to socks. University students buy t-shirts and gym shorts with their logos, mascots, and slogans emblazoned everywhere. In recent years, however, many students have been shocked to discover that these items were stitched together by workers paid mere pennies a day for 16- to 20-hour shifts, often in dangerous and even violent work environments. In the mid-1990s, students at Duke University staged a sit-in, demanding that the university implement a code of conduct for all companies that manufactured Duke apparel. Students at universities across the nation followed Duke's lead and took action to bring the anti-sweatshop movement to light. Students went on hunger strikes, staged sit-ins, and held press conferences to protest university contracts with known violators of labor rights.

The protests were also often highly innovative. At the University of Wisconsin, students held a press conference where they presented their chancellor with a jumbo check for 16 cents—the hourly wage of workers in a Nike factory making Badger gear. Students at Yale hosted a "knit-in," while students at other schools hosted fashion shows describing the working conditions where university apparel was made.[35] These events generated media attention, putting even more pressure on university officials.

Partly in response to these and other protests, the Clinton administration brought together a group of human rights organizations, labor unions, and representatives from the garment industry in the Apparel Industry Partnership. They created a framework to guide corporate codes of conduct. Many believed, however, that it did not go far enough to protect workers abroad. Several universities put together codes of conduct for their licensees to follow, including key provisions like a safe work environment, right to unionize, and laws forbidding the use of child labor. Although these were small steps in protecting workers' rights worldwide, the college anti-sweatshop movement established the precedent that garment companies must responsibly carry out all stages of the manufacturing process, both at home and abroad.

Human rights advocates, business leaders, and consumers have become more attuned to sweatshop labor and other abuses in the supply chains that produce the goods we buy each day, but much work remains to better understand the conditions under which local communities and companies can work together in ways that are just, sustainable, and socially responsible (Hertel, 2019). Consumers are a critical part of this work, and the anti-sweatshop movement continues today on college campuses, most prominently through the work of United Students Against Sweatshops. Some universities are even becoming Fair Trade Certified campuses. Is yours?

THE ANTI-TRAFFICKING MOVEMENT. Similar to the anti-sweatshop movement, the anti-trafficking movement began in the late 1990s. It gained serious momentum on college campuses, however, at the turn of the 21st century. Human trafficking refers to the "act of recruiting, transporting, transferring, harboring or receiving a person through a use of force, fraud or coercion, for the purpose of exploiting them."[36] Human trafficking is a form of modern-day slavery, ranging from adult and child sex tourism; forced domestic, restaurant, agricultural, and factory labor; debt bondage; forced marriage through the mail-order bride industry; and forced prostitution. Exploiters often forcibly deliver victims to brothels or coerce them to mine minerals in dangerous regions. Traffickers use a range of techniques to capture victims, including abduction, deceit, seduction, and promises of a better life. The clientele and consumers drive the trafficking market, making it one of the most lucrative industries in the modern era.

Over the past few years, students and lawmakers have become increasingly aware of the scope and magnitude of the issues. So far, the anti-trafficking movement on college campuses focuses on a select group of offenders with whom they are already familiar. For example, Nike and Gap, both targets of the anti-sweatshop movement, continue to come under fire for using slave labor in their factories. Further investigation has found that many garment factories are not simply underpaying workers—the workers are unable to leave or quit if they so desired. This use of force to keep workers in the factories changes the crime from a violation of worker's rights to an instance of human labor trafficking. Students, in conjunction with labor activists from the National Guestworker Alliance, are also targeting Hershey for their use of foreign student workers in chocolate bar production and are boycotting the sale of the chocolate bars across the country.[37]

Campaigns against known brands and their manufacturers are relatively easy for students to undertake because of familiarity. These companies may be uncertain whether their contractors utilize slave labor, but once student letter-writing campaigns or media attention calls them out, the companies feel pressured to act. The situation is far more difficult, however, when the traffickers are not associated with well-known brands. In these cases, they are criminal agents, working below the media spotlight or our social radar, and student organizations work to raise awareness on their campuses and in their communities, discussing risk factors for trafficking victims and prevention measures, all the while pushing for legislation through their organization or asking their community members to get involved. National student coalitions like I Am a Student and the Campus Coalition Against Trafficking provide networks and larger institutional structures under which students can organize.

STUDENTS AND INTERNATIONAL HUMAN RIGHTS MOVEMENTS. Students also play a role in larger human rights movements. Amnesty International, one of the largest international human rights NGOs, has a program specifically designed for college students in their annual campaigns. If a group registers with the national office, it receives Amnesty resource packages, invitations to their annual conferences, and conference voting rights. Amnesty encourages these student groups to work collectively against human rights abuses. In early 2012, for example, they encouraged their student groups to participate and take action as part of Death Penalty Awareness Week. They hosted an interactive online event to brainstorm ideas and actions that these groups can take. As Map 12.5 illustrates, this activism coincides with a global trend of gradual increases in national

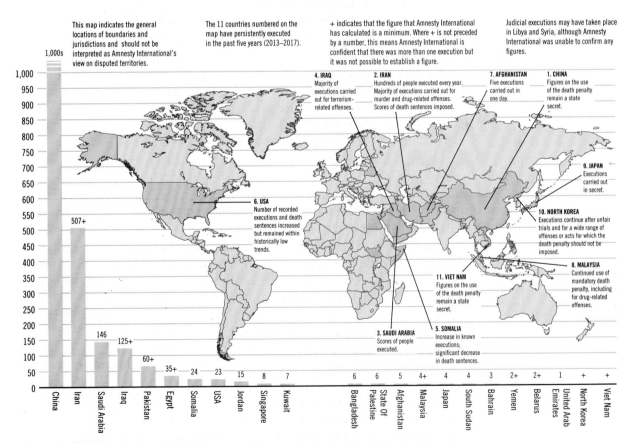

Map 12.5 EXECUTING COUNTRIES IN 2017. According to Amnesty International, the death penalty is legal in only about one-quarter of the world's countries. In the last 25 years, 67 governments have abolished the death penalty, 5 have abolished it for ordinary crimes, and an additional 35 have abolished the death penalty in practice if not by law per se. For some, this trend reflects an emerging abolitionist norm toward the death penalty. This norm is by no means universal, however, with countries like the United States still regularly executing people as sentence for their crimes.

The March for Our Lives movement is a student-led protest turned movement in support of legislation to prevent gun violence in the United States. The first protests took place in over 800 cities throughout the U.S. and around the world. The movement was initially spearheaded by a group of students from Marjory Stoneman Douglas High School in Parkland, Florida, in the wake of the school shooting that left 17 dead in 2018.

laws prohibiting the death penalty. Currently, Amnesty International student campaigns in the United States are focused on gun violence and changing gun laws.

Ultimately, it is important to understand that the promotion and protection of human rights are not just the business of elected officials, international diplomats, and global organizations. Ordinary people, especially the world's young, should be aware of the relevance and importance of making human rights progress. The UN or large global NGOs cannot be the sole purveyors of human rights promotion. A small group of students on a college campus can create—and have created—a difference. Whether it is fundraising for a larger organization or raising awareness of a local human rights issue, higher education and the academy have an important role to play in understanding and advancing equal rights for all.

Chapter Summary

- Human rights are the moral principles that are universal to all human beings. These inalienable rights are basic freedoms and protections we need in order to live a life with dignity. Many human rights are now codified in national, regional, and international laws that shape the way social institutions like the state interact with individuals and communities. The founding and most far-reaching legal document outlining the fundamental human rights is the UDHR.

- Political theorists have long been thinking and writing about human rights, particularly those derived from natural law, as inherent duties that people had to one another and to God. With the Enlightenment, however, these natural rights that emerged from the laws of nature increasingly focused on the secular origins of individual freedoms and liberties rather than a divine moral order.

- First-generation rights focus on civil and political rights and for many people serve as the core of a rights system based on equality and nondiscrimination. Some classify these rights as proscriptive rights, or those policies and actions that governments cannot do to groups.

- Second-generation rights are largely centered on economic and social rights, such as economic subsistence, education, nutrition, sanitation, work, housing, and health care. These prescriptive rights include the essentials that a society and its government are arguably obligated to try to provide in order to assure certain qualitative standards of life for everyone in the community.

- Third-generation rights, or those focused on the communal aspects of being human, refer to solidarity rights unique to certain groups in a particular context. These group rights can be wide-ranging, from self-determination rights to the right to development to the right to a healthy environment.

- The modern human rights movement has been catalyzed by a combination of powerful events like the Holocaust, the growth and influence of IGOs and NGOs, the leadership of key individuals and grassroots movements, the expansion of international human rights law, and the developments in information technology connecting these various actors across the globe.

- Criticisms of the universal approach embedded within the human rights movement include arguments concerned with cultural relativism, modern forms of imperialism, and feminist activism.

- Although the human rights movement has many notable achievements, barriers to progress still exist. Gaps in treaty interpretation and failures in law enforcement as well as political selectivity highlight the fundamental (and often problematic) nature of the human rights regime—namely, that sovereign states are the primary enforcers for international human rights.

- Individuals, from students to world leaders, and NGOs, from the local to the global, continue to play a critical role in the full realization and implementation of international human rights for all.

Critical Thinking Questions

1. Review the basic human rights principles codified in the UDHR (see Table 12.1), and consider the various ways that your state might interpret these rights and translate them into policy. Then, select one principle, and compare and contrast at least two different interpretations for this right (e.g., right to life, right to marry, or right to be free from torture). Why are these different interpretations significant, and what does this difference imply about actual implementation of these basic moral principles in real-world political systems?

2. What do you see as the most significant barrier to human rights promotion and protection in the world today and why? Discuss at least one possible way to realistically address this barrier.

3. Why are measuring and monitoring important for human rights advocacy?

4. What do you believe is the most urgent human rights issue of the 21st century and why? If you wish to get involved with this issue, what can you do as an activist for human rights?

Key Terms

Chapter VII
Convention on the Rights of the Child
cultural relativism
customary law
first-generation rights
human rights
human trafficking
internally displaced persons
International Bill of Human Rights

International Covenant on Civil and Political Rights
International Covenant on Economic, Social, and Cultural Rights
legal positivism
lesbian, gay, bisexual, transgender, queer, asexual and ally
natural law

Office of the United Nations High Commissioner on Human Rights
prescriptive rights
proscriptive rights
refugees
Responsibility to Protect (aka R2P)
second-generation rights
sweatshop

third-generation rights
UN High Commissioner for Refugees
UN Human Rights Council (UNHRC)
Universal Declaration of Human Rights
Universal Periodic Review
universalism

13

Global Political Ecology

Global climate change. As that phrase implies, climate change is likely the most "global" of the issues the world community confronts today. Climate does not observe national boundaries. Typhoons, hurricanes, snowstorms, or dust storms impact countries and regions in ways that fly in the face of independent national action. Nevertheless, the international community has struggled to address global environmental challenges. The UN Framework Convention on Climate Change (UNFCCC), discussed in this chapter, enjoys widespread international participation but has in fact shown little progress. From the perspective of realist theory, the lack of legally binding international standards regulating state behavior, which encourages countries to send their problems to others "downstream," is to be expected. Indeed, the contemporary state-based political system does not lend itself to the resolution of cross-border environmental disputes, especially when the involved countries have limited economic resources. As a result, agreements aimed at achieving the UNFCCC's objectives in summits from Kyoto, Japan (1997) to Katowice, Poland (2018), lack enforceability. Although the **Intergovernmental Panel on Climate Change (IPCC)** has successfully developed a high degree of consensus about the science of climate change and its policy demands, most recently expressed in a 2018 Summary for

This image is sadly descriptive of too many human-environment interactions. In January 2019, an olive ridley sea turtle was found dead on an Indian beach with ropes from fishing nets around its neck.

Policy-Makers, that consensus has yet to generate global policy action with any real teeth.

In the absence of such action, as realism would predict, many countries have engaged in their own unilateral approaches to climate mitigation (reducing greenhouse gases to slow climate change), and to adaptation (coping with the impacts of climate change). European countries have been particularly progressive on climate change policy on both mitigation and adaptation. In the United States, where climate change remains hotly debated, states and localities have taken the lead, even moreso now that the Trump administration has withdrawn US support for the 2015 Paris climate agreement. California, Connecticut, and other states, as well as many individual cities and towns, have developed their own independent policies to combat rising sea levels, storm surge, and smog—expressing their commitment through the "We Are Still In" movement.[1]

Intergovernmental Panel on Climate Change (IPCC)
A UN-sponsored organization created to study and scientifically assess climate change.

Strict adherence to state sovereignty poses a challenge to those seeking to respond to global environmental problems. Yet this chapter's discussion also supports the assertions of liberal international relations theorists that cooperation is on the rise in global politics. Earth Summits and other multilateral negotiations have put environmental problems on the global policy agenda. As a result, a norm of state responsibility to avoid "doing harm" to other states has emerged, launching the push for environmental sustainability. These normative changes have also led to a series of multilateral discussions about the effects of climate change, among other transnational environmental challenges.

By definition, transboundary challenges such as climate change pose collective action problems—situations where members of a group (often states in global politics) would be better off cooperating but fail to do so because of conflicting interests that discourage joint action. Collective action problems like climate change are not solely caused (and cannot be solved) by the individual action of any one country. In this way, the types of global environmental challenges profiled in this chapter are perfect illustrations of what the ecologist and philosopher Garrett Hardin called the "tragedy of the commons"[2]—that is, the likelihood that shared resources will be degraded because of a lack of commitment by individual users to care for them.

Learning Objectives

Explain different perspectives on global environmental issues and the ways those perspectives shape thinking about environmental problems and possible solutions.

Discuss the impacts of human activity on the natural environment and the ways in which those impacts differ according to the lifestyle choices of those living in the developed and developing worlds.

Identify the factors that point toward the urgency for a global policy response to climate change

An Ecological State of the World

Just as the US president delivers an annual State of the Union address, a regular evaluation of the state of the global **ecosystem** is a worthwhile exercise. There are both positive and negative developments about the Earth's environmental health, and interpreting these environmental data remains a question of significant debate. To understand the roots of those debates, we first focus briefly on the theoretical perspectives applied to ecological analysis by prominent individuals involved in the global political process.

Theoretical Perspectives on Political Ecology

The *Thinking Theoretically* feature illustrates the need to confront the reality of divergent perspectives about how to respond to environmental problems. **Neotraditionalists** tend to be more pessimistic in their assessments of the state of the world and believe that humans are causing serious, even irreversible damage to the environment. They worry that environmental damage will increasingly cause human suffering: devastating storms due to global climate change, skin cancer due to ozone-layer depletion, warfare over scarce natural resources, and other problems. Representing this position, a Worldwatch Institute study warned in 2005 that "depending on the degree of misery and biological impoverishment that we are prepared to accept, we have only one or perhaps two generations in which to reinvent ourselves." It is imperative to do so, the study continued, because "by virtually every broad measure, our world is in a state of pervasive ecological decline."[3]

Some analysts even foresee environmental issues or resource scarcities as the cause of future warfare among states desperate to sustain their economies and quality of life. Oil is one obvious example, but countries may increasingly clash over water or even such other matters as "invasions" of acid rain and similar pollutants from other countries.

The neotraditionalist perspective is also deeply rooted in systems thinking. **Systems thinking** emphasizes the study of the whole over the component parts of a system, relationships among the parts more than the parts

ecosystem A biological system consisting of all the living organisms in a particular area and the nonliving components with which the organisms interact, such as air, minerals, soil, water, and sunlight.

neotraditionalists Those who believe in ecological limits and the need to reduce ecological stress, thereby emphasizing conservation and the search for environmental solutions that reduce humanity's impact on ecosystems. Neotraditionalists are sometimes referred to as inclusionists because they view humankind as part of nature.

systems thinking A wholistic approach to the analysis of socio-political-economic-ecological phenomena. It focuses attention on the complexity of relationships, processes, and actors and how small changes in one part of a system can lead to large changes throughout a system.

▲   **THINKING THEORETICALLY**

Your World, Your Worldview

Each theory we apply to international relations yields a different analysis of the political challenges facing decision-makers. Building on our practice in previous chapters, we suggest that you consider what insights realism and liberalism can provide for our understanding of global environmental politics. We also apply a political ecology perspective here, allowing us to think more directly about humanity's relationship with nature and how the costs and benefits of environmental change are distributed both among and within states and communities.

Realism is valuable for understanding environmental politics because it focuses our attention on the power that states continue to possess in contemporary international affairs, despite the fact that many environmental problems transcend political boundaries. When air pollutants enter the atmosphere in the northern United States, those pollutants are often carried into Canada and even further. If chemicals are dumped into the Nile River in Uganda, those chemicals negatively affect the soil, water, and people in the Sudan and Egypt and eventually may flow into the Mediterranean Sea.

Environmental degradation can become the root of conflict as countries "export"—intentionally or not—their environmental problems to their neighbors. For instance, the Mekong River in Southeast Asia encompasses a river basin that borders six countries: Cambodia, China, Laos, Myanmar, Thailand, and Vietnam. But China and Myanmar do not belong to the Mekong River Commission that monitors water quality. As this example illustrates, the fact that ecosystems do not abide by national boundaries highlights the problems caused by the state-centric international political system—especially as it focuses on environmental challenges.[4]

These problems in turn urge us to consider what liberal analysis can provide for our understanding of the growing incidence of transnational environmental cooperation. Although policy change is indeed slow in coming, much has been achieved in terms of scientific consensus about environmental problems, and few countries are able to ignore environmental problems in the way they did even 20 years ago. For instance, the Convention on Long-Range Transboundary Air Pollution, signed in 1979 by 32 countries, now has 51 parties that have ratified the agreement. Although this agreement and its secretariat have not eliminated air pollution, they have provided a mechanism to limit and monitor air pollution and to enhance compliance amongst its members.[5] Agreements such as this one also demonstrate that states are willing to cede authority, in some instances, to international organizations.

From a different angle, contending views of political ecology also affect the ways different policy-makers approach environmental challenges. To quote one of the foundational scholars in this area, political ecology "focuses on the relationships of humans . . . and the biological and physical environment in which we live" (Hughes, 1985:27). Humans and natural ecosystems are coupled in ways that require us to recognize human impacts on the environment in almost all political decision-making (Willig & Scheiner, 2011).

The value of thinking about political ecology as a theoretical perspective is that it helps us better understand the divergent policy stands taken in the political realm, such as the modernist/neotraditionalist schools discussed in this chapter.[6] As you might assume, each school advocates different solutions to environmental problems, with modernists committed to the optimistic view of technological "quick fixes" for social and environmental problems (e.g., the dramatic increases in food production through the so-called Green Revolution) and neotraditionalists emphasizing the realities of carrying capacity and ecological limits and the need for substantially reducing humanity's impact on local and global ecosystems. Where would you place yourself? Are you a modernist or a neotraditionalist?

themselves, and processes over structures (Klotz, 2016). Systems thinking dominates research by ecologists (Meadows, 2009) and focuses our attention on how small, seemingly insignificant changes or actions can have system-wide impacts. For instance, Figure 13.1 shows the impact of the wolf as a primary predator in the Yellowstone National Park ecosystem. Rather surprising to nonecologists like the authors of this book, the reintroduction of the wolf to Yellowstone in 1995 actually led to *increased* biodiversity in that ecosystem. As the figure shows, the reintroduction of the wolf led to a decline in the primary herbivore, the elk, and a secondary predator, the coyote, thus allowing greater growth in the remaining plant and animal species in the ecosystem. Research studies of single-variable changes such as this provide evidence that ecological systems are extremely fragile and sensitive. This perspective tends to emphasize limited **carrying capacity** (the maximum capacity of an ecosystem to sustain organisms dependent on it at prevailing rates of resource consumption) and points policy

Figure 13.1   The food web of Yellowstone National Park shows a striking example of the systemic implications of what seem like small, and sometimes even apparently logical, changes to an ecosystem. Somewhat ironically in this case, the ecosystem is significantly healthier with the wolf in the food web.

responses in the direction of the **precautionary principle** (the concept that preventative remedial action is warranted in situations where consequences are high).

Another example of this approach to understanding global environmental problems focuses on **ecosystem services** in the biophysical and social sciences (Boyd et al., 2014). At the most fundamental level, ecosystem services are the human benefits generated by the ecosystems that host and surround human communities. For instance, although we might think of swamps primarily as breeding grounds for mosquitoes and other annoying insects, wetlands (the more technical name for swamps) provide habitat for many animals and serve as natural filters for water in the environment. This filtration service is one of the primary reasons why environmental agencies pay so much attention to wetlands protection. When one of the authors of this book built his family's home in 1994, he had to obtain a special town permit to allow construction because of a very small wetland in the front

carrying capacity   The largest number of organisms that an global ecosystem can sustain indefinitely at current per capita rates of consumption of natural resources and discharges of pollution and other waste.

precautionary principle   The approach holding that measures are warranted to reduce or mitigate risks to human health and/or the environment even if cause-and-effect relationships are not fully established scientifically.

ecosystem services The many and varied benefits that humans gain from the natural environment and from properly functioning ecosystems. These can be grouped into four broad categories: provisioning (production of food and water), regulating (control of climate and disease), supporting (through nutrient cycles and oxygen production), and cultural (spiritual and recreational benefits).

modernists Those who believe in humankind's mastery of the environment and possess great faith in technology to solve existing and future environmental problems. Modernists contend that ecosystem carrying capacity can be extended through technological advances.

biosphere Earth's ecological system (ecosystem) that supports life—its land, water, air, and upper atmosphere—and the living organisms, including humans, that inhabit it.

ecological footprint A tool used to assess and measure human impact on nature—meaning the quantity of nature it takes to support a person, community, nation, or economy, both in terms of consumption of natural resources and pollution and other negative outputs.

corner of the property. The permit required installation of a silt fence that would prevent runoff of construction waste, silt, and disturbed soil into the wetland, thus preserving its ability to provide the longer-term ecosystem service of water filtration.

As discussed in the *Thinking Theoretically* feature, **modernists** differ in offering more optimistic views of the global environment and its future. Optimists like Bjørn Lomborg (2007) have tended to chastise the ecology movement for alarmism by promoting "green guilt."[7] Accordingly, the modernist school of thought looks to technological innovation to solve most **biosphere** problems. They believe, for example, that new technology can find and develop additional oil fields. Synthetics can replace natural resources. Fertilizers, hybrid seeds, and mechanization can increase crop yields. Desalinization and weather control can meet water demands. Nuclear, solar, thermal, wind, and hydroelectric sources can produce energy.

One example of this modernist approach is reflected in an ambitious land reclamation project undertaken by Singapore. A very small country in terms of geographical size, Singapore is aggressively reclaiming land from the surrounding ocean to create more living space for its people and economic development. According to one government official, "We're already reclaiming in water that is 20 meters deep. Maybe it would be viable to reclaim in 30 meters, if land prices go up. But 40 and 50 meters would be very difficult. It's physically difficult and economically unviable."[8] Using debris from subway and other construction projects, the government is actively working to defy physical laws and push the limits of what can be a stable structure in the reclaimed ocean with enough money, time, and will. Only time will tell if this approach is physically sustainable.

Regardless of whether one adopts a neotraditional or a modernist perspective, the goal for humanity is to find ways to live sustainably for years into the future, even if we hold different views on how to do so. In the next section, we will focus on different views of sustainability.

The Challenge of Sustainable Development

Throughout most of history, the Earth has provided humans with the necessities of life, absorbed their waste, and replenished itself. Now, the mounting human population and its **ecological footprint** have changed this, and neotraditionalists warn that we are straining Earth's carrying capacity. Map 13.1 provides the World Wildlife Federation's measure of the relative ecological footprint produced by countries around the world. The countries in the Global North have a decidedly larger ecological footprint than those in the Global South. This "North-South divide" is correlated with levels of economic development (see Chapters 10 and 11), but for our purposes here, it also reflects the clear disparity in ecological stress from the North to the South. It is worth keeping this image in mind as we proceed throughout the chapter, because North-South tension pervades global environmental concerns.

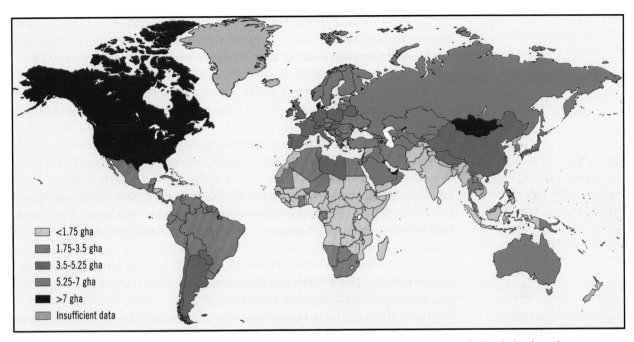

Map 13.1   The Global North has a much heavier ecological footprint than does the Global South. But as the South develops, that may change, a reality that doesn't bode well for overall global ecological stress.

Not only are more than six times as many people living on our planet as there were just a little over 200 years ago, but technological progress has multiplied our per capita resource consumption and our per capita waste and pollutant production. Whether technological wizardry can eventually provide solutions remains uncertain, but if that does not happen soon, the world is approaching, or may have even reached, a crisis of carrying capacity—the potential of no longer being able to sustain its population in an adequate manner or absorb its waste. To put this as an equation that illustrates what can happen when we push the boundaries of carrying capacity:

Crowding in the Global South is particularly acute in urban areas. This photo of a busy market in Lagos, Nigeria, shows both human and vehicular gridlock choking the streets.

Expanding population × Increasing per capita resource consumption
× Mounting waste and pollutant discharges = Biosphere catastrophe

The Earth is Full

If this equation is correct, then a primary environmental goal should be to ensure we do not reach—or even approach—full carrying capacity. That will not be easy, however, because another fundamental goal of humans has been and remains an increase in their economic well-being and the acquisition of other benefits, such as better health, that come with prosperity. The Global North has largely achieved that goal; not surprisingly, the Global South largely intends to follow suit.

Industrialization and science are key elements of development, but they have both positive and negative impacts on the relationship between the environment and the quality of human life. On the positive side, industrialization has allowed global wealth to expand, especially in the Global North. And scientific research has created many substances that enhance our lives, like vaccines that prevent outbreaks of disease or synthetic fibers used to make lightweight and durable clothing. On the negative side, industry consumes natural resources and creates pollution. Moreover, decreased infant mortality rates and increased longevity (positive developments) have been major factors in global population growth (a negative development).

Given the ubiquity of these features of modern life, the dilemma is how to achieve **sustainable development** in order to protect the biosphere while simultaneously advancing socioeconomic well-being. Sustainable development was first defined and introduced by the World Commission on Environment and Development (known as the Brundtland Commission for its chair, Gro Harlem Brundtland of Norway) in 1987: "development that meets the needs of the present without compromising the ability of future generations to meet their own needs."[9] Focusing on prioritizing the essential needs of the world's poor in concert with recognizing ecological limits, advocates of sustainable development wonder: Can the biosphere survive if we bring the more than 6 billion people who live in the Global South up to the standard of living—with all its cars, air conditioners, throwaway plastic containers, and other biosphere-attacking amenities—enjoyed by the 1 billion people in the Global North? Here, we discuss these tensions, as well as the history of the Earth Summits and their contribution to sustainability.

THE CONUNDRUM OF SUSTAINABLE DEVELOPMENT.   Central to the discussion in the rest of this chapter is if and how we can meet the legitimate but resource-consuming and waste-creating modernization goals of countries in the Global South without further damaging the environment. For example, what would consumption be like if India, with its 1.3 billion people, reached the same level of economic development as the United States—including the same resource use and waste patterns? There are now about 65 million cars in India. If Indian citizens owned cars at the same rate as Americans, there would be more than 530 million. One impact would be astronomically increased pressure on global petroleum supplies. The additional cars and other accoutrements of a developed economy would put India on the road to consuming as much petroleum per capita as Americans. Since the United States currently uses about 20 times more petroleum per capita than does India, annual oil consumption in India would also skyrocket.[10]

sustainable development
The ability to continue to improve the quality of life of those in the industrialized countries and, particularly those in the less developed countries while simultaneously protecting Earth's biosphere.

While much progress has been made toward reducing pollution in the Global North, weaker environmental regulations throughout much of the Global South remain. The emissions from this steel plant in the eastern Indian city of Jamshedpur are a case in point.

In addition to the drain on the world's oil supply, this surge of cars in India would increase pollution enormously. Carbon dioxide (CO_2) emissions would rise ominously. Americans discharge about 15 times more CO_2 per capita than do Indians, but India already emits over 2 billion metric tons of CO_2 annually.[11] That figure would rise to about 34 billion metric tons, escalating the threat to the environment. If India were to achieve the same level of economic prosperity as the United States and also have similar resource consumption and waste patterns as Americans today, it would be detrimental to the ecological future of the planet. Similar comparisons apply to China, especially considering that China has occupied the dubious distinction of the world's largest emitter of CO_2 since 2007.[12]

Further, if you were to bring the rest of the Global South up to the US level of resource use and emissions discharge, you would hyperaccelerate the depletion of natural resources and the creation of pollution. At current rates of increase, emissions of CO_2 from the Global South will surpass those of the Global North in only a few years, and if the Global South discharged CO_2 at the same per capita rate as the Global North, current world emissions would be more than double the current level, which is already too high. Clearly, such an escalation is not acceptable. Less clear, however, is what to do.

HISTORICAL CONTEXT: EARTH SUMMITS AND THE POLITICS OF SUSTAINABLE DEVELOPMENT.   Many environmentalists would argue that future economic development must occur in ways that reduce our impact on the planet. But what to do and who is responsible for doing it are much more difficult questions. Moreover, the international community has yet to develop a robust approach to protect our global environmental commons. Although we can identify international environmental agreements as far back as the 1300s, such as those establishing access to fisheries and control over

United Nations Conference on Environment and Development Often called Earth Summit I or the Rio Conference, this gathering in 1992 was the first to bring together most of the world's countries, a majority of which were represented by their head of state or government, to address the range of issues associated with sustainable development.

Convention on Biological Diversity A multilateral treaty introduced at the Earth Summit I in Rio de Janeiro in 1992, which entered into force in 1993. The three main goals of the Convention are the conservation of biodiversity, the sustainable use of it, and the fair distribution of benefits accruing from that use. The treaty calls upon states to develop strategies to pursue and achieve these three goals.

United Nations Framework Convention on Climate Change The UN body that meets annually as the Conference of the Parties (COP) to the Framework Convention. These annual meetings seek to negotiate multilateral agreements over the management of climate change.

Simulation:
Negotiating the
Lisbon Protocol

riverways, most concrete international measures to preserve ecosystems did not emerge until the late 20th century.[13] As the international community has come to realize, the Earth's resources are finite, and individual state regulation is not enough.

The most comprehensive efforts have focused on the pursuit of sustainable development, as promoted by the United Nations (UN)–sponsored Earth Summits in 1992, 2002, and 2012. Although each summit drew a vast array of countries and nongovernmental organizations (NGOs), the legacies of each summit illustrate the tension between environmental protection and economic growth and the ways that state sovereignty can limit progress in this issue area. The nature of a state-based international system constrains efforts to solve global environmental problems that are fundamentally transboundary in nature.

The 1992 **UN Conference on Environment and Development**, popularly dubbed Earth Summit I, in Rio de Janeiro symbolized the growing concern with the environment and sustainable development. Most of the 178 countries in attendance were represented by their head of state. Additionally, 15,000 representatives of NGOs attended a nearby parallel conference. The official conference produced Agenda 21 (a 112-topic, nonbinding blueprint for sustainable development in the 21st century); two treaties, the **Convention on Biological Diversity** and the **UN Framework Convention on Climate Change** (UNFCCC); and the annual review process that continues today.

Earth Summit I also featured the often-divisive politics of environmental protection. In particular, the North and the South were at odds on many issues:

- The Global South argued that the burden of sustainable development should fall substantially on the countries of the Global North, because they were responsible for most of the pollution and depletion of resources.

- The Global South contended that they should be exempt, either wholly or in part, from environmental restrictions because the Global North had already developed, and it was unfair to ask the Global South not to achieve the same national standards as the Global North. Indeed, some in the Global South suspected that efforts by the Global North to restrict their development might really be a neocolonial effort to keep the Global South poor, weak, and dependent.

- The Global South maintained that they were too poor to develop their considerable resources in an environmentally sustainable way; therefore, the Global North should significantly increase aid to help the Global South do so.

For their part, most of the Global North, especially the United States, disagreed with each of these positions.

Not surprisingly, a standoff occurred. The Global North averted efforts by the Global South to set binding timetables for the North to reduce its emissions of CO_2 and other gases that contribute to global warming. The North also resisted making major financial commitments. "We do not have an open pocketbook," President George H. W. Bush observed.[14] Similarly, the South avoided restrictions on such activities as deforestation. "Forests are clearly a sovereign resource. . . . We cannot allow forests to be taken up in global forums," Malaysia's chief negotiator asserted.[15]

Given the various divisions, it was not surprising that legally binding mandates on biodiversity and climate change proved elusive. It would be an overstatement to call the conference a failure, however, because important global initiatives normally gestate for an extended period. In addition, the two treaties previously mentioned, Agenda 21, and the attention the conference generated globally all helped to firmly plant the environment on the world political agenda. This first summit also illustrated the degree to which solutions to environmental issues can successfully be framed in economic terms. That is, with the "right" language and enough money, environmental problems can be solved, at least for those countries that have already climbed the economic development ladder and have the "luxury" to pursue sustainable development.

A decade later, in 2002, delegates from almost all of the world's countries and representatives from some 8,000 NGOs gathered in Johannesburg, South Africa, at the **World Summit on Sustainable Development** (WSSD), or Earth Summit II, to address what then–UN Secretary-General Kofi Annan of Ghana called the "gap between the goals and the promises set out in Rio and the daily reality [of what has been accomplished]."[16] The political disputes, however, that had bedeviled Earth Summit I also afflicted the WSSD, creating what an Indonesian diplomat portrayed as "a battle, a conflict of interest between developed and developing countries."[17]

The United States and some others in the Global North were unwilling to provide the Global South with substantially increased aid for sustainable development or to accept environmental restrictions that did not also apply at least partly to the Global South. The North also opposed the creation of international agencies to monitor conditions and enforce mandatory standards. Articulating this view, one US official insisted that the only path to progress was that "both developing and developed nations" agree to mutual restrictions.[18] Taking the opposite view, the Secretary-General asserted, "The richest countries must lead the way. They have the wealth. They have the technology. And they contribute disproportionately to global environmental problems."[19]

At the end of the Summit, the Global North did announce new funding commitments, and the conference also adopted some new, albeit voluntary targets for reducing pollution and resource depletion and for easing other biosphere problems. Although these were modest steps, it would be wrong to judge the WSSD a failure. Providing some perspective, the UN Secretary-General advised, "I think we have to be careful not to expect conferences like this to produce miracles. It is not one isolated conference that is going to do this whole thing." Instead, he suggested, "What happens is the energy that we create here, the commitments that have been made, and what we do on the ground as individuals, as civil society, as community groups and as governments and private sector [are what matters]."[20]

World Summit on Sustainable Development
Often called Earth Summit II, this conference was held in Johannesburg in 2002. It was attended by almost all countries and by some 8,000 NGOs, and it established a series of calls for action and timetables dedicated to the promotion of environmentally sustainable economic and social development.

100 Solutions to
Reverse Global
Warming

The preparations for the **UN Conference on Sustainable Development** in June 2012, popularly referred to as Rio+20 or Earth Summit III, centered on seven critical themes in sustainable development. They were:

1. *Jobs:* focusing attention on the impact of the global economic crisis.
2. *Energy:* a central variable in the environment-development relationship.
3. *Cities:* focusing on the unique environmental challenges of urbanization in the developing world.
4. *Food:* centering on rethinking how food is grown, shared, and consumed.
5. *Water:* access to freshwater and wastewater treatment is critical to personal and environmental health.
6. *Oceans:* care of our oceans has an array of impacts on health, weather, food, air, and beyond.
7. *Disasters:* coping with disasters is a recurrent challenge for humankind and is a special challenge in the developing world.

The Summit concluded by issuing "The Future We Want," a report stating that the parties "renew our commitment to sustainable development and to ensuring the promotion of an economically, socially, and environmentally sustainable future for our planet and for present and future generations."[21] The member-states also decided to develop a set of **Sustainable Development Goals** (SDGs)[22] that would build from the Millennium Development Goals.[23] The SDGs established a path forward for sustainable development, but they did not directly engage the fundamental tension between the Global North and Global South. As the subsequent sections in this chapter will illustrate, this remains a central challenge.

🌍 Global Carrying Capacity

There are multiple dimensions to understanding global carrying capacity. One, based in neotraditional thought, focuses on the finite number of people and other organisms that the Earth can sustain. A second, based in modernist thought, focuses on the ways we can manage and expand the Earth's carrying capacity. In many ways, these views are at odds with each another, but some visionaries argue for a middle ground that seeks solutions drawing from both perspectives.

Energy development provides a useful example. Since the start of the Industrial Revolution, economic development has been based on fossil fuel consumption in both commercial and residential sectors of the world economy. But as analysts predict the eventual end to fossil fuel resources, renewable energy sources like solar, wind, and geothermal have grown in use and cost competitiveness. In this way, technological advances in renewable technologies (arguably a modernist approach) contribute to lower stress on Earth's resources (something advocated by neotraditionalists). Here, we focus on human population challenges, followed by a brief assessment of human impact on global environmental quality.

Human Population Pressures

Although a full and nuanced discussion of demography is beyond the scope of this text, it is impossible to consider global environmental issues without taking population dynamics into account. In April 2017, the world population passed the 7.5 billion mark. That is a stunning number, especially when placed in historical context. Humans in their modern form date back about 200,000 years, and their number did not reach 1 billion until 1804. It took only another 213 years to get to the 7.5 billion mark in 2017—and the leap from 5 billion to 7.5 billion only took 29 years. Simply, the world is awash in people, with China's current population

Human population growth continues to pressure the Earth's carrying capacity. Growth rates in many Global South countries, as illustrated by the crowded streets of New Delhi, India, shown here, will continue to increase global population through the 21st century.

alone greater than that of the entire plant in 1800. The exponential growth in the world's population has begun to slow, but only slightly. Current UN projections, as Figure 13.2 depicts, show the world population continuing to grow to 11 billion by 2100.

Given a reasonably finite amount of resources and ability to absorb waste, this growing population presents a challenge to Earth's carrying capacity—a point emphasized as long ago as the 18th century by the theologian and philosopher Thomas Robert Malthus in his *Essay on the Principle of Population* (1798). Demographic pressures especially complicate environmental problems in some re-gions of the world, given forecasts of continued and rapid rates of growth. Sub-Saharan Africa will likely be the most troubled. Statisticians noted that its population grew annually by 2.43% between 2005 and 2015, while the rest of the world population grew at an annual rate of just over 1%.

The acceleration of population growth beginning about 1950 occurred for several reasons:

1. *High fertility rates:* Between 1950 and 1970, the average woman had five children, with an average between six and seven children per family in the Global South. That overall rate has fallen, but the world's population continues to grow.

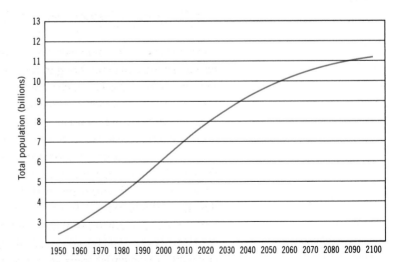

Figure 13.2 The UN expects global population to be about 11 billion by 2100. This growth, even if leveling off in the next century, will continue to stress global ecosystems and further pressure global carrying capacity. (Source: Data from United Nations, Department of Economic and Social Affairs, Population Division, 2015.)

2. *Fewer deaths:* An increasingly important factor, better health care around the globe, means that more infants survive and that adults live longer. In 1950, 20 of every 1,000 people worldwide died each year; now, only 9 of every 1,000 do.

3. *Population base multiplier effect:* During the next decade, more than 3 billion women will enter their childbearing years. At the current fertility rate, these women will have more than 7.5 billion children, who in turn will have yet more children. Thus, the population is projected to grow until the world fertility rate falls to 2.1, the approximate replacement rate at which each set of parents has two surviving children.

GLOBAL RECOGNITION OF THE POPULATION PROBLEM.   Unchecked population growth puts extreme pressure on carrying capacity, further complicating and worsening environmental problems. Consequently, the UN has led the effort to address global population growth. Among the involved UN divisions and associated agencies, the UN Population Fund (UNFPA) is the largest. It began operations in 1969 and focuses on promoting family planning services and improving reproductive health in the Global South. During its history, the UNFPA has provided over $6 billion to support population programs in the vast majority of the world's countries.

In addition to its own programs, the UNFPA helps coordinate programs of other related intergovernmental organizations (IGOs) and national governments. Its efforts are further supplemented by and often coordinated with NGOs such as the International Planned Parenthood Federation. Founded in 1952, this British-based organization operates its own international family planning programs and also links with the individual Planned Parenthood organizations of about 150 countries. In 2016, the UNFPA provided a range of health care services to people in the Global South, including worldwide distribution of 275 million condoms.[24]

The need to address the environmental and social problems associated with global population growth have led the UN to sponsor three world population conferences. Given the importance of population growth, it may be surprising that the most recent was the 1994 **UN Conference on Population and Development** in Cairo, Egypt. This event brought together delegates from over 170 countries and a large number of NGOs and focused on population planning and reproductive health. Each year, for example, about 529,000 women (99% of whom live in the Global South) die from pregnancy and childbirth complications. Abortion was the most controversial issue at the conference. Abortion is widely available in about 60% of countries, fairly restricted in another 15%, and very restricted or unavailable in the remaining 25%. According to the **World Health Organization** (WHO), induced abortions (those that occur for other than natural causes) end about 22% of pregnancies in the Global South. Abortions performed in unsafe conditions, either in countries where it is illegal or severely restricted or in countries with an inadequate health care system, are a major threat to women's health. The WHO estimates that about 68,000 women a year die from unsafe abortions. In some countries that both restrict abortions

---

United Nations Conference on Population and Development A United Nations–sponsored conference that met in Cairo, Egypt, in September 1994 and was attended by delegates from more than 170 countries. The Conference called for a program of action to include spending $17 billion annually by the year 2000 on international, national, and local programs to foster family planning and improve the access of women in such areas as education.

World Health Organization A United Nations–affiliated organization created in 1946 to address world health issues.

and are exceptionally poor, more than half of maternal mortality is the result of illegal abortion.[25]

Controversy at the conference centered on how far it should go toward supporting abortion as a health measure—or even as an approach to controlling population growth. Predominantly Muslim countries were strongly opposed to the conference's support of abortion, with the Sudanese government charging that this would result in "the spread of immoral and irreligious ideas."[26] The Roman Catholic Church was also critical, with the Pope warning the conference not to "ignore the rights of the unborn."[27] Representing an alternative view was Norway's Prime Minister Gro Harlem Brundtland, who charged, "Morality becomes hypocrisy if it means accepting mothers' suffering or dying in connection with unwanted pregnancies and illegal abortions and unwanted children."[28]

The result was a compromise, with the language in the conference report promoting safe abortion qualified by the phrase "in circumstances in which abortion is legal" and the caveat "[i]n no case should abortion be promoted as a method of family planning."[29] The 1994 Cairo conference unanimously approved a "Program of Action" calling for spending $5.7 billion annually by the year 2000 on international programs to foster family planning. Funding never reached that goal, but the heightened awareness of the population problem and the closely associated issue of women's reproductive health, along with the delegates' and others' postconference activity, did help to increase funding for many of the poorest countries of the world.[30] Most importantly, maternal mortality declined by 44% (at a rate of 2.3% annually) from 1990 to 2015, even if that decline has plateaued in recent years.[31] In addition, the UN General Assembly voted to create the Commission on Population and Development, as a means to continually monitor population challenges and develop policy to address the ongoing concerns.

APPROACHES TO REDUCING THE BIRTH RATE. There are two broad approaches to reducing the birth rate. Social and educational approaches provide information about birth control and encouragement to practice it by making birth control devices and pills, sterilization, and in some cases, abortion programs available. The combined efforts of national governments, the UNFPA, and other IGOs and NGOs have had an impact as well. During the early 1960s, the contraceptive prevalence rate (the percentage of couples practicing contraception) in the Global South was only 9%. Now, it is about 60%. This contraceptive prevalence rate falls off drastically, however, in the least developed countries in the Global South, where the rate is only 40%.

Providing quality women's health care remains a challenge throughout much of the Global South. These pregnant women in Uganda are waiting patiently for ultrasound exams being administered by German physicians who are there to train local doctors in the latest approaches to prenatal care.

fertility rate The average
number of children who
would be born to a woman
over her lifetime.

Economic approaches to limiting population growth also can have an impact. There is a clear relationship between poverty and birth rates. The **fertility rate**, the average number of children a woman will have, is 1.7 in most of the Global North, 2.1 in middle-income countries, and 3.7 in much of the Global South. How does one explain the link between population and wealth? One view is that overpopulation causes poverty. This view argues that with too many people, especially in countries that are already poor, there are too few resources, jobs, and other forms of wealth to go around. This view is only part of the story, however, because it is also true that poverty causes overpopulation. The low-income countries tend to have the most labor-intensive economies, making children economically valuable because they help their parents with farming or, when they are somewhat older, provide cheap labor in mining and manufacturing. As a result, cultural attitudes in many countries have come to reflect economic utility. Having a large family is also an asset in terms of social standing in many societies with limited economic opportunities.

Further, women in the Global South have fewer opportunities to limit the number of children they bear. Artificial birth control methods and counseling services are less readily available, and efforts to limit educational access for girls and women also make it harder to convey birth control information (especially written information) to women. Additionally, fewer opportunities for paid employment and status roles beyond that of motherhood contribute to reproductive decisions, with respect to both the use of contraception and the fertility rate.

The relationship between poverty and population growth has spurred efforts to advance the economic and educational opportunities available to women. This realization was one of the factors that led the UN to designate 1975 as International Year of the Woman and to kick off the Decade for Women. That year, the UN also convened the first World Conference on Women. In 1976, the UN Development Fund for Women (UNIFEM, after its French name) was established. UNIFEM worked through 10 regional offices to improve the living standards of women in less developed countries by providing technical and financial support to advance the entry of women into business, scientific and technical careers, and other key areas.

In 2011, UNIFEM was merged with other UN agencies, such as the International Research and Training Institute for the Advancement of Women, into UN Women (the UN Entity for Gender Equity and the Empowerment of Women), which continues to lead the way in incorporating women into the international and national planning and administration of development programs and to ensure that issues of particular concern to women, such as food, security, human rights, and reproductive health, remain on the global agenda. Among other recent endeavors, in 2013 UN Women launched a systematic review of national constitutions with a particular emphasis on gender equity, and since 2015, it has been working to promote a stand-alone addition to the SDGs focusing on gender equality and women's empowerment.

THE EFFECT OF INTERNATIONAL POPULATION PLANNING EFFORTS.   The effort to address overpopulation is somewhat of a success story. Part of the credit goes to the work of IGOs, NGOs, and national governments. Improved economic conditions in much of the Global South as well as the slowly improving economic and educational status of women in many countries have also played a role. As a result, the average global fertility rate has declined dramatically, as Figure 13.3 illustrates. The generally accepted fertility rate goal is 2.1, which is about the stable replacement rate. The UN expects the global population to reach that standard by the middle of the 21st century. Indeed, after that date, the UN expects the fertility rate to drop below the replacement rate, which could result in a temporary decrease in the world population late in this century.

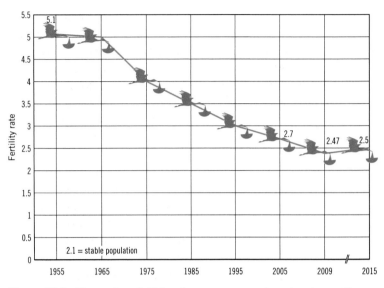

Figure 13.3   The number of children the average woman bears has dropped by over 50% since the 1950s. This change is the result of numerous factors, including the work of international agencies to improve educational and economic opportunities for females and to provide information and other forms of assistance to women who wish to practice family planning. (Source: https://ourworldindata.org/fertility-rate.)

As recently as 1994, the population was expanding at 94 million a year, and the UN was estimating that it would reach 11.6 billion by 2150. Now, the UN projects the population to peak at about 11 billion people. That is significant news and global progress, but it merits two cautions. First is that demographic trends are hard to predict. One worst-case scenario projects the population at 14 billion at the end of this century and peaking at 36 billion in 2300.[32] Also, despite the slowdown, the substantial population increase that still looms will challenge Earth's carrying capacity, especially in areas of the Global South least able to cope with the environmental stress of such population increases.

Assessing Global Environmental Quality

In the carrying capacity equation shown earlier, the expanding world population and its increasing consumption of resources are only part of the story. Another part of that equation is the degree of ecological stress foisted upon the biophysical world by more than 7 billion people, by the billions of domestic animals they keep for food or companionship, and by the negative outputs (human waste, litter, and other environmental stressors) produced by everyday human activity.

When considering the impact of humans on the global environment, environmental scientists use the term **Anthropocene** (in which human activity has been the dominant influence) to describe the current geological age in which we live. From that perspective, humans are the first species that can create enormous physical changes to the Earth. For example:

- We physically alter the world by cutting down forests for grazing and cropland.

- We build enormous hydroelectric facilities that flood large valleys and dramatically change the ecosystems in those areas.

Anthropocene Denotes the current geological age; viewed as the period during which human activity has been the dominant influence on climate and the environment.

- We strip-mine in ways that literally remove mountains so that we can access the coal underneath to power our economic and heating needs.
- We produce chemicals that help us grow food, but those same chemicals also accumulate in bodies of water, creating dead zones and other pollution-related problems.

And we do many more things that transform the world in ways that we believe are positive but that may ultimately prove to have harmful outcomes. As the next several sections will show, current assessments reveal a mix of significant concern, some reason for optimism, and inconsistent progress toward solving the environmental challenges of the Anthropocene.

Although assessing the state of the biophysical environment within which humans live and work is complex, we authors attempt such an assessment in the following sections in order to provide a general sense of the scale of global ecological stress and the health of the global ecosystem. Even though we use imperfect classifications, we roughly divide this assessment across land, air, water, and the biome—that is, the collection of biological organisms that exist within the global ecosystem. Any effort to split this assessment into categories runs into conceptual troubles rather quickly, and that reality makes us recall the discussion of systems theory from earlier in the chapter. Perhaps of all the issue areas that are encountered in global politics, environmental concerns are likely the most complex and systemically integrated.

LAND. Land use changes all the time. Suburban housing developments are built on what was once farm land. Urban areas in decline are sometimes left to decay until a conscious effort is made to reclaim and rebuild those areas. And entropy (gradual decline or decay) leads to the eventual reclaiming of land by the biophysical world through reforestation and other natural forms of decay that allow the environment to become natural once again, even if built artifacts remain. Recall the example of Singapore's attempt to reclaim portions of the ocean for expanding land. China has been undertaking similar efforts in the South China Sea as it builds islands in an effort to expand territorial claims in that strategically important waterway.

Perhaps the most significant, and potentially troubling, land use change is the growing urbanization of the global population. Maps 13.2 and 13.3 dramatically illustrate this point with a stylized map of the world. In 1960, nearing the end of the first wave of decolonization, the US population was about 70% urban, and the Chinese population was only about 16% urban (Map 13.2). By 2020, those statistics, along with those of many other countries, will have changed dramatically, as the United States grows to 85% urban and China to 55% urban.

With this migration from rural to urban comes growing stress on urban infrastructure. Both water delivery and waste disposal necessitate the building of infrastructure as well as the funding to maintain it. And as we can see in Map 13.3, the highest levels of urban growth have come in the Global South. As a result, countries around the world must engage in concerted efforts to plan

The Case for Optimism on Climate Change

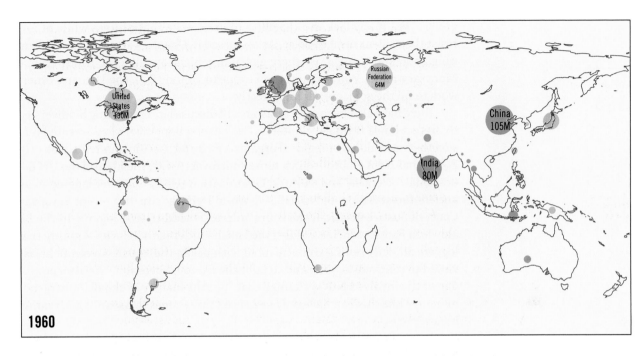

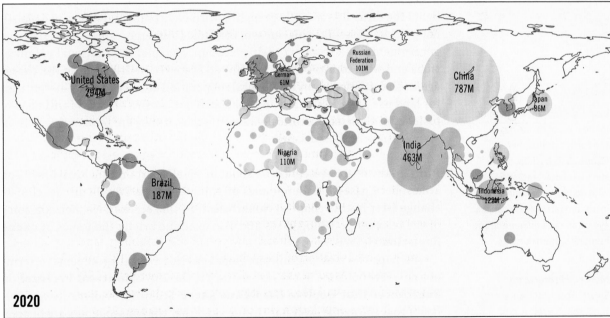

Maps 13.2 and 13.3.   Growing Urbanization: The world is becoming more urbanized, as these two maps show. This will also bring with it a greater need for urban infrastructure, including waste removal, water treatment, and more. Those needs will be acute in the Global South, where urbanization will be most dramatic.

growth, but many lack the expertise to undertake that process while others resist the evident need to do so. As discussed in Chapters 10 and 11, this planning and expertise gap is where global organizations like the International Monetary Fund, World Bank, the European Union (EU), the UN, and others work to fill the void, even if imperfectly.

There have also been efforts, as we will discuss later regarding biodiversity, to protect lands from development. Such protection efforts have created tensions between global or regional organizations and specific countries. Recently, Poland has been embroiled in a tense controversy with the EU and the UN Educational, Scientific and Cultural Organization (UNESCO) over logging in an ancient forest designated a UNESCO World Heritage site. In a recent European Court of Justice decision, the court ordered Poland to stop logging in the Białowieża Forest, which straddles the Polish border with Belarus. Arguing that loggers are only felling trees infested with pests, the Polish government has vowed to continue logging and to fight the EU court decision. The attorney for one of the involved NGOs claimed that "[i]n the history of the EU, emergency measures like this ban have only been used three times in nature conservation issues."[33]

As with so many other issues in this book, the struggle between national policy and global or regional policy is at the heart of this controversy and highlights the difficulty of easily grappling with environmental issues in a globalizing world. Cases like this one will continue to emerge, especially as national governments seek to assert their sovereignty against international organizations and with countries like the United States currently leading the charge against international environmental cooperation and action. And as demands for land use grow, especially in urban areas, countries and IGOs will need to plan better than has historically been the case, if they are to manage environmental stress in those locales.

AIR.   Many of today's concerns about air quality around the world focus on atmospheric gases and their impact on climate change. We will discuss climate change later in this chapter. Nonetheless, in this section, we mention some of the relevant polluting gases and also examine briefly the issues of **ozone depletion** and acid rain.

Perhaps the most significant global environmental agreement in terms of a concrete outcome in the last century is the 1987 **Montreal Protocol on Substances that Deplete the Ozone Layer**. Scientific evidence leaves little doubt that the ozone layer has thinned and that the consequences are of great concerns to living organisms. Chlorofluorocarbons (CFCs), a chemical group prevalent in refrigerators, air conditioners, products such as Styrofoam, many spray-can propellants, fire extinguishers, and industrial solvents, deplete the ozone layer by turning ozone into atmospheric oxygen, which does not block ultraviolet rays. The thinning of this ozone layer increases the penetration through the atmosphere of ultraviolet-B (UV-B) rays, which cause cancers and other mutations in lifeforms on Earth.

ozone depletion A "thinning" in the layer of ozone gas in the Earth's stratosphere. Ozone absorbs most of the sun's ultraviolet radiation, with depletion resulting in increased rates of skin cancer, eye cataracts, and genetic and immune system damage.

Montreal Protocol on Substances that Deplete the Ozone Layer A 1987 treaty designed to protect the ozone layer by phasing out the production of numerous substances that scientists have proved are responsible for ozone depletion.

At the UN Environment (UNEP)–sponsored 1987 conference in Montreal, 46 countries agreed to reduce their CFC production and consumption by 50% before the end of the century. Further, in Montreal in 2007, to commemorate the 20th anniversary of the convention, signatories agreed to accelerate phasing out CFCs, as there is belief that CFC reduction also plays a role in combating climate change. As a result of the original 1987 agreement, there is relatively good news on ozone depletion. The annual buildup of CFC concentrations reversed itself from 5% in the 1980s to a slight decline beginning in 1994, only seven years after the Montreal Convention. The CFC buildup had increased so rapidly in the years before 1987, however, that it will take many decades before the damage substantially reverses.

And that reversal is far from certain. The most important caveat has to do with the economic advancement of the Global South. The substitutes for CFCs in refrigerants and other products are expensive, and the estimates of phasing out CFCs worldwide range up to $40 billion. Therefore, the Global South will be hard-pressed to industrialize and provide their citizens with a better standard of living while simultaneously abandoning the production and use of CFCs. Nonetheless, by 2015, all UN members had ratified the protocol and were making efforts to replace the chemical in both residential and commercial uses. As a major success story, in the more than 25 years since signing, according to the UN Environment Programme, the world has phased out 98% of the ozone-depleting chemicals worldwide.[34] It is worth noting, however, that with every policy triumph come some unintended consequences: By the early 2000s, the ban had sparked illegal trafficking in CFCs to such an extent that it rivaled cocaine in global smuggling.

The quality of the air we breathe has deteriorated dramatically since the beginning of the Industrial Revolution. Currently, air pollution from sulfur oxides (SO_x), nitrogen dioxide (NO_2), and particulate matter such as dust and soot cause about 7 million deaths a year, according to the WHO. The largest share of those deaths are in Asia, where many major cities (Beijing, Delhi, and Kuala Lumpur, among others) exceed WHO guidelines for air quality.

Using SO_x as an illustration, we can look more closely at air-quality issues. Sulfur is common in raw materials such as petroleum, coal, and many metal ores. SO_x is emitted when we burn such materials for energy or during such industrial processes as petroleum refining, cement manufacturing, and metal processing. SO_x has numerous deleterious effects. It can cause or aggravate respiratory problems, especially in the very young, the sick, and the elderly. The sulfurous gas in the atmosphere forms an acid when combined with water, and the resulting **acid rain** contaminates water resources and harms forests. The United States, Canada, and Europe were the first to suffer, largely because of their earlier industrialization. The northern United States and the Canadian border region have suffered extensive damage to trees, and many lakes became so acidified that it killed most of the fish. About a quarter of Europe's trees have sustained moderate to severe defoliation, again resulting from transboundary effects of air pollution.

acid rain Rainfall made acidic by atmospheric pollution, typically caused by the industrial burning of coal and other fossil fuels. Such rainfall causes significant environmental harm to forests and bodies of water.

On a more positive note, there has been progress on acid rain reduction. Most European countries abide by a 1979 treaty to reduce acid rain, and the Canada-US Air Quality Agreement (1991) further addressed this issue. These types of agreements could be broadened to other regions and should also serve as models of cross-border environmental agreements.

In our discussion of climate change later in the chapter, much of that focus will be on emissions of CO_2, as is the case in the popular debate about the causes of climate change. But other gases also classify as pollutants and contributors to climate change. In fact, in the landmark US Supreme Court ruling in 2007 on *Massachusetts v. Environmental Protection Agency*, the Supreme Court confirmed that greenhouse gases, including CO_2, methane, and NO_2, are air pollutants and must be regulated under the 1970 U.S. Clean Air Act. This ruling changed the legal context of the climate change debate, and also placed climate change inside efforts to reduce air pollution more generally.

As with CO_2, levels of methane and nitrous oxide have steadily increased in atmospheric concentrations. These gases are produced in a variety of ways, but mostly from agricultural and industrial sources.[35] These data are shown in Figures 13.4 and 13.5. Thus, although CO_2 remains the rhetorical focus in the climate change debate, it is also essential that the world reduce the production of these global public "bads," as they diffuse around the world. In this way, atmospheric pollutants have truly become the most global environmental problem we face, both because of their widespread dispersal and because of the irony that the producers of these pollutants are essentially exporting the negative consequences of their production to everyone else.

WATER. Access to water is essential to all forms of life. In terms of physical realities, 71% of the Earth's surface is covered by water, but 97% of that is saltwater and another 2% is frozen in the polar ice caps. Thus, only 1% is readily available for drinking, watering livestock, and irrigating crops. Because of this

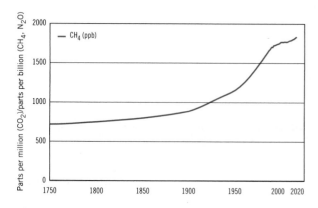
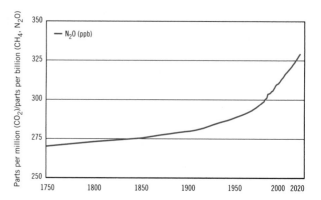

Figures 13.4 and 13.5 As Figures 13.4 and 13.5 show, CO_2 is not the only greenhouse gas increasing in the global atmosphere. Methane and nitrous oxide also pose risks and exacerbate global climate change as well.

scarcity and the stress that humans have placed on freshwater supplies and water resources more generally, water is now considered the "new oil" by many commentators.[36] Disputes over access to water supplies, especially in arid areas such as the Middle East and North Africa, have long been a source of conflict in global politics.[37] Moreover, pollution is depleting or tainting some of the freshwater supply that exists. After tripling between 1940 and 1975, freshwater use has slowed its rate of growth to about 2% to 3% percent a year—but growth in demand is still growth in demand, even if slowed.

Complicating matters even further, many countries show high levels of water risk as measured by the World Resources Institute and shown in Map 13.4. This level of risk is especially concerning for many countries in the Global South. Per capita availability around the world is over 8,500 cubic meters, but it is unevenly distributed. Indeed, about 20% of countries have an annual availability of less than 1,000 cubic meters of water per person. Given the fact that Americans annually use 1,682 cubic meters of water per capita, the inadequacy of less than 1,000 cubic meters is readily apparent. To make matters worse,

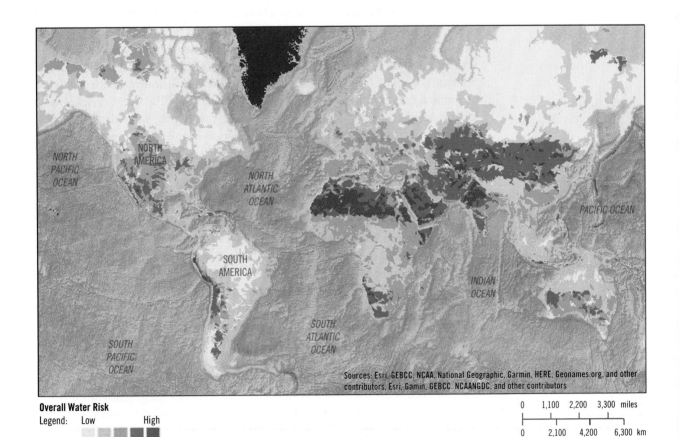

Sources: Esri, GEBCC, NCAA, National Geographic, Garmin, HERE, Geonames.org, and other contributors, Esri, Gamin, GEBCC, NCAANGDC, and other contributors

Overall Water Risk

Legend: Low   High

0   1,100   2,200   3,300 miles

0   2,100   4,200   6,300 km

Map 13.4 Overall water risk around the globe. For those of us living in the Global North, even in places like the southwestern United States, we rarely have to worry about the availability of water for drinking or other daily uses. That is much less true outside the North where water risk is much higher as shown by the areas in the darkest red on this map. (Source: https://www.wri.org/our-work/project/aqueduct.)

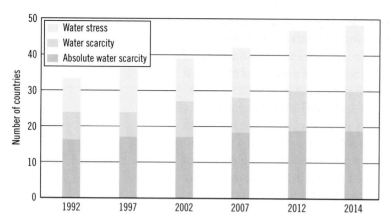

Figure 13.6   Water is a source of concern for a growing number of countries each year. That trend is unlikely to change direction in the near term.

water usage in the Global South will increase in conjunction with economic development. These increases will either create greater pressure on the water supply or limit a country's development potential.

It is also worth noting the number of countries exhibiting some form of water stress and the rise in the volume of that stress over the past 20 years. Figure 13.6, based on data from the UNEP, shows that the number of countries in each of three categories—water stress, water scarcity, and absolute water scarcity—has steadily increased. Such an increase does not bode well for human health or economic development in the coming years.

Thinking about water scarcity in a global political context also raises human rights concerns. If access to water is a human right, an idea around which there is much consensus, then everyone should have that access regardless of his or her ability to pay for it. But, as we know from the news and social scientific research, water delivery is not always a given—and in fact is often a weapon in political struggles. This is particularly true in the Global South, where problems of water access are most acute. As one scholar puts it, "The water crisis is very local; it affects different countries in different ways. At the same time, its greatest humanitarian impact is in water-scarce areas in the developing world."[38]

In light of this concern about water, the United States and Mexico recently reached an agreement to re-establish a higher level of flow to the Colorado River. Before being dammed for agriculture, commercial, and residential use in the United States, the Colorado River flowed more freely across the border, creating a lush delta in northern Mexico. The new pact will allow greater river flow into Mexico, helping to restore the delta ecosystem and provide greater freshwater access to those living in the area. The agreement also allows scientists, environmentalists, and governmental officials to consult annually about the river flow and the ecosystem restoration project. And at least thus far, the Trump administration has not expressed concerns about this environmental agreement (Cornwall, 2017).

Even with this incremental progress, threats to water quality around the world continue. Recently, the largest "dead zone" ever identified was found in the Gulf of Mexico. A dead zone occurs when nutrients produce algae blooms that then die and decompose, drawing oxygen from the water. Largely produced by nitrogen and phosphorous runoff from agricultural fertilization (sometimes called "nonpoint" pollution) in the upper Midwest of the United States, this area in the Gulf largely devoid of life now covers an area about the size of New Jersey, or roughly 8,800 square miles. As Dan Scavia, one of scientists studying the zone, has stated: "You know, it's 8,000 square miles of no oxygen. That can't be good!"[39]

This environmental disaster underscores the urgent need for greater national and global control of pollutant runoff. Even though the pollutants come from the United States, the dead zone spreads to countries throughout the Gulf region. It negatively affects fishing, tourism, and other forms of commerce. It also highlights the ways that freshwater pollution directly harms the seas and oceans. Beyond the Gulf example, the Baltic, Black, and Mediterranean seas, among others, have been heavily afflicted with eutrophication, which encourages the growth of algae, and even ocean areas such as the northeast and northwest coasts of the United States have seen a significant increase in the number of algae blooms over the past quarter-century. Given that 99% of all commercial fishing takes place within 200 miles of continental coasts, such pollution is especially damaging to fishing grounds.

Marine pollution has other sources beyond nonpoint pollution runoff. Spillage from shipping, ocean waste dumping, offshore mining, and offshore oil and gas drilling—a centerpiece of the current US energy strategy—account for a significant part of the pollutants that pour into the oceans, seas, and other international waterways. Petroleum is a particular danger. Spills from tankers, pipelines, and other vessels of transportation are a recurrent threat, as we know from news coverage of events like the *Deepwater Horizon* disaster in 2010, a human and technical failure that produced the largest oil spill in history, dumping over 5 million barrels of petroleum into the Gulf of Mexico. The flow of oil from seepage and dumpsites on land and oil discharge into inland waters are yet other large, human-induced sources of contamination, annually adding more than 40,000 tons of oil to the marine environment.

Still another recent revelation on ocean pollution comes in the form of plastic pellets. One recent study found that 73% of beaches in the United Kingdom contained plastic pellets that had washed ashore. The pea-sized pellets, called nurdles, are primarily used for the industrial manufacture of plastics, but some also come from plastic waste that has been partially broken down.[40] These pellets engender a health threat to wildlife, releasing toxins into the animals that ingest them and creating health concerns both for those primary consumers and for humans further up the food chain.

These examples strongly suggest that the world needs revitalized efforts to create stronger environmental laws about waterways. One such effort regarding the law of the sea was discussed in Chapter 9, but that comprehensive legal structure has unfortunately not met its original promise. These common resources will require collective solutions to cope with such fundamentally transboundary problems.

THE BIOME. Although the other categories discussed earlier illustrate transboundary policy challenges, the biome likely includes the most acute examples. Put simply, living organisms (excluding humans) do not recognize political boundaries. Thus, their normal migratory movements, their collective and individual health, and their protection are not well served by policy solutions based primarily at the state level. Moreover, as our knowledge of systemic relationships suggests, we still lack a full understanding of their interrelationships

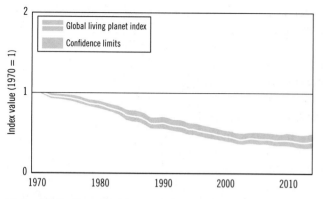

Figure 13.7   Since 1970, the Living Planet Index shows a 58% decline in vertebrate populations globally. This is a disturbing loss of biodiversity, especially when you recall the systemic relationships discussed earlier in this chapter.

and interactions. This last point makes clear that a great deal of care must be taken to preserve the fragile balance of species within the biome.

One assessment of the overall health of the global biome is shown in Figure 13.7. Based on work published by the World Wildlife Fund (2016), this figure shows a decline of 58% in the abundance of species populations globally from 1970 to 2012. Included in that overall figure, the report found that terrestrial populations have declined by 38%, freshwater populations by 81%, and marine populations by 36%. These numbers are troubling not only because of their sheer volume, but also because they include the extinction of entire species as well as declines in species populations. Some of these changes are the result of human encroachment on natural habitat, and some (like those of declining amphibian populations) are the result of toxins leeching into water and the landscape, poisoning those creatures within their biome, promoting starvation, and preventing others from reproducing. Regardless of the exact causes, most of the overall decline is indeed due to human activity, direct and indirect, intended and unintended.

Importantly, some efforts have been made to protect the biome and its biodiversity. One notable endeavor was the 1992 Convention on Biological Diversity, an outcome of the first Earth Summit. This convention had three primary goals: (1) the conservation of biological diversity (or biodiversity), (2) the sustainable use of its components, and (3) the fair and equitable sharing of benefits arising from genetic resources.[41] As of 2016, all UN members with the exception of the United States had signed and ratified the convention. Under the current US administration, a change in that stance is unlikely, further isolating the country on global environmental issues.[42] On most of these issues, concerns emphasize that adherence to a treaty like this will negatively affect potential economic gains from the "mining" of biodiversity.

There have been other global efforts to protect biodiversity—for example, the **Convention on International Trade in Endangered Species of Wild Fauna and Flora** (CITES)—each with varying degrees of impact.[43] One specific case where CITES has had some influence is the protection of African elephants, which are hunted and slaughtered for the ivory in their tusks. Many countries have been working for several decades to ban the ivory trade. In 2016, for example, at a CITES review conference in South Africa, 182 countries agreed to close legal ivory markets in their countries. Tougher penalties for countries failing to clamp down on poaching were also put in place, even if a number of other proposals regarding the disposition of ivory stockpiles were left undecided. With about a third (i.e., about 140,000) of the African elephant population killed by poachers from 2007 to 2014, the threat to this species is very real. But the demand for ivory remains high in some global markets, especially in Asia, and eliminating that element of the problem continues to pose difficulties. Many

Convention on International Trade in Endangered Species of Wild Fauna and Flora A multilateral treaty to protect endangered plants and animals, originally drafted by the International Union for Conservation of Nature in the 1960s and entering into force in 1975.

conservationists view the situation as a "tragedy for elephants . . . when we are seeing such a dramatic increase in the slaughter of elephants for ivory."[44]

At a more micro level, there are increasing calls to protect local and regional areas, their biota, and the ecosystem services they provide to human society (McPherson & Boyer, 2016). Such local protection efforts have the advantage of requiring agreement of fewer parties for their implementation. But they also tend to be more limited in their geographic scope and, thus, in the breadth of their impact. As with the more global protection efforts, these geographically limited protection efforts face opponents who cite the negative economic impacts that will result. For example, when President Obama more than quadrupled the size of the Papahānaumokuākea Marine National Monument to 582,578 square miles of land and sea in the northwestern Hawaiian Islands, fishing interests in the region were vocal about the negative effects this newly protected area would have on their livelihood.[45] As we have noted throughout this chapter and others, the degree to which policy decisions affect economic interests is often a driving force behind the eventual outcome. And as we shall see in the final sections of this chapter, economic calculations weigh heavily in attitudes and decisions about climate change.

Illegal hunting of endangered species, like the rhino, is a serious threat to species conservation. These rhino horns were seized by South African officials before they could be exported to places where people believe the horns can do everything from curing cancer and hangovers to enhancing sexual experiences.

Global Climate Change: The Looming Macrochallenge

Over the past two decades, **global climate change** has become the leading environmental concern, and at the same time a dramatic point of political controversy. Global climate change's place at center stage was symbolized in 2007 by former Vice President Al Gore, Jr., as he stepped up to claim his Oscar award for the documentary *An Inconvenient Truth*. Gore told the Hollywood audience and several hundred million television viewers that addressing global climate change is not just a political issue, but a moral one. "We have everything we need to get started," he urged, "with the possible exception of the will to act." As if to second the call to action, singer Melissa Etheridge also received an Oscar for the movie's theme song, "I Need to Wake Up." There is little doubt that Earth is warming, but the *political* controversy centers on the degree to which anthropogenic causes, or human activities, are the primary factors. For one dramatic side effect of the heated political debate over climate change, see the *Personal Narratives* feature focusing on the experiences of one well-known climate scientist, Michael Mann.

There exists, however, very little *scientific* controversy on this topic. As the 2013 statement from the IPCC clearly states: "It is extremely likely that more than half of the observed increase in global average surface temperature

global climate change   The significant and lasting change in the distribution of weather patterns over periods ranging from decades to millions of years. Both anthropogenic (human induced) and natural causes have been identified by climate scientists.

The Politics of Science and Michael Mann's Push for Climate Truth

Few college professors receive death threats because of the research they do. In fact, most of us work in relative anonymity throughout our careers. But Michael Mann, Penn State University Distinguished Professor of Atmospheric Science, has received death threats and more, as he has engaged with the politically charged atmosphere surrounding climate change research and its rejection by climate change deniers.

In recent decades, there has been a high degree of agreement among climate scientists about human impact on rising global temperatures. As part of this body of scientific work, Mann and several colleagues published two articles in the late 1990s showing the rapid rise of global temperatures in the 20th century. Using what is a now-famous graph, shown in Figure 13.8, named the "hockey stick," their data showed the sharp upward turn in temperature in the 20th century and argued persuasively that the upward bend was primarily the result of human (or anthropogenic) activity.[46]

Quickly after publication, Mann and his colleagues became the targets of threats and intimidation against them, their families, and their jobs. As Mann put it, "The critics, funded by fossil fuel interests, are hoping that their attacks will dissuade scientists from participating in the public sphere and we have to make sure that that is not the case."[47]

The efforts to debunk the work of climate scientists like Mann and others have been launched by members of Congress, private foundations and think tanks, and most recently, by members of the Trump administration, including former Environmental Protection Agency Director Scott Pruitt. In a March 2017 statement, Pruitt was clear in his views about climate science: "I think that measuring with precision human activity on the climate is something very challenging to do and there's tremendous disagreement about the degree of impact. So no, I would not agree that it's a primary contributor to the global warming that we see."[48] But what Pruitt fails to mention is that "tremendous disagreement" does not exist among climate scientists, only among those without the scientific expertise to systematically assess the biophysical impacts of climate change.

This level of hostility from the US executive branch toward scientific inquiry leads Mann to "fear an era of McCarthyist attacks on our work and our integrity." Adding to the worry about increased hostility toward climate scientists are President Trump's statements calling global warming "a Chinese hoax" and a "big scam for a lot of people to make a lot of money."[49] In the meantime, scientists like Mann continue their work in the midst of this threat-filled environment. They are also creating data backups in an effort to preserve their research outside the eyes of current governmental watchdogs who might want to see their climate data disappear. This certainly is not what academic scientists in the United States would call normal ways of going about their business.

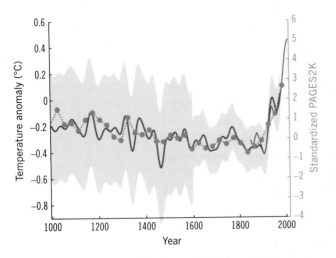

Figure 13.8 Commonly referred to as the "hockey stick" diagram, this figure shows the dramatic temperature rise due largely to increased CO_2 concentrations brought on by the advent of the Industrial Revolution. While there was CO_2 variation prior to industrialization, the rapid increase since cannot be explained away.

from 1951 to 2010 was caused by the anthropogenic increase in greenhouse gas concentrations and other anthropogenic [factors] together."[50] Thus, the accumulation in the upper atmosphere of CO_2 and other **greenhouse gases (GHGs)** generated mostly by human activity have exacerbated the natural temperature cycles of the Earth's climate. These gases create a blanket, trapping heat and preventing the cooling of Earth. This process, called the **greenhouse effect**, is similar to the way that an agricultural greenhouse builds up heat by permitting incoming

Even in the developed Global North, control of natural events is problematic. Although Houston, Texas, is a large, prosperous city in the wealthiest economy in the world, the flood waters from Hurricane Harvey still inundated much of the city in August 2017.

solar radiation to come in, but hinders the outward flow of heat. Rising global temperatures are also linked to increased incidents of severe weather around the world, from hurricanes and typhoons to tornadoes and flooding. One recent study published in *Science* shows that climate change has produced a change in the annual timing of river flooding in Europe; a change in flood timing can also have a cascading effect on river ecosystems, salmon spawning, agricultural production, and hydroelectric power generation.[51]

Global Climate Change: What We Know

The issue of global climate change has taken a central role on the international stage, and debate surrounding the issue has both political and scientific aspects, as further analyzed by scholars (Dessler & Parson, 2006). Scientifically, three things are abundantly clear.

First, as shown in Figures 13.9 and 13.10, global emissions of GHGs have risen significantly. The primary cause has been a huge increase in the emissions of GHGs from burning fossil fuels because of industrialization and the need of the growing world population to warm itself, cook food, and produce economic output. The rate of increase has accelerated in recent decades. For example, CO_2 emissions more than tripled between 1960 and 2006 alone. Deforestation accelerates the buildup of CO_2 in the atmosphere because it destroys trees, which are necessary to convert CO_2 into oxygen by the process of photosynthesis.

One way to calculate this conversion is to compare the CO_2 impacts of an SUV and a big tree. Based on the amount of CO_2 discharged by a large SUV, which burns 800 gallons of gas to go 12,000 miles a year (at 15 miles per gallon), and the amount of CO_2 a large tree can absorb and convert to oxygen, it takes 333 trees to absorb the CO_2 emitted annually by each SUV.

Second, atmospheric CO_2 concentrations have risen, as is clear in Figure 13.10. That most of this added CO_2 comes from human intervention is evident in the fact that the start of the increase coincides with the beginning of the Industrial Revolution in the mid-1700s. Not only did factories and other commercial uses of fossil fuels put more CO_2 into the atmosphere, but

greenhouse gases Carbon dioxide, methane, chlorofluorocarbons, and other gases that create a blanket effect by trapping heat and preventing the cooling of Earth.

greenhouse effect The process by which the accumulation of carbon dioxide and other gases in Earth's upper atmosphere causes an increase in temperature by creating a thermal blanket effect.

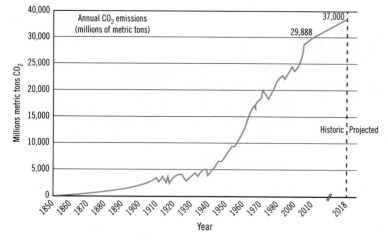

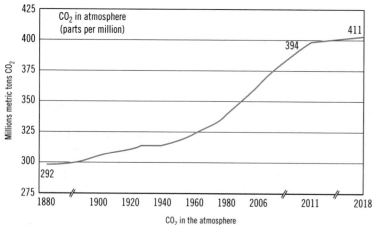

Figures 13.9 and 13.10 Consider Figures 13.9 and 13.10 in tandem with Figure 13.8. Figure 13.9 shows that since the growth of industrialization, carbon dioxide (CO_2) emissions increased dramatically. These increased emissions caused a significant buildup of CO_2 in the atmosphere. Almost all scientists believe that the increase in atmospheric CO_2 (in combination with other atmospheric chemicals like methane and nitrous oxide) has created a greenhouse warming effect that is responsible for the steady increase in Earth's average temperature. Source: World Resources Institute.

mitigation Action to reduce greenhouse gas emissions to slow or stop global warming.

Issue Navigator: Climate Change

the GHGs emitted into the atmosphere linger there for up to 200 years before dissipating. As a result, CO_2 concentrations have increased dramatically over the past 250 years. The increase was slow at first and then gradually grew faster, before accelerating even more beginning in the 1950s. Of the overall increase between 1750 and 2006, half occurred after 1975. Global environmental concern was piqued in April 2015 when atmospheric CO_2 breached the 400 ppm level with no reversal of this trend in sight.

Third, there is no doubt that the global temperature is rising; that is, global climate change is occurring. Between 1880 and 2006, the Earth's average temperature rose 0.7°C/1.3°F. The first decade of the 21st century was the hottest decade since the mid-1800s when temperature records began. Because experiments can show that a CO_2 buildup traps heat, there is certainly a strong case that the causality chain is greater CO_2 emissions → a buildup of atmospheric CO_2 → global climate change. Most people understand that this causal chain is valid—but not all people, as the discussion of Michael Mann's experience in the *Personal Narrative* feature unfortunately makes clear. And the *Challenge Your Assumptions* feature presents one policy scenario for you to ponder regarding GHG **mitigation**. In many situations, policy decisions like the one in this feature are based on how much you personally are willing to pay for a collective benefit.

Global Climate Change: Policy Challenges

Climate change is here and confronts us not only with short-term but also long-term policy and ecological challenges. One challenge is understanding the full range of the ecological consequences of climate change. A second set of challenges centers on the economic consequences of global climate change. A third challenge makes clear the necessary economic and lifestyle changes needed to halt, or at least significantly slow, the rate of global climate change.

CHALLENGE YOUR ASSUMPTIONS

Would You Pay More at the Pump?

Americans make up less than 5% of the world population, yet they consume about 25% of its petroleum. With a private passenger vehicle for every two Americans, the largest single item (45%) in US petroleum consumption is gasoline. Private vehicles use about two-thirds of all gasoline in the United States; Americans drive their private vehicles about 10,000 miles a year per capita, or over 25,000 miles a year per household.

This freedom of movement comes at a price. US dependence on foreign petroleum imports is significant (11% of total petroleum consumption) and expensive ($25 billion in 2018 for oil imports). Pollution is another cost. Carbon dioxide (CO_2) is one of several pollutants produced by motor vehicles, and CO_2 is a primary GHG contributing to climate change. Given Americans' driving habits and long-standing preference for large vehicles such as SUVs, it is not surprising that the United States emits about 24% of all the world's CO_2. Private (non-commercial) driving by Americans generates one-fifth of that, or about 5% of world CO_2 emissions.

American motorists could thus make a major contribution to reducing CO_2 emissions and easing global climate change by driving less and with more fuel-efficient cars. One way to impact the driving habits of Americans would be to drastically hike gasoline taxes. Such an approach to energy conservation, though, might face stiff opposition in the American political system, given the rise of anti-tax movements spearheaded by the Tea Party and other groups seeking limited governmental intervention in our daily lives.

Figure 13.11 shows that per capita gasoline consumption is significantly higher in the three countries with the lowest gasoline taxes, Canada, the United States, and Venezuela. But where the price per gallon of gasoline and the associated tax rate is higher, per capita consumption is substantially lower. These lower consumption levels are also reflected by the many small vehicles driven in Europe. The SUV craze that took the United States by storm in 1990s and early 2000s never hit Europe, and the tendency of Europeans to purchase smaller cars is manifest in the consumption patterns shown.

Historically, Venezuela has been an interesting case to note because of its negative tax structure. The

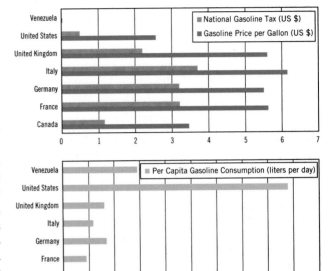

Figure 13.11   Gasoline prices, taxes and consumption. (Source: Data from: https://www.bloomberg.com/graphics/gas-prices/#20162:United-States:USD:g; http://www.keepeek.com/Digital-Asset-Management/oecd/taxation/consumption-tax-trends-2014_ctt-2014-en#page136; http://www.globalpetrolprices.com/articles/52/.)

Venezuelan government has long subsidized gasoline consumption so that it remains inexpensive to consume gas in this rapidly developing, oil-producing country. And even though Venezuela is not considered as industrialized as any of the other countries in this figure, it has the third highest per capita consumption of the countries shown. But it is likely that, as Venezuela's oil production peaks, those consumption patterns may need to change for the economy to prosper. This may obviously be changing with the ongoing turmoil in Venezuela.

What would YOU do? Based on the apparent relationship between gasoline tax rates and per capita consumption, do you think countries should raise their taxes to provide incentives for energy conservation and the development of alternative energy supplies? How much more would you be willing to pay for a gallon of gas? What policy outcomes might convince you to pay more for gasoline? Given that oil supplies are indeed declining globally, what other approaches to energy policy do you suggest? Which ones do you support and why?

ENVIRONMENTAL IMPACTS OF GLOBAL CLIMATE CHANGE.   Neotradition-alists predict dire consequences from global climate change. The IPCC esti-mates that the world's average temperature could rise several more degrees Celsius by the year 2100, about doubling the temperature increase since the last ice age.[52] They believe this change has already altered rainfall, wind cur-rents, and other climatic patterns, and that the deleterious effects, such as the melting of the polar ice caps and the rise of sea levels, will escalate during the coming century as temperatures continue to rise. These climate changes also affect animal migration patterns, the prevalence of disease vectors like mosquito populations, coral reefs around the world, agricultural production, and much more.

One recent study published in *Science Advances* predicts that millions of people in South Asia "will experience temperatures close to the limits of surviv-ability by 2100, without emissions reductions."[53] The authors further argue that adhering to the provisions of the Paris Climate Agreement (discussed later) is the only path that promises to reduce the dangerous heat and humidity levels in South Asia and other places around the globe. But as we will discuss, with President Trump's decision to withdraw from the Paris accord, achieving these reductions to avoid such a future is increasingly uncertain.

Destructive weather changes are yet another possible peril because global climate change affects ocean temperatures and currents as well as upper at-mospheric wind patterns, which in turn control rainfall, temperature, and other climatic variables. Droughts could occur in some places; other areas could see much heavier precipitation, including periods of torrential rainfall. An important factor in such weather changes are the El Niño/La Niña (un-usual warming/cooling) conditions that are natural, but have been occurring with increasing frequency and intensity in the equatorial Pacific Ocean. Just one impact, according to the head of the US Bureau of Land Management's weather program, is the increased likelihood of wildfires due to increasingly arid conditions—as we have seen in recent years in California, for example, which in 2018 experienced its worst fire season on record.[54] The US govern-ment's Fourth National Climate Assessment (released in 2018 and more than 1,600 pages) predicts expansion of the annual fire season to the Southwest, with agricultural yields decreasing significantly and major negative implica-tions for U.S. exports.[55]

Moreover, as the most recent IPCC Assessment Report states, "Many as-pects of climate change and associated impacts will continue for centuries, even if anthropogenic emissions of greenhouse gases are stopped. The risks of abrupt or irreversible changes increase as the magnitude of the warming increases" (IPCC, 2013). As the report bluntly states, the only real ambiguity regarding climate change research is that we won't know the extent of impacts until they actually happen.

Some modernists downplay the damage from climate change. Moreover, optimists predict that some areas could benefit and most could adapt to the changes brought on by global climate change. Drought in some regions would damage their present agricultural areas, but the creation of new arable areas could create prosperity in other regions. Farmers in colder regions might have their growing seasons and bounty increased. And optimists contend that the world can use its technological and financial resources to deal with whatever climate change does occur without causing major changes to our economies or lifestyles. Optimists believe, for example, that nuclear power plants can safely replace environmentally unfriendly coal- and oil-fueled power plants. France and Great Britain have similar economies, yet Great Britain, which generates only 25% of its electricity from nuclear power, emits 50% more CO_2 per capita than does France, where nuclear plants generate 75% of its electricity. Such perspectives lead some scientists to conclude that technology alone can significantly mitigate climate impacts without requiring lifestyle changes.

ECONOMIC IMPACTS OF GLOBAL CLIMATE CHANGE.

Projections of what climate change **adaptation** will cost vary widely. Different studies make different assumptions about how much danger there is from flooding, violent weather, loss of agricultural land to arid conditions, and many other factors that environmental pessimists stress and environmental optimists minimize. Another problem is reaching a cost estimate of preventing or repairing damage. In 2018, Working Group III of the IPCC concluded that ensuring GHG concentrations do not exceed a level that would offer a 66% chance of avoiding global warming of more than 2°C would mean losses in global consumption of 1% to 4% in 2030, 2% to 6% in 2050, and 3% to 11% in 2100.[56] As this projection suggests, the costs of action are not insignificant—and will only grow with delay.

> **adaptation** The process or outcome of a process to adjust to and cope with climate change impacts.

Governments around the world are just beginning to accept and take action on the impacts to their jurisdictions and the costs that they must bear in coming years as they seek to cope with them. In the Global North, the work on climate adaptation will range across infrastructure, health, agriculture, and more, but it also concerns the relative wealth held within those countries. In other words, when they need to adapt, they have the financial resources to do so. In the Global South, climate impacts may well go unaddressed because of the lack of financial resources in those regions of the world. This is one of the reasons why the Global South has repeatedly raised the issue of "loss and damage" so forcefully, beginning at the Copenhagen climate conference in 2009.

THE COSTS OF TAKING ACTION ON GLOBAL CLIMATE CHANGE.

Projections of what it will cost to adapt to global climate change also differ widely, with neotraditionalists saying that the cost will be high and modernists predicting lower costs. It would take volumes to cover the different cost estimates, and resolving them is impossible because they rest on vastly different assumptions, just as do the estimates of the economic impact of climate change. However, it is clear that there will be significant costs, and that they will have an impact on people's wallets, lifestyles, or both.

Consider, for example, one existing proposal for a US tax on CO_2 emissions of $14 a ton to promote conservation and raise money to combat global climate change.[57] That equation translates to an added tax of about 12 cents a gallon on gasoline. Since Americans drive about 10,000 miles a year per capita and the US government estimates that the average private vehicle gets just over 20 mpg, the added annual tax would be about $60 per person, or $240 for a family of four. The cost of electricity from coal- and oil-fueled plants would also increase, and people would pay more for many goods because of the added cost of producing and delivering them. Whether this seems expensive to you or not likely depends on your own income level.

Surely, such costs will be lower than the expense of dealing with the damage from climate change, but only if we act soon. Regarding the economic realities of responding to climate change, there seems to be a wisdom in the observation offered by environmental law and policy professor Dan Esty that "[i]t's important for the people arguing for action to make the case that it's worth it, rather than the promise that it will be free."[58]

The Global Response to Climate Change

The early movement toward addressing global climate change came at the World Climate Conference in 1990, at which most in the Global North other than the United States made nonbinding pledges to stabilize or reduce GHG emissions, and at Earth Summit I's Global Warming Convention or, more formally, the UNFCCC in 1992, whereby virtually all countries, this time including the United States, agreed to ease pressure on the climate and work toward a global solution through annual meetings to discuss policy.

Kyoto Protocol

A supplement to the 1992 UN Framework Convention on Climate Change that requires economically developed countries to reduce greenhouse gas emissions by specified targets tied to 1990 emissions levels and encourages, but does not require, less developed countries to reduce emissions.

THE KYOTO PROTOCOL. During the 1997 round of these discussions in Kyoto, Japan, delegates drafted a supplement to the agreement called the **Kyoto Protocol**. This agreement was the result of intense negotiations, often divided along familiar North-South lines. The Global South wanted the Global North to cut GHG emissions by 12% to 15% by 2012 and to provide the South with massive new aid to cut pollution. Most representatives from the North found neither of these proposals acceptable. For its part, the Global North wanted the Global South to commit to upper limits on future emissions, but the South rejected this idea, arguing, "Very many of us are struggling to attain a decent standard of living for our people. And yet we are constantly told that we must share in the effort to reduce emissions so that industrialized countries can continue to enjoy the benefits of their wasteful lifestyle."[59]

The compromise was to require the Global North to reduce GHG emissions by about 7% below their 1990 levels by 2012 and to urge—but not require—the Global South to do what they can to restrain GHG emissions. The protocol specified that it would go into effect when ratified by at least 55 countries representing at least 55% of the world's emissions of GHGs at that point. Some participants met those standards in 2005, and by early 2019, a total of 192 countries are parties to the treaty (meaning they have formally ratified, accepted, approved, or otherwise acceded to it).[60]

In this context, the continued absence of the United States is conspicuous. Although Vice President Al Gore was the chief US negotiator in Kyoto and signed the protocol on behalf of the United States, President Bill Clinton did not send it to the Republican-controlled Senate for ratification, knowing it had no chance of approval. Among other indications, the Republican leader in the Senate condemned the Kyoto Protocol as a "flawed treaty" that would cripple the U.S. economy.[61] The election of President George W. Bush in 2000 ended any immediate chance of US adherence to the treaty. One reason he cited for his opposition was the lack of requirements for the Global South. "It is ineffective, inadequate, and unfair to America," he told reporters, "because it exempts 80% of the world, including major population centers such as China and India, from compliance."[62] Bush also argued that complying with "the Kyoto treaty would severely damage the United States' economy." Placing himself squarely in the camp of environmental optimists, he argued, "We can grow our economy and, at the same time, through technologies, improve our environment."[63]

MORE RECENT DEVELOPMENTS.   Since 2007, the climate debate has witnessed many twists and turns. On the scientific side, as noted earlier, the IPCC has been increasingly certain and emphatic in its research findings explaining that global climate change is largely human induced and that potential climate impacts are increasingly dire. Many celebrities have also worked to highlight climate change through such events as the Live Earth concerts held around the world in July 2007, featuring entertainers including Bon Jovi, Madonna, and Snoop Dogg. Then, with President Barack Obama's election victory in 2008, which followed the Democratic recapture of Congress in 2006, the time appeared ripe for climate action with a receptive American government. That optimism, however, was short-lived.

Among other initiatives, in 2007 the United Kingdom introduced global climate change for the first time as a topic in the UN Security Council, arguing that it presented a threat to world security. British Foreign Secretary Margaret Beckett contended, "Our responsibility in this Council is to maintain international peace and security, including the prevention of conflict. An unstable climate will exacerbate some of the core drivers of conflict, such as migratory pressures and competition for resources."[64] However, the ongoing North-South divide stymied the British effort, with China's representative rejecting the initiative on the grounds that "[t]he developing countries believe that the Security Council has neither the professional competence in handling climate change, nor is it the right decision-making place for extensive participation leading up to widely acceptable proposals."[65]

In part, all such efforts were skirmishes leading up to the 2009 round of UNFCCC climate talks held in Copenhagen, Denmark. Beginning with this annual meeting among the Conference of the Parties (COP) and continuing in those following, the concept of loss and damage has become a focal point for discussion across the North-South divide. In fact, at Copenhagen, the Global Climate Fund was established, with a $100 billion pledge from the North to provide climate adaptation funding to Global South countries. As the COP process moves forward, this fund will need to be greatly expanded for the Global South to cope effectively with the climate impacts it will increasingly confront.

The Paris COP meeting in 2015 saw the development of what is arguably the most significant climate agreement to date. The major components include:

- Holding the increase in the global average temperature to well below 2°C above pre-industrial levels and pursuing efforts to limit the temperature increase to 1.5°C above pre-industrial levels, recognizing that these restrictions would significantly reduce the risks and impacts of climate change;

- Increasing the ability to adapt to the adverse impacts of climate change and to foster climate resilience and low-GHG development in a manner that does not threaten food production;

- Making financial flows consistent with a pathway toward low GHG emissions and climate-resilient development.

Although agreement on these general principles was indeed path-breaking, the mechanisms for implementation were left undetermined, and decisions about national contributions to GHG reductions were left to the discretion of each party to the agreement. In this way, the Paris agreement represented a significant achievement regarding goals, but it did not create an enforcement mechanism for their achievement. This has remained a central issue in subsequent COPs, including the most recent (COP-24) held in Katowice, Poland, in December 2018. With over 20,000 delegates seeking to clarify the "rulebook" for implementing the Paris agreement, progress was made in terms of reporting procedures, though many NGOs were disappointed at the lack of more forceful measures.

The COP process absorbed significant damage when President Trump announced in June 2017 that the United States would withdraw from the agreement, an act that threatens much of the progress accomplished to this point. That announcement came immediately in advance of the Group of 20 (G-20) Summit in Hamburg, Germany, where US isolation from the other G-20 countries on climate and many other issues was on view for the world to see. German Chancellor Angela Merkel summed up the feeling of many present when she stated at the summit's conclusion, "Unfortunately—and I deplore this—the United States of America left the climate agreement."[66]

This act was only compounded by the Trump administration's dismantling of the Obama-era Environmental Protection Agency's Clean Power Plan, as well as its elimination of US contributions to the UN Green Fund. All of these actions reflect an openly hostile attitude toward climate science—and the very idea of climate change—on the part of the Trump administration. Such a perspective leads people to casually dismiss climate change on the basis of whatever weather they might be personally experiencing in the present moment. For example, in January 2019, while parts of the northern United States and Canada were experiencing record cold, the world outside of North America was experiencing temperatures well above normal (see Map 13.5).

Whether or not these US actions signal growing isolation and a decline in American global leadership will be determined as this and other developments

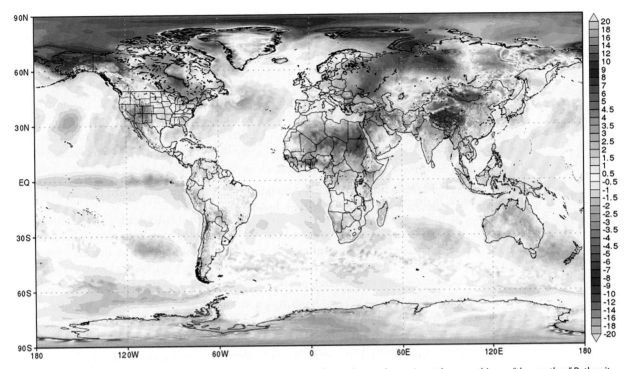

Map 13.5 As this map of temperature anomalies at the end of 2017 reflects, climate change is not the same thing as "the weather." Rather, it is a global phenomenon, and it unfolds over time. Here, we see that one part of the world (North America) can experience temperatures below normal (bluer shades) while the rest of the world (redder shades) is significantly above. This serves as a reminder that even on a day when it is colder than average where you live, the world as a whole is frequently warmer than average.

play out in the coming years in global affairs. Certainly, the current policy approach of the Trump administration indicates that isolation defines the day. The 2020 election cycle may be pivotal to see if proposals like the Green New Deal will redirect attention in more proactive ways regarding climate change.

Chapter Summary

- This chapter focuses on international ecological concerns and international cooperation to address those concerns. Each of these requires systems thinking to better understand the linkages among diverse components of the environment and the interactions between humans and the environment.

- A wide range of views exists about how serious the threats to the biosphere are and

what can and should be done to address them. Broadly, these differing views can be classified as modernist or neotraditional.

- A key concept—and goal—is sustainable development. A key question is how to ensure that the Global South develops economically while simultaneously protecting the environment. Given the justifiable determination of the Global South to develop economically, the potential for accelerated resource depletion and pollution production is high.

- Several large, multilateral Earth Summits have been launched over the last 25 years to address sustainable development. They have achieved some limited gains, with perhaps their greatest success being the recurrent placement of environmental issues on the global agenda.

- There are multiple dimensions to understanding global carrying capacity. One dimension, based in neotraditional thought, focuses on the finite number of people and other organisms that the Earth can sustain for the long term. A second dimension, based in modernist thought, focuses on the ways we can manage and expand the Earth's carrying capacity.

- Continuing expansion of the world's population has begun to slow, but only slightly. Given a reasonably finite amount of resources and ability to absorb waste, population growth presents a challenge to Earth's carrying capacity. This problem is and will be especially acute in some regions, such as sub-Saharan Africa, because their populations continue to grow at a relatively rapid rate.

- Another part of the carrying capacity equation is the degree of ecological stress foisted upon the biophysical world by more than 7 billion people, by the billions of domestic animals they keep for food or companionship, and by the negative outputs (human waste, litter, and other environmental stressors) produced by human society.

- Environmental scientists use the term *Anthropocene* (the age of humans) to describe the current geological age in which we live. From this perspective, we humans are the first global species that can create enormous physical changes to our world, including land, air, water, and the biome.

- Over the past two decades, global climate change has become the leading global environmental concern and a sometimes dramatic catalyst for political controversy.

- The IPCC states that the accumulation in the upper atmosphere of CO_2 and other GHGs generated mostly by human activity has exacerbated the natural temperature cycles of the Earth's climate.

- The annual COP meetings of the UNFCCC process remain the focal point of collective policy-making about climate change. The concept of loss and damage has become a focal point for discussion of climate change across the North-South divide. The degree of global consensus on climate action is high, even if a number of significant carbon-emitter countries are reluctant to take strong action.

Critical Thinking Questions

1. Do you think that the concept of sustainable development is being applied fairly to all countries around the world?

2. Are multilateral organizations and conferences effective ways to pursue environmental quality? Why or why not?

3. How urgent is the need for action to preserve or remediate environmental quality around the globe?

4. Which environmental issues are the most pressing for the global community to engage? Explain your answer.

5. What have been the major roadblocks to global environmental cooperation historically, and what will they be in the years ahead?

Key Terms

acid rain
adaptation
Anthropocene
biosphere
carrying capacity
Convention on
    Biological Diversity
Convention on Inter-
    national Trade in
    Endangered Species
    of Wild Fauna and
    Flora (CITES)
ecological footprint
ecosystem

ecosystem services
fertility rate
global climate change
greenhouse effect
greenhouse gases
Intergovernmental
    Panel on Climate
    Change (IPCC)
Kyoto Protocol
mitigation
modernists
Montreal Protocol on
    Substances that De-
    plete the Ozone Layer

neotraditionalists
ozone depletion
precautionary principle
sustainable
    development
Sustainable Develop-
    ment Goals
systems thinking
UN Conference on
    Environment and
    Development
UN Conference on
    Population and
    Development

UN Conference
    on Sustainable
    Development
UN Framework
    Convention on
    Climate Change
    (UNFCCC)
World Health
    Organization
World Summit
    on Sustainable
    Development

Glossary

acid rain Rainfall made acidic by atmospheric pollution, typically caused by the industrial burning of coal and other fossil fuels. Such rainfall causes significant environmental harm to forests and bodies of water.

adaptation The process or outcome of a process to adjust to and cope with climate impacts.

adjudication Referral of an ongoing dispute to an impartial third-party tribunal (either a board of arbitrators or a standing court) for a binding legal decision.

aggression Tensions between states that produce arms races, militarized interstate disputes, and war. An unprovoked military attack by one state on another is a commonly understood act of aggression.

alliances Formal political associations between two or more parties, made in order to advance common goals and to secure common interests.

anarchy A fundamental concept in global politics identifying the lack of a governing authority in the global system and the implications it has on global interactions.

Anthropocene Denotes the current geological age; viewed as the period during which human activity has been the dominant influence on climate and the environment.

Anti-Personnel Mine Ban Convention (Ottawa Treaty) A treaty drafted and signed in 1997 that aims at eliminating anti-personnel landmines around the world by requiring parties to cease production of anti-personnel mines, destroy existing stockpiles, and clear away all mined areas within their sovereign territory.

arms control Ranges from restricting the future growth in the number, types, or deployment of weapons to the reduction of weapons to the elimination of some types (or even all) weapons on a global or regional basis.

arrearages The state of being behind in the discharge of obligations, often an unpaid or overdue debt.

Asia-Pacific Economic Cooperation A regional trade organization founded in 1989 that now includes 21 countries.

asymmetric warfare A strategy of conflict employed by a weaker actor in contending with a stronger one, in an attempt to "level the playing field." Terrorism is the most commonly cited example of asymmetric warfare.

authoritarian A type of restrictive governmental system in which people are under the rule of an individual, such as a dictator or king, or a group, such as a party or military junta.

balance of power A concept that describes the degree of equilibrium (balance) or disequilibrium (imbalance) of power between and among powerful actors in the global or regional system.

balancing The act of states responding to the threat of an emergent (international) power or coalition of powers by banding together to balance against that emergent state or states.

bandwagoning The act of a weaker sovereign state or states joining a stronger (international) power or coalition as a subordinate partner with the expectation of deriving gains by riding on the "coattails" of that rising power.

behavorialism A strand of intellectual study of global politics that focused on employing scientific methods to the study of social phenomena. Behavioral analysts believe that social science can be studied in ways similar to those employed in the biological and physical sciences.

biological weapons Living organisms or replicating entities (viruses and other pathogens) that reproduce or replicate within their host victims. Employed in various ways to gain a strategic or tactical advantage over an adversary, either by threats or by actual deployments.

biosphere Earth's ecological system (ecosystem) that supports life—its land, water, air, and upper atmosphere—and the living organisms, including humans, that inhabit it.

bipolar system A type of international system with two roughly equal actors or coalitions of actors that divide the international system into two "poles" or power centers.

bounded rationality A concept that rational choices of individuals are bound or limited by time pressures, imperfect information, and biases that influence those choices.

Brexit Refers to the 2016 UK referendum and follow-on negotiations with the EU so that the UK can leave EU membership.

BRICS This term indicates the group of countries comprised of Brazil, Russia, India, China, and South Africa that all exhibit a somewhat higher level of development than many in the Global South, but also continue to face large development-related challenges.

bureaucracy The bulk of the state's administrative structure that continues to serve the public even when political leaders change.

capitalism An economic system based on the private ownership of the means of production and distribution of goods, competition, and profit incentives.

carrying capacity The largest number of organisms that an ecosystem can sustain indefinitely at current per capita rates of consumption of natural resources and discharges of pollution and other waste.

cartel An international agreement among producers of a commodity that attempts to control the production and pricing of that commodity.

center/core The focal points of global politics according to world systems theory, which encompasses Global North countries around which global economic and political power revolve as a result of an overwhelming concentration of capital.

Chapter VII Part of the Charter of the United Nations that deals with action regarding threats to peace, breaches of the peace, and acts of aggression.

chemical weapons Devices that use chemical agents to inflict death or harm to human beings. They are classified as weapons of mass destruction.

classical liberalism A branch of liberal thought that attributes cooperation to human nature and the understanding that people can achieve more collectively than individually.

classical realism A branch of realist thought that believes the root cause of conflict is the aggressive nature of humans.

cognitive consistency The tendency of individuals to hold fast to prevailing views of the world and to discount contradictory ideas and information in the process.

cognitive dissonance A discordant psychological state in which an individual attempts to process information contradicting his or her prevailing understanding of a subject.

Cold War A term used to describe the relations between the United States and the Soviet Union from about 1945 to about 1990. During that period, the two countries avoided direct warfare but remained engaged in very hostile interactions.

collective security Holds that an act of aggression against one state constitutes an act of aggression against all members in good standing of the international community and therefore is deserving of a collective response. Underpins the peace and security strategies and operations of the United Nations, other international organizations, and some states.

colonialism The policy or practice by which a powerful and often distant state acquires political and territorial control over a territory and society, creating a dependent relationship through occupying it with settlers and exploiting it economically.

complex interdependence The broad and deep dependence of issues and actors in the contemporary global political system that many scholars believe is a by-product of globalization.

complex peacekeeping International, multidimensional operations comprising a mix of military, police, and civilian components to lay the foundations of a sustainable peace. Tasks include monitorand ceasefire enforcement as well as the monitoring of democratic elections, disarmament programs, and human rights documentation.

Comprehensive Test Ban Treaty Bans all nuclear explosions in all environments for military or civilian purposes. Adopted by the United Nations General Assembly on September 10, 1996, but has yet to enter into force.

compulsory jurisdiction A state's acceptance of the authority of an international tribunal, thereby creating an obligation for that state to abide by tribunal decisions.

Concert of Europe The balance of power arrangement in Europe from the end of the Napoleonic Wars (1815) to the outbreak of World War I (1914). The chief function was maintaining stability and averting major wars between the powers of the Continent while also policing skirmishes and disputes.

conditionality The policy of the International Monetary Fund, the World Bank, and others to attach conditions to their loans and grants. These conditions may require recipient countries to devalue their currencies, lift various controls, and cut their budgets.

conflict management An approach to security provision that focuses on containing the use of violence in interstate and intrastate conflicts and disputes. Conflict management efforts, which often take the form of third-party mediation or peace operations, are best understood as a necessary prelude to conflict resolution.

constructivism The view that changing ideas, norms, and identities of global actors shape global politics.

containment doctrine A cornerstone of US foreign policy during the Cold War, devised by George Kennan, that sought to prevent the spread of communism through a mix of coercive diplomacy, strong alliances, and military strength.

Convention on Biological Diversity A multilateral treaty introduced at the Earth Summit I in Rio de Janeiro in 1992, which entered into force in 1993. The three main goals of the Convention are the conservation of biodiversity, the sustainable use of it, and the fair distribution of benefits accruing from that use. The treaty calls upon states to develop strategies to pursue and achieve these three goals.

Convention on Cluster Munitions Adopted by 107 states in Dublin, Ireland, on May 30, 2008, this treaty prohibits all use, stockpiling, production, and transfer of cluster munitions (a form of air-dropped or ground-launched explosive weapon that releases or ejects smaller munitions).

Convention on International Trade in Endangered Species of Wild Fauna and Flora A multilateral treaty to protect endangered plants and animals, originally drafted by the International Union for Conservation of Nature in the 1960s and entering into force in 1975.

Convention on the Rights of the Child A human rights treaty setting out the civil, political, economic, social, health, and cultural rights of children.

cosmopolitanism An understanding and appreciation of the shared human experience and the ties that bind people together across nations, borders, and cultures.

crimes against humanity Can include murder, extermination, torture, rape, and other inhumane acts. These are not isolated events but rather official government policy or a systematic practice tolerated or condoned by a government or *de facto* political authority.

critical (or radical) feminism The belief that gender equality is best achieved when we restructure the system in order to change what society values in terms of work, leadership, and politics and what society constructs as normal.

cultural relativism The principle that an individual human's beliefs and activities are understood by others in terms of that individual's own culture.

customary law In international law, a reference to the Law of Nations or the legal norms that have developed through the customary exchanges between states over time, whether based on diplomacy or aggression.

decolonization The undoing of colonialism, or the unequal relation of polities in which one people or nation establishes and maintains dependent territory over another.

defensive realism An explanation of war and conflict in international relations rooted in the realist appreciation of states, power, and anarchy. Defensive realists contend that war is a by-product of the anarchic nature of the international system: States and their leaders typically do not choose war, but the mutual and sometimes incompatible quest for security by states inherently produces armed conflict.

democracy A system of government that at minimum extends to citizens a range of political rights and a range of civil liberties that are important to free government.

democratic peace The proposition, supported empirically to some degree, that democracies do not engage in war with one another. Those who accept this proposition view democracy promotion as the key to containing war and expanding the "zone of peace."

dependency theory The view of global politics as an economic system in which the Global South is dependent upon and disadvantaged by the Global North as a perpetuation of the imperialist relationships established in previous centuries.

deterrence Persuading an opponent not to carry out an undesirable action by combining both sufficient capabilities and credible threats so as to forestall that action.

diplomatic immunity The notion that official diplomatic emissaries of a sovereign state are to be largely immune from prosecution under the laws and procedures of the foreign country to which they are dispatched.

diplomatic recognition The formal recognition of one state's sovereignty by another, extended through the establishment of an embassy and/or consular relations. Diplomatic recognition is a key criterion of state sovereignty, suggesting its relational and subjective nature.

disarmament The act of reducing, limiting, or abolishing a category of weapons.

diversionary theory of war A thesis that a war is instigated by a country's leadership in order to distract its population from their own domestic strife.

Doha Round The ninth and latest round of global trade negotiations to reduce barriers to international free economic interchange.

due process The legal principle that the state must respect in full the rights of the individual within the legal system, allowing judges to define matters of fundamental fairness and justice.

dumping Predatory pricing, especially in the context of international trade, where manufacturers export a product to another country at a price either below the price charged in its home market, or in quantities normal market competition cannot explain.

ecological footprint A tool used to assess and measure human impact on nature—meaning the quantity of nature it takes to support a person, community, nation, or economy, both in terms of consumption of natural resources and pollution and other negative outputs.

economic nationalism The realpolitik theory that the state should use its economic strength to further national interests.

ecosystem A biological system consisting of all the living organisms in a particular area and the nonliving components with which the organisms interact, such as air, minerals, soil, water, and sunlight.

ecosystem services The many and varied benefits that humans gain from the natural environment and from properly functioning ecosystems. These can be grouped into four broad categories: provisioning (production of food and water), regulating (control of climate and disease), supporting (through nutrient cycles and oxygen production), and cultural (spiritual and recreational benefits).

Enlightenment An 18th- and 19th-century Western social and intellectual movement focused on the advancement of science, knowledge, and human rationality.

ethnonationalism The desire of an ethnic community to have full authority over its political affairs—often marked by the pursuit of self-determination by that community.

Euro The official currency of the Euro zone, used by 19 of the 28 member-states of the EU.

European Commission A 28-member commission with shared executive power that serves as the bureaucratic organ of the European Union.

European Court of Justice A supranational court that serves as the "high court" in the European Union (astride the Court of First Instance and Court of Auditors) and is responsible for the enforcement of European Union "community law" and ensuring its application across and within all 28 current EU member-states.

European Parliament The 751-member legislative branch of the European Union. Representation is determined by population of member-countries and is based on 5-year terms.

European Union The European regional organization established in 1993 when the Maastricht Treaty went into effect that encompasses the still legally existing European Communities, including the European Coal and Steel Community, the European Economic Community, and the European Atomic Energy Community.

exceptionalism The belief of some that their nation or group is better than others.

exchange rates The values of two currencies relative to each other (e.g., how many yen equal a dollar or how many yuan equal a euro).

failed states Countries in which the state is unable to effectively maintain order and provide public goods due to political upheaval, economic instability, crime and lawlessness, violence, ethnic and cultural divides, and other destabilizing forces.

fascism An ideology that advocates extreme nationalism, with a heightened sense of national belonging or ethnic identity.

feminist theory A collection of theoretical approaches that analyze the role of gender in global politics.

fertility rate The average number of children who would be born to a woman over her lifetime.

first-generation rights Based on the principles of individualism and noninterference, these are "negative" rights based on the Anglo-American principles of liberty. Developed under a strong mistrust of government, they have evolved into "civil" or "political" rights.

former Soviet republics (FSRs) These are 15 independent states that seceded from the Union of Soviet Socialist Republics in its dissolution in December 1991. They include Armenia, Azerbaijan, Belarus, Estonia, Georgia, Kazakhstan, Kyrgyzstan, Latvia, Lithuania, Moldova, Russia, Tajikistan, Turkmenistan, Ukraine, and Uzbekistan.

functionalism A theoretical perspective that explains cooperation between governance structures by focusing on the necessity of people and states to interact on specific issue areas, such as communications, trade, travel, health, or environmental protection activity.

fundamentalism A particular, literalist interpretation of and approach to one's faith tradition that seeks a return to traditional religious attitudes and beliefs as well as the introduction of such attitudes and beliefs into the social, political, and legal realms.

fungible The idea that power of one type (e.g., military power) is not necessarily transferable or applicable to other policy areas. Thus, military power might not prove helpful in the financial or environmental sector.

gender opinion gap The difference in attitudes on various issues between those identifying as male and those identifying as female along any one of a number of dimensions, including foreign policy preferences.

General Agreement on Tariffs and Trade A series of multilateral trade negotiations that reduced tariffs after World War II and continued into the early 1990s. Became enforced by the World Trade Organization beginning in 1993.

global civil society The realm of ideas, values, institutions, organizations, networks, and individuals located between the society, the state, and the market and operating outside and apart from the confines of national societies, polities, and economic structures.

global climate change The significant and lasting change in the distribution of weather patterns over periods ranging from decades to millions of years. Both anthropogenic (human induced) and natural causes have been identified by climate scientists.

global governance The multiple structures and processes that regulate the behavior of state and nonstate actors on a wide range of global norms, from the laws of the sea to the protection of civilians in armed conflict.

Global North Refers to the 57 countries with high human development. Most, but not all, of these countries are located in the Northern Hemisphere.

Global North–Global South divide (or North-South divide) The economic disparities between the developed North and underdeveloped South that are the roots of tension in global forums. To a large degree, this cleavage is a legacy of colonialism.

global politics Who gets what, how, and when around the globe. Used to describe the substantive focus of this book. Signifies that many interactions in today's world no longer fit with the term *international*, which implies that states remain the sole purveyors of global political activity.

global security The efforts taken by a community of states to protect against threats that are transnational in nature. The responses to these threats are usually multilateral, often involving regional and/or international organizations.

Global South Countries that have medium or low economic and human development. The Global South is made up of some 133 countries out of a total of 197. Most of them are in South and Central America, Asia, and Africa.

globalization A multifaceted concept that represents the increasing integration of economics, communications, and culture across national boundaries.

greenhouse effect The process by which the accumulation of carbon dioxide and other gases in Earth's upper atmosphere causes an increase in temperature by creating a thermal blanket.

greenhouse gases Carbon dioxide, methane, chlorofluorocarbons, and other gases that create a blanket effect by trapping heat and preventing the cooling of Earth.

gross domestic product A measure of economic activity within a country including activity by both domestic and foreign-owned sources.

gross national product A measure of the sum of all goods and services produced by a country's nationals, whether they are in the country or abroad.

Group of 20 A standing forum for economic summitry amongst sectoral policy officials (finance, environment, etc.) and heads-of-state from the world's largest and fastest growing economies.

Group of 77 (G-77) The group of 77 countries of the South that cosponsored the Joint Declaration of Developing Countries in 1963 calling for greater equity in North–South trade. This group has now come to include 134 members and represents the interests of the less developed countries of the South.

Group of Seven/Eight The seven economically largest free market countries (Canada, France, Germany, Great Britain, Italy, Japan, and the United States) plus Russia (a participant since 1998, suspended in 2014).

Hague Convention Name given to the peace conferences held in the Netherlands in 1899 and 1907 where the global community issued the first formal statements of the laws of war and war crimes.

hard power The use or threatened use of material power assets by an actor to compel one or more other actors to undertake or not undertake a desired action. Hard power relies on coercion.

hawk/hawkish In foreign policy, a term used to describe individuals and/or attitudes that favor a more aggressive, coercive, "hard-line" position and approach often predicated on military strength.

head-of-state immunity The notion that a person's conduct as the head of state or a high-ranking political official renders that person "above the law" and not culpable for any criminal activity carried out in the dispatch of his or her responsibilities.

hegemony A systemic arrangement whereby one predominantly powerful actor possesses both the disproportionate material capabilities and the will to enforce a set of rules to lend order and structure to that system.

heuristic devices A range of psychological strategies that allow individuals to simplify complex decisions.

high-value, low-probability problems The nature of most problems or threats, in which the likelihood of a given individual being impacted is very low but the consequences if it occurs are very serious.

Holy Roman Empire The domination and unification of a political territory in western and central Europe that lasted from its inception with Charlemagne in 800 to the renunciation of the imperial title by Francis II in 1806.

"homegrown" terrorism A thesis that contends the most recent wave of transnational terrorism is being advanced by "homegrown" actors living in, and citizens of, Western countries with only loose ties to groups such as ISIS and al-Qaeda.

human rights Inalienable fundamental rights to which a person is inherently entitled simply because he or she is a human being. Conceived as universal and egalitarian, these rights may exist as natural rights or as legal rights in both national and international law.

human security An emerging paradigm for understanding security vulnerabilities that challenges the traditional notion of national security by arguing the proper referent for security should be the individual rather than the state. Human security holds that a people-centered view of security is necessary for national, regional, and global stability.

human trafficking The illegal trade of human beings for the purposes of reproductive slavery, commercial sexual exploitation, forced labor, or a modern-day form of slavery.

ideological/theological school of law A set of related ideas in secular or religious thought, usually founded on identifiable thinkers and their works, that provides a coherent legal framework.

IGO secretariat The executive body that manages the organization.

imperialism A term nearly synonymous with *colonialism*, recalling the empire building of the European powers in the 19th century. The empires were built by conquering and subjugating Southern countries.

individual-level analysis Emphasizes the ways in which people shape the conduct of global politics.

information and communication technology An umbrella term referring to any communication device or application encompassing radio, television, cellular phones, computer and network hardware and software, satellite systems, and various services and applications.

intergovernmental organizations (IGOs) Organizations that are global or regional in membership and scope and whose members are states.

Intergovernmental Panel on Climate Change (IPCC) A UN-sponsored IGO to study scientifically and assess climate change.

Intermediate-Range Nuclear Forces Treaty A 1987 agreement between the United States and the Soviet Union signed by President Reagan and General Secretary Gorbachev that eliminated nuclear and conventional ground-launched ballistic and cruise missiles with intermediate ranges.

intermestic Characterized by interconnectedness of international and domestic concerns. In decision-making, used to signify the merger of international and domestic concerns.

internally displaced persons People forced to flee their home but who remain within that country's borders.

International Atomic Energy Agency The world's center of cooperation in the nuclear field. Established in 1957 as the world's "Atoms for Peace" organization within the United Nations family. The Agency works with its member-states and multiple partners worldwide to promote safe, secure, and peaceful nuclear technologies.

International Bill of Human Rights An informal name given to one United Nations General Assembly resolution and two international treaties, including the Universal Declaration of Human Rights (adopted in 1948), the International Covenant on Civil and Political Rights (1966) with its two Optional Protocols, and the International Covenant on Economic, Social, and Cultural Rights (1966).

International Court of Justice Serves as the primary judicial organ of the UN and is headquartered in The Hague (Netherlands). Consisting of 15 judges serving rotating nine-year terms, its main function is to settle international legal disputes and to provide advisory opinions on legal matters.

International Covenant on Civil and Political Rights A multilateral treaty the United Nations General Assembly adopted on December 16, 1966, and in force from March 23, 1976. It commits the parties to respect the civil and political rights of individuals, including the right to life, freedom of religion, freedom of speech, freedom of assembly, electoral rights, and right to due process and a fair trial.

International Covenant on Economic, Social, and Cultural Rights A multilateral treaty the United Nations General Assembly adopted on December 16, 1966, and in force from January 3, 1976. It commits the parties to work toward the granting of economic, social, and cultural rights to individuals, including labor rights, the right to health, the right to education, and the right to an adequate standard of living.

International Criminal Court The first permanent global tribunal established to try individuals for war crimes, genocide, crimes against humanity, and crimes of aggression.

international law The body of principles, customs, and rules regulating interactions among and between states, international organizations, individuals, and in more limited cases, multinational organizations.

International Monetary Fund The world's primary organization devoted to maintaining monetary stability by helping countries to fund balance-of-payment deficits.

international nongovernmental organizations Organizations with an international membership, scope, and presence whose members are nonstate actors of various types drawn from the private and nonprofit sector.

international organizations Organizations with an international membership, scope, and presence. There are essentially two types of international organizations—intergovernmental and nongovernmental organizations.

international regime Sets of implicit or explicit principles, norms, rules and decision–making procedures around which actors' expectations converge in a given area of international relations.

internationalism A theoretical approach holding that entities should and can conduct international economic relations cooperatively.

intersectionality Refers to the ways in which multiple institutions of oppression (e.g., racism, sexism, homophobia, transphobia, ableism, xenophobia, and classism) are interconnected and cannot be understood separately from one another.

iron triangle A close, mutually beneficial arrangement between interest groups, the bureaucracy, and legislators within a given political system that forms the basis for the military-industrial complex.

jus ad bellum From the Latin as "just right to wage war"; the primary decision-law of just war theory that is intended to provide the minimal moral and legal criteria necessary to justify a resort to war.

jus in bello From the Latin as "justice in war"; theory that is intended to provide the minimal moral and legal criteria necessary to govern proper conduct in war.

jus post bellum From the Latin as "justice after war"; the third and least developed component of just war theory that is intended to provide the minimal moral and legal criteria necessary to define and assess just outcomes after war.

Kyoto Protocol A supplement to the 1992 UN Framework Convention on Climate Change that requires economically developed countries to reduce greenhouse gas emissions by specified targets tied to 1990 emissions levels and encourages, but does not require, less developed countries to reduce emissions.

League of Nations The first attempt to establish an intergovernmental organization with global reach in terms of membership and issue areas. It existed between the end of World War I and the beginning of World War II and was the immediate predecessor of the United Nations.

least developed countries Those countries in the poorest of economic circumstances. In this book, this includes those countries with a per capita GNP of less than \$400 in 1985 dollars.

legal positivism A philosophy of law that emphasizes the conventional nature of law—that it is socially constructed and even codified. According to legal positivism, law is synonymous with positive norms, that is, norms made by the legislator or considered as common law or case law.

lesbian, gay, bisexual, transgender, queer, asexual and ally In use since the 1990s, and then amended, the term is intended to emphasize diversity of sexuality and gender identity–based cultures and sometimes refers to anyone who is nonheterosexual instead of exclusively to people who are homosexual, bisexual, or transgender.

levels-of-analysis approach A social scientific approach to the study of global politics that analyzes phenomena from different perspectives (system, state, individual).

liberal (or orthodox) feminism The belief that gender equality is best achieved through political and legal reform so that women have equal access and equal opportunity in the workplace, politics, and other public spaces.

liberal internationalism A theoretical perspective that seeks to transform international relations to emphasize peace, individual freedom, and prosperity by replicating models of liberal democracy globally through various foreign policy objectives.

liberalism The view that people and the countries representing them are capable of cooperating to achieve common goals, often through global organizations and according to international law.

limited membership council A representative organizational body of the United Nations that grants special status to members who have a greater stake, responsibility, or capacity in a particular area of concern (e.g., the Security Council).

majority voting A system used to determine how votes should count. This system has two main components: (1) each member casts one equal vote, and (2) the issue is carried by either a simple majority or, in some cases, an extraordinary majority (commonly two-thirds).

manufactured goods Items that require substantial processing or assembly to become usable. Distinct from primary goods, such as agricultural and forestry products, that need little or no processing.

Marxist theory The philosophy of Karl Marx that the economic order determines political and social relationships. Thus, history, the current situation, and the future are determined by the economic struggle, which is termed *dialectical materialism*.

merchandise trade The import and export of tangible manufactured goods and raw materials.

microstates Countries with small populations that cannot survive economically without outside aid or that are so weak militarily that they are inviting targets for foreign intervention.

militarism The belief or desire of a government or people that a country should maintain a strong military capability and be prepared to use it aggressively to defend or promote national interests.

military-industrial complex A term coined by President Dwight Eisenhower that refers to political and economic relationships between legislators, national armed forces, and the defense industrial base that supports them. These relationships include political contributions, political approval for defense spending, lobbying to support bureaucracies, and beneficial legislation and oversight of the industry.

Millennium Development Goals (MDGs) In 2000, 189 nations made and committed to eight global goals aimed at poverty reduction, education, public health, and human rights. This pledge encompassed eight specific goals to achieve by 2015.

Millennium Summit A meeting among many world leaders at the UN headquarters in New York City in 2000 to discuss the role of the UN at the turn of the 21st century. World leaders ratified the United Nations Millennium Declaration.

mitigation Action to reduce greenhouse gas emissions to slow or stop global warming.

modernists Those who believe in humankind's mastery of the environment and possess great faith in technology to solve existing and future environmental problems. Modernists contend that ecosystem carrying capacity can be extended through technological advances.

monarchism A political system that is organized, governed, and defined by the idea of the divine right of kings, or the notion that because a person is born into royalty, he or she is meant to rule.

monetary relations The entire scope of international money issues, such as exchange rates, interest rates, loan policies, balance of payments, and regulating institutions.

Montreal Protocol on Substances that Deplete the Ozone Layer A 1987 treaty designed to protect the ozone layer by phasing out the production of numerous substances that scientists have proved are responsible for ozone depletion.

moral absolutism A philosophical viewpoint that contends that the ends alone cannot and should not justify the means, or that morality should be the absolute guide for human decisions and actions.

moral pragmatism The idea that a middle ground exists between amorality and moral absolutism that acts as a guide to human actions, particularly in regard to international law.

moral relativism A philosophical viewpoint that contends ascertaining the morality of human actions or decisions requires careful appreciation of the context in which said actions or decisions take place.

multinational corporations Private enterprises that have production subsidiaries or branches in more than one country.

multipolar system A world political system in which power is primarily held by four or more international actors.

mutually assured destruction (aka MAD) A situation in which each nuclear superpower has the capability of launching a devastating nuclear second strike even after an enemy has attacked it. The crux of the MAD doctrine is that possessing an overwhelming second-strike capacity prevents nuclear war due to the rational aversion of the other side to invite massive retaliation.

nation A group of culturally and historically similar people who share a communal bond and desire self-government.

nation-state A politically organized territory that recognizes no higher law and whose population politically identifies with that entity.

national security The goal of maintaining the survival of the state through all available means. Originally (and still largely) focused on amassing military strength to forestall the threat of military invasion, national security now also encompasses a broad range of factors related to a nation's nonmilitary or economic security, material interests, and values.

nationalism The belief that the nation is the ultimate basis of political loyalty and that nations should have self-governing states.

nativism A political attitude demanding favored treatment for established inhabitants of a nation-state and resisting the presence or claims of newer immigrants.

naturalist school of law A system of law that is purportedly determined by nature, and thus is universal. Classically, natural law refers to the use of reason to analyze human nature—both social and personal—and to deduce binding rules of moral behavior.

neofunctionalism A theoretical perspective that explains cooperation between governance structures by focusing on the basic needs of people and states to interact on specific issue areas, such as communications, trade, travel, health, or environmental protection activity.

neoliberal institutionalism Embraces and builds on the liberal school of thought that states are rational-unitary actors and that they can cooperate through international regimes and institutions. The focus is on long-term benefits instead of short-term goals.

neoliberalism The branch of liberalism that recognizes the inherent conflict in an anarchic global system but asserts it can be eased by building global and regional organizations and processes that allow actors to cooperate for their mutual benefit.

neorealism A branch of realist thought that attributes the self-interested struggle for power among countries to the anarchic nature of the global system.

neotraditionalists Those who believe in ecological limits and the need to reduce ecological stress, thereby emphasizing conservation and the search for environmental solutions that reduce humanity's impact on ecosystems. Neotraditionalists are sometimes referred to as inclusionists because they view humankind as part of nature.

New International Economic Order (NIEO) A term that refers to the goals and demands of the South for basic reforms in the global economic system.

new security environment A catch-all term referring to the emergence of a multiplicity of "new" (or perhaps newly recognized) threats to the security of states, individuals, and the global system in the contemporary (post–Cold War) world.

"new" wars Identity-fueled, intrastate conflicts that are waged by a wide range of official and irregular combatants and are sustained and fueled by remittances, organized crime, and transnational networks moving money, arms, and people.

new world order An emphasis on maintaining and promoting peace, democracy, and human rights. The "new world order" referred to a Western-led international system in which particular norms and laws favored liberal democracy, civil and political rights, and market-led economic globalization.

newly industrializing countries (NICs) Less developed countries whose economies and whose trade now include significant amounts of manufactured products. As a result, these countries have a per capita GDP significantly higher than the average per capita GDP for the Global South.

nongovernmental organizations Formal legal entities distinct from the state, often operating not for profit, and primarily composed of individuals.

nonproliferation Limitation of the production or spread of any form of weaponry. Higher-profile non-proliferation efforts concern nuclear, chemical, and biological weapons.

nontariff barriers (NTBs) A nonmonetary restriction on trade, such as quotas, technical specifications, or lengthy quarantine and inspection procedures.

norms Ideas that come to be shared by the majority of the population in a given society, such that they become the basis for assessing and regulating social conduct and behavior.

North American Free Trade Agreement (NAFTA) An economic agreement among Canada, Mexico, and the United States that went into effect on January 1, 1994.

Nuclear Utilization Theory This theory asserts that it is possible for a limited nuclear exchange to occur and that nuclear weapons are simply one rung on the ladder of escalation.

nuclear weapons Explosive devices that derive their destructive force from nuclear reactions, either fission or a combination of fission and fusion.

offensive realism An explanation of war and armed conflict in international relations rooted in the realist appreciation of states, power, and anarchy. Offensive realists contend that war is a result of the inherently aggressive tendencies of states and their leaders, who capitalize on the condition of anarchy and purposefully choose war as a tool of advancing their interests and amassing greater power.

Office of the United Nations High Commissioner on Human Rights Established by a United Nations General Assembly resolution in 1993 and mandated to promote and protect the enjoyment and full realization, by all people, of all rights established in the United Nations Charter and in international human rights laws and treaties.

official development assistance (ODA) Often referred to as foreign aid, ODA refers to concessional financial flows from the Global North to the Global South. It can take the form of grants or loans with interest rates below normal market rates (thus, it is considered concessional and not commercially driven).

"old" wars Wars fought by and through the state and its organized, professional, standing armies in pursuit of the national interest. Key distinctions typifying the "modern" state (disaggregated civil and military authority, distinctions between combatants and noncombatants, etc.) shaped the conduct of such wars.

operational code How an individual acts in a given situation, based on a combination of one's fundamental world-view and understanding of the nature of politics.

optimistic bias The pyschological tendency of individuals—particularly those in power—to overrate their own potential for success and underrate their own potential for failure.

optional clause All United Nations member-countries must sign the *optional clause*, agreeing to be subject to the International Court of Justice's compulsory jurisdiction. About two-thirds of all countries have not done so, and others that once were adherents have withdrawn their consent.

Organization for Economic Cooperation and Development An organization that has existed since 1948 (and since 1960 under its present name) to facilitate the exchange of information and otherwise promote cooperation among the economically developed countries.

overstretch A concept developed by historians that suggests a recurring tendency of powerful actors to overextend themselves by taking on costly foreign policy commitments that deplete their finances and generate domestic discord.

ozone depletion A "thinning" in the layer of ozone gas in the Earth's stratosphere. Ozone absorbs most of the Sun's ultraviolet radiation, with depletion resulting in increased rates of skin cancer, eye cataracts, and genetic and immune system damage.

pacta sunt servanda From the Latin as "treaties are to be served/carried out"; an important international norm that treaty agreements between states should be considered to have binding legal force.

particularistic identity politics A zero-sum conception of political identity that tends to generate fragmentation and intercommunal violence along national, ethnic, religious, or linguistic lines. Identity politics employed by elites to consolidate power through zealous appeals to one identity group and derogation of the "other."

patriarchy The system of gender-based hierarchy in society that assigns most power to men, uses male(ness) as the norm, and places higher value to masculine traits.

peace enforcement The use of military means in a semi-coercive posture by an international organization such as the United Nations to introduce and enforce peace in an ongoing conflict setting. Peace enforcement operations relax some of the restrictions on peacekeeping, allowing more expansive rules of engagement and deployment without full consent of the warring parties.

Peace of Westphalia The peace agreement signed in 1648 to end the Thirty Years War, effectively removing papal authority for dispute settlement in Europe. Viewed as the starting point for the modern nation-state system.

peacekeeping The use of military means in a noncoercive posture by an international organization such as the United Nations to prevent a recurrence of military hostilities, usually by acting as a buffer between combatants in a suspended conflict. The international force is neutral and must be invited by the combatants before deployment.

periphery Countries in the Global South that are exploited by the countries in the Global North (center/core) for their cheap labor, natural resources, or as dumping grounds for pollution or surplus production.

Permanent Five (P5) Refers to the five permanent members of the UN Security Council who have the power to veto resolutions. These include China, France, Russia, the United Kingdom, and the United States.

plenary body A session that is fully attended by all qualified members.

polarity The number of predominantly powerful actors in the global system at any given point in time.

political communities As defined by the political scientist Karl W. Deutsch (1957), social groups with a process of political communication, some machinery for establishing and enforcing collective agreements, and some popular habits of compliance with those agreements.

political culture A concept that refers to a society's long-held and fundamental practices and attitudes. These are based on a country's historical experiences and the values (norms) of its population.

popular sovereignty A political doctrine holding that sovereign political authority ultimately resides with the citizens of a state, to whom a state's rulers are accountable.

positive-sum game A contest in which gains by one or more players can be achieved without being offset by losses for other players.

positivist school of law Social and cultural contexts necessitate a legal standard and set of rights and obligations that are consistent with the norms and values of the people living in those states and societies.

precautionary principle The approach holding that measures are warranted to reduce or mitigate risks to human health and/or the environment even if cause-and-effect relationships are not fully established scientifically.

preemption A strategy of warfare predicated on the legitimacy and desirability of using military force against an evident security threat from an adversary prior to one's own state or interests being attacked.

prescriptive rights A right that has existed for so long that it is as effective as a law.

preventive war The use of offensive military force against a potential adversary in order to eliminate a perceived threat before it ever materializes.

primary goods Agricultural products and raw materials, such as minerals. Distinct from manufactured goods, which require substantial processing or assembly to become usable.

primordial identities The view of some political and social theorists that a given identity may be deeply embedded or "hardwired" in a person's consciousness. Such identities override other possible sources of identity, which can produce extreme intolerance and violence toward members of other identity groups.

proscriptive rights Obligations on a society and its government to try to provide a certain qualitative standard of life that, at a minimum, meets basic needs.

protectionism Using tariffs or nontariff barriers, such as quotas or subsidies, to protect a domestic economic sector from competition from imported goods or services.

Protestant Reformation The religious movement initiated by Martin Luther in Germany in 1517 that rejected the Catholic Church as the necessary intermediary between people and God.

public goods Goods that are nonrivalrous and nonexcludable. Nonrivalrous means that consumption of the good by one individual does not reduce availability of the good for consumption by others; nonexcludable means that no one can be excluded effectively from using the good.

purchasing power parity A measure of the relative purchasing power of different currencies. Measured by the price of the same goods in different countries, translated by the exchange rate of that country's currency against a base currency, usually the US dollar.

quotas Quotas are used to create balanced (e.g., gender, race, ethnicity, region, etc.) representation within legislative bodies of national governments and can be mandated by the constitution or electoral laws.

rational actors The idea that people in general aim to maximize their utility and profit from action taken rather than acting against their self-interest.

real dollars Dollars that have been adjusted for inflation.

realism The view that world politics is driven by competitive self-interest and that the central dynamic of the global system is a struggle for power among states as each tries to preserve or improve its military security and economic welfare.

realpolitik A realist interpretation of "power politics" where material and practical factors matter and ethical or moral values do not.

refugees People who are outside their country of origin or habitual residence because they have suffered persecution on account of race, religion, nationality, or political opinion or because they are a member of a persecuted "social group."

regime theory Regime theory argues that international institutions or regimes affect the behavior of states or other international actors on a specific issue, such as nuclear weapons or human rights, by promoting and upholding norms and rules governing behavior.

regime type The type of government prevailing in a given society.

regional trade agreement A broad term the World Trade Organization uses to define bilateral and cross-regional agreements as well as multilateral regional ones.

relative deprivation A condition wherein one gauges what they do not have by comparing themselves with others who are materially better off.

remittances A transfer of money by an expatriate to persons in his or her home country.

resource curse theory Focuses on the difficulties experienced by many resource-rich countries in benefiting from their resource wealth.

Responsibility to Protect (aka R2P) A global policy doctrine, endorsed by the United Nations in 2005, based on the idea that sovereignty confers responsibilities on states and their leaders—first and foremost, to ensure the well-being of their citizens. Among other things, R2P seeks to afford the international community the authority to address threats to human security in the event that a given state and its leaders are unwilling to do so themselves or are responsible for them.

rogue state(s) A state that is perceived to be in noncompliance with the majority of prevailing rules, norms, and laws in the global system and therefore constituting a threat to order.

rules of engagement Rules defining acceptable conduct by members of the armed forces engaged in a theater of conflict during operations or in carrying out the course of their duties. Typically, the rules of engagement are clearly stipulated by political leaders and military commanders and are formulated to advance strategic goals while ensuring compliance with the laws of war.

salience The degree of which an issue, question, or problem can be said to resonate with or "matter" to the general public.

sanctions Economic, diplomatic, or military actions put in place to punish a state in an attempt to coercively force states to comply with legal obligations.

second-generation rights Based on the principles of social justice and public obligation, these tend to be "positive" rights associated with continental European conceptions of liberty and equality. The notion has evolved into what is now called "social" or "economic" rights.

securitization A highly politicized process by which policy issues across various sectors and domains (military, political, social, economic, environmental, etc.) are identified and prioritized as "security threats." This process tends to result in the devotion of greater attention and resources to the securitized issue or problem.

security dilemma Given anarchy, the tendency of states and other actors to undertake actions to enhance their own security in a "self-help" system may result in posing a threat to other states or actors who are uncertain of the original state's intentions. This is a dilemma in that the original action, intended to make the state or actor more secure, has the opposite effect.

self-defense A measure that involves defending oneself, one's property, or the well-being of another from harm. The right of self-defense is available in many jurisdictions as a legal justification for the use of force in times of danger, but the interpretation varies widely.

self-determination The concept that a people should have the opportunity to follow their own political destiny through self-government.

semi-periphery Those countries that do not occupy a commanding position in the global economy but that serve an important function or fill an important niche in the global system, supporting the primacy of the center/core countries.

services trade Trade based on the purchase (import) or the sale (export) to another country of intangibles, such as architectural fees; insurance premiums; royalties on movies, books, patents, and other intellectual properties; shipping services; advertising fees; and educational programs.

Smoot-Hawley Tariff Act Senator Reed Smoot and Representative Willis C. Hawley proposed this act in 1930. The act raised U.S. tariffs on over 20,000 imported goods to record levels.

social contract A concept associated with liberal political philosophy referring to an implicit understanding between citizens and government detailing their mutual obligations.

soft power The use or prospective use of material or ideational power assets by an actor to induce another actor or actors to undertake a desired action or not undertake an undesirable one. Soft power relies on persuasion.

Southern Common Market (aka Mercosur) A regional organization established in 1995 that emphasizes trade relations among countries in South America.

sovereignty The most essential defining characteristic of a state and perhaps the global system. The term strongly implies political independence from any higher authority and also suggests at least theoretical equality.

special drawing rights Reserves held by the International Monetary Fund that the central banks of member-countries can draw upon to help manage the values of their currencies.

Special Tribunal for Sierra Leone A judicial body established by the government of Sierra Leone and the United Nations with the authority to prosecute persons bearing responsibility for violations of international humanitarian law and/or Sierra Leonean law during the civil war in Sierra Leone.

state A political actor that has sovereignty and a number of characteristics, including territory, population, organization, and recognition.

state building The process of creating both a government and other legal structures of a country and fostering the political identification of the inhabitants of the country with the state.

state of nature A theoretical time in human history when people lived independently or in family groups and there were no societies of nonrelated individuals or governments.

state sovereignty A central tenet of global politics first established in the Treaty of Westphalia, which holds that the administrative unit of the state has the sole right to govern its territory and people, free from outside interference.

state-level analysis Emphasizes the characteristics of states and how they make and implement foreign policy choices.

state-sponsored terrorism Terrorism sponsored by nation-states. In general, state-sponsored terrorism is associated with providing material support and/or sanctuary to terrorist or paramilitary organizations.

statecraft The use of military, economic, diplomatic, and ideational tools in the pursuit of clearly defined foreign policy interests and objectives.

Strategic Arms Reduction Treaties (START I and II) START I (1991) and START II (1993) provided for large cuts in the nuclear arms possessed by the United States and the Soviet Union (later the Russian Federation). START I was the first arms control treaty to reduce, rather than merely limit, the strategic offensive nuclear arsenals of the United States and the Soviet Union. START II established nuclear warhead and bomb ceilings of 3,500 for the United States and 2,997 for Russia by the year 2003 and also eliminated some types of weapons systems.

strategic-range delivery vehicles Delivery vehicles for nuclear weapons, such as land- or submarine-based ballistic missiles and long-range heavy bombers, capable of attacking targets at distances greater than 5,500 kilometers. These delivery systems confer tremendous strategic advantage to states possessing them and have often been a great source of instability as well as a target of arms control efforts, such as those between the United States and USSR/Russia.

subsidies Assistance paid to a business or economic sector. Most subsidies are made by the government to producers or distributed as subventions in an industry to prevent the decline of that industry or an increase in the prices of its products or simply to encourage it to hire more labor.

supermajority voting A majority (such as two-thirds or three-fifths) that is greater than a simple majority.

supranational organization An organization that is founded and operates, at least in part, on the idea that international organizations can or should have authority higher than individual states and that those states should be subordinate to the supranational organization.

sustainable development The ability to continue to improve the quality of life of those in the industrialized countries and particularly those in the less developed countries while simultaneously protecting Earth's biosphere.

Sustainable Development Goals Adopted by the UN in 2015 as a roadmap for peace and prosperity for humanity and the global ecosystem now and into the future.

sweatshop A negative term for any working environment that is unacceptably difficult or dangerous. Employees often work long hours for very low pay, regardless of laws mandating overtime pay or a minimum wage.

system-level analysis Focuses on identifying and assessing the constraints and opportunities that the global system imposes on state and nonstate actors alike. Also focuses analysis on how different system structures can shape behavior of actors within a system.

systems thinking A holistic approach to the analysis of socio-political-economic-ecological phenomena. It focuses attention on the complexity of relationships, processes, and actors and how small changes in one part of a system can lead to large changes throughout a system.

tariffs A tax, usually based on a percentage of value, that importers must pay on items purchased abroad. Also known as an import tax or import duty.

terrorism A form of political violence carried out by individuals, nongovernmental organizations, or covert government agents or units that specifically targets civilians using clandestine methods.

theory An interconnected set of ideas and concepts that seeks to explain why things happen and how events and trends relate to one another. Theories allow us to explain and even predict the occurrence of various phenomena.

third-generation rights Remaining largely unofficial, this broad spectrum of rights includes group and collective rights, rights to self-determination, rights to economic and social development, rights to a healthy environment, rights to natural resources, rights to communicate, rights to participation in cultural heritage, and rights to intergenerational equity and sustainability.

Thirty and Eighty Years Wars Two partly concurrent periods of declared and undeclared warfare during the 16th and 17th centuries throughout Europe involving the Holy Roman Empire and various opponents of its centralizing imperial rule.

totalitarianism A political system in which the ruling regime recognizes no limit to its authority and seeks to regulate and control all aspects of public and private life.

transaction costs Impediments to commercial or other cooperative ventures stemming from a lack of trust between and among involved parties rooted in concerns about the enforceability of agreements.

transitional justice Judicial and nonjudicial processes and mechanisms associated with a society's attempts to redress the legacies of massive human rights abuses and work toward accountability, justice, and reconciliation.

transnational Social, political, economic, and cultural activities and processes that transcend and permeate the borders and authority of states.

transnational advocacy networks A group of relevant actors bound together by shared values, a common discourse, and a dense exchange of information. TANs are organized around promoting principles and ideas with the goal of changing the behavior and policy of states and IGOs.

transnational crime The accelerated and illicit movement of drugs, counterfeit goods, smuggled weapons and small arms, laundered money, trafficked humans and organs, and piracy from the high seas to cyberspace.

transnational terrorism Terrorism carried out either across national borders or by groups that operate in more than one country.

Treaty on the Nonproliferation of Nuclear Weapons A multilateral treaty concluded in 1968, then renewed and made permanent in 1995. The parties to the treaty agree not to transfer nuclear weapons or to "assist, encourage, or induce any nonnuclear state to manufacture or otherwise acquire nuclear weapons" in any way. Non-nuclear signatories of the NPT also agree not to build or accept nuclear weapons.

UN Charter Signed on June 26, 1945, the Charter serves as the foundational treaty of the United Nations. All members are bound by its articles. The Charter also states that obligations to the United Nations prevail over all other treaty obligations.

UN Conference on Trade and Development (UNCTAD) A UN organization established in 1964 and currently consisting of all UN members plus the Holy See, Switzerland, and Tonga that holds quadrennial meetings aimed at promoting international trade and economic development.

UN Development Programme (UNDP) An agency of the UN established in 1965 to provide technical assistance to stimulate economic and social development in the South. The UNDP has 48 members selected on a rotating basis from the world's regions.

UN General Assembly The main representative body of the United Nations, composed of all 192 member-states and in which each state has one vote.

UN Global Compact UN Initiative launched in 2000 to guide corporate behavior globally in ethical and sustainable ways.

UN Secretariat The administrative organ of the United Nations, headed by the Secretary-General.

UN Secretary-General The head of the Secretariat of the United Nations who also serves as the UN spokesperson. Many other international organizations also use the term secretary-general to designate their organizational leader.

UN Security Council The main organ of the United Nations charged with the maintenance and promotion of international peace and security. The Security Council has 15 members, including 5 permanent members.

UN Trusteeship Council Suspending operation on November 1, 1994, with the independence of Palau, its major goals were to promote the advancement of the inhabitants of Trust Territories and their progressive development toward self-government or independence.

unanimity voting A system used to determine how votes should count. In this system, in order for a vote to be valid, all members must agree to the proposed measure. Abstention from a vote may or may not block an agreement.

unipolar system A type of international system that describes a single country with complete global hegemony or preponderant power.

United Nations A global intergovernmental organization with near universal membership of the world's sovereign states; established in 1945 after WWII.

United Nations Conference on Environment and Development Often called Earth Summit I or the Rio Conference, this gathering in 1992 was the first to bring together most of the world's countries, a majority of which were represented by their head of state or government, to address the range of issues associated with sustainable development.

United Nations Conference on Population and Development A United Nations–sponsored conference that met in Cairo, Egypt, in September 1994 and was attended by delegates from more than 170 countries. The Conference called for a program of action to include spending $17 billion annually by the year 2000 on international, national, and local programs to foster family planning and improve the access of women in such areas as education.

United Nations Conference on Sustainable Development Also known as Rio 2012, Rio+20, or Earth Summit III, this was the third international conference on sustainable development aimed at reconciling the economic and environmental goals of the global community.

United Nations Framework Convention on Climate Change The UN body that meets annually as the Conference of the Parties (COP) to the Framework Convention. These annual meetings seek to negotiate multilateral agreements over the management of climate change.

United Nations High Commissioner for Refugees Established December 14, 1950, by the United Nations General Assembly and mandated to lead and coordinate action to protect refugees and resolve refugee problems worldwide. Its primary purpose is to safeguard the rights and well-being of refugees.

United Nations Human Rights Council An intergovernmental body within the United Nations system responsible for strengthening the promotion and protection of human rights around the globe and for addressing situations of human rights violations and making recommendations.

United States–Mexico–Canada Agreement The follow-on trade agreement to NAFTA signed in 2018, but not yet approved by the US Congress.

Universal Declaration of Human Rights Adopted by the UN General Assembly in 1948, it is the most fundamental internationally proclaimed statement of human rights in existence.

Universal Periodic Review A unique process that involves a review of the human rights records of all 193 United Nations member-states once every four years.

universalism A belief that human rights are derived from sources external to society, such as from a theological, ideological, or natural rights basis.

Vienna Convention on the Law of Treaties Defines a treaty as "an international agreement concluded between states in written form and governed by international law," and affirms that every state possesses the capacity and right to conclude treaties.

war crimes Violations of the laws of war (e.g., international humanitarian law), including the murder or mistreatment of prisoners of war; wanton destruction of cities, towns, villages, or other civilian areas; the murder or mistreatment of civilians; and the forced deportation of civilian residents of an occupied territory to internment camps.

weapons of mass destruction Often referring to nuclear weapons, but also including biological and chemical weapons. Weapons of mass destruction warfare refers to the application of force between countries using biological, chemical, and/or nuclear weapons.

weighted voting A voting formula that counts votes depending on what criterion is deemed to be the most significant, such as population or wealth.

World Bank Group Four associated agencies that grant loans to less developed countries for economic development and other financial needs.

World Health Organization A United Nations–affiliated organization created in 1946 to address world health issues.

World Summit on Sustainable Development Often called Earth Summit II, this conference was held in Johannesburg in 2002. It was attended by almost all countries and by some 8,000 NGOs, and it established a series of calls for action and timetables dedicated to the promotion of environmentally sustainable economic and social development.

world systems theory The view that global politics is an economic society brought about by the spread of capitalism and characterized by a hierarchy of countries and regions based on a gap in economic circumstance.

World Trade Organization Implements and enforces the General Agreement on Tariffs and Trade (GATT) and mediates trade-related disputes between and among states-parties to the GATT.

xenophobia Fear of foreigners or other "out-groups."

zero-sum game A contest in which gains by one player can only be achieved by equal losses for other players.

Endnotes

CHAPTER 1

1. For the full report, see http://www.p3.pr.gov/assets/pr-draft-recovery-plan-for-comment-july-9-2018.pdf.
2. For an up-to-date count on the world population, see http://www.worldometers.info/world-population/.
3. https://www.un.org/development/desa/publications/graphic/wpp2017-global-population.
4. *Reason in Common Sense, The Life of Reason*, Vol.1, Dover Press, 1980.
5. http://www.hani.co.kr/arti/english_edition/e_northkorea/870329.html.
6. For the full report, see http://visionofhumanity.org/app/uploads/2017/10/Positive-Peace-Report-2017.pdf.

CHAPTER 3

1. http://www.cnn.com/2017/02/24/politics/trump-interview-nuclear-weapons/.
2. https://www.washingtonpost.com/news/made-by-history/wp/2018/08/01/the-distortion-of-islam-that-drives-terrorism/?noredirect=on&utm_term=.f369536c1652.
3 http://www.bbc.com/news/world-europe-37574307.
4. Richard Brookhiser, "The Mind of George W. Bush," *Atlantic Monthly*, April 2003, pp. 55–69.
5. https://www.washingtonpost.com/world/national-security/fbi-director-to-testify-on-russian-interference-in-the-presidential-election/2017/03/20/cdea86ca-0ce2-11e7-9d5a-a83e627dc120_story.html.
6. Transcript of joint press conference, October 21, 2001. Available at the American Presidency Project, University of California, Santa Barbara. http://www.presidency.ucsb.edu/.
7. https://www.sipri.org/databases/milex.

8. https://foreignpolicy.com/2019/03/10/pentagon-eyes-windfall-as-trump-seeks-750-billion-defense-budget-military/
9. http://data.worldbank.org/indicator/MS.MIL.TOTL.P1?year_high_desc=true.
10. http://www.fao.org/statistics/en/.
11. https://data.worldbank.org/indicator/sp.pop.totl.
12. https://www.nytimes.com/2015/10/30/world/asia/china-end-one-child-policy.html.
13. http://data.uis.unesco.org/index.aspx?queryid=154.
14. https://www.unicefusa.org/stories/infographic-education-crisis-syria-statistics.
15. "Scientific Balance of Power," *Nature*, 439 (February 9, 2006), pp.646–647.
16. https://data.worldbank.org/indicator/ne.exp.gnfs.zs.

CHAPTER 4

1. *New York Times*, October 6, 1995.
2. *New York Times*, October 6, 1995.
3. Comment by anthropologist Eugene Hammel in the *New York Times*, August 2, 1994.
4. *New York Times*, April 10, 1994. https://www.nytimes.com/1994/04/10/world/serbs-take-key-area-above-bosnia-town.html
5. *New York Times*, April 10, 1994. https://www.nytimes.com/1994/04/10/world/serbs-take-key-area-above-bosnia-town.html .
6. Statement in "Report of the Secretary-General on the Work of the Organization," quoted in the *Hartford Courant*, September 9, 1999.
7. *Time*, March 12, 1990. http://content.time.com/time/magazine/0,9263,7601900312,00.html
8. Address to Congress by President Woodrow Wilson, February 11, 1918.
9. Political scientist Rupert Emerson of Harvard University, quoted in Wiebe (2001:2).

10. *Business Insider,* 2011. https://www.business insider.fr/us/sudan-oil-production-2011-2
11. *New York Times,* February 26, 1992. https://www.nytimes.com/1992/02/26/world/san-marino-journal-after-1600-years-is-it-time-to-join-the-world.html

CHAPTER 5

1. Pankaj Ghemawat. 2017. "Globalization in the Age of Trump," *Harvard Business Review* (July-August). Available at https://hbr.org/2017/07/globalization-in-the-age-of-trump.
2. Pankaj Ghemawat and Steven A. Altman. 2017. "Is American Enriching the World at Its Own Expense? That's Globaloney," *The Washington Post* (Feb. 3). Available at https://www.washingtonpost.com/posteverything/wp/2017/02/03/globaloney/?utm_term=.614a02863612.
3. https://www.businessinsider.com/world-population-mobile-devices-2017-9.
4. https://www.statista.com/statistics/617136/digital-population-worldwide/.
5. http://www.latimes.com/world/middleeast/la-fg-arab-spring-recap-hml-20151009-html-story.html.
6. https://thediplomat.com/2018/01/google-stumbles-back-to-china/.
7. http://money.cnn.com/gallery/technology/2016/05/23/banned-china-10/11.html.
8. https://www.bbc.com/news/blogs-trending-38156985.
9. https://www.wired.com/2016/10/internet-finally-belongs-everyone/.
10. http://wir2018.wid.world/files/download/wir2018-summary-english.pdf.
11. https://www.who.int/news-room/fact-sheets/detail/obesity-and-overweight
12. https://ec.europa.eu/eurostat/statistics-explained/pdfscache/1151.pdf
13. https://www.nytimes.com/1996/04/14/weekin review/computer-speak-world-wide-web-3-english-words.html?mtrref=www.google.com&gwh=AAE68C9E389DE4D44E0E753383672085&gwt=pay
14. https://www.washingtonpost.com/archive/politics/2000/01/29/english-is-the-talk-of-japan/51052f5c-9a85-4055-9f62-fa2a17570740/?utm_term=.77ecc54c5f6e15
15. https://www.washingtonpost.com/archive/politics/2000/01/29/english-is-the-talk-of-japan/51052f5c-9a85-4055-9f62-fa2a17570740/?utm_term=.77ecc54c5f6e
16. State of the Union message transcript, *Washington Post,* January 28, 2000. https://www.washingtonpost.com/wp-srv/politics/special/states/docs/sou00.htm
17. https://www.brookings.edu/blog/africa-in-focus/2018/09/27/figures-of-the-week-progress-on-the-sustainable-development-goals-in-sub-saharan-africa/
18. https://www.latimes.com/archives/la-xpm-1996-02-23-ls-38942-story.html
19. https://www.womeninpeace.org/i-names/2017/5/16/esther-ibanga.
20. https://rk-world.org/news_archive_show.aspx?archiveid=1714
21. https://www.pri.org/stories/2015-01-14/its-not-about-you-being-muslim-and-me-being-christian-says-one-nigerian-activist.
22. http://nonprofitaction.org/2015/09/facts-and-stats-about-ngos-worldwide/.
23. http://csonet.org/.
24. Randall L. Tobias, Director of U.S. Foreign Assistance and USAID Administrator Address before the U.S. Conference of Catholic Bishops, Washington D.C., December 13, 2006.
25. https://sustainabledevelopment.un.org/content/documents/9486ANilo%20Civil%20Society%20&%20Other%20Stakeholders.pdf.
26. https://www.weforum.org/agenda/2015/09/what-are-the-sustainable-development-goals/.
27. https://www.independent.co.uk/news/uk/politics/eu-brexit-european-union-citizens-feel-like-eurobarometer-survey-results-a7872916.html.
28. https://www.globalfundforwomen.org/womens-movements-a-critical-moment-for-global-womens-rights/#.Wx7iDnovzcs.
29. https://www.hrw.org/news/2017/10/11/globally-girls-struggle-rights.
30. https://www.washingtonpost.com/news/democracy-post/wp/2017/11/21/rape-is- still-being-used-as-a-weapon-of-war-right-now-today/?noredirect=on&utm_term =.166834176afa.
31. https://www.weforum.org/reports/the-global-gender-gap-report-2017
32. https://www.politico.com/story/2018/03/08/women-rule-midterms-443267.

33. https://www.nytimes.com/1995/09/16/world/forum-on-women-fragile-consensus.html?mtrref=www.google.com&gwh=395F49DDABD6FE0DA20BAB3D8DF54516&gwt=pay&login=smartlock&auth=login-smartlock

34. http://www.unwomen.org/en/news/stories/2017/2/take-five-chidi-king-equal-pay.

35. http://fortune.com/2019/05/16/fortune-500-female-ceos/

36. https://www.ipu.org.

37. https://www.undispatch.com/first-time-history-full-gender-parity-top-leadership-united-nations/.

CHAPTER 6

1. https://www.americanforeignrelations.com/A-D/Collective-Security-Early-history.html

2. http://www.historiasiglo20.org/europe/monnet.htm

3. "The History of the European Union and European Citizenship" on www.historiasglo20.org.

4. Yearbook of International Organization, https://uia.org/sites/uia.org/files/misc_pdfs/pubs/yb_2017_vol5_lookinside.pdf.

5. Churchill made the widely quoted statement on June 26, 1954, while visiting the United States. For example, see https://www.dailykos.com/stories/2015/11/29/1455064/--To-jaw-jaw-is-always-better-than-to-war-war.

6. Address to the General Assembly, July 16, 1997, UN Document SG/SM/6284/Rev.2.

7. https://www.un.org/depts/los/convention_agreements/texts/unclos/unclos_e.pdf

8. https://www.wto.org/english/tratop_e/dispu_e/dispu_e.htm

9. World Federalist Movement, https://www.wfm.org

10. Permanent Mission of Germany to the United Nations at http://www.new-york-un.diplo.de/Vertretung/newyorkvn/en/Startseite.html.

11. International Monetary Fund, January 9, 2012, IMF Members' Quotas and Voting Power. http://www.imf.org/external/np/sec/memdir/members.aspx.

12. https://www.theatlantic.com/international/archive/2018/09/antonio-guterres-united-nations/570130/.

13. Address to the Council on Foreign Relations, New York, January 19, 1999, UN Document SG/SM/6865.

14. http://iknowpolitics.org/en/learn/video/major-general-kristin-lund-leading-change-paving-way-many.

15. http://iknowpolitics.org/en/learn/video/major-general-kristin-lund-leading-change-paving-way-many.

16. http://www.nordiclabourjournal.org/artikler/portrett/portrait-2016/article.2016-03-03.2551063647.

17. http://www.unwomen.org/en/news/stories/2017/10/announcer-un-women-convenes-champions-group-to-support-wps-agenda.

18. http://iknowpolitics.org/en/learn/video/major-general-kristin-lund-leading-change-paving-way-many.

19. http://iknowpolitics.org/en/learn/video/major-general-kristin-lund-leading-change-paving-way-many.

20. https://www.un.org/gender/content/un-secretariat-gender-parity-dashboard.

21. https://www.un.org/press/en/2017/gaab4270.doc.htm

22. https://www.everycrsreport.com/reports/R45206.html

23. https://www.un.org/en/sections/un-charter/un-charter-full-text/

24. https://peacekeeping.un.org/sites/default/files/dpko-brochure-2018v17_1.pdf.

25. https://peacekeeping.un.org/sites/default/files/dpko-brochure-2018v17_1.pdf.

26. http://www.undp.org/content/undp/en/home/about-us/results-at-a-glance.html.

27. UN Press Conference, December 6, 2006. https://www.un.org/press/en/2006/sgsm10809.doc.htm

28. https://www.cnn.com/2018/08/18/africa/kofi-annan-obit-intl/index.html.

29. http://documents.worldbank.org/curated/en/918311468316164759/pdf/541650WDI-0200610Box345641B01PUBLIC1.pdf

30. http://www.pewresearch.org/fact-tank/2016/09/20/favorable-views-of-the-un-prevail-in-europe-asia-and-u-s/.

31. https://www.newsweek.com/john-bolton-loves-war-and-detests-diplomacy-even-more-trump-864469

32. *New York Times*, January 8, 1997. https://www.nytimes.com/1997/01/08/world/christopher-and-un-chief-discuss-differing-agendas-for-change.html

CHAPTER 7

1. BBC, 2017. http://www.bbc.com/news/world-middle-east-35806229#orb-footer

2. *Saturday Evening Post* (27 March 1954)

3. https://www.democracynow.org/2015/4/27/no_to_violence_yes_to_dialogue. April 27, 2015.

4. https://www.nobelprize.org/prizes/uncategorized/heroines-of-peace-the-nine-nobel-women-2

5. START, 2017. https://www.start.umd.edu/pubs/START_AmericanTerrorismDeaths_FactSheet_Oct2015.pdf

6. US Centers for Disease Control and Prevention, 2015. https://www.cdc.gov/nchs/fastats/injury.htm

7. START, 2017. https://www.start.umd.edu/pubs/START_AmericanTerrorismDeaths_FactSheet_Oct2015.pdf

8. *PBS NewsHour*, 2017. http://www.pbs.org/newshour/bb/u-s-sees-300-violent-attacks-inspired-far-right-every-year/

9. New York Times, 2015. https://www.nytimes.com/2015/06/16/opinion/the-other-terror-threat.html?_r=0

10. *Washington Post*, April 24, 2002.

11. Julian Borger, "Civilian Deaths from US-Led Strikes on ISIS Surge Under Trump Administration," *The Guardian*, June 6, 2017, https://www.theguardian.com/us-news/2017/jun/06/us-syria-iraq-isis-islamic-state-strikes-death-toll.

CHAPTER 8

1. *Labor*, September 6, 1947. See: https://www.norway.no/en/missions/UN/norway-and-the-un/norways-rich-history-at-the-un/trygve-lies-seven-years-for-peace---a-bio/

2. Congressional Research Service, 2018. "Mexico: Organized Crime and Drug Trafficking Organizations." Report prepared by June S. Beittel, July 3, 2018. Available online at: https://fas.org/sgp/crs/row/R41576.pdf.

3. Schwartz, Peter, and Doug Randall. 2003. *An Abrupt Climate Change Scenario and its Implications for United States National Security*. (New York: Environmental Defense).

4. A special issue of *Security Dialogue* (2004, vol. 35, no. 3) examines the controversial aspects of this concept theoretically, analytically, and in practice.

5. *New York Times*, May 29, 1998. Available online at: https://www.nytimes.com/1998/05/29/world/nuclear-anxiety-overview-pakistan-answering-india-carries-nuclear-tests-clinton.html

6. Homer, *The Odyssey* with an English Translation by A.T. Murray, PH.D. in two volumes. Cambridge, MA., Harvard University Press; London, William Heinemann, Ltd. 1919. Book 16, line 266.

7. *The Hindu*, May 13, 1998. https://www.thehindu.com/topic/From_the_Archives/

8. *The Pakistan Observer*, May 31, 1998. https://pakobserver.net/category/articles/

9. https://www.un.org/womenwatch/osagi/wps/

10. Quoted in BBC, February 17, 2011. https://www.bbc.co.uk/history/worldwars/coldwar/pox_weapon_01.shtml

11. John M. Deutch, quoted in the *New York Times*, February 25, 1996. https://www.nytimes.com/1996/02/25/world/huge-chemical-arms-plant-near-completion-in-libya-us-says.html

12. https://www.nytimes.com/2017/04/04/world/middleeast/syria-gas-attack.html?_r=0.

13. http://www.cnn.com/2017/08/08/politics/north-korea-missile-ready-nuclear-weapons/index.html.

CHAPTER 9

1. http://law2.umkc.edu/faculty/projects/ftrials/conlaw/RopervSimmons.htm

2. https://www.independent.co.uk/news/world/americas/us-politics/donald-trump-laughter-united-nations-general-assembly-claim-iran-patriotism-un-a8554571.html.

3. http://www.internationalcrimesdatabase.org/case/1107

4. https://www.icj-cij.org/en/list-of-all-cases/introduction/desc.

5. https://www.straitstimes.com/world/united-states/john-bolton-calls-un-world-court-politicised-us-to-limit-exposure

6. https://www.un.org/law/icjsum/9623.htm

7. https://www.centcom.mil/MEDIA/NEWS-ARTICLES/News-Article-View/Article/884292/obama-declares-justice-has-been-done/

8. https://home.ubalt.edu/ntygfit/ai_04_distinguishing_perspective/ai_04a/ai_04a_tell/machiavelli_prince18.htm

9. https://founders.archives.gov/documents/Jefferson/01-25-02-0562-0005

10. All quotes from President George W. Bush in this section taken from his Address to the Nation, March 17, 2003.

11. CNN.com, February 24, 2003.
12. *New York Times*, March 11, 2003.
13. Quoted at http://www.why-war.com/news/2002/10/12/iraqwarn.html.
14. Phyllis Bennis of the Institute for Policy Studies, quoted in Margot Patterson, "Beyond Baghdad: Iraq Seen as First Step to Extend U.S. Hegemony," *National Catholic Reporter,* December 12, 2002.
15. Radio Free Europe release, April 9, 2003.
16. https://www.theguardian.com/law/2016/jun/05/fatou-bensouda-international-criminal-court-tyrants.
17. https://www.aljazeera.com/news/africa/2012/06/2012615163252565966.html.
18. https://www.theguardian.com/law/2016/jun/05/fatou-bensouda-international-criminal-court-tyrants.
19. https://www.theguardian.com/law/2016/jun/05/fatou-bensouda-international-criminal-court-tyrants.
20. International Criminal Tribunal for the Former Yugoslavia 2012, *About the ICTY* [Homepage of UN ICTY], [Online]. http://www.icty.org/sections/AbouttheICTY.
21. CNN.com. June 1, 2000.
22. *New York Times,* August 13, 1997.
23. https://www.cfr.org/blog/international-criminal-court-and-trump-administration
24. https://www.telegraph.co.uk/news/2018/09/10/trump-administration-threatens-sanctions-against-international/
25. *New York Times,* June 15, 1998.
26. *Washington Post,* April 12, 2002.
27. Interview of April 29, 2002, in Judicial Diplomacy on the Web. http://www.diplomatic judiciaire.com/UK/ICCUK7.htm.
28. http://www.aljazeera.com/news/africa/2012/04/201242693846498785.html.
29. Statement of the Islamic Resistence Movement, Hamas-Palastine, issued December 17, 2001, in reaction to the speech of President Arafat. http://www.jmcc.org/new/01/dec/hamasstate .htm ©©/

CHAPTER 10

1. http://whitehouse.blogs.cnn.com/2011/11/02/obama-faces-tall-order-at-g-20/.
2. https://cei.org/blog/tracking-public-opinion-trump-tariffs-and-trade.
3. https://www.sanders.senate.gov/download/the-trans-pacific-trade-tpp-agreement-must-be-defeated?inline=file.
4. https://www.migrationpolicy.org/article/international-students-united-states; https://www.iie.org/Why-IIE/Announcements/2018/11/2018-11-13-Number-of-International-Students-Reaches-New-High.
5. https://www.census.gov/foreign-trade/Press-Release/current_press_release/exh1.pdf.
6. https://www.nytimes.com/2018/06/10/us/politics/trump-trudeau-summit-g7-north-korea.html.
7. https://www.bea.gov/international/di1usdbal.
8. https://www.esa.gov/sites/default/files/FDIU-S2017update.pdf.
9. https://www.nytimes.com/2018/06/05/technology/facebook-device-partnerships-china.html.
10. https://www.nytimes.com/2019/05/29/business/huawei-us-lawsuit.html?searchResultPosition=1
11. https://www.marketwatch.com/story/this-is-how-much-money-exists-in-the-entire-world-in-one-chart-2015-12-18.
12. https://www.doughroller.net/banking/largest-banks-in-the-world/.
13. As quoted in Robert A. Pastor, *Congress and the Politics of U.S. Foreign Economic Policy, 1929–1976,* (Berkeley: University of California Press, 1981), p. 86.
14. For additional reading, see the following books:
    - Barry Eichengreen, *Globalizing Capital: A History of the International Monetary System,* 2nd ed. (Princeton, NJ: Princeton University Press, 2008).
    - Charles Kindleberger, *A Financial History of Western Europe* (London: Routledge, 2006).
    - Charles Kindleberger, *The World in Depression, 1929–1939* (Berkeley: University of California Press, 1986).
    - Robert Solomon, *The International Monetary System, 1945–1981* (New York: Harper & Row, 1982).
15. https://www.ft.com/content/225bf402-03b1-11e9-9d01-cd4d49afbbe3.
16. https://www.nytimes.com/2017/09/22/business/economy/military-industrial-complex.html.

17. https://www.nytimes.com/2018/06/18/us/politics/trump-says-us-may-impose-tariffs-on-another-200-billion-worth-of-chinese-goods.html.

18. https://www.wto.org/english/tratop_e/dda_e/dda_e.htm#development.

19. https://www.wto.org/english/res_e/booksp_e/anrep_e/anrep16_chap6_e.pdf.

20. http://www.imf.org/en/About/Factsheets/IMF-at-a-Glance; https://www.cfr.org/backgrounder/imf-worlds-controversial-financial-firefighter.

21. For a timeline (1974–2018) on Greece's debt crisis, see https://www.cfr.org/timeline/greeces-debt-crisis-timeline.

22. https://www.nytimes.com/reuters/2019/04/06/business/06reuters-egypt-economy-imf.html.

23. Walden Bello, from "Justice, Equity and Peace Are the Thrust of Our Movement," acceptance speech at the Right Livelihood Award ceremonies, Swedish Parliament, Stockholm (December 8, 2003).

24. See http://www.imf.org/external/np/pp/eng/2010/070710.pdf, p. 6; https://www.imf.org/external/np/sec/memdir/members.aspx.

25. Johan Norberg, "Three Cheers for Global Capitalism," *American Enterprise Online* (June 2004).

26. http://pubdocs.worldbank.org/en/982201506096253267/AR17-World-Bank-Lending.pdf.

27. http://pubdocs.worldbank.org/en/982201506096253267/AR17-World-Bank-Lending.pdf.

28. https://www.nytimes.com/2018/01/25/business/world-bank-jim-yong-kim.html.

29. Professor John Kirton of the University of Toronto G-8 Information Centre, quoted by the BBC, July 12, 2005.

30. Nicholas Bayne, "Impressions of the Evian Summit, 1–3 June 2003," *2003 Evian Summit: Analytical Studies*, G-8 Information Centre, University of Toronto, http://www.g7.

31. https://www.nytimes.com/2018/06/07/us/politics/trump-allies-g7-summit-meeting.html.

32. https://www.thestar.com/news/canada/2018/01/16/justin-trudeau-confident-in-progressive-approach.html.

33. https://www.nytimes.com/2018/06/07/us/politics/trump-allies-g7-summit-meeting.html.

34. https://www.nytimes.com/2018/06/11/world/canada/canada-milk-dairy-industry-trudeau-trump.html.

35. https://www.odi.org/sites/odi.org.uk/files/resource-documents/12274.pdf

36. https://www.huffingtonpost.com/lori-wallach/nafta-at-20-one-million-u_b_4550207.html

37. Gary Hufbauer of the Institute for International Economics, quoted in the *Virginian-Pilot*, January 14, 2004.

38. https://www.nytimes.com/2018/06/06/us/politics/trump-nafta-businesses-frustrated.html.

39. https://www.usatoday.com/story/news/2018/10/01/comparison-nafta-and-usmca-trade-agreements/1487163002/.

40. Apec.org.

41. https://www.cfr.org/backgrounder/what-trans-pacific-partnership-tpp.

42. *New Zealand Herald,* January 14, 2004.

CHAPTER 11

1. Note that these statistics use World Bank rather than UN definitions.

2. https://fivethirtyeight.com/features/big-business-is-getting-bigger/.

3. http://www.globalissues.org/article/26/poverty-facts-and-stats.

4. https://data.worldbank.org/indicator/SH.MED.PHYS.ZS?locations=XD.

5. https://data.worldbank.org/indicator/sh.sta.mmrt.

6. http://databank.worldbank.org/data/reports.aspx?source=2&series=SP.DYN.LE00.IN.

7. http://databank.worldbank.org/data/reports.aspx?source=2&series=SP.DYN.LE00.IN#

8. https://www.theguardian.com/world/2008/aug/07/china.olympics2008.

9. http://www.oecd.org/newsroom/development-aid-stable-in-2017-with-more-sent-to-poorest-countries.htm.

10. http://ec.europa.eu/trade/policy/countries-and-regions/regions/west-africa/.

11. https://data.oecd.org/oda/net-oda.htm.

12. https://www.nytimes.com/2018/08/18/obituaries/kofi-annan-dead.html.

13. https://www.nytimes.com/2018/08/18/obituaries/kofi-annan-dead.html.

14. https://www.un.org/press/en/1999/19990201.sgsm6881.html.

15. http://fortune.com/change-the-world/list.

16. https://www.unglobalcompact.org/news/4399-08-18-2018/.

17. https://sustainabledevelopment.un.org/post2015/transformingourworld.

18. http://unctad.org/en/PublicationsLibrary/iss2016d1_en.pdf.

19. http://www.unctad.org/Templates/Page.asp?intItemID=1530&lang=1.

20. G-77 at www.g77.org/southsummit2/en/intro.html.

21. https://www.theguardian.com/global-development/poverty-matters/2012/may/15/developing-world-of-debt; http://www.cadtm.org/Crisis-deepens-as-global-South-debt-payments-increase-by-85.

22. https://www.bbc.co.uk/news/business-45350218.

23. NORC, annual survey, www.norc.org.

24. https://www.bp.com/en/global/corporate/energy-economics/statistical-review-of-world-energy/country-and-regional-insights/china.html.

25. https://www.eia.gov/tools/faqs/faq.php?id=87&t=1.

26. BBC online, March 25, 2007, http://news.bbc.co.uk/2/hi/business/6492833.stm.

27. https://www.nytimes.com/2018/08/14/world/asia/china-trade-war-trump-xi-jinping.html.

28. https://www.wto.org/english/res_e/booksp_e/tariff_profiles18_e.pdf.

29. https://www.nytimes.com/video/business/100000005788184/what-bananas-tell-us-about-trade-wars.html.

30. https://www.nytimes.com/2018/06/03/opinion/a-trade-war-primer.html.

31. http://food-studies.net/foodpolitics/agricultural-subsidies/jades-sample-page/.

32. https://www.nytimes.com/2019/05/23/us/politics/farm-aid-package.html

33. See the video story at https://www.cbsnews.com/news/us-fight-against-china-espionage-ensnares-innocent-americans-60-minutes-bill-whitaker/.

34. W. Michael Cox and Richard Alm, "2002 Annual Report: The Fruits of Free Trade," US Federal Reserve Bank of Dallas. https://www.dallasfed.org/fed/~/media/documents/fed/annual/2002/ar02.pdf

35. *New York Times,* November 2, 1996; https://www.nytimes.com/1996/11/02/business/mickey-kantor-gutsy-campaigner-has-smoothed-clinton-s-path.html

36. https://www.oecd-ilibrary.org/development/oecd-international-development-statistics-volume-2017-issue-1/official-development-assistance-as-a-percentage-of-gross-national-income-gni_dev-v2017-1-table3-en; https://www.oecd-ilibrary.org/development/data/oecd-international-development-statistics/oda-official-development-assistance-disbursements_data-00069-en?parentId=http%3A%2F%2Finstance.metastore.ingenta.com%2Fcontent%2Fthematicgrouping%2Fdev-aid-stat-data-en.

37. Frank J. Gaffney Jr., "China's Charge," *National Review,* June 28, 2005.

38. https://www.nytimes.com/2019/05/09/us/politics/china-trade-tariffs.html?searchResultPosition=1

39. https://www.nytimes.com/2018/08/08/business/trump-trade-china.html.

40. https://www.nytimes.com/2017/11/01/world/americas/cuba-un-us-embargo.html.

41. https://www.nytimes.com/reuters/2018/08/16/sports/16reuters-usa-russia-sanctions-en-group.html; https://www.nytimes.com/2019/01/27/us/politics/trump-russia-sanctions-deripaska.html?searchResultPosition=1

CHAPTER 12

1. https://www.unhcr.org/en-us/news/stories/2018/6/5b222c494/forced-displacement-record-685-million.html

2. For up-to-date interactive data on displaced people, see http://popstats.unhcr.org/en/overview.

3. http://popstats.unhcr.org/en/overview.

4. For the full text, go to http://www.un.org/en/universal-declaration-human-rights/.

5. https://constitutioncenter.org/interactive-constitution/amendments/amendment-v

6. The idea of the generation of rights was coined by Karel Vasak in the 1970s to reflect the rallying cry of the French Revolution—liberty, equality, and fraternity.

7. For a more activist approach to human rights and the environment, see https://www.hrw.org/news/2018/03/01/case-right-healthy-environment.

8. For the most recent human rights cases being litigated at national levels, see https://ijrcenter.org/cases-before-national-courts/.

9. http://indicators.ohchr.org/.

10. https://www.washingtonpost.com/world/national-security/us-expected-to-back-away-from-un-human-rights-council/2018/06/19/a49c2d0c-733c-11e8-b4b7-308400242c2e_story.html?utm_term=.4f22aa4127d2.

11. For an excellent video reflection of the UNHRC and OHCHR over the last decade, see http://www.ohchr.org/EN/HRBodies/HRC/Pages/HRCAt10.aspx.

12. For an excellent list of key human rights NGOs, see http://www.humanrights.com/voices-for-human-rights/human-rights-organizations/non-governmental.html.

13. https://www.ft.com/content/18b9b194-fb98-11e8-aebf-99e208d3e521.

14. https://www.bbc.com/news/world-europe-33986738.

15. Tharoor, Ishaan, "Slovakia Will Take in 200 Syrian Refugees, but They Have to Be Christian," *Washington Post*, August 19, 2015.

16. For more information on Invisible Children and the global campaign, see http://invisiblechildren.com/kony-2012/.

17. http://www.pbs.org/newshour/rundown/obama-to-disclose-how-many-civilians-died-in-u-s-drone-attacks/.

18. https://www.people-press.org/2018/11/29/conflicting-partisan-priorities-for-u-s-foreign-policy/

19. For the most recent data on this reality, see https://interactive.unwomen.org/multimedia/infographic/violenceagainstwomen/en/index.html#nav-1.

20. https://data2.unhcr.org/en/situations/mediterranean

21. https://www.newswire.ca/news-releases/national-survey-reveals-the-canadian-public-opinion-about-immigration-has-remained-stable-or-grown-more-positive-over-the-past-year-598322281.html

22. https://www.cicnews.com/2019/04/majority-of-canadians-maintain-positive-views-of-immigration-new-survey-finds-0412240.html

23. https://www.weforum.org/agenda/2018/12/canada-wants-to-take-in-more-than-1-million-new-immigrants-in-the-next-3-years/.

24. For more information, see https://www.hrw.org/topic/childrens-rights.

25. http://www.warchild.org/.

26. https://www.hrw.org/topic/childrens-rights/child-soldiers.

27. https://foreignpolicy.com/2016/06/29/syrias-refugee-children-have-lost-all-hope/?utm_content=buffer3ee27&utm_medium=social&utm_source=facebook.com&utm_campaign=buffer.

28. https://www.unicef.org/media/media_94417.html.

29. http://www.migrationpolicy.org/news/us-record-shows-refugees-are-not-threat.

30. https://www.nytimes.com/2015/06/25/us/tally-of-attacks-in-us-challenges-perceptions-of-top-terror-threat.html?_r=0.

31. https://www.aauw.org/research/the-simple-truth-about-the-gender-pay-gap/

32. https://polarisproject.org/human-trafficking/facts

33. https://www.nytimes.com/2018/03/05/us/student-protest-movements.html.

34. www.hpalliance.org/what_we_do.

35. see http://prospect.org/article/campus-anti-sweatshop-movement.

36. http://www.unodc.org/unodc/en/human-trafficking/what-is-human-trafficking.html.

37. http://www.guestworkeralliance.org/tag/hersheys/.

CHAPTER 13

1. https://www.wearestillin.com/.

2. https://science.sciencemag.org/content/162/3859/1243.full

3. Christopher Flavin et al., *State of the World 2003* (Worldwatch Institute: Washington, DC, 2005), p. 5.

4. http://www.riob.org/IMG/pdf/Dominique_Fougeirol_RIOB_Debrecen_Mekong.pdf.

5. http://live.unece.org/env/lrtap/welcome.html.

6. Dennis Pirages (1989) uses the terms *exclusionists* and *inclusionists* instead of modernists and neotraditionalists, respectively.

7. https://www.wsj.com/articles/SB10001424052702304765304577478470785293702

8. "How Singapore Is Creating More Land for Itself," *New York Times,* June 20, 2017, on-line edition, https://www.nytimes.com/2017/04/20/magazine/how-singapore-is-creating-more-land-for-itself.html?searchResultPosition=1.

9. https://web.archive.org/web/20131103112536/http://grawemeyer.org/worldorder/previous-winners/1991-the-united-nations-world-commission-on-environment-and-development.html.

10. https://www.eia.gov/tools/faqs/faq.php?id=709&t=6

11. https://ourworldindata.org/co2-and-other-greenhouse-gas-emissions

12. https://ourworldindata.org/co2-and-other-greenhouse-gas-emissions

13. See Ron Mitchell's International Environmental Agreements Project at http://iea.uoregon.edu/page.php?file=home.htm&query=static for an extensive database of international environmental agreements starting at 1300.

14. *Hartford Courant*, June 8, 1992.

15. *Hartford Courant,* June 6, 1992.

16. September 2, 2003, on the WSSD site at http://www.un.org/events/wssd/.

17. Reuters, June 7, 2002.

18. Undersecretary of State for Global Affairs Paula Dobriansky, on the website of the U.S. Embassy in Indonesia at http://www.usembassyjakarta.org.

19. September 2, 2003, on the WSSD site at http://www.un.org/events/wssd.

20. September 4, 2003, on the WSSD site at http://www.un.org/events/wssd.

21. https://sustainabledevelopment.un.org/rio20.

22. https://sustainabledevelopment.un.org/index.php?menu=1300.

23. http://www.un.org/millenniumgoals/.

24. http://www.unfpa.org/, 2017.

25. http://www.who.int/reproductivehealth/topics/unsafe_abortion/article_unsafe_abortion.pdf.

26. *New York Times,* August 31, 1994.

27. *L'Observatore Romano,* n.d.

28. *New York Times,* September 6, 1994.

29. https://www.prb.org/whatwascairothepromiseandrealityoficpd/

30. http://www.who.int/pmnch/topics/maternal/app_maternal_health_english.pdf.

31. http://www.who.int/mediacentre/factsheets/fs348/en/.

32. http://www.un.org/esa/population/publications/longrange2/WorldPop2300final.pdf.

33. http://www.bbc.com/news/world-europe-40756784.

34. http://web.unep.org/ozonaction/who-we-are/about-montreal-protocol.

35. https://www.epa.gov/ghgemissions/overview-greenhouse-gases.

36. https://www.ft.com/content/fa9f125c-0b0d-11e7-ac5a-903b21361b43.

37. See, e.g., the International Water Event Database at Oregon State University (https://transboundarywaters.science.oregonstate.edu/content/international-water-event-database).

38. Quote taken from Herrera interview at http://today.uconn.edu/2017/05/dangerous-brew-politics-water/.

39. http://www.npr.org/sections/thesalt/2017/08/03/541222717/the-gulf-of-mexicos-dead-zone-is-the-biggest-ever-seen.

40. https://www.theguardian.com/environment/2017/feb/17/tiny-plastic-pellets-found-on-73-of-uk-beaches.

41. https://www.cbd.int/. Last accessed June 2, 2018.

42. https://qz.com/872036/the-us-is-the-only-country-that-hasnt-signed-on-to-a-key-international-agreement-to-save-the-planet/.

43. https://www.cbd.int/brc/.

44. Damian Carrington, "Bid for Strongest Protection for all African Elephants Defeated at Wildlife Summit," *The Guardian*, October 3, 2016; https://www.theguardian.com/environment/2016/oct/03/bid-for-stronger-protection-for-all-african-elephants-defeated-at-wildlife-summit.

45. https://www.washingtonpost.com/politics/obama-to-create-the-largest-protected-place-on-the-planet-off-hawaii/2016/08/25/54ecb632-6aec-11e6-99bf-f0cf3a6449a6_story.html?utm_term=.6b1df511374e.

46. https://climatesciencedefensefund.org/2017/07/20/perspectives-of-scientists-who-become-targets-michael-mann/.

47. https://climatesciencedefensefund.org/2017/07/20/perspectives-of-scientists-who-become-targets-michael-mann/.

48. https://www.washingtonpost.com/news/energy-environment/wp/2018/02/07/scott-pruitt-asks-if-global-warming-necessarily-is-a-bad-thing/?noredirect=on&utm_term=.ce36a93b9ed4

49. https://www.washingtonpost.com/opinions/ this-is-what-the-coming-attack-on-climate-science-could-look-like/2016/12/16/e015cc24-bd8c-11e6-94ac-3d324840106c_story .html?tid=ss_mail&utm_term=.6a38d03154a3.

50. https://www.ipcc.ch/site/assets/uploads/ 2018/02/AR5_SYR_FINAL_SPM.pdf

51. BBC, "Climate Change has Shifted the Timing of European Floods," August 10, 2017.

52. https://www.ipcc.ch/site/assets/uploads/ 2018/02/AR5_SYR_FINAL_SPM.pdf

53. BBC, "Warming to Boost Deadly Humidity Levels Across South Asia," August 2, 2017.

54. https://www.washingtonpost.com/nation/ 2018/11/25/camp-fire-deadliest-wildfire-californias-history-has-been-contained/?utm_ term=.073531d754d9.

55. https://nca2018.globalchange.gov/.

56. http://www.lse.ac.uk/GranthamInstitute/ faqs/how-much-will-it-cost-to-cut-global-greenhouse-gas-emissions/.

57. The proposal was made by Harvard economist Richard Cooper.

58. Yale environmental law and policy professor Dan Esty quoted in the *Washington Post,* October 31, 2006, A18.

59. Mark Mwandosya of Tanzania, head of the LDC caucus in Kyoto, quoted in the *New York Times,* November 20, 1997.

60. https://treaties.un.org/Pages/ViewDetails.aspx-?src=TREATY&mtdsg_no=XXVII-7-a&chapter= 27&clang=_en.

61. *New York Times,* December 12, 1997.

62. *New York Times,* December 13, 1997. Bush's remark was made while he was still a presidential hopeful.

63. *Washington Post,* June 5, 2002.

64. *New York Times,* April 7, 2007.

65. *New York Times,* April 7, 2007.

66. http://www.cnn.com/2017/07/08/europe/ g20-merkel-trump-communique/index.html.

References

Abbott, K. W., and D. Snidal. 1998. "Why States Act Through Formal International Organizations." *Journal of Conflict Organization*, 42(1):3–32.

Abrahms, M. 2006. "Why Terrorism Does Not Work." *International Security*, 31(2):42–78.

Acemoglu, D., and J. A. Robinson. 2013. *Why Nations Fail: The Origins of Power, Prosperity, and Poverty*. Danvers, MA: Currency.

Acharya, A. "Global International Relations (IR) and Regional Worlds: A New Agenda for International Studies." *International Studies Quarterly* 58.4 (2014): 647–659.

Ackerly, B., and J. True. 2010. *Doing Feminist Research in Political and Social Science*. New York: Palgrave Macmillan.

Agah, Y. F. 2012. "WTO Dispute Settlement Body Developments in 2010: An Analysis." *Trade, Law and Development*, 4(1):241–250.

Akande, D., and S. Shah. 2010. "Immunities of State Officials, International Crimes, and Foreign Domestic Courts." *European Journal of International Law* 21(4): 815–852.

Almond, G. A., R. S. Appleby, and E. Sivan. 2003. *Strong Religion: The Rise of Fundamentalisms around the World*. Chicago: University of Chicago Press.

Al-Tamimi, A. J. 2014. "The Dawn of the Islamic State of Iraq and ash-Sham." *Current Trends in Islamist Ideology*. Washington, D.C.: Hudson Institute.

Alter, K. J. and L. Hooghe. 2016. "Regional Dispute Settlement Systems" in *Oxford Handbook of Comparative Regionalism*, Tanja A. Börzel and Thomas Risse (eds.), pp. 538–558. Oxford: Oxford University Press.

Altman, S., Ghemawat, P., and P. Bastian. (2018). "DHL Global Connectedness Index 2018—The State of Globalization in a Fragile World." Available online at: https://www.logistics.dhl/content/dam/dhl/global/core/documents/pdf/glo-core-gci-2018-full-study.pdf.

Amstutz, M. R. 2005. *International Ethics: Concepts, Theories, and Cases in Global Politics*. Lanham, MD: Rowman & Littlefield.

Anderson, B. 1991. *Imagined Communities: Reflections on the Origin and Spread of Nationalism*. New York/London: Verso.

Anderson, M. J. 2016. *Windows of Opportunity: How Women Seize Peace Negotiations for Political Change*. New York: Oxford University Press.

Andrade, L. M. 2003. "Presidential Diversionary Attempts: A Peaceful Perspective." *Congress & the Presidency*, 30:55–79.

Anghie, A. "The Evolution of International Law: Colonial and Postcolonial Realities." *Third World Quarterly* 27.5 (2006): 739–753.

Anheiner, H., M. Glasius, and M. Kaldor. 2004. *Global Civil Society*. Cambridge, UK: Polity Press.

Anheiner, H., M. Kaldor, and M. Glasius. 2012. "The Global Civil Society Yearbook: Lessons and Insights 2001–2011." In *Global Civil Society 2012*. London: Palgrave Macmillan.

Appiah, K. 2006. *Cosmopolitanism: Ethics in a World of Strangers*. New York: W. W. Norton.

Arend, A. C. 2003. "A Methodology for Determining an International Legal Rule." In *International Law: Classic and Contemporary Readings*, 2nd ed., eds. C. Ku and P. F. Diehl. Boulder, CO: Lynne Reinner.

Axelrod, R. 1984. *The Evolution of Cooperation*. New York: Basic Books.

Axworthy, L. 2001. "Human Security and Global Governance: Putting People First." *Global Governance*, 7:19–23.

Azar, E. E. 1990. *The Management of Protracted Social Conflict: Theory and Cases*. Aldershot, UK: Dartmouth.

Baaz, M. E., and M. Stern. 2013. *Sexual Violence as a Weapon of War? Perceptions, Prescriptions, Problems in the Congo and Beyond.* London: Zed Books.

Baele, S. J., and C. P. Thomson. 2017. "An Experimental Agenda for Securitization Theory," *International Studies Review*, 19(4):646–666, https://doi.org/10.1093/isr/vix014.

Bajpai, K. 2000. "Human Security: Concept and Measurement," Kroc Institute Occasional Paper 19. South Bend, IN: Kroc Institute, University of Notre Dame.

Baldwin, D. A. 1979. "Power Analysis and World Politics: New Trends Versus Old Tendencies." *World Politics*, 31(2):161–194.

Baldwin, D. A. 1980. "Interdependence and Power: A Conceptual Analysis," *International Organization*, 34(4):471–506.

Baldwin, D. A. 1997. "The Concept of Security," *Review of International Studies*, 23(1):5–26.

Baradat, L. P. 2003. *Political Ideologies*, 8th ed. Englewood Cliffs, NJ: Prentice-Hall.

Baran, P. A., and P. M. Sweezy. 1966. *Monopoly Capital: An Essay on the American Economic and Social Order.* New York: Monthly Review Press.

Barash, D. 2011. "Why We Needed Bin Laden Dead," *Chronicle of Higher Education*, 57(37):B14–B15.

Barber, B. R. 1992. "Jihad vs. McWorld," *The Atlantic Monthly*, May 1992.

Barber, B. R. 1996. *Jihad vs. McWorld: How Globalism and Tribalism Are Reshaping the World.* New York: Ballantine Books.

Barber, J. D. 1985. *Presidential Character*, 3rd ed. Englewood Cliffs, NJ: Prentice-Hall.

Barnett, M., and R. Duvall. 2005. "Power in International Politics," *International Organization*, 59:39–75.

Barnett, M., and M. Finnemore. 2004. *Rules for the World: International Organizations in Global Politics.* Ithaca, NY: Cornell University Press.

Bartelson, J. 2016. "Blasts from the Past: War and Fracture in the International System," *International Political Sociology*, 10(4):352–368, https://doi.org/10.1093/ips/olw019.

Bassiouni, C. 2007. "Ceding the High Ground: The Iraqi High Criminal Court Statute and the Trial of Saddam Hussein." *Case Western Reserve Journal of International Law*, 39(1):21–97.

Baylis, J. 2001. "International and Global Security in the Post–Cold War Era." In *The Globalization of World Politics*, 2nd ed., eds. J. Baylis and S. Smith. Oxford, UK: Oxford University Press.

Beard, S., and J. A. Strayhorn. 2018. "When Will States Strike First? Battlefield Advantages and Rationalist War," *International Studies Quarterly*, 62(1):42–53, https://doi.org/10.1093/isq/sqx080.

Bell, S. R., M. E. Flynn, and C. Martinez Machain. 2018. "UN Peacekeeping Forces and the Demand for Sex Trafficking," *International Studies Quarterly*, 62(3), pp. 643–655.

Bellamy, A. J. 2009. *Responsibility to Protect.* London: Polity.

Bellamy, A. J., P. Williams, and S. Griffin. 2010. *Understanding Peacekeeping*, 2nd ed. Cambridge, UK: Polity.

Bengtsson, R., and O. Elgström. 2012. "Conflicting Role Conceptions? The European Union in Global Politics," *Foreign Policy Analysis*, 8(1):93–108, https://doi.org/10.1111/j.1743-8594.2011.00157.x.

Bennett, S., and A. C. Stam. 2004. *The Behavioral Origins of War.* Ann Arbor: University of Michigan Press.

Berdal, M. 2003. "How 'New' Are 'New Wars'? Global Economic Change and the Study of Civil War." *Global Governance*, 9(4):477–502.

Bergen, P. L. 2016. *United States of Jihad: Investigating America's Homegrown Terrorists.* New York: Crown.

Berman, M. (1985), *All that is Solid Melts into Air: The Experience of Modernity.* Verso: London.

Betsill, M. M., and H. Bulkeley. 2004. "Transnational Networks and Global Environmental Governance: The Cities for Climate Protection Program." *International Studies Quarterly*, 48(2):471–487.

Bhagwati, J. 2004. *In Defense of Globalization.* Oxford, UK: Oxford University Press.

Bieler, A., R. Higgott, and G. Underhill, eds. 2004. *Non-state Actors and Authority in the Global System.* Routledge.

Bigo, D. 2014. "Security, IR and Anthropology: Encounters, Misunderstanding and Possible

Collaborations." In *The Anthropology of Security*, eds. C. Frois, M. Maguire, and N. Zurawski. Basingstoke, UK: Palgrave.

Bilder, R. B. 2007. "Adjudication: International Arbitral Tribunals and Courts." In *Peacemaking in International Conflict: Methods and Techniques*, rev. ed., ed. I. W. Zartman. Washington, DC: US Institute of Peace Press.

Blagden, D. 2018. "Two Visions of Greatness: Role-play and Realpolitik in UK Strategic Posture," *Foreign Policy Analysis* https://doi.org/10.1093/fpa/ory011.

Bob, C. 2012. *The Global Right Wing and the Clash of World Politics*. Cambridge, UK: Cambridge University Press.

Bobrow, D. B. 1996. "Complex Insecurity: Implications of a Sobering Metaphor: 1996 Presidential Address." *International Studies Quarterly*, 40(4):435–450.

Boehmer, C. 2006. *Neoliberal Institutionalism*. El Paso: University of Texas El Paso. Available at http://utminers.utep.edu/crboehmer/Neo-Liberal%20Institutionalism.pdf.

Bohas, H.-A. 2003. "A New Middle Age: A Post-Westphalian Approach to the European Union." Paper presented at "Challenge and Prospects for the European Union in a Globalizing World," Research Conference of the European Union Center of California, Claremont, CA.

Bonner, M.D. 2007. *Sustaining Human Rights: Women and Argentine Human Rights Organizations*. Pennsylvania State University Press, PA.

Bonner, M. D. 2014. "'Never Again': Transitional Justice and Persistent Police Violence in Argentina." *International Journal of Transitional Justice* 8(2):235–255.

Booth, K. 1991. *New Thinking About Strategy and International Security*. London: HarperCollins.

Booth, K. 1994. "Security and Self: Confessions of a Fallen Realist." Prepared for presentation at the conference *Strategies in Conflict: Critical Approaches to Security Studies,* York University, Toronto Ontario, 12-14 May 1994. Available online at: https://yorkspace.library.yorku.ca/xmlui/bitstream/handle/10315/1414/YCI0073.pdf?sequence=1&isAllowed=y.

Booth, K. 2005. *Critical Security Studies and World Politics*. Boulder, CO: Lynne Rienner.

Booth, K., and N. Wheeler. 2008. *The Security Dilemma: Fear, Cooperation, and Trust in World Politics*. Basingstoke, UK: Palgrave Macmillan.

Bottke, W. 1989. "Rule of Law or Due Process as a Common Feature of Criminal Process in Western Democratic Societies." *U. Pitt. L. Rev.* 51: 419.

Boulding, K. E. 1956. "General Systems Theory—The Skeleton of Science." *Management Science*, 2(3):197–208.

Bower, A. 2015. "Norms Without the Great Powers: International Law, Nested Social Structures, and the Ban on Antipersonnel Mines," *International Studies Review*, 17(3):347–373, https://doi.org/10.1111/misr.12225.

Boyd, J., P. Ringold, A. Krupnick, R. Johnson, M. Weber, and K. M. Hall. 2015. "Ecosystem Services Indicators: Improving the Linkage between Biophysical and Economic Analyses." *Resources for the Future Discussion paper*: RFF-DP 15-40. Washington, D.C.: Resources for the Future.

Boyer, M. A., and M. J. Butler. 2005. "Public Goods Liberalism: The Problems of Collective Action." In *Making Sense of International Relations Theory*, ed. J. Sterling-Folker. Boulder, CO: Lynne Rienner.

Boyer, M. A., N. F. Hudson, and M. J. Butler. 2012. *Global Politics: Engaging in a Complex World*, 1st ed. New York: McGraw-Hill.

Brecher, M., and J. Wilkenfeld. 2000. *A Study of Crisis*. Ann Arbor: University of Michigan Press.

Breuning, M. 2003. "The Role of Analogies and Abstract Reasoning in Decision-Making: Evidence from the Debate over Truman's Proposal for Development Assistance." *International Studies Quarterly*, 47:229–245.

Brewer, P. R., K. Gross, S. Aday, and L. Willnat. 2004. "International Trust and Public Opinion about World Affairs." *American Journal of Political Science*, 48(1):93–109.

Brooten, L., A. I. Syed, and N. A. Akinro. 2015. "Traumatized Victims and Mutilated Bodies: Human Rights and the 'Politics of Immediation' in the Rohingya Crisis of Burma/Myanmar," *International Communication Gazette* 77(8):717–734.

Brown, M., ed. 1996. *The International Dimensions of Internal Conflict.* Cambridge, MA: MIT Press.

Brown, O., A. Hammill, and R. McLeman. 2007. "Climate Change as the 'New' Security Threat: Implications for Africa." *International Affairs,* 83(6):1141–1154.

Brown, S. 1998. "World Interests and the Changing Dimensions of Security." In *World Security: Challenges for a New Century,* 3rd ed., eds. M. T. Klare and Y. Chandrani. New York: St. Marin's Press.

Brysk, A. 2009. *Global Good Samaritans: Human Rights as Foreign Policy.* Oxford, UK: Oxford University Press.

Bueno de Mesquita, B. 2002. "Domestic Politics and International Relations." *International Studies Quarterly,* 46:1–10.

Bueno de Mesquita, B., and A. Smith. 2016. "Competition and Collaboration in Aid-for-Policy Deals, *International Studies Quarterly,* 60:413–426.

Bueno de Mesquita, E. 2005. "The Quality of Terror." *American Journal of Political Science,* 49(3):515–531.

Bull, H. 1977. *The Anarchical Society: A Study of Order in World Politics.* London: Macmillan.

Bullough, O. 2018. "The Dark Side of Globalization." *Journal of Democracy,* 29(1):25–38.

Bunch, C., and N. Reilly. 1994. *"Demanding Accountability: The Global Campaign and Vienna Tribunal for Women's Human Rights."* Rutgers University, Center for Women's Global Leadership.

Burton, J., and F. Dukes. 1990. *Conflict: Practices in Management, Settlement, and Resolution.* New York: St. Martin's Press.

Butler, M. J. 2012a. *Selling a "Just" War: Framing, Legitimacy, and US Military Intervention.* New York: Palgrave Macmillan.

Butler, M. J. 2012b. "Ten Years After: (Re) Assessing Neo-Trusteeship and UN Statebuilding in Timor-Leste." *International Studies Perspectives,* 13(1):85–104.

Butler, M. J., ed. 2019. *Securitization Revisited: Contemporary Applications and Insights.* London: Routledge.

Buzan, B., O. Wæver, and J. De Wilde. 1998. *Security: A New Framework for Analysis.* Boulder, CO: Lynne Rienner.

Calin, C., and B. Prins. 2015. "The Sources of Presidential Foreign Policy Decision Making: Executive Experience and Militarized Interstate Conflicts." *International Journal of Peace Studies,* 20(1):17–34.

Caporaso, J. A. 2005. "The Possibilities of a European Identity." *Brown Journal of World Affairs,* 12(1):65–75.

Caprioli, M. 2004. "Feminist IR Theory and Quantitative Methodology: A Critical Analysis." *International Studies Review,* 6(2):253–269.

Caprioli, M., and M. A. Boyer. 2001. "Gender, Violence and International Crisis," *Journal of Conflict Resolution,* 45(4):503–518.

Cardoso, F. H., and E. Faletto. 1979. *Dependency and Development in Latin America.* Berkeley: University of California Press.

Carlsnaes, W., T. Risse, and B. A. Simmons, eds. 2002. *Handbook of International Relations.* Beverly Hills, CA: Sage.

Caron, D. 2006. "Towards a Political Theory of International Courts and Tribunals." *Berkeley Journal of International Law,* 24(2):401–422.

Carpenter, R. C. 2006. "Recognizing Gender-Based Violence against Civilian Men and Boys in Conflict Situations." *Security Dialogue,* 37(1):83–103.

Carr, E. H. 1939. *The Twenty Years' Crisis, 1919–1939: An Introduction to the Study of International Relations.* London: Macmillan.

Carter, R. G. 2003. "Leadership at Risk: The Perils of Unilateralism." *PS: Political Science & Politics,* 36(1):17–22.

C.A.S.E. Collective, 2006. "Critical Approaches to Security in Europe: A Networked Manifesto." *Security Dialogue,* 37(4):443–487.

Castells, M. 2008. "The New Public Sphere: Global Civil Society, Communication Networks, and Global Governance." *Annals of the American Academy of Political and Social Science,* 616(1):78–93.

Cederman, L.-E., A. Wimmer, and B. Min. 2010. "Why Do Ethnic Groups Rebel? New Data and Analysis." *World Politics,* 62(1):87–119.

Center for Systemic Peace, 2017. Integrated Network for Societal Conflict Research (INSCR) Data Page. Available online at: http://www.systemicpeace.org/inscrdata.html.

Council on Foreign Relations. 2018. "The International Criminal Court and the Trump Administration." Blog Post by Guest Blogger for Stewart M. Patrick, March 28, 2018. https://www.cfr.org/blog/international-criminal-court-and-trump-administration.

Chan, S. 2004. "Influence of International Organizations on Great-Power War Involvement: A Preliminary Analysis." *International Politics,* 41:27–143.

Chayes, A., and A. H. Chayes. 1995. *The New Sovereignty: Compliance with International Regulatory Agreements.* Cambridge, MA: Harvard University Press.

Checkel, J. 1998. "The Constructivist Turn in International Relations Theory." *World Politics,* 50(2):324–348.

Checkel, J. T. 1999. "Social Construction and Integration." *Journal of European Public Policy,* 6(4):545–560.

Cheng, C. 2012. "Charles Taylor Trial Highlights ICC Concerns." *Al Jazeera,* April 27, 2012. Available at http://www.aljazeera.com/indepth/opinion/2012/04/20124268513851323.html.

Chernoff, F. 2004. "The Study of Democratic Peace and Progress in International Relations." *International Studies Review,* 6(1):49–65.

Chittick, W. O., and L. A. Pingel. 2002. *American Foreign Policy: History, Substance and Process.* New York: Seven Bridges Press.

Clausewitz, C. von. 1976. *On War,* ed. and trans. M. Howard and P. Paret. Princeton, NJ: Princeton University Press.

Clunan, A. L. and H. A. Trinkunas (eds.). 2010. *Ungoverned Spaces: Alternatives to State Authority in an Era of Softened Sovereignty.* Stanford University Press.

Coate, R., and J. Fomerand. 2004. "The United Nations and International Norms: A Sunset Institution?" Paper presented at the annual meeting of the International Studies Association, Montreal, Canada.

Coates, N. 2005. "The United Nations Convention on the Law of the Sea, the United States, and International Relations." Paper presented at the annual meeting of the International Studies Association, Honolulu, HI.

Cogan, J. K., I. Hurd, and I. Johnstone (eds). 2016. *The Oxford Handbook of International Organizations,* Oxford University Press.

Cohn, C. 1987. "Sex and Death in the Rational World of Defense Intellectuals." *Signs,* 12(4):687–718.

Collier, P. 2008. *The Bottom Billion.* Oxford, UK: Oxford University Press.

Commons, J. R. 2017. *Legal Foundations of Capitalism.* Routledge.

Conversi, D., ed. 2004. *Ethnonationalism in the Contemporary World.* Oxford, UK: Routledge.

Conway, D. 2004. *In Defense of the Realm: The Place of Nations in Classical Liberalism.* Aldershot, UK: Ashgate.

Cooper, A. 2009. *Taking Celebrity Diplomacy Seriously in International Relations.* Available at http://www.e-ir.info/2009/09/14/taking-celebrity-diplomacy-seriously-in-international-relations/.

Cornwall, W. 2017, "U.S.-Mexico Water Pact Aims for a Greener Colorado Delta," *Science,* Vol. 357, Issue 6352, pp. 635, https://science.sciencemag.org/content/357/6352/635.summary.

Cotton, J. 2007. "Timor-Leste and the Discourse of State Failure." *Australian Journal of International Affairs,* 61(4):455–470.

Cozette, M. 2008. "What Lies Ahead: Classical Realism on the Future of International Relations." *International Studies Review,* 10:667–679.

Crenshaw, M. 1988. "Theories of Terrorism: Instrumental and Organizational Approaches." In *Inside Terrorist Organizations,* ed. David Rapoport. New York: Columbia University Press.

Cunningham, K. J. 2003. "Cross-Regional Trends in Female Terrorism." *Studies in Conflict.* DOI: https://doi.org/10.1080/10576100390211419

Cutler, C. 2001. "Critical Reflections on the Westphalian Assumptions of International Law and Organization," *Review of International Studies,* 27, 133–150.

Daalder, I. H., and J. M. Lindsay. 2003. *America Unbound: The Bush Revolution in Foreign Policy.* Washington, DC: Brookings Institution Press.

Dag Hammarskjöld Library. 2012. *Dag Hammarskjold: The UN Years.* United Nations, New York. Available at http://www.un.org/depts/dhl/dag/index.html.

Dahre, U. J. 2017. "Searching for a Middle Ground: Anthropologists and the Debate on the

Universalism and the Cultural Relativism of Human Rights." *The International Journal of Human Rights*, 21(5):611–628.

Danspeckgruber, W. 2002. *The Self-Determination of Peoples: Community, Nation, and State in an Interdependent World*. Boulder, CO: Lynne Rienner.

Davis, C. L and J. C. Morse. *International Studies Quarterly*, Volume 62, Issue 4, December 2018, Pages 709–722, https://doi.org/10.1093/isq/sqy022.

De Bary, W. T. 2004. *Nobility and Civility: Asian Ideals of Leadership and the Common Good*. Cambridge, MA: Harvard University Press.

de Hoop Scheffer, J. 2005. "Keynote Address by NATO Secretary-General." Victoria University Institute of Policy Studies and New Zealand Institute of International Affairs, Wellington, New Zealand. Available at http://www.nato.int/docu/speech/2005/s050331a.htm.

Delahunty, R. J., and J. Yoo. 2005. "Against Foreign Law." *Harvard Journal of Law & Public Policy*, 29(1):291–329.

de Nevers, R. 2006a. "The Geneva Conventions and New Wars." *Political Science Quarterly*, 121(3):369–396.

de Nevers, R. 2006b. "Modernizing the Geneva Conventions." *The Washington Quarterly*, 29(2):99–113.

Dessler, A. E., and E. A. Parson. 2006. *The Science and Politics of Global Climate Change: A Guide to the Debate*. Cambridge, UK: Cambridge University Press.

Deutsch, K. W., et al. 1957. *Political Community and the North Atlantic Area: International Organization in the Light of Historical Experience*. Princeton, NJ: Princeton University Press.

Dietz, M.G. 2003. "Current Controversies in Feminist Theory," *Annual Review of Political Science*, June 2003, Vol. 6: 399–431.

DiIulio, J. J. 2003. "Inside the Bush Presidency: Reflections of an Academic Interloper." Paper presented at the conference The Bush Presidency: An Early Assessment, Woodrow Wilson School, Princeton University, Princeton, NJ.

Dinan, D. 2004. *Europe Recast: A History of European Union*. Boulder, CO: Lynne Rienner.

Donnelly, J. 1989. *International Human Rights*. Boulder, CO: Westview.

Donnelly, J. 2013. *Universal Human Rights in Theory and Practice*. Ithaca, NY: Cornell University Press.

Doyle, M. W. 1983. "Kant, Liberal Legacies, and Foreign Affairs." *Philosophy and Public Affairs*, 12(3):205–235.

Dreher, A., A. Fuchs, B., Parks, A., Strange, and M. Tierney. 2018. "Apples and Dragon Fruits: The Determinants of Aid and Other Forms of State Financing from China to Africa," *International Studies Quarterly*, 62:182–194.

Druckman, D. 1994. "Nationalism, Patriotism and Group Loyalty: A Social Psychological Perspective." *Mershon International Studies Review*, 38:43–68.

Dunne, T., M. Kurki, and S. Smith. 2013. *International Relations Theories: Discipline and Diversity*, 3rd ed. New York: Oxford University Press.

Dyson, S. B. 2006. "Personality and Foreign Policy: Tony Blair's Iraq Decisions." *Foreign Policy Analysis*, 2(3):289–306.

Dyson, S. B., and T. Preston. 2006. "Individual Characteristics of Political Leaders and the Use of Analogy in Foreign Policy Decision Making." *Political Psychology*, 27(2):265–288.

Eatwell, R. 2006. "Explaining Fascism and Ethnic Cleansing: The Three Dimensions of Charisma and the Four Dark Sides of Nationalism." *Political Studies Review*, 4(3):263–278.

Ehrlich, P. R., and J. Liu. 2002. "Some Roots of Terrorism." *Population and Environment*, 24(2):183–192.

Elliott, L. 2004. "The Global Politics of the Environment," In *The Global Politics of the Environment*. London: Palgrave.

Elms, Deborah Kay. 2007. "Intellectual Property Rights, Drug Access, and the Doha Round." Case #297. Georgetown University, Institute for the Study of Diplomacy. Washington, D.C.

Emerson, M. O., and D. Hartman. 2006. "The Rise of Religious Fundamentalism." *Annual Review of Sociology* 32:127–144.

Enloe, C. 1989. *Bananas, Beaches, and Bases: Making Feminist Sense of International Politics*. Berkeley: University of California Press.

Enloe, C. 2004. *The Curious Feminist: Searching for Women in a New Age of Empire*. Berkeley: University of California Press.

Enloe, C. 2014. *Bananas, Beaches, and Bases: Making Feminist Sense of International Politics*, 2nd ed. Berkeley: University of California Press.

Erskine, T. 2003. *Can Institutions Have Responsibilities? Collective Moral Agency and International Relations*. New York: Palgrave Macmillan.

Etheredge, L. S. 2001. "Will the Bush Administration Unravel?" *The Government Learning Project*. http://www.policyscience.net/harding27.601.pdf.

Etzioni, A. 2004. "A Self-Restrained Approach to Nation-Building by Foreign Powers." *International Affairs*, 80(1):1–17.

Federation of American Scientists. 2018. "Status of World Nuclear Forces." Available at https://fas.org/issues/nuclear-weapons/status-world-nuclear-forces/.

Ferguson, N. 2004. "A World Without Power." *Foreign Policy*, 143(July/August):32–40.

Ferguson, Y. H. 2005. "Institutions with Authority, Autonomy, and Power." *International Studies Review*, 7(2):331–333.

Ferguson, Y. H., and R. W. Mansbach. 1996. *Polities: Authority, Identities, and Change*. Columbia: University of South Carolina Press.

Finnemore, M. 2004. *The Purpose of Intervention: Changing Beliefs About the Use of Force*. Ithaca, NY: Cornell University Press.

Finnemore, M., and K. Sikkink. 1998. "International Norm Dynamics and Political Change." *International Organization*, 52(4):887–917.

Foot, R., S. N. MacFarlane, and M. Mastanudo, eds. 2003. *US Hegemony and International Organizations*. New York: Oxford University Press.

Foreign Policy/Fund for Peace Fragile States Index. 2019. https://fundforpeace.org/2019/04/10/fragile-states-index-2019/.

Forsythe, D. P. 2006. "United States Policy Toward Enemy Detainees in the 'War on Terrorism.'" *Human Rights Quarterly*, 28(2):465–491.

Forsythe, D. P. 2012. *Human Rights in International Relations*, 3rd ed. New York: Cambridge.

Foster, D. M., and G. Palmer. 2006. "Presidents, Public Opinion, and Diversionary Behavior: The Role of Partisan Support Reconsidered." *Foreign Policy Analysis*, 2(3):269–290.

Foster-Carter, A. 1973. "Neo-Marxist Approaches to Development and Underdevelopment," *Journal of Contemporary Asia*, 3(1):7–33.

Foulon, M. 2015. "Neoclassical Realism: Challengers and Bridging Identities," *International Studies Review*, 17(4):635–661.

Fox, J. 2004. "The Rise of Religious Nationalism and Conflict: Ethnic Conflict and Revolutionary Wars, 1945–2001." *Journal of Peace Research*, 41:715–731.

Fox, J., and S. Sandler. 2004. *Bringing Religion into International Relations*. New York: Palgrave Macmillan.

Freedom House. 2007. *Freedom in the World: The Annual Survey of Political Rights & Civil Liberties, 2005–2006*. New Brunswick, NJ: Transaction.

Freedom House. 2018. "Freedom in the World." Available at https://freedomhouse.org/report/freedom-world/freedom-world-2018.

Friedberg, A. L. 2010. "Implications of the Financial Crisis for the US–China Rivalry." *Survival* 52(4):31–54.

Friedman, T. 2005. *The World Is Flat: A Brief History of the Twenty-First Century*. New York: Farrar, Straus and Giroux.

Friedman, Thomas L. 2007. *The World is Flat* (Release 3.0). New York: Picador.

Friedman, T. 2012. *The Lexus and the Olive Tree: Understanding Globalization*. New York: Farrar, Straus and Giroux.

Fukuda-Parr, S., T. Lawson-Remer, and S. Randolph. 2015. *Fulfilling Social and Economic Rights*. New York: Oxford University Press.

Fukuyama, F. 1989. "The End of History?" *The National Interest* (Summer).

Fukuyama, F. 2004. *State-Building: Governance and World Order in the 21st Century*. Ithaca, NY: Cornell University Press.

Gallie, W. B. 1956. "Essentially Contested Concepts." *Proceedings of the Aristotelian Society*, 56:167–198.

Galtung, J. 1994. *Human Rights in Another Key*. Cambridge, UK: Polity Press.

Gartzke, E., and Q. Li. 2003. "War, Peace, and the Invisible Hand: Positive Political Externalities of Economic Globalization." *International Studies Quarterly*, 47(4):561–586.

Geisler, M., ed. 2005. *National Symbols, Fractured Identities.* Hanover, NH: University Press of New England.

Geller, D. S., and J. A. Vasquez. 2004. "The Construction and Cumulation of Knowledge in International Relations: Introduction." *International Studies Review,* 6(4):1–12.

Gellner, E. 1983. *Nations and Nationalism.* Ithaca, NY: Cornell University Press.

George, A. L. 1969. "The 'Operational Code': A Neglected Approach to the Study of Political Leaders and Decision-Making." *International Studies Quarterly,* 13(2):190–222.

Ghosn, F., G. Palmer, and S. Bremer. 2004. "The MID3 Data Set, 1993–2001: Procedures, Coding Rules, and Description." *Conflict Management and Peace Science,* 21:133–154.

Gibler, D. M., T. J. Rider, and M. L. Hutchison. 2005. "Taking Arms against a Sea of Troubles: Conventional Arms Races during Periods of Rivalry." *Journal of Peace Research,* 42:131–147.

Gigerenzer, Gerd. 2004. "Dread Risk, September 11, and Fatal Traffic Accidents," *Psychological Science* Vol 15, Issue 4, pp. 286–287.

Gilpin, Robert. 1996. "Economic Evolution of National Systems." *International Studies Quarterly* 40 (3): 411–431.

Gitlin, T. 2003. "America's Age of Empire." *Mother Jones* (January/February).

Glahn, G. von, and J. L. Taulbee. 2007. *Law Among Nations: An Introduction to Public International Law,* 9th ed. New York: Pearson.

Glasius, M., and Doutje Lettinga. "Global Civil Society and Human Rights," in *Human Rights Politics and Practice* edited by Michael Goodhart. Oxford: Oxford University Press.

Glenny, M. 2008. *McMafia: A Journey Through the Global Criminal Underworld.* New York: Penguin Books.

Global Civil Society Yearbook. 2001. Conflict and Civil Society Research Unit, London School of Economics and Political Science. Available at http://www.lse.ac.uk/international-development/conflict-and-civil-society/past-programmes/global-civil-society-yearbook.

Goldberg, J. 2003. "The Neoconservative Invention." *National Review,* May 20. Available at http://www.nationalreview.com/article/206955/neoconservativism-paleoconservatism-jews-arguing-world.

Goldsmith, J. L., and E. A. Posner. 2005. *The Limits of International Law.* New York: Oxford University Press.

Goldstein, Joshua S. 2011. *Winning the War on War: The Decline of Armed Conflict Worldwide.* Plume/Penguin.

Goldstone, P. R. 2007. "Pax Mercatoria: Does Economic Interdependence Bring Peace?" *MIT Center for International Studies, The Audit of the Conventional Wisdom,* 1–3.

Gomez-Mera, L., and A. Molinari. 2014. "Overlapping Institutions, Learning, and Dispute Initiation in Regional Trade Agreements: Evidence from South America." *International Studies Quarterly,* 58(2):269–281, https://doi.org/10.1111/isqu.12135.

Goodhart, M. 2009. *Human Rights: Politics and Practice.* Oxford, UK: Oxford University Press.

Grauvogel, J., A. Light, and C. von Soust. 2017. "Sanctions and Signals: How International Sanction Threats Trigger Domestic Protest in Targeted Regimes," *International Studies Quarterly,* 61:86–97.

Gray, C. 1994. "Force, Order, and Justice: The Ethics of Realism in Statecraft." *Global Affairs,* 14:1–17.

Gray, C., and B. Kingsbury. 1993. "Developments in Dispute Settlement." In *The British Year Book of International Law,* Vol. 63. New York: Oxford University Press.

Greenhill, B. 2010. "The Company You Keep: International Socialization and the Diffusion of Human Rights Norms." *International Studies Quarterly,* 54(1):127–146.

Gregory, T. 2015. "Drones, Targeted Killings, and the Limitations of International Law," *International Political Sociology,* 9(3):197–212, https://doi.org/10.1111/ips.12093.

Gruenberg, L. 1996. "The IPE of Multinational Corporations." In *Introduction to International Political Economy,* eds. D. N. Balaam and M. Veseth. Upper Saddle River, NJ: Prentice-Hall.

Gulmohamad, Zana Khasraw. 2014. "The Rise and Fall of the Islamic State of Iraq and Al-Sham (Levant) ISIS." *Global Security Studies* 5(2): 1–11.

Gunder, F. A. 1967. *Capitalism and Underdevelopment in Latin America.* New York: Monthly Review Press.

Gurr, T. R. 1998. "Terrorism in Democracies: Its Social and Political Bases." In *Origins of Terrorism: Psychologies, Ideologies, Theologies, States of Mind,* ed. W. Reich. Baltimore, MD: Johns Hopkins University Press.

Haas, P. M., ed. 1997. *Knowledge, Power, and International Policy Coordination.* London: Reaktion Books.

Hafner-Burton, E. M. 2005. "Trading Human Rights: How Preferential Trade Agreements Influence Government Repression," *International Organization,* 59(3):593–629.

Hafner-Burton, Emilie M. 2008. "Sticks and Stones: Naming and Shaming the Human Rights Enforcement Problem." *International Organization* 62(4): 689–716.

Haftel, Y. Z. 2004. "From the Outside Looking In: The Effect of Trading Blocs on Trade Disputes in the GATT/WTO." *International Studies Quarterly,* 48(1):121–149.

Haftel, Y. Z., and A. Thompson. 2006. "The Independence of International Organizations: Concept and Applications." *Journal of Conflict Resolution,* 50(2):253–275.

Halperin, S. 1998. "The Spread of Ethnic Conflict in Europe: Some Comparative-Historical Reflections." In *The International Spread of Ethnic Conflict: Fear, Diffusion, and Escalation,* eds. D. A. Lake and D. Rothchild. Princeton, NJ: Princeton University Press.

Hameiri, S., L. Jones, and A. Sandor. 2018. "Security Governance and the Politics of State Transformation: Moving From Description to Explanation," *Journal of Global Security Studies,* 3(4):463–482, https://doi.org/10.1093/jogss/ogy024.

Hamill, J. 1998. "From Realism to Complex Interdependence? South Africa, Southern Africa, and the Question of Security." *International Relations,* 14(3):1–30.

Harding, J. 1994. *Small Wars, Small Mercies: Journeys in Africa's Disputed Nations.* London: Penguin.

Heasley, J. E., III. 2003. *Organization Global Governance: International Regimes and the Process of Collective Hegemony.* Lanham, MD: Lexington Books.

Heater, D. 2004. *Citizenship: The Civic Ideal in World History, Politics, and Education.* Houndsmills, UK: Palgrave Macmillan.

Heather, D., and K. De Ceuster. 2008. *North Korean Posters: The David Heather Collection.* New York: Prestel.

Hechter, M. 2000. *Containing Nationalism.* Oxford, UK: Oxford University Press.

Held, D., and A. G. McGrew. 2000. *The Global Transformations Reader: An Introduction to the Globalization Debate.* London: Polity.

Helleiner, E. 1996. *States and the Re-Emergence of Global Finance: From Bretton Woods to the 1990s.* Ithaca, NY: Cornell University Press.

Helleiner, E., and A. Pickel, eds. 2005. *Economic Nationalism in a Globalizing World.* Ithaca, NY: Cornell University Press.

Henderson, E., and J. D. Singer. 2002. "New Wars and Rumors of New Wars." *International Interactions,* 28(2):165–190.

Henkin, L. (1979). *How Nations Behave: Law and Foreign Policy.* Columbia University Press.

Henry, C. M., and R. Springborg. 2010. *Globalization and the Politics of Development in the Middle East,* Vol. 1. Cambridge, UK: Cambridge University Press.

Herrmann, R. K., and J. W. Keller. 2004. "Beliefs, Values, and Strategic Choice: US Leaders' Decisions to Engage, Contain, and Use Force in an Era of Globalization." *Journal of Politics,* 66(2):557–580.

Hertel, S. 2019. *Tethered Fates: Companies, Communities, and Rights at Stake.* New York: Oxford University Press.

Hertel, S. and L. Minkler (eds). 2007. *Economic Rights: Conceptual, Measurement and Policy Issues.* Cambridge University Press.

Herz, J. H. 1950. "Idealist Internationalism and the Security Dilemma." *World Politics,* 2:157–180.

Hewitt, J. J., J. Wilkenfeld, and T. R. Gurr. 2010. *Peace and Conflict 2010.* Boulder, CO: Paradigm.

Hicks, D. L., J. H. Hicks, and B. Maldonado. 2016. "Women as Policy Makers and Donors: Female Legislators and Foreign Aid." *European Journal of Political Economy,* 41:46–60.

Hiskes, R. P. (2009) *The Human Right to a Green Future.* Cambridge: Cambridge University Press.

Hobbes, T. 1651 (1994). *Leviathan,* ed. E. Curley. Indianapolis: Hackett.

Hobson, J. M. 2005. "The Enduring Place of Hierarchy in World Politics: Tracing the Social Logics of Hierarchy and Political Change." *European Journal of International Relations,* 11(1):63–98.

Hoffman, B. 2006. *Inside Terrorism,* rev. and expanded ed. New York: Columbia University Press.

Hoffmann, S. 2003. "World Governance: Beyond Utopia." *Daedalus,* 132:27–35.

Holsti, K. 1996. *The State, War, and the State of War.* Cambridge, UK: Cambridge University Press.

Holsti, K. 2004. *Taming the Sovereigns: Institutional Change in International Politics.* New York: Cambridge University Press.

Holsti, O. R. 2004. *Public Opinion and American Foreign Policy.* Ann Arbor: University of Michigan Press.

Honke, J. 2018. "Transnational Clientelism, Global (Resource) Governance, and the Disciplining of Dissent," *International Political Sociology,* 12:109–124.

Hook, S. W., and J. G. Rumsey. 2916. "The Development Aid Regime at Fifty: Policy Challenges Inside and Out," *International Studies Perspectives,* 17:55–74.

Hopf, T. 1998. "The Promise of Constructivism in International Relations Theory." *International Security,* 23(1):171–200.

Horowitz, M., R. McDermott, and A. C. Stam. 2005. "Leader Age, Regime Type, and Violent International Relations." *Journal of Conflict Resolution,* 49(45):661–685.

Hudson, N. F. 2009. *Gender, Human Security, and the United Nations: Security Language as a Political Framework for Women.* New York/London: Routledge.

Hudson, V. M. 2005. "Foreign Policy Analysis: Actor-Specific Theory and the Ground of International Relations." *Foreign Policy Analysis,* 1(1):1–11.

Hudson, V. M., B. Ballif-Spanvill, M. Caprioli, and C. F. Emmett. 2012. *Sex and World Peace.* New York: Columbia University Press.

Huff, C., and R. Schub. 2018. "The Intertemporal Tradeoff in Mobilizing Support for War," *International Studies Quarterly,* 62(2):396–409, https://doi.org/10.1093/isq/sqx062.

Hughes, B. 1985. *World Futures: A Critical Analysis of Alternatives.* Baltimore: Johns Hopkins University Press.

Human Rights Watch. 2018. "South Sudan: Warring Parties Break Promises on Child Soldiers." Available online at: https://www.hrw.org/video-photos/video/2018/02/05/south-sudan-warring-parties-break-promises-child-soldiers. Last accessed 4 February 2018.

Human Security Centre. 2010. "Human Security Brief 2009/10." Human Security Centre, Simon Fraser University. Available at http://www.hsr-group.org/human-security-reports/20092010/overview.aspx.

Huntington, S. P. 1991. *The Third Wave: Democratization in the Late Twentieth Century.* Norman: University of Oklahoma Press.

Huntington, S. P. 1993. "The Clash of Civilizations." *Foreign Affairs,* 72(3):56–73.

Huntington, S. P. 1996. *The Clash of Civilizations and the Remaking of World Order.* New York: Simon & Schuster.

Hurst, R., T. Tidwell, and D. Hawkins. 2017. "Down the Rathole? Public Support for US Foreign Aid," *International Studies Quarterly,* 61:442–454.

Ikenberry, G. J. 2001. *After Victory: Institutions, Strategic Restraint, and the Rebuilding of Order after Major Wars.* Princeton, NJ: Princeton University Press.

Intergovernmental Panel on Climate Change. (2013) *Climate Change 2013: The Physical Science Basis.* Working Group I Contribution to the Fifth Assessment Report of the Intergovernmental Panel on Climate Change. http://www.climatechange2013.org/report/full-report/

International Criminal Tribunal for the Former Yugoslavia (ICTY). 2017. "About the ICTY." Available online at: http://www.icty.org/en/about.

International Social Survey Programme. 2013. "National Identity III." Available at https://www.gesis.org/issp/modules/issp-modules-by-topic/national-identity/2013/.

Isaak, R. A. 2000. *Managing World Economic Change: International Political Economy* (3rd ed.). London/New York: Pearson.

Jackson, Robert H. 1993, *Quasi-states: Sovereignty, International Relations and the Third World*. Vol. 12. Cambridge University Press.

Jackson, R., and G. Sørensen. 2003. *Introduction to International Relations: Theories and Approaches*, 2nd ed. Oxford, UK: Oxford University Press.

Jacques, M. 2009. *When China Rules the World: The End of the Western World and the Birth of a New Global Order*. New York: Penguin Press.

James, P. 2002. *International Relations and Scientific Progress: Structural Realism Reconsidered*. Columbus: Ohio State University Press.

Jaquette, J. S. 1997. "Women in Power: From Tokenism to Critical Mass." *Foreign Policy*, 108:23–97.

Jayawickrama, N. 2003. *The Judicial Application of Human Rights Law: National, Regional and International Jurisprudence*. Cambridge, UK: Cambridge University Press.

Jervis, R. 1976. *Perception and Misperception in International Politics*. Princeton, NJ: Princeton University Press.

Jervis, R. 1978. "Cooperation under the Security Dilemma." *World Politics*, 30:167–214.

Johansen, R. C. 2006. "The Impact of US Policy toward the International Criminal Court on the Prevention of Genocide, War Crimes, and Crimes against Humanity." *Human Rights Quarterly*, 28(2):301–331.

Johnson, D. D. P. 2004. *Overconfidence and War: The Havoc and Glory of Positive Illusions*. Cambridge, MA: Harvard University Press.

Johnson, J. T. 1999. *Morality and Contemporary Warfare*. New Haven, CT: Yale University Press.

Johnston, D., ed. 2003. *Faith-Based Diplomacy: Trumping Realpolitik*. New York: Oxford University Press.

Johnston, N. 2001. "Peace Support Operations." In *Inclusive Security, Sustainable Peace: A Toolkit for Advocacy and Action*. Denver, CO: Hunt Alternatives Fund.

Jok, J. M. 2011. "Diversity, Unity, and Nation Building in South Sudan." USIP Special Report 287. Washington, DC: United States Institute of Peace.

Jones, B. T. 2017. "Altering Capabilities or Imposing Costs? Intervention Strategy and Civil War Outcomes," *International Studies Quarterly*, 61(1):52–63, https://doi.org/10.1093/isq/sqw052.

Jones, L. 2018. "Theorizing Foreign and Security Policy in an Era of State Transformation: A New Framework and Case Study of China." *Journal of Global Security Studies*, https://doi.org/10.1093/jogss/ogy030.

Jones, S. 2010. "In the Pursuit of Justice: A Comment on the Arrest Warrant for President Al Bashir of Sudan." *Eyes on the ICC*, 6(1):13–42.

Joseph, S., and M. Castan. 2013. *The International Covenant on Civil and Political Rights: Cases, Materials, and Commentary*. Oxford University Press.

Joyner, C. C. 2000. "The Reality and Relevance of International Law in the Twenty-First Century." In *The Global Agenda: Issues and Perspectives*, eds. C. W. Kegley, Jr., and E. R. Wittkopf. Boston: McGraw-Hill.

Joyner, C. C. 2005. *International Law in the 21st Century: Rules for Global Governance*. Lanham, MD: Rowman & Littlefield.

Juergensmeyer, M. 2003. *Terror in the Mind of God*. Berkeley: University of California Press.

Jung, D., ed. 2003. *Shadow Globalization, Ethnic Conflicts, and New Wars*. London: Routledge.

Jung, H. Y. 2002. *Comparative Political Culture in the Age of Globalization*. Lanham, MD: Lexington Books.

Jutta, J. 2003. "Framing Issues and Seizing Opportunities: The UN, NGOs, and Women's Rights." *International Studies Quarterly*, 47:247–274.

Kaarbo, J. 2015. "A Foreign Policy Analysis Perspective on the Domestic Politics Turn in IR Theory." *International Studies Review* 17(2):189–216.

Kahler, M. 2018. "Global Governance: Three Futures," *International Studies Review*, 20(2):239–246, https://doi.org/10.1093/isr/viy035.

Kahneman, D. 2011. *Thinking, Fast and Slow*. New York: Macmillan.

Kahneman, D., and J. Renshon. 2007. "Why Hawks Win." *Foreign Policy*, 158:34–38.

Kaldor, M. 1999. *New and Old Wars: Organized Violence in a Global Era.* Stanford, CA: Stanford University Press.

Kant, I. 1785. *Groundwork for the Metaphysics of Morals.* Edited and translated by Allen W. Wood. New Haven: Yale University Press.

Kant, I. 1795 (1905). *Perpetual Peace: A Philosophical Essay,* trans. M. Campbell Smith. London: S. Sonnenschein.

Karns, M. P., and K. A. Mingst. 2012. *International Organizations: The Politics and Processes of Global Governance,* 2nd ed. Boulder, CO: Lynne Rienner.

Keck, M., and K. Sikkink. 1998. *Activists Beyond Borders: Advocacy Networks in International Politics.* Ithaca, NY: Cornell University Press.

Kellett, P. 2006. *Conflict Dialogue: Working with Layers of Meaning for Productive Relationships.* Thousand Oaks, CA: Sage.

Kennan, G. F. 1951. *American Diplomacy: 1900–1950.* Chicago: University of Chicago Press.

Kennan, G. F. 1954. *Realities of American Foreign Policy.* Princeton, NJ: Princeton University Press.

Keohane, R. O. 1998a. "Beyond Dichotomy: Conversations Between International Relations and Feminist Theory." *International Studies Quarterly,* 42:193–198.

Keohane, R. O. 1998b. "International Institutions: Can Interdependence Work?" *Foreign Policy,* 110:82–96.

Keohane, R. O., and J. S. Nye, Jr. 2001. *Power and Interdependence: World Politics in Transition,* 3rd ed. New York: Addison-Wesley.

Keohane, R. O., and J. S. Nye. 2012. *Power and Interdependence,* 4th ed. Boston: Little Brown.

Kertzer, J. D., and K. M. McGraw. 2012. "Folk Realism: Testing the Micro Foundations of Realism in Ordinary Citizens," *International Studies Quarterly,* 56(2):245–258.

Keshk, O. M. G., B. M. Pollins, and R. Reuveny. 2004. "Trade Still Follows the Flag: The Primacy of Politics in a Simultaneous Model of Interdependence and Armed Conflict." *Journal of Politics,* 66(4):1155–1182.

Keynes, J. M. 2017. *The Economic Consequences of the Peace.* New York: Routledge.

Kindleberger, C. 1973. *International Economics.* Homewood, IL: R. D. Irwin, Inc.

Kindleberger, C. 1986. *The World in Depression, 1929–1939.* Berkeley: University of California Press.

King, G., and C. J. L. Murray. 2001. "Rethinking Human Security." *Political Science Quarterly,* 116(4):585–610.

King, S. J. 2009. *The New Authoritarianism in the Middle East and North Africa.* Bloomington: Indiana University Press.

Kirby, P. 2013. "How Is Rape a Weapon of War? Feminist International Relations, Modes of Critical Explanation and the Study of Wartime Sexual Violence." *European Journal of International Relations* 19(4): 797–821.

Klabbers, J. 2006. "The Right to Be Taken Seriously: Self-Determination in International Law." *Human Rights Quarterly,* 28(1):186–206.

Klotz, L. (2016) *Sustainability through Soccer.* Berkeley: University of California Press.

Knox, J., and R. Pejan. 2018. *The Human Right to a Healthy Environment.* Cambridge, UK: Cambridge University Press.

Koh, H. H. 1997. "Why Do Nations Obey International Law?" *Yale Law Journal,* 106(8):2599–2659.

Kolstø, P. 2006. "National Symbols as Signs of Unity and Division." *Ethnic and Racial Studies,* 29(4):67–701.

Kraidy, M. 2017. *Hybridity, or the Cultural Logic of Globalization.* Philadelphia: Temple University Press.

Krasner, S. D. 1983. *International Regimes.* Ithaca, NY: Cornell University Press.

Krause, K., and M. Williams. 1996. "Broadening the Agenda of Security Studies: Politics and Methods." *Mershon International Studies Review,* 40(2):229–254.

Krause, K., and M. Williams, eds. 1997. *Critical Security Studies.* Minneapolis: University of Minnesota Press.

Kristof, N. D., and S. WuDunn. 2009. *Half the Sky: Turning Oppression into Opportunity for Women Worldwide.* New York: Knopf.

Kugler, J., A. Fisunoğlu, and B. Yeşilada. 2015. "Consequences of Reversing the European Union Integration." *Foreign Policy Analysis* 11(1): 45–67. Kugler, Fisunoglu, and Yesilada. 2015.

Kuziemko, I., and E. Werker. 2006. "How Much Is a Seat on the Security Council Worth? Foreign Aid and Bribery at the United Nations." *Journal of Political Economy,* 114(5):905–930.

Kydd, A. H., and B. F. Walter. 2006. "The Strategies of Terrorism." *International Security,* 31(1):49–79.

Lake, M. 2018. *Strong NGOs and Weak States.* Cambridge, UK: Cambridge University Press.

Lal, D. 2004. *In Praise of Empires: Globalization and Order.* New York: Palgrave Macmillan.

Landman, T. 2004. "Measuring Human Rights: Principle, Practice and Policy." *Human Rights Quarterly,* 26(November):906–931.

Landman, T. 2006. *Studying Human Rights.* New York: Routledge.

Lang, A. 2013. "Global Constitutionalism as a Middle-Ground Ethic." In *Ethical Reasoning in International Affairs.* London: Palgrave Macmillan.

Langlois, C. C., and J.-P. P. Langlois. 2006. "When Fully Informed States Make Good the Threat of War: Rational Escalation and the Failure of Bargaining." *British Journal of Political Science,* 36(4):645–669.

Lanskoy, M., and D. Myles-Primakoff. 2018. "Power and Plunder in Putin's Russia." *Journal of Democracy,* 29(1):76–85.

Laqueur, W. 2004. *No End to War: Terrorism in the Twenty-First Century.* New York: Continuum International.

Larémont, R. R. 2005. *Borders, Nationalism, and the African State.* Boulder, CO: Lynne Rienner.

Larrain, J. 2013. *Theories of Development: Capitalism, Colonialism and Dependency.* New York: Wiley.

Larson, D. W. 2018. "New Perspectives on Rising Powers and Global Governance: Status and Clubs," *International Studies Review,* 20(2):247–254, https://doi.org/10.1093/isr/viy039.

Lasswell, H. D. 1936. *Politics: Who Gets What, When, How.* New York, London: Whittlesey House, McGraw-Hill.

Law, R. D. 2009. *Terrorism: A History.* Cambridge: Polity Press.

Layne, C. 2012. "This Time It's Real: The End of Unipolarity and the Pax Americana." *International Studies Quarterly* 56(1):203–213.

Le, N. "Are Human Rights Universal or Culturally Relative?" *Peace Review* 28.2 (2016): 203–211.

Lektzian, D., and Patterson, D. 2015. "Political Cleavages and Economic Sanctions: The Economic and Political Winners and Losers of Sanctions." *International Studies Quarterly,* 59:46–58.

Lenin, V. I. 1916 (1963). "Imperialism, the Highest Stage of Capitalism." In *Lenin's Selected Works,* vol. 1. Moscow: Progress Publishers.

Leonard, E. K. 2007. "Establishing an International Criminal Court: The Emergence of a New Global Authority?" GUISD/Pew Case Studies Center, Case 258. Washington, DC: Georgetown University Institute for the Study of Diplomacy.

Levy, J. S. 1988. "Domestic Politics and War." *Journal of Interdisciplinary History,* 18(3):653–673.

Lobell, S. E. 2004. "Historical Lessons to Extend America's Great Power Tenure." *World Affairs* (Spring). 166(4): 175–184.

Locke, John. 1948. *The Second Treatise of Civil Government and a Letter Concerning Toleration.* Oxford: B. Blackwell.

Lomborg, B., ed. 2007. *Solutions for the World's Biggest Problems: Costs and Benefits.* Cambridge University Press.

Longman, P. 2004. "The Global Baby Bust." *Foreign Affairs,* 83(3):64–79.

Lopez, G. 2004. "Containing Iraq: Sanctions Worked." *Foreign Affairs,* 83(4):90–103.

Luck, E. 2016. "The Security Council at Seventy: Ever Changing or Never Changing " in *The UN Securiy Council in the Twenty-First Century,* edited by Sebastian von Einsiedel, David M. Malone, and Bruno Stagno Ugarte, Boulder, CO: Lynne Rienner Publishers, pp. 195–216.

Mackenzie, M. 2009. "Securitization and Desecuritization: Female Soldiers and the Reconstruction of Women in Post-Conflict Sierra Leone." *Security Studies,* 18(2):241–261.

MacKinnon, C. A. 2017. "Rape, Genocide, and Women's Human Rights," in *Genocide and Human Rights,* Lattimer, Mark (ed.). pp. 133–144. London: Routledge.

Mann, M. 1993. *The Sources of Social Power: Volume 2, The Rise of Classes and Nation States 1760–1914.* Cambridge, UK: Cambridge University Press.

Mann, Michael, 1994. "The Autonomous Power of the State: Its Origins, Mechanisms and Results."

In: John Hall (ed.). *The State: Critical Concepts.* London: Routledge. pp. 331–385.

Mann, M. 2012. *The Hockey Stick and the Climate Wars: Dispatches from the Front Lines.* New York: Columbia University Press.

Mansfield, E. D., and J. Snyder. 1995. "Democratization and the Danger of War." *International Security,* 20(1):5–38.

Marshall, M. G., and T. R. Gurr. 2005. *Peace and Conflict, 2005: A Global Survey of Armed Conflicts, Self-Determination Movements, and Democracy.* College Park, MD: Center for International Development and Conflict Management, University of Maryland.

Martin, A., and G. Ross, eds. 2004. *Euros and Europeans: Monetary Integration and the European Model of Society.* Cambridge, UK: Cambridge University Press.

Marx, A. W. 2003. *Faith in Nation: Exclusionary Origins of Nationalism.* New York: Oxford University Press.

Marx, K., and F. Engels. 1848 (2004). *Manifesto of the Communist Party.* Marxists Internet Archive. Last accessed January 14, 2018. https://www.marxists.org/archive/marx/works/download/pdf/Manifesto.pdf.

Mastanduno, M. 1998. "Economics and Security in Statecraft and Scholarship." *International Organization,* 52(4):825–854.

Maternal Health. 2016. https://www.thelancet.com/pb/assets/raw/Lancet/stories/series/maternal-health-2016/mathealth2016-exec-summ.pdf.

Mathews, J. T. 1989. "Redefining Security." *Foreign Affairs,* 68(2):162–177.

Mathiason, J. 2007. *Invisible Governance: International Secretariats in Global Politics.* Bloomfield, CT: Kumarian.

Matijasevic, N. 2015. *Celebrity Diplomacy.* Available at http://foreignpolicynews.org/2015/01/12/celebrity-diplomacy/.

McCants, W. 2015. *The ISIS Apocalypse: The History, Strategy, and Doomsday Vision of the Islamic State.* New York: St. Martin's Press.

McGrew, A. 1997. *The Transformation of Democracy: Globalization and Territorial Democracy.* London: Polity Press.

McKeil, A. C. 2013. *International Relations as Historical Political Theory.* Available at https://www.e-ir.info/2013/08/05/international-relations-as-historical-political-theory/. Last accessed June 24, 2019.

McPherson, T. and M. A. Boyer. (2016) "Transboundary Conservation Collaboration: Navigating the Political-Economy of Biodiversity in the Guiana Shield," *International Studies Perspectives,* 17(1), 17–33.

Meadows, D. 2009. *Thinking in Systems: A Primer.* White River Junction, VT: Chelsea Green Publishing.

Mearsheimer, J. J. 1990. "Back to the Future: Instability in Europe after the Cold War." *International Security,* 15(1):5–56.

Mearsheimer, J. J. 2001. *The Tragedy of Great Power Politics.* New York: W. W. Norton.

Meernik, J., and M. Ault. 2005. "The Diverted President: The Domestic Agenda and Foreign Policy." Paper presented at the annual convention of the International Studies Association, Honolulu, HI.

Melander, E. 2005. "Political Gender Equality and State Human Rights Abuse." *Journal of Peace Research,* 42:149–166.

Melander, E., T. Pettersson, and L. Themnér (2016). "Organized Violence, 1989-2015," *Journal of Peace Research* 53(5):727–742.

Meunier, S. 2000. "What Single Voice? European Institutions and EU–US Trade Negotiations." *International Organization,* 54(2):103–135.

Mill, J. S. 1848. *Principles of Political Economy.* Batoche,

Mill, J. S. 1859 (1873). "A Few Words on Non-Intervention." In *Dissertations and Discussions.* New York: Holt & Company.

Miller, B. 2010. "Democracy Promotion: Offensive Liberalism Versus the Rest (of IR Theory)." *Millennium: Journal of International Studies,* 38(3):561–591.

Miller, T. 2007. *Cultural Citizenship: Cosmopolitanism, Consumerism, and Television in a Neoliberal Age.* Philadelphia: Temple University Press.

Mingst, K. A., M. P. Karns, and A. J. Lyon. 2016. *The United Nations in the 21st Century,* 5th Ed., Dilemmas in World Politics Series. London: Routledge.

Mistry, D. 2004. "Military Technology, National Power, and Regional Security: The Strategic Significance of India's Nuclear, Missile, Space, and Missile Defense Forces." *In South Asia's Nuclear Security Dilemma,* ed. L. Dittmer. New York: M. E. Sharpe.

Mitchell, S. M., and B. C. Prins. 2004. "Rivalry and Diversionary Uses of Force." *Journal of Conflict Resolution,* 48(6):937–961.

Mitrany, D. 1946. *A Working Peace System.* London: Royal Institute of International Affairs.

Monshipouri, M. 2004. "The Road to Globalization Runs through Women's Struggle: Iran and the Impact of the Nobel Peace Prize." *World Affairs,* 167(1):3–14.

Moore, W. H., and D. J. Lanoue. 2003. "Domestic Politics and US Foreign Policy: A Study of Cold War Conflict Behavior." *Journal of Politics,* 65:376–397.

Moravcsik, A. 1997. "Taking Preferences Seriously: A Liberal Theory of International Politics," *International Organization,* 51(4):513–553.

Moravcsik, A. 1998. *The Choice for Europe: Social Purpose and State Power from Messina to Maastricht.* Ithaca, NY: Cornell University Press.

Morgan, T. C., and L. E. Reyes. 2018. "Getting the Law on Your Side: State Legal Frameworks and the Enforcement of Economic Sanctions." Paper presented at the joint ISA-FLACSO conference Quito, Ecuador, July 2018.

Morgenthau, H. J. 1945. "The Evil of Politics and the Ethics of Evil." *Ethics,* 56(1):1–18.

Morgenthau, H. J. 1946. *Scientific Man Versus Power Politics.* Chicago: University of Chicago Press.

Morgenthau, H. J. 1948. *Politics Among Nations: The Struggle for Power and Peace.* New York: Alfred A. Knopf.

Mortensgaard, L. A. 2018. "Contesting Frames and (De)Securitizing Schemas: Bridging the Copenhagen School's Framework and Framing Theory," *International Studies Review,* https://doi.org/10.1093/isr/viy068.

Mousseau, M. 2003. "Market Civilization and Its Clash with Terror." *International Security,* 27(3):5–29.

Mueller, J. 1989. *Retreat from Doomsday: The Obsolescence of Major War.* New York: Basic Books.

Mueller, J. 2004. *The Remnants of War.* Ithaca, NY: Cornell University Press.

Münkler, H. 2004. *The New Wars.* London: Polity.

Nacos, B. L. 2007. *Mass-Mediated Terrorism: The Central Role of the Media in Terrorism and Counterterrorism,* 2nd ed. Lanham, MD: Rowman & Littlefield.

Natural Resource Governance Institute. 2015 *The Resource Curse: The Political and Economic Challenges of Natural Resource Wealth.* NRGI Reader, March 2015. Available at https://resourcegovernance.org/sites/default/files/nrgi_Resource-Curse.pdf.

Neier, A. 2018. "'Naming and Shaming': Still the Human Rights Movement's Best Weapon." *OpenGlobalRights,* July 11. Available at https://www.openglobalrights.org/Naming-and-shaming-still-the-human-rights-movements-best-weapon/.

Neumann, I. B. 2016. *Russia and the Idea of Europe: A Study in Identity and International Relations,* 2nd ed. London/New York: Routledge.

Norris, P., and R. Inglehart. 2009. *Cosmopolitan Communications: Cultural Diversity in a Globalized World.* Cambridge, UK: Cambridge University Press.

Nussbaum, B. 2001. *International Law in Antiquity.* Cambridge, MA: Cambridge University Press.

Nye, J. S., Jr. 2000. *Understanding International Conflicts,* 3rd ed. New York: Longman.

Nye, J. S., Jr. 2002. "Globalism versus Globalization." *Globalist,* April 15. Online.

Nye, J. S., Jr. 2004. *Soft Power: The Means to Success in World Politics.* New York: Public Affairs.

Oneal, J. R., and B. M. Russett. 1997. "The Classical Liberals Were Right: Democracy, Interdependence, and Conflict, 1950–1985." *International Studies Quarterly,* 41:267–294.

Onuf, N. G. 1989. *World of Our Making: Rules and Rule in Social Theory and International Relations.* Columbia: University of South Carolina Press.

Onuf, N. G. 2013. *Making Sense, Making Worlds: Constructivism in Social Theory and International Relations.* London/New York: Routledge.

Opello, W. C., Jr., and S. J. Rosow. 2004. *The Nation-State and Global Order: A Historical Introduction to Contemporary Politics.* Boulder, CO: Lynne Rienner.

Orford, A. 2003. *Reading Humanitarian Intervention: Human Rights and the Use of Force in International Law.* Cambridge: Cambridge University Press.

Organization for the Prohibition of Chemical Weapons. 2017. "Report of the OPCW Fact-Finding Mission in Syria Regarding an Alleged Incident in Khan Shaykhun, Syrian Arab Republic." S/1510/2017. Available at https://www.opcw.org/sites/default/files/documents/Fact_Finding_Mission/s-1510-2017_e_.pdf.

Organski, A. F. K., and J. Kugler. 1980. *The War Ledger*. Chicago: University of Chicago Press.

Page, M. E., and P. M. Sonnenburg. 2003. *Colonialism: An International, Social, Cultural, and Political Encyclopedia*. Vol. 1. Santa Barbara, CA: ABC-CLIO.

Paine, T. 1791. *The Rights of Man: Being an Answer to Mr. Burke's Attack on the French Revolution*. Cambridge: Cambridge University Press, 2012.

Paquette, L. 2003. *Analyzing National and International Policy: Theory, Method, and Case Studies*. Lanham, MD: Lexington Books.

Park, S. 2005. "How Transnational Environmental Advocacy Networks Socialize International Financial Institutions: A Case Study of the International Finance Corporation." *Global Environmental Politics,* 5(4):95–119.

Peksen, D. 2017. "How Do Target Leaders Survive Economic Sanctions? The Adverse Effect of Sanctions on Private Property and Wealth," *Foreign Policy Analysis*, 13:215–232.

Peoples, C., and N. Vaughn-Williams. 2014. *Critical Security Studies: An Introduction*. New York: Routledge.

Perry, M. et al. 1992. *Western Civilization: Ideas, Politics, and Society*, 4th ed. Boston: Houghton Mifflin.

Peterson, V. S., and A. S. Runyan. 2010. *Global Gender Issues in the New Millennium*, 3rd ed. Boulder, CO: Westview Press.

Petras, J., and H. Veltmeyer. 2013. *Imperialism and Capitalism in the Twenty-First Century: A System in Crisis*. Farnham, UK: Ashgate.

Pettersson, T., and K. Eck. 2018. "Organized Violence, 1989–2017." *Journal of Peace Research*, 55(4):535–547.

Pew Research Center. 2016. "Where Americans and Europeans Agree, Disagree on Foreign Policy." Available at http://www.pewresearch.org/fact-tank/2016/06/14/where-americans-and-europeans-agree-disagree-on-foreign-policy/.

Pew Research Center. 2018. "U.S. Foreign Policy Views by Political Party." 29 November 2018. http://www.people-press.org/2018/11/29/conflicting-partisan-priorities-for-u-s-foreign-policy/.

Piazza, J. A. 2006. "Rooted in Poverty? Terrorism, Poor Economic Development, and Social Cleavages." *Terrorism and Political Violence*, 18(1):159–177.

Piazza, J. A., and J. I. Walsh. 2010. "Terrorism and Human Rights: Editors' Introduction." *PS: Political Science & Politics* 43(3): 407–409.

Piccone, T. 2016. "Ten Years Later: The Status of the UN Human Rights Council." Brookings Institution: Washington, D.C. Available online at: https://www.brookings.edu/testimonies/ten-years-later-the-status-of-the-u-n-human-rights-council/.

Pilch, F. 2005. "Developing Human Rights Standards in United Nations Peacekeeping Operations." Paper presented at the annual meeting of the International Studies Association, Honolulu, HI.

Pirages, D. 1989. *Global Technopolitics*. Dallas: Wadsworth.

Posen, B. R. 1984. *The Sources of Military Doctrine: France, Britain, and Germany between the World War*. Ithaca, NY: Cornell University Press.

Post, J. M. 2008. *The Mind of the Terrorist: The Psychology of Terrorism from the IRA to al-Qaeda*. New York: St. Martin's Press.

Powell, R. 2006. "War as a Commitment Problem." *International Organization,* 60(1):169–203.

Price, R., and C. Reus-Smit. 1998. "Dangerous Liaisons? Critical International Theory and Constructivism." *European Journal of International Relations,* 4(3):259–294.

Pye, L. W., and S. Verba. 1965. *Political Culture and Political Development*. Princeton, NJ: Princeton University Press.

Ralph, J. 2005. "International Society, the International Criminal Court, and American Foreign Policy." *Review of International Studies,* 31(1):27–44.

Ratner, S. R. 1998. "International Law: The Trials of Global Norms." *Foreign Policy,* 110:65–81.

Raunio, T. 2011. "The Changing World of EU Governance," *International Studies Review*, 13(2):314–317, https://doi.org/10.1111/j.1468-2486.2011.01030.x.

Rehn, E., and E. J. Sirleaf. 2002. *Women, War and Peace: The Independent Experts' Assessment on the Impact of Armed Conflict on Women and Women's Role in Peace-Building.* New York: United Nations Development Fund for Women.

Reid, J. 2013. "Interrogating the Neoliberal Biopolitics of the Sustainable Development-Resilience," *International Political Sociology*, 7:353–367.

Reimann, K. D. 2006. "A View from the Top: International Politics, Norms and the Worldwide Growth of NGOs." *International Studies Quarterly*, 50(1):45–68.

Renan, E. 1995. "Qu'est-ce Qu'une Nation?" In *Nationalism*, ed. J. Hutchinson and A. D. Smith. New York: Oxford University Press.

Rengger, N. 2011. "The World Turned Upside Down? Human Rights and International Relations after 25 Years." *International Affairs*, Vol. 87, No. 5, pp. 1159–1178.

Renshon, S. A. 1995. "Character, Judgment, and Political Leadership: Promise, Problems, and Prospects of the Clinton Presidency." In *The Clinton Presidency: Campaigning, Governing, and the Psychology of Leadership,* ed. S. Renshon. Boulder, CO: Westview.

Renshon, S. A., and D. W. Larson, eds. 2002. *Good Judgment in Foreign Policy: Theory and Application.* Lanham, MD: Rowman & Littlefield.

Ricardo, D. 1817. *On the Principles of Political Economy and Taxation.* Cambridge: Cambridge University Press, 2015.

Rice, E. E. 1988. *Wars of the Third Kind: Conflict in Underdeveloped Countries.* Berkeley: University of California Press.

Richards, D. L., and J. Haglund. 2015. *Violence Against Women and the Law.* Boulder, CO: Paradigm Publishers.

Richardson, L. 1960. *Statistics of Deadly Quarrels.* Pittsburgh: Boxwood Press.

Robertson, G. 2011. "Why It Is Absurd to Claim That Justice Has Been Done." *The Independent.* Available at http://www.independent.co.uk/opinion/commentators/geoffrey-robertson-why-its-absurd-to-claim-that-justice-has-been-done-2278041.html.

Robinson, William I. 2006. "What Is Critical Globalization Studies? Intellectual Labor and Global Society," in Judith R. Blau and Keri Iyall-Smith, *Public Sociologies Reader*, Rowman and Littlefield. pp. 21–36.

Rodin, D. 2005. *War and Self-Defense.* New York: Oxford University Press.

Rocha de Siqueira, I. 2017. "Development by Trial and Error: The Authority of Good Enough Numbers," *International Political Sociology*, 11:166–184.

Rodrigues, M. G. M. 2004. *Global Environmentalism and Local Politics: Transnational Advocacy Networks in Brazil, Ecuador, and India.* Albany: State University of New York Press.

Rodrik, D. 2011. *The Globalization Paradox: Democracy and the Future of the World Economy.* New York: W. W. Norton.

Roht-Arriaza, N. 2015. "After Amnesties Are Gone: Latin American National Courts and the New Contours of the Fight Against Impunity." *Human Rights Quarterly*, 37(2):341–382.

Rosato, S. 2003. "The Flawed Logic of Democratic Peace Theory." *American Political Science Review*, 97(4):585–602.

Rose, G. 1998. "Neoclassical Realism and Theories of Foreign Policy." *World Politics*, 51(1):144–172.

Rosen, S. P. 2004. *War and Human Nature.* Princeton, NJ: Princeton University Press.

Rosenau, J. N. 1994. "New Dimensions of Security: The Interaction of Globalizing and Localizing Dynamics." *Security Dialogue*, 25(3):255–281.

Rosenau, J. N. 2000. *Thinking Theory Thoroughly: Coherent Approaches to an Incoherent World.* Boulder, CO: Westview Press.

Rosenau, J. N. 2004. "Understanding World Affairs: The Potential of Collaboration." *Globalizations*, 1(2):326–339.

Ross, M. L. 2015. "What Have We Learned About the Resource Curse?" *Annual Review of Political Science*, 18:239–259.

Rothschild, E. 1995. "What Is Security?" *Daedalus: Journal of the American Academy of Arts and Sciences*, 124(3):53–90.

Rousseau, J.-J. 1750. *Discourse on the Arts and Sciences [The First Discourse].* Geneva: Barillot & Fils.

Rousseau, J-J. 1762. *The Social Contract; or, Principles of Political Right,* trans. G. D. H. Cole; Available online at: https://oll.libertyfund.org/titles/rousseau-the-social-contract-and-discourses. Last accessed 14 June 2019.

Ruane, A. E. 2011. "Pursuing Inclusive Interests, Both Deep and Wide: Women's Human Rights and the United Nations." In *Feminism and International Relations*. 3rd ed., ed. L. Sjoberg and J. A. Tickner. New York: Routledge.

Ruggie, John. (1983) "International Regimes, Transactions and Exchange: Embedded Liberalism in the Post-War Economic Order," in Stephen Krasner, ed., *International Regimes*, Ithaca: Cornell University Press, pp. 195–232.

Runyan, A. S., and V. S. Peterson. 2013. *Global Gender Issues in the New Millennium*, 4th ed. Boulder, CO: Westview Press.

Russett, B. M., and J. R. Oneal. 2001. *Triangulating Peace: Democracy, Interdependence, and International Organizations*. New York: W. W. Norton.

Sachs, J. D., and A. M. Warner. 2001. "The Curse of Natural Resources," *European Economic Review*, 25:827–838.

Sagan, S. D., and B. A. Valentino. 2018. "Not Just a War Theory: American Public Opinion on Ethics in Combat." *International Studies Quarterly*, 62(3):548–561, https://doi.org/10.1093/isq/sqy033.

Sageman, M. 2008. *Leaderless Jihad: Terror Networks in the Twenty-First Century*. Philadelphia: University of Pennsylvania Press.

Samuels, R. J. 2006. "Japan's Goldilocks Strategy." *The Washington Quarterly*, 29(4):111–127.

Schafer, M., and S. G. Walker. 2006. "Democratic Leaders and the Democratic Peace: The Operational Codes of Tony Blair and Bill Clinton." *International Studies Quarterly*, 50(3):561–583.

Schiff, B. N. 2008. *Building the International Criminal Court*. New York: Cambridge University Press.

Schmidt, B. C. 2004. "Realism as Tragedy." *Review of International Studies*, 30:427–441.

Schmitter, P. C. 2005. "Ernst B. Haas and the Legacy of Neofunctionalism." *Journal of European Public Policy*, 12(2):255–272.

Schmitz, H. Peter. 2004. "Domestic and Transnational Perspectives on Democratization." *International Studies Review*, 6(3):403–421.

Schneewind, J. B. 2009. "Kantian Unsocial Sociability: Good Out of Evil." In *Essays on the History of Moral Philosophy*. Oxford University Press, Oxford Scholarship Online. Available at http://www.oxfordscholarship.com/view/10.1093/acprof:oso/9780199563012.001.0001/acprof-9780199563012-chapter-17.

Scholte, J. A. 2002. "Civil Society and Democracy in Global Governance." *Global Governance*, 8(3):281–304.

Schweller, R. L. 2004. "Unanswered Threats: A Neoclassical Realist Theory of Underbalancing." *International Security*, 29(2):159–201.

Senese, P. D. 2005. "Territory, Contiguity, and International Conflict: Assessing a New Joint Explanation." *American Journal of Political Science*, 49(4):769–791.

Shah, T. S., and M. D. Toft. 2006. "Why God Is Winning." *Foreign Policy*, 155:38–43.

Shaikh, A. 2005. "The Economic Mythology of Neoliberalism." In *Neoliberalism: A Critical Reader*, eds. A Saad-Filho and D. Jonston. London: Pluto Press.

Shaw, M. 1999. "War and Globality: The Role and Character of War in the Global Transition." In *The New Agenda for Peace Research*, ed. Ho Won Jeong. Aldershot, UK: Ashgate.

Sheehan, M. 2005. *International Security: An Analytical Survey*. Boulder, CO: Lynne Rienner.

Sheehan, M. 2008. "The Changing Character of War." In *The Globalization of World Politics: An Introduction to International Relations*, 4th ed., eds. J. Baylis, S. Smith, and P. Owens. New York: Oxford University Press.

Shepherd, L. J. 2015. *Gender Matters in Global Politics*. New York: Routledge.

Shue, H. 1980. *Basic Human Rights: Subsistence, Affluence and US Foreign Policy*. New Jersey: Princeton University Press.

Sikkink, K. 2011. *The Justice Cascade: How Human Rights Prosecutions Are Changing World Politics*. New York: W.W. Norton.

Sikkink, K. 2018. *Evidence for Hope: Making Human Rights Work in the 21st Century*. Princeton, NJ: Princeton University Press.

Simmons, B. A. 2009. *Mobilizing for Human Rights: International Law in Domestic Politics*. Cambridge: Cambridge University Press.

Simmons, B. A., and Z. Elkins. 2004. "The Globalization of Liberalization: Policy Diffusion in the International Political Economy." *American Political Science Review,* 98(1):171–189.

Simmons, B. A., and D. J. Hopkins. 2005. "The Constraining Power of International Treaties: Theory and Methods." *American Political Science Review,* 99(4):623–631.

Simmons, M., and P. Dixon, eds. 2006. "Introduction." In *Peace by Piece: Addressing Sudan's Conflicts.* London: Conciliation Resources.

Simmons, R. 2011. *Odd Girl Out.* New York: Mariner Books.

Simon, H. 1957. "A Behavioral Model of Rational Choice." In *Models of Man, Social and Rational: Mathematical Essays on Rational Human Behavior in a Social Setting.* New York: Wiley.

Simon, H. 1976. *Administrative Behavior,* 3rd ed. New York: The Free Press.

Sinclair, A. 2004. *An Anatomy of Terror: A History of Terrorism.* New York: Palgrave Macmillan.

Singer, J. D. 1961. "The Level-of-Analysis Problem in International Relations." *World Politics,* 14(1):77–92.

Singer, J. D., and M. Small. 1972. *The Wages of War 1816–1965: A Statistical Handbook.* New York: Wiley.

Sjoberg, L. 2010. "Gendering the Empire's Soldiers: Gender Ideologies, the US Military and the 'War on Terror.'" In *Gender, War, and Militarism: Feminist Perspectives,* eds. L. Sjoberg and S. Via. Santa Barbara, CA: ABC-CLIO.

Sjoberg, L. 2012. "Toward Trans-Gendering International Relations?" *International Political Sociology,* 6(4):337–354.

Sjoberg, L. 2017. "Revealing International Hierarchy Through Gender Lenses." *Hierarchies in World Politics.* ed. A. Zarakol. Cambridge, UK: Cambridge University Press.

Sjoberg, L, and C. E. Gentry. 2007. *Mothers, Monsters, Whores: Women's Violence in Global Politics.* London: Zed Books.

Skjelsbaek, I. 2001. "Sexual Violence and War: Mapping out a Complex Relationship." *European Journal of International Relations* 7(2): 211–237.

Slaughter, A.-M. 2003. "The Global Community of Courts." *Harvard International Law Journal,* 44:217–219.

Small Arms Survey. 2011. Graduate Institute of International, Development Studies (Geneva, & Small Arms Survey, Geneva. (2012). *Small Arms Survey 2012: Moving Targets.* Cambridge University Press.

Smidi, A., and S. Shahin. 2017. "Social Media and Social Mobilization in the Middle East: A Survey of Research on the Arab Spring." *India Quarterly,* 73(2):196–209.

Smith, Adam. 1776. *The Wealth of Nations.* New York: Bantam Classics (reprint edition).

Smith, A. D. 1994. "Gastronomy or Geology? The Role of Nationalism in the Reconstruction of Nations." *Nations and Nationalism,* 1(1):3–23.

Smith, A. D. 2004. *Chosen Peoples: Sacred Sources of National Identity.* Oxford, UK: Oxford University Press.

Smith, S., T. Dunne, and A. Hadfield. 2016. *Foreign Policy: Theories, Actors, Cases.* New York: Oxford University Press.

Snow, D. M. 1996. *Uncivil Wars: International Security and the New Internal Conflicts.* Boulder, CO: Lynne Rienner Publishers.

Snyder, J. 1991. *Myths of Empire: Domestic Politics and International Ambition.* Ithaca, NY: Cornell University Press.

Snyder, J. 2019. "The Broken Bargin" *Foreign Affairs.* (March/April).

Stein, J. G. 2001. "Image, Identity, and the Resolution of Violent Conflict." In *Turbulent Peace: The Challenges of Managing International Conflict,* eds. C. A. Crocker, F. O. Hampson, and P. Aall. Washington, DC: United States Institute of Peace Press.

Stein, J. G. 2002. "Psychological Explanations of International Conflict." In *Handbook of International Relations,* eds. W. Carlsnaes, T. Risse, and B. A. Simmons. London: SAGE.

Sterling-Folker, J. 1997. "Realist Environment, Liberal Process, and Domestic-Level Variables." *International Studies Quarterly,* 41:1–26.

Sterling-Folker, J. 2002. "Realism and the Constructivist Challenge: Rejecting, Reconstructing, or Rereading." *International Studies Review,* 4:73–97.

Stiehm, J. H. 1982. "The Protected, the Protector, the Defender." In *Women's Studies International Forum*, 5(3–4):367–376.

Stiglitz, J. E. 2002. *Globalization and Its Discontents.* New York: W. W. Norton.

Stipp, D. 2004. "Climate Collapse: The Pentagon's Weather Nightmare." *Fortune Magazine*, January 26, 2004.

Stockholm International Peace Research Institute. 2018. *SIPRI Yearbook 2018: Armaments, Disarmament, and International Security.* New York: Oxford University Press.

Stockholm International Peace Research Institute. 2019. "Press Release: Global Arms Trade—USA Increases Dominance; Arms Flows to the Middle East Surge." Available online at: https://www .sipri.org/media/press-release/2019/global-arms- trade-usa-increases-dominance-arms-flows- middle-east-surge-says-sipri.

Strange, S. 1996. *The Retreat of the State: The Diffusion of Power in the World Economy.* Cambridge: Cambridge University Press.

Strange, S. 2015. *Casino Capitalism.* New York: Oxford University Press.

Strauss, K. 2011. "Globalization and the Service Workplace: Citizenship, Entitlement, and the Future of UK Occupational Pensions." *American Behavioral Scientist* 55(7): 902–919.

Stroup, S. S., and W. H. Wong. 2016. "The Agency and Authority of International NGOs." *Perspectives on Politics* 14(1):138–144.

Stroup, S. S., and W. H. Wong. 2017. *The Authority Trap: Strategic Choices of International NGOs.* Ithaca, NY: Cornell University Press.

Subotic, J. 2009. *Hijacked Justice: Dealing with the past in the Balkans.* Ithaca, NY: Cornell University Press.

Subotic, J., and B. J. Steele. 2018. "Moral Injury in International Relations," *Journal of Global Security Studies,* https://doi.org/10.1093/jogss/ogy021.

Sullivan. C. M . 2014. "The (In)effectiveness of Torture for Combating Insurgency," *Journal of Peace Research* 51(3): 388–404.

Swaine, A. 2018. *Conflict-Related Violence Against Women.* Cambridge, UK: Cambridge University Press.

Sylvester, C. 1994. *Feminist Theory and International Relations in a Postmodern Era.* Cambridge, UK: Cambridge University Press.

Tabb, W. K. 2004. *Economic Governance in the Age of Globalization.* New York: Columbia University Press.

Thomas, D. C. 2001. *The Helsinki effect: International Norms, Human rights, and the Demise of Communism.* Princeton University Press.

Thompson, A. 2006. "Coercion Through IOs: The Security Council and the Logic of Information Transmission." *International Organization,* 60(1):1–34.

Tickner, J. A. 1992. *Gender in International Relations: Feminist Perspectives on Achieving Global Security.* New York: Columbia University Press.

Tickner, J. A. 2001. *Gendering World Politics: Issues and Approaches in the Post–Cold War Era.* New York: Columbia University Press.

Tir, J., and M. Jasinski. 2008. "Domestic-Level Diversionary Theory of War: Targeting Ethnic Minorities." *Journal of Conflict Resolution,* 52(5):641–664.

Trindade, A.A. C. 2011. *The Access of Individuals to International Justice.* Vol. 18. Oxford University Press.

Tripp, A. M. 2010. "Toward a Comparative Politics of Gender Research in Which Woman Matter." *Perspectives on Politics* 8(1):191–197.

True, J. 2003. "Mainstreaming Gender in Global Public Policy." *International Feminist Journal of Politics,* 5(3):368–396.

Trumbore, P. F. 2003. "Victims or Aggressors? Ethno-Political Rebellion and Use of Force in Militarized Interstate Disputes." *International Studies Quarterly,* 47:183–201.

Truschke, A. 2016. *Culture of Encounters: Sanskrit at the Mughal Court.* New York: Colombia University Press.

Tryggestad, T. L. 2009. "Trick or Treat? The UN and Implementation of Security Council Resolution 1325 on Women, Peace and Security." *Global Governance,* 15:539–557.

Tsingou, E. 2014. "Power Elites and Club-Model Governance in Global Finance," *International Political Sociology,* 8(3):340–342, https://doi.org/10.1111/ ips.12066.

Turner, M., and F. P. Kühn, eds. 2017. *The Politics of International Intervention: The Tyranny of Peace.* New York: Routledge.

Ugur, M. 2013. "Europeanization, EU Conditionality, and Governance Quality: Empirical Evidence on Central and Eastern European Countries," *International Studies Quarterly,* 57(1):41–51, https://doi.org/10.1111/isqu.12035.

Ullman, R. 1983. "Redefining Security." *International Security,* 8(1):129–153.

UN General Assembly, *International Covenant on Economic, Social and Cultural Rights,* 16 December 1966, United Nations, Treaty Series, vol. 993, p. 3, available at: https://www.refworld.org/docid/3ae6b36c0.html [accessed 19 June 2019].

UN General Assembly, *Convention Against Torture and Other Cruel, Inhuman or Degrading Treatment or Punishment,* 10 December 1984, United Nations, Treaty Series, vol. 1465, p. 85, available at: https://www.refworld.org/docid/3ae6b3a94.html [accessed 19 June 2019].

UN General Assembly, *Vienna Declaration and Programme of Action,* 12 July 1993, A/CONF.157/23, available at: https://www.refworld.org/docid/3ae6b39ec.html [accessed 19 June 2019].

United Nations Commission on Human Security. 2003. *Human Security Now: Protecting and Empowering People.* New York: United Nations Publications.

United Nations, Department of Economic and Social Affairs, Population Division. 2015. *World Population Prospects: The 2015 Revision.* New York: United Nations.

United Nations Development Program. 1994. *Human Development Report 1994: New Dimensions of Human Security.* Available at http://hdr.undp.org/en/reports/global/hdr1994/. Last accessed November 11, 2011.

United Nations Educational, Scientific and Cultural Organization. 2001. "What Agenda for Human Security in the Twenty-First Century?" UNESCO Division of Human Rights, Democracy, Peace and Tolerance, Social and Human Sciences Sector. Paris.

United Nations High Commissioner on Refugees. 2017. Population Reference Database.

United Nations High Commissioner on Refugees. 2018.

United Nations Office for Coordination of Humanitarian Affairs. 2019. South Sudan Humanitarian Bulletin. Available at https://www.unocha.org/south-sudan.

Uppsala Conflict Data Program. 2012. UCDP/PRIO Armed Conflict Dataset. Uppsala University Department of Peace and Conflict Research. http://www.pcr.uu.se/research/ucdp/datasets/ucdp_prio_armed_conflict_dataset/.

Urquhart, B. 2011. "Learning from Hammarskjold." *New York Times.* Available at http://www.nytimes.com/2011/09/17/opinion/learning-from-hammarskjold.html?_r51.

Uzonyi, G., and Hanania, R. 2017. "Government-Sponsored Mass Killing and Civil War Reoccurrence," *International Studies Quarterly,* 61(3): 677–689, https://doi.org/10.1093/isq/sqx050.

Vasquez, J. A. 1995. "Why Do Neighbors Fight? Proximity, Interaction, or Territoriality." *Journal of Peace Research,* 32(3):277–293.

Veltmeyer, H. 2005. "Development and Globalization as Imperialism." *Canadian Journal of Development Studies* 26(1):89–106.

Veseth, Michael, and David N. Balaam, eds. 1996. *Readings in International Political Economy.* Prentice-Hall.

Voeten, E. 2004. "Resisting the Lonely Superpower: Responses of States in the UN to US Dominance." *Journal of Politics,* 66:729–754.

Volgy, T. J., and A. Bailin. 2002. *International Politics and State Strength.* Boulder, CO: Lynne Rienner.

Von Hippel, K., and M. Clarke. 1999. "Something Must be Done." *The World Today,* 55(3):4–7.

von Stein, J. 2005. "Do Treaties Constrain or Screen? Selection Bias and Treaty Compliance." *American Political Science Review,* 99(3):611–622.

Wæver, O. 1995. "Securitization and De-Securitization." In *On Security,* ed. R. Lipshultz. New York: Columbia University Press.

Wakabi, W. 2009. "Aid Expulsions Leave Huge Gap in Darfur's Health Services." *The Lancet,* 373(9669):1068–1069.

Waldorf, L. 2009. "A Mere Pretense of Justice: Complementarity, Sham Trials, and Victor's Justice at the Rwanda Tribunal." *Fordham Int'l LJ* 33: 1221.

Walker, R. B. J., R. Shilliam, H. Weber, and G. Du Plessis. 2018. "Collective Discussion: Diagnosing the Present," *International Political Sociology*, 12(1):88–107, https://doi.org/10.1093/ips/olx022.

Walker, S. G., M. Schafer, and M. D. Young. 1998. "Systematic Procedures for Operational Code Analysis: Measuring and Modeling Jimmy Carter's Operational Code." *International Studies Quarterly*, 42(1):175–189.

Wallace, G. P. R. 2014. "Martial Law? Military Experience, International Law, and Support for Torture," *International Studies Quarterly*, 58(3):501–514, ttps://doi.org/10.1111/isqu.12092.

Wallensteen, P., and K. Axell. 1994. "Conflict Resolution and the End of the Cold War, 1989–93." *Journal of Peace Research*, 31(3):333–349.

Wallerstein, I. 2004. *World-Systems Analysis: An Introduction*. Durham, NC: Duke University Press.

Walt, S. M. 1985. "Alliance Formation and the Balance of World Power." *International Security*, 9(4):3–43.

Walt, S. M. 1987. *The Origins of Alliances*. Ithaca, NY: Cornell University Press.

Waltz, K. N. 1959. *Man, the State, and War*. New York: Columbia University Press.

Waltz, K. N. 1979. *Theory of International Politics*. Reading, UK: Addison-Wesley.

Walzer, M. 1977. *Just and Unjust Wars: A Moral Argument with Historical Illustrations*. New York: Basic Books.

Walzer, M. 2006. *Just and Unjust Wars: A Moral Argument with Historical Illustrations*, 4th ed. New York: Basic Books.

Weber, C. 1999. *Faking It: US Hegemony in a "Post-Phallic" Era*. Minneapolis: University of Minnesota Press.

Weber, M. 1918 (1946). "Politics as a Vocation." In *Max Weber: Essays in Sociology*, ed. and trans. H. H. Gerth and C. Wright Mills. New York: Oxford University Press.

Weinberg, L. 1991. "Turning to Terror: The Conditions Under Which Political Parties Turn to Terrorist Activities." *Comparative Politics*, 23(4):423–438.

Weiss, T. G. 2009. "What Happened to the Idea of World Government?" *International Studies Quarterly*, 53(2):253–271.

Weiss, T. G., T. Carayannis, and R. Jolly. 2009. "The 'Third' UN." *Global Governance: A Review of Multilateralism and International Organizations*, 15(1):123–142.

Welsh, J. M., ed. 2004. *Humanitarian Intervention and International Relations*. Oxford, UK: Oxford University Press.

Wendt, A. 1992. "Anarchy Is What States Make of It: The Social Construction of Power Politics." *International Organization*, 46(2):391–425.

Wendt, A. 1999. *Social Theory of International Politics*. Cambridge, UK: Cambridge University Press.

Wendt, A. 2004. "The State as Person in International Theory." *Review of International Studies*, 30:289–316.

Whitworth, S. 2004. *Men, Militarism, and UN Peacekeeping*. Boulder, CO: Lynne Rienner.

Wiebe, R. H. 2001. *Who We Are: A History of Popular Nationalism*. Princeton, NJ: Princeton University Press.

Wilkinson, D. 2004. "Analytical and Empirical Issues in the Study of Power–Polarity Configuration Sequences." Paper presented at a Conference of a Working Group on Analyzing Complex Macrosystems as Dynamic Networks, Santa Fe Institute, Santa Fe, NM.

Wilkinson, P. 2005. *Terrorism Versus Democracy: The Liberal State Response*, 2nd ed. London: Routledge.

Williams, M. C. 2004. "Why Ideas Matter in International Relations: Hans Morgenthau, Classical Realism, and the Moral Construction of Power Politics." *International Organization*, 58(4):633–665.

Williams, P. D., ed. 2008. *Security Studies: An Introduction*. New York/London: Routledge.

Williamson, J. G. 1996. "Globalization, Convergence, and History." *The Journal of Economic History* 56(2):277–306.

Willig, M. R., and S. M. Scheiner. 2011. "The State of Theory in Ecology." In *The Theory of Ecology*, eds. S. M. Scheiner and M. R. Willig. Chicago: University of Chicago Press.

Wohlforth, W. C. 1999. "The Stability of a Unipolar World." *International Security*, 24(1):5–41.

Wood, D. 2016. *What Have We Done: The Moral Injury of Our Longest Wars*. New York: Little Brown & Company.

World Bank. 2019a. "World Bank Open Data: GDP per Capita." Available at https://data.worldbank.org/indicator/NY.GDP.PCAP.CD?locations=SS.

World Bank. 2019b. "World Bank Open Data: Life Expectancy at Birth." Available at https://data.worldbank.org/indicator/sp.dyn.le00.in.

World Bank. 2019c. "World Bank Open Data: Imported Goods and Services as a Percentage of US GDP." Available at https://data.worldbank.org/indicator/NE.IMP.GNFS.ZS?end=2016&locations=US&start=1960&view=chart.

World Bank. 2019d. "World Bank Open Data: Literacy Rate, Adult Female." Available at https://data.worldbank.org/indicator/se.adt.litr.fe.zs.

World Bank. 2019e. "World Bank Open Data: Maternal Mortality Ratio." Available at https://data.worldbank.org/indicator/SH.STA.MMRT.

World Wildlife Fund. 2016. *Living Planet Report 2016: Summary*. Gland, Switzerland: World Wildlife Fund.

Wyn Jones, R. 1996. "Travel Without Maps: Thinking About Security After the Cold War." In *Security Issues in the Post-Cold War World*, ed. M. J. Davis. Cheltenham, UK: Edward Elgar.

Wyn Jones, R. 2001. *Critical Theory and World Politics*. Boulder, CO: Lynne Rienner.

Xu, B. 2014. China's Environmental Crisis, (25 April 2014), online: Council on Foreign Relations, http://www.cfr.org/china/chinas-environmental-crisis/p12608.

Yarger, H. R. 2010. *Short of General War: Perspectives on the Use of Military Power in the 21st Century*. Carlisle, PA: US Army War College, Strategic Studies Institute.

Yassin-Kassab, R. and L. al-Shami. 2016. *Burning Country: Syrians in Revolution and War*. London: Pluto Press.

Zagare, F. C. 2013. "Game Theory." In *Security Studies: An Introduction*, 2nd ed., ed. P. D. Williams. London/New York: Routledge.

Zakaria, F. 1993. "Is Realism Finished?" *National Interest*, 32:21–32.

Zalewski, M. 2007. "Do We Understand Each Other Yet? Troubling Feminist Encounters With(in) International Relations." *The British Journal of Politics & International Relations*, 9:302–312.

Zartman, I. W. 2008. "Introduction: Toward the Resolution of International Conflicts." In *Peacemaking in International Conflict: Methods & Techniques*, rev. ed., ed. I. W. Zartman. Washington, DC: US Institute of Peace Press.

Zenko, M. 2012. "Americans Are as Likely to Be Killed by Their Own Furniture as by Terrorism," *The Atlantic*, June 6, 2012. Available online at: https://www.theatlantic.com/international/archive/2012/06/americans-are-as-likely-to-be-killed-by-their-own-furniture-as-by-terrorism/258156/.

Credits

PHOTOS

CHAPTER 1

p. 2: AP Photo/Moises Castillo; p. 5: JORGE Muniz/EPA-EFE/Shutterstock; p. 6: REUTERS/US State Department/Handout via Reuters; p. 8: (Photo by Michael Brochstein/SOPA Images/Sipa USA)(Sipa via AP Images); p. 9: Sascha Steinbach/EPA-EFE/; p. 10: Free Wind 2014; p. 12: Korea Summit Press Pool via AP; p. 15: Hans-Maximo Musielik/AP/Shutterstock.

CHAPTER 2

p. 20: Filip Fuxa/Shutterstock; p. 27: AP Photo/Xinhua, Zha Chunming; p. 35: Paul Hilton/EPA/Shutterstock; p. 37: Nanda Kusumadi; p. 39: guy oliver/Alamy Stock Photo; p. 41: KNCA/Shutterstock; p. 42: FARID TAJUDDIN; p. 45: Ryan Remiorz/The Canadian Press via AP; p. 46: Guide to Women Leaders, official sites, AFP photos.

CHAPTER 3

p. 52: Julian Simmonds/Shutterstock; p. 59: Sabah Arar/Shutterstock; p. 63: Karim Sahib/AFP-Getty Images; p. 64: Leslie Priest/AP/Shutterstock ; p. 67: Yaw Bibini/Reuters; p. 69: Alexander Zemlianichenko/AP/Shutterstock; p. 71: AP Photo/Susan Walsh.

CHAPTER 4

p. 90: Kyodo via AP Images; p. 93: Shawn Thew/EPA/Shutterstock; p. 95: AP Photo/Rajesh Kumar Singh; p. 98: Glasshouse Images/Shutterstock; p. 116: Chema Moya/EPA/Shutterstock; p. 121: Denis Balibouse/REUTERS.

CHAPTER 5

p. 124: AP Photo/Kirsty Wigglesworth; p. 127: Yoan Valat/EPA; p. 128: Geof Kirby/Alamy Stock Photo; p. 131: Vincent Thian/AP; p. 133: UN in collaboration with Project Everyone; p. 144: Benoit Tessier/Reuters; p. 145: AP Photo/Victor R. Caivano; p. 147: Soe Than WIN/AFP/Getty Images.

CHAPTER 6

p. 156: Xinhua/Alamy Stock Photo; p. 159: AP Photo/Richard Drew; p. 161: The Postal Museum; p. 165: UNODC; p. 167: nairobiwire.com; p. 177: Dag Hammarskjold Foundation; p. 179: New Zealand Defense Force; p. 186: AP Photo/Ramon Espinosa.

CHAPTER 7

p. 192: AP/Shutterstock; p. 195: C. Peter Chen/World War II Database; p. 200: Reuters/Enrique Marcarian; p. 201: Pictorial Press Ltd/Alamy Stock Photo; p. 208: Copyright © 2014 by John Shea; p. 210: Mioljub Jelesijevic/AP/Shutterstock; p. 212: JUNIOR D.KANNAH/AFP/GettyImages; p. 213: WESH Orlando; p. 214: CARMEN TAYLOR, AP File Photo; p. 217: Yannis Kolesidis/AP; p. 220: SOCIAL MEDIA WEBSITE/REUTERS.

CHAPTER 8

p. 224: AP Photo/Wong Maye-E, File; p. 230: Heather and DeCeuster, 2008; p. 233: AP Photo/Ariana Cubillos; p. 239: AP Photo/Evan Vucci; p. 247: Imaginechina via AP Images; p. 250: AFP/Ameer Alhalbi.

CHAPTER 9

p. 256: AP Photo/Fred Ernst; p. 261: CSPAN/National Cable Satellite Corporation; p. 262: Sang Tan/AP/Shutterstock; p. 271: EPA/BAS CZERWINSKI; p. 276: Pierre Hazan; p. 278: Everett Collection Historical/Alamy Stock Photo; p. 288: Adel Hana/AP/Shutterstock.

CHAPTER 10

p. 292: Xu Jinquan/Xinhua/Alamy Live News; p. 299: Matt Wuerker/Politico/Universal Uclick; p. 301: Sipa Asia/Shutterstock; p. 311: Ahn

Young-Joon/AP/REX/Shutterstock; p. 316: © The White House; Jesco Denzel/German Federal Government via AP; p. 318: THE CANADIAN PRESS/ Riley Smith; p. 325: Marjorie Kamys Cotera/Bob Daemmrich Photography/Alamy Stock Photo; p. 328: MAST IRHAM/EPA-EFE/Shutterstock.

CHAPTER 11

p. 332: AP Photo/Cedar Attanasio, File; p. 335: AP Photo/Petar Petrov; p. 337: Imaginechina via AP Images; p. 338: Sandra Gätke/picture-alliance/ dpa/AP Images; p. 342: AP Photo/Richard Vogel; p. 345: AP Photo/Themba Hadebe; p. 354: Federico Rios Escobar for The New York Times; p. 357: Imaginechina via AP Images; p. 359: Liu Xiang/ Xinhua/Alamy Live News; p. 365: AP Photo/ Cooper Inveen, File.

CHAPTER 12

p. 372: Aleppo Media Center; p. 378: Asia News; p. 380: Jurgen Schadeberg; p. 387: © Mohammed Badra, European Pressphoto Agency; p. 390: AP Photo/Bernat Armangue; Invisible Children; p. 400: Lana H. Haroun; p. 404: Joseph Sohm/ Shutterstock.com.

CHAPTER 13

p. 406: Soren Andersson/Agence France-Presse — Getty Images; p. 413: ariyo olasunkanmi/Shutterstock; p. 415: Hari Mahidhar/Shutterstock; p. 419: Sumit.Kumar.99/Shutterstock; p. 421: Dennis Wegewijs/Shutterstock; p. 433: AP Photo/ Kin Cheung, File; p. 435: AP Photo/David J. Phillip, File.

FIGURES

CHAPTER 1

p. 9: Howard the Duck/Wikimedia Commons/Creative Commons.

CHAPTER 3

p. 73: Federal Reserve Bank of St. Louis, US Department of the Treasury, Fiscal Service; p. 82: Spring 2016 Global Attitudes Survey, Pew Research Center; p. 83: Spring 2016 Global Attitudes survey. US survey conducted April 12-19, 2016. Pew Research Center.

CHAPTER 4

p. 107: Spring 2016 Global Attitudes survey. US survey conducted March 17-27, 2016. Pew Research Center; p. 120: Freedom House.

CHAPTER 5

p. 127: The World Bank; p. 130: We Are Social, © Statista 2019.

CHAPTER 6

p. 168: Union of International Associations, 2018; p. 172: United Nations Global Marketplace; p. 176: securitycouncilreport.org; p. 182: Council on Foreign Relations.

CHAPTER 7

p. 204, 205: Uppsala Conflict Data Programme/ Peace Research Institute Oslo.

CHAPTER 8

p. 227: SIPRI 2019; p. 235: SIPRI Arms Transfers Database, Mar. 2019; p. 237: Data from the Federation of American Scientists, the UN Department for Disarmament Affairs, and the US Department of State; p. 242: Global Peace Operations Review.

CHAPTER 9

p. 267: Spring 2015 Global Attitudes Survey, Pew Research Center.

CHAPTER 10

p. 308: Stockholm International Peace Research Institute, 2018; p. 315: The World Bank.

CHAPTER 11

p. 336: The World Bank; p. 340: The World Bank; p. 353: Organization for Economic Cooperation and Development; p. 358: International Monetary Fund; p. 363: The World Bank.

CHAPTER 12

p. 384: Global Attitudes Survey 2015, Pew Research Center; p. 395: Spring 2018 Global Attitudes Survey, Pew Research Center; p. 399: Freedom House.

CHAPTER 13

p. 419: UN Population Division; p. 423: UN Population Division; World Fertility Patterns 2015,

UNICEF; p. 428: European Environment Agency; p. 430: Living Planet Report 2016: Summary. World Wildlife Fund: Gland, Switzerland, page 54; p. 432: WWF Living Planet Report 2018 page 90; p. 434: Klaus Bittermann/Wikimedia Commons; p. 436: World Resources Institute; p. 437: Global-PetrolPrices.com.

MAPS

CHAPTER 1

p. 12: "Colonial Affiliations before 1945," adapted from Kishinksy et al., *Civilization in the West*, 5th edition, 2003.; p. 16: The Lancet.

CHAPTER 3

p. 74: UNCTAD.

CHAPTER 4

p. 100: Adapted from Perry et al., *Western Civilization: Ideas, Politics, and Society*; p. 108: onlinemaps.blogspot.com; p. 120: Freedom House; p. 122: © 2018 The Fund for Peace.

CHAPTER 5

p. 153: United Nations Office on Drugs and Crime (2010). The Globalization of Crime: A Transnational Crime Threat Assessment. Vienna: UNODC, page 2.

CHAPTER 7

p. 203: Uppsala Conflict Data Program/Uppsala University.; p. 207: Institute for the Study of War,

LiveUAMap; p. 217: Global Terrorism Database, START.; p. 221: Conflict Monitor by IHS Markit.

CHAPTER 8

p. 252: Adapted from Deadly Arsenals: Tracking Weapons of Mass Destruction from Carnegie Endowment for International Peace; p. 253: Adapted from Deadly Arsenals: Tracking Weapons of Mass Destruction from Carnegie Endowment for International Peace.

CHAPTER 10

p. 304: Alinor/Wikimedia Commons/Creative Commons.

CHAPTER 12

p. 383: Database of the United Nations Office of Legal Affairs (OLA); p. 394: Operational Data Portal by UNHCR; p. 397: World Without Genocide at Mitchell Hamline School of Law.; p. 403: Amnesty International and Death Penalty Information Center.

CHAPTER 13

p. 413: WWF Living Planet Report 2018 page 32; p. 425: © 2012 UNICEF.; p. 429: World Resources Institute; p. 443: © Karsten Haustein.

Index

Page numbers in **bold** refer to key terms. Page numbers in *italic* refer to photos. Page numbers followed by *f, m,* and *t* refer to figures, tables, and maps, respectively.

Vienna Convention on Consular Relations, 271
Vienna Convention on Diplomatic Relations, 265
Vienna Convention on the Law of Treaties, **260**
Vienna World Conference on Human Rights, 387
Vietnam, 56, 71, 80, 327, 340*f*, 410
Vietnam War, 80, 205
violence
  in global politics, 194
  measuring intensity of, 205–6
  in "new" wars, 211
  right to avoid, 378
  in terrorism, 213
Volkswagen, 337*t*
voluntary compliance, with international law, 267
voting
  majority, **175**
  supermajority, **175**
  unanimity, **176**
  in United Nations, 175–76, 175*f*, 176*f*
  weighted, **175**–76
  See also democracy

W

"wagging the dog," 199–200
Wales, 110
Wallensteen, P., 207
Wallerstein, Immanuel, 36, 37
Wall Street Journal, The, 125
Walmart, 337, 337*t*, 401
Waltz, Kenneth, 29, 59, 61, 198, 200
war(s), 13, **195**–212
  abstract, 209
  causes of, 198–202
  child soldiers in, 395–96
  conduct in, 278–80
  decision to go to, 277–78
  defining, 194–95, 205
  diversionary theory of, 115, **199**–200
  as economic engine, 308
  and education, 77

as effective political instrument, 202
  extrastate, 204
  feminist view of, 44
  gender opinion gap on, 65
  and international law, 260, 261, 277–84
  interstate, 194, 204, 205*f*
  intrastate, 204–5, 205*f*
  "new," **208**–12
  "old," 207–9, **208**
  persistence vs. obsolescence of, 196–98
  preventive, **196**
  rape as weapon of, 149
  real, 209
  total, 206
  types of, 195–96
  See also armed conflict; terrorism
war crimes, 187, 216, **273**, 390
  individuals wanted for, 276
  international law and, 268
  justice for individuals accused of, 274
  prosecution of, 260, 287
  Charles Taylor's conviction for, 257
  tribunals, 280–84
warfare, asymmetric, **213**
War on Terror, 375
Washington, DC, inauguration of Barack Obama in, *93*
Washington Post, 125
water quality and access to clean water, 341, 375, 428–31, 429*m*
WCW. *See* World Conference on Women
wealth inequality, 134, *299*, 340–41, 340*f*, 362
Wealth of Nations, The (Smith), 298
weapons of mass destruction (WMDs), 88, 110, **248**–54
  biological weapons, 248–50, **249,** 253*m*
  chemical weapons, 193, *250*, 250–51, **250**–51, 253*m*
  as justification for military intervention, 278

See also arms control; nuclear weapons
"We Are Still In" movement, 408
weather control, 412
Weber, Max, 114–15, 194
"we-feeling," 94, 105, 141
weighted voting, **175**–76
Weimar Republic, 60
Weiss, Thomas, 187
well-being needs, 378
Wells Fargo, 305
Wendt, Alexander, 41
WEOG. *See* Western European and Others Group
Western Europe
  "homegrown" terrorism in, 217–18
  "old" wars in, 208
Western European and Others Group (WEOG), 9*f*
Western Sahara, 116, *116*
Western societies, influence of, on international law, 273–75
West Germany, 111, 320. *See also* Germany
Westphalia, Treaty of. *See* Peace of Westphalia
WFM. *See* World Federalist Movement
"What It Tkaes to Be Truly 'One of Us'" (poll), 106
"Where are the lions of war?" (Abdul Hasan al-Muhajir), 216
Whitworth, Sandra, 184
WHO. *See* World Health Organization
WikiLeaks, *52–53*, 53, 54, *59,* 62, 69, *69,* 80
wildfires, 438
wildlife, 188
Wilkinson, D., 218
Williams, Betty, 215
Wilson, Woodrow, 32, *98,* 105, 109, 110
win-win situations, 31
WMDs. *See* weapons of mass destruction
wolves, 411, 411*f*